FROM MY BONES

FROM MY BONES

Memoirs of **Col. Gurbakhsh Singh Dhillon**
of
the Indian National Army

(Including 1945 Red Fort Trial)

Aryan Books International
New Delhi

From My Bones

ISBN: 978-81-7305-148-7

First Published: 1998

Reprinted: **2025**

Published by:

Aryan Books International

Pooja Apartments, 4B, Ansari Road, New Delhi-110 002 (India)

Tel.: 23255799, 41099562

E-mail: aryanbooks@gmail.com

www.aryanbooks.com

Printed in India

FROM MY BONES

Memoirs of **Col. Gurbakhsh Singh Dhillon**
of
the Indian National Army

(Including 1945 Red Fort Trial)

Aryan Books International
New Delhi

From My Bones

ISBN: 978-81-7305-148-7

First Published: 1998

Reprinted: **2025**

Published by:

Aryan Books International

Pooja Apartments, 4B, Ansari Road, New Delhi-110 002 (India)

Tel.: 23255799, 41099562

E-mail: aryanbooks@gmail.com

www.aryanbooks.com

Printed in India

To

Myanmar

Her

People and Pagodas

at

Myingyan, Nyaungu, Bagan,

Mount Popa, Kyaukpadaung

Magwe

and

the Holy Irrawaddy

CONTENTS

Foreword *ix*

Preface *xi*

Acknowledgements *xvii*

Chapters

1. Beginnings and Endings 1
2. Heritage 5
3. Childhood 10
4. Education 17
5. The Army 29
6. The Surrender 93
7. The Changi Garrison 105
8. Shaping the INA 175
9. Netaji Arrives 203
10. The 5th Guerrilla Regiment 216
11. To Burma 220
12. I Meet Netaji 229
13. The Nehru 237
14. "The Nehru" Holds the Irrawaddy 271
15. Mount Popa and Kyauk Padaung 299
16. The Retreat 318
17. The Last Clash 339
18. Interrogation 350

19. Hospitalisation 365
20. Rangoon Jail 370
21. To Delhi 389
22. The Red Fort 402
23. The Trial 428
24. The Verdict 499
25. Aftermath 507
26. Memorabilia 534
27. Netaji 552
28. Afterword 572
Index 579

Maps

1. Myingyan Setting 243
2. The Battle of Nyaunga and Pagan 275
3. The Retreat 323

Foreword

A historian's perspective of an event or series of historical events differs from the more intimate subjective view of a participant in the same event or series of events. As a historian of the Indian National Army (see *Jungle Alliance; Japan and the Indian National Army,* Singapore : Asia Pacific Press, 1970), I had the rare opportunity of meeting the three national heroes of the INA tried by the British in the Red Fort at the end of World War II : Gen. Shah Nawaz Khan, Col. P.K. Sahgal, and Col. Gurbakhsh Singh Dhillon. I spent many enjoyable hours in the company of the latter two in particular and gained valuable insights from their recollections. Shah Nawaz, the first of the three whom I met was actually in Tokyo when in 1955 he was there to inquire into the circumstances of Subhas Chandra Bose's death, was the first of the three to write his recollections of his role in the INA (*My Memories of the INA and its Netaji*, Delhi : Rajkamal Publications, 1946).

Nearly fifty years later in 1993, Professor Peter Fay's work *The Forgotten Army : The Indian National Army* (University of Michigan Press) appeared, centred around the roles of Col. Sahgal and his wife Col. Lakshmi Swaminadhan Sahgal, Commander of the Rani of Jhansi Regiment, the women's unit of the INA. Fay's account is based on many months spent in the company of this illustrious couple, during which he taped their detailed recollections. Col. Sahgal unfortunately died several months before Fay's book appeared.

Now Col. Dhillon is the only survivor of this heroic trio. I have been particularly anxious that the record of his experiences that contributed so signally to India's independence may not to be lost to history. Dhillon has the advantage in recording his recollections of several decades, during which he has often shared his memories in vivid and generous detail at the annual seminars held every 23rd

January at the Netaji Research Bureau in Calcutta. At these seminars and on numerous other occasions at Meerut, Jhansi, Gwalior, Kurukshetra, Hisar and elsewhere he has captivated audiences with his spellbound eloquence and his own Urdu poems rendered in fiery rhetoric. While English is not Col. Dhillon's first language, his early education in English and his distinctive gift with words imbue his account with historic value and vivid realism.

Col. Dhillon's memoirs reveals to the reader his unshakable principles, patriotic dedication to the cause of independence, courage under fire, historical sense, as well as his humanity and sense of humour, just as in his struggle they contributed so vitally to India's independence.

It was my great privilege to have Col. Dhillon as a personal friend for many years, and it is a pleasure to be invited to provide this preface. My hope is that the means to publish this historical memoir be found to ensure that it will be available to coming generations in India and elsewhere.

Jai Hind !

Gwalior **Joyce C. Lebra**

PREFACE

The Indian struggle for freedom from the British Raj covers more than one and a half century of sustained effort in various ways. On the eve of World War II the Indian soldier in the British Indian Army had reached a stage of political awareness to think for and do something for the national liberation. What they lacked was an army of their own. The so-called Indian Army at the time was in fact an Army of occupation of India by a foreign nation. The personnel of the Indian army owed allegiance to the British Crown and not to India. The Indian soldier, one of the best in the world, took pride in his fighting skill and loyalty. He would die rather than go against his word. He loved his honour the most. He was however oblivious of the fact that his loyalty to the foreign Crown was the cause of perpetuation of a foreign nation's domination over India. Thus he was the protector of the slavish status of his own.

During World War II early victories of Germany and Italy in the West followed by the Japanese victories in the East created a combination of circumstances that favoured the formation of India's Army of Liberation. This army came to be known as the Indian National Army (INA) or Azad Hind Fauj. This army waged war against the British for emancipation of the Indian nation. Out of its sixty thousand soldiers, I was one.

Ever since the end of the war, friends and well wishers irrespective of their nationality urged me to write my memoirs. Writing memoirs I thought was an exercise in egoism. Hence I could not persuade myself to recount my past, which I held was part of my day-to-day mundane activities in the discharge of my duties as a soldier. Gradually it dawned on me that action and the fate of an individual cannot be isolated from those of his country and the people, and what is more, an individual cannot understand his own self without historical awareness and proper perspective of history. Almost all thoughts and actions of an individual are determined by the collective fate of the nation. Thus when I look back, I discover that my past does not belong to me alone. It is the joint past of those amongst whom I was called upon to work—my men, ny junior and senior colleagues and commanders, my leaders and the Supreme Commander. It was because of our collective action that history gave us a role to play which it gives rarely and to very few.

The story narrated in the following pages is not the history of the INA. That history cannot be compiled as memoirs of an individual because of the size of the movement which was spread out over more than a dozen countries of Asia and Europe, whose shores are washed by three oceans—the Atlantic, the Indian and the Pacific. My narrative is of the event which concerned my person or were to my knowledge in connection with my duties and status in the movement. It is more like an account of my actions. The diaries and records of the events were thrice burnt and destroyed by me during the operations, when I was encircled by the enemy and my capture looked imminent.

The following narrative has been compiled out of memory and from those records which were produced by the prosecution and the defence counsels during the INA's first trial by General Court—Martial in the Red Fort of Delhi in 1945. In that trial I was one of the accused. The main charge against us was waging war against the King. I am grateful to Basant, my wife who carried those records with her from place to place after the partition of India. Her last will was that I write my memoirs. Basant died at Gwalior Jaya Arogya Hospital on 19th March 1968.

I am also grateful to my eldest brother Sardar Gurdial Singh Dhillon who kept and gave me newpaper cuttings of the trial days, which helped me to refresh my memory. Brother Gurdial Singh died at Bulsar (Gujarat) in January 1969.

I confess that I found it more difficult to write than to fight on the battelfield fifty years ago. I had to question myself everytime I wrote about an event, "Did I, could I do it? Was it possible?" I had to judge each statement before putting it on paper. I chose not to follow any set and precise method of narrating my memoirs. I had to relive the past in my imagination. Different pictures of the bygone days did not appear before my mind's eye for my asking. They took time to emerge at odd intervals and hours of their liking, at times even in my sleep. They were like twinkling little flames of different colours which the wind of time (passage) would blow off. And next morning I was left without any light. I am indebted to Prof. Bashir Badar who through his poetry showed me the path, "Let the hand of words secure them before the wind blows them off."

Wadiay zehan mein hain rang brang ke diay,

Dast-e-ilfaz mehfooz kar lay inhain,

Chal rahi hai hawa bhuj na jaen kaheen.

So I often kept a paper and pencil handy beside my pillow. I would get up at night whenever a picture of my past visited my mind and secured it in words on paper. Despite all these methods and sincere intentions I could not make any headway in writing. Yet I was often, nay always, surprised that if I had to talk to an audience, my memory never failed me. But then spoken language does differ from the written one. What I needed was assistance of a typist. That would not be possible since my son-like comrade Ram Labhya Sarin's untimely death in January 1974. Even otherwise struggle for existence was difficult ever since my release from the Red Fort on 3rd January, 1946. The partition of India in 1947 made things worse because of my becoming a refugee having lost all movable and immovable assets overnight. Ultimately on 21st October in 1952, I came to settle down at Hatod, a village in Shivpuri district in Central India—Madhya Bharat, presently in the state of Madhya Pradesh.

Migration from Punjab - the place of my birth—to Madhya Pradesh demanded a pioneering spirit. Rehabilitation on an unreclaimed territory infested with tigers and dacoits was a challenge in itself. Here I was to discover that the poor, half-clad local people especially the Sehrias were richer in heart than the so-called rich and the wild beasts more human than men. By and large the people had fellow-feelings and were of a helping nature. Government officials were responsive and eager to solve citizens' problems.

In the INA I had learnt to live on land by developing the ability to improvise. Yet a life of paucity and privation was not easy to put up with. Not so when there was a family along with eleven members to support and a past to live up to. I was obliged to live on loans. The experience was bitter. My own family consisted of Basant, my wife, five-year old daughter, Amrita and two sons, Amarjit of four and Sarvjit of two and a half years. Besides, we had three dogs—Billo, Pashi and Tiger, five chickens with Moti as their leader, and Mano the cat. All these animals lived in harmony amongst themselves and gave us an impression that they were as important members of our family as any one of the humans.

Raising of loans was a difficult job. I was obliged to face many disappointments. Depression was a frequent visitor. But in the end Iqbal's poetry came to my rescue, when I read :-

Nahin tera nasheman Qas-re-Sultani ke gumbad par,

Tu shaheen hai basera kar paharon ki chatanon mein.

(Your abode is not on the dome

Of an imperial palace.

You are an eagle,

You roost amongst the mountain rocks.)

And it was there amid the rocks of Hatod Hill by the Barai Nadi (rivulet), that I found a genuine specimen of humanity. There my life was enriched with a passion to live with faith in the people. I owe my well-being to them who dwell in the villages of Barai valley and in Shivpuri district as well as to my mother, my wife and my children.

In mid-eighties Dr. Joyce Lebra and Prof. Bernier of the University of Colorado in the U.S. arranged a three-month visit for me to Boulder. With the help of their colleagues they made arrangements to assist me to complete my manuscript and undertook to get it typed and published at the earliest. When all arrangements were complete and I was about to leave for the U.S., I received a call from the Ministry of Home Affairs, Government of India. I was asked if I could accept to be member of an INA. Committee which was to scrutinise and recommend the pending cases of INA veterans for the grant of Freedom Fighters' pension by the Government. The welfare of the INA men demanded my acceptance of Government's proposal. I was obliged to cable to Boulder to get my visit cancelled. The grace

Her Majesty's Stationery Office - *The Transfer of Power 1942-47*, Volume VI, *The Post-War Phase: New Moves by the Labour Government,* 1 August 1945 - 22 March 1946, printed in England by Vivian Ridler at the University Press, Oxford, 1976.

Lt. General S.L. Menezes, PVSM, SC, *Fidelity & Honour - The Indian Army - From the Seventeenth to the Twenty First Century,* Viking Penguin India, 1993.

A Beacon Across Asia, edited by Sisir K. Bose, Alexander Werth and S.A. Ayer, published by Orient Longman.

H.N. Pandit - *Netaji Subhas Chandra Bose: From Kabul to Battle of Imphal,* Sterling Publishers Private Limited.

Peter Ward Fay - *The Forgotten Army*, Rupa & Co.

Leonard A. Gordon - *Brothers Against The Raj,* Viking Penguin Books (India) Limited.

with which Prof. Bernier, Dr. Joyce Lebra and their colleagues agreed to my backing out of all the arrangements they had made was indeed magnanimous. I shall ever remain under a debt of gratitude to them.

Again, a similar invitation was given by Poonam Sibbal and her parents, Col. & Mrs. M.C. Sibbal from Dehra Dun and yet another standing invitation from my son-like J.K. Agarwal from Meerut. But I could not avail myself of their golden opportunities due to my poor health and unfavourable circumstances.

But for Dr. Joyce Lebra's insistent advice and encouragement, my memoirs would not have seen light of the day. I value the foreword by her the most for which I shall ever remain beholden to her.

I am grateful to Prof. Harbans Lal Agnihotri for his afterword. I owe special thanks to Mrs. Chand Agnihotri and their sons, Sundeep and Maneesh for their warm hospitality during my stay with them at Hisar.

My special thanks are due to Kataria daughters, Archana, Sumedha and Rashmi for their secretarial assistance and overwhelming hospitality during my stay at Kurukshetra. I am indebted to Prof. K.L. Johar and Prof. K.C. Yadava for their kind interest in my work. Yadava lent me photos of some of the historical personalities.

Dr. B.R. Mani, L.S. Mamani and my son-in-law Rajendra Nath Mehrotra made the three maps for me. Shri Kashmiri Lal Arora typed the first copy of the manuscript. After certain changes by me Dr. Pradeep Mishra and my grandson Maneesh Mehrotra retyped the whole manuscript. I am grateful to them all. Maneesh's proximity was of great help to me in many ways.

Finally the fair copy was typed by Dr. Jyoti Bindal. She burnt midnight oil to complete the job not withstanding her busy life due to clinical and teaching work and household chores to boot. She was helped by all the Bindals, especially Amar, her husband, daughter Jyotsana and son Aditya who loves typing. Jyoti has a flair for the English language, and enjoys exactitude in expression. I found her suggestions objective, hence valuable.

The credit for suggesting the title, FROM MY BONES, to this book goes to a recent friend, Mr. Roger White A. Brit. He hails from Wales, the famous principality of Great Britain. We were chance co-travellers to Singapore by an Air India flight from Delhi on 14th December, 1995. I shall ever remember him and his good turn with gratitude.

I am indebted to the past and present doctors of Gwalior Medical College from whom I received regular medical care. Presently I am being looked after by Dr. S.B. Gupta, Dr. S.M. Tiwari, Captain Dr. Uday Bhonsle and Mrs. Bhonsley, Dr. Satish Setiya, Dr. Satya Sao, Dr. Purshotam Dutta and doctors at the Goel Dental Clinic. Similarly I owe my gratitude to doctors at Shivpuri in general and particularly to Dr. D.C. Chaudhary, Dr. R.N. Dhingra and at village Hatod to Dr. Pritam Singh Sandhu for providing medical cover with care and warmth.

My children and their children call me Tatu. This title of endearment was bestowed on me by my daughter Amrita, when she was a baby and was learning to speak, little knowing that in Sanskrit father is called Taat and Tatu becomes its natural derivative. I love the word. Tatu family is an ever growing unit of mankind. It comprises of high and low, irrespective of their station in life. The grace with which good wishes, love, respect and help have been showered on me by them notwithstanding their distance in space and time from me, obliges me to remain under their debt of gratitude for ever. I do not want to decrease this obligation by counting their names or saying thanks. I bless them all and wish them happy and glorious future. Hope they may enjoy reading the following pages of their Tatu's past.

I shall ever remain indebted to Shrimati Shyama and Shri G. Sagar Suri and the member of Suri family for their overwhelming hospitality to make me feel at home during my various visits to Delhi. I am grateful to my publishers M/s Aryan Books International for bringing out the book in an elegant manner and within very short time.

With best wishes to my readers,

Jai Hind!

G.S. Dhillon

Dhillon's Den
Village Hatod
Shivpuri - 473551
Madhya Pradesh (India)

ACKNOWLEDGEMENTS

I am and shall ever remain gratefully indebted to the following for their kind and objective observation of some of my actions during the war by name or by reference to the period or the area of operations of the 4th Guerrilla Regiment of the Indian National Army which I had the honour to command in the service of my country and thereafter facing the trial for waging war against His Majesty the King Emperor :-

Bhulabhai J. Desai - *INA Defence,* published by Rajkamal Publications at the Albion Press Delhi, 1946.

Moti Ram - *Two Historic Trials in Red Fort,* printed by M.L. Sabharwal at the Roxy Printing Press, New Delhi, 1946.

S.A. Ayer, *Unto Him a Witness - The Story of Netaji Subhas Chandra Bose in East Asia*, Bombay, 1951.

Hugh Toye, *The Springing Tiger - A Study of Subhas Chandra Bose,* Allied Publishers Private Ltd., 15 Graham Road, Ballard Estate, Bombay 1, 1959.

Report to the Combined Chiefs of Staff by the Supreme Allied Commander, South-East Asia 1943-45, Vice Admiral The Earl Mountbatten of Burma, The English Book Store, 7-L, Connaught Circus, New Delhi - 1, 1960.

Field-Marshal Sir William Slim - *Defeat into Victory,* Four Square Books Limited, 173, New Bond Street, London, Reproduced, 1960.

Joyce C. Lebra, *Jungle Alliance: Japan and the Indian National Army,* Singapore, Asia Pacific Press, 1970.

General Mohan Singh - *Soldiers' Contribution to Indian Independence,* published by S. Attar Singh, Army Educational Stores, New Delhi - 28, 1974.

1

Beginnings and Endings

The scene is the Punjab in August 1947. Roads and routes are sodden from incessant rains which are lashing the land in all their fury. Travel is difficult and dangerous.

Condemned to an uncertain future, driven out of their native homes, dishonoured, displaced and dispossessed of their entire belongings, millions are on the move from east to west and west to east, constantly being attacked, harassed, hunted and hounded by bloodthirsty fanatic mobs on both sides of the newly drawn international border which has divided the subcontinent of India and split the Punjab—the land of five rivers and granary of India. Punjab, the original home and cradle of all Indo-Aryan cultures, Punjab- 'the Sword Arm of India', lies broken and prostrate.

Civility and compassion, the very inherent part of the Punjabi nature, seem to have taken wings. Humanity has run amok. Humans act worse than wild beasts.

In the prevailing chaos, urged by the sheer natural instinct of self-preservation, bewildered and dazed, people move off in disordered haste, carrying some hurriedly salvaged wherewithal on their bullock-carts, on animals or on themselves. They know not where to go to. After drifting hither and thither, the uprooted and homeless people merge into unorganized and irregular columns called caravans - kafila - of fellow refugees.

Along a caravan, plodding through the mud, leading her grandchildren and daughters-in-law and various other kin, is a gentle old lady. She carries her seventy years lightly and with rare grace and fortitude. Beside her riding on a horse is her husband suffering from arthritis. His personal arms have been confiscated by the police. A man proud of his firearms is now unarmed and insecure. Their progress is slow. They are passing through the worst days of their life. At this crucial hour none of their sons is with them; they are all away at different posts unaware of the disaster at home.

'Misfortunes never come alone', she thinks. On the second day after the move, their bullock-carts are bogged down in the mud. By nightfall they are attacked by fearful Fanatic mobs and are forced to abandon most of their carts along with their loaded effects. Raiders abducted a number of screaming young girls who could not be saved. One of the girls was a newly-wedded niece of the lady - the daughter of her husband's younger brother. She could never be recovered.

Next day a baby is born in the family under the shelter of a bullock- cart which is the only protection against wind and rain. There is neither a doctor nor midwife nor any medicines. The old lady is the only help under those helpless conditions. With abounding sorrow, suffering and shame, drenched to the skin in the pouring rain, the old lady, though exhausted, cares less for herself but for others. Children are crying for food. Elders find it difficult to walk but camping for rest is fraught with danger. The caravan has to continue moving onward and forward; that is the only option. It is a forced march into the unknown. The march continues.

On the fourth night, the rain relents a bit. The following morning the sun rises in all its glory, yet there is gloom all around. In the dark of night they have crossed the border and entered India - that is, Bharat.

In the light of day, the lady is pleasantly surprised as she recognises some familiar ground seen after a lapse of about half a century. And lo! approaching those houses she sees her ancestral village. This is the place where she was born and brought up. She recalls her childhood and girlhood, carefree days under the shadow of parental love and affection. For a moment she enjoys blissful memories of the past, her father lavishing unbounded adoration on her, she being the only daughter, a precious sister of four affectionate brothers. Even in the days when a daughter was considered a debt and liability, her parents felt proud of her. Her father gave her an auspicious name Bhago - meaning good luck. He had brought her up to be a strong, hardworking, determined, fearless and courageous person. She used to love to carry her father's midday meals to his fields where he would be ploughing. He used to collect seasonal vegetables and fruits for her to carry back home, which she would share with others. He taught her horse-riding and she could ride any horse well and with confidence.

She remembers her girlhood with her, *sahelees* - girl friends. She recalls the old songs and folklore when she could sing, swing on the swings under village trees, dance, laugh and cry without feeling ashamed. She thinks of their continuous *charkha*-spinning sessions along with devotional songs unbroken for days on end until a brother would bring sweets and pray that they break their fast and stop spinning. The faces of her *sahelees* separated long ago return vividly before her eyes. She recalls their wedding and her own marriage and the sad farewell songs.

We are a flock of sparrows.

O father, we must fly away.

(Chirian da chamba ve, babal asan ud janan)

Bitter sweet memories give her a feeling of nostalgia. She is transported into the past, into the lap of her mother. This changes helplessness and hopelessness into hope and confidence. With assurance that she will now be able to get some food and a respite for her children, she steps out of the caravan. Her pace quickens as she makes for the nearest big house where a woman standing in a partly open door watches her approach. The old lady has yet to make a request, when the door is shut in her face with stinging words, "Go, you old mother, go. Go away, we can't feed you millions passing this way everyday." The old lady is stunned. She tries to swallow the insult of not having been recognized even at her own ancestral village, which though she had left when she was young. With a lump in her throat, controlling her tears, she quickly and silently falls back into the caravan, unable to share the terrible tragedy with any one.

That is her "Tryst with Destiny". Oh! what a tryst and at what price ?

The lady is my mother.

The village is Algon.

Here I was born at noon on Wednesday, the 18th of March 1914. Algon was in Lahore district before Partition. Presently it is in Amritsar district of Punjab in India. However, my date of birth as recorded in my school leaving certificate and the subsequent official documents was shown as April 4, 1915.

Acknowledgements

I am and shall ever remain gratefully indebted to the following for their kind and objective observation of some of my actions during the war by name or by reference to the period or the area of operations of the 4th Guerrilla Regiment of the Indian National Army which I had the honour to command in the service of my country and thereafter facing the trial for waging war against His Majesty the King Emperor :-

Bhulabhai J. Desai - *INA Defence,* published by Rajkamal Publications at the Albion Press Delhi, 1946.

Moti Ram - *Two Historic Trials in Red Fort,* printed by M.L. Sabharwal at the Roxy Printing Press, New Delhi, 1946.

S.A. Ayer, *Unto Him a Witness - The Story of Netaji Subhas Chandra Bose in East Asia*, Bombay, 1951.

Hugh Toye, *The Springing Tiger - A Study of Subhas Chandra Bose,* Allied Publishers Private Ltd., 15 Graham Road, Ballard Estate, Bombay 1, 1959.

Report to the Combined Chiefs of Staff by the Supreme Allied Commander, South-East Asia 1943-45, Vice Admiral The Earl Mountbatten of Burma, The English Book Store, 7-L, Connaught Circus, New Delhi - 1, 1960.

Field-Marshal Sir William Slim - *Defeat into Victory,* Four Square Books Limited, 173, New Bond Street, London, Reproduced, 1960.

Joyce C. Lebra, *Jungle Alliance: Japan and the Indian National Army,* Singapore, Asia Pacific Press, 1970.

General Mohan Singh - *Soldiers' Contribution to Indian Independence,* published by S. Attar Singh, Army Educational Stores, New Delhi - 28, 1974.

Her Majesty's Stationery Office - *The Transfer of Power 1942-47*, Volume VI, *The Post-War Phase: New Moves by the Labour Government,* 1 August 1945 - 22 March 1946, printed in England by Vivian Ridler at the University Press, Oxford, 1976.

Lt. General S.L. Menezes, PVSM, SC, *Fidelity & Honour - The Indian Army - From the Seventeenth to the Twenty First Century,* Viking Penguin India, 1993.

A Beacon Across Asia, edited by Sisir K. Bose, Alexander Werth and S.A. Ayer, published by Orient Longman.

H.N. Pandit - *Netaji Subhas Chandra Bose: From Kabul to Battle of Imphal,* Sterling Publishers Private Limited.

Peter Ward Fay - *The Forgotten Army*, Rupa & Co.

Leonard A. Gordon - *Brothers Against The Raj,* Viking Penguin Books (India) Limited.

from Wales, the famous principality of Great Britain. We were chance co-travellers to Singapore by an Air India flight from Delhi on 14th December, 1995. I shall ever remember him and his good turn with gratitude.

I am indebted to the past and present doctors of Gwalior Medical College from whom I received regular medical care. Presently I am being looked after by Dr. S.B. Gupta, Dr. S.M. Tiwari, Captain Dr. Uday Bhonsle and Mrs. Bhonsley, Dr. Satish Setiya, Dr. Satya Sao, Dr. Purshotam Dutta and doctors at the Goel Dental Clinic. Similarly I owe my gratitude to doctors at Shivpuri in general and particularly to Dr. D.C. Chaudhary, Dr. R.N. Dhingra and at village Hatod to Dr. Pritam Singh Sandhu for providing medical cover with care and warmth.

My children and their children call me Tatu. This title of endearment was bestowed on me by my daughter Amrita, when she was a baby and was learning to speak, little knowing that in Sanskrit father is called Taat and Tatu becomes its natural derivative. I love the word. Tatu family is an ever growing unit of mankind. It comprises of high and low, irrespective of their station in life. The grace with which good wishes, love, respect and help have been showered on me by them notwithstanding their distance in space and time from me, obliges me to remain under their debt of gratitude for ever. I do not want to decrease this obligation by counting their names or saying thanks. I bless them all and wish them happy and glorious future. Hope they may enjoy reading the following pages of their Tatu's past.

I shall ever remain indebted to Shrimati Shyama and Shri G. Sagar Suri and the member of Suri family for their overwhelming hospitality to make me feel at home during my various visits to Delhi. I am grateful to my publishers M/s Aryan Books International for bringing out the book in an elegant manner and within very short time.

With best wishes to my readers,

Jai Hind!

G.S. Dhillon

Dhillon's Den
Village Hatod
Shivpuri - 473551
Madhya Pradesh (India)

with which Prof. Bernier, Dr. Joyce Lebra and their colleagues agreed to my backing out of all the arrangements they had made was indeed magnanimous. I shall ever remain under a debt of gratitude to them.

Again, a similar invitation was given by Poonam Sibbal and her parents, Col. & Mrs. M.C. Sibbal from Dehra Dun and yet another standing invitation from my son-like J.K. Agarwal from Meerut. But I could not avail myself of their golden opportunities due to my poor health and unfavourable circumstances.

But for Dr. Joyce Lebra's insistent advice and encouragement, my memoirs would not have seen light of the day. I value the foreword by her the most for which I shall ever remain beholden to her.

I am grateful to Prof. Harbans Lal Agnihotri for his afterword. I owe special thanks to Mrs. Chand Agnihotri and their sons, Sundeep and Maneesh for their warm hospitality during my stay with them at Hisar.

My special thanks are due to Kataria daughters, Archana, Sumedha and Rashmi for their secretarial assistance and overwhelming hospitality during my stay at Kurukshetra. I am indebted to Prof. K.L. Johar and Prof. K.C. Yadava for their kind interest in my work. Yadava lent me photos of some of the historical personalities.

Dr. B.R. Mani, L.S. Mamani and my son-in-law Rajendra Nath Mehrotra made the three maps for me. Shri Kashmiri Lal Arora typed the first copy of the manuscript. After certain changes by me Dr. Pradeep Mishra and my grandson Maneesh Mehrotra retyped the whole manuscript. I am grateful to them all. Maneesh's proximity was of great help to me in many ways.

Finally the fair copy was typed by Dr. Jyoti Bindal. She burnt midnight oil to complete the job not withstanding her busy life due to clinical and teaching work and household chores to boot. She was helped by all the Bindals, especially Amar, her husband, daughter Jyotsana and son Aditya who loves typing. Jyoti has a flair for the English language, and enjoys exactitude in expression. I found her suggestions objective, hence valuable.

The credit for suggesting the title, FROM MY BONES, to this book goes to a recent friend, Mr. Roger White A. Brit. He hails

2

Heritage

The Indo-Aryan stock is tall, sturdy, strong, handsome, industrious and adventurous. Though varying in religious beliefs and practices, the Jats predominantly inhabit areas falling in Pakistan, Punjab, Haryana and Western Uttar Pradesh of India. Besides constituting the finest peasantry of the subcontinent, the Jat community has produced valiant warriors, poets, patriots, great administrators, eminent scholars, saints and sages throughout the ages. Their clans are named after their gotras, sub-castes or clans. My father and mother were descendants of the Dhillon and Dhariwal Sikh Jat clans, respectively.

The Dhillons enjoy recognition and a status among their Jat brethren. They are often addressed as 'Dhillon Padshah' - Dhillon Majesty. This courtesy shown by a Jat to a Jat is gratifying, for a Jat, though simple and straightforward, is sensitively self-respecting and proud of his birth irrespective of his station in life but choosy in bestowing praise on others. The Dhillons owe their happy position to the outstanding exploits of their forefathers in the field of war and statecraft, apart from their generally easy-going and genial nature.

Early in the eighteenth century during the decline of the Mughal empire, four Dhillon Hindu Jats—Chaudhuries Chhaja Singh, Bhim Singh, Mala Singh and Jagat Singh—of Panjwar, a village eight miles from Amritsar, embraced Sikhism. Under the command of Sardar Chhaja Singh they set up a Dal comprising a force of twelve thousand strong. It was the first of the twelve Sikh Misls which came into being during that period. It was named the Panjwarya Misl but more commonly called the Bhangi Misl, because they were fond of bhang, an intoxicating drink made of the leaves of hemp.

After the death of Sardar Chhaja Singh, Sardar Bhim Singh led the Misl successfully with ability, making it a well equipped, organized and disciplined force. With Amritsar as their base, they operated far and wide. The capture of the big gun, the **Zamzama** at Ramnagar and the occupation of Lahore which they held for thirty years, are some of their outstanding exploits. **Zamzama** is displayed as a showpiece of history in front of the Museum at Lahore. It is popularly called "Bhangion ki Tope" after the name of the Misl. The Misl held sway over most of the Mahjha region of the Punjab till the advent of Maharaja Ranjit Singh of the Sukerchakya Misl who occupied Lahore in 1799 and set up his Raj as the sole sovereign of the Punjab.

But more important than the military and political exploits are the attainments of a simple peasant - an old man—the venerable Baba Buddha. He was held in such a high esteem by the successive Sikh Gurus that he is believed to have enjoyed the unique honour of having been called to install six out of the ten Gurus on the spiritual throne, the **Gaddi,** though actually he did install five Gurus for Guru Nanak had not been formally installed by anybody. He spent much of his active life in the jungles around Jhabal (Beer) near Amritsar, where he reared his herd of cattle. A simple and pious Randhawa Jat, Baba Buddha was the pride of all Sikh Jats and the Sikhs.

Far from pretending any claim to the great Dhillon dynasties, I have enjoyed being just a Dhillon right from my childhood. This natural sense of belonging to the lineage has been responsible to an extent in moulding my own character.

My family was of a humble origin. Narwar, our ancestral village, is in Lahore district today as it was before the partition of India. It is about 28 kilometres from Amritsar across the border. My grandfather, Sardar Jawahar Singh was of an ascetic temperament and devoted all his time to prayers and to the service of the Sikh temple (gurudwara). The granthi (Sikh priest) was so much enamonred of him that he married his daughter, his only child to Jawahar Singh. Out of this wedlock were born two sons, Sardar Harbhajan Singh and Sardar Natha Singh.

Sardar Harbhajan Singh was my grandfather. He learnt Urdu and

Persian and was employed as a Patwari, the lowest revenue official. As a mark of appreciation of his diligence and creditable service, he was promoted as Kanungo, land revenue inspector. Towards the end of the nineteenth century with the advent of canals when new colonies were opened in the Punjab, he was awarded a *murabba,* 25 acres of land, under the Upper Bari Doab canal in Chak No. 32 near Chhanga Manga in Chunian tehsil of Lahore district. After retirement, he migrated to the new land. In those days it was quite a challenge to reclaim a virgin forest.

Incidentally, my grandfather lost his eyesight. My recollections of him are that of a blind old man walking with a stick holding someone's hand. He had a terrible temper and it was not a pleasant job to lead him but somehow I loved his company on long evening walks along the canal bank near our village. Once I asked him, "Babaji. How did you lose your eyesight?". He said, "One day as I was crossing the canal over the bridge, I saw some women bathing naked in the canal. I stood there to watch them. They got annoyed and cursed me, so I got blind". I asked, "Babaji I have seen pictures of Lord Krishna hiding in a tree with women's clothes and the women concealing their bodies in the river water. Didn't they curse Krishna? Why didn't He go blind like you?" The grandpa replied, "You see, it is the intention of an act which determines the ethics of it. Bhagwan Krishna was the greatest Master, a Divine Teacher. He intended to teach those girls a lesson not to take naked bath in the open. Krishna was holy. I was wicked, so l got blind". My grand- father died in 1928 when I was just a student of the 7th standard.

My father Sardar Thakar Singh was the first child of his parents. He was three days old when his mother died and was brought up by his mother's younger sister Har Kaur, called Haro, whom my grandfather married. Since she remained childless, grandfather contracted another marriage with Maalaan, who gave birth to three sons and two daughters, all very much younger than my father. As the eldest son, my father shared with grandfather the responsibility of bringing up his younger brothers and sisters. Bebe Maalaan died early. I do not remember seeing her.

As far as we children were concerned, Bebe Haro was our grandmother. She always lived with my parents. We fondly addressed her as Bebe. Short of stature but lofty in ideas, she offered a wonderful company. As I look back, I can still visualize being cuddled up in her warm bed along with other children listening to the bedtime stories as she quietly distributed dried fruit, candy or sweets and parched corn or gram which she saved for us out of her own share. I have always cherished the heavenly bliss that tenderly enveloped us in complete fearlessness and sense of sublime security under her wings.

The Bebe had a kind heart. She loved animals and each morning would be seen feeding small birds, sparrows and doves, filling little bowls with water for birds and dogs. During the hot summer noon, she would personally water and bathe little calves. She enjoyed excellent health. I never saw her ill. She was her own doctor, prescribing simple treatments. Her curative agents were hot or cold water and milk, sugared or salted curds, butter or mustard oil massage, hot or cold bath, alum, camphor, asafoetida, garlic, onions and honey taken in different doses and in different ways.

She had a great sense of humour and would make us laugh with her anecdotes narrated in a poetic vein. Amrik, my younger brother, once remarked, "If Bebe had been to school she would have become a great poet". She lived a long life spanning over 90 years and died in 1944 of sheer old age, the only disease for which there is no cure. My mother often used to say, "I owe all my happiness and prosperity to Bebe's blessings. May god bless her soul ! She never scolded me as mothers-in-law would".

My father started his education rather late. There was no school in the village. He had to go all the way to Lahore even for primary education, where he lived in a rented room shared by other boys from the village. They had to cook for themselves and would come home on weekends.

My father got married when he was still a child: he passed his 4th class after his marriage. Being a bright student, he wished to go in for higher education but grandfather decided otherwise, which would save him two rupees a month. Fourth class was considered a standard of qualification good enough for getting a clerical job. My father had just attained his majority and it was considered proper that he should start earning for himself and for the family. My father did not wish to have an office job because he wanted to be a soldier. Accordingly, he presented himself before the Recruiting Officer at Lahore for enlistment in a cavalry unit. To his disappointment, his chest was found two inches too small. He was told to go back, build up his chest and report thereafter.

Back at the village, some one advised him to take plenty of milk and ghee and to exercise his chest muscles with a pair of dumb-bells. He purchased an old acacia (babool) tree from his neighbour's field and himself cut it down; then with the help of the village carpenter he fashioned two heavy dumb-bells. The remaining wood was sold as timber and fuel. In this bargain he got his dumb-bells free and made some profit too. Till the partition of India, those dumb-bells were preserved in the family.

During the days when my father was building up his chest, he had a lot of spare time which he utilized in salvaging clay from the bottom of the village pond. He kneaded it and moulded it into bricks and got them sun-baked. Thus by the time he was fit to be recruited, he had single-handedly got enough bricks made to construct a decent mud house of his own. Then he went to the Recruiting Officer and got enlisted as a sowar in the 8th K.G.O. (King George's Own) Light Cavalry. A sowar's pay in those days used to be seven rupees per month plus free rations and kit. If a sowar at the time of joining the service paid three hundred rupees as the price of his horse, it was considered a sort of status symbol, and the sowar enjoyed the privilege of taking the horse fully harnessed to his home while going on long leave. He could wear his uniform and the village headmen en route were obliged to provide food and fodder. It gave the soldier pride in his uniform and boosted his morale. As a child, I used to listen to father's accounts of riding all the way from Bangalore and Secunderabad in the south to Lahore in the north, marvelling over the vastness of India and varieties of her people and their cultures.

The payment for the horse and his educational qualification gave my father a good start in service. He got an early promotion and was selected to be trained as a veterinary surgeon. He happened to be stationed at Ferozepur when I was born.

3

CHILDHOOD

"Isn't he a scraggly, skinny, dark little creature ? What an ugly specimen of a boy!" were my father's opening remarks on seeing me for the first time. I must have been a great disappointment to him. He had travelled all the way from Ferozepur to Algon just to have a look at me.

I was the fourth child of my parents. My elder siblings were brother Gurdial Singh, sister Tej Kaur - (Tejo), who expired as a teenager, and brother Balwant Singh. I was named Gurbakhsh Singh, normally called Bakhshi or Bashki. My father would call me Chappan, meaning a round lid of an earthen pot. I resented being addressed by this name except by my father and mother. My resentment often landed me in little combats with my siblings.

My earliest recollections are of living under a huge tent at the slope of a hillock which I loved running up and down. I would often fall while trying to compete with other children especially while climbing down. My hands and knees often got badly injured which would smart when treated with tincture-iodine. Injuries apart, my greater regret used to be the imposition of a ban on my climbing the hill. The ban was seldom lifted. I was always obliged to break it and in the process repeat the story again and again.

This place was at Deolali in the Bombay Presidency, now in Maharashtra. Here the Army Remount Base Depot was set up during World War I. It was a big establishment occupying a vast area of land spread over many miles, with long sheds, stables, horse ponds, big enclosures and riding schools with deep sawdust to break a fall. Hundreds of men and women were employed to look after the place, horses and mules.

Train loads of horses and mules untouched by man from the ranches of various parts of the British Empire, were brought here in thousands to be broken—to make them obey and get accustomed to the saddle and the bridle before drafting them to different theatres of war. On their arrival at the Depot, these remounts especially Waler horses from Australia were violent wild beasts that hated the very sight of man and would react against any approach in a hostile manner by snorting and baring teeth viciously, biting and kicking into the air.

The horse-trainers had a challenging job that demanded courage, patience, resourcefulness and great experience in horsemanship. Treating the sick and injured animals was an even more difficult and dangerous job. There was a big team of veterinary surgeons, dressers, syces (stablemen or grooms) to do this duty. My father was the head veterinary surgeon at the Depot.

It was at Deolali that my younger sister and brother Amrik Singh were born. There was an old Maratha lady, Tara Bai, who was our ayah-nurse. She was so much respected by my parents and loved by us children that my sister was given her name Taro Bibi by this lady and the suggestion was accepted to perpetuate Tara Bai's memory in the family.

I learnt horse-riding very early. As young horses could not accompany their mothers going to the war, when a mare was due to be sent to the front, her foal was destroyed by shooting it in the head. The rules were so strict that the British Officer Commanding the Depot had to be present to watch personally the destruction of foals. One day I saw a foal being taken to be shot. Out of compassion I ran up to the Commanding Officer and pleaded with him to spare the life of the foal. The Commander called father and told him that as a special case, he would give the foal to me provided that it was well cared for and not sold off.

My father took the responsibility and I got the young horse which grew to be a graceful animal with lovable manners. It was on this very horse that I learnt riding. A British farrier, Mr. Green, used to be my instructor. Green Sahib, as I used to call him, loved Indian food. It is amazing how little things remain embedded in one's memory. Once

I had a fall from the horse and was reluctant to ride again. Green got hold of the horse, pulled one of its ears close to his mouth and acted as if saying something. Then he got hold of horse's mouth close to his own ear, the horse nibbled at Green's ear and hair. Green turned to me and remarked that the horse was friendly and had promised not to be rash again. Encouraged thus, I rode the horse.

I remember a pilgrimage to Panchavati at Nasik on the banks of the sparkling waters of the river Godavari. The place is hallowed by the association of Lord Rama who spent some of the eventful days in his exile in the company of his consort Sita and brother Lakshmana.

Once my father took us on a trip to Bombay where I saw the sea and ships for the first time. An unforgettable scene that shows sister Tejo sitting on a rock laughing and playing with the waves splashing against the seashore close to the Gateway of India remains embedded in my memory. She died soon after returning to the Punjab. Ever since it has been a regular feature of my schedule to visit the spot whenever I happened to be in the city.

Under the Depot arrangement, a dresser called Mohammad Bakhsh ran a school for the children of the Camp. I did not like attending the school because the teacher often beat the pupils. One day when I failed to recite numerals in the correct order he raised his cane to hit me but before he could do that, I hurled my slate at his face and ran away.

Afraid of going back home, I went to my grand uncle, father's uncle, Baba Natha Singh who lived in a room at the end of the Depot hospital. He gave me a drink and some sweets which I relished. When I asked for more sweets, Baba gave me drinks also. Soon I was drunk. I tumbled out of his room and went to a water tap in front of the hospital. There were several buckets near the tap. I sat in a bucket and got stuck in it. All my efforts to extricate myself failed. The hospital had closed for the noon and there was nobody around to help me. It was hot sunny day. I was forced to spend the whole afternoon in the metal bucket without any shade.

When the hospital was to open for the evening shift at 4 o' clock and dressers came to collect their buckets, a dresser rescued me. He took me home where my long absence had created quite an anxiety.

The school episode was forgotten. I started fearing Baba Natha Singh and took to going to the school regularly. After the school hours, I loved watching horses being tamed and trained. Soldiers in uniform impressed me much.

After the death of sister Tejo, my mother went back to the Punjab taking along with her my brother Balwant Singh, my sister Taro Bibi, and my brother Amrik Singh. I was left at Deolali to remain with father. By that time the Great War had ended. The Depot was to be closed. Everyone was planning to go back home. Every soldier was in the grip of homesickness. In the evening my father often recited the poem of Josef and Zulekha. It was believed that the regular recitation of the poem would hasten the reunion of soldiers with their beloved ones in the same manner as Josef had been reunited with Zulekha and his folk. Incidentally, the poem recounted how Josef, the estranged son of Jacob, had returned after a long exile from Egypt where he had been sold off as a slave. Since my father had good voice, it was a treat to hear him recite. He got me an air-gun with which I loved to play a soldier.

In 1919 we left Deolali. My father got an appointment at home in the Army Remount Department which looked after the breeding and rearing of fresh horses and mules by farmers who were given twenty-five acres of land for keeping a pedigreed mare approved by the Department. The land thus granted was known as "Ghoripal Murrabba"- land for keeping a mare. The grown-up foals reared on such fields were purchased by the Government for the Army. The farmers chosen for the award were ex-servicemen with their distinguished record of war service. If the awardee of a Ghoripal Murrabba did not look after his mare and her progeny well, he was liable to be fined or to forfeit the awarded land.

With his headquarters fixed at his village Chak No. 32, commonly called Batti Chak (Batti means 32 in Punjabi), my father's jurisdiction covered the area falling under the tehsil (sub-division) of Chunian in the district of Lahore. This special facility was extended to my father in recognition of his services during the war and also in view of my grandfather's blindness.

Batti Chak was a lovely little village. It was a typical new village. Its broad streets were all of equal width of about sixty feet each. One main street ran in the middle connecting the eastern end to the western part of the village. It was crossed at right angles by three equally broad streets from north to south. Even as a child standing in a street I could easily point out the Pole star and main geographical directions without the help of a compass.

There was a big pond in the east and another on the west of the village. These ponds which came into being in the process when earth had to be dug out for raising houses in the village formed a vital part of the village environment. They presented a wonderful sight at sunrise and particularly at sunset when the cattle came home slowly, sipping water en route and raising dust before rushing to their fodder-filled mangers. The dust, thus raised, had an aroma of its own. Its very thought has always reminded me of my village and often made me homesick irrespective of distance in time and space.

There was a well in the centre of the village. It served the entire village comprising of about five hundred people belonging to different communities. There was a metre high brick platform around the well on which four wooden hand-wheels with ropes were fixed for drawing water buckets. The members of the lower caste were not allowed to draw water on their own from this platform. The curse of untouchability was taken for granted by all including the poor souls who would place their pitchers at the ground level and wait for some member of an upper caste to pour water from above.

Normally this job was performed by water carriers called Mehras amongst the Hindus and the Sikhs and their Muslim counterparts called Bihisthi or Mashki. When I was big enough to draw water, I took pleasure in serving these folks. Notwithstanding the curse of untouchability, all communities lived in harmony. Due respect was shown to the elderly and the aged irrespective of their caste, creed or station in life. An elderly person would normally be addressed in a manner as if he or she were an adult relative or a friend of one's parents.

Quite close to the well there was a big wooden platform approximately a metre high, three metres broad and six metres long. There were also a few old tree trunks placed around the platform spread out to serve as benches to sit upon. It was a meeting place where after hard day's work men would come to relax and chit-chat. A visiting

The author, Col. Gurbakhsh Singh Dhillon

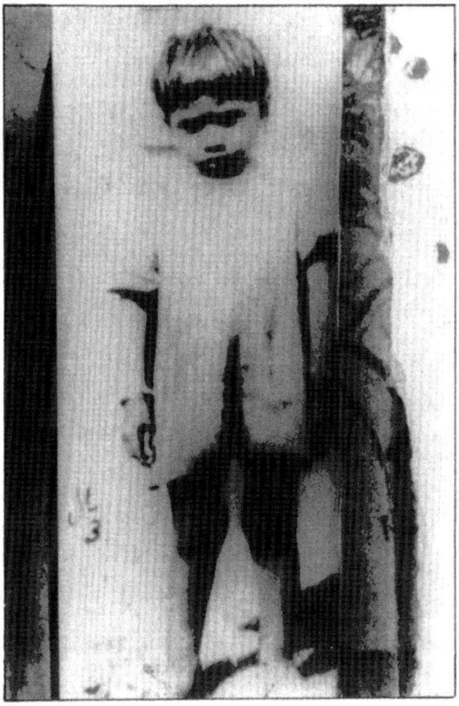

The author at the age of 4

At the age of 6

With his mother (1977)

Sardar Thakar Singh Dhillon
(Author's Father)

Father and eldest brother Gurdial Singh

With his eldest brother Gurdial Singh Dhillon

With wife Basant (1960)

With wife (1966)

As 2nd Lieutenant (1941)

In INA'S 4th Guerrilla Regiment

With wife and children (1956)

With mother, wife and children (1966)

government officer would be received at this spot. It was also a meeting place for the village Panchayat.

A Panchayat was not an elected body before the independence. It was a fraternal assembly of leading respectable elders of the village community irrespective of their religion or caste. A member of this body was called Panch. It was an institution with age-old traditions for collectively sorting out disputes and common problems and also for safeguarding the village common land called Shamlat and other interests of the community. By and large, the decisions of the village panchayat used to be fair and unanimous so long as the interest of the the upper caste were not in jeopardy.

Towards the north of the village about five hundred yards away, there flowed a canal from east to west. It irrigated our fields. Except for the rainy season its water was clear and clean and refreshingly fit for human consumption. Its proximity to the village was a boon to the people and the cattle alike. There was a well maintained motorable track on its left bank that was used by the canal inspecting officers. Others, except the government officials, had to get permission to use the track. It was good for a road walk and running practice.

There was a railway bridge of steel over the canal in the north-westerly direction and a masonry bridge for a road crossing in the north-easterly direction from the village. Both these bridges were about a mile apart from each other and made prominent landmarks. There were also popular washing, bathing and swimming spots. While quite young, I learnt diving and swimming. Near the eastern bridge there was a rare specimen of a botanical wonder. Lala Ruldu Ram, one of the pioneer settlers of the village, had planted two saplings of two different trees belonging to the fig family, a pipal, *Ficus religiosa*, regarded sacred by most Indians and especially by the Buddhists, for it was under a pipal tree that Lord Buddha attained enlightenment and a banyan, *Ficus benghalensis*, having large and thick oval leaves, reddish fruit, and many aerial roots that develop with age into additional trunks.

At the time of planting these saplings Lala Ruldu Ram had entwined the two saplings so well that they had embedded into each other to form a single trunk grown together as one beautiful umbrella-shaped canopy of lighter green and dark green leaves. A passer-by crossing the bridge could not help stopping there to admire this wonder of nature. During hot summer days, birds, cattle and men would love to spend their long lazy afternoons under the shady tree made cooler by the blowing wind that brushed against the foliage after it had kissed canal water on its way.

During summer vacation our parents allowed us to go to this shady place to spend some afternoons on the condition that we would not swim and thus avoid drowning. Children were strictly prohibited to go there. Once my youngest brother Dalip Singh, who was about five years old, stole out of the house and stealthily followed me. Instead of bringing him back to home, I told him to remain under the tree and not to enter the water. I, however, enjoyed diving from the highest point of the bridge feeling confident that Dalip was resting under the tree. I had warned him by cooking a story not to go near the water as there were crocodiles in the canal which carried away young children.

I remained merrily engaged in diving and swimming. Once when I was just going to dive from the top of the bridge, I saw a bunch of hair carried down by the current as a head bobbed in the water. It was about fifty yards distant from me. Without knowing whose head it was, spontaneously I rushed to the bobbing head. As I raised it above the water, I was stunned to find that it was Dalip. Nervously he clung to me and I brought him to the bank. Luckily, he did not suffer any injury. I asked him why he had entered the water. His reply was, "As I came to drink water from the canal, I slipped into the water and a crocodile took me away". Bidding him not to talk about the accident to anybody, we quietly came back home. Dalip grew to a handsome young man of 18 years when he died of jaundice in 1937. His death drastically affected my life which I have refrained from narrating in these memoirs.

4

Education

There was no school in our village. The parents desirous of sending their sons to school had to send them two miles away to Chhanga Manga. Educating girls was something unheard of in that part of the country in those days. Chhanga Manga was a station on Multan line of the North Western Railway connecting Lahore and Karachi. It is famous for its forest of rosewood of the genus of Delbergia commonly called Sheesham (*Tali* in Punjabi) and mulberry (*Toot* in Punjabi). These trees were planted by the Punjab Forest Department in an area of 144 square miles. It is irrigated by perennial canals.

The Government primary school at Chhanga Manga had no building of its own. Classes were held under trees or under somebody's shed or in a gurudwara or in an old caravanserai of the Mughal period. It was not a satisfactory arrangement at all. I was sent to Patoki nine miles away but the arrangement did not work and I had to return to Chhanga Manga. In the meantime, my father managed to get a Government primary school established in our village by providing land and building free of charge for ten years till the village Panchayat could allot a common land to the school.

My youngest brother Dalip Singh was born when I was in the third standard. After passing 4th class, I attended a number of schools, namely, Government High School, Chunian in district Lahore; Government High School, Dipalpore in district Montgomery; Vernacular Middle School, Raiwind in district Lahore; Victoria Dalip High School, Solan in Baghat State of Simla Hills; Dayananda Anglo Vernacular (D.A.V.) High School, Montgomery and lastly Gordon Mission College, Rawalpindi. Whatever I am, I owe to these institutions.

When I joined the Government High School in the fifth class at Chunian, my elder brother Balwant Singh was already there as a student of the 7th class. He was always very kind to me. We lived in the school boarding house and came home on holidays. Chunian was famous as the birthplace of Raja Todar Mal, the giver of the land revenue laws to India. He was one of the nine jewels of Emperor Akbar the Great.

Boy Scouts Association

At Chunian, brother Balwant Singh and I enrolled ourselves in the Boy Scouts Association. I joined as a cub. We went to participate in the great Jamboree held at Lahore. Here we met Lord Baden-Powell, the father of the worldwide organization which he founded in England in 1908 for the youth to develop character, practical skills, self-reliance and resourcefulness. By inculcating in the scouts the spirit of helping the needy, we were taught to imbibe the maxim of doing "one good turn a day". Lord Baden-Powell's simple, jovial and friendly nature was impressive and pleasing. He would sing and dance with us. The movement left an overwhelming impact on me.

Gurudwaras Reform Movement

As a child I was very religious. I loved going to the gurudwara. The first half of the decade 1920 witnessed the Gurudwaras Reform Movement when the Sikhs under the leadership of Baba Kharak Singh peacefully struggled for the emancipation of their Gurudwaras and shrines from the clutches of the corrupt hereditary Mahants, the custodians of the shrines. The Government lent its support to the Mahants and the movement turned out to be as much against the Government as against the Mahants. It was a non-violent movement and so well-disciplined that the Hindus and the Muslims equally appreciated the cause and the conduct of the Sikhs. Even Mahatma Gandhi was thrilled with the deeds and achievements of the Sikhs. As a child, I used to see the Jathas (bands) of Sikh volunteers passing through our village on their way to Nankana Sahib, the birthplace of Guru Nanak Dev, the founder of Sikhism. The success of the movement was perhaps the most glorious and proud moment in the history of the people. It was but natural that I too should feel proud and happy.

I was fortunate in being schooled by teachers belonging to various religions. This made me appreciate the teachings of the Masters of mankind like Rama, Krishna, Mahavira, Buddha, Christ, Mohammad, Nanak, Kabir, Guru Gobind Singh, Swami Vivekananda, Swami Dayananda and Swami Ram Tirath. Not that I understood all their teachings but I learnt this much that a religion, whatever its name, is meant to make us love one another and live in harmony.

Whenever I studied any religion I did so with respect. Once reading about Prophet Mohammed I was overwhelmed to learn how his daughter Fatimah had to daily pluck out thorns and rubbish which a woman used to throw on the Prophet's head as the Prophet passed the street in front of her door. And the Prophet would not retaliate. Once when the woman did not turn up for three days consecutively, the Prophet was worried as to what was wrong with her. When he found out that she was ill, he served her with medicines and milk. The story made me cry. Some one asked me the cause of my crying. My answer stunned him and he said, "Why do you cry, you are not a Muhammadan?" My reply was, "But I am a human being and compassion has no religion". I can narrate at length similar experiences arising out of my encounter with various religions. Suffice it to say that unknowingly I was being groomed for a future in which I was destined to play a role as a nationalist quite distinct from any kind of communal approach.

My father was stationed at Dipalpore in Montgomery district and I was in the 7th class when he fell ill. He was suspected of having contracted tuberculosis whereupon Doctor Jeevan Ram of Lahore advised him to go immediately to a hill station. My mother took him to Solan in the Simla Hills. Amrik and Dalip, being young, accompanied them. Brother Balwant Singh and I were then at the school boarding house.

At times, our father could not send us funds in time to pay our school and hostel dues. The superintendent of the hostel was very strict and would allow us to have only one meal a day till the dues were cleared. Balwant Singh would then let me have the morning meal and himself ate in the evening and would steal some chapatis so as to feed me in secrecy. This way I had my two meals but Balwant Singh could have only one meal a day. He stole for me but I could not reciprocate. My conscience did not allow me to do what I was abetting him to do for me. I was too weak to commit the crime as well as to stop the crime being committed for my benefit. I wish I had higher moral and physical courage to resist the act.

The very first summer spent in the hills amongst the cool fragrance of the pine trees had a miraculous effect on father's health. He spent two more summers in the hills, but instead of living in the town of Solan he lived in a village, Barog, about a mile away from the railway station bearing the same name. With a view to augment his resources, my father took up a temporary job as manager of the Hindu refreshment room at Barog railway station. During summer vacations the whole of our family used to be together with parents at Barog.

Barog, midway between Kalka and Simla on a narrow gauge railway line, is situated at the end of a mile long tunnel. The emergence of a train out of the smoke-filled tunnel used to be a welcome relief to the passengers. Refreshingly cool mineral water gushing out of the mountain and fragrant cool breezes blowing all over the place gave one an impression of having come to an altogether different world. There were three refreshment rooms which catered each for the English, the Hindus and the Muslims.

Apart from these refreshment rooms, there were various food-stalls. The service provided at all these places used to be excellent. Simla was the summer capital of India. During the summer season special trains were run to cope with the rush of passengers. Each train normally stopped for a period ranging from half an hour to three-quarters of an hour so as to enable the running staff and the passengers to have their meals. Sometimes the catering staff was not adequate enough to serve the passengers in time. My father put me to work as a bearer on such an occasion. He was a great believer in the dignity of labour.

After my promotion to the 8th class I got admitted in the Victoria Dalip High School, Solan which was run by the Baghat State. Its ruler Raja Durga Singh was a person of very noble character. His was one of the most progressive states of Simla Hills. He had employed well-qualified teachers in the school. His uncle taught us English. I walked to the school daily from Barog, a distance of about five miles. At this school I learnt Persian as an optional subject. Urdu and English were among the compulsory subjects. It was at this school that I started understanding Urdu poetry.

Of poets, I appreciated Maulana Iltaf Hussain "HALLI" of Panipat for his two verses the most :

Never did God alter

That nation's lot

Who neither cared nor strove

To better her own lot.

(*Khuda ne aaj tak us kaum ki halat nahin badli,*

Na ho.jis ko fikr khud apni halat ke badalne ka).

In another couplet, addressing India, Halli says,

How could the Westerner invade thee ?

Thou got punished for thy disunity.

(*Tu kahan aur ahl-e-maghrah ke bhala hamle kahan*

Balke is na-ittefaqi ki mili tujh ko szaza).

Again at Solan, looking at the great Himalayan mountains as I stood there learning Iqbal, my young heart was thrilled by the eloquence of his poem, "Himalaya", in which the opening stanza makes one feel blessed to be alive and proud of being an Indian, sharing the possession of the mighty Himalayas with one's countrymen. Iqbal hails Himalayas thus:

O Himalayas!

O the rampart!

Of the soil

Of Hindustan

The Sky does bow

To kiss thy brow.

(*Ay! Himala ay fasil-e-kishwar-e-Hindustan!*

Choomta hai teri peshani ko jhuk kar aasman).

Further in the poem his description of the glory of the Ganges is not only captivating but patriotic too. Iqbal's "*Bache ki Dua*"— A child's prayer, "*Naya Shiwala*" — New temple, "*Hindustani Buchaun ka kaumi Geet*" — National song of the Indian children, and "*Tirruna-e-Hindi — Sare Juhan se Achha Hindustan Hamara*," are some of his poems which have left an indelible stamp on my mind and inspired me to love my country. Other poets have also contributed to the growth and development of my thoughts but to Iqbal I owe something special for I did try to live up to his ideals pertaining to patriotism, self-respect, love of nature and freedom, as presented in his poems.

D.A.V. High School

After passing the 8th class I came to Montgomery. By now father had recovered his health and rejoined his duties at the Army Remount Veterinary Hospital, Montgomery. I got admission in 9th class in the D.A.V. High School. At D.A.V. High School, Montgomery special emphasis was laid on building the national character of the students without inviting the Government's adverse attention. Our Headmaster Shri Karam Chand used to call me on special functions where I was asked to recite "*Naya Shiwala*". Often I bagged an award apart from applause. In this poem, Iqbal makes an immediate appeal to the heart when he addresses the Brahman:

God is in figures of stone you think:

Each particle of the dust of the native land is a god to me.

(*Pathar ki moorton main*

Samjha hai tu khuda hai

Khake-wattan ka mujh ko

Har zarra devta hai).

Iqbal's eloquent message of religious harmony, beautifully expressed in his Tarana-e-Hindi, has ever inspired me with the sentiments of national unity. I always felt happy to recite,

Religion does not teach hatred.

We are all Indians and

India is our motherland.

(*Mazhab nahin sikhata appas mein ber rakhna,*

Hindi hain ham, wattan hai Hindostan hamara)

In another poem, *Tasvir-e-Dard*, Iqbal's crying on the sight of India and his prophetic warning to his countrymen is as relevant today (1998) as it ever was. Iqbal says:

O ignorant fellow! think of the country

A calamity is in the offing.

There are talks of your destruction in the skies.

(*Wattan ki fikar kar nadan! Museebat ane wali hai,*

Teri barbadion ke mashware hain asmano mein).

In that very poem Iqbal makes bold to say,

Distinctions of community and creed

Ruined nations.

Do my countrymen have the concern

Of their country in their hearts ?

(*Ujara hai tameez-e-millat-o-aayin ne kaumon ko,*

Mere ahle watan ke dil mein kuch fikr-e-wattan bhi hai)

Whenever the making of a decision posed any difficulty, Iqbal has enlightened my path with the observation:

O bird of the heights,

Death is better than food

That hampers thy flight.

(*Ay taire-e-lahooti, us rizk se maut acchi*

Jis rizk se aati ho parwaz mein kotahi)

Our Second Master at Montgomery, Gianchand, called me to his home one day and dictated a poem of Hafeez Jalandhri "*Koonj ki Sada*" - Cry of the crane - (*Ik Sarson ka Kafla*). He asked me to memorize it and then recite. This was one of the greatest gifts which I got. It sustained me through many a difficult day.

Our science teacher used to take extra classes, as was done by the Headmaster, without charging any tuition fee. Our most revered teacher Master Nathu Ram used to teach us Urdu and Persian. He had retired after forty years of meritorious service from Government High School in Multan and then offered his honorary services to the D.A.V. High School. He was an example of simple living and high thinking. Once he wrote a Persian verse on the blackboard and called for a non-Persian student to explain its meaning. Persian was not my subject then, but I explained the meaning. Pleased, he called me, left his chair and asked me to sit on it. I was flabbergasted and did not know what to do. I could not imagine to occupy a teacher's chair even in his absence. Finding me hesitant, the teacher said in a royal tone, "We are pleased to honour you and you have the audacity to disobey us?" I quietly sat down on the chair. He patted me and thanked as I went back to my seat. Such was Master Nathu Ram's style of teaching and creating self-confidence.

I was never an outstanding student yet I was not poor either. My weakest subject was Mathematics. In Arithmetic and Algebra I seldom got pass marks but I was good at Geometry. Since the three branches of Mathematics were considered as one subject, I used to pass it in aggregate. I did my Matriculation in a good second division and aspired to be a doctor of medicine.

While at Montgomery, my father's Commanding Officer, Captain J.F.L. Taylor allowed me to use his laboratory for conducting experiments in practical science. He was a very simple and kind-hearted person. Seeing me wearing European clothes he said, "Why do you try to ape the British? If as a student you cannot contribute actively to India's freedom struggle the least you can do is to wear *khadi*, hand-spun cloth". Actually, I was wearing borrowed clothes from brother Balwant Singh in order to impress the officer. I returned those clothes and by spending two rupees borrowed from my brother, I got a pair of *khadi shalwar* (Punjabi trousers) and a *kamiz*, shirt, stitched by his wife, my sister-in-law, Bhabi Kartar Kaur. The next day when father saw me wearing *khadi*, he slapped me and rebuked, "Do you want me to continue in service or don't you like the bread and salt which I earn?" That was the abrupt end of my honeymoon with *khadi* at least for the time being.

His Holiness Satguru Partap Singh

One day in December 1930, His Holiness Satguru Partap Singh, the Head of *Namdhari* (*Kuka*) Sikhs came to visit the stables of the Army Remount Department at Montgomery. His Holiness the Satguru was a great lover of horses and cattle. He was proficient in the knowledge of breeds and breeding animals. He had come to see a particular stallion recently brought from His Majesty's stables in England.

Satguru Partap Singh's forefather Shri Guru Ram Singhji had led the Kuka movement against the British rule, in which a large number of Kukas were blown to death with cannons in 1872. It was one of the foremost organized movements of resistance put up by the people in the Punjab after the First War of Independence in 1857.

A saintly tall figure, Satguru Partap Singh carried an aura of nobility around him. He wore white home-spun *khadi* clothes. He was simple and polite and a staunch nationalist. I have always cherished my first meeting with him.

Martyrdom of the Trio

By then the whole country was stirred with the news of the death sentence passed against Sardar Bhagat Singh, Rajguru and Sukhdev. The country was so agitated over the impending executions that there were demonstrations against the British Raj everywhere. Though my father, being a Government servant, could not and did not take part in the agitation, he did at times take me to watch demonstrations in the town. There I saw the police brutally beating the unarmed demonstrators with lathies, long wooden clubs. It moved me. My father admired the tenacity of the demonstrators.

Bande Mataram

One day I saw a thin, skinny Congress man with a Tricolour hoisted on a crude little pole. He was shouting "*Bande Mataram*"—Hail the motherland. Even this simple salutation of one's land of birth was considered too revolutionary and dangerous to be tolerated by the British Raj. The English Superintendent of Police ordered the Congress man to stop shouting "*Bande Mataram*". Inspired by the attention the poor man had received single-handedly from the representative of the Crown, he shouted still louder "*Bande Mataram*", and incurred the wrath of the Raj in the form of a lathi charge.

Seven policemen snatched the flag away from the little man and rendered him semi-conscious with their beatings. After the policemen had left, the man came back to life and again shouted, "*Bande Mataram.*" He was attacked again and again but did not give up shouting "*Bande Mataram*". Here was a contest, Raj versus one Indian. Ever since I saw that episode, *Bande Mataram* has meant much to me. So much so that whenever I hear it being played, a thrill runs through my spine reminding me of the Indian independence struggle when the expression "*Bande Mataram*" was the sole weapon.

Greatness Requires no Robes

Another occurrence that impressed me deeply was my meeting with a man moaning as he lay on the road. His groans invited my attention. Though I was in a hurry to attend a class, I approached the helpless man and asked him what I could do for him. He asked for water. I ran back home and brought a glass of water for him which he drank hurriedly by cupping his hands. He refused to take it direct from the glass. He was running a high fever. I went back home and brought some aspirin and quinine tablets along with a glass of milk. The medicine and milk brought him some relief. Then he said, "Would you mind pressing and massaging my body a bit ? It is aching a lot. But you are a Sikh and I am a Mussulman".

Remembering the lesson of doing one good turn a day taught by the Scout Master, I gave his body a good rub and a massage not minding his body perspiring profusely, of which he was very conscious. Surprisingly, he took very little time to look relieved. He said, "Son, you have done me a good turn without knowing me and without caring about my religion; that is true humanity. I shall ever pray for you". I was surprised to learn that he was a saint and an eminent member of a shrine about twenty miles away from Montgomery. Reverently I took leave of the saint. He gave me an open invitation to visit his shrine whenever possible where I would be the honoured guest of the whole village. We never met again but ever since I have felt that true greatness lies not in robes but in humanity and humility.

Gorden College

In the month of March 1931 I got my school leaving certificate from D.A.V. High School, Montgomery. My father sent me for higher education to Rawalpindi. I was sent so far away from home because my elder brother Balwant Singh was at that time working as an apprentice fitter in the Army Heavy Repair Workshop at Chaklala about five miles away from Rawalpindi. In spite of my brother's meagre emoluments, he and his wife Kartar Kaur accepted the responsibility of my boarding and lodging. Next to my parents, I owe my education to them.

I got admission in the first year F.Sc., (Faculty of Science) as it was then called, in Gorden College at Rawalpindi. Gorden College was run by an American Christian Mission and was affiliated with the Punjab University. Our teachers were masters of their subjects. They were Americans as well as Indians but not necessarily Christians. They made the college a great seat of learning.

I took up subjects of Medical group, Biology, Chemistry, Physics and English. There were Bible classes also which left a deep imprint on my mind in respect of life and teachings of Lord Jesus Christ. I have often felt sad to think how little ethics preached by one religion differs from those of another and yet human history teems with religious wars. Gorden College had good playing fields and usually our football and hockey teams put up a good show during inter-college tournaments. We had a coach to train us in various events. He was an all-rounder sportsman. I learnt pole-vaulting from him.

We had a college hall which was commodious enough for large gatherings. It was very well-furnished having a raised platform with a pulpit. Normally, our teachers sat on the platform. They behaved with such decorum that we were inspired to conduct ourselves with propriety. I can vividly recall our Principal Rev. Dr. Porter speaking to us in pin-drop silence in the hall. It used to be a delightful experience listening to an honoured guest speak.

We were encouraged to go on trips arranged by various departments to show us the practical application of science and technology. I enjoyed going on such trips. Once Professor Gupta of Chemistry took us to show Kheora salt mines, where we saw awe-inspiring columns of stalagmites and stalactite white like snow; and a twenty feet thick wall of crystal clear salt so transparent that if light was shown on one side we could read a paper on the other side of the wall. The mine had a canopy-like ceiling hundreds of feet higher than the ground level which was shown to us by sending up balloons. And there was a lake within that cave of an enormous area. We had a joy-ride on the railway trolleys pulled by an engine. Close by, we also saw the temple of Katasraj where the Pandavas of Mahabharata fame had spent some of the days of their exile in disguise.

Prof. R.C. Lacy of Botany led another trip via Abottabad to the mountain resort of Murree. We made it to Abottabad by bus and then travelled on foot witnessing various plant life en route to Nathiagalli and Ghorgalli up to Murree. It was amazing how pine trees had adapted their branches to escape the strong prevailing winds. There were marvellous wild flowers and various ferns which we collected on the way. From Murree we were brought back to Rawalpindi by bus.

There was another trip undertaken to show us the cement factory at Hassanabdal near the holy Sikh shrine of Panja Sahib. I was so much enamoured with the scenic beauty of the blue water streams with orchards of peach trees on both sides and many kinds of fish in the water that I made two visits to that holy place on my own. Once when I visited those orchards in the spring, they were blooming with flowers. I spent more than a week at the Gurudwara Panja Sahib and took part in doing *Kar Seva* while the old edifice was being pulled down to build the new one of greater size. I did the journey up and down from Rawalpindi on a push-bike. Similarly, I took a team of five college mates on bicycles from Rawalpindi to Murree. I found the people of Rawalpindi very courteous and sweet-tongued. They used "ji" with practically every sentence they spoke. I have never forgotten their one expression of appreciation, "*dahdee shay vain*" - you are par excellence. Actually those people are excellent.

I remain indebted to those people and especially to Gorden College and my teachers for they opened up new horizons of knowledge before me. How encouraging was the motto of Gorden College, "SEEK AND YE SHALL FIND".

5
The Army

I failed to qualify for the F.Sc. (Faculty of Science) examination of the Punjab University in 1933. It was ironic that I failed in Botany which was my favourite subject. With it ended my dream of becoming a doctor. Early that year my father had retired from service. He had yet to bring up my three younger siblings and an equal number of my eldest brother's children. Ours was a joint family. My father had heavy responsibilities to shoulder. He also deserved some rest after a long service of thirty-two years.

Now that I was of age and already married, I felt I had no right to continue being a burden on my parents. It was high time that I started an independent livelihood. Afraid of broaching the subject direct with father, I approached my mother. She gave me a patient hearing and was sympathetic, but her response was outright refusal of my proposal: "Education is the greatest wealth that we can give you provided you try to take it. Leave our worries to us, we are not as weak as you think. Don't be timid. Try again and work harder. Continue your studies. I shall talk to your father".

The spring of I933 was a gloomy one for me. I had lost interest in further studies and was in a quandary. I did not know what to do. Matriculation was not the qualification adequate enough to get me any good job. At that time my father received a letter from his friend and previous superior officer Captain J.F.L. Taylor. At the moment I could little guess how momentous that letter was going to be in my life. Taylor had proposed that I should join the Indian Army as a combatant in the lowest rank of a sepoy (Private). I was advised to improve my educational standard and general knowledge. I should work hard and strive to be selected for the I.M.A. (Indian Military Academy), Dehra Dun. If successful, I would become an I.C.O. (Indian Commissioned Officer) starting in the rank of 2nd Lieutenant in His Majesty's Indian Land Forces.

The Indian Military Academy was established at Dehra Dun in 1932. Here a G.C. (Gentleman Cadet) had to undergo a training course in two and a half years in five half-yearly terms. Each term (class) started with thirty cadets. Of these cadets, fifteen were recruited on the basis of an All India open competition. The remaining fifteen cadets were selected out of the entire Indian Army and the Indian State Forces by a Board of Selection. In those days Burma, too, formed a part of India. Thus a cadet coming out of the Indian Army entered the I.M.A. as one of the fifteen chosen ones from an army over half a million strong. It was quite a contest.

The I.M.A. at Dehra Dun was run on the lines of the Royal Military College, Sandhurst in England. The officers passing out of Sandhurst were granted a commission by His Majesty the King. These officers were known as K.C.Os - King's Commissioned Officers in case of their British nationality, and K.C.I.Os - King's Commissioned Indian Officers in case of Indians. The officers passing out of Dehra Dun were granted a commission by the King addressing the recipient, "Our Trusty and well beloved ..." but signed by the Viceroy in India and were called I.C.Os. (Indian Commissioned Officers).

Apart from certain differences in their emoluments, K.C.Os, K.C.I.Os and I.C.Os enjoyed an equality of status under a common code of conduct and service rules. They lived in the British style of the "Ruling Race" as the Great Sahib Bahadurs. As aptly described by Sir Winston Churchill, "Princes could live no better than us".

So, here was something to aspire to, a career that offered plenty of challenge. I decided to give myself a try. My parents' response to this decision was favourable. Now the question at issue was which arm of service I should join, the cavalry or the infantry. As an ex-cavalryman, my father was rather a strict judge; he felt that I did not have making of a good cavalier. My mother was of the view that training could make me a good horseman, but the drudgery involved in looking after the horse, the saddlery and the other equipment was so time consuming that I would be left with very little time to prepare myself for various tests and examinations to qualify for selection to the Indian Military Academy. Their considered opinion was that I should join an infantry battalion.

Early one day in the last week of May 1933, my father and I boarded a Lahore-bound train at Chhanga Manga. Just after sunrise we detrained at Lahore Cantt. railway station, commonly called Mianmeer. We made for the nearest barracks located on the east of the station hardly at a distance of one mile. Both of us wore khaki shirts and shorts with stockings. My father displayed his Webley and Scott revolver with a bandolier full of polished cartridges. He could easily be made out as a veteran military man who had seen some good service. He carried a thick well-maintained file of testimonials and letters from British officers under whom he had served and from V.I.P.s whose animals, especially dogs and horses, he had treated.

When we arrived at a road crossing, my father spotted a British Captain who was mounting the Regimental Guards of the day. Directing me to stay where I was, my father rushed to see the Captain. When the Captain had marched off the Guards and was going towards the nearby office building, my father approached him with a smart salute. From a distance of about two hundred yards I saw father showing his credentials and certificates from the file and pointing towards me. Within a few seconds, my father saluted the Captain and came to where I was waiting for him. He said, "Bakshi, you are very lucky".

Enrolled as a Recruit

The Captain who happened to be the Battalion Adjutant was pleased to meet my father. He told my father to take me to the Recruiting Officer at Lahore and ask the Recruiting Officer to get me enrolled in the Fourth Battalion of the 14th Punjab Regiment. My father took me to Lahore where I was enlisted the same day. My father was paid two rupees for having brought a recruit. That was the usual reward paid by the Government to a person who brought a young man for recruitment in the armed forces of the Empire. My father was happy to get that small reward for it carried a great value as a proof of his loyalty to the British crown. I was given a railway warrant from our railway station Chhanga Manga to Ferozepur Cantt. to travel at the

Government expense.

That very evening we came back home to collect my clothes and certain items of daily use. Everybody was happy that I had joined the Army to become an officer. My mother gave me a tin of ghee prepared by her at home and some *gur* (raw sugar). She also gave me five rupees as pocket money. On the 29th of May, 1933 early in the morning my father took me to the training centre of the 14th Punjab Regiment (10/14 Punjab). On the way, father pointed out to me a King's Commissioned Indian Officer riding on a bicycle. At that time little did I know that I and that officer would be in the same unit one day, and he would be one of my heroes. He was Lieutenant S.P.P. Thorat who later retired in 1961 as a Lt. General, just short of becoming Army Chief.

Father's Advice

After certain formalities, my father and I were guided to a barrack where I was to stay during my training as a recruit. Being a retired Jemadar, a V.C.O. (Viceroy Commissioned Officer), my father was lodged in a V.C.O. quarters where he stayed for the night and left the next day. I recall his parting advice before he left for the village: "Your regimental number is 12249. From now onwards always think that the recruit whose number is 12248 is senior to you and better than you. He is made of gold and you are made of dust. Respect him and all your seniors".

His second advice was, "Never quarrel with anybody even when you are right and the other fellow is in the wrong, for in the Army a quarrelsome person is never appreciated and two quarrelling persons are punished equally and once your record is spoiled you will not be selected for the I.M.A." Thirdly, he advised, "Never drink". Fourthly, "Keep away from women. Apart from losing your character you may catch a venereal disease which will spoil your character-sheet".

Advising me once again not to fight with anybody he said, "Even if somebody calls you bad names and uses abusive language against your mother, don't get provoked. None will have guts to go all the way to Battichak (our village) to attack her, and if anybody at all dares to come that far, remember, *Ke tumhara baap wahan hai. Main use dekh loonga* - that your father is there, I shall see to it. If you remember my advice and work hard you are bound to go to Dehra Dun. Hard work is the shortest cut to success".

After giving me twenty rupees, my father urged me to read an English newspaper and take half a litre of milk everyday. His parting words were: "This is the last money I am giving to you. From now onwards don't expect me to give you any financial aid and never ask me nor try to borrow any money from any source. Stand on your own feet. God bless you! *Sat Siri Akal!"* He moved his hand over my head and as I touched his feet, he hastened to go away. I could feel his emotions as we parted. I returned to the barracks with a lump in my throat. For once I felt lonely in the whole world.

What a Beginning

When I joined the Training Battalion, the 10/14 Punjab Regiment, my Company No. 4, or the D Coy, was on annual leave. There were barely five or six persons in my Platoon No. 4. The Platoon Havildar (Sergeant) was on leave and the Platoon was being looked after by Naik (Corporal) Mohan Singh.

Small in stature, Naik Mohan Singh was very smart. Having joined the Army during World War I, he had seen active service in Mesopotamia (Iraq) and was in the siege of Kut-al-Amara. After seeing my father off as I entered the barrack, Mohan Singh shouted, "Yesterday you asked me where your 'seat' was. How dare you use an English word: Couldn't you say *charpoy* (bed)? Don't be proud of your education. My *ustad* (Instructor) used to be very strict with me, and I am going to see that I am with you stricter than he was with me. I understand that you have come here to go to Dehra Dun?" I had just uttered, "Yes Naik" that Mohan Singh cried out, "Say Havildar Sahib, that is how a Naik is addressed by a junior. You are just a recruit. Don't forget I am your Platoon Havildar. You shall have to obey all my orders. As you are the only recruit in the Platoon I will see that you keep the barrack clean other-wise I may have to derail your train leading to Dehra Dun" (*Tumhari Dehra Dun wali gari ulta doonga).*

Outside the barrack on the verandah were two big earthen pitchers for drinking water. There was a pit in front of the verandah where we could wash our hands and eating utensils. In the pit were broken pieces of bricks to soak up the water and avoid mosquito breeding. There was about a cart-load of bricks in the pit which used to be emptied twice a week so that it could dry. Mohan Singh told me to empty the pit. The process of emptying the pit was time consuming because each piece of brick was picked up one by one by hand and spread out for drying. It took me about two hours to do the job, which could normally be done by about ten men in a few minutes. When I came into the barrack after emptying the pit, I lay down on my cot to stretch my legs.

Mohan Singh came and struck my feet with a cane and said, "What are you doing?" I replied that I was taking a little rest. He shouted, "Get up. You have not come here to rest, and I will see to it that you do not rest. My Havildar never allowed me any rest. I will do the same with you." He told me to climb up to the barrack roof and clean the glass ventilators of the barrack. The barrack had about twenty ventilators on each side.

During May and June Ferozepur is extremely hot. The metal frames of the ventilators were very hot at noon time and they had not been cleaned for some days. It took me all the afternoon to clean the ventilator panels and frames. When I climbed down to report that I had done the job, Mohan Singh was not satisfied. He sent me up again to clean some frames again and when I came down after cleaning the frames he said, " Now why are you sitting ? Who will fill up the pit, your mother ?" *(Gadha teri maan bharegi?)*

Putting the bricks back into the pit took about an hour. Mohan Singh did not show any sign of satisfaction with my work, but other sepoys and instructors who were present were sympathetic. For about a fortnight I remained the only recruit in the Platoon which should have had over forty men. Then new recruits started coming, instructors and general duty personnel also returned from their annual leave and by the middle of June our Platoon reached its full complement. Among the new recruits many were educated far higher than I. There were four graduates among them and they were not as docile as I had been. It was then that Mohan Singh started telling other recruits that they should try to emulate me.

Training as a Recruit

Our Training Platoon was called Q Platoon and our Company

No. 4 was responsible for its training from the start to the end, a period of nine months.

My Section Commander as well as the training instructor L/Nk Teja Singh, was a soft-spoken person of amiable nature. The training was hard and tedious. In the beginning I often experienced weakness owing to lack of food. Our *Langar* man (the sepoy on kitchen duty) used to serve us a regulated number of *chapaties.* He saw to it that chapaties were served cold. Every sepoy was addressed by recruits as 'USTAD' (teacher/instructor). Once I asked the Langarman, "Ustad why don't you serve us hot chapatics ?" He replied, "Because you recruits eat hot chapaties more than cold ones".

I was lucky to get Proficiency badge for general training and Marksman's badge for riflery. I didn't do well in academics. I could not pass the 2nd class English examination. It took me two attempts to pass the Roman-Urdu examination and also two attempts to pass the lowest standard of English examination. I was not an outstanding player in hockey or in football, the two most popular games in the training centre. Sulakhan Singh was our Company Havildar Major during the training. A veteran of World War I, he was a very efficient and strict instructor. Being fearless and just he was respected by officers and men alike. The recruits not only respected but also feared him. His only weakness was that he was addicted to taking opium. He was in overall charge of training in the Company. One afternoon he came to where "Q" Platoon was drilling. Not satisfied with our rifle drill, he ordered the whole Platoon to sit in two lines facing inward. Then he told us to ask each other why our mothers gave us birth if we would not do even rifle drill properly. His language was filthy and abusive, too obscene to be put on paper.

After the parade most of the recruits got together and asked me, the senior-most recruit, to report against Sulakhan Singh. By that time I had learnt that making a joint complaint in the Army was tantamount to hatching a conspiracy and fostering disaffection. It was a normal procedure that in the evening we had roll call where all four Platoons of the Company - Dogras, Pathans, Punjabi Mussalmans and Sikhs - were present in a square formation. The Havildar Major received the roll call and reports from each Platoon Havildar after which he reported "all correct" to one of the four Platoon Commanders, a V.C.O. (Viceroy Commissioned Officer)— a Subedar or a Jemadar who attended every evening by turn. Before reporting to the V.C.O., the Havildar Major used to ask, *"Koi arz report hai?"* (Is there any report or a request?) On that evening when Hav. Maj Sulakhan Singh asked that question, I took a step forward, "Yes Sir: I have a report to make against the Hav. Maj." Everybody was stunned.

The V.C.O. on duty that evening was Subedar Jai Singh, an upright Dogra. He was the senior-most V.C.O. in the Company. Out of decorum he did not listen to anything against the Hav. Maj. in front of all ranks of the Company. He ordered the Hav. Maj. to bring me to his Dehra (residence). There Sub. Jai Singh asked me what I had to say against the Hav. Maj. I narrated all that had happened that afternoon on the parade ground. When asked whether I was right, Hav. Major Sulakhan Singh said, "Recruit Gurbakhsh Singh is right and I am sorry that due to not having had my dose of opium I could not control myself." And the matter ended there. Back at the barrack, everyone was happy and satisfied.

The next day Sulakhan Singh met me alone. I was afraid that he would be annoyed with me, but I was surprised when he said, "Gurbaksh, I am happy with you. These days we have Dogra Sardars (officers) in the company. They are neutral towards the Sikhs and they will appreciate your courage and straightforwardness, but frankness will not help you when you go to the active Battalion under your own Sikh Sardars because they will always support men coming from their own districts and clans. These days there is no Sardar from your district." I was grateful for his advice and it helped me greatly in my future career.

It was in the first week of March 1934 that "Q" Platoon completed its training. We attended an attestation parade where we took an oath of allegiance to the British King in the presence of our respective religious teachers, the Hindu Pandit, the Mussalman-Mullah, and the Sikh-Garanthi. Now we had become full-fledged sepoys fit for service in our respective active Battalion. On the same day, I was drafted to my active Battalion, the 4/14th Punjab Regiment at Lahore. I commanded the draft. I was posted to "B" Company consisting of three Sikh and one Pathan platoons.

I Become a Sepoy

As a recruit my pay used to be fifteen rupees per month. After certain deductions, I was paid thirteen rupees, seven annas and six pies. Even as a sepoy our pay and deductions remained the same. Over and above this, we were fed, clothed (uniform only), equipped and accommodated, transported and medically treated at the public expense. After two years, a sepoy was considered to be fully trained and our pay was increased by two rupees. During the early two years we were considered and treated as recruits by the old soldiers who did their utmost to ridicule us in every possible way.

As I have already stated I had not been able to pass the English and Roman-Urdu examinations during my training as a recruit at Ferozepur. I had to work harder to attend the English classes which were held under a British Sgt. Major in British Battalion school. I was happy to avail myself of this opportunity. These classes were held from four to six in the evening under Brigade arrangements. I had just started attending these classes when my Platoon Commander Subedar Kartar Singh transferred me to the Light Machine, gun section of the Platoon.

A Mule Driver

I was put in charge of the mule of the Section. So, for all practical purposes, I became a mule driver. My mule, number 24, was known to be a very uncontrollable animal. While grooming, it would not allow me to touch its neck or back, to say nothing of scrubbing or brushing. Since the brushing and grooming of the mules were done at four o'clock onward in the afternoon, I could not attend classes at the Brigade school. When the result of the examination was announced in the Battalion routine orders my name was not included. My Platoon Commander asked me, "Why is your name not here?" I replied, "Sir, I could not sit for the examination as I had to look after the mule". He asked me, "Why the hell didn't you inform me ? I would have transferred you to another Section."

He did transfer me the same day but I had to wait for another full year to sit for the examination. In any case, I started attending the classes. This poor deal reminded me of Hav. Maj. Sulakhan Singh's advice. Actually, my Platoon Havildar Sarup Singh, a very saintly and a kind man, had approached Sub. Kartar Singh regarding my examination but the Subedar had ignored Sarup Singh's recommendation. Though Kartar Singh never showed any apparent hostility towards me, he always gave preference to the educated sepoys belonging to his own district in other platoons, though I was the only educated person in his own Platoon.

Basant Enters My Life

As I was already married when very young, I had never lived with my wife. By now both of us were of age but dealt with each other as strangers. At Lahore our Battalion used to provide a guard at the Punjab Governor's house for two weeks at a time. Platoons were detailed by turns from different Companies to perform this duty. Once when I was part of Governor's Guard, my father came to visit me and while leaving told me that Nikki, as he used to call my wife, was bitten by a mad dog and had to be in Lahore for some weeks to receive anti-rabies injections. The dog which had bitten Basant (my wife) had also bitten three children of an assistant registrar of co-operative societies who was then stationed in our village. Since the three children and Basant needed the same treatment, my father had left Basant at the registrar's home in Lahore. This registrar was a Muslim gentleman, a Sayed. We used to call him Sayed Sahib.

My father gave me his address and casually told me, "Do look up Nikki when you are off duty if you can". Till that time Basant and I used to avoid each other. For about four days after father's visit I did not go to visit her. I was so careless that I had not even written down the address of the registrar. The only thing I remembered was that it was near an Unchi Masjid, a high mosque. After about a week, as I was standing on sentry duty, it occurred to me that if any other person from our village had been getting treatment at Lahore I would definitely have gone to look him up. Why shouldn't I go to look up Basant, if not as my wife, at least as a person from my village ?

So the next day when I was off duty I took leave to go to the town. I borrowed ten rupees from Lance Naik Arjun Singh, my Section Commander. I hired a tonga, a light two-wheeled horse-drawn carriage, and asked the driver to take me to Unchi Masjid. To my disappointment I found that there were many Unchi Masjids in the town. Having spent five rupees on going to different localities, disappointed and tired, I returned after sunset to the Governor's house. Everybody was keen to know about the welfare of my wife, and when they learnt that I had failed to find the place where she was staying I was advised to take another day's leave. A sepoy, Karnail Singh, of my Section offered to stand guard in my place on the following day.

This time I hired a bicycle for the full day and had to spend only eight annas (half a rupee). I went to the Mayo Hospital where persons bitten by dogs were given anti-rabies injections. I sat on the verandah of the hospital building from eight in the morning till two in the afternoon. Basant never came. When all the patients were gone, the hospital attendant asked me whom I had come to see. I said I was looking for three children and a young girl. He told me that their turn to receive injections was the next day. I returned and had to take another leave the next day. I went to the hospital early and sat there till mid-day. The attendant told me that they would be coming any moment. I sat there very anxiously, and then I saw a girl along with an elderly man and three children coming slowly towards the hospital. I thought the girl was too beautiful to be my wife. For the first time I found Basant was beautiful. I rose from the bench where I was sitting and went forward to greet her and Sayed Sahib. Basant was happy to see that I had come and thanked me. Her courtesy made me ashamed of my carelessness.

After getting their treatment they were to return to Sayed Sahib's residence. I was invited to accompany them. I gladly accepted the offer. On the way, I purchased a basketful of fruit with five additional rupees I had borrowed from my Section Commander. There was so much fruit that it was difficult to carry on the bicycle. Sayed Sahib was happy but did not appreciate my having spent that much money for fruit for his family. They treated me as an honoured guest. As purdah was observed in their home, Basant was asked to bring refreshments for me. Their drawing room had heavy curtains. When I wanted to sit near Basant she said that though the curtains were heavy we were being watched, so we sat at a distance from each other. After sometime I was served lunch and was asked to rest.

At four o'clock Sayed Sahib took Basant, me and his children for a walk to the famous Shalimar Gardens of Lahore which were within walking distance of their house. Coming to a lonely spot in the Gardens near a bed of zinnias, Sayed Sahib asked me and Basant to sit down on the lovely grass while he would walk around the Gardens with the children. That was the first time that we talked to each other intimately. Basant thanked me over and over again for my visit. She told me that she was finding it very difficult to explain to the ladies of the house why I had not come to visit her. She said that my visit had saved her honour. I asked if she would like to be with me longer. Her answer was that she would love to live with me. The mutual love, thus generated, was to grow ever stronger and intenser.

Before I left her that evening she told me that my father had advised her not to tell my mother that she was dining with a Muslim family. She was happy that I had taken a meal with her. I told her that I had no prejudice about eating with any community so long as the food was clean. Sayed Sahib belonged to a very noble Muslim family. I owed it to my father that from my very childhood we had no communal prejudices. Ours was a God-fearing religious-minded family. That Basant could share that mentality was, I felt, a very beneficial thing for me when I became an officer.

I asked Basant if she would like to come to live with me when married quarters were available. She liked my proposal. By that time, I had learnt that an officer after getting his commission was not allowed according to rules to marry within two years of getting his commission. I was already married and Basant's name had gone on my sheet roll as next-of-kin along with my mother's name. The snag was that my living with her might adversely affect my career.

The Jemadar Head Clerk of our Battalion was a Muslim gentleman, Sayed A.M. Khan. He knew the type of treatment I was receiving from Platoon Commander, Sub. Kartar Singh. In due course of time the Head Clerk became friendly with my father, and I was lucky to have won his sympathies. He was a very influential V.C.O. whom British officers admired for his all-round knowledge and efficiency. At the request of father he used to teach me English. My father had told me to approach him if I had any problem. I casually asked him one day if I could bring my wife to stay with me in married quarters. He said it was no problem. Basant, thus, came to live with me and we got on very well. It was during her stay that I was again working as a mule driver.

Mule Driver Again

As already mentioned, my mule number 24 was an uncontrollable and aggressive beast. It had already killed two men. I was the only educated person doing such menial work in the Battalion. Most of the men working with me used to joke about my doing the drudgery after twelve years of education. Our animal transport lines were close to a common road. My colleagues used to stop passers-by and ask, "Have you ever seen a person scrubbing a mule after twelve years of education ? Can there be such a fool ?" they would ask. My colleagues would say, "Yes, we have one. Would you like to see the specimen ?" And I was pointed at. The situation would be so absurd and ludicrous that I had no other choice but to laugh it away. I did feel humiliated on such occasions.

The mule driver next to me was very sympathetic. His name was Jagat Singh but was nicknamed, Moora meaning an idiot. He feared going on parades and I feared driving a mule-cart. So we used to swap our duties. The Transport Havildar who had lost an eye during World War I was a very strict man. He used to swear like rapid-fire. I found it very hard, nay impossible, to satisfy him with my work. One day as I was leading the mule back from the water trough the mule kicked and I fell down. The mule broke away from the rope and rolled on the ground, gathering dust and hay. It was with great difficulty that I managed to bring it to the manger. I was able to catch the rope and tie it to the peg. On finding the animal so filthy, the Transport Havildar shouted abuses at me. "Why don't you clean your mother ? If you can't do the job why don't you leave the service and go home ?" cried the Havildar.

In the evening when I returned to my quarters Basant made tea for me, and when she offered me the cup she saw my tears. She asked, "What's wrong ?" I told her the whole story and started sobbing. I said I would resign and go back home. If I had to look after such an animal here and bear such abuses why shouldn't I go and look after our own land and the cattle at home ? Basant argued that if I did that, my father and the whole family would blame her for having made me resign.

Father Enters

We were discussing the subject and the cup of tea had gone cold in my hands when I heard a knock at the outer door of the yard. I wiped my tears and went to open the door. I was surprised to find my father there. I brought him into the verandah of the one-room house and offered the only chair we had. I went into the room and with folded hands begged Basant in a whisper not to tell father that I was going to resign. I myself left to bring milk from the canteen, as father did not drink tea.

The old soldier in my father had guessed my intention. While I was away, Basant confirmed it to save her own skin. When I returned with the milk, there transpired an unhappy dialogue between my father and me.

Father : I didn't know I had such a cowardly son who is afraid of a mule. I have spent all my life among horses and mules. I am ashamed of you.

I : Father, it has already killed two Jawans.

Father : So what ? What's the use of having a cowardly son ?

I : It will be you who will cry if I die.

Father : I won't cry at a coward's death. I have four more sons. If you resign my door will be ever closed on you. You must learn to tame the animal. Nikki, give this fellow a bit of gur (unrefined sugar) or a couple of chapatis when he goes to the Transport Lines. Come along, you coward, take me to the mule. I will show you how it can be tamed.

I : Father, please, don't do that. If I take you to show you the mule, the whole Battalion will be talking that I took my father to show him the mule.

Father : What's wrong with that ?

I : Everybody has already a low opinion of me.

Father : All right; I will stay for the night. Take me in the early morning while it's dark.

Taming the Mule

The next morning at about five o'clock I took father to the Transport Lines. He offered the mule a piece of bread and gur. Then he made me do likewise. When I was offering the bread, father said, "Now pat it on the back and stroke its snout." I did as told. The mule which used to kick at my touch appeared to enjoy being patted and stroked. Then my father patted me and went away. He had some work in the town.

In the evening when I went to scrub the animal I gave the mule a piece of bread and some gur and kept some in my pocket. From that time onwards whenever I went near the mule I always took gur and bread or both. That stubborn and hostile mule started behaving like a pet dog. It would wait for my arrival. When I went near it and if I would not immediately feed it, it would sniff my pocket and put its snout on my shoulder and breathe and sniff as if begging me for a treat. Now I was the talk of the Battalion and everyone said that Gurbakhsh Singh knows how to tame an animal.

During his visit father also told Basant that to save my time from the drudgery of cleaning and polishing the saddlery and other pieces of equipment, she should do the job so that I could spend that time preparing for my academic examinations. Basant's presence, thus, greatly helped me to study. Her soft little hands suffered and the skin cracked. Her loss was my gain. The one-eyed Transport Havildar had now started appreciating my work. I felt at home in the Transport Lines.

N.C.Os Training Cadre

Soon after I had tamed the mule, a three-months N.C.Os training course started. I was one of the thirty sepoys chosen from all the Companies of the Battalion for this course. Again there was a whisper-mongering against me as to how I could fare while living in the family quarters. The course was not only difficult but also time-consuming. For the first time there were majority of the trainees who were highly educated. There were about ten graduates, all aspiring to go to Dehra Dun.

The syllabus of this course included practically all the subjects concerning an infantry section and weapons of an infantry battalion.

Our day started early in the morning with physical training followed by drill, weapon training, tactics and general knowledge. In each class, our uniform and weapons were thoroughly inspected. There was a lot to learn. We had to prepare notes and give lectures. We had to take command of a Section. A lot of reading and writing was required. Our progress was watched by all the Company Commanders, Company Officers and Platoon Commanders. A trainee had to be on the alert all the time.

After the training period, a trainee had to spend a long time to clean his uniform and equipment for the next day and check that every thing was well polished and shining. In my case all this work was done by Basant.

In the last week of the course we were tested. The first test was for P.T. (Physical Training) and the examiner was my own Platoon Commander, Sub. Kartar Singh. For all other tests examiners were either Company Commanders or Company Officers, all of whom were British. The last test for tactics carried the highest marks. The Battalion Commander, Lt. Col. C. Hungerford Jackson assisted by his 2nd-in-Command, Major D.P.T. Dean and two Company Commanders was the Chief Examiner. My name incidentally was in the lot that was to be examined by him. When the result of the course was published in the Battalion orders, everybody including myself was surprised as I topped the list. I got ninety-six marks out of a possible hundred. The only four points I lost were on the first day in P.T. All the same, I was congratulated by Subedar Kartar Singh, my Platoon Commander.

My success was eminently due to Basant. Not only did she volunteer herself to do the drudgery for me, she also goaded me to burn midnight oil to study my subjects and write notes. Had I lived in a barrack, I could not have worked after the last post, the bugle call blown as a signal for the hour for retiring to bed, when lights had to be put out.

Family Lines Life

It was not easy to get accustomed to living in the family lines. The wives of Other Ranks had to abide by very strict and orthodox conventions. Purdah was rigidly observed. A veiled woman wrapped in a broad white cotton sheet from top of her head to the ground level looked an inanimate statue on the move like a robot. She would always be behind the husband at a distance of about four paces. It was considered the pride of the community that their womenfolk were neither seen nor heard. The living quarters were one-room accommodation. The room was approximately fifteen feet by ten feet with a seven feet verandah in front of it. A hearth in the verandah served as a kitchen. There was an open-air bathroom with walls around it. The latrines were on one side. The courtyard was hardly adequate to allow space for two bedsteads placed in the shape of letter L.

The Family Welfare Centre was next door to us, accommodated in a similar quarter. It was under the charge of a Lady Health Visitor. Mrs. Jackson, the wife of the Battalion Commander, visited the Centre regularly every week. She was a motherly person. She would come walking from her bungalow about a mile away, carrying a light umbrella to protect herself from sun. The umbrella was a status symbol also. Indians in those days were not supposed to use it within the cantonment area. Accompanied by a maid servant (ayah), she was normally escorted by the Colonel's Orderly, in uniform. These visits gave her an opportunity to get acquainted with Sardaranis (wives of Sardars) and families of Other Ranks and their problems. She often distributed wool among the women and showed them how to knit socks and sweaters. Most of the women enjoyed this informal get-together which was, however, not compulsory.

Being small, young and fair, Basant was quite likable. She was intelligent for her age and she could speak a little English. Mrs. Jackson's attitude was by nature patronising. Whenever she came a bit early she would ask the Lady Health Visitor to call Basant in case she did not happen to be there already. She would make Basant to sit next to her on a chair and showed her to knit some new design in sweaters. This was not tolerable to the wife of the senior-most Sikh Sardar Subedar Bahadur Singh. One day she was so enraged that she shouted at Basant, "You bitch, woman of a mere sepoy; how dare you sit on a chair meant for us Sardarnis?" Before Basant could say anything, Mrs. Bahadur Singh pulled her out of the chair and pushed her towards a bench saying, "That is your place, you bitch." Basant quietly sat down on the bench and kept her cool fearing that any retaliation on her part might have an adverse effect on my service. When I learnt about this ugly episode, I made up my mind not to take the *beizzati* (dishonour) lying down.

In the evening I went to report the incident to Jemadar Gurbaksh Singh, then officiating for Subedar Kartar Singh who was on leave. Jemadar Gurbaksh Singh was a fearlessly just Sardar. He immediately took me to Subedar Bahadur Singh's Dehra. As I waited outside, Gurbaksh Singh went in to see Bahadur Singh. After about twenty minutes, both Sardars came out. Bahadur Singh was prudent enough to apologize. He asked me to call on them the next day so that his wife and my wife could make it up. Later I learnt that Gurbaksh Singh had threatened Bahadur Singh that if his wife did not apologize, he would surrender his sword which meant resigning his Viceroy's Commission.

Next evening, when Basant and I turned up at Bahadur Singh's Dehra (quarters), Gurbaksh Singh and his wife were also there. The ladies were ushered in while men sat outside on chairs. We were served refreshments and treated with courtesy. We returned to our quarters satisfied, though not happy for Mrs. Bahadur Singh had not apologized. She was an illiterate, crude and proud person, so unlike a Sardarni who was supposed to be an example of courtesy, compassion and dignity. However, the story went round the Family Lines that Basant had emerged a victor in that affair of honour. There was always a little bird which would have carried the news to Mrs. Jackson for she was as kind to Basant as ever when she met her during the next week. That was enough of a consolation for a mere sepoy and his spouse.

Though Educated More Proficient at Work than the Uneducated

During winter each Company went out for field training to a camp about ten miles from Lahore Cantt. at Niazbeg. During this camp we lived in tents under field conditions. Our Company Commander Major A.B. Miller, a veteran of World War I, never called us by name. He remembered each of us by our Regimental numbers and was fond of prefixing or suffixing it with the word *Bakri* meaning goat. One day from behind my tent I heard the following conversation between Major Miller and Sub. Kartar Singh:

Miller: *Subedar Sahib Bakri No. 12249 Kaisa hai ?*

(Subedar Sahib, how is goat No. 12249 ?)

Kartar Singh: *Hazoor! Ek dam bahut achaa hai.*

(Sir! he is very good indeed).

M: *Kaisa achha kam karta hai ?*

(How good is he at work ?)

K.S.: *Hazoor! hai to parha likha lekan kam karne mein unparhon se bhi ziada laik hai.* (Sir though he is educated, he is more proficient at work than an uneducated person).

M: *Kiya aap is Bakri ko tarraki dena mangta ?*

(Do you want to promote this goat ?)

K.S. *Hazoor ! Mangta hun. Yeh achha section leader banega. N.C.O. course mein bhi awwal aya hai.* (Yes Sir, I do want it. He will make a good Section Leader. He has also stood first in the N.C.O. course).

The next day I was promoted Acting (unpaid) Lance Naik. I was happy to get this desirable promotion. I was happy too that I had gained the confidence of my Platoon Commander, Subedar Kartar Singh. Thereafter, he always gave me a good report.

Jumps in Dreams

A few days after getting promotion, one afternoon I was preparing myself to participate in pole vaulting. I had just cleared eight feet six inches when the Company Commander Major Miller happened to come that way. He asked, "12249, how high did you jump ?" I replied, "Eight feet six inches, Sir." Miller said, "I would like to see you take another jump." When I tried I couldn't clear the bar. He gave me another chance and still another, but each time I failed. He asked me to put it at eight. Again I failed. I couldn't clear even seven feet six inches. By that time most of the Company jawans had gathered around the vaulting pit to watch. In the end Major Miller asked, "Did you really clear eight feet six inches ?" I said, "Yes Sir, I did". He retorted, *"Khawab mein kuda hoga!* (You might have jumped in your dream)" and he went away. After that, people in the Company started taunting, "Oh, there goes the man who jumps in his dreams".

After return from Niazbeg we started preparing for the annual sports tournament among companies. The winning Company was awarded the Battalion Sports Banner which was hoisted atop their barracks till the next year. The Headquarters Company having the pick of jawans from all communities had won the banner successively for the past several years. In December 1935, B Company was trying to emerge as the winner.

I was no good in any sport but pole vault was the only one where I could hope to be in my Company team. I had coached one Sepoy Santa Singh of the 7th Platoon who had learnt to clear seven and a half feet. Humorously called 'Tangewala' because he had been running a tonga before joining the Army, Santa Singh was a jovial fellow. The Dogra and the Pathan Companies had little better pole valuters. C Company of the P.Ms (Punjab Mussalmans) had one sepoy, Ali Mohammad, an all-rounder, highly educated and well-qualified to enter the I.M.A. He could easily clear nine feet but his team mate was as good as Santa Singh. The Headquarters Company's Sepoy Gian Singh and his mate were the ones who had been taking part in the Brigade tournaments.

After the Niazbeg incident I had lost self-confidence. Howsoever hard I might try, I could not clear higher than eight feet. Actually the people would laugh at me when they saw me carrying a vaulting pole. "Are you going to jump in a dream?" they would say. So I would go for practice late in the evening or early morning when there was no one around the ground. Sepoy Karnail Singh of my own Platoon (6th Pl.) and Santa Singh used to help me to carry poles and stands to the ground. For ten successive days I kept on failing to clear even eight feet in the proper way. On the eleventh day late in the evening I cleared the bar at eight feet six inches with perfect ease and landed in style. I had grasped the skill and regained the lost confidence. With revived hopes I went to sleep that night.

The next day was the final day of the tournament. The only two events left to be contested were the tug-of-war and the pole vault. The tie was between the Headquarters Company and the B Company. A very close competition, indeed!

Basant was not then with me and I was living in the barrack. On the final day of the tournament, early at dawn, I heard a gentle knock at the barrack door next to my bed. I got up and opened the door. I was pleasantly surprised to find that the visitor was none other than my father. He was on his way to Lahore and had thought he would see how I was. My father was the first man I saw that morning. I was overjoyed. As I touched his feet, I felt blessed. He further added to my joy by handing over a letter from Basant and a tin of ghee, some parched grams, pop-corn and gur from mother. He told me that all was well at home and in the village. I told him about the tournament and requested him to come and watch me do pole vaulting. He promised to come and left immediately.

The tug-of-war was a fine display of strength, skill and stamina between the two Companies, the Headquarters and B. They were so evenly matched that many a time they went back and forth pulling each other close to the deciding line. They perspired even in that chilly winter afternoon. It was a test of patience as the spectators watched the show breathlessly for some time and then suddenly yelled to buck up their respective teams. It seemed as if the tussle would go on forever. Eventually the Headquarters Company won the event. Even so the main contest remained to be decided by the outcome of the pole vault.

All the officers and men now moved over to the pole vaulting field. Some of the men ran to the nearby Muslim shrine to offer prayers for the victory of their respective teams. Some men took grains to feed the holy pigeons at the shrine irrespective of their own religion. I saw Karnail Singh was one of them.

With the consensus of the competitors, the judges got the crossbar raised to the starting height of seven feet. C Company and Headquarters Company opted to wait until a higher bar. Most of the competitors who tried failed to clear the bar even at that low level. Santa Singh and I took no chances and both of us cleared seven feet six inches. Santa Singh could not go higher than that. I continued to get the bar raised successively by three inches at a time. When I cleared nine feet, C and Headquarters Companies sprang up to vault. Unfortunately, one contestant from each of the two Companies failed to clear the bar. Ali Mohammed from C, Gian Singh from Headquarters and I from B Company were the only three left in the field. The whole Battalion was watching. The atmosphere was tense. The bar was raised to nine feet three.

Both Ali Mohammed and Gian Singh who used to clear above eleven feet failed even to clear that low height. I had never before cleared that height. With my steady gait as I proceeded towards the starting point I saw father enter. He had come to see me win, I thought. I vaulted and cleared the bar. Hurrahs greeted me. I was lifted on shoulders by my Company men. I was the hero of the day. It was a moment of triumph for B Company because we got the banner. The Battalion Commander congratulated my father and I got lot of SHABASH, well-done, from all the officers and Sardars of the Battalion. When Major Miller congratulated me, I said, "Sir this is the highest I have ever done. It looks like a dream". He smiled, patted me on the back and went to congratulate my father.

After the tournament I started receiving the attention and kindness of most of the Battalion Officers. By then Sulakhan Singh had rejoined the Battalion after completing his tenure at the Training Centre. He was now the Battalion Havildar Major. He took me as his assistant and saw to it that I devoted most of my time to studies.

Nomination for Kitchner College

During June 1936, I was enjoying my annual leave at Battichak when I received a telegram that the Battalion Commander had nominated me as a candidate to undergo a training course as prospective cadet at Kitchner College, Nowgong. I was instructed to proceed immediately for an interview by the General Officer Commanding, Lahore Area at his summer headquarters in Dalhousie for the selection of this course.

On my arrival at Dalhousie, I stayed for the night at the local gurudwara. The next morning I duly reported at the Area Headquarters. A British Sergeant Major received me and asked me to wait as the General would be arriving presently. Within a few minutes a Major General followed by his A.D.C. arrived on a horse. The Sergeant Major reported to the General that I had arrived for my interview. Without entering his office the General ordered up my file and standing in the porch of his office went through it.

He said, "Your Commanding Officer Colonel Jackson is very

proud of you. He says that you are his best athlete. What is your favourite sport?" I replied, "Sir I happened to do well in pole vaulting." He asked the Sergeant Major to bring a piece of paper and a pencil and told him to give me some dictation. The Sergeant Major had hardly given me two lines to write when the General said, "O, you write good English. Your handwriting is clear. Thank you very much. You may go." The General spoke to me so informally that before I could utter any word, he said, "Good-bye", to which I responded with, "Thank you, Sir, good-bye" and gave a smart salute. That was the end of the interview. A week later I was informed that I had been selected for the course at Nowgong.

Soon after my selection, C Company Commander who was at the time officiating for the Brigade Major called for me. He congratulated me on my selection to Kitchner College, Nowgong and then he said that if Ali Mohammed of his Company did not go at that time he would be overage and not able to go at all, whereas I was younger and could afford to wait another year. He promised that if I gave Ali Mohammed the chance he would see to it that I would go in the next batch of thirty. I agreed. As luck would have it, the Army Headquarters decided to start a long course of two years duration. I was sent for the first long course and Ali Mohammad for the last short course of six-month duration. It suited both Ali Mohammad and me. We went to Nowgong simultaneously though he had the advantage of being selected for the IMA earlier than I by a year and a half.

At Nowgong

With the start of the long course, Kitchner College was upgraded. Prior to that it was commanded by an officer of the rank of a Major. When I went there it was commanded by Lt. Col. Emerson of the Frontier Force Rifles. He was a very strict disciplinarian. He had an awe-inspiring personality gifted with competence of the highest order. Out of my class of thirty probationers, only fifteen were to be selected for the Indian Military Academy. I was not an outstanding candidate and for the first few months I found the going tough because of the focus on academic part of the training. Most of our academic instructors were British Sergeants and Officers. They were such good teachers that it did not take me long to start feeling at home with my studies.

As mentioned above, I was not a good sportsman but I had good physique. To improve it further after the morning P.T. period, instead of going straight to barracks for a change of uniform I would run to the swimming pool and plunge into the cold water even during winter. One day, curious to see where I was going, Colonel Emerson followed me on horseback. He saw me jump into the icy cold water. I swam and ran back to the barrack to be in time for the next period.

At Kitchner College in those days there existed separate messes for Hindus, Sikhs and Muslims. Colonel Emerson arranged a debate as to whether we should have separate messes or a single mess. I was not one of the speakers picked up for participation in the debate. Colonel Emerson acted like a speaker in a parliament. There were about five students each to speak for and against the proposition. All the rest of the students as well as officers and staff were the audience.

At the end of the debate Colonel Emerson asked if any one in the audience had any thing to say. I raised my hand. When he called on me to speak I made my maiden speech like an orator. I ended saying, "Let us be the pioneer of the social reform. When we have a single common mess at Dehra Dun why should we hesitate to start one here at Nowgong ?" I was greeted with an applause. All officers, especially Emerson, were so impressed that in the following debates on other subjects, I was never asked to speak. Once some VIP was being shown round the campus. I was surprised when Colonel Emerson said, "Meet Gurbakhsh Singh. He is my best speaker in English."

The Colonel was fond of duck shooting during the winter season and he used to invite some of us to join him on week-ends. Only those students who had their own sports guns were invited. During the first Christmas vacation I asked my father to get me a gun. Basant's father, Wassan Singh Sidhu, was there when I made this request. My father said, "I can get you a licence." Basant's father added, "And I will give you my gun." He had gone vegetarian and did not like carrying the gun any more.

So when I returned to Nowgong after the Christmas I had my own gun which was quite a distinction. One day, the Colonel invited me to accompany him for duck shooting. He had some English guests. On that day, the Colonel bagged fifteen ducks. I bagged nine while all other guests could not shoot more than two or three ducks each. After that, the Colonel never took me along, but would let me go on my own. At times he asked me to take along some of his guests.

Two months before the end of the course, we were taken to visit the Navy at Bombay. One of the cadets was detailed to look after the mess arrangements. The Adjutant of Kitchner College, Major Fairbank, a Cavalry Officer, was in charge of that trip. On the return journey it fell to my lot to be responsible for the mess. When we arrived back at Jhansi, the bogies in which we were travelling were separated from the train and taken to the platform from which we were to leave the next morning for Harpalpur, the road station for Nowgong. At the previous night, the Subedar Major and the Jemadar Adjutant reported to Major Fairbank that morning tea and breakfast would not be possible because of non-availability of fuel and milk. I was, however, determined to see to it that tea and breakfast were served.

Very early the next morning I took two mess servants with me and, after inquiring at the station tea stalls about the place where fuel for kitchen and milk were available, I went to Sipri Bazar. I returned with a tonga-load of fuel wood and two bucketsfuls of fresh milk. Fairbank was surprised when he got bed tea served to him in his special compartment. He was further surprised when he got his breakfast. I was glad to find that Fairbank relished the hot crisp *parathas* and a mugful of tea. After he had eaten two *parathas* I asked him if he would like to have another. He accepted the offer and asked for another mug of tea.

After the breakfast was over, the mess servants cleaned the place where we had been cooking under the trees on the platform. The cooking utensils had been cleaned and loaded on the train. I was standing under a tree feeling happy and satisfied that tea and breakfast had been a success. Maj. Fairbank was having a short walk along the platform. After sometime he came to me and said slowly, "Gurbakhsh, I hope you will be very happy at the end of the term." I understood that I had won his favour. Though I felt elated, I kept the secret to me so as not to provoke any jealousy among my classmates.

Generally speaking, I had by then won the goodwill of most of my instructors and teachers. I had also passed the qualifying examination called "The Special Examination in English" essential for appearing before the Selection Board for the IMA. At the end of the final term, we had to appear before the Selection Board. The President of the Board was Brigadier Kingsley, the Commandant of the Indian Military Academy at Dehra Dun. Colonel Emerson was one of the five members.

An English Sergeant Advises

A few days before the Board meeting I was called by an English Sergeant who gave me a few tips for appearing before the Board. It was something like this. He told me that I must go before the Board with the feeling that I was the most deserving candidate and had come to get my right and was not begging for any favour. He said that such mental attitude was very essential. Then he advised me to shampoo my hair the morning I was to appear before the Board, with soap of good quality like Pears. I should not use any scent or strong smelling oil. If I smelt of a good soap they would think that I like cleanliness. If there was any scent they would think I was fond of girls.

My uniform of course was always clean but on that day I should be doubly sure that my shoes were shining. I should take an extra handkerchief with me and just before going in I should wipe my shoes again. Above all, I must take special care to tie the turban neatly and have the beard well-pressed so as to give a smart appearance. I should adopt an upright natural pose. While answering the questions I should be brief and to the point. If I did not know the answer to a certain question I should not hesitate to say so.

The Board Selected Me

The result of the Board's interview was told by the Commandant Colonel Emerson himself to each one of us individually after about a week of the selection. The only other officer in the Commandant's office at that time was his Adjutant, Major Fairbank. We were called in one by one. As I saluted the Colonel he shouted in his typical way stressing on each word, "Gurbakhsh Singh, the Board has selected you. I do not know why?" I said, "Sir, I know it." "Tell me why ?" he asked. I replied, "Sir you would have recommended me." He answered, "Oh, yes I had to, I had to, I did!" He congratulated me, shook hands, and I left. I was one of the fifteen lucky ones.

A Cursed Man

During my last term at Nowgong I was selected President of the College Gurudwara Committee. Throughout the year we were allowed to observe only three religious holidays. Those were Janam Ashtami, the birthday of Lord Krishna, the giver of Geeta; Eid at the end of the month of Ramazan (the ninth month of the Muslim year, spent in fasting from sunrise to sunset); and the birthday of Guru Nanak Dev, the founder of Sikhism. The last festival fell during my tenure of presidency. Previously we used to celebrate Guru Nanak's birthday purely as a religious function in gurudwara where all the communities attended and we had a **Guru ka Langer**, a common meal sitting down in a row. We also used to have a big fireworks display at night. So many poor people used to partake of food with us that even five bags of wheat flour (each bag of a quintal weight) did not suffice.

I felt the fireworks display was a waste of money. In response to my proposal, the Committee decided to do away with the fireworks display altogether. The money, thus saved, was spent on feeding the poor. We also innovated and staged a drama in English to which guests were invited from outside the College campus. Dignitaries from far and near of the district attended the show. It turned out to be such a success that I received over a hundred congratulatory letters of thanks of appreciations of that rare treat at such a remote place like Nowgong. It was considered an achievement which made me happy.

During Christmas we used to have a ten-days vacation when we went to our homes.

A few days before leaving Nowgong I had gone all alone on a long bicycle ride on a Sunday. As I was returning in the evening at a distance of about five miles from Nowgong, an old man stopped me and asked if I could carry him on my bicycle to Nowgong. I obliged. On the way, we started talking. The old man was very grateful that I had given him a lift for he was getting late for a function at the residence of an officer in connection with the birth of his child. The old man manufactured and displayed fireworks.

I happened to ask him how his business was getting on. He replied, "Fairly well. By the grace of God Almighty there are people who appreciate fireworks. They are not like your President of the

College Gurudwara who is so miserly. If everyone was like him we would have no chance of a livelihood." He went on condemning the President in that derogatory vein using forceful adjectives all through the journey. I kept listening to him curse the President. When I dropped him in front of the College gate and was going to take leave of him I asked if he would like to see the President. He said, "I would not like to see the face of that cursed man."

I apologized and told the old man that I was that very person. I had thought that I was doing good to the poor but he opened my eyes. I would leave behind a proposal that in future fireworks should not be cancelled. I offered two rupees to the man which he accepted with great reluctance and we parted. The incident taught me that before taking any decision concerning others in future as a responsible officer, I would have to consider how the decision was going to affect all the parties concerned.

IMA Dehra Dun

From Nowgong I was sent back to my parent unit, the 4/14 Punjab Regiment, which had moved from Lahore to Chaman near the Afghan border and from there I was sent to Dehra Dun. In between I had a month's leave, which was a period of rejoicing and equipping myself for the Academy.

After the leave I went to the Indian Military Academy, Dehra Dun, where I began two and a half years' training. It was there in the Chetwode Hall that I read engraved in block letters in gold an extract from the inaugural speech made by Field Marshal Sir Philip Chetwode, the Commander-in-Chief of India in 1932:

THE SAFETY, HONOUR AND WELFARE OF YOUR COUNTRY

COME FIRST ALWAYS AND EVERY TIME.

THE HONOUR, WELFARE AND COMFORT OF THE

MEN YOU COMMAND COME NEXT.

YOUR OWN EASE, COMFORT AND SAFETY COME LAST,

ALWAYS AND EVERY TIME

This motto has been the guiding inspiration of my military career and life thereafter.

I was the 487th Gentleman Cadet to enter the I.M.A. As such, my GC number was 487. There were four Companies A, B, C, and D. I belonged to D Company commanded by Major Bamfield. We, the cadets, lived in independent rooms. There was one common mess. The food served there was of the English and continental variety which was good and wholesome. It did not take me long to acquire its taste but as the Indian food was not to be served in the mess, craving for my own native food awakened in me. At that time I could little foresee that the absence of Indian dishes from the menu of the Officers Mess would be the seed of disaffection against the "Ruling Race" in the British Indian Army.

Liquor other than beer was forbidden. Even beer was taken rarely in the form of shandy, a drink of beer mixed with lemonade or ginger beer. Most of the cadets came from well-to-do families. We had the Crown Prince of Cooch Bihar in our term but we were all treated on equal footing. Ragging the Ist-termers for about three days before the formal beginning of training was a step towards fostering a sense of equality and curbing any false sense of dignity among the would-be defenders of the country.

I found the training tough. We were kept on our toes from reveille to last post. Our day started with a period of P.T. at five in the morning before which we were expected to take our bath and a hurried cup of tea with a couple of ginger nuts (biscuits spiced with ginger). We did P.T. bare bodied wearing a pair of shorts. P.T. shoes were worn without socks. P.T. instructors drove us hard enough to make us perspire even when it snowed on the nearby Mussoorie hills.

After P.T. we would run back to our rooms, change into full uniform, draw our rifles from the armoury within a duration of fifteen minutes and be on time for drill at the parade ground. We could run while in P.T. kit but in full uniform, running was not done. In those days wearing of putties was part of the uniform which were wound spirally around each leg from ankle to the knee in a precise way. It was a skill and task which took quite a bit of time.

Apart from our trainers in horsemanship, all our teachers and instructors, whether Officers or N.C.Os, were British drawn from various units of the British Army. The Sergeants at times did upbraid us in their choice Army language but would always hasten to prefix or suffix a title of courtesy by adding Mr. or Gentleman in order to show that they meant no ill-will. As regards the Officers, they were mostly of high ethical standards and ability worthy of being respected and emulated.

I often thought of the Chief Instructor, a Colonel who never asked a cadet the reason for coming late to his class. He held the view that a cadet's career depended so much on his goodwill that no cadet would afford to be late unless there was cause beyond his control. He did not like to add to a cadet's embarrassment even by putting him a question. Then there was a Captain who taught us Mathematics. At the beginning of the first term, after welcoming us to his class, he told us that ever since his arrival at the Academy he had not punished any cadet for an act of indiscipline, a fact of which he was proud. "I seek your co-operation gentlemen to help me to maintain my record," said he.

Sergeant Major Crofts was another lovable person. He had his own way of making us feel at ease while learning to do certain difficult P.T. feats. I was not so good at jumping over the long horse. He told me to forget about my body and let my eyes and mind guide my movements. It was because of him that I could do well in P.T. He had a great sense of humour. Once while exhorting us to put in our best during a P.T. show, he said, "Gentlemen! You are going to be watched by His Excellency the Commander-in-Chief and your parents along with many V.V.I.Ps. And remember, above all, there will be my wife watching you to judge me. Please don't let me down."

Games and sports formed an essential part of our life at the Academy. Our D Company (The Dawn) was always the champion company during my stay at the Academy. P.T. being the backbone of physical fitness, efficiency and strength, an extra special attention was paid to it by alloting a special period of so-called voluntary P.T. which in practice, was compulsory. During the period intervening the lunch hour and the compulsory P.T., we had to attend swimming pool to learn and practise swimming and diving. The voluntary P.T. was followed either by hockey or football and after that boxing and cross-country race when the Cadet Captains would take us for their share of training and exercise. They would let us off so late that we were lucky if we got twenty or thirty minutes to take a shower and dress up into mess kit to be in time to assemble in the Company ante-room to proceed to the Mess for dinner at eight.

Putty Parade

At the dining table, a first termer had to be very careful to keep an Officer-like posture and decorum otherwise he might earn a "Putty Parade" after the dinner. The Putty Parade was a punishment in which a G.C. had to change into review order, full uniform and report to the G.C. Duty N.C.O. of the day for inspection and drill. It depended on the whims of the G.C. N.C.O. how long he kept us winding and unwinding our putties or drilling us. However, we had one consolation, that the day was bound to end by the sounding of the last post. During my first term I was lucky to have got only two puttee parades. Giving punishment to a G.C. was also a part of training so as to let the would-be officer know how men under his command would feel when punished, specially when it was unjust or unduly excessive.

Towards the end of my first term, I was surprised when the Company Sergeant on a very minor excuse during a drill period asked me to report at the Company office. When I was produced before the Company Commander Major Bamfield, the Sergeant Major gave out a long list of irregularities and faults, though not committed by me. The Company Commander asked, "What have you to say Mr. Gurbakhsh Singh ?" "Nothing Sir," was my reply for we were not supposed to give an excuse or any justification against a charge. I got three days C.B. confinement to barracks. It meant no going out during the week-end which happened to fall within those three days. During those days of the punishment, one had to remain in uniform and attend extra drill parades as well as puttee parades after dinner. This was the only instance when I was hauled up before the Company Commander.

It was at the I.M.A. that I met Colonel Prem Kumar Sahgal. He was in his final (5th) term when I entered the Academy as a first termer. Both of us belonged to D Company. It was there that I met his father Mr. Justice Achhru Ram who in those days was a practising advocate at the Punjab High Court at Lahore. Perchance I was detailed to entertain him to tea during a cricket match. Little did I know that one day he would be one of our defence counsels along with Bhulabhai

Desai during the first INA trial at the Red Fort, Delhi, in 1945.

A Long Vacation

We used to have a long 3-month summer vacation while undergoing training at the Academy. During my first such vacation, I looked forward to having some good rest and leisure. As was his wont, my father came all the way walking to receive me at the railway station in spite of his very busy day. He was at the time getting built a pucka brick house. He had employed a number of masons and labourers. In the afternoon on the very first day of my vacation, I dressed up in a clean white half-sleeve shirt, shorts and socks and shoes to match and wore a neat dark blue pugree. I thought my father would be pleased to see me in that smart outfit.

On the contrary, he curtly asked me what I was up to in that 'fancy dress'. He told me to change into some simple working kit and get down to work with other labourers. My mother came to my rescue and intervened, "By the grace of God our son is going to be an officer. It is his first day at home. Let him have some rest." My father spoke, "Son ? Is he from us or are we from him ?" Then pointing towards me he continued, "You, my dear son, either remove your good clothes, take a spade, get into that mud heap and knead it to the satisfaction of the head mason and having done that bring those bricks near the wall which is being built, or if you wish to rest, go and sit in your dear mother's lap."

I quietly left the scene and within no time returned dressed up only in a small waist cloth to cover my under dress. I picked up a spade and bare-footed started kneading the mud. My father said to mother, "Now look at our son. Doesn't he look handsome and strong while working rather than doing nothing in those swanky clothes?" Apparently pleased to see my well-developed muscles, she hastened to say, "You have had your way but please do not praise the boy's body lest an evil eye should cast its influence on his health."

Father's Most Precious Gift

I confess that I did feel at the moment that father was a bit too exacting but during my later life I found that the training that he imparted made me feel at ease during some of the most difficult days when I had no wherewithal except my two hands to do the manual labour. It is my considered opinion that one of the most precious gifts my father gave me was the notion of dignity of labour and the will to labour hard. During that vacation I had to work as an unskilled labourer from dawn to dusk. My father gave me only two days to prepare myself before returning to Dehra Dun.

Good Old Sher Dil and Lahore

I was just an average cadet at the I.M.A. World War II cut short my stay in the Academy by one term. The final (5th) term and our fourth term were combined and we graduated in March 1940. My I.C.O. Number was 336. I was posted to the Ist Battalion of the 14th Punjab Regiment (19th Punjabis) which was called, "Sher Dil Paltan"- the Battalion with a Lion's Heart. It was considered to be the best Battalion in the British Indian Army, Being one of the early Indianized units, it had a distinguished cadre of K.C.I.Os and I.C.Os. I joined my Battalion on the last day of March 1940 at Lahore in the same barracks where I had been a sepoy in the 4th Battalion of the 14th Punjab Regiment. It was from here that I had been selected to go to the Kitchner College, Nowgong. The place reminded me of the bitter-sweet past. It never let me forget that, basically, I was a sepoy. This background went a long way to temper my character that has always cared for the jawan.

On arrival at Lahore Cantt. Railway Station I and my bearer Bansi Lal were received by an N.C.O. and three sepoys. They had brought an A.T. Cart to carry my baggage to an allotted accommodation. The N.C.O. and his party along with Bansi Lal made for the bungalow while I, knowing the geography of the place, pushed on my own to the Adjutant's Office. In spite of late office hours (5.30 p.m.) Capt. S.P.P. Thorat (later Lieut. General) was waiting to receive me. It was a pleasant coincidence that Thorat was the first K.C.I.O. whom I had seen when I joined the 14th Punjab Regimental Centre at Ferozepur in 1933. He was then a Company Officer in A Company. He had been my examiner too in Roman Urdu and English subjects. He was the only Indian Officer then in the Centre and we used to look up to him as, "*Apna Kala Sahib Bahadur*"— our own black officer Bahadur.

Seeing him again on the very first day of joining my new Battalion augured well, I thought. There were two more K.C.I.O's with him at the time, Capt. Sant Singh (later Lt. General) and Capt. Vir Singh. Vir Singh, unfortunately, was killed in action on the Western front during the war. Mrs. Vir Singh, a very noble person took up a job with the Cottage Industries' Emporium at Connaught Place in New Delhi. I was posted to A, the Dogra Company, commanded by an I.C.O., Lieut. Hardial Singh Randhawa (later Brigadier). He was a very hard taskmaster and a dependable friend as I was to know him later more and more.

A sepoy had already been detailed as my batman, who took me to a bungalow where I was to live. It was beside the Officers' Mess across a road. This bungalow used to be the residence of my previous Battalion Commander of the 4th Battalion of the 14th Punjab Regiment. Now I was to share it with Lieutenant R.N. Nehra who was living with his family. One of the last batch from Sandhurst, I found him and his wife very good neighbours to live with, reserve, non-interfering and courteous. We had independent entrance to our respective parts of the bungalow. The door of my drawing room opened into the main porch which I rarely used on the occasion of receiving a formal guest. Within a couple of months, Nehra got his posting at Dehra Dun as an Instructor at the I.M.A.

I was lucky to have employed Bansi as my bearer. From the very first day of my joining the Sher Dil, he took care of my uniform and clothes with knowledge and experience. He saw to it that I was always dressed properly according to the occasion, checking my tie or bow and belt etc. before letting me go out. He handled my money with thrift and loyalty. He was a perfect waiter in mess and irrespective of long hours would be ready with bed-tea at the appointed early morning time and laid bath and uniform so that I could be punctual for my appointments and parades. His relationship with my batman was cordial.

Public Indifference to War

At Lahore we were busy in training for the war. The public indifference to the war was apparent: whenever German forces won any victory, they rejoiced in the British setbacks. Soon after the outbreak of World War II on 3rd September 1939, Congress ministries in the provinces gave up office in October and November. In the Punjab though there was a non-Congress ministry in office, there was a general lack of goodwill for the British. Lahore, being the capital city of the Punjab, was often a centre of anti-war and anti-government demonstrations. We were kept in readiness for rushing to the aid of the civil administration at a moment's notice. We were also sent on flag marches in distant villages to boost up people's morale.

Once when my Company went across the Ravi for a week long flag marches, I noticed that the villagers showed little interest in our exercise. When we passed through their various lanes with our Regimental band playing ahead of us with all the show of arms, children ran after us but the elderly people simply stared at us without betraying any feeling of pride expected of a people whose young men go to war. Once an elderly lady asked, *"Beta kidhar ja rahe ho ?"* (Sons! where are you going?) When told that we were going to war, she added, "What for ? For the country or for the British who are keeping us in bondage, or only for the few coins they give to you ?"

Some villagers simply cried as we passed along. An old man, when asked why he was crying, said, "I lost my son in the last World War I and what did I get? What did the country get? Jallianwala Bagh?" An old mother cried, "What have the Germans done against India?" We soldiers were supposed to listen but not to speak. We officers did not even discuss politics. What my Company Commander might have reported to the Battalion Commander, I did not know. But I do confess that for days I pondered over the episode reflecting whether we had boosted up the morale of the villagers or the simple farmers had sown a seed of disaffection against the Raj in the hearts of the simple soldiers.

What has Happened to My Son the Khalsa?

A few weeks after the aforesaid flag march, all the British and Indian Officers, the Sikh Sardars (V.C.O.s) and all the other Sikh Ranks were assembled in the Battalion school hall. At 10.00 A.M. our Battalion Commander, Lt. Col. L.V. Fitzpatrick, ushered into the hall A.E. Barstow, a serious looking Colonel (later Brigadier). As Barstow entered, he hailed the assembly in the typical Sikh style,

Wahguru ji ka Khalsa

Wahguru ji ki fateh !

(The Khalsa are the chosen of God,

Victory be to God).

He addressed us in chaste Punjabi and in a deliberate manner which was somewhat as under:

Khalsaji ! Kuchh din hoay Jangilat Sahib Bahadur
Ne mainoo Shimlay saddya. Jaad hazar ho ke main
Fateh gajaie, Jangilat boley, "Merey Khalse putr
noo ki ho gaya? Ki ho gaya mere Khalse noo ?"

(Khalsa ji ! Some days ago the Commander-in-Chief called me to Simla. When I presented myself and saluted, the Commander-in-Chief said, "What has happened to my son, the Khalsa ? What has gone wrong with my Khalsa ?")

Barstow talked in that vein at some length and narrated the incident in which a Sikh Company of the Royal Indian Army Service Corps (RIASC) refused to load ammunition boxes on the pretext that they were not coolies. He also told us about some Sikh soldiers of the 3rd Battalion of the 1st Punjab Regiment who had deserted. The incident which hurt the most was the refusal of the Sikh Squadron of the Central India Horse to embark when ordered to go to Egypt. Barstow explained to us that the Commander-in-Chief had shown him various charts depicting all communities who were enlisted in the Indian Army. He felt ashamed when the C-in-C showed him maximum number of black spots on the face of the Khalsa and said, "I am ashamed of this son who has failed to live up to the name of the Khalsa and I am hard put to decide whether to disown such a troublesome son or not."

Then pointing to the senior-most Sardar, Subedar Hazara Singh, Barstow said, "Subedar Sahib! What will you do if your son was so rebellious ? Won't you disown him and throw him out of your house ?" The Subedar answered, *"Hazoor nahin. Main baap haan. Put kaput ho sakday han, par mape kamape nahin ho sakde. Main usnoo maaf kar dwanga te ohnoo sudharan di koshash karanga"* (No Sir. I am a father. A son may be undutiful and disobedient but how can parents ignore their duty and grace. I shall pardon him and try to redeem him). Barstow who had spent all his life among the Sikh soldiers told us that he would try to plead for the Khalsa who had played in the hands of the various political parties, since the end of the World War I. He specially warned us against the Kirti Kisan movement and the communists and took pains to explain their modus operandi. Before leaving he asked questions at random from the Other Ranks to ascertain that his message had been understood. He shook hands with all the Officers and Sardars and said, "*Wahguru ji ki Fateh*," as he left.

The Government, however, continued its efforts to placate the Sikhs. The Sikh leadership on their part wanted that they should win over the goodwill of the Government so that they might retain their prestige and privileges and get the ban on the enrolment of the Sikhs in the Army lifted. Much later I learnt that four men of the Central India Horse were executed and over a hundred were transported for life while many others got various terms of rigorous imprisonment. Similarly, law took its course without mercy in dealing with the personnel indicted of mutinous offences.

I Own a Car

Earlier in May I received a letter from my elder brother Havildar (later Subedar) Balwant Singh Dhillon who was serving in the Heavy Repairs Workshop at Chaklala near Rawalpindi. His Section Commander, a British Sergeant under whom he had worked for about a decade, was going home on transfer. He had a 1927-model two-seater Morris car with an open dickey seat at the back. The Sergeant was prepared to sell it to my brother for a throw-away price of three hundred and fifty rupees. My brother had neither the money nor the need to keep a car. He advised me to purchase it. He told me that notwithstanding the old model of the car, it was a very well-maintained machine with a sturdy body, new tubes and tyres and most of its parts replaced by the most up-to-date components available in the country. It had a new battery and a magneto in addition, which could run the car without a battery. It was very economical on fuel with an average of forty-five to fifty miles per gallon (4.55 litres) of petrol.

It was a very attractive proposition but I had no ready money. My brother had written that the Sergeant was in an immediate need of money and he had much higher offers. Knowing that my brother was a gifted mechanic and thrifty by nature and observing that his proposal was sound, I decided to get the car. So I sent my bearer to call the Battalion shop-owner commonly called Regimental Bania. The canteen system of today was not common then. He came to my bungalow and I requested him for a loan of four hundred rupees. He was good enough to give me the money without charging any interest thereon. I gave him four advanced dated cheques for a hundred rupees each to be encashed on the following consecutive four months. I was in no position to do him any favour but I remained under a debt of gratitude to him ever since.

I sent the money immediately by a telegraphic money-order. Four days later brother Balwant Singh brought the car to me with all its necessary tools and spare parts. It had been duly transferred in my name before its owner left Rawalpindi. It was the only car I ever owned and I enjoyed driving it. I learnt driving on it. It never gave me any trouble and was the most dependable vehicle I ever had during my various walks of life except once when I had to cut a sorry figure due to my own fault.

Basant was ailing and I had brought her to Lahore for treatment. As I was not allowed married quarters, I had hired a room for her in the Canal Park where her father looked after her. My father came to see her and as usual came to me first. He did not approve of my having a car but now that I had got one he kept quiet. When I was driving him to Basant's place of residence and had yet gone only about five hundred yards away from my bungalow, the car stopped. When I checked the cause, I found the petrol tank dry. My father admonished, "When you don't have money enough to feed it, why are you keeping a car ? Again who told you to buy this rotten second-hand cart ?" It was not for me to reason why. I ran to my bungalow and sent a man to fetch some petrol. I slowly walked back to where my father was standing beside the car. As soon as the car got petrol it started without any trouble. I drove to the nearest petrol station and got the tank filled up. I learnt a lesson of life, and then onward never forgot to check the fuel whenever I used a vehicle.

Once when I was dining in the mess, some six brother Officers took away my car for a joy-ride. They were in their Regimental dinner jackets and were in hilarious mood. At a little distance from our barracks they encountered another car from the opposite direction with blazing headlight. The occupants of both the cars shouted at one another in an offensive language. The occupants of the oncoming car were all Britishers in their formal civilian dinner jackets and appeared to be some important officers. So what ? Our Officers would not yield simply because of their nationality. Both the cars stopped and both sides started blaming one another for rash driving.

The situation grew hot. Arguments would have led to a fistic scuffle when another car pulled up and an elderly gentleman got down to ask what the matter was. The Officer at the steering wheel of my car said, "They did not dip their light." The elderly man spoke, "And Sir, may I ask why didn't you dip your light ? Look ! it is still blazing." "But I don't know how to dip the damn thing," answered our brother Officer. There was a sudden roar of laughter from all sides. They shook hands with one another and introduced themselves. The Britishers were Officers who belonged to the political department of the Central Government. They were invited to our Mess to cement the newly founded friendship with drinks. The hospitality was reciprocated by both sides many a time during our stay at Lahore.

Local Officer's Club

When I joined my Battalion at Lahore, one day I found a notice along with application forms inviting officers to join the Local Officer's Club. It had a swimming pool which was an attraction for me. I filled out a form, and showed it to the Mess President, the 2nd-in-Command of the Battalion, a British Major. He very politely advised me not to apply. I did not ask him the cause for such an advice but asked my Company Commander, Lieut. (later Brigadier) Hardial Singh Randhawa why the 2nd-in-Command had advised me not to apply for the membership of the Club. Haridal Singh became very angry and said, "Don't you know that we Indians, in spite of our rank and all the show of equality, are not allowed membership of the Club ? That is an exclusive white men's Club. We are Sahib Bahadurs only to work but not to share the privileges of the 'Ruling Race'. You have humiliated not only yourself but all the Indian officers. All said and done, socially we are bloody niggers and you better be careful."

Lieut. Randhawa warned me not to speak about this incident to any-body, not even to fellow Indian Commissioned Officers, for they would have a low opinion of me. After this incident I felt that we Indian Officers whether K.C.I.Os or I.C.Os were submitting to the national humiliation for the sake of remaining in service. This was an early seed of disaffection sown in my mind. The pride and aspiration with which I had decided to join the Army received a big jolt.

Apart from the afore said incident, my stay at Lahore was, otherwise, a happy one. Naik Babu Ram and Lance Naik Surat Singh who were my Instructors at the Regimental School at Ferozepur had now become Subedar and Jemadar, respectively. They had taught me elementary map-reading, Military geography and Roman-Urdu. Some men who were either instructors or recruits at Ferozepur were good enough to remember me from those days. Their courtesy and affection were overwhelming. It was something to be with them again during the war. These Regimental ties persevered through good and bad days which the future had in store for us.

Secunderabad

In September 1940, our Battalion left Lahore for Secunderabad. In spite of her illness Basant came to see us off at the railway siding. Lt. Col. Fitzpatrick was kind enough to approach her to ask about her health and wish her "get well soon." Thorat who was then Bn. Adjutant also met her for the first time, and so did most of the brother Officers of the Battalion. These small courtesies meant so much at that emotional moment of parting.

Secunderabad was one of the oldest and the biggest British cantonments situated close to the city of Hyderabad, the capital of the state bearing the same name. In the centre of Deccan plateau of Southern India, Hyderabad was the largest state with an overwhelming Hindu population ruled by a Muslim ruler hailing from a time-honoured dynasty. The Nizam of Hyderabad was the only Indian ruler who had the distinction of being addressed as His Exalted Highness. He had an up-to-date army with modern artillery and aircraft. Some of his officers were Graduates from the Indian Military Academy, Dehra Dun.

Our Battalion was accommodated in Bawanpally lines beyond which lay miles and miles of vast open plains, fields and forests dotted with hillocks commanding their surroundings. It was an ideal training ground for all types of military exercises and manoeuvres. Secunderabad was our mobilization station. We were kept busy to put ourselves on to war footing as per War Establishment (W.E.). The Commanding Officer and the Battalion staff officers had to work late into the night to check, recheck and demand the required number of officers and men of all categories as well as arms, stores and equipment and also to plan the disposal of personal and regimental property and documents etc., which were to be sent to the Regimental Centre for safe-keeping during the Battalion's service overseas. In the process we got six Emergency Commissioned British Officers, 2nd Lieutenants MacCarthy, Morrey, Graer, Dicky, Longwill and Corfield. They were raw subalterms with little experience of military life. We also got fresh recruits to complete our strength as per War Establishment. Major Ingle, the Battalion 2nd-in-Command, was promoted Lt. Col. and sent to raise 6/14th Punjab Regiment near Ferozepur. Some V.C.Os and N.C.Os were sent with him for raising the 6th Battalion.

Major Anderson, who was at the time commanding 'B' Company where I was one of his Company Officers, was impressed with my work and had been grooming me to take over the command of the Company. One day he got the Sikh V.C.Os together and asked their opinion. Subedar Hazara Singh said, *"Hazoor! sano taan koi topi wallah deo* (Sir! Give us some topi wallah)." So the command of the Sikh Company was given to 2nd Lient. MacCarthy and I was transferred to the Headquarters Company, and was appointed the Bn. Signal Officer. An N.C.O. Bara Singh was detailed to instruct me in signalling. At that time Captain (later Colonel in the INA) C.J. Stracey, the Bn. Quartermaster had to proceed on leave and during his absence I acted as the Battalion Quartermaster. This experience, though of a short duration, greatly helped me in my later career in the INA and in life thereafter.

MacCarthy was a good lad. He had earlier been a labour officer in a tea garden in Assam. His only drawback was that he at times treated and talked to his men as if they were labourers which did not suit the soldier's psyche. The Sikh V.C.Os felt distressed but had to blame none other than themselves for having preferred a topi to a puggaree.

From A.T. to M.T.

The most significant change which took place at Secunderabad was the replacement of age-old mule and mule cart, A.T. (animal transport) by M.T. (motor transport). Instead, we got a few light weight 15-cwt. trucks. Bicycles used by despatch riders were replaced by motor cycles. The officers' chargers and horses were completely withdrawn. The Bn. Commander got a station wagon which could carry his Command Group. Mohan Singh was appointed the M.T.O. (Motor Transport Officer). It was here that I learnt to drive a motor cycle but I confess I have always missed horse-riding.

Secunderabad was a beautiful place with moderate climate where living was economical. The commodities of daily necessities as well as labour were cheap. One could always have a feeling of plenty. People were peace-loving. Basant who had come to see our Regiment off straight from hospital on the day we left Lahore, was still undergoing some treatment. While at Secunderabad I felt very lonely and worried about Basant's health, yet according to prevalent regulations I could not ask for married accommodation. During a dinner at my Company Commander's bungalow Dr. Mrs. Leela Thorat having observed that I was looking sad, called me aside and asked why I was so sad. I told her that Basant was not well and according to regulations I could not ask for married quarters till I had completed two years of commissioned service. This meant separation till the period of the war.

She said, "Don't worry. Come to our bungalow at 4 tomorrow and have tea with us. I will talk to the 'Tree Rat'. What is he there for ? He must help." Thorat was our Adjutant. The following day when I went to tea at the Thorat's, he drafted a letter for the Commander-in-Chief in India through proper channel, that the regulations prohibiting young officers from living with their families were all right for peace time, but as I was married before joining the Army and was ready to move overseas at any moment I felt the regulations had to be changed. I did not know where I would be sent or whether I would return at all after the war. Therefore, I requested that I be allowed to live with my wife and given married accommodation.

Basant Joins Me

The next day I took the letter to Colonel Fitzpatrick who agreed with me and said that these regulations must be changed at least for the duration of the war. He sent the letter to Simla. Within ten days of the despatch of my letter, my request was granted and I was allotted married quarters. Subedar (later Captain INA) Santa Singh had been on leave at his home. I contacted him who agreed to escort my wife to Secunderabad at the end of his leave. Accordingly Basant joined me on the 19th of January, 1941. I was happy that a person who had lived with me for a few months in one-room quarter in the married lines was now living with me in an Officer's bungalow.

Some days before Basant's arrival I received a letter from my father informing me that Major J.F.L. Taylor to whose suggestion and advice I owed my entry into the Army was in a cantonment about ten miles from Bawanpally where we were stationed. My father advised me to go and call on him and get his advice whenever I needed it. One afternoon I rode to his bungalow on a charger. He met me with warm courtesy. I told him that my wife was coming to join me. I sought his advice as to how to furnish my bungalow.

He said, "The trouble with you Indians is that you like to ape the British and compete with them in furnishing your bungalows in an expensive manner. I want to tell you that if a friend or a colleague calling on you is not happy to sit on a hard bench or even a box with you he is not going to become friendly if you offer him a soft sofa. I learnt from your father to get ordinary cotton bed-sheets costing only a rupee, while other officers would pay five or ten times more for fancier ones. When you furnish your windows and doors with curtains don't buy expensive cloth. You can buy any coloured piece. Nobody will care about its quality as long as it looks clean and tidy. If I were you I would go for cloth costing only two annas a yard produced in Ludhiana (Punjab) and furnish my whole bungalow with curtains with ten or fifteen rupees only."

Following Major Taylor's advice when I returned to my residence I sent for the Battalion shopkeeper and asked for the cheapest available cloth in his shop. He showed me a sample of a green cloth which cost a rupee for three and a half yards. I had my entire bungalow furnished with curtains with twenty rupees. For me it was a lesson to live within my means and yet to enjoy a feeling of plenty.

As our mobilization neared completion, our leaving for overseas came closer. Though I acted on Major Taylor's advice to be thrifty, yet I thought, that was the only time when I could let Basant have an experience of living the life of an Army Officer's wife. I owed much to her for having helped me to be where I was. She had shared some of the most arduous days of my life. Before her arrival, Bansi Lal had already engaged a cook and a *misalchi* (dish-washer). A few days later after Basant's arrival, one Sunday morning a neatly dressed middle-aged man turned up seeking for a cook's job. When I told him that we already had a cook, he said, "Sir! whether you employ me or not I request you to kindly have a look at my testimonials so that you may like to recommend me to some other officer. Here is a certificate of Mrs. Sarojini Naidu."

The moment we heard the great Indian lady's name who besides being one of the top national leaders, was known for her taste of cuisine, we employed the man. Thus, we had a bearer, two cooks, a dish-washer to serve us. In addition to these servants we had a *dhobi* (washerman), *mali* (gardener) and a sweeper as part-time helpers whose services were shared with two officers residing in the adjacent bungalow, Captain Mohammad Zaman Kiani (later Major General INA) and Lieut. (later Colonel INA) Ali Iqtadar Shah Dara, the famous Olympian hockey player, a team-mate of the renowned hockey wizard, Major Dhian Chand.

On principle, we never used the orderly for any domestic work other than sending him on errands. He looked after my personal arms and saw to it that my bearer kept my uniform and kit in order. The new cook taught Basant how to prepare various dishes. I believe that our style of living at Secunderabad, though of a short duration, was a period of learning and imbibing certain cosmopolitan habits, which broadened our outlook.

In those days we were supposed to pay courtesy call on all the married Officers of the Battalion and Flag Staff House in the station, the senior civil officers who held the status of a representative of the Crown like the Collector/Deputy Commissioner of a district, a Resident or a Political Agent or the higher ones and rulers of the Indian states, as well as on all the Officer's Messes. Our senior officers also visited married officers of their respective units, regardless of their seniority. It meant respect to ladies, one of the high points of the British culture.

When Basant joined me at Secunderabad I expected that the Colonel and other senior British Officers would pay a courtesy visit to my wife. It was not done. I felt bad. It was a reminder of our mercenary or slavish standing because of our colour. It hit me hard because otherwise I had found the Colonel and the 2nd-in-Command very considerate in my official life. Major Taylor, however, did pay a courtesy visit and was kind enough to come when invited to a dinner. He had no anti-Indian complex. He was from Ireland.

During the middle of January in 1941, the whole Brigade of which our Battalion 1/14th Punjab Regiment was a part had to go for training on manoeuvres for a month. Colonel Fitzpatrick chose me to be Commander of the Battalion Depot during his absence on manoeuvres. I was the only Officer of the Battalion left in the cantonment. Similarly, in the Brigade Headquarters just one Field Officer, Major Sarda Nand (later Lieutenant General) was left to officiate for the Brigade Commander. Colonel Fitzpatrick paid only a few flying visits during that period to check and help to handle certain important matters.

Punishment should be the Barest Minimum

It was during that period that I caught a sentry sleeping during my night rounds. I took it very seriously and intended to award an exemplary punishment to the delinquent. In view of my junior rank as an Officer I could not authorise more than fourteen days' confinement. I thought the matter was too serious. It became a bit sensitive when the Hindu religious teacher, the Pundit, visited my bungalow and approached Basant to let the sepoy off. When Basant conveyed Pundit's request to me, I warned her never to entertain outside requests or interfere in any official matter. It was simply not done and was not appropriate either. The incident of Punditji's approach annoyed me so much that I thought of giving the maximum punishment to the sepoy.

During Colonel Fitzpatrick's next visit, I requested him to

enhance my powers of punishment. Like a teacher Col. Fitzpatrick told me that we should not be too strict in awarding punishments. "Don't you think, the man has already suffered enough while waiting for the trial ?" asked the Colonel. He added, "It is not fair to be too harsh in giving punishment when you intend to correct a man's behaviour and restore discipline." I understood the Colonel's point of view. I owe it to him that later on whenever judging a defaulter, I recalled his advice that punishment should be the barest minimum to correct a man but it should not be vindictive. This advice helped me a lot all through my Army career and in later life.

Though I missed going on Brigade manoeuvres I did get an experience of commanding the Battalion Depot which was akin to independent command. I owe my gratitude to General Sarda Nand, then a Major, who commanded the Brigade Depot because he helped me in the performance of my day-to-day duties. He often would call on me after the forenoon office hours and we would lunch together. When his wife joined him we found in her a very graceful lady. Basant and she got on very well. General Thorat visited us and gave us a feeling of belonging to one family. As already mentioned, Col. Fitzpatrick visited me in the office or the Mess whenever he could snatch some time from the training during Brigade manoeuvres. He never came to my bungalow.

Subhas Chandra Bose's Escape

Once on a Sunday Col. Fitzpatrick came early in the morning. I went to the Mess and had breakfast with him. During breakfast he seldom talked. On that day all the daily newspapers flashed on the front page in the banner headlines the news of Subhas Chandra Bose's escape from his Elgin Road house in Calcutta. Bose was awarded in absentia two rigorous punishments of some long terms to run concurrently. The Colonel read out the news to me and said, "Don't you think such a dangerous man deserves no leniency and the terms of punishment should have been ordered to run consecutively instead of concurrently?" "Yes Sir," was my reply. Little did I know then that one day Bose would be my Netaji, a revered leader, and that I would be one of his followers to fight against and cause the end of that very Raj which had punished him.

Orders to move Overseas

Soon after the second week of February 1941, we received orders to move overseas. That day Mohan Singh, my Company Commander, came to drop me at my bungalow. It was afternoon tea-time. I requested him to join us over a cup of tea. He very kindly accepted my request. We sat down on the stairway of the bungalow. Basant served us tea. When we broke the news of our move, Basant said that she had already dreamt of it. She looked sad. "Are you afraid of our going to the deadly war?" I asked. "No, not at all. I am destined to be a fortunate wedded woman. Hence nothing untoward can happen to you. *Main suhagan hi rehna hai.* What worries me is that you have started drinking. You may not take to heavy drinking, for I understand that drinks are very low-priced in war." "Do you want me to give up drinking when I go abroad ?" I asked. She replied that she would be very happy if I gave up all those drinks which were in our stock.

Vow not to Drink while Abroad

I solemnly assured Basant with a promise that I would never take any of the those drinks until my return to the motherland. I called Bansi and told him to bring a bottle each of every drink which were in stock and line them up before us. There were various brands of whisky, rum, gin, beer, stout, sherry, port, madeira, apple cider and creme de mentha of which I made a mental list. I confess that despite Major Taylor's advice I was lavish in my style of living. Parting is always sad. Along with Mrs. Mohan Singh, Mrs. Hardial Singh Randhawa and Bansi Lal, Basant left for the Punjab on the 2nd of March, 1941. The bungalow which was full of life looked a desert. I felt as if I would never be able to bear separation from her.

Baggage Officer

We left Secunderabad on the following day, the 3rd of March, 1941. During the move I was given the duty of the Baggage Officer which meant loading all the heavy luggage, stores and vehicles of our Battalion in a goods train at Secunderabad, getting them unloaded at Bombay Port, reloading them in the hold of the ship by which we were to sail and again unloading and reloading in a ferry and then a train which was to take us to our destination. It was a strenuous and time consuming but responsible job.

At Bombay Harbour when I was supervising the loading of the ship S.S. Cynthia from its upper deck, a British Sergeant on the embarkation staff shouted at me as if I were his subordinate. I disliked his intolerable conduct. He called upon me to come down to him at the shore. I did not go down and told him to come up to me. When he shouted again, I warned him to behave. He was obliged to come up to where I was working. He got my signatures and went away after handing over certain papers to me.

The ship, having been loaded, left the Bombay Harbour to get into position in a convoy of about ten troop ships. The sun was setting on the fifth of March as we waited in the open sea. I looked at the Gateway of India, the Taj Mahal Hotel and the Bombay skyline. Wondering at the beauty of the scene, I felt homesick and I thought how long it would be before I saw that skyline again! I went to the bar of the ship. There I saw most of the brother Officers enjoying their drinks in order to make the departure as pleasant as they could. When I checked at the bar, I could not order a drink. I was disappointed to find that most of the common long drinks were the same as I had in my house at Secunderabad.

Feeling sad and lonely, I went to the top deck to be alone to enjoy the solitude. I found Mohan Singh was already there sitting alone on a deck chair. He had just been promoted to the rank of Major. I congratulated him. He was drinking something. He asked me what I would have. I told him that I had already been to the bar and I could not find any drink to order that I did not have at my home. He said. "Surely you didn't have the variety that is available on this boat ?" Then he said, "Oh, forget about it. Basant won't know." I said, "I want to keep my promise." While we were talking, a steward approached to ask Mohan Singh if he would like to order another drink. Mohan Singh said, "Yes, a brandy and ginger ale." I shouted, "Oh, I didn't have brandy in my house. I'll also have the same drink." Hence onwards I drank brandy and ginger ale during the voyage.

It was on the third day of the voyage that in the presence of all the Officers of the Battalion, the Colonel opened a sealed secret envelope in which our destination along with instructions was given. Then alone we learnt that we would go to Penang Island and from there to Ipoh, north of Kuala Lumpur in Malaya. Till that day our convoy had sailed to the West. Now it changed its direction to go to the East.

Colonel's Criticism

At the end of the conference Col. Fitzpatrick mentioned the trouble between me and the Embarkation Sergeant at Bombay Port. He criticized me and advised all Officers to be careful and co-operate with the embarkation staff irrespective of their rank. I did not appreciate Col. Fitzpatrick's strict remarks against me before all the Officers, since I had not complained to him about the Sergeant's misbehavior which was so insulting. The Colonel's criticism without having asked me any explanation hurt my feelings. When the Officers dispersed I went to the Colonel and told him how I felt and how the Sergeant had insulted me and shouted and bullied me. I had not caused any trouble except asking him to come up to me as I was so busy. I had ignored the incident as nothing had gone wrong at Bombay. The Colonel remained silent and after this episode my dealings with the Colonel were very formal throughout the voyage.

On the night before the last day of the voyage Col. Fitzpatrick asked me to come to him in his cabin on the following day to get instructions about unloading the baggage. The next day after breakfast I went to his cabin and knocked at the door. Colonel shouted, "Who is it?" "Sir, I am Dhillon. You wanted me to see you." "Oh, not this early." His tone was very harsh.

So I came away and did not care to go to him until about eleven, when he himself came to me where I was standing with most of the Officers looking towards the beautiful island of Penang which we were about to approach. He quietly gave me instructions for unloading baggage from the ship, reloading it on a ferry boat, unloading it again and then reloading it on to a train that was to go to Ipoh. As he was giving these instructions, it appeared as if nothing untoward had occurred. He was wonderfully cool and calm. When we arrived at Ipoh, Col. Fitzpatrick took great care to help me check railway goods bogies and the Battalion baggage. At times, I felt pity for the old man who was working very hard. I was happy that our entire baggage arrived safe and intact.

Ipoh

Ipoh, the capital of Perak state, was a beautiful clean town. People looked happy and prosperous. There were many amusement parks and lot of night life. The picture houses ran their shows throughout the night. There were excellent dance halls for ball-room dancing where one could go without a partner and hire a professional dancer called "Taxi-girl." The payment was made for each dance of about three minutes by offering a coupon which the gentlemen purchased from the dance hall establishment.

It was a good opportunity to learn ball-room dancing which offered entertainment and healthy exercise but I was so much in love with Basant that my attitude towards dancing was rather orthodox and anti-dancing. Those were the beautiful girls who were normally chaperoned by their parents or guardians. I was much impressed by the fluorescent lights of various hues which lit the public places and roads. They dazzled not only the eyes but the mind too and created a feeling of complacency and tranquillity. The war seemed to be a distant thing.

Our men were billeted in the buildings of the Perak Turf Club. The Officers were lodged in a five-star hotel, Hotel Majestic. Here food was excellent and drinks were cheap as 'STINGA', half a peg of Scotch whisky, cost only nine cents while a lemonade or any aerated soft drink cost at least forty cents. It was so because alcoholic drinks were given to us on NAAFI rates prescribed by British Navy, Army and Air Force institute, which ran a canteen for service personnel and their families. A Malayan dollar was equal to one and a half rupees. As per my promise made to Basant, I carried on with my brandy and ginger-ale whenever I wished. We were busy training for war.

On a Saturday I took my Signal Platoon on a long route-march. That very morning I had written a letter to Basant that I was keeping my promise made to her. After returning from the route-march, I took a bath and went down to have a cup of tea and post the letter. On the way to the post box I saw a forlorn British Lieutenant. We introduced ourselves to each other. I invited the Lieutenant to tea and told him that after tea I would go to see a picture, *'The Thief of Baghdad'*. This officer had come from home and was one of the 33,000 Allied troops who were evacuated from the beaches of Dunkirk in the face of the German attack during 1940.

During tea he talked about the debacle at Dunkirk. Our brother Officers returning after games kept joining us and after tea I offered drinks to everybody. And then each one of the Officers stood drinks to the assemblage in turn. At about eleven at night we had our dinner and we went to see the picture. The letter remained unposted. On Sunday morning I meditated and concluded that though I was keeping the promise but not the spirit of it. I tore off the letter and wrote another one that from that day onwards I would not drink except when I stood on the native soil again.

Being a raw signaller I devoted most of my time to train myself. Nk. Ajmer Singh was my instructor who was assisted by Hav. Mohammad Ashraf, the Signal Platoon Havildar. During our stay at Ipoh we were visited by most of the General Officers. Once when Air Chief Marshal Sir Robert Brooke-Popham, Commander-in-Chief, Far East, visited us, we were stunned when he asked Major Mohan Singh, "Do you understand English ?" The gross ignorance of the Commander-in-Chief was, indeed, shocking. We spent about two months in long route marches and weapon training. Normally, we had our evenings free. It was here that I met Sardar Gurdial Singh Dhillon of Padhri from Amritsar district. He had a sports goods shop. Gurdial Singh was a graduate of Chiefs' College, Lahore. His uncle Sardar Sampuran Singh was the first Deputy High Commissioner of India in Pakistan after independence. Presently Gurdial Singh lives in tehsil Pauhri of Shivpuri district in Madhya Pradesh. Whenever we wanted to have our Indian food, he and his wife played generous hosts.

Another friend close to him was Rattan Singh. He joined the INA as early as December 1941. He was a Captain in the INA and worked on General Mohan Singh's personal staff. He remained with the General during his imprisonment under the Japanese and later under the British. He and Chhatra Bahadur served the General selflessly. In appreciation of their services, the General treated them as equal members of his family.

Importance of Proper Expression

As the Battalion Signal Officer, I was normally in touch with the Battalion Commander in connection with my duties. Mohan Singh was the Headquarter Company Commander. As such, I came under

Mohan Singh's command. One day while at Ipoh I approached Mohan Singh and confided in him that though I did everything to the satisfaction of the Colonel, I had a feeling that he was not very happy with me. Mohan Singh told me that my feeling was correct but the fault was not of the Colonel.

Mohan Singh explained that the fault lay with my language and its misplaced expression. Teaching me as a sympathetic senior colleague, he said: "For instance, when the Colonel gives you some instructions or information you always reply, 'I know'. Actually what you mean is that you follow what he tells you or you understand what he says. If you are careful of your language, everything will be all right". Mohan Singh's advice helped me a lot not only in understanding the Colonel but throughout my life. I saw to it that I never gave a chance to the Colonel to be annoyed with me on account of my improper expression. I was glad to find a marked change in his attitude towards me.

As Officiating Battalion Adjutant

After about two months' stay at Ipoh, our Battalion moved to Sungei Pattani in South Kedah as a part of the 5th Indian Infantry Brigade under Brigadier Garrett. A few days after our arrival at Sungei Pattani, Major (later Maj-Gen. in the INA) Mohammad Zaman Kiani, our Bn. Adjutant, fell ill. The following day I was surprised when Col. Fitzpatrick came to my room very early in the morning. He said, "Gurbakhsh ! Zaman has been hospitalized. Here are keys of his papers. Will you please help me in his place as my Adjutant. I am running to a conference at the Div. Headquarters and shall be back by the afternoon." Our Brigade was a part of the 11th Indian Division which was commanded by Maj. Gen. Murray Lyon.

The Colonel left the keys and went out. Everybody including me was surprised that Col. Fitzpatrick had chosen me to do that important staff job. Normally in our Battalion this job was given to the senior-most Captain while I was still a 2nd Lieut. After breakfast I went to Major Mohan Singh and informed him about my appointment. Though surprised, he was happy and said, "Be very careful. Let this appointment not go to your head. See that you don't provoke the jealousy of your senior subalterns or Captains and whenever you are in any difficulty or you don't understand a problem, don't hesitate to come to me for guidance. You have got a very good opportunity. Congratulations and good luck."

One of the officers who was very happy at my appointment was Captain Hardial Singh Randhawa, my previous Company Commander in 'A' Company at Lahore. He liked playing difficult and was a very hard task-master. He loved his men and they loved him. He was very proud of his Dogras as the 'A' Company was a Dogra Company. When I told him about my appointment his remark was, "You bloody toady!"

The C.Os office had an independent entrance. There was also a door through my office. One day while going to his office, the Colonel passed through my room and said, "Mr. Dhillon, turnout of the Regimental Quarter Guard is not good. I want to see it up to the SHER DIL standard. Send a circular round to all the Companies that I want Company Commanders to pay special attention to the turnout of the Guard." I did what I was told. On the top of the circular, I wrote A Company followed by other companies in the customary alphabetical order. The next day Capt. Hardial Singh came to me and said, "Why did you put my Company on top of the circular?" "Because A comes always on top," I replied. "Not in bad turnout," he added and went away.

On another occasion the C.O. wanted me to congratulate all the Company Commanders for the good show put up during a Brigade exercise. So while addressing the Company Commanders, I wrote, "All Companies." Hardial Singh again turned up and scolded me for having put him at par with other Company Commanders. As a result when I sent another circular I reversed the order and put the Headquarters Company on top. He came to me again and said, "You bloody toady, you try to please Mohan Singh, your Company Commander, and the two white-skinned 2nd Lieut. boys whom you put above me to show to the C.O. that I am no good." It was not with me alone that he behaved in this way. He liked being tough for the sake of fun. As for an instance, one day he came to the Mess when English music was going on the radio. He tuned it to Indian music. The 2nd-in-Command Maj. Anderson walked in. Since he did not like the Indian music, he tuned it back to English music. Hardial objected and went to the radio and tuned it back to the Indian music again.

Problem of Indian Food

In those days we missed Indian food the most because in the Officers' Mess only English food was served. We had to fight hard to get Indian food in the Mess. The food issue was one of the causes of disaffection against the British. One day Hardial heard a senior British Officer say, "I don't like this wretched Indian food." Hardial paid him back in the same coin and ordered the Mess waiter, "Take that bloody porridge away. I don't like the look of it." Hardial simply could not tolerate listening to or being done anything against an Indian by anybody especially the English.

I learnt later that during the war Hardial was transferred sixteen times to different Units. He could not be punished because he was a good Commander and good fighter who knew how to go according to the book and not violate the law. He was a very self-respecting man. During his tenure as Commander of "A" Company, he made the Dogras win the sports banner in the annual tournament. I requested him to be my "friend of the accused" during the Red Fort trial about which I shall write later.

A Case of Colour Bar

During my adjutancy at Sungei Pattani, one day while we started to go on a tactical exercise during which our Battalion was commanded by the 2nd-in-Command, Major Anderson, and Col. Fitzpatric acted as a referee, the C.O's station wagon was allotted to the acting Bn. Commander Major Anderson. Before Major Anderson's arrival, the Battalion command group had occupied their respective seats in the CO's (Bn. Commander's) station wagon. Being the senior-most Company Commander during that exercise Captain Mohammed Akram sat in a seat in front of the two white 2nd Lieut. Company Commanders who sat in the rear seat and waited for Maj. Anderson's arrival. When he arrived and saw the white Officers sitting in the rear of Capt. Mohammad Akram, he shouted at Akram, "How dare you sit in front of the Officers ? Get Back." Akram obeyed. Then Anderson made the two White Officers occupy the front seat vacated by Capt. Akram.

Stunned by Major Anderson's action, I remained out of my

elements throughout the exercise. At the end of the exercise as we reached our camp, Akram came to me and told me that he wanted to resign from the service. I begged him to give me a day to report to the Colonel. Since I was the Adjutant it was my responsibility to inform the Colonel about such a happening. Akram was one of highly respected Officers in our Battalion by virtue of age and experience. He had been in the Unit much longer than any of the Commissioned Officers. We used to call him Lala, elder brother.

The next day when Col. Fitzpatrick passed through my office, I told him about the unhappy incident. The Colonel took me to his office, made me draw a sketch of the station wagon (staff car) and narrate the story in detail. During my narration I said that I felt hurt when I heard Maj. Anderson shouting at Capt. Mohammed Akram. The Colonel advised me, "Keep your feelings aside. I do not need your opinion. You narrate the episode as you saw it." When he understood the whole story, the Colonel let me go and called Major Anderson alone. They were closeted for over four hours.

As usual, I returned very late from my office. When I did return to my room that evening I found Captain Akram waiting for me. As I have already said, Akram was an elderly person with twenty-five years of service. He came to my room and told me that Major Anderson went to his (Akram's) room and begged his pardon. Anderson was so repentant that he cried before Akram, stayed with him for about an hour and apologized. Akram thanked me profusely for having restored his honour and prestige as an Indian and as an individual. I was naturally happy at the pleasant outcome of an unpleasant episode.

Though rash at times, Major Anderson was a good hearted man. When I went to the Mess late that evening, he showed extraordinary courtesy to me and showed no signs of annoyance with me for having reported the matter to the Colonel. This incident was talked about among most of the Indian Commissioned Officers in all the Units of the 11th Division and I got a lot of appreciation from them. After about three months of stay at Sungei Pattani I was selected and sent to undergo a two-month signal course at Puna (now Pune) in India. I handed over the Signal Platoon to Hav. Mohammad Ashraf. The night before I left, Col. Fitzpatrick offered me a drink. When I told him that I had taken a vow not to drink on a foreign soil he offered me a *nimbu-*

pani, lime with soda. On the day of my departure for home when I went to hand over the keys of my office, Col. Fitzpatrick gave me a warm hearted send-off and said, "Gurbakhsh, you have done much better than my expectations. I hope you will do your Signal Course with distinction. I will be happy to see you back."

An Acknowledgement

I feel that what I learnt during the period of my acting adjutancy under Colonel Fitzpatrick cannot be repaid fully in routine expressions of gratitude. It was because of his training that I was later able to serve in the Indian National Army with distinction as a Staff Officer and as a Commander. Fitzpatrick was a man of few words. I remember once I took a letter to him for his signatures. The letter had been typed by the Head Clerk during the night on the previous day's date. Fitzpatrick read through the draft and showed his satisfaction at my wording but pointed with his pen at the date and said, "The letter is already a day late. What sort of impression will it make at higher headquarters about the staff of this Battalion ?" I said, "Sorry, Sir, it won't happen again." Ever since that day I have never forgotten to check my letters from beginning to end. In my office work I got help from our Head Clerk, Havildar (later Lieutenant in the INA) P.P. Singh. He always improved upon my wordings for which I got the credit.

On my return voyage, I got accommodation on the same ship S.S. Cynthia on which our Battalion had come. Instead of going to Bombay we landed at Madras. From there I went to report at my Regimental Depot at Ferozepur and after enjoying three days casual leave proceeded to the Signal School, Puna. When I finished the course I got a month's leave. During that time I took Basant to Lahore and got her admitted to Hans Raj Mahavidyalay, a Girls College. The Principal, Premvati Thapar, was kind enough to admit Basant to her college, though Basant had never been to any school. She could not be admitted to any class but as a special favour Principal Thapar admitted Basant in a special class where she was the only student and was tutored in Hindi, Punjabi and English.

After my leave I joined the Regimental Depot at Ferozepur. I had to stay there for eleven days before my departure to Malaya. Basant came to stay with me for those eleven days. It was a happy coincidence that we met Major and Mrs. Joginder Singh Dhillon normally known as "Jogi". He became a Lieut. General in independent India. During my stay overseas Basant had some trouble in receiving the monthly allotment of two hundred rupees from me. Jogi very kindly got it restored.

During my stay at Ferozepur I met some of my old Instructors and colleagues of the recruitment days and also of the period when I was with them at Lahore in the 4/14 Punjab Regiment. They wanted me to dine with them in their barrack. Instead I invited them to my bungalow. Their condition was that they would play the host. They brought a bottle of country liquor distilled at Faridkot. I was not accustomed to taking the countryliquor. When I refused to drink the stuff, Basant said, "Sahib, you are an officer to day because of them. Don't forget your past." I took the stuff. It was a very warm send-off. Before leaving Ferozepur I called on Lt. Col. Ingle who was raising a new Battalion, the 6/14 Punjab. This Unit later joined us in Singapore as late as the first week of February 1942 and had to surrender having seen a little action. I also called on Mrs. Anderson and am sad to recollect that Major Anderson died in action during the war in Malaya. The Regimental ties are amazingly strong.

Easier Vow

I left Ferozepur for Delhi on my way to Madras to catch a boat for Malaya on 11th November 1941. When I went to see off Basant at the railway station, Basant said, "Let me make your vow a bit easier. From today on you may take two chhotas (half a peg) of any drink within a period of twenty four hours." I thanked her for her leniency and we parted trying to put up a brave face. At Delhi I spent the day calling on Thorats and Misri Chand who were working in the General Headquarters. They said that they would look forward to welcoming us back at the end of the war. From them I learnt about the whereabouts of Major Adams and Lieut. Gurucharan Singh (an old colleague of my sepoy days) at Kabul Lines. Then I visited the Qutab Minar and had my tea at Thorats. Dr. Mrs. Leela Thorat showed their little baby, Kusum.

Thereafter, I went to the Red Fort. As I stood on the ramparts of the Fort, I heard the call sign of the A.I.R. (All India Radio). This tune enchanted me so much that whenever I heard it, I was reminded of my country and the Red Fort. I still had four hours at my disposal before catching the G.T. Express. I went to spend this time in a cinema hall at Chandni Chowk after my pilgrimage of the Gurudwara. I saw the picture, *Naya Sansar*. In this picture, Ashok Kumar, the hero of the story, sang *chal chal re naujawan*. With some variations, this song was destined to become one of the most popular marching songs of the INA

I again boarded S.S. Santhia at Madras during my return voyage to Malaya. S.S. Santhia was a merchant ship. It carried civilian passengers. This time it carried the 3rd Cavalry which landed at Penang. Unfortunately, the Unit's armoured fighting vehicles did not accompany it. Those were supposed to follow, later. That shows how poor was the planning of the War Office in London. This was the only mechanized Unit sent to Malaya. They were little better than a motorized Unit. This deficiency was there because of the demand of troops and resources on the Western theatres of war. The 3rd Cavalry formed a part of the 11th Indian Division and was allotted the defence of the Island of Penang. I disembarked at Singapore and reported at 7 MRC, Mixed Reinforcement Camp at Bidadari. From Singapore I was sent to Jitra situated on the main road to Thailand, sixteen miles south of the border. I arrived there on the 5th of December in the afternoon. Now the war looked imminent.

Alternative Plans of Action

There were two alternative plans — one defensive and the other offensive. The defensive plan envisaged a defensive line to be put up from Kota Bharu on the east coast of northern Malaya to Jitra on the west. This line of defence was to make use of natural obstacles like jungles and marshes. The offensive plan, "Matador", called for attacking the enemy on the Thai territory as soon as they landed on the eastern coast of Thailand, beaches of Singora, Sangkla and Patani. The Royal Air Force based at the aerodromes at Alor Star, Kota Bharu and Sungei Patani was to support the ground forces.

"Matador" could be launched by the Commander-in-Chief, Far East on orders from London. Hence the G.O.C. Malaya, Lt. Gen. Percival, the 3rd Indian Corps Commander, Lt. Gen. Sir L.M. Heath, and the 11th Indian Division Commander Maj. Gen. Murray Loyan, were helpless to take initiative on their own. The British Government were still trying to avoid war with the Japanese. No wonder, the civilian population were caught unaware in the war when the undeclared war broke out with an attack on Pearl Harbour and the bombing of Singapore on the early morning of the 7th December. On 8th December, the Japanese forces landed on the north-eastern coast of Malaya at Singora, Patani and Kota Bharu. Simultaneously, the British Air Force was destroyed completely at Sungei Patani, Alor Star and Kota Bharu airfields.

The Japanese enjoyed complete control of the skies in northern Malaya. The initiative slipped away from the hands of the Field Commanders on the very first day of the war in Malaya for no fault of their own. The Commanders and their troops were to suffer because of the delayed decision of the British Government in London. But then the British Empire had grown too extensive to be defended at all places. It is natural to guard one's home first than to look after the far-off acquired colonies. Politicians err and the soldiers pay with their lives because of mistakes committed by the politicians.

We had been waiting at Alor Star railway station since the 8th of December ready to move at a moment's notice into Thailand as per plan, "Matador", which was never to be. It was then that the 5th Brigade under Brigadier Garret and the 6th Brigade under Brigadier Lay were ordered to hold the Jitra defences. Two Companies of the 1/8th Punjab Regiment were hurriedly moved up to destroy road bridges within the Thailand territory in order to delay the enemy's advance. They did that job successfully and then fell back to their allotted position along the Jitra defences.

The 1/14th Punjab Regiment was ordered to go up north to the Thailand frontier and delay the enemy's advance between the frontier and the Asun line and then fall back to form the Brigade Reserve in Jitra. We advanced with speed and delayed the enemy's advance for full three days in spite of the heavy rains. On the 10th of December the Prince of Wales and the Repulse, two destroyers, the pride of the British Navy, were sunk by the Japanese Air Force off Kota Bharu coast. This was a great blow to the defenders of Malaya and Singapore.

On the 11th, 1/14th Punjab fought a pitched battle at Changlun near the Thai frontier. Our advance Company was ably led by Captain Mohammad Akram. Being the Battalion Signal Officer, I was always with my C.O. Col. Fitzpatrick who remained nearest to the front line where the battle was waging. He cared neither for the fire nor relaxed even for a moment. It was a lesson to be with him and watch him command and control the battle. He was calm as if it were an exercise during peace time manoeuvres. My signallers worked successfully to his satisfaction in maintaining telecommunication with all the Companies, the Light Battery supporting our Battalion and with the Division and Brigade Headquarters.

The battle of Changlun went on for about eight hours. There were casualties on both the sides. At times, the C.O. sent me to contact Company Commanders to maintain a personal touch. Many a time bullets whizzed by my head. It was my first battle inoculation. The good old SHER DIL lived up to its name,

At 2 p.m. our Battalion was ordered to withdraw to the north of the Asun and wait for further orders. Brigadier Garret called a conference of all the Commanders including the Company Commanders. Habibur Rehman, then our Bn. Adjutant and I fell back to the given line just north of the Asun. Habib allotted areas to Companies. I got busy establishing contact and was happy to talk to Captain Hargreeves at the Division Headquarters. I gave him a report of the situation as it was. Satisfied I came to the place where Habib stood by the main highway. Just then at about 4.30 P.M. we were surprised by the Japanese tanks which tore through us with their fire power. They threw incendiary bombs on our vehicles which were parked under trees, and put them on fire. As the vehicles burnt, the enemy tanks wreaked havoc on both sides of the highway with their fire power.

I rushed to my phone to warn the Brigade and the Division headquarters of the enemy advance. The enemy aimed at my taping rod and destroyed it. My phone went dead. The bursts of machine-gun bullets from a tank followed my movements as I tumbled about on the ground trying to avoid being hit. However, the tanks rolled on towards the Asun. They crossed a bridge over the marshes of Asun. This bridge was to be blown up by our engineers but the Japanese were on time to cut off the fuse wires. The bridge remained undetonated and thus in tact. The Units of the 6th and 15th Brigades got bombed.

My Signal truck was burnt with all our equipments and effects. I felt bereaved of the two carrier pigeons and my wife's photo which went to flames along with the truck. There followed an utter panic which caused a stampede in our rear. Habib and I ordered a withdrawal of the men of our Unit who ran helter-skelter. It was with great difficulty that by nightfall we could manage to collect about four hundred men and Officers, British, Gurkhas and Indians of different Units and camped on the railway line near the first station north of Alor Star.

At the dawn of 12th December a train from the North came and halted about half a mile away from us where the bridge had been destroyed earlier by our sappers. The Japanese troops detrained and fired at us. We were taken unaware. Habib shouted, "Take position." None obeyed except some men of our own Unit. There followed another stampede when men rushed into deep water paddy fields like animals. It took us all a long time to collect some of the stragglers again.

Alor Star Fell

Avoiding direct routes we approached a place south of Alor Star. There we learnt that Alor Star had fallen and the Japanese flag was hoisted on the Sultan of Kuala Kehdah's palace. We escaped with about four hundred men of different Units to the Island of Penang in small local boats during an overnight voyage. It was in the afternoon of the 13th December that we arrived Miami Beach near Penang. The coastal guards fired at us. The fire was only due to nervousness, mistaking us for Japanese. We hoisted a white flag. When we were identified we were allowed to land and were taken to 3 M.R.C. in Penang.

Penang Evacuated

We had just reported our arrival when the evacuation of Penang was ordered. The C.O. of the 3 M.R.C. gave Habib and me a Company each to command. We left the M.R.C. Camp without having eaten anything. We were in a hurry to catch a ferry to the mainland of Malaya. We had no food for the previous two days. A sepoy told me that there were a lot of chapatis and dal left in the Muslim kitchen. I ran to the kitchen and found heaps of nice hot chapatis and tasty hot dal. Apparently, that food had been abandoned because of panic. I filled a mug with dal and took about twenty chapatis to share with Habib and kept some in my haversack which came very handy during the next twenty-four hours. By the next dawn we reached the mainland and were ordered to go to guard a railway bridge at Nibong Tabol.

Colour Bar even in War

Habib and I were given this duty though there were a number of British Officers in the 3 MRC. We remained in position for three days, after which the bridge was blown up by engineers. We guarded the bridge for another two days till the arrival of the Japanese. Then we were ordered to withdraw to Ipoh where I fell ill with malaria. I was hospitalized and removed to Singapore. After discharge from the hospital I was sent to 7 MRC which was stationed at Bidadri Camp. It was commanded by an English Lt. Colonel who had recently come from England. He appointed me Adjutant under him. That was the first time that I had to deal with Australian and English troops. I did not find much difference between the mentality of the Australians and the Indians but the English had a bias against me as their coloured Adjutant.

It was during those days that I heard a story about an Indian Captain commanding a Company who was travelling with two English Lieutenants. The Indian Captain was asked by the railway guard to leave the first class compartment in which he was travelling. The English Officers objected and told the guard that the Indian Captain was their Commander and they were his subordinates. The guard replied, "Sir I have to abide by the Malayan Federated States Railways rules. A coloured man cannot travel with the white man." The Indian Captain was forced to leave the coach. The story went round the Indian Officers. We wondered why we were serving in the war to support such a system of discrimination ! Weren't we in the Army as mercenaries to defend the British Empire ? Where was the much-talked-about fidelity and honour ?

By the dawn of 9th February, almost two Divisions of the Japanese had landed on the soil of Singapore. On 10th February, 7 MRC was moved to Raffles Square, a business area. By that time it was apparent that the surrender of Singapore was imminent. Besides scarcity of water, we were living only on dry rations of hard Army biscuits. The Japanese were bombing the city with heavy guns. Intensive bombardment was exchanged from both sides across Johore Bharu Channel. En route to Raffles Square we saw that the civilian population had gathered in a large open space under the Indian National Congress Tricolour Flag.

The English Colonel asked me what flag was that. When I told him that it was the Indian national flag and the Indians had gathered to avoid being bombed by the Japanese, the Colonel replied, "I can't blame them. When we cannot protect them, they have to look after themselves." The Indians had been influenced by leaflets air-dropped by a Japanese organization called the Fujiwara Kikan and signed by Capt. Mohan Singh designated as the GOC of the Indian National Army. Such leaflets were being dropped throughout the Malayan campaign after Mohan Singh and Captain Mohammad Akram had met Maj. Fujiwara and Giani Pritam Singh, an Indian revolutionary in the jungles of Kuala Kedah State. The existence of an Indian National Army's Company on an island attacking Singapore and dropping leaflets had a great demoralizing effect on the Indian troops.

On 13th February Raffles Square was bombed. We suffered heavily with about three hundred killed and many more wounded. The 2nd-in-Command of 7 MRC, a very kind experienced English Major, and I had a difficult job disposing of the corpses. We just dropped them in the ocean. There were no religious functionaries available to perform the last rites. We did whatever we could for all the communities alike. Evacuation of the wounded was a very difficult job. Under that hopeless situation, the Red Cross Society of Singapore came to help us. The British Major gave me a helping hand in that predicament. To keep up the morale of the men he kept on recounting, *"Thanda dil, mushkil men rakho thanda dil, thanda dil"*—In crises keep your cool.

Singapore Falls

Late on the night of 15th February we learnt that Singapore had capitulated. Lt. Gen. A.E. Percival, the G.O.C. of the British Forces, surrendered unconditionally to the Japanese Commander, Lt. Gen.

Tomoyuki Yamashita. I was asked by the O.C. 7 MRC to collect all arms and be prepared to take all the Indian troops to a place called Farrer Park. With a heavy heart I took leave of the English Commanding Officer and his Second-in-Command who had been really good to me and marched off to Farrer Park not knowing what the future held in store for us.

6
THE SURRENDER

Farrer Park

Farrer Park was a big spacious ground off Serangoon Road by Kenden Kerbau Maternity Hospital in Singapore. It was otherwise known as Old Race Course. On the western precincts was a big double-storey club building with a verandah facing east, which could be used as balcony.

Defeated and demoralized, Indian soldiers were now without their traditional leaders, "The White Sahibs". Here and there were a few Indian Officers, who were their only hope. Shabbily dressed, carrying extremely meager belongings, they collected themselves in this area of about two square miles, converging from all corners of the Singapore battlefield where they and their comrades had fought and lost their lives in vain. They never looked like soldiers. Only a miracle could remake them fighting sons of the soil again.

After midday Major Iwaichi Fujiwari, a Japanese officer, Giani Pritam Singh and Captain Mohan Singh, Captain Mohammad Akram of 1st Battalion, 14th Punjab Regiment, accompanied by some Japanese and Indian Officers appeared on the balcony of the Fareer Park club building Lt. Colonel Hunt, a British Staff Officer of the Malayan Command, had come to hand over to the Japanese all the Indian troops who had now become Prisoners of War. He looked crestfallen and frightened. He was one of the vanquished. After saluting Major Fujiwara, he ordered all of us over the microphone to come to attention. Saluting Major Fujiwara once again, he spoke a few words and handed us over to him, and saluting again, stepped back. The white man's prestige was at its lowest ebb in Asia.

The microphone was then taken over by Major Fujiwara. Besides him stood Lieutenant Kunizuka, a Japanese interpreter, and Lieut. Col. Naranjan Singh Gill, the senior-most Indian Combatant Officer amongst Indian Prisoners of War in Malaya. Major Fujiwara spoke in the Japanese language. He looked impressive and dignified. Tall and medium built, dressed in a Staff Officer's uniform with gold-lace epaulettes, he looked a towering personality among the Japanese. In a commanding voice, he said "You have been handed over to us as prisoners. You are Asians and so are we, the Japanese. As such, we are brethren. How can a brother be a prisoner of the brother ?" He explained at length the Japanese war aims, and the Japanese policy towards the Asiatic countries. He dwelt on the Japanese objective of forming a Co-prosperity Sphere in Greater East Asia on the basis of equality and reciprocity.

Maj. Fujiwara expressed his firm belief that world peace and the liberation of Asia could not be achieved and maintained without a free and independent India. He condemned the British for having kept India enslaved for the last three centuries. He further said that if Indian Prisoners of War in Malaya were prepared to fight the British Imperialism for the noble cause of achieving the independence of their motherland, the Imperial Japanese Government and their mighty fighting forces would advance all out support. He suggested the formation of the Indian National Army, and announced that he was handing over all the Indian Prisoners of War in Malaya to Capt. Mohan Singh, the G.O.C. of the Indian National Army. Major Fujiwara's speech was translated sentence by sentence into English and Hindustani by Lieut. Kunizuka and Lt. Col. N.S. Gill, respectively. It was well received by all those who were present there.

At this stage Capt. Mohan Singh moved over to the microphone and spoke at length in Hindustani. He said that the British were being defeated on all Fronts, and the time was ripe for all Indians abroad to serve four hundred million Indians inside India by pushing the British out of India. While Capt. Mohan Singh was speaking on the microphone, there was a sudden and spontaneous outburst of joy and enthusiasm accompanied by different slogans. Soldiers threw their caps and pugrees up in the air. Some even jumped upward. There appeared to be a storm raging in that ocean of human beings of which individuals were the waves. Observing this enthusiasm Capt. Mohan Singh said, "Slogans alone will get us nowhere. What we need is disciplined and an organized power."

Appreciating the help promised by the Japanese Government, he stressed that at that moment he was not in a position to paint bright pictures, for the forming of a real Indian National Army was a difficult task for which time and planning were essential factors. Success could only be possible by the combined efforts of all those present there. He concluded, by saying: "All of us and our forefathers have been fighting for the British Raj. Now we have got a chance, so let us fight for our own independence". Capt. Mohan Singh's speech was greeted with acclaim of Inqilab Zindabad from all sides. In the British surrender at Singapore could be seen a new light and a new hope for the future of our great country, our dear India.

Giani Pritam Singh, a civilian from Bangkok, got up to speak. He acquainted us with his activities outside India, particularly in Siam and especially since the time hostilities broke out in the Far East. He said that he had accompanied the Japanese from Bangkok with the only object of saving Indian lives, property and all that was dear to them. He was happy to have achieved success in his object thus far. He showed pleasure at our having survived the campaign and the interest shown by us in the proposed Indian National Army, for which he placed all his services at our disposal. His speech was followed by an informal introduction of some officers to Major Fujiwara. Later a musical programme presented by Jemadar Ram Singh of the Gurkha Regiment (later Major in the Indian National Army) and his party entertained the troops. Uncertainty and gloom had vanished. The erstwhile Prisoners of War were now to become the soldiers of India's Army of Liberation, the Army that was to fight under its own leadership, with a real and just cause to wage war. A new era had dawned. All were happy.

That night was spent in Farrer Park. Friends met friends; relatives met relatives. Those who had been lost were mourned. The happy reunions were cheered. The pleasant and unpleasant surprises were witnessed. Discussions and an exchange of views on the formation of the Indian National Army continued throughout the night. More information was needed, more clarifications were desired. Officers, in particular, were carefully weighing the pros and cons of this new situation. I knew Mohan Singh well as we belonged to the same Unit. He was one of my close friends. I had confidence in him. However, I had a long mental struggle throughout the night and eventually decided to volunteer for the Indian National Army. It was during that night of 17-18th February, 1942 that I took a vow, NOT TO DRINK TILL INDIA BECAME FREE

Next morning orders were issued by Capt. Mohan Singh to march off all the Units to various camps on the island where the Units were to occupy their allotted accommodation. My Unit was to proceed to Neesoon Camp. The defeated and demoralized troops once again appeared to be regaining their lost confidence. A comparatively good command and organization could be witnessed amongst the ranks. The depressed and gloomy were happy. The dispersal to our respective camps was done in a manner which showed itself in marked contrast to the gloom and indiscipline found in us at the time of our arrival at Farrer Park. The Officers appeared to have had a better hold on their men.

Early Formation of the INA

Before leaving Farrer Park I had a talk with Capt. Mohan Singh and learnt that during the Malayan Campaign he had formed the Indian National Army at Kuala Lumpur as early as the beginning of January 1942. It was at Kuala Lumpur that Mohan Singh was joined by a number of Officers prominent amongst whom were Captain Habib-ur-Rehman (later Col.) and Deputy Chief of General Staff of the INA who accompanied Netaji in his last journey, Captain Ehsan Qadir (later Col.) and Member of Netaji's Cabinet, Captain Gulzara Singh (later Colonel), Commander of Azad Brigade and Member of Netaji's Cabinet, Captain Talib Din (later Major), a Medical Officer, Captain Mahboob Ahmed (later Colonel) and Netaji's Military Secretary and Captain Ram Sarup (later Colonel) who during 1944 campaign was awarded the medal of Sardar-e-Jung.

From the very start the ranks of the Indian National Army set up traditions of service and sacrifice which brought them popularity and praise from Indian nationals and respect from the local population. Revolutionary changes were introduced on national lines, abolishing all differences of class and creed. Separate kitchens for Hindus, Muslims, Sikhs, Christians and Gurkhas were abolished. They worked, lived and ate together in complete harmony. That was the nucleus around which grew the Indian National Army.

Before the battle of Singapore, these volunteers had done commendable work by affording protection to civilians' life and property from looters, dacoits and hooligans who normally spring up in countries which have the misfortune of becoming theatres of war. Some of these volunteers moved in parties along the Japanese advance collecting Indian soldiers who were wounded or had become stragglers and those civilians who had gone homeless.

First Action by INA

The morale and fighting spirit and skill of this newly raised Indian National Army was tested in the battlefield when the Japanese agreed to let a party of two Companies, each one hundred strong, take part in the battle of Singapore. The honour of commanding that party was given to a Gunner Officer, Captain Allah a former Subedar. They were given an important task of seizing the island of Pulau Ubin opposite to the Changi naval base.

And After

After the conclusion of this historic meeting at Farrer Park, 45,000 Indian Prisoners of war, moved into different camps, each commanded by the senior-most officer designated as Station Commander. Capt. Mohan Singh set up his own Headquarters, generally known as Supreme Headquarters, at Mount Pleasant, a European residential area in Singapore where mostly the British police officials lived before the capitulation of Singapore. This area was "white-man's paradise". No Asiatic could take on rent any accommodation in this locality. The Supreme Headquarters discharged all such duties and obligations as are the responsibility of any High Command concerning general policy, supplies, administration, accommodation, medical care, transfers, routine welfare, propaganda and discipline of troops.

These headquarters were organized from the very start in different branches dealing with separate subjects so as to ensure the smooth running of the administration connected with all Indian Prisoners of

War located in Singapore and another 10,000 spread out all over the mainland of Malaya. At this time the Japanese occupation forces had enforced 'movement restrictions', pending the re-establishment of military administration. The means of transportation and communications throughout the Malayan peninsula were not yet restored. These difficulties were magnified all the more when an insufficient number of motor vehicles and an insufficient quantity of petrol were placed at the disposal of the Supreme Headquarters. Along with the Supreme Headquarters, in a nearby house was located the office of the Fujiwara Kikan, a Japanese organization under Major Fujiwara established with the object of promoting liaison between the Japanese authorities and the Supreme Headquarters. Its immediate aim was to help the Indian independence movement.

The daily routine now consisted mainly of providing fatigue parties to work under the Japanese. The sense of discipline among men was still unsatisfactory. When told to do something, men would often answer back to their superiors, "I am a prisoner and so are you." But they disobeyed only those Officers who had lost all respect in the eyes of their men in one way or another. The Officers who had discharged their duties properly during the Malayan war and after and still felt their responsibilities towards the men were respected and looked up to as leaders. It was due to these Officers and the G.O.C's personal character and influence that this mob of an army could be handled under unprecedentedly difficult circumstances, and later organized into an Army, otherwise second to none in the world in spirit and the art of fighting. Therefore, to facilitate the day-to-day routine of administration and command, separate Prisoners of War Headquarters at Singapore Island and the mainland of Malaya were set up at Neesoon and Kuala Lumpur, respectively.

Capt. Mohan Singh called meetings of senior Officers from time to time to discuss the problems of raising the Indian National Army. He desired that on such vital question, each individual, irrespective of his rank and seniority, should be given the right to express his views, and that Officers commanding Units would collect such suggestions from troops under their command and forward them to the Supreme Headquarters. He made it absolutely clear that membership of the Indian National Army would be strictly on a voluntary basis. He advocated freedom of political thought so far unknown in the Indian Army under the British. The imparting of political education in the form of lectures by senior Officers was started. I took up this work in Neesoon Camp.

The initiative and responsibility for raising the Indian National Army rested on the shoulders of Captain Mohan Singh and senior Officers. Certain Officers were over enthusiastic and prepared to do or die in the cause of Indian independence. Those holding extreme opposite opinion were the Officers who thanked their stars for having survived the Malayan campaign and said, "*Jaan bachi, lakhon pae*". The safety of their life meant everything to them. They had lost all courage and the spirit of adventure. No cause, British or Indian, could make them fight once again. Cowardly and timid, they had become useless. Nothing could make their blood boil, the blood that had gone cold even to the sense of self-respect. There were others who genuinely believed that the Indian National Army could serve no useful purpose, and thus they would have nothing to do with it. They made no secret of their views. These were honourable people, with guts and character with the good of their mother-land and of their men at heart.

And there was another category that comprised a set of men who regarded themselves as more British than the British themselves with the only difference that the British Officers looked after their men while those aping the Britishers looked after themselves alone. When anyone of them, owing to personal irregularities and indiscipline, got into trouble with the Japanese authorities, Capt. Mohan Singh had to come to their rescue. These were the people who owe their lives to Capt. Mohan Singh and the Indian National Army.

In return, these people gave their saviours a kick when the latter appeared to be tumbling over the high walls of the Red Fort. What for ? Only to curry favour with the British Government in India and to get some decorations or obtain dignified appointments or a reward. These were the people who in their hour of difficulties used to run to the Indian National Army for help, but when there was a loop around our necks they promptly came forward to tighten it. I admire them for their "guts" for were they not opposing the wishes of four hundred million people of India who got us free once again ?

Neesoon Camp

Up-to-date in every respect, this recently built three-storey tall camp was fitted with modern sanitation. Its big sprawling lines covered a vast area of approximately two square miles. Thirteen miles away from the main town of Singapore it was situated next to a Chinese village by the name of Neesoon where one could always buy all the necessities of life. While the men lived in spacious barracks, the married Officers were provided with entirely modern bungalows. The bachelor Officers were accommodated in the Officer's Mess, the only one of its type in Asia where luxury was in abundance. An open air swimming pool was a great attraction, apart from spacious playgrounds for outdoor exercise. This camp was the Regimental Centre of the Hong Kong and Singapore Royal Artillery, commonly known as H.K.S.R.A. Besides this camp, just outside its perimeter, was an artificial lake converted from a catchment area. This was an ideal place for picnics and evening strolls. But this was the Neesoon Camp of pre-surrender days.

Though it had survived the battle of Singapore, this camp was badly scarred. Originally meant to accommodate 2,000 Indian soldiers only, it had to put up 20,000 Indian Prisoners of War. The water system had been completely wrecked by the repeated Japanese bombing. The sanitary arrangements had broken down and electricity connections damaged. It was really an unhealthy place to live in. It was a problem for all of us to be prepared to fight all types of diseases, which would flourish under similar circumstances, particularly when the vitality of our soldiers would be going down from day to day due to improper ration supplies and the unexpectedly heavy fatigues under the Japanese.

"This is the first case of dysentery that ever passed away in my hands. I am afraid this is the beginning only. Unless good water-discipline is maintained there may be no end to it", thus spoke Col. B. Chaudhury, I.M.S., with tears in his eyes, when he watched the dead body of a prisoner, first victim of dysentery, removed from his Hospital. He preached hard, and he worked hard to stem the outbreak of this epidemic.

An Indian soldier has never been a good water disciplinarian. Leaving aside their own latrines, men would go all over the place and make the whole area filthy. Something had to be done. Some really strong measures were required to correct these bad habits in our men. "Use of force" alone was the remedy. A Company of Pathans of the 1st Battalion 14, Punjab Regiment, under the command of Capt. Abdul Rashid Khan (later Major in the Indian National Army, convicted to seven years, rigorous imprisonment after his Court Martial trial in the Red Fort of Delhi) was detailed on this duty. These troops had to use a lot of physical force to start with, but in a very short time water discipline was rigidly enforced and sanitation of the camp considerably improved. Thus many lives were saved which otherwise might have been lost.

The vitality of the men was declining visibly. It was a matter of grave concern. Rations were insufficient and not of the required type and standard. Practically no vegetables were supplied and rice mixed with lime (a preservative) was issued. The Japanese were ignorant of our needs. Often they issued *atta* but no pulses and *vice versa*. The same was true of salt and spices and various other commodities. In fact, the Japanese knew nothing about Indian rations. Once our fatigue party, while working in Seletar Aerodrome, found some Japanese soldiers using ghee to lubricate their rifles and polish boots. Our fatigue party Commander was clever and sensible. He would never let this chance go. By a clever mixture of Indian-English and gestures, he was able to convince these Japanese soldiers that the 'lubricant' was an item of Indian ration. He was, thus, able to salvage many tins of this valuable commodity. When no *atta* was available for issue to Indian Prisoners of War, the Japanese fed their horses on wheat. But their ignorance was too costly for us. Our rations had to be improved and supplemented.

Large scale gardening was started. The Units were encouraged to grow vegetables. A central garden was started under the Station Commander's orders. But bad surface, lack of manure and seeds handicapped our efforts. Something was, nevertheless, better than nothing. This was a great encouragement to our men. In three camp hospitals, sick and war-wounded numbered over 2,000. Milk was of urgent necessity for them at least. The Fujiwara Kikan was approached. They pleaded helplessness in respect of milk of any kind — whether fresh, condensed or powdered. After extreme pressure they promised to get us some cows to start our own dairy farm. Our Supreme

Headquarters promptly detailed Officers and men to run this establishment. But we were disappointed when on a bright morning a Japanese Officer turned up with forty bulls instead of cows. One is amazed at what was either quaint sense of humour or gross ignorance.

Under orders from the Supreme Command, I was detailed to deliver lectures to various Units to improve discipline, to inculcate communal harmony and national unity and to arouse a keen desire in the heart of every Indian to fight for the sacred cause of winning freedom for our enslaved country even if it meant the supreme sacrifice of laying down one's life. The response was encouraging, though there existed amidst us a few "British watch-dogs" who could not appreciate my enthusiasm. Close by us, there lived some Japanese soldiers, preachers of "Tojo Gandhi Sama Sama"—Tojo and Gandhi are alike. They became very friendly towards us. They were simple-minded folks. Knowing little about the Indian religious idiosyncrasies, they were pleased to add to their knowledge that beef was prohibited to Hindus and Sikhs and pork was prohibited to Muslims.

The Move

Early one night in the first week of March, tired and worried, I lay in my bed looking at the sky through a window. I was thinking of certain unpleasant happening in the camp. Apart from the unpleasant past and an uncertain present, the future of our proposed Indian National Army appeared gloomy. We were neither free men nor prisoners. During these musings I heard somebody shout my name. It was Captain S.M. Hussain (later Col. in the Indian National Army). I went down to meet him. He informed me that Lt. Col. N.S. Gill wanted me immediately at his bungalow. Hussain could not tell me the reason. Trying to imagine the reason of this sudden call I quietly accompanied him to Col. Gill's place, which was hardly 200 yards away.

Col. Gill was sitting alone in his drawing room. As I set my eyes upon him, I felt that he was worried and upset. He received me in his usual charming way and informed me that he was faced with a problem which I could help him solve. It took him some time before coming to the point. He told me that the Japanese Headquarters had asked the Supreme Headquarters to provide 200 Officers and men to guard the British and Australian Prisoners of War at Changi Camp. He was of the opinion that it was a very dirty job but, at the same time, if we wanted help from the Japanese we on our part had also to help them. Naturally nothing could be more unpleasant and dishonourable for one than to guard one's own comrades-in-arms when they happened to be someone else's prisoners.

Col. Gill added that he had asked many Officers but nobody seemed to be willing to come forward to do this job. He had already detailed 200 Junior Officers and men along with Subedar Santa Singh of 1/14th Punjab Regiment. Since Subedar Santa Singh had no knowledge of English it would be very difficult for him alone to deal with the Japanese on one side and the British on the other. Col. Gill wanted me to volunteer myself for the job but at the same time pointed out the value of work I was then doing directly under Supreme Headquarters. It seemed that while sending me on this duty he would not take the responsibility of detailing me. There was an air of half-heartedness in his ways. Perhaps his conscience was hurting him. But someone had to go. I took the risk and volunteered my services for this unpleasant task. The Colonel felt relieved.

This was followed by a short discussion on various administrative details. I was surprised to find that though being sent on guard duty we were to be issued no firearms. Wooden sticks were going to be our weapons. Col. Gill was not in a position to answer all my queries as he himself appeared to be in the dark. But he assured me that he would try and keep in touch with me and would advance all possible help. In fact, I had to depend wholly on myself. Col. Gill said that he was not happy to see me doing that job and would get me relieved within a week or so.

Our move was to take place by sunrise next morning. As it was getting late, we wished good-bye to each other and parted. On my return I woke up Mehar Singh, my batman, and informed him about our move. Before retiring we finished packing our brief possessions which Mehar Singh had managed to collect from here and there after surrender. I had lost practically all of my belongings during the Malayan campaign. Early next morning I met Capt. Shah Nawas Khan, 1/14th Punjab Regiment (later Major General in the Indian National Army). He was at that time in command of Neesoon Station and had already received information about my party's move. He gave me some advice which proved greatly useful during my stay at Changi. He assured me of his whole-hearted support. His was a most encouraging attitude though he considered it to be a very bad job which we should not have taken up. It was not proper, he thought.

Mehar Singh and I left our bungalow. Brother Officers and their orderlies wished us good-bye. Feelings of separation md sorrow arose within me. How strong are the Regimental ties ! On arrival at the Station Commander's offices which was our starting point, I found 200 Officers and men under Subedar Santa Singh waiting for me. Along the road also waited a convoy of eight 3-ton lorries under Mr. Itoh, a Japanese interpreter. Short-statured, bespectacled and cute, he spoke good English.

Here I must introduce Subedar Santa Singh to my readers. This Officer belonged to the same Indian Army unit as I. We had both worked together previously in India and had great respect for each other. This respect was to increase further during the days to come. After taking "all-correct" from Subedar Santa Singh, I addressed my party and asked if anybody wanted to stay back. All of them showed keenness and willingness to accompany me on this strange and adventurous mission. Thus, I ordered "Embus". Our move had been kept secret. It came as a surprise to many soldiers who learnt about our going away only on seeing us. They gathered around us and, bidding us farewell, gave us whatever articles of food and of daily necessity they could spare. They thought we were parting for ever.

The lorries had just started and had not yet gathered speed when one of my old Battalion signaller, Naik Ajmer Singh, ran towards my vehicle and threw in a pair of navy blue woollen trousers saying, "Sir, you need it more than I do." It was an expensive and useful gift. In haste I decided to accept it. This piece of clothing served me for the following three years and always reminded me of a soldier's generosity towards his Officer in time of need. As we were moving out of Neesoon Camp, Ajmer Singh's words kept on ringing in my ears, "Sir, you need it more than I do". Our lorries gathered speed and Neesoon was left behind.

7

The Changi Garrison

The Arrival

From Neesoon Camp we proceeded by a tarmac road, winding through rubber estates, via Seletar naval base, where another Camp for Indian Prisoners of War, under Major M.S. Brar of 1st Bahawalpur Infantry Regiment was being set up. Col. Brar joined the Indian National Army and then became a P.O.W. when the Indian National Army was dissolved by orders of General Mohan Singh. A hospital for the Indian Prisoners of War was also being set up at Seletar under Lt. Col. B. Chaudhury, I.M.S. (later Major General in the Indian Army). He rose to be the Director General of Medical Services. He was a very conscientious doctor and an excellent surgeon.

The fine drive and the sight of old comrades cheered us up and we never felt that we would be absolutely cut off from our people. After Seletar we passed through crowded bazars at Payalebar. Seeing civilians once again was a welcome change. On arrival in Changi area, we were directed to a Camp comprising of small huts under a rubber plantation near the junction of Tempinis and Changi roads. We were received by a Japanese Officer, Lieut. Okazaki, and his staff at the entrance to the Camp. Though rigidly formal, it was, nevertheless, a warm reception.

Lieut. Okazaki was a Liaison Officer between the Japanese Headquarters in Singapore and the Allied Prisoners of War. For all intents and purposes I was going to be under him. About five and a half feet tall, he had thinnish face more like the Chinese than the Japanese. Dressed in a khaki tunic and a loose-fitted breeches, with black top-boots on, he wore a light pith hat. Of course, a Japanese sword dangled on his left side. He wore a white armband with some Japanese characters in black on it which displayed his identity. Throughout the meeting I found him standing stiff with legs sometimes closed and sometimes apart. Whether talking or listening, he would twist, squeeze and press his lips in a strange manner. Educated at the Japanese Imperial University in Tokyo, he spoke fairly good English and looked an intelligent Officer, though without that grace which belongs to the Officer class. He gave me the impression of an efficient and clever Sergeant Major. From the very start, there was something in him I liked and something I disliked.

A member of Lieut. Okazaki's staff, Mr. Sunasawa, was introduced to me as an interpreter, who looked rather tall for a Japanese. He had a charming personality of a gentleman. Hardly thirty-five years of age, he wore spectacles through which showed his remarkably observant eyes. His features were like those of an Indian. I learnt afterwards that he had been a Professor of Philosophy at the University of Kobe in Japan before the war broke out in Asia. He spoke good and expressive English. He had left his country and profession in order to serve his Emperor and the nation by his knowledge of English. The rest of the Japanese staff at Changi will be introduced to my readers in their turn in order of importance in relation to the Changi Garrison.

Standing at the entrance to the Camp, Lieut. Okazaki told me that was going to be our Camp, and we should settle down as quickly as possible and be prepared for visits from Japanese high ranking officers who frequently came to see Allied Prisoners of War in the Changi area. Apart from his office, which was about 500 yards away and a few civilian shops adjacent to the Camp boundary, the rest of the area was to remain out of bounds for us until further notice. He was going to get in touch with his Headquarters in order to get detailed instructions for us. Meanwhile, he promised us full help. With these preliminaries, Lieut. Okazaki left for his office.

The Camp

Okazaki had gone. I ordered my men to "Debus". They unloaded all the baggage from the lorries. Mr. Itoh was now free to take them away. Meanwhile, I started to have a hurried look round the Camp.

The Camp was divided into two parts, of huts and without huts, each sub-Camp was approximately 150 yards long and 100 yards wide. A double-apron barbed wire fence, which required repairs at places, was stretched all round the Camp. The entrance to the part without huts lay through the hutted area.

For the time being, it was the area of the huts that I was concerned with, because that was going to be our residence. The Camp was unpleasantly filthy and in a neglected condition so much so that one had to put a handkerchief to one's nose while passing through it. The whole of the Camp was stinking due to decomposed and improperly buried human bodies lying about in slit trenches. These bodies had been thrown there wrapped in ground sheets or blankets, while very little earth was thrown on them. Those seemed to have been hurried burials during a battle.

Ah! the fate of soldiers! They were brave men who sacrificed their all in the name of their respective countries and people. Of whatever nationality, humanity demanded from us to give these dead bodies a proper burial. That was the first thing we did, though no religious rites could be performed at the time. It was after some four months that some British Prisoners of War, who were under my custody, approached me to ask permission to erect a wooden cross on those graves, for they knew their dead comrades. Their request was granted.

In the Camp with huts there were seven big huts which could be used as barracks and five small ones where Officers, stores and the Quarterguard had to be accommodated. Apart from the huts, there was a shed which was meant to serve as a kitchen. The huts were made of "attap" leaves. The roofs were in serviceable condition but the walls made of leaves required repairs. It was feared that leaves had been removed and perhaps burnt as fuel. Around the walls of each hut there were drains to keep rain water away. But these drains had been ignored for sometime past and had been swept away at places, thus flooding each hut and making their inside ground wet and muddy when it rained. Because of the uneven surface in the Camp, water had collected in holes and pits where mosquitoes bred.

The most obnoxious thing of all was that practically each hut, inside as well as outside, was littered with human excreta, pieces of bread, unused tinned foodstuffs, rags and all sorts of dirty articles rotting about. Food tins had been bayonetted and left. Added to this was water which had made a mess of everything, so repulsive to human senses. Clearing meant a job which would take time. Latrines were in the unhutted area which had four seats only. Their pans were overflowing with the contents and were covered with flies, insects and worms of different kinds, which greeted one with their loathsome buzzing sound.

There were no arrangements for lighting in the Camp and we had little equipment in this respect. Though not a serious problem, it needed attention before an emergency might arise. In spite of all these bad points, there were some other factors which gave one hope that conditions could be improved within a reasonable time. The Camp was at a sloping ground, and higher than the surrounding area. The soil was hard which, if properly maintained, would give a smooth surface. Taps were in good order and water supply was in abundance. The accommodation was just sufficient, though touching the congestion point.

After allotting accommodation to different sub-units, men were ordered to start cleaning their respective areas. They remained busy throughout the day with practically no rest, and then alone the Camp looked a bit tolerable. Rubbish was collected in heaps and was buried or burnt. One of these heaps happened to contain some small arms ammunition which started going off during the middle of our first night in the Camp. This caused a slight commotion and it looked as if our Camp had been fired upon by a light automatic weapon. An alarm was sounded, but the cause was discovered almost simultaneously.

Tired and fed up, our men returned to their beds. They must have been swearing at the Camp and at their fate. It must have been very uncomfortable for them to sleep on ground which had been reclaimed from water and filth a few hours earlier. A very unpleasant beginning, indeed! As for myself, Mehar Singh had managed to get hold of a wooden plank from some where and made an elevated bed by placing four bricks underneath. Though hard, it was a cosy bed. I could not, however, sleep well.

Settling Down

On the day following our arrival Lieut. Okazaki paid us a courtesy call and asked if he could do anything for us. He was surprised to observe a noticeable improvement in the Camp overnight. Appreciating our labour, he said that he would approach Col. Sugita, Head of the Intelligence and Information Branch in General Yamashita's General Headquarters to pay us a visit. I was not even a little satisfied in any way with our surroundings. Before I could ask Okazaki to meet our needs, he said that we looked more comfortable in our new surrounding than the Japanese soldiers putting up in Changi area. Considering this remark, I decided not to ask for anything. I kept quiet thinking that I had to depend on my own resources and improvisation. We got busy in cleaning the Camp and preparing ourselves for Col. Sugita's visit.

Col. Sugita was punctual. As he arrived, I recognised him right away because his photographs had often appeared in various newspapers in Malaya. His photograph was particularly noticeable when General Percival signed the unconditional surrender documents at Ford Factory, Singapore in the presence of General Yamashita. Of medium build, Col. Sugita had a big, prominent moustache and appeared to be very cute and observant. Though he did not speak English, I could make out that he understood every word spoken long before the interpreter translated it. I learnt from him that he had been in India for some time. From his talk I could feel that he understood the Indian mentality quite well.

On arrival in the Camp my Sikh Officers and men had approached me to allot some accommodation for a "gurudwara", but considering the shortage of accommodation I had declined their request. Eventually from their own allotment, they had used an N.C.O's small bunk for the same purpose. They had decorated this place so well that while going round the Camp, it could not escape Col. Sugita's eyes. He at once asked me as to what it was. "A temple", I replied. He asked me how many temples there were in the Camp. I replied, "Only one". "Do you belong to one religion?" was his next question. I found myself in a fix. I replied that though we belonged to different religions we had only one temple. I could imagine that he did not believe in what I said. To save me from embarrassment he did not pursue this point any further. His attitude was magnanimous.

I had been always broad-minded where religion was concerned. But on that day I made up my mind that in our Garrison, religion was going to be a personal and a purely personal affair. To outsiders we must appear as Indians only.

Col. Sugita was very pleased with our Camp, and while addressing our Garrison, he praised us and informed us that he would very soon arrange to get us issued with arms, equipment and clothing. Accompanying Col. Sugita was a long train of about a dozen officers, most of whom wore gold lace epaulettes showing that they were staff officers. They showed great interest in us and our affairs.

We had arranged to offer them a cup of tea. Mehar Singh had managed to produce a China cup from somewhere in which we served Col. Sugita. But for others we could not provide cups. We offered them tea in cups made out of empty food tins. They all relished the tea, which was apparent by their way of noisy sipping. However, the Colonel did not ignore our poor belongings, and before leaving the Camp instructed Lieut. Okazaki to provide us with some furniture, crockery and utensils. In the evening Lieut. Okazaki called on me and told me that the Colonel had gone back more than satisfied with the inspection of our Camp.

During the following week our Camp was visited daily by several Japanese Officers. Perhaps we were on trial. Nay, free Indians were on trial. During this period we did our best to keep on improving the condition of our Camp. Ultimately we reached a stage when, inspections or no inspections, it made little difference to us. We were ever ready in our Camp, clean and tidy.

Though promised, we were provided with no furniture, crockery or cooking utensils. Without crockery and cooking utensils we could somehow manage but I could never bear my men sleeping on the wet ground. And it happened to be raining heavily at that time of the year. One day an idea occurred to me. Improvisation was the only solution. There existed deep slit trenches in our Camp, dug during the British days. These trenches were lined inside with thick wooden planks. I got these planks pulled out and converted them into sleeping boards. We had no carpenter's tools but a few Chinese civilians residing in the Changi area lent us a few saws and the rest of the job was done with an axe. I was very happy when each man of my Garrison had a board to sleep on.

During the first week after our arrival in the Camp, Swaran Singh (later a Lieutenant in the Indian National Army) joined us. His arrival was greatly welcomed, specially because he brought with him a large kit bagful of tinned foodstuffs, God knows from where. He was a Transport Havildar in 1/14 Punjab Regiment and was captured by the Japanese near Alorstar in north Malaya after the battle of Jitra, along with his Commanding Officer, Lt. Col. L.V. Fitzpatrick, Captain Mohan Singh, Captain Mohd. Akram and others. Swaran Singh remained with Captain Mohan Singh until the surrender of Singapore and served him as his most trusted subordinate. Many a time he had taken risks in dangerous situations while carrying out his orders.

Standing six feet tall, Swaran Singh was handsome, well-built and had an attractive personality. He had been to school but I could never judge what standard he had passed. He spoke a jumble of languages including Hindustani, Punjabi, Pushtu, English Malaya, and Japanese, but somehow he always succeeded in making himself understood. When he failed to find a suitable word to express himself, he would use his hands, head and other limbs to convey his thought. People who knew him well would always make it a point to stand at a respectable distance from him because while conversing he was in the habit of patting others and his pat used to be something like a hammer blow. With regard to his seniors, Swaran Singh always knew his position. He was capable of working hard without a break for any length of time provided his efforts were appreciated. Long working hours made no difference to him. Because of his qualities and resourcefulness, he had been promoted to the rank of 2nd Lieut. by our Supreme Headquarters. In him I found a useful subordinate and I gladly appointed him my Camp Adjutant.

Forty 3-ton lorries, ten trucks and eight cars were issued to us. This transport was meant for supplying rations to the British and Australian Prisoners of War and to carry them for fatigues outside the Changi area. A car was specially placed at my disposal. Subedar Lal Din was appointed M.T.O. (Motor Transport Officer), with Jemadar Khushi Ram as his second-in-command. Both of them belonged to 40th

Transport Company and knew their job well.

Subedar Lal Din had been an Army Instructor at the Armoured Fighting Vehicles School, Ahmednagar. Tall and dark, he looked every inch an instructor. On parade he would be very strict. Off parade he was the most humorous person in the Garrison. He was a very conscientious Officer. Once told to do a thing he would not rest until his job was completed. I depended upon him fully. Communal prejudices were unknown to him. He rose to the rank of Captain in the Indian National Army and finally commanded the Armoured Fighting Vehicles Battalion.

Jemadar Khushi Ram was a small man with a very serious nature. I always found him overworking. His men loved him and he always placed their interests before his own. His spirit of sacrifice and energy for work were great. Many a time, I found him working even when running a high temperature. Once while going round on my night check-up, I found him standing as a sentry. This surprised me. Later I found that to punish his Platoon, which had complained against sentry duty, he took this duty on himself. The result was that all his men literally fell at his feet and never made any complaint in future.

For the time being, in the absence of any definite duties, we continued to perform the maintenance of our transport vehicles. Uneven parts of the Camp were levelled and used as parking place for our vehicles. A workshop lorry was salvaged from amongst a collection of broken down vehicles in the vicinity of our Camp. Thus, our boys opened a workshop of our own. The N.C.O. in charge of this workshop was Hav. Harnam Singh. An efficient and a hard-working mechanic, he had a set of very useful persons around him. They belonged to various communities and religions and were the first to start a common mess.

Towards the end of March 1942, one day Lieut. Okazaki asked me to detail a fatigue party to collect firearms and ordnance equipment for the Garrison from the Japanese stores. As I broke this news to my Officers and men they went mad with joy. These were very arms which we had surrendered on 15th February 1942. Getting them back was indeed a matter of pride. When our fatigue party brought a lorry load of rifles, revolvers, shot-guns and ordnance equipment, men rent the sky with shouts of '*Inquilab Zindabad*' and other national slogans. When these arms were distributed among the men, they kissed them saying that this time they were handling these weapons for the sacred cause of using them against the British in order to win freedom of their motherland. These very arms had been used to build the British Empire. They took them to destroy that very Empire.

Drilling and Words of Command

Arms and equipment had now been issued to us. But this gave rise to a very unpleasant problem. One day Lieut. Okazaki asked me to give up the British drill and words of command and adopt Japanese ones. This was no small a problem. I was not in a position to accept any basic change unless rulings were obtained from our Supreme Headquarters at Mount Pleasant. Capt. Mohan Singh, G.O.C. of the Indian National Army in the making, had been away from Singapore on a goodwill mission to Japan. In his absence nobody was in a position or even prepared to take this responsibility of a basic change for we were yet volunteers of the Indian National Army. I was left to use my own discretion.

Lieut. Okazaki was of the opinion that by using the Japanese methods, many misunderstandings arising out of linguistic difficulties would be avoided. He said that it was not possible for the Japanese Headquarters to detail a permanent Garrison for Changi, as their troops were constantly moved from one place to another due to operations. It would be very difficult for incoming Units to pick up our ways and when they had understood they would be transferred, leaving us to deal with a new lot. This would definitely result in waste of time and energy. He also asserted that the Japanese troops, by instinct, hated anything British. If we, claiming to be fighting for freedom from the British, still used the British ways, it would cause suspicion in the mind of a Japanese soldier. Thus, it would mar the efficient running of both the Indian and the Japanese Garrisons at Changi.

This problem gave me a big headache. Amongst the Officers under my command, Subedar Santa Singh was the only one with whom I could discuss such an important issue. We agreed that the British ways were not our ways. For us, the Japanese and the British were equally foreign. We wanted Indian ways, but unfortunately they had not yet come into existence. Had we had our own drill and words of command, this problem would not have arisen. If it had arisen, one would take it as a national insult. At a time when our Goodwill Mission was visiting Japan it could have been unwise on my part to show a non-cooperative spirit, for the Changi Garrison was in itself a gesture of our goodwill towards the Japanese. The important point to remember at this time was that if we started yielding to the Japanese, we might in the long run be left to play the second fiddle in their hands. But something had to be decided and decided pretty quickly. At last I took the initiative and came to a provisional understanding with the Japanese Headquarters through Lieut. Okazaki. I told them that as soon as the Indian National Army came into being, Indian drill and words of command would be introduced. Until then, as there were no Indian words of command in force, I was prepared to adopt Japanese ones.

Then arose the question of training, for which Lieut. Okazaki detailed five instructors from his own Unit. They were: Sergeant Kawanishi, Corporal Tamamori, Lance-Corporal Undo and Privates Taniguchi and Okamura. Sgt. Kawanishi had a bad temper and often betrayed his quarrelsome mood. He became very unpopular with my men due to his bad temper. Tall and well-built, Corporal Tamamori had typical Japanese features. He was a fine figure of health and humanity. Obedient and respectful, he would talk in an innocent childlike way which was charming. He was an efficient and hardworking N.C.O. who had been through many battles in different theatres of war. He had in him a farmer's simplicity, a soldier's grace and experience blended with practical wisdom. When I met him first he knew little English. Since he had to deal with us, he worked hard, and within a few days we were able to understand him fully as he would pour out a jumble of words accompanied by gestures. Sgt. Kawanishi appeared to have many responsibilities elsewhere and his dealings with us were nominal. Thus we were left to deal with Cpl. Tamamori who soon became greatly attached to the Garrison.

Within a fortnight we learnt the Japanese drill and words of command. We felt at home. In a way it was quite interesting, for the Japanese words of command were more forceful than the British ones but the drill was on the softer side and one would not get tired as quickly as by the British drill. Of course, "Goose-step" was an exception. The Japanese position of "standing-at-ease" was very impressive. Instead of placing the left foot about 12 inches to the left, they would place it about the same distance forward in the left-inclined direction. This position showed the chest prominently and it was definitely more comfortable. Another point to my liking was the looking of the men, whilst standing at attention, in the eyes of the Officer being saluted, irrespective of the direction where he stood.

Thus the Japanese drill and words of command were adopted, which were a constant reminder to us of the need for having our own drill and our own words of command.

The Changi Area

A big chunk of land covered with hillocks and rubber plantations about sixteen square miles in area jutting out into the sea, situated at the north-eastern extremity of Singapore Island, was the Changi Area. Tempinis and Changi roads connected it with the main town, fifteen miles away. Before the outbreak of war, it used to be a cantonment where the British and the Malay troops lived. Apart from this, there was the notorious Changi jail. At Changi point there were two naval posts, where 16" coastal guns, huge monsters, guarded the entrance to the Naval Base of Singapore. The place was dotted with small fishing and farming villages here and there, where the Chinese, Malays and South Indians lived. They had been issued individual permits without which they could not move in and out of the area. Since the Japanese guarded the main roads only, it was not very difficult to escape.

Here in this area were kept the Allied Prisoners of War in five separate Camps — Australian Camp, Hospital area, 9th Indian Division Camp, 11th Indian Division Camp and 18th British Division Camp. Though the area was big and the buildings thereon large in number, overcrowding was still a great problem. Some tents had been pitched and several huts created to minimise this congestion. Still it was in no way satisfactory. The sanitation of the place was bad due to the breakdown of lavatory arrangements. Added to this, the bad water discipline then prevailing amongst the troops resulted in outbreak of dysentery which took a heavy toll of life. When I came to Changi there were only ten graves. But by the time I left Changi Camp after four months, there were over six hundred. Another reason for the outbreak of dysentery was the abrupt change of diet. It could not be easy for bread, butter and meat eating people to adapt themselves to boiled rice and vegetables, which they did not know how to prepare.

To supplement their meals, prisoners used to escape from their Camps to buy foodstuffs from civilians living nearby. These civilians had stored large quantities of foodstuffs looted from the British stores, which they now sold at very high price, not because they wanted to help prisoners but because they wanted to make a fortune out of their misfortune. A packet of ten cigarettes was sold for five dollars. The same was true of other articles. Prisoners had a lot of money on their persons especially the British, for they had several 'field-cashiers' amongst them who were handling large amounts before the surrender and had managed to keep some of it. The Indians and the Australians were not so fortunate in this respect. Thus, when the British troops bought these deteriorating foodstuffs, they purchased dysentery too.

Once a British Major, a friend of mine since 7 MRC days, came to see me with the object of getting something to eat and naturally to get whatever information he could regarding our movement. We ate together. When we had finished our meals, two "chapaties" were left on the table. My friend asked me if he could take them with him. On my consent he put them away in between his sweating body and his shirt. I warned him that those chapaties would be spoiled and asked him to put them in his pocket. He did not accept my suggestion and informed me that his fellow prisoners might snatch them away if they happened to know what he was carrying. He told me that they had reached a stage when an Officer would not hesitate to steal a man's rations, and a man his Officer's belongings.

I had always liked and respected that British Officer and he had often shown kindness and courtesy towards me. I was moved to learn these unpleasant facts from him. I offered him some more chapatis and the only tin of milk I had with me. It gave me pleasure and satisfaction that I was in a position to do a good turn to an old friend. When he was gone, my men who had been watching us eating gave a loud roar of laughter and said, "The Sahib ate twenty-three chapatis". I asked them as to how many I had eaten. "seven", they replied. We wondered how hungry he was ! Being a British, many a time he would have hated the very sight of those "bloody chapatis" which "niggers" used to eat. But this time he relished them and was grateful that he could get them. He was a prisoner !

Each Camp was commanded by its own Officer, usually a General residing in the Camp. Within their respective camps, prisoners were left entirely to themselves. They were not allowed to come outside their Camps between the hours of sunset and sunrise. During the day they were allowed certain movements as long as they wore distinctive signs such as armbands or if they carried distinctive flags. The Medical Officers and Camp Commanders had better facilities. A prisoners' unarmed guard was posted at the inside of each sub-Camp gate, whilst on the outside stood a Japanese guard. The latter was to be taken over by us along with perimeter patrols.

In the 18th British Division area, a ration issue point was opened from where prisoners would carry their Unit rations to their respective lines. In order to facilitate carriage, the Japanese had issued chassis of motor vehicles with engines removed. With ropes tied to front axles, prisoners were often seen pulling and pushing this new means of moving load from one place to another. My Garrison provided them transport when it was required for going to Singapore for collecting rations or buying medicines.

Apart from Prisoners of War Camps, the Allied civilians were interned in the Changi jail, where they were guarded by the Japanese. Some Generals and senior officers were put up in bungalows where formerly the Changi jail staff used to live. These Generals, when brought out for interrogation by the Japanese, were well-guarded.

Our Problems

From the very day of our arrival at Changi we were faced with certain problems, which concerned us as members of the Garrison, and as Indians. Too much was expected overnight from those soldiers who had joined the British Indian Army for the sake of earning their daily bread. These were the soldiers who for generations together had known the British as their all-powerful white sahibs. Now they were going to treat their old masters as inferiors. This was going to be a real revolution but before it could be brought about, the deep-rooted inferiority complex in the mind of an Indian soldier had to be removed.

While doing this, it was also to be borne in mind that, though prisoners, the British were human beings and required to be treated as such. It was rather a difficult problem for an illiterate soldier to judge the correct standard of treatment. We had also to remember that they were not our prisoners, but of the Japanese, with whom we did not have so far an equal standing and status. We were neither Prisoners of War nor the soldiers of an Independent Army, at least not yet.

There was a big difference between our mentality and the Japanese mentality. Before we could understand them we could not afford to carry on as we wished. A little bit of kindness shown by us towards the Allied prisoners might be easily misunderstood by the Japanese as well as the British, which actually did happen at times. The Indian National Army was yet to be organized. If the Japanese became suspicious from the very beginning, the Indian National Army might never come into existence. They were conquerors drunk in feelings of victory and a sense of superiority, and naturally would not submit to anything which did not suit them. Yet we could not afford to play as puppets is their hands.

The Changi area was, strictly speaking, under the military control of the Japanese as well as ours. In case we ill treated the civilian population in this area, our name would be blemished and civilians, irrespective of their nationality, could never sympathize with our movement that was taking shape. And yet we had to see that these civilians did not rob the prisoners of their possessions.

My men were not getting any pay or pocket money. They were living on dry rations, on the same scale as other Prisoners of war. There was a temptation to beg, borrow or steal, specially when both civilians as well as the prisoners were much frightened to approach the Japanese. The British Prisoners of War showed a superiority complex while dealing with us. They still took us as their good old slaves and always showed us a hostile attitude. They were justified to some extent because they had not surrendered to us but to the Japanese. The mentality of a people cannot be changed overnight. But for the good of this world as a whole, their mentality had to be changed; the fact that, white or coloured, we were all human beings, had to be brought home.

My Garrison included Officers and men of different religions. If not properly handled, they would have spoiled the whole show. The essence of national unity had to be brought home to them, which had long been crushed by the Divide and Rule policy of the British Raj. Our problems called for strict discipline, a keen sense of duty and responsibility. For all this, men were to be educated and made to feel that they were members of a nation, a great nation; and to make it greater still they should ever be prepared to make any sacrifices called for. This spirit was inculcated by daily lectures, personally delivered by me and issuing definite orders for dealing with each problem. Soon I found that men started taking a keen interest in their new and heavy responsibilities and looked like a national unit in the real sense. Mr. Suna Sawa once remarked, "The Indian Garrison is a spectacle through which I see a powerful and united India."

Our Duties

Our problems became more clearly defined as we started performing the duties assigned to us. These duties included:

1. Providing guards and sentries at different places in the Changi area, to stop Prisoners of War from escaping and civilians from contacting Prisoners of War in Camps.
2. Patrolling the Changi area so that prisoners could not escape, loot or destroy vegetable farms and other property belonging to civilians living in that area.
3. Carrying Prisoners of War out of the Camp and back during their movements.
4. Carrying civilian internees of European nationalities to hospitals for treatment.
5. Carrying civilian internees to the town for purchase of canteen goods on week days.
6. Maintenance of M.T. vehicles under our charge.
7. Maintenance of general discipline and order in the area. POWs were supposed to pay compliments to us irrespective of ranks.

The Allied Prisoners of War were informed of our duties before we had actually taken charge. But owing to the slackness and inefficiency of the Camp staff, and the superiority complex against the coloured races, these instructions were ignored. In the beginning they would not pay any heed to us and I too did not mind being ignored either. They appeared determined to continue this attitude towards us. But as far as the Japanese were concerned, the Prisoners of War saluted them all very promptly irrespective of their ranks. My attitude had to be changed now, for I could not put up with it indefinitely. Yet I can remember today only one incident where I had shown some high-handedness, otherwise I feel I was always fair and just. There was some background also to this incident.

One day I happened to pass through an area where some British Gunner Officers belonging to the Regiment of Major S were living. These Officers had once lived with us in our Regimental Mess at Sungei Pattani in Malaya. We had often found them discourteous to our senior Indian Officers. As I approached them, all of them remained seated nicely after a hearty breakfast. I had seen their men in a very poor condition but to find these Officers enjoying at the cost of the poor soldiers was a loathsome sight. They paid no heed to me. When I asked them for the senior, most Officer present there, they refused to reply me even that much. They were still proud of their imperialistic attitude. They looked vain and ignorant of the changing times the world had changed. The sun had started setting on the British Empire; Britannia no more ruled the waves. But there sat the Officers who refused to face the facts and I had a complex of my own.

Capt. A, an old man, then advanced and asked me, "On what authority have you entered this Camp ?" I told him to accompany me so that I could show him the authority. But he refused to do that. Giving him blow with a baton, I ordered him to accompany me. My escorts got round him and he was put in my car. At this juncture, all the Prisoners of War, residing in that locality, gathered around us. Lieut. X, whom I knew, came forward and started talking to me:

Lieut. X : Do you remember me ?

I : Yes. You were giving us covering fire at Jitra.

Lieut. X : You mind letting Capt. A go this time ? I request you please to leave him. Have you forgotten that I used to be a member of your mess?

I : That is no qualification.

Lieut. X : Why do you do this job?

I : Because I have volunteered my services for it.

Lieut. X : Do you like it?

I : No, but someone had to do it.

Similar questions were put to me by other Officers and they were all answered in the same spirit. Afterwards I sat in my car and ordered my driver to drive on. Capt. A begged of me to let him go. His old age and gray hair moved me; the Indian in me took pity on his old age. Showing him a letter of authority, written in the Japanese script, I said to him, "This is my authority. Do you understand what is written here ?" "No", he replied. I said, "Nor do I" and told him to get down. He looked happier and I drove away.

In the evening I told Lieut. Okazaki all that had happened. He showed me a long letter written by Prisoners of War complaining about the same incident. Most of it was true but I was surprised to see that there had been an effort made by the Prisoners of War to create suspicion in the Japanese mind against me by telling them that I did not like to do the job and had my sympathies with the British. I wondered what would have happened to the British Empire if there were a few more sympathisers like me ! Anyway, I explained everything to Lieut. Okazaki plainly admitting that I had shown high-handedness. Lieut. Okazaki immediately made for the Japanese General Headquarters. On his return I was informed not to go into the Camp areas until further intimation.

Meanwhile, I learnt that General Percival had written a letter to General Yamashita asking the latter not to employ Indian Prisoners of War for guarding the British Prisoners of War camps. General Percival detested that a Captain who held the same category of Commission as himself, who was once his subordinate and had turned traitor, should be saluted by him and his other senior officers. Appealing to the Japanese "Bushido spirit", General Percival added that after the war this would not be beneficial for their international relations. I waited with interest and concern the outcome of this letter. General Yamashita had given a long reply to it. As far as I was concerned, the conqueror had refused to alter the statusquo.

A day or two later, I was issued with an armband, sewn of white cloth with blue lining, bearing two words "GUARDS COMMANDER" in English. A similar flag was issued for my car. All the Camp Commanders were called at the Liaison Office and I was introduced to them. My duties were read out to them. They were told to obey me implicitly. They were given twenty-four hours to acquaint their men with those instructions, after which no excuse was to be accepted for disobedience of those instructions. And during these twenty-four hours I was not to enter any Camp areas.

After the lapse of twenty-four hours, I started my rounds on duty. Many Prisoners of War still failed to salute me to the annoyance of Cpl. Tamamori and his companions who often used to accompany me. They would stop and slap all those who were found negligent in paying compliments. Thus they would slap hundreds of them in a day. I hated all this and told Cpl. Tamamori to stop it. But he would reply that he could not see me being ignored. He wanted me to be respected. I informed him that it was more of an insult than respect to me if prisoners were to salute me because of fear of slaps from him. I further told him that I would make them do so myself if need be. The Japanese stopped slapping Prisoners of War in my presence. But at times my men had to perform the same unpleasant job with regard to those Prisoners of War who would refuse to understand any language other than that of force. As time passed, this need lessened gradually and I found them prompt and smart in saluting, even at the sight of my car whether I was in it or not. They would even salute from their quarters while sitting, eating, bathing or even while answering the call of nature in open latrines. I am sure, they must have cursed me in the filthiest possible language. Sometimes my arms would get tired and I would detail one of my juniors or orderlies to take the salute for me. At times I would decide not to visit camps simply to avoid being saluted. There was no grandeur in being saluted by the English when the "White Sahibs" superiority complex had waned, though only apparently.

A Change

Though the Allied Prisoners of War had given up that air of superiority and had started realizing that they were as much human beings as the coloured people, my men had still an inferiority complex towards them. They would make the British salute all right, but at times while standing at their posts, they would instinctively come to attention at the approach of the British Officers under whom they had served. This was a great weakness and had to be remedied. In order to prepare our men to fight against the British in the battle-field, we had to create anti-British feeling in the minds of the men. You cannot fight a battle unless you hate your enemy. My daily evening lectures served the required purpose.

Slowly and steadily, my men changed. I recall an amusing incident. One day, when a sentry was approached by his former Commanding Officer, the sentry promptly told him to keep away by the movement of his hand, but what the sentry actually said all the while was: "Come on, come on." Not understanding what to do, the Colonel hesitatingly approached closer and closer. When he came within reach, the sentry gave him a slap, shouting at him in Punjabi: "I am saying come on, come on and yet you are drawing closer and closer". Afterwards when I told the sentry the meaning of 'come', the sentry replied, "Sir! I have heard the white people calling like that to their dogs. So I also treated him only as a dog".

Another time, a Pathan N.C.O. was asked by his former Company Commander, "Have you joined the Japanese ?" The N.C.O. promptly replied, "It's a pity that this was the only army I could join. It would have given me a greater pleasure to join the German Army and be able to attack the British Isles. Now I can only attack a few British forces which are occupying India, my mother country". The Officer said, "Don't you realize that you are proving disloyal to the salt that you have been eating?" The N.C.O. said, "I cannot recollect having gone to England to eat your salt but I do know you people having come to our country as guests and eat our salt". I wonder how that Officer liked that naked truth coming out of an illiterate Indian soldier.

It is interesting to note how the human brain reacts under different environments. There used to be a question hour after my evening lectures. One would be surprised to hear really intelligent questions and answers coming out of those men who had never been to school or had never known the word of freedom. Amongst them were found those who began to compose poems in their different languages. Those who did not know how to read and write started making an attempt and their progress was amazing. There was a time when these very men were looked down upon. Now it was their turn to look down upon those who had detested them in the past. One was convinced that our men were in no way inferior to any people of the world, if trained in the right way. Behind this evolution was hidden the real revolution.

And Another Change

While patrolling the Changi area we used to come across moneyed Prisoners of War who managed to escape through barbed wire in order to buy foodstuffs. To start with, we used to let them off and merely send them back to their respective camps. But it resulted in more and more Prisoners of War coming out of their camps. This indiscipline was an indirect challenge to our authority. We began to arrest them and keep them in our Garrison for about three days before they were allowed to return to their respective camps. Even this practice failed to create the desired effect and the Prisoners of War started coming out in ever increasing numbers. Thus we were compelled to keep them in our Garrison for longer periods.

In the beginning I used to lodge them in my own hut where they would eat with me as equals, irrespective of their ranks. But as their number increased, there arose the problem of boarding and lodging them separately. An open air cage about thirty feet in length by twenty feet in breadth with a tentage accommodation to stop rain water from wetting the prisoners was erected. It was a poor accommodation in those tropical rains. For eating, prisoners were attached to different Platoons and were given the same food as my men ate. On top of this they were given no labour or fatigue work. This hospitality became known to the inmates of different camps with the result that the number of our 'guests' kept on increasing daily and their reception became a serious problem.

I asked Lieut. Okazaki to supply separate rations for them but he refused to take any action on my demand. He was of the opinion that no food should be provided to them as a punishment during their stay at the Garrison Camp. I frankly told him that it would not be possible for me to do so. "It goes against our nation to keep a prisoner without food. As for myself, I can never let a person go without food under my roof, be he a prisoner or a friend". Lieut. Okazaki maintained that their rations were already being issued for them to their respective camps. It was not proper that those soldiers who escaped, looted and plundered should be issued rations at two places, while the civilian population starved. It would be no punishment to them. In this long discussion Lieut. Okazaki, however, agreed with my idea and allowed me to carry on feeding them as long as I did not demand any surplus rations from him, though he would try to get some extra rice supply if possible. I got the shock of my life one day when for fifty-seven Prisoners of War I was given just two hundred pounds of rice only, for a period of one month.

My strength lay in my own men and in their spirit of sacrifice. I asked them for help and told them that we might even starve but the British and Australian Prisoners of War in our Camp were to be fed. They responded to my call and began to observe fast once a week so that rations could be saved for prisoners and they could be fed throughout the week. The problem was further eased when Lieut. Swaran Singh managed through Sgt. Hirao to smuggle in some extra bags of rice from time to time. For the sake of Allied Prisoners of War detained in our cage, we had to exaggerate our demand which boiled down to telling a lie.

Sgt. Hirao was the N.C.O. in charge of supplying rations to the Changi area. Of medium build, he wore spectacles through which could be observed his ever-scrutinizing eyes. He hardly knew any English but was, nevertheless, intelligent enough to understand through gestures. He seldom made a mistake and was a terror among the Japanese soldiers because of his strict disciplinary ways. I always wondered how Lieut. Swaran Singh could make friends with him. It was Sgt. Hirao's generosity and Lieut. Swaran Singh's cleverness by which we were able to continue to feed our 'unwanted guests'.

The food provided to the Allied Prisoners of War under our custody was cooked by our men in the Indian style. The prisoners liked it much better than their own food cooked in their camps and most of them preferred to stay with our Garrison. In order to discourage this influx of P.O.Ws at times we used to give them a good dose of beating when they were caught escaping or breaking Camp rules. Those who happened to be our victims must be having some bitter memories. But after such an unpleasant reception they used to get exactly the same treatment as the members of my Garrison. The Allied Prisoners of War were determined to continue being caught and thus undergo so-called confinement under us. At times we used to capture as many as twenty of them during one night.

Ambushing prisoners at night used to be a fun which greatly added to my experience of night operations. It provided me an excellent change to study the British mentality. The prisoners used to break out of their camps to buy foodstuffs from civilians living in the Changi area or even from outside as far away as eight to nine miles. In any case they had to pay very high price as I have previously written. Some enterprising young men used to collect money from their fellow prisoners and take the risk of being captured and given 'allied' entertainment. Once when we had laid an ambush, a party of about fifty Prisoners of War collided with us. We were only ten. As we ran forward to capture them, they ran away in different directions and were lost from our sight in the thick undergrowth. As we were retuning, having given them up as a lost bargain, I saw a dog standing all alone in the jungle. Suspecting that the dog belonged to the prisoners and that they were hiding somewhere close by, we started searching the area. But we could find nobody. This time they had scored a point against us.

Disappointed, as we started back, my foot struck against something solid hidden in long grass. When I kicked it again, there was not the slightest movement. I had very nearly given it up when curiosity made me touch it. To my surprise, it was a man. We started another search and within a radius of ten yards discovered nine of them. Considering that it was a full moon night, it was praiseworthy that these British soldiers had managed to take such an excellent cover. Seldom does a dog betray his master but here the poor animal was helpless. Having brought these prisoners to the Garrison, I asked them all their reasons for leaving their Camp during the hours of darkness. Most of them gave silly excuses. But an old man said, "For the sake of adventure, Sir." His straightforward reply came in such a manly way that he was excused a beating and throughout his stay with us was accorded courtesy and special treatment worthy of old age.

Another prisoner who impressed me the most was an Australian, over six feet tall and with an attractive personality. He was caught by me one afternoon. As I brought him to our Camp and asked why he had come out of his Camp, he replied, "I wanted to be caught by you".

"Did you not know that I give a beating to those who are captured by us?", I asked. He said, "Yes, I know. Many a time I saw you all alone and could have shot you dead if I wanted to. But I have been told that apart from being strict you are kind-hearted and generous. Can you guess how many times you have passed by me within an arm's length?" "But what has this to do with your present captivity?" I asked. He replied, "I have come to make a complaint against a civilian who robbed me of my wallet containing fifty dollars. When I was buying some fruits from him, some of your sentries made an appearance. I had to run away leaving my wallet behind. When I returned the old man refused to give me my wallet."

I was so much impressed by the frankness of the man that I took him to show me the civilian in question. Though the wallet could not be recovered, the civilian was made to return the money. I sent this man back to his Camp after he had stayed with me for three days. He told me that he had no money on the day of surrender, but ever since he had been literally playing in it. He would take the risk of coming out and buying foodstuffs and other commodities and then reselling them to the fellow prisoners at good profit. He informed me that he had always eaten well and was very happy with his adventurous life.

One day just after noon, as I happened to go on a round unaccompanied by my personal escort, I found two Australian Prisoners of War escaping from their Camp in a very stealthy manner taking cover in a nullah. I followed them by stages. As they approached a forest, I challenged them to stop. One of them obeyed while the other ran away and stood about forty yards from me. By now I had drawn out my revolver, and pointing it at the nearer person called the other one to come back or his companion would be shot. But he would not come. It took me about half an hour to make him understand. If he walked ten paces towards me, he would bolt away fifteen paces. At last I asked the captured man to tell his friend to come back.

The captured man shouted, "O' Joe, come back. This fellow is going to shoot me." His appeal worked and the runaway companion approached us slowly and reluctantly. Pointing them to a path I told them to walk ahead of me and I followed covering them with my revolver. The fellow caught first, a younger lad hardly twenty years old, was nearest to me. He would stop every now and then and would ask me questions with an implied request to be released. He addressed me as 'O Joe' and it preceded almost all his sentences. We had hardly gone ten paces when he started questioning me:

He : O Joe! Where are you taking me to ?

I : To the Indian Garrison.

He : O Joe! But what for ?

I : Just for a treat.

He : O Joe! Do you mean you will hand me over to the Japanese?

I : No, now then keep quiet and look in front.

He : O Joe. How can I when you are pointing that frightful thing at my back ?

I : Don't talk.

He : O'Joe! Do you know I am married ?

I : No I don't.

He : I have a baby too. A nice little one.

I : So what ?

He : O Joe! What will happen to them if you kill me ?

I : But what makes you feel that I will kill you ?

He : O Joe! Then why don't you return your revolver ? I don't like it.

Continuously talking, we arrived at the Garrison. It was evening. Mehar Singh had got food ready for me which we offered to the two new captives. The food was served but the younger of the two would not touch it. At last he said:

He : O Joe! What is this fun feeding first and then killing ?

I : But what makes you think that you will be killed ?

He : O Joe! Do you say that on your honour ?

I : Yes, I do.

He : O' Joe! Then let us shake hands.

We shook hands and he started eating. After he had finished eating I said.:

I : O'Joe! Why did you leave the Camp ?

He : To get Po Po for my brother.

Luckily we had a papaya which was offered to him. Then I asked him if he wanted anything else. He told me that his brother was ill in the hospital and he had also come out to get a tin of milk for him. A milk tin was given and he was again asked if he needed anything else. He showed a desire for coconuts. As luck would have it, my men had collected some coconuts that very day. So I told him and his friend to carry as many as they could. Having done so I took them to the place from where they had come out of their Camp. Before letting them go I told them not to tell their friends that I had given them those things. But the younger man promptly replied, "O Joe! How can we tell lies when you have been so kind to us?" They had hardly entered their Camp when hundreds of fellow Prisoners of War gathered around them. As they started explaining their experience, I came away. If the Japanese had come to know of it, they might have misunderstood me. My security lay in secrecy. But till today I remember and love the childlike innocence of that Australian soldier and him.

When we captured prisoners, we used to confiscate all articles on them, which we would hand over to the Japanese, who in turn would send them to the Prisoners of War hospitals. At times, we did retain certain articles for the use of these arrested guests. Money on their persons was also taken, but deposited in the name of its respective owner and on release from our Camp it was handed back to him and a proper receipt obtained thereof.

During their stay in our Garrison, the prisoners used to quarrel at times. Some would take the side of Mr. Churchill and others would attack him saying, "But why are we here? For bloody tin and rubber? What does Mr. Churchill do except smoke a cigar and here we are without even a cheap quality cigarette." Sometimes these quarrels would go too far and our sentries had to intervene in order to restore peace, astonishing that we had to do that very duty which they were supposed to perform in India.

Some prisoners used to discuss politics with me, and almost all of them got convinced of our Indian point of view. In any case, I found little difference between their mentality and that of an average Indian under those circumstances. Actually they were worse off than the Indians. They were often found dirty and were made to bathe by order. Many of them could not read and write even their own names. I had always thought and believed that the British soldiers were literate but here I found them different. Again, there appeared to be innumerable differences among them. Captivity brings out the worst in a people.

In the morning they used to go round our barracks collecting cigarette butts which had been thrown by my men during the night. While doing so, they would start fighting with each other and often sentries had to be harsh with them. It reminded me of a British Colonel E. whom once I saw in India throwing a few coins to some poor Indians. When they started quarrelling over them, the Colonel started beating them all. Poor fellows, they were no more rulers. They were prisoners. What a change!

A Shooting Case

To the north of the Changi area was situated a small fishing village, about a mile or two away from the nearest POW Camp. The inhabitants of this village had been constantly complaining against the Allied POWs who, armed with sticks, would organise raids at night and get food from the villagers by force. The limit was reached one day when one of the inhabitants of this village reported to me of a rape case. His own daughter was the victim. An end had to be put to this once for all.

I increased patrol duty in that area, but prisoners could still escape when the sentries were a distance away on their beats. A standing day-and-night patrol was posted near the village which achieved the desired effect. But as soon as this patrol was withdrawn, prisoners started giving the same old trouble. One evening during the month of April 1942, we paid a surprise visit to this area. The sun had set. When I was returning to the Garrison, I left behind Subedar Santa Singh with my driver and my escort to do another round. A truck was left behind at their disposal. I returned alone driving the car myself. On arrival at the Garrison I proceeded to the Liaison Office to submit my daily report.

On my return from the Liaison Office I was surprised to find that Subedar Santa Singh had returned to the Garrison with a dead body and a wounded British prisoner. I ordered the Garrison Medical Officer, Jemadar Sucha Singh, to attend to the wounded, who had a bullet shot through the joint of his right shoulder. I started an immediate inquiry into this shooting incident personally. Naik Didar Singh, who had fired the bullet, stated that he and L/Nk Tara Singh were returning home. On arrival near the gate of the Camp situated near the old Changi Post Office, about fifteen Allied Prisoners of War attacked them with sticks and had very nearly carried away L/Nk Tara Singh. Thus, he fired an aimed round from a kneeling position to save his comrade. The bullet passed through the right shoulder of the wounded man and struck at the heart of the dead POW, who happened to be standing at a higher level and killed him instantaneously.

On hearing the sound of firing, the British guard at the Camp gate had fled away. Fearing that the British Prisoners of War might make a combined effort to snatch away the dead body and the wounded soldier, Subedar Santa Singh had brought them both to the Garrison. He was also of the opinion that this attack was meant for me. But because of darkness, prisoners completely misjudged and attacked the wrong person. Since I had come away all alone driving the car myself, the interpretation or explanation of event made some sense to me. I was in no way popular among the British POWs in the Changi area. In fact, my very sight used to hurt their pride.

After obtaining complete facts about the shooting incident, I immediately made for the Liaison Office to report the matter to the Japanese Headquarters. Lieut. Okazaki was not present there. I intimated all the facts to one of his juniors. After hearing my story be advised me to kill the wounded man and bury both the dead bodies. I might have done so if both were dead. Killing a wounded person was too much to do. I told him that I could never do that because it would be a very inhuman act on my part and against the Geneva Convention. However, I was fully prepared to face all the consequences. I was determined not to commit that brutal crime. Having replied thus I returned to the Garrison and inquired about the wounded soldier, who was still unconscious.

I was still in the hospital hut when Mr. Sunasawa called on me and informed that a Japanese Platoon was going round through POW camps with a view to finding out if they were making any preparations to attack the Indian Garrison during the night. Meanwhile, the Japanese had mounted two machine-guns to protect the flanks of my Camp, which were nearest to the POW camps. I was surprised to mark the speed with which the Japanese had taken this action. The Garrison remained alert during the night. But nothing untoward happened. Next day the Japanese waited for a report from the British but there was not a word coming from them. At long last this particular British Camp Commander was asked to submit a report on this incident. The report was lodged at about 2.30 P.M. whereas the incident had occurred at about 8.30 P.M. on the previous evening. The Japanese always used to make POW Camp Commanders and senior officers responsible for everything which their men did.

Early in the morning I sent Lieut. Swaran Singh by car to report to Col. Chaudhury at Seleter Hospital, with a request for him to come and attend the wounded prisoner. The evacuation of this particular prisoner was not permitted by the Japanese authorities who wanted to make further investigations into the whole affair. Col. Chaudhury was kind enough to come to our Garrison. He was a Surgical Specialist. I felt relieved when he communicated to me that the wounded soldier was out of danger, unless complications developed later on. Col. Chaudhury kept on visiting the patient daily. He got him X-rayed and gave him the best possible treatment under those circumstances.

Meanwhile, the case had been taken up for investigation by the Japanese military police, under Mr. Murata. I have been interrogated by many British and Indian Officers before my trial in the Red Fort of Delhi, but I have yet to meet an interrogator who would show greater intelligence, patience and energy than Mr. Murata. For nine days he continuously kept on interrogating my men. He used to begin in the morning and break for about half an hour only towards the evening for a cup of tea after which he would start again and continue late into the night. During those days Mr. Murata did not talk to me at all except greeting good morning and good night. Apart from a cup of tea he did not eat anything in my Camp.

Col. Chaudhury had forbidden Mr. Murata to disturb the patient until he was declared out of danger. During this period Mr. Murata had been interrogating my men and the British guards who were on duty on the day of this incident as well as some British Officers. The dead body had already been handed back to the POW Camp. But it was not recognized by any, either intentionally, or unintentionally. There seemed to be some difference in the story told by my men and the British guards.

I found it difficult to stand the suspense of not knowing whether the story narrated by Tara Singh and Didar Singh was true or false. At the end of his interrogation Mr. Murata told me he would interrogate the wounded British prisoner on the following day. This information was given to the prisoner. Before leaving my Camp that night Mr. Murata surprised me by congratulating me that my men had stood their interrogation well and had told the truth. I felt happy and relieved as I saw him off that night. But as soon as I entered my hut, a fearful thought overwhelmed me that the wounded prisoner was going to be found guilty of having attacked my men. This was a serious crime. The prisoner had survived his wounds but now he might have to face a firing squad.

But then it was no part of my job to defend him. And then there was no one else who could do so either. I tried to detach myself from this case but however hard I tried, sleep would not come to me. At last I got up from my bed and began to stroll about, thinking hard on the ways and means to save this unfortunate British POW.

It was 2.00 a.m. when I stealthily entered the Hospital hut. I found the patient wide awake. He was all alone. I asked him to go to sleep but he said that he could not. His worried look showed that he was mentally tortured. When I asked him if I could do anything for him, he kept quiet with tears flowing down from his eyes. The spectacle pained me immensely and I came back. I could not go to my bed either. After some time I went back to him. He still had not gone to sleep. In order to console him I started talking. He picked some courage and said, "Sir can you tell me the version of the story as stated by your men ?" I told him all what I knew. He said, "Pardon me, Sir, your men have not told the truth but then who will believe in my version of the story? I better agree with what your men have said otherwise the Japanese may torture me. How can you save me Sir ?" And he started crying.

Now, I was caught on the horns of a dilemma. I found that I could save either my men or the wounded soldier. After thinking hard for about another two hours, I came to the conclusion that if the prisoner was to be saved, the story had to be distorted to some extent to prove that the wounded man was not one of the attackers but had appeared on the scene, attracted by curiosity and got shot.

I thought that if by telling a lie, the life of an innocent POW could be saved, it was worth it. But how could I depend upon a prisoner to do so without giving away the secret that I had tutored him and thus endanger my honour and future relations with the Japanese. It was great personal as well as a national risk. I decided to take it. I told the prisoner what I wanted him to do. I gave him a plan to pursue. He appreciated my concern to save his life. Satisfied that he had fully understood my plan, I said "Good morning and happy day to you. Cheer up. All will be well."

The sun was just rising when I returned to my hut. Another day of suspense followed as Mr. Murata started interrogating the man early in the morning. I felt triumphed at the end of the day when Mr. Murata declared the man innocent and I was asked to release him. The next day I took him to Seletar Indian POW Hospital for a check-up by Col. Chaudhury and also to thank him for his treatment. Col. Chaudhury got him X-rayed and declared him fit. The prisoner was an honourable man. Once he had asked me to get him fried eggs and beacon which I had no means to provide. On the way back from Seletar to Changi I offered him this treat at a small wayside coffee stall. When we approached the Garrison Camp, he suddenly embraced me and gave me a kiss on the cheek. Astonished as I looked at him he said, "Pardon me, Sir I love you like my father. I did not realize what I was doing. You have given me a new life." That was the biggest reward he could give me. The next day he was sent back to his Camp.

Later I learnt that the Camp Commander of this particular Camp, a General Officer, was punished and awarded imprisonment for a few days. I saw this wounded soldier a month after his release from my Camp. He greeted me happily. I offered him a packet of cigarettes. I could see that he was indebted to me and remembered the good done to him.

The Hut

Our duties took a smoother course. The number of arrested prisoners increased. New additions were further made to this lot by the Japanese military police, who apprehended and caught Allied POWs in the act of escaping as far away as hundreds of miles from Singapore. All such POWs caught while attempting to escape were handed over to us. Some of these soldiers brought with them chits bearing 'Starve until death'. I used to show them those chits and would afterwards feed them all the more. There was little work for them to do. Now labour had to be found for them. An idea struck me. There was insufficient accommodation in the Garrison. Some huts had recently fallen. I wanted a hut for myself. Some building material was available from the damaged buildings at the Changi naval post. This was brought to the Garrison in lorries.

One of the prisoners, Sgt. J., an Australian, was fond of carpentry. He appeared to be a responsible man. I put him in charge of buildings and works, while I personally designed the model. In twenty days we were able to get a nice little hut constructed for me, with double-lined wooden walls, and elevated from the ground on cylindrical concrete blocks. My hut had a verandah, a drawing room, a sleeping-cum-dressing room, a store, an orderly's bunk and another small verandah in the rear. It was very well-ventilated and lighted by the sun.

The vacant land all around the hut was reclaimed from a rubber plantation after prisoners had removed the trees from it for fuel. This was allotted to sub-units for growing vegetables. A kuchha (unlined) well was dug to irrigate our vegetable gardens. My workshop personnel offered their services to electrify the Garrison Camp if the Japanese gave permission. An approach was made to the Japanese and they promptly agreed. Thus we had electricity in our Camp. The availability of fans and lights was a boon in that tropical climate.

One day the Japanese Liaison Staff invited all officers of the Indian Garrison to a dinner party. After the meals, the hosts and the guests were asked to sing songs alternately. The Japanese songs were full of martial spirit. After listening to a few of our Indian songs, which were mainly love songs, the Japanese remarked, "Do you sing love songs only ? Haven't you got any martial songs ?" I felt ashamed of myself for having failed to create a good impression. I requested Subedar Lal Din to give us a Punjabi ballad, "*O khuti Khattan giya, khat hey Liaanda tota,* etc." Even before I translated it, the Japanese felt so much inspired by Subedar Lal Din's loud and noisy singing that a spirit of competition could be seen starting between the hosts and the guests. When Subedar Lal Din's pitch of singing could not be surpassed, the Japanese decided to entertain us with a sword dance.

It was only proper for us that we should have returned their hospitality. But we had no funds. I had only five dollars on me and with this capital we undertook to entertain them to a dinner. About four hundred yards away from our Camp lived an old Chinese lady, who used to distill "Shamshu", a kind of country-made liquor from rice. She agreed to sell us five bottles of this stuff for two and a half dollars. The rest of the capital was used in buying a few ingredients for preparing meals. Tea water was mixed with "Shamshu" to give it a colour of liquor. This was to be served to our men while for the Japanese, Lieut. Swaran Singh had procured a bottle of whisky from some friends in Singapore town.

My men agreed to forgo two days' tea rations in order to make sugar available for preparation of a sweet dish. Some rice was bartered for vegetables and chickens with local civilians. Cups, saucers, and crockery of all designs were borrowed from about twenty houses for the evening. Anyway, it appeared to be a right royal dinner, particularly when speeches were made and toasts proposed. It was not for Officers only. All my men down to the junior-most person took part in it without any distinction of class, creed and religion. The Japanese Officers used to mix with their men on an equal basis. They were really surprised to find the spirit of cordiality between our Officers and men.

Insults

Our life in the Changi Garrison was becoming increasingly comfortable and pleasant everyday but one evening an unpleasant incident took place. I heard somebody being slapped near the Camp entrance. On approaching I found that my sentry was being beaten by Cpl. Tamamori. On seeing me, he stopped beating my sentry. It was far too much to be tolerated or overlooked. We had got ready to go on a patrol duty. I called it off and instead went straight to Lieut. Okazaki to make a complaint. As I was talking to him, Cpl. Tamamori entered the Office and started putting forward his side of the case. It took him about ten minutes.

Lieut. Okazaki was enraged after hearing Cpl. Tamamori. He asked me at the top of his voice who could have dared to insult his N.C.O. He told me to clear off and report to him after investigation of the whole incident. For the time being, I obeyed him and came back to the Garrison, where my Officers and men waited for me with great anxiety. Without talking to anybody I made for my hut. After waiting there for about half an hour I went back to inform Lieut. Okazaki that nobody had insulted Cpl. Tamamori. I did not make any investigations nor was I prepared to do so.

Lieut. Okazaki thundered back in English saying, "Your sentry....". He waited to search for a suitable word, which I supplied — "made a mistake". But he continued looking through his dictionary and shouted, "No, not made a mistake but insulted my N.C.O. by not saluting him when he was told to do so. It is not N.C.O's insult, it is my insult, whose representative he is; not my insult, it is the Imperial Japanese Army's insult; it is a Japanese National insult. As such, there can be no excuse for such a crime." I waited for a while. Many thoughts crossed my mind. What could I say ? We were no army yet; we were not a nation even, though we were trying hard to become one.

Suddenly I got a brainstorm. I said, "Mr. Okazaki...." The moment I had called him Mr., he roared at me, "Not Mr. Okazaki— Lieut. Okazaki, Changi Commandeer". I replied, "Lieut. Okazaki, Changi Commander, if my sentry is beaten by your N.C.O. in my presence, it is not my sentry's insult; it is my insult because he happens to be my man. Not my insult but of the Fujiwara Kikan who has sent me here; not Fujiwara Kikan's insult but of the Japanese Army whose organisation that Kikan is. So you may take it anyway you like, it is a Japanese national insult. My nation does not come in nor do I feel so."

Lieut. Okazaki waited for some time. Throwing out his right hand towards me he stood up saying, "Let us shake hands for the sake of the Greater East Asia". I waited and then grasped his hand. Outwardly it appeared that we had made up. But from then onward that cordiality which had existed disappeared for ever. Cpl. Tamamori formally apologised to me. In fact, he was hurt and had made a habit of picking quarrels with my men so often that I began to hate him unlike the past when I liked him so much.

There were more incidents of beating and slapping my men and Officers approached me many a time so that I might allow them to retaliate. They would argue that when they had rifles and ammunition and were in a position to hit back why they should not do so. But I drew their attention to Mahatmaji's principle of non-violence. I would tell them that courage lay in controlling the force which one possessed. I would even say to them that I wanted them to withhold force even if they were provoked to the extent that I was slapped right in their presence. It was not because we were afraid to fight, but because that was not the right time and place to take up arms. Negotiations were going on at the top regarding the expansion of the Indian National Army and it would be mere foolishness on our part to take a serious view of an individual's actions and thus endanger the outcome of bigger issues. My men listened to me carefully and they carried on making the best of a bad job.

I gave up visiting Lieut. Okazaki's office as often as I had been doing in the past. Even on important occasions I would detail some junior officer as my representative to answer for me. The co-operation which I used to extend lessened. My present mentality, on the contrary, resulted in a more sympathetic attitude towards the Allied POWs. This indifference towards the Japanese on my part became noticeable but Lieut. Okazaki who had earlier praised my work before his higher Headquarters so much that he could not say anything against me without making his own position awkward. At last he showed some signs of forgetting the unpleasant past. But before he did so, he tried his best to create a split amongst us, particularly among the Officers of my Garrison, through special favours to some by presenting them articles of food as a bait. But we were so united that his very best efforts met with an utter failure. My Officers would refuse to take any notice of such instructions as were issued by him directly. Our strength was established. It was a strength that lay in our unity and national awakening.

Religion

Before going to Changi I used to be very religious-minded, though not communal. I must observe everything religious and I would offer prayers regularly thrice a day. But this was purely my personal affair. As Garrison Commander I felt that even my personal self belonged to my men. While offering prayers, often my mind would start thinking of my duties and my responsibilities towards my command. Thus I forgot the links in my prayers and had to start them all over again. In this way more time had to be spent than was actually required for offering prayers. This wasting of time in duplicity of thought continued for about a month. I failed to make up my mind whether to stop offering prayers or to continue in the present state. Any decision would have been all right as long as I could satisfy my conscience.

Religion had given me self-confidence and strength of character. It was because of my religion that I had answered to the national call of the moment. My prayers had been responsible for keeping religion alive in me. I wanted my religion but could not afford to spend any time on it; it was the time which could be better employed in the performance of my duties. When my thoughts wandered away from my duties while offering prayers, I thought that it was nothing less than cheating God and my conscience. What I did need was meditation to guide me in practical humanitarianism, nationalism and my duties. I thought it would make little difference in the eyes of God if I were to give up formal or customary practices as long as I believe in Him. So I decided to forego all my daily prayers except the last one before going to sleep and a brief morning prayer.

Confidence in one's self and faith in God to my mind are one and the same thing. God or nature has given each one of us a brain. If we use it and our plans are decided after a deliberate rational exercise, then it gives us boldness in action. Then if we fail we can always analyse and I have always come to the conclusion that the fault lay in planning. So instead of blaming God, Qismat, Nature or others I would try to improve upon my actions and would be invariably successful and victorious and then I would be grateful to God and be happy with myself, and with my Qismat and colleagues and would love my environments.

I was happy but was not prepared to impart my ideas to others. I sincerely believed that for a simple-minded soldier, who had some daily routine to perform, there must be some religious ceremonies to cultivate in him meditation and the spirit of patriotism. In fact, I wanted him to be very regular in offering his prayers. I was pleased to notice an increasing number of men who had started offering prayers in their own way. Religion was everybody's personal affair.

National unity had to be cultivated. Religious bars against eating a certain type of meat were a great concern to me. My evening lectures were a great help in tackling these problems. Luckily, we were not issued any kind of meat, except tinned fish; as such the question of '*jhatka*' and '*halal*' did not arise. Though belonging to different religions, my men would eat together. A common kitchen could not be started due to lack of sufficiently large cooking utensils. All those things, which did more harm than good, had to be done away with. My men developed a better understanding and gave up their prejudices regarding food and religion. They respected each other's feelings and had become very broad-minded human beings.

At times the Japanese supplied preserved meat from the Singapore cold storage to the Allied Prisoners of War. Once they offered some beef to the Changi Garrison. The Muslim members of my Garrison refused to take it. These were the days when we had been living on dry rations only, issued from the Japanese supplies. Anything to supplement the dry rations was welcome, especially meat which our soldiers had not eaten for the past so many months. To refuse to accept such an important item of diet at a time when the human body needed it so badly was a great sacrifice. I collected all my men and asked the non-Muslims if they could allow their Muslim friends cooking beef in the Garrison and *viceversa*. Without exception all of them agreed to allow each party to cook and eat meat of their choice with full freedom. I am putting this down here with a sense of pride that there never arose any controversy over diet in the Changi Garrison.

I have already mentioned that on our arrival in Changi, Sikhs had asked me for allotment of some accommodation for their gurudwara, which I had frankly refused. My refusal was mainly due to the insufficiency in accommodation. Again, if Sikhs were allotted accommodation for their gurudwara it would be only fair and proper that Muslims, Hindus and Christians were also allotted separate accommodation for their respective places of worship. I could not imagine having four different places of worship in a small Camp of two hundred men. I even discouraged Sikhs to continue with their gurudwara which they had made in their own accommodation. They happened to be the largest in number and could afford to spare a bunk for this purpose. But what was to be done by others who were small in number and hence could not spare any accommodation for their places of worship. To my mind it was unfair that one community should have a place of worship and the others should not. Being a Sikh, I was in a better position to ask Sikhs to show greater broad-mindedness.

Another allied problem was of a great concern to me. During Sunday services, the Sikhs would approach me to give them a special quota of sugar and ghee for cooking 'Prashad'. The Japanese had presented the Garrison with three bags of sugar and one bag especially for me. I had been using this bag on special occasions to entertain the Garrison on festivals or when men did something good. Twice out of this reserve I had issued sugar to the Garrison on Sundays. The Sikhs had used their share for their Sunday service while others did as they thought best. The bag could not last long and I could not afford to make this special concession every Sunday. Thus, I called all Sikh Officers and acquainted them with my point of view. Subedar Santa Singh was in complete agreement with me. Of course, Lieut. Swaran Singh was far too broad-minded to need even to discuss this matter. He left everything to Subedar Santa Singh and me. But some Sikh Officers did not like my views in the beginning. Later, realising the benefits which we would all derive as a national unit, they also decided in favour of my views.

The accommodation which could have been allotted to religious institutions was reserved for the Garrison Hospital under Dr. Sucha Singh, a simple-minded, kind-hearted and unassuming officer. With his painstaking habits and kindness, he soon became popular among civilians residing in the Changi area. It was very difficult during those days for civilians to get any medical treatment. Dr. Sucha Singh would often approach me to ask for permission to admit some civilians in the Garrison Hospital. He was successful in curing such patients as had given up all hope of recovery. I found in him a courageous doctor who was never impatient or nervous. He was a good Surgeon. In the beginning I took him to be an irresponsible type of an Officer. But as the time progressed I gained so much confidence in him that I would prefer even serious patients to be left under his care than to get them admitted in any POW or civilian hospital. He was resourceful and would often manage to get medicines for the Garrison Hospital through the Japanese. Initially he was intolerant of criticism, but he was a changed man as the time passed. It was a blessing to have a small hospital run under an efficient doctor like Sucha Singh.

A Desertion

The Garrison latrines were dug in the unhutted area of the Camp. During daytime the Allied Prisoners-of-War detained under our custody were allowed to move about freely in the hutted as well as the unhutted area of the Camp. For night use, if need be, a large bucket was placed in their cage. Two prisoners used to carry this bucket in the morning to empty its contents in a covered pit in the latrine area. The prisoners carried out this duty in turn and it was left to themselves to arrange their own reliefs. The senior-most prisoner was detailed as the cage commander who was required to report to me daily. Two of my men, who always acted as my personal escort during my rounds outside the Garrison, were also detailed to look after the prisoners.

I was shocked to learn one morning from Nk. Didar Singh that two prisoners who had gone to dispose of the night-soil in the latrine area had deserted. These two British soldiers — Privates Peter and Martin — along with their third companion, Private David, had been handed over to me by the Japanese Military Police only two days earlier. They had been caught deserting four times before this, once as far away as two hundred miles from Singapore. The Privates Peter and Martin were caught this time trying to make a get-away in a small country boat.

Brave lads! Ever since their recapture they had been kept in chains. I had received written orders from the Japanese Headquarters to keep them in chains throughout their detention in my Garrison. They were not supposed to be given any food. I learnt from them that they had been given nothing to eat for the last four days when they were captured. On my own responsibility I gave them food and removed their chains after the first day of their arrival in my Garrison. They were to be treated like the other POWs undergoing detention in my Garrison. They had given me their word of honour, but they let me down.

What was I to do? Lieut. Okazaki had just shown a little improvement in his attitude. Now he would have the upper hand once again. My position was made very awkward. Immediately I ordered all my men present in the Garrison to go out to make a thorough search in the adjoining rubber plantations and woods. Meanwhile, I went to report to Lieut. Okazaki who received the news very badly. He was personally responsible to the Japanese Military Police for those prisoners. He felt that I had let him down purposely. Shouting at me, he told me to leave his office and search for the deserters.

We searched throughout the day. There was no clue available. We had neither rest nor any food. We went on and on. At last a civilian gave some information, but it proved to be of no use to us. Lieut. Okazaki was furious. He sent Cpl. Tamamori with a squad of Japanese soldiers to search for the deserters in conjunction with us. All the Japanese soldiers had their different plans. They would take men from the Garrison as they wished. When any of my Officers or men gave an excuse by saying that Capt. Dhillon had issued instructions differently, the Japanese would shout out, "No Dhillon. Dhillon no good. He no Commander. Lieut. Okazaki Commander". It seemed that I had been summarily dismissed from my command. My Officers and men continuously asked my permission to retaliate against the arrogant attitude of the Japanese soldiers. But I had to calm them pointing out that it was not the time to do so. They must wait and put up with all those insults for my sake, if not for the bigger cause.

The Japanese had their way for two days and two nights during which we neither had rest nor sleep. The whole of Singapore Island was thoroughly combed, yet there was no clue. It seemed that in spite of his temper Lieut. Okazaki had not reported the case of desertion to his Headquarters and the Japanese Military Police. He was equally keen to save the situation and his face. He said, "I give you seven days and within this period the prisoners must be apprehended and caught. Otherwise your sentry who was on duty when the prisoners deserted will he handed over to the Japanese Military Police". He detailed Mr. Saji and Cpl. Tamamori's squad to help me during the search. With the exception of Mr. Saji, I found others more of a nuisance than help. Every time I suggested a plan they would say that Lieut. Okazaki would not like it. In fact, I was fed up with this interference. Once when I happened to call a Japanese L/Cpl. by name, he said, "No Undo. I His Imperial Majesty's non-commissioned officer L/Cpl. Undo." I decided to put up with no nonsense any more.

Mr. Saji was an interpreter. Obviously, he was well educated. He was a refined person who paid me proper respect. It appeared that he liked my plans. At last I told him that, if proper search was to be made, I must be alone and free to make any decisions. I had regained my former confidence. I felt that I was the Commander of the Changi Garrison and from then onward I would put up with no nonsense from any quarter and I would brook no interference. If the Japanese had lost confidence in me I would gladly go. When I intimated my feelings to Mr. Saji, we were about ten miles from Changi. Cpl. Tamamori would not yield an inch. He would argue that he had to obey Lieut. Okazaki's orders. Thus we returned to the Liaison Office and placed the matter before Lieut. Okazaki. There was an exchange of tempers. I refused to command the Garrison. Finding himself in an awkward position, Lieut. Okazaki left me alone and agreed that Cpl. Tamamori and others would remain with me only if I needed their help.

Lieut. Swaran Singh obtained my permission to use third degree methods to extract information out of Private David, the third companion of the two deserters. Private David was put in chains immediately. Lieut. Swaran Singh had hardly given him a slap when Private David started talking and gave the information so far withheld. He intimated that an old woman, Mrs. Farah, who was a woman of low repute, always gave protection to Privates Peter and Martin whenever they escaped from the POW Camps. He admitted that before they deserted, Privates Peter and Martin had discussed with him their plans to escape. He was of the opinion that the deserters must be staying somewhere within knowledge of Mrs. Farah.

David further informed us that the deserters had hatched a plan to leave the Island as soon as arrangements could be made to procure some rations and money for the journey. This would take them at least a week. This was valuable information. An important clue had been found, provided Private David was not telling a lie. It seemed that Lieut. Swaran Singh's initiative had solved our problem which two days of intensive interrogation had failed to do. Private David was intimate with an Eurasian girl, Miss Rosy, who was a maid-servant to Mrs. Farah. Miss Rosy had given him shelter for two months prior to his recent capture by the Japanese Military Police.

To make full use of such an important information, an intelligent plan was essential. It was an exercise in a sort of a secret mission. There was no difficulty in locating Mrs. Farah's place. All possible precautions were necessary to ensure that our identity was not disclosed and nobody could suspect or entertain any suspicions with regard to our activities. Mrs. Farah and the deserted Prisoners of War had to be dealt with on their own terms. After going through all pros and cons and judging the situation, we started on our mission in the right earnest.

Mr. Saji was dressed like a Chinese merchant, whereas Tamamori looked like a Malay servant. I had put on clothes befitting an Indian cloth merchant, in a Punjabi attire with a flowing beard, which otherwise I kept tied and pressed. Private David remained as he was. We pretended to be his old friends, who were sheltering him from the Japanese Military Police and the Indian guards at Changi. Three of us had tied revolvers on our bodies. hiding them carefully so that no suspicion could arise, yet at the same time to be handy for use in case of an emergency. All four of us got in my car. My driver looked like a typical taxi-wala. A squad of Japanese soldiers followed us in a truck for help, if required.

We left the car in a rubber plantation and walked up to the shop, belonging to Mrs. Farah, situated in Payalebar, where she ran a brothel. Mrs. Farah was not present. She had gone to her house, which was about a mile away in a small village. We proceeded to her house. Miss Rosy was standing at the gate. She greeted Private David. We were introduced to her as Private David's friends. There was a glitter in her eyes and she looked very happy to see Private David a free man once again. By now our eyes fell on gray-haired Mrs. Farah, who was seated in the verandah of her house with a two-year-old child in her lap. She smoked in a carefree manner and drank coffee which she offered to us as well. The coffee served in a clean set of crockery tasted excellent.

Private David performed the introduction ceremony once again. Mrs. Farah asked him about his present place of refuge. He informed her that I was giving him protection in my house in the town. She desired to know the story of Private David's recapture and his subsequent escape, to which the latter made suitable answers and asked about whereabouts of Privates Peter and Martin. She said, "They are planning to leave this island as soon as I can arrange some money and provisions for them.:" At this stage Mr. Saji got impatient and he started inquiring about their whereabouts. I was afraid lest he should undo the whole show. I frowned at him and he managed to restrain himself.

Mrs. Farah replied that she did not know the whereabouts of Privates Peter and Martin during the day but they would come to eat with her after dark (it was midday at that time). Knowing so much about the deserters, Mr. Saji and Cpl. Tamamori showed greater impatience. Luckily for us, at this stage Mrs. Farah went inside her house to get something. I advised both my Japanese companions to leave the place so that Mrs. Farah should not become suspicious. Apologising this time, they left. I stayed behind to collect more information if possible.

Continued talking to Mrs. Farah for about another hour. Private David got a chance to talk to Miss Rosy at length. I decided to leave that place. Addressing Private David, I said, "Mr. David, you better stay on and meet your friends at night. I must go to my shop". Having understood our pre-arranged cue, Private David replied, "I would not like to take the risk of staying with Mrs. Farah for the night. In case the Japanese Military Police should smell my presence here, I would be back in the cage once again and Mrs. Farah might find herself in hot waters". Thus both of us left Mrs. Farah with a promise to call on her some other time.

Private David and I went to Mrs. Farah's house the same evening. We had hardly wished her 'good evening' when she started bombarding us with the filthiest expressions of abuse. To digest abuse is pretty hard for a soldier but it is worse still when it comes from a female of ill-repute. She thundered that she knew who I was and as such would have nothing to do with me. I had to put up with all these insults. But when she would not stop, addressing Private David, I said,

"Look here, Mr. David, I did not shelter you in the face of so many risks from the Japanese Military Police and my countrymen to get this reception from your friends. I have had enough of it. Now you better stay and I go."

Private David apologised and Mrs. Farah too controlled her temper and tone. Suddenly she said, "Can you swear by God that you are Mr. David's friend ?" I replied, "Yes. by God he is my friend." After this she was a changed person. She said, "All right, sit down. They will be arriving here in half an hour's time." I was offered coffee and it really tasted well after all that stormy scene. David got another chance to meet Miss Rosy. We waited and waited but Peter and Martin did not arrive. At last we took leave at about 2 A.M. and rejoined the Japanese escort which had been waiting for us some distance away from that village. David was happy to have met his girl friend. I was disappointed for having missed Peter and Martin and my two dollars which I had to offer to Mrs. Farah for her hospitality. Two dollars meant so much during those days. What an experience!

On the following day David and I paid another visit to Mrs. Farah's place. She informed us that Peter and Martin had left her place only fifteen minutes ago. She also told us that they could not risk turning up on the previous night as they suspected that somebody was watching them. In fact, Cpl. Tamamori had made another mistake. He had laid a cordon round the village. Apart from being very sure of capturing the deserters, he was nervous about my personal safety too. It was good of him to have thought of me in this way but the result was that suspicion was created in the minds of Peter and Martin, and very rightly too. Once again we had lost the game. I abstained from paying any visits to Mrs. Farah on the next day lest she should again become suspicious.

Meanwhile, I received a message from the G.O.C. Mohan Singh. He wanted to see me at Mount Pleasant. I had not seen him ever since his return from Tokyo, where he had gone on a Goodwill Mission; nor had I the nerve to face him, having failed in my duty.

Six days had elapsed. One day more and Lieut. Okazaki should submit a report to the Japanese Military Police. Only two nights and a day of hope and toil remained at our disposal. Another effort was made to contact Mrs. Farah. Perhaps she had come to know what we were after and she was trying her best to outwit us. Hoping against hope, after dark in the evening, Private David and I entered Mrs. Farah's house, leaving a party of 12 men half a mile away with instructions. Mrs. Farah was away. Miss Rosy sat by a small oil lamp which threw its dim rays to display her worried looks.

As she saw us, her face suddenly beamed with joy. Before we could greet her she said, "You have come only five minutes too late. Madam Farah has gone to see them off. She suspects your intentions. The boys too have their suspicions. They are going to leave the island by tomorrow. Madam Farah has got them some money, rice and eggs. But I do know where they are going to stay for the night." She described to us the location of a deserted house which was hardly half a mile away from Madam Farah's residence. On my request Miss Rosy came half the way to point out the house to me.

It was a moonlit night. Leaving Private David and Miss Rosy in the shade of a tree— I am sure they liked it too—I made for the house where our deserters were supposed to stay that night. This house was built on wooden stilts. Crawling stealthily, I went underneath the house. I could hear the stamping of the heavy tread of army boots. I grew hopeful. But soon my hopes were to be dashed to the ground though temporarily. I heard a man talking in Hindustani, "What a joke! How can sparrows kill hawk or jackal a lion?" That house appeared to be definitely occupied by some Indians. Perhaps Mrs. Farah had given the wrong location to Miss Rosy.

I came back to the tree where David and Rosy sat talking in shade. They must have desired my absence as long as possible. But for me it was a very serious problem. When I asked Miss Rosy if she was definite about the house, she swore at me and told me, that was the house she meant. I asked a few more questions, but she did not approve of my action. She did not like any interference in her short-lived romance.

I was still hesitant. I did not believe that it was the house where Peter and Martin were going to put up for the night before they left Singapore Island. I felt that my patience was at an end. I was not accustomed to such treatment as Miss Rosy had given me. I made up my mind for a final attempt. Signalling to my party which was waiting for me and explaining my plan to them, I ordered them to encircle that house. My men were impatient like those hounds who on sight of a game would wish to break their leads if they could. Slowly and cautiously they closed on the house. I entered the house by the rear staircase holding a loaded revolver in my right hand and a torch in the left. Naik Didar Singh and Cpl. Tamamore followed me.

In our way, lay an Indian barber, who was swearing at someone. I recognised that it was the same voice I had heard when I had called underneath the house a short time ago. This man needed no threats. As soon as I asked him he informed me of the two men I was after. At the same time he pleaded with me that he had been forced to sleep there under threats from those British soldiers. I advanced towards the room where Peter and Martin were sleeping under a mosquito net. They were startled by our sudden appearance. I warned them not to move. When I asked them if they had recognised me, they uttered, "Captain Dhillon."

Cpl. Tamamori and Nk. Didar Singh overpowered both the deserters. By now, others had also come up. They wanted to beat the two captives but they were stopped from so doing. Ordering my men to take the prisoners to our motor vehicles, I hurried towards the "Lovers tree". Collecting David and conveying my sincerest thanks to Miss Rosy, we departed happily. Before our departure Miss Rosy asked if I could bring David to her on the following or another day. I readily gave her my word. By now she knew my identity and profusely apologised for her swearing at me.

Immediately we made for the Garrison. Peter and Martin were put in chains and a report was sent to Lieut. Okazaki. He was surprised at our success, and in recognition of my efforts presented me a bottle of beer, a rare gift in those days of scarcity, which as I did not drink, I kept for Miss Rosy.

On the following day Lieut. Okazaki called on me to thank us formally and presented us a purse containing ten dollars as a reward for our efforts. The Indian in me moved once again. Adding another five dollars to it, I returned the same to Cpl. Tamamori and his squad. Refusal on both sides resulted in a common plan that we should have a community dinner, which came off very successfully. David also attended this dinner, for I had sworn in the presence of Mrs. Farah that he was my friend! Speeches and songs on both sides marked the occasion.

A few days later, I honoured my word when I took David to meet Miss Rosy. Both these lovers enjoyed that bottle of beer which Lieut. Okazaki had presented to me. I gave a sum of five dollars to Miss Rosy for her help rendered to us. Everybody appeared to be happy once again. I wonder how Mrs. Farah felt about this episode! Poor woman ! The fate of Peter and Martin remained to be decided. My men and the Japanese had treated them very badly, so much so that marks of lashes were clearly visible on their backs, but they deserved it. Had they not let us down while we had given them full freedom on their word of honour to freely move about within the Garrison ?

A few days later Lieut. Okazaki informed me that the Japanese authorities had decided to try Privates Peter and Martin. Lt. Col. Ogami, with my assistance, was to conduct a court of inquiry as to their escape. Lt. Col. Ogami was an old man who had braved sixty summers. He was well-built and appeared aristocratic. He could speak good English easily enough to make himself understood. After going through the case he remarked that there could be no punishment for Privates Peter and Martin other than death. I explained that it was a Prisoner of War's right and duty to escape if he could, and the Geneva Convention recognised it. These soldiers had let me down and I felt extremely bitter against them. But after capturing them personally, my anger against them had vanished. I showed him their backs covered with lashing marks and suggested to him, that was enough punishment for the poor devils. Col. Ogami promised to convey to me his decision on the following day. He was a kind-hearted Japanese Officer.

His decision was a mild one. Privates Peter and Martin were left under my charge to undergo simple confinement for an indefinite period. Col. Ogami had shown the real "Bushido" spirit. The culprits got a pleasant surprise when the news of their punishment was broken to them. And once again they were set free in the Changi Garrison Camp area. A week later, it was discovered that Private Martin had contracted venereal disease. He was admitted in the British Prisoners-of-War Hospital. Private Peter remained with us. In due course he became a favourite of the Garrison. He learnt our language and was often seen moving about freely in our kitchens to get whatever he could. My men enjoyed his speaking in Hindustani. They would gladly help him with foodstuffs. Private David lived with us and was treated as an equal. But one day he too lost my favour. He stole some articles of food from my hut. I was compelled to put him back in the Prisoner's cage.

Sometime later I fell seriously ill. During my prolonged illness Private Peter served me faithfully. He used to spend lot of time in making my bed and decorating my hut with wild flowers. I started liking him immensely. Once he said that I should take him with me and he would serve me even in the Indian National Army. Often I have thought that kindness can result in relations which know no barriers of communities, religion or nationality. Humanity overcomes all barriers.

I Meet the G.O.C.

Short-statured and of thin build, Captain Mohan Singh, the G.O.C. of the Indian National Army was very unassuming in his appearance. I would not call him handsome but he had something in him which would attract any sincere and good-hearted person and repel those who were insincere and cunning. He was a good speaker on the stage and could spellbind his audience for hours on end. While speaking he became forceful and lively as if there were springs in his body. His very presence would be an inspiration to the masses. Once on the stage, he knew how to control and play on an audience. After joining the Indian Army as an ordinary soldier, he had worked his way up to the Indian Military Academy and was one of the first to join it in 1932.

Having been through the mill, he knew exactly the feelings of soldiers, whatever their ranks might be. I had been his colleague in the Ist Battalion, 14 Punjab Regiment, where I found him in the habit of drinking and enjoying other amusements like an average British Indian Army Officer. But ever since he conceived the idea of raising the Indian National Army, he was a changed man. He had given up all his old habits. All his time, energy and thoughts were devoted to the Indian National Army. One day I asked him whether he had ever thought of his wife and folks. Showing me a heap of about seventy unopened letters, he said, "I do not have the time to think of them. Look, I could not even open these letters. My soldiers are my people and I cannot afford to use a moment out of their time for things personal. I belong to them." When I reminded him of the death of his son and of my son, he said, "Let us rejoice over it and congratulate each other for having got rid of a burden and thus be better placed to serve the Movement."

Mohan Singh was popular among the men and was often seen paying surprise visits to Camps at odd hours of the day and night in order to look into their welfare and know their exact feelings personally. A leader of soldiers who acted like a soldier. He had guts unsurpassed. Though he was not a polished diplomat, he was the only person among us who could handle the Japanese, for they always respected a sincere and strong character.

Since he was junior in age, experience and service in the Indian Army, many of his senior colleagues were jealous of his position. Cliques and intrigues hindered his progress. The age-long slavish mentality of our people was always there to thwart his way. But undaunted, he advanced onward and worked hard day and night to overcome all those hurdles that came in the way of raising the Indian National Army. He was on his way to becoming a top class leader of men.

One evening I thought of paying him a visit. On arrival at Mount Pleasant I found that he had not yet returned from his office. I waited and waited in the Visitors' Room till it was midnight. At long last he came but made straight for his room. One of his secretaries informed him that I had come. Immediately he called me in. On entering his room I found that he was seated in a low arm chair and was knocking his head against a small table placed in front of him as if trying to recollect an idea. I stood in the doorway for a few seconds, but he was unaware of my presence. At last I greeted him, or in other words aroused him from his deep thinking. Poor G.O.C.!

We had not seen each other ever since his departure on the Goodwill Mission to Tokyo in March 1942. Captain Mohd. Akram of Ist Battalion 14 Punjab Regiment was then alive. He was Mohan

Singh's best friend and the most trusted colleague from amongst the Officers around him. Captain Mohd. Akram, Giani Pritam Singh and Swami Satya Nand had met their end in an air crash en route to Tokyo. They were the first martyrs of the Indian National Army. I uttered the name of Akram and, failing to control my emotions, burst into sobs. Mohan Singh got up to meet me, and as my elder brother, tried to console me.

For about fifteen minutes, utter grief had come over me and I could not speak a word. Crying made me lighter and at last I started talking to Mohan Singh. I asked him the cause of his worried look. He informed me that the Japanese had asked for a Company of Indian Gunners. Accordingly, he had approached some gunners who had agreed to go on this duty. But just that night when the Japanese wanted to take them to an island, they had refused to go due to some unpleasant incident or experience with the Japanese. The Japanese had now taken it as a breach of trust. The G.O.C. was then in a very awkward position. He had to look after the interests of his men and at the same time he could not afford to adopt a hostile attitude towards the Japanese at that juncture.

With great concern suddenly he said, "Gurbakhsh! are you quite happy in Changi or have you any complaints? Do tell me if you have any. I must know the exact situation". I came out with all my hurt feelings and related one by one all the incidents which had taken place at Changi. The G.O.C. was surprised for he had always been told that I was very happy and so were the Japanese with me. When he heard my version of the story, he became furious and said that he would ask the Japanese to return the Changi Garrison by the next day. He would no longer put up with any nonsense when his troops were insulted. He asked me for more details. Having burdened him with more worries I returned to Changi.

Some days later I learnt that the G.O.C. had put up this matter to the Fujiwara Kikan, who had taken a serious view of it. With a view to patch up our relationship, Lieut. Okazaki was called to Mount Pleasant to explain to the G.O.C. in person. The G.O.C. must have given a real good ticking off to Okazaki, for after a few days he called me in his office, and when I was directed to the Conference Room, Lieut. Okazaki, dressed in review-order uniform, appeared with a few members of his staff and an interpreter. He formally informed me that I had approached my G.O.C. without any prior warning to him. Taking this as a breach of discipline, he said that I had no right to report to my Headquarters directly. He dared to ask me for an explanation. He was talking to me loudly as if he were addressing a gathering of thousands of people.

I was reminded of the Farrar Park meeting when Major Fujiwara addressed us but then Fujiwara's attitude was warm and courteous. When he finished talking, I said, "Lieut. Okazaki, I have often reported to you about your own misbehaviour and the high-handedness of your men towards me and my Garrison. Since you never cared to listen to me, I had to approach my own Headquarters, for I expected no justice or sympathy from you." He thought that I might be frightened by his hustling ways. When he saw the reverse effect of his bullying behaviour, he politely asked, "I know that you have asked for your transfer but I have requested your G.O.C. that you should not be relieved from the command of the Changi Garrison as long as I do not agree. I do not want you to leave me. Perhaps you do not know that I have been talking very highly of you to my Headquarters as well as to your Headquarters. If you insist on your transfer it will go against us both." The change in his tone changed me too. Once again we made up but only for the sake of formality.

On the following day I again visited Mount Pleasant to see the G.O.C. and I informed him in detail about what had transpired between me and Okazaki. The G.O.C. advised me to carry on for some time. He said that a conference of the representatives of Indians from all over Asia was going to take place in the near future at Bangkok. After that conference we should know exactly whether the Indian National Army could be organised or not. No decisive steps could be taken before that time. Thus I continued to command the Changi Garrison. The relations between Okazaki and me remained strictly formal. But I was heartened for I knew that the G.O.C. fully understood how and where to put his foot down and get things done.

Officers' Mess

The differences between me and Lieut. Okazaki continued increasing, but there were certain things for which we commanded mutual respect. Soon another incident occurred. Cpl. Tamamori quarrelled with one of my N.C.Os. Normally I would have made a verbal report to Lieut. Okazaki, but this time, due to our strained relations, I lodged a written report. Lieut Okazaki took a very serious view of it and the result was that Cpl. Tamamori and his squad were removed from my Garrison. My Officers and men who had watched my activities with keen interest and concern were so pleased that they congratulated me on this success. From then onwards Lieut. Okazaki left us alone. The absence of interference gave me an opportunity to devote more time to my men. There were certain problems which had often troubled me, and I began to tackle them in the right earnest.

On my arrival at Changi I had started an Officers' Mess, which had been a failure thus far. I wanted to try again. I believed that separate messing arrangements for Officers and men were essential to maintain good military discipline. Apart from providing a teaching ground, as an Officers' Mess always provides a common stage where seniors and juniors can live together and generate comradeship and fraternity, so essential in a revolutionary army. My men had failed to appreciate these higher points of view, specially because of their newly-born sense of independence. They seemed to have a wrong notion of freedom. Freedom to them meant all-round equality, irrespective of rank and responsibility. This type of freedom would not work in an army, especially of a revolutionary type. Besides starting our Mess, it was of great importance that the men had to be made to realize that it was just the proper thing to do. At last a Mess was started.

And was not it a real mess of everything? We had no servants, no furniture and no utensils. Added to this peculiar state of affairs, our rations were so meager that there was no fun and dignity in eating boiled rice and dal in a formal congregation at every meal. At last I was compelled to give up this idea of running an Officers' Mess and we adopted a new system which suited us better still, particularly from the point of view of our men. Apart from a few messing nights when officers would dine together, each Officer ate with his men.

Men are Generous

My evening lectures continued, more as an entertainment than for education. I thought that my men no longer needed any spiritual training. But one evening I got the shock of my life when I was approached by some of my men with a request that I should try to get their rations of sugar increased. They knew that I had been trying; not only that, I did actually get some for them from the Japanese over and above their normal rations. They also knew that I never took any sugar for myself from the normal rations, but instead I used to get it from certain friends outside the Garrison. A reminder to me to do what I was already doing for them came to me as a feeling of their no-confidence in me. I advised them to cut their requirements and start having tea once a day instead of twice. Hardly had I spoken these words when a man stood up and said, "But Sir, why do you have it more than once a day?"

Yes, he was right, but considering that I used to have only one meal a day, that I used to work daily from dawn till after midnight, that I had to entertain some Japanese and Indian Officers visiting our Camp, that the Japanese supplied me with a special quota of sugar for this purpose, I had taken it as a proper thing to take tea whenever I had to entertain a guest. Men in a sense are the best judges of their Officers. You cannot please them all, but at the same time you cannot ignore them either. I said, "It has given me pain to realise that while I am the most hardworking and worried individual living on one meal a day, having no other form of amusement, I should be denied even an extra cup of tea which I liked so much". The speaker apologised to me and immediately took his words back. But I continued, "Because your observation is correct, from today onward I will give up taking tea even once a day and will not resume it until I can get your sugar rations increased."

The moment I made this statement, all the men started begging of me to continue my tea, but I would not listen to any of them. Two days had passed. I had taken no tea. Admittedly, I missed it very much. The next evening after the roll call it was reported to me that all the members of the Garrison had taken no tea for the last two days either, and they had made up their mind not to take it until I resumed taking tea. The sugar they had thus saved was offered to me as a gesture to show that they were prepared to give up their tea but would not see their Commander going without it. Their sincerity moved me. I told them that the most I could do was to start having one cup a day only.

A long and interesting discussion followed. At last they agreed to my proposal and said that they would also have it only once a day.

Poor fellows, how sincere and simple were their thoughts and actions, and how generous ! I was especially struck by their action of providing tea to the prisoners when they themselves did not have it. Oh, how I wish to be with such men again, those boys whom I used to call my spiritual sons, irrespective of their age, and I their spiritual father, though so young?

Our Neighbours

A fairly large number of civilians lived in Changi area. There were mainly Indians, Malays and Chinese. The Indians were either Tamils or the Punjabis. The former were mostly rubber tappers and menial labourers, and had little standing in any society except their own. Non-Indians would scornfully call them "Klings" which meant blackies. They were the ones who formed the backbone of INA in times to come. The Punjabis were mostly employed in the Singapore police, and in the jail guards. They were commonly called "The British Watch-dogs." These slurs always reminded me of our slavery for the last three centuries. How could slaves be respected at all and that too on a foreign soil? Fortunately, the Indian independence movement in Asia was raising their prestige nicely. The national awakening in them was coming to their assistance. They had started feeling that they also were a nation. Their respect towards the Officers and the men of the Garrison was increasing gradually.

At times, they would invite us to their celebrations of different festivals. We would take these opportunities to preach them the spirit of independence. In the beginning they were very backward but eventually their national consciousness awakened. Their faith in me grew gradually, so much so, that they would refuse to approach the Japanese if they had any dispute, among them to be settled. Instead, they would come to me and I had to act as their intermediary. I also settled their civil suits amounting to several hundreds of dollars. I was always successful in satisfying both the contesting parties who brought their cases before me.

The Malays were mainly farmers and fishermen who possessed very small holdings of arable land. In the beginning they did not know us, our independence movement or our aim. With the passage of time they came to understand us and they started showing us respect and were prepared to give us any help we wanted. In return, we also offered our hand of assistance whenever they wanted. In them we found very amiable neighbours.

The Chinese were the most prosperous of all the communities. They were farmers, fishermen and shopkeepers. To start with, they were reserved towards us but as time passed they became our friends, and very dependable friends, indeed. All the communities would approach us, particularly when they needed any medical aid for their sick or wanted our protection against any undesirable elements in the Changi area, whether they be the Japanese, POWs or any others. To promote cordiality, strict orders were enforced in the Garrison, prohibiting the sale, purchase or accepting of any articles from our neighbours.

At a stone's throw from our Camp's northern boundary lived a Chinese family. With the passage of time, this family became very much attached to our Garrison. An old lady about seventy years old was the head of this family. Her tiny little feet were always donned in small shoes of embroidered cloth. The family consisted of three sons, two daughters-in-law and three grand-children. They respected the old lady as if she were their goddess. Though she had spent over twenty years of her life in Malaya, she could hardly speak Malay. She used to treat me as her son and I always addressed her as "Amman", the name by which she came to be called by all the members of the Garrison.

The old lady was very particular to offer me coffee and boiled eggs whenever I happened to call on them. If ever I refused their offer, she would snub me in a motherly way. On every Chinese festival, and it appeared that they had many festivals in a year, she would send me "Makan basar', i.e. a big dinner. Her eldest son, Mr. K. used to grow vegetables which we bartered with rice. Mr. K. had a few months old small baby daughter who became very friendly with me. Whenever I called for the baby, they always used to dress her as cleanly as possible in a farmer's family.

On our arrival in the Changi Camp in the month of March, this

Chinese family decided to evacuate their home on the ground that they did not like to stay next door to the "Bengalis". In Malaya, the "Bengalis" was a strange name they had given to the Sikhs. Perhaps it was somehow related to the fact that the fist Sikh immigrants in Malaya had sailed from Calcutta. The Sikhs did not have much of reputation in Malaya due to their being members for the Singapore Police and Straits-Settlement Police. Thus, they had failed to develop harmonious relations with other nationalities of Malaya.

The majority of Sikhs were employed as *"Jagas"*, i.e. watchmen. These watchmen were normally very poorly paid. They made their fortune by lending money at exorbitant rates of interest. Some of them were actually worth lakhs, but their standard of living remained extremely poor and their social life amounted to nil. A *jaga* would be commonly seen sitting on an old charpoy (cot) in front of a shop with a dirty kettle of tea and a cup beside. A long stick would be his only weapon. Thus he would spend the best years of life doing very little of the job for which he was enlisted. His very appearance ensured security.

Yet there was another class, of taxi drivers, who by their bullying tactics had damaged the name of their community irreparably. We approached "Amman" to request her to stay on and she agreed rather reluctantly. When they found us well-behaved, they changed their opinion regarding the Sikhs as a community. They would say "Bengalis banyan Bagus", i.e. the Sikhs are very good. It is amazing that what a good or a bad name a few individuals can earn for their communities by their behaviour. If ever I were in a position to influence our National Government, the first thing I would do would be to stop every man and woman leaving our shores unless it could be guaranteed that their professions abroad would not tarnish the name and the prestige of our country.

My Illness

Non-interference from the Japanese decreased my work and worries to a great extent. The period of my hard work was over. Now a stage had reached when I had to create work for myself. As far as the junior officers and the men were concerned, they had sufficient routine work to keep them busy. My hut was an ideal place for reading and writing. Since no books could be made available, I commenced writing a few things about my Garrison. Meantime, I composed a long poem in Hindustani, titled, "*Malaya ki Kahani*", The Story of Malaya. In this poem I traced the conditions prevailing in Malaya before and during the Malayan campaign; the weakness of the British might and strategy; the Japanese bravery and overwhelming military superiority; the fate of the Malay Peninsula and the future role of an Indian. It took me twenty days to compose it. When finished, it was in good rhyme. It became very popular among the troops. In recitation, it would take quarter of an hour.

To get into the writing mood I used to chop wood. In those days, a dozen of prisoners were undergoing detention in our Garrison who fell rubber trees and saw them into logs. They worked from 8 in the morning to 4 in the evening, with an hour's break for lunch. Exactly at 4 P.M. I would be out to split those logs into small pieces of wood for fuel in our kitchens. With two axes I could finish that job in one hour. During this one hour, I kept six men busy placing logs in front of me and piling chopped wood into stacks. Thus all the fuel which was required in the Garrison kitchens those days was procured in this way.

Sometimes, when chopping wood failed to tire me enough, I would do physical training in the form of groundwork and pole vaulting. Those were the days when I felt fittest in Malaya, though I looked thin. Vaulting poles were cut from a forest close by. They were sufficiently strong and heavy when green but as they dried up they became nice and light. I believed they were still strong enough to support eleven stones, but in fact they were not. One day when I was trying to vault at ten feet, my pole broke into two while I was still in the air over the bar. I fell down and hurt my back. My men rushed to pick me up. I did not take my fall seriously and took a cold bath as per my usual practice. Normally I would go to sleep after midnight, but that night, the night of 28-29th June 1942, I could snatch a few moments of sleep early in the morning only.

Sometime during the night, I felt very thirsty. Dreaming that I was at home in India, I called for my wife. There was no response. I called for my mother and then for my father, but no one replied. By now I was awake, I felt homesick. Thus I sat up and began crying. In a short time I realised that my sheets, pillows and under clothes were wet with perspiration. I felt I was running a fever. Feverish, gloomy and thirsty, I lay down and tried in vain to sleep. Sleep would not come to me. I could hear the hourly beat of sentry's going. That night appeared to me unending. It was a night of excruciating pain, agony and depression.

In the morning Mehar Singh came to wake me up. On finding me running a high temperature, he called Dr. Sucha Singh who looked after me for the following two days. My temperature would not come down to normal. On top of that, signs of blood appeared in my sputum though there was no pain in my chest or back. Dr. Sucha Singh was worried. I had taken it as an ordinary fever but the doctor's mind saw something else. In spite of my foolish unwillingness, Dr. Sucha Singh and other Officers made arrangements to call Col. B. Chaudhury.

Col. Chaudhury examined me thoroughly for about half an hour and asked me several questions. Perhaps there was something serious. Did this fall hurt my lungs or some other vital organ ?

I could not understand. I was instructed to take a complete rest. A number of medicines were administered to me. For seven days I remained very ill. Only then my temperature showed a downward trend. My case sheet had been so far kept hidden from me. On perusal I learnt that I had been through an acute attack of pneumonia. During this period I had been put on S.I. (seriously ill) and D.I. (dangerously ill) lists. During my sickness, all the Officers and men of my Garrison remained greatly concerned. Subedar Santa Singh looked after me like my own father. Under the directions of Col. Chaudhury who paid visits daily, Dr. Sucha Singh nursed me admirably well.

Col. Chaudhury's gentle and saintly ways, coupled by his professional skill, attracted me so much that I always looked forward to his visits. His kind words used to soothe me a lot. Lieut. Gurcharan Singh of the 2nd Battalion, 12 Frontier Force Regiment specially came to stay at Changi in order to look after me during those critical days. He served me with brotherly affection and friendly devotion. But above all, I must say that Mehar Singh, my batman, served me with the faithfulness and sincerity of a true comrade. Though there were so many others to look after me, Mehar Singh refused to leave my side even for a moment's rest. For seven days and seven nights he kept awake, always standing by my side, ready to answer my call and also to ensure that the doctor's instructions were strictly followed. What a sacrifice and devotion in the name of comradeship ! At last there is a limit to human endurance. Exhausted, he fell ill and had to be removed to the Garrison Hospital. Even there he was more worried about me than for himself.

On learning about my illness, Col. Ogami paid me a visit. He kept on enquiring about my health through his doctor (a Captain) and his Adjutant, who visited me regularly. As a mark of his goodwill, he often sent me sweetened condensed milk and flowers wrapped in attractive coloured papers. His junior officers and men also called on me a number of times. But as visitors were not allowed, they would hover round my hut enquiring about my health from my men. When I was allowed to receive visitors, these innocent soldiers were overjoyed to come and in a respectful way they would enquire about my health. I was so much amused by their simplicity that often I would allow them to visit me more frequently than Col. Chaudhury had allowed. On such occasions Dr. Sucha Singh would come rushing and tick me off and send soldier-visitors away. Bowing again and again they would leave saying, 'Odaijini', meaning wishing health and recovery.

Once two Japanese soldiers came to see me. They went round and round my hut. Dr. Sucha Singh had posted a sentry who would stop any visitor coming to see me. Some Japanese Generals even were unable to see me when they saw the notice board prohibiting interviews. They enquired about my health from Dr. Sucha Singh and went away leaving a message, "Get Well soon." But these two soldiers would not go. Lying inside I could see them begging the sentry to let them go in. Taking pity on them, I asked the sentry to allow them in. Against Dr. Sucha Singh's instructions they were allowed in. After bowing to me, for many times, one of them kept on feeling my pulse, while the other kneeling besides his comrade looked at his watch. They continued this way for about five minutes.

I could not keep quiet and I burst out into laughter. They produced a small bottle containing some tablets and advised me to take them daily thrice a day. To show me, one of them immediately swallowed a pill and said, "You see, very good". Though I was receiving proper medical treatment I could not say 'No' to them. I took their bottle just to please them and kept in my medicinal chest for the following three years as a remembrance of their unalloyed kindness and concern.

When the news of my illness reached my brother Officers living in different Camps, they started coming to see me and to enquire about my health General M.Z. Kiani, Colonels Habib-ur-Rehman, M.S. Brar, Balwant Singh, Jaswant Singh, A.I.S. Dara, Bishan Singh and Malhotra I.M.S. were some of them whom I can remember presently. They were all so very kind and concerned about me. The day Col. Jaswant Singh came I was sitting up in my bed against a bed rest. He was very worried about my illness. It took me a lot of time to persuade him to go back. He wanted to stay behind and look after me.

A Christmas Cake

Towards the beginning of the second week of July 1942, we got some pocket money. My share was fourteen dollars, while each sepoy got ten dollars. One evening, one of my Pathan N.C.Os came to see me and presented me with a tin of Christmas cake, which he had bought for nine dollars. I asked him to take it back. But he said, "Sir, if you don't accept it, I will throw it away". I accepted it. How generous was this Naik to me ! Five months after surrender he had got ten dollars, yet he had the heart to spend nine out of ten to get a gift for me. At the same time, I proposed to members of the Garrison to raise a fund for our Garrison Hospital. They collected a decent sum of two hundred dollars in response to my appeal. It was really heartening to be in the midst of such men who were selfless and sincere with hearts of gold.

Baba Budh Singh

One day during my illness, I felt greatly honoured when Baba Budh Singh, generally known as the 'Malayan Gandhi' paid me a visit. His charming personality, graced by his old age, long grey beard and affectionate smile, touched my heart. I felt elated by his visits. He was the only Indian patriot who had taken up voluntarily the difficult task of looking after the Indian Prisoners of War stationed at Kuala Lumpur and elsewhere on the mainland of Malaya, prior to the British surrender of Singapore. It was said that he would arrange medicines and rations for our Camps, while at times he would go without food in his own home. The amount of stores he had collected for our welfare lasted us for over a year.

I remember with a feeling of great appreciation the way those British and Australian Prisoners of War under my custody used to enquire about my health. They would come to me every morning and evening and talk to me in a very friendly manner. Some of them, specially Private Peter, used to take pains in making my bed and cleaning my room. Their kind thoughts remain a living memory with me.

Lieut. Okazaki paid only one visit to me, though he used to write to me that a very high ranking Japanese doctor would come to see me in the near future. That doctor never came, but Okazaki's men were very regular in calling on me. Mr. Sunassawa and Mr. Saji, Cpl. Tamamori, in particular, used to be so much concerned that they would often break into tears on seeing my weak condition.

A British Officer, Major James, was attached to the Japanese Liaison Office. He worked as an interpreter and spoke very good Japanese. He was an old man. I always felt pity for him because his fellow countrymen took him as a traitor, but he always tried his best to do whatever he could for them. Many a thing would never have been done for the British Prisoners of War if this old man had not been there with his knowledge of the Japanese language, his tact and resourcefulness. He was very kind to pay me a visit along with Sgt. I. Hirao.

"Amman" showered an unbounded kindness on me during those days. She sent me milk, fruits, vegetables, eggs and chickens regularly without accepting anything in return. Under the best possible medical care and with the kindness shown to me by all those who had known me intimately or casually, I made a speedy recovery. Once again I looked strong and healthier.

It was the middle of July 1942. I was recovering steadily, though still not allowed to move about or even leave my bed. In the middle of June 1942 Bangkok was the venue of a Conference attended by Indian delegates from all over East Asia. The Indian POWs who were in favour of the Indian Independence Movement had also sent their thirty delegates, together with sixty proxy votes. By now the delegates from Bangkok Conference were returning. Subedar Major Babu Ram of my old Unit (later a Major in the INA) paid me a visit. He had attended the Conference and was in a position to give me first-hand information which was both interesting and encouraging.

Those were the days of rapid changes. General Mohan Singh had returned from Bangkok. The organisation establishment of the INA was being discussed and planned. Staff Officers got busy in working out the details of arms, equipment, strength, organisation and establishment. The Indian National Army was being organised. The training of officers and men was receiving all possible attention. New drill and words of command were being thought of. In this connection three officers, i.e. Captain Mohd. Azim Khan Rana, Capt. Jang Bahadur Singh Grewal and Lieut. Madan Mohan Khurana were attached to the Garrison in order to study the Japanese drill and advise the Indian National Army Headquarters if anything useful could be borrowed from them. The arrival of these three Officers was greatly welcomed by me, for in them I found good company.

Capt. M.A.K. Rana (later a Lt. Col. in the INA) started looking after me as an elder brother. Before joining the Indian National Army he belonged to the Kapurthala Light Infantry. A sincere and straightforward person, he was always apt to be blunt. I was surprised to learn about his knowledge of the Sikh religion and Guru Granth Sahib. Capt. J.B.S. Grewal (later Major in the INA) of the 5th Battalion, 2nd Punjab Regiment, was an old friend of mine since my days at the Indian Military Academy. He stayed with us for only a few days. Col. N.S. Gill, who had been deputed to proceed to Burma with a party, wanted the services of this young officer.

Lieut. M.M. Khurana (later Major in the INA) was one of the most well-read and educated young officers. During those days he used to keep himself busy by reading books, drinking coconut milk or taking exercise. It used to be a treat and an experience listening to him when he debated with Capt. Rana practically every evening. Though I was not allowed by doctors to talk, I could not help taking part in their discussions on subjects which ranged from personal to international and spiritual.

Pala Singh's Boldness

During one of those days, Sgt. Hirao, while driving one of the Garrison trucks in charge of L/Nk Pala Singh, met with an accident in front of the Headquarters of the Japanese Military Police in Shonan town (Singapore). The victim of this accident was an N.C.O. of the Japanese Military Police itself. Sgt. Hirao was not a trained driver. As such, he had no driving licence but was trying to learn driving. He was immediately put under arrest by the Japanese M.P. (Military Police). Pala Singh was left to come back to the Garrison. In the evening Sgt. Hirao was also released. He came to me and said that he could be saved only if we helped him.

As a responsible N.C.O., he ought to have known the regulations. The wounded man was lying in a precarious condition in a hospital. If he died Sgt. Hirao's punishment would be very heavy. The only way to save Sgt. Hirao was for Pala Singh to admit that he was responsible for the accident and that it was he who was at the wheel when the accident took place. Sgt. Hirao said that even if Pala Singh was found guilty he would not be punished, being an Indian. I called for Pala Singh and asked him if he was prepared to take the risk.

Bold as he was, he agreed and falsely admitted Hirao's crime as his own. On the following day, Pala Singh was removed from the Garrison by the Japanese Military Police, who, having known the exact story, would not accept his statement. He was given the third degree treatment but to no purpose. When Sgt. Hirao came to learn about this, he did not have the heart to keep on telling a lie. He admitted his crime but Pala Singh would not. At last Sgt. Hirao came to me and said that I should send a message to Pala Singh to change his statement and tell the real truth. This was done. Pala Singh obeyed my instructions.

The Japanese authorities in Changi area as well as in the Military Police were astonished at the brave action of a soldier of having carried out the instructions of his Commander knowing that they were wrong. Sgt. Hirao, who was supposed to be one of the most strong-hearted persons came to apolgise for having put Pala Singh in difficulties. But when I told him that he (Sgt. Hirao) had helped me whenever I wanted rice for prisoners under my custody and thus saved so many of them from starvation, it was just natural that I should have such a high regard for him and that my men should take his crime on them. Sgt. Hirao could not utter a word. He sat beside my bed for about two hours. His sentiments found expression in his tears.

General Mohan Singh Visits

Then one bright morning Jemadar Sadhu Singh of the Ist Battalion 14 Punjab Regiment (later a Captain in the INA) came with a pleasant message. General Mohan Singh was coming to visit the Garrison that very day. The Garrison went mad with joy at the thought that the founder of the Indian National Army was coming. All the possible strength which could be mustered was collected to greet and to listen to the General. Against medical advice, I got up and took him round the Garrison and even went to the extent of making a short speech of welcome. He addressed us all for about two hours and explained in detail all that was happening. He hoped that soon the INA would be expanded, for which he required true and sincere volunteers who were prepared to follow him unconditionally.

On his way to the Garrison, General Mohan Singh met Lieut. Okazaki. From his talk it appeared that Lieut. Okazaki had praised the work of the Garrison. Appreciating our work, General Mohan Singh remarked that in Changi Garrison he found the best material for the INA. As a mark of appreciation he awarded us five hundred dollars, which were equally distributed amongst all the members of the Garrison, after allotting 100 dollars for the Garrison Hospital. Thus everybody received two dollars per head. General Mohan Singh had his lunch with us during which I kept on talking and placing before him report concerning the Garrison. After lunch he left us. I was feeling tired. Again I had a temperature followed by another attack of pneumonia. Once more I was confined to bed. From the second attack I recovered after about a week but not satisfactorily. I grew weak. Even little things used to upset me and I would get a fever. Once again the doctors were worried. They wanted to remove me from the Garrison but the very idea of removal pained me more than the illness.

Prisoners of War

During the relapse of my illness, I had plenty of time to think of the past and the present. The future worried me little for things were taking shape nicely. I had the happiness which usually accompanies optimism. Sitting or lying alone in my bed, I would often sit in judgement on my actions performed during my command of the Garrison. I had been harsh, strict, as well as mild and considerate. One man had been shot by men during this period, but considering that more had been saved from death and starvation. I felt satisfied.

Never had I been saluted by more people than when I commanded this Garrison though I did not deserve it. I would often remember Lt. General Sir L.M. Heath. The old man was always very punctual and smart in saluting on the few occasions he happened to pass me. I would recall his brave deeds during the Malayan campaign. I had always respected and still admire this General. Once he was kept in a separate bungalow at Changi. The responsibility of the guard for this bungalow had been entrusted to my Garrison. My soldiers used to tell me how the General behaved. He was living in the upper storey while the Guards put themselves up in a verandah of the ground floor.

Once or twice the General approached my Guards for a cup of tea, but the Guards declined him even that much courtesy mistaking his request as a move to get them into trouble. What a shame! Once Lieut. Swaran Singh had a long conversation with him. They argued about the Indian political situation. How strange that a Havildar of the British Indian Army should be able to argue with a General ! At times, General Heath was taken to visit Lady Heath, who was ill in a hospital. Whenever I approached his bungalow I found him disappearing into his inner room prior to my arrival perhaps to avoid a salute, poor fellow ! He would have shone as one of the leading British Generals of this war if he had not been a prisoner.

I remember having seen Lieut. General A.E. Percival. Tall, thin and gentle, General Percival, the G.O.C. Malaya Command, was confined for some-time in a bungalow in front of the Liaison Office. I always felt pity for the General who had always done his best to save his men and the civilian population. He might have done better if the War Office in London had placed better resources of men and material at his disposal. He was one of the most brilliant and kind-hearted commanders. While surrendering to Gen. Yamashita, one of the deciding factors was to save the civilian population of Singapore.

I also remember having seen so many British Generals, Brigadiers, Colonels and other Officers whose names I fail to recollect.

The British Other Ranks often told me how they had been ignored. They would say, "Well Sir! These are officers because of whom we are here. Yet they consider themselves so high that they refuse to eat with us. They get the same scale of rations as we do yet they run their messes in lavish ways. They would not even let us sit near them, let alone cigarettes and the treatment you accord to us." Many a time some of them would refuse to go back to their Camps and would prefer staying with us. Once when Col. Chaudhury had come to visit me, he asked two prisoners who were making my bed, "Do you feel happy here?" They replied, "Yes, Sir, because we get better food here than in our own camps." And we used to get the same scale of rations as they did ! Surely, there was something wrong with their Camp administration, or in other words with their Officers. But then the times were difficult indeed. And again the majority of the Officers were not bad but then one black sheep lets the majority the bad name.

When Captain Bishan Singh (later a Col. in the I.N.A.) of the 3rd Battalion 16th Punjab Regiment came to see me, two British Captains also called on me on that day to beg some chapatis and dal. We had just finished our meals. They were told to wait until chapatis were made and dal cooked. As they entered my room, they removed their shoes before entering the room. God knows how many times they sirred me just to get dal and chapatis'. Their efforts did not go waste, for they were given four bottles full of dal and pack-load of chapatis. Saluting over and over again, they thanked us. It reminded me of beggars in our own country. Now they were beggars and we were givers ! Oh, captivity !

I invariably liked the British men, for a soldier is a soldier whatever be his nationality. They had some dignity of their nation and even in that distressing status, they had not lost their sense of humour. They hated Mr. Churchill for having got them in that plight. But leaving aside this common feeling, we liked their simplicity and lack of that complex which at times would make us hate their Officers. In spite of all these feelings, we could not afford to be too friendly with them for often their Officers would misrepresent our ideas to the Japanese with a view to causing suspicion in order to harm our Movement.

Then there were the good old, brave and bold, "Aussies or the Diggers". They had fought well during the Malayan Campaign and were still in high spirits. Simple and straightforward, they were more akin to us than any other soldiers we had seen so far. Their large-heartedness was perhaps due to the vast size of their country. Australia had never been a colonial power. In them we found typical Indian farmers. They never tried to misconstrue anything in order to cause misunderstanding between us and the Japanese. It used to be a pleasure to help them and talk to them.

Their Camp Commandant whom I will never forget was a typical Australian. We never had any complex while approaching each other or any of the members of the Garrison. Their senior-most Medical Officer, a Brigadier, was a nice man. It was from, him that I learnt how to flavour tea in the absence of milk with fresh lime. He was a noble personality. They were people who demanded respect from us and often made us overlook the mistakes of their men because of the goodness of these two officers. Once or twice, they wanted certain person to be released from my Garrison. Their wishes were fulfilled. Simple and straightforward as they were, once they thanked me through the Japanese for having shown kindness towards some of their men. It gave me a real pleasure to learn that they were pleased with me, though the Japanese did not like it and told me to be a bit stricter with them. But how could one be strict to those whom one admired so much because of their good ways !

Whatever be the behaviour of the British or the Australians, I would often ask myself the question, "What right have I to treat these prisoners like this ?" Then I would start thinking as to who was not a prisoner in this world, especially among the enslaved nations. If stronger nations could keep weaker nations as virtual slaves for generations together, what difference did it make if my men guarded these vanquished POWs for the duration of the war? Someone had to do the unpleasant job. Perhaps I was making it less displeasing. Again, how could a nation be prepared to fight against their traditional enemy, if we could not even dare to guard them at that stage?

Leaving aside the Australians, the British were our enemies. Though they were prisoners, yet the fact could not be ignored that they were still our enemies. One might say that they were helpless. The very struggle for existence was based on the fact that the stronger lived on the weaker. We were doing nothing against the very law of existence, the law of nature, the only law by which life is maintained in this world, leaving aside the righteousness of the cause. It was a very unpleasant job indeed. A dirty job.

The Garrison in Retrospect

Punishments

Barring our first week at Changi when a few persons had to be removed to our Cage on disciplinary grounds, no man of the Garrison was ever punished during my command of the Garrison. Discipline and efficiency were maintained not through fear of punishment but by explaining it to Officers and men and thus appealing to their sense of responsibility and duty through reason.

Equality

In order to inculcate a feeling of pride and friendship among ourselves, even an individual had to salute his superiors on first meeting during a day. Thus even our sepoys used to take and give salutes to each other. Leaving aside this formality, which ultimately became our second nature, off duty we treated each other on the basis of equality. Whether a fellow was cook or a barber or a water carrier or a sweeper, he would be offered a chair, when he came to my room or went to any other Officer's or N.C.O's bunk. On formal occasions we always ate together as one community.

No Provincialism

There were nineteen South Indians in the Garrison. In the beginning they did not want to be one of us. It was not their fault. In the Indian Army we had always been kept separate by provinces and classes by the British for their own ends. When these men developed a better understanding, they became so much attached to the Garrison that once when I wanted to transfer two of them from the Garrison, they said, "Sir, you better shoot us than send us away." We were all Indians, one happy family!

Establishment

There was only one sweeper in the Garrison. Once when he fell ill we used to clean the latrines ourselves. There was no clerk in our establishment. There would be no red-tapism. Officers' or men's words used to be taken as good as orders in black and white.

Visitors

Apart from the visits of personalities I have already mentioned, Lt. Col. G.Q. Gilani of the First Bahawalpur Infantry (later a member of the Council of Action) visited me twice. Once Lt. Col. M.I.M.S. who did not join the INA came to visit us. I took him round the Changi area in my car. The poor fellow was too frightened to be seen by his British masters. He left his comfortable seat and sat down, ducking his head so that he could not be recognised. I learnt that he was awarded a decoration by the British after the war. In those days this gentleman used to flatter me a lot, but it appeared that he later went about saying that he was very bold throughout and resisted the I.N.A.

Entertainment

At times we used to have small spontaneous concerts. Our guests, the British prisoners, also took part in them. Once the I.N.A. Dramatic Party came to Changi to give us a performance. It was good entertainment. Lieut. Okazaki had presented me with a .22' rifle. Subedar Santa Singh was very good at it. Often he would shoot fish in the clear sea-water. I used to kill birds with it. Of course, Mehar Singh was an excellent cook.

Character

Once a British Captain of the 5th Bn. of the 14th Punjab Regiment was brought before me on a charge of having failed to pay compliments to our sentry. He was detained in our Garrison for a couple of days. During this period, a sepoy of his own old Unit guarded him on a fatigue duty. As luck would have it, a snake appeared on the scene. Naturally the Captain was startled and as he moved aside, the sepoy said, "*Dushmn dekh kar mat bhago*' (Don't run away at the sight of an enemy). Swearing at the Captain, the sepoy told him to kill the snake. As the Captain was going to give a strong blow to the snake to kill it, the sepoy said, "Wise men say that you should kill your enemy by slow torture". Giving a light blow to the snake and another to the Captain, the sepoy said, "For me both of you are enemies. Here is a black snake and you are a white snake".

In the evening the Captain asked for permission to see me. Accordingly, I invited him to have his dinner with me. Before the dinner I was informed by Sub. Santa Singh that the sepoy on duty had earlier served the Captain as his orderly and the Captain was known as an Indian-hater; he had at times spit at and kicked this sepoy. The Captain was brought by the sepoy only to avenge the ill-treatment he used to receive from the British Officer.

After dinner, the Captain and I talked late into the night. The Captain's version was that he had been brought by the sepoy because he had once punished him for some act of indiscipline. I tried to pacify him by my talk. Then we started discussing war and politics. The Captain asked me why I was doing that "dirty job" for the Japanese. I told him that I was not doing that job for anybody but for the independence of my country. We had a long discussion. When I told him about the I.N.A. and its aim of achieving the independence of India, he readily concurred with my views. Then he asked me whether I would take him to the Japanese. My reply was in the negative which pleased him. He said, "Thank you very much, for I fear facing them. Now how long will you keep me in your Garrison?" "As long as you wish" I said. He said that he would like to he back at the earliest.

The next day after breakfast, he asked for my permission to leave. I gave him some tea leaves, sugar, a tin of milk and some cigarettes. As he was not in a position to carry these articles, I went to drop him personally to his Camp. At the Camp gate, he thanked me and before we could say good-bye, he said, "Captain Dhillon ! If you don't mind, let me tell you that I do not agree with your aim and actions." "Well, you won't be British if you did", was my reply. We shook hands as we parted. In the evening during my talk to my Garrison I narrated this episode to my men. We had a lesson to learn that how determined and honest was the Captain towards his country. That was an example of the British national character which we were to inculcate among us.

Our Glorious Dead

Many of my comrades of Changi Garrison are no more today. I do not have even a record of their demise, except that of two Officers.

Subedar Santa Singh (who was a Lieutenant and then a Captain in the INA) during the crisis he preferred to go to the South Pacific and died in New Guinea. I feel that his loss was not to the INA alone but to India as well. He was a brave soldier. Subedar Lal Din (who was a Lieutenant in the INA) took part in the Imphal Campaign and died a soldier's death on the road to Delhi, the road to freedom, the road to which he gave his blood, flesh and bones to build.

Long live our Glorious Dead — the known and the unknown!

Vive La Garrison

My indifferent health continued. At last Col. Chaudhury was compelled to recommend my release from the command of the Changi Garrison and removal to hospital. His decision came to me as a painful blow, but I had to go. Captain Rana was the next senior-most officer present in the Garrison. The command was formally handed over to him in the first week of August 1942. Prior to my departure, I addressed the Garrison, my own Garrison, with some advice and a few words of thanks.

I paid a round of courtesy calls on all my friends. With tears in her eyes, "Amman" blessed me with maternal love, when I wished her good-bye. As a mark of friendship, Col. Ogami presented me flowers and tins of condensed milk. Lieut. Okazaki met me with tears in his eyes as he spoke, "I respect you. You did your duty. Look after your health. May God bless you!" The Japanese soldiers who were connected with the Garrison in one way or the other kept on coming to me with their autograph books. In return, they presented me with their photographs. Sentiments and sincere feelings were displayed on both sides. It was so human.

At the time of my departure, a large crowd of Japanese soldiers, local civilians and my own men gathered to give me a hearty send-off. The Japanese called out to me "Odaijini", the civilians bowed to me as a mark of homage. My own men shouted slogans of '*Inquilab Zindabad*' and '*Dhillon Zindabad*'. With a heavy heart I left them behind.

8

SHAPING THE INA

Convalescence

From Changi Garrison I came straight to Seletar Camp and was admitted to the Prisoners-of-War Hospital commanded by Lt. Colonel B. Chaudhary. Mehar Singh accompanied me. Apart from being an excellent surgeon, the Colonel was an equally good physician. I was very weak and my power to resist any infection was low. Col. Chaudhary knew that I needed long time for recuperation. He got a special tent put up at an open, secluded at distant corner of the Camp so as to keep me away from other patients. Here was plenty of fresh air and sunshine.

I was provided meals from the hospital kitchen, which Mehar Singh brought fresh and hot along with two green chillies with seeds removed. These were to make up for deficiency of vitamin C. Food here was slightly better than the one served at Changi Garrison. In the beginning I was not allowed to receive any visitors. When my health showed some signs of improvement, this restriction was lifted. I gathered from friends who visited me that events of far-reaching consequences occurred during the period when I was away at Changi.

Tokyo Conference

Early in March 1942, Shri Rash Behari Bose, a great pioneer of the Indian revolution and an exile residing in Tokyo since 1915, called a conference of Indian leaders from all parts of East-Asia. In order to select a representative delegation from Malaya, Singapore and Thailand, Giani Pritam Singh convened a meeting of the prominent Indian leaders from these countries at Shri S.C. Goho's residence in

Singapore. It was attended by about twenty leaders of the Indian Independence League (I.I.L.) and Officers of the INA Swami Satyananda Puri and Baba Arnar Singh came all the way from Bangkok and took part in the deliberations of this meeting. They unanimously chose the following delegation for the Tokyo Conference:

(*a*) K.P.K. Menon, N. Raghvan, Nilakanta Aiyer, S.C. Goho from Malaya and Singapore.

(*b*) Swami Satya Nanda Puri and Giani Pritam Singh from Thailand.

(*c*) Captain Mohan Singh, Capt. Mohammed Akram and Lt. Col. Niranjan Singh Gill from the INA

The delegates left Singapore by two separate planes for Tokyo. The plane carrying Captain Mohammad Akram, Swami Satya Nanda Puri, Giani Pritam Singh, Nilakanta Aiyer and Otaguro, of Fujiwara Kikan crashed en route on 24th March, 1942. Everybody aboard the plane perished along with the crew. They became the first martyrs of the Indian Independence and were given a funeral service in their memory at Hongenji temple in Tokyo. Their bodies could never be recovered. It was an irreparable loss to the Indian Independence Movement.

Under the shadow of the tragedy, the Tokyo Conference was held at Sanno Hotel in Tokyo from 28th to 30th March, 1942. It was presided over by Shri Rash Behari Bose. Besides the delegation from Malaya and Bangkok there were two delegates from Hong Kong, two from Shanghai and eight from Japan. General Tojo sent a message to the Conference assuring all possible help to the Indian Independence Movement. Major Fujiwara and Colonel Iwakuro also addressed it. Iwakuro who was to replace Fujiwara soon after expressed his intention to help the Indians in their noble mission.

The Tokyo Conference was marked with friction between the delegates who had come from South-east Asia and the Indians residing in Tokyo. However, it was unanimously decided that a bigger and far more representative meeting of Indians residing in the Far East be called in Rangoon or in Bangkok to elect a governing body of the Indian Independence Movement which would be responsible for running the Movement.

Bidadari Conference

By far the most important meeting from the point of view of us, soldiers of the INA, was the one called by Captain Mohan Singh, the G.O.C. at Bidadari Camp in Singapore on 24th April, 1942. It was attended by over thirty important senior officers from among the Indian Prisoners of War. I attended this conference. This meeting which came to be known as the Bidadari Conference was in fact a heart-to-heart talk among the participants. Lt.-Col. A.C. Chatterji asked Capt. Mohan Singh to state on oath that he was neither playing nor would ever play in the hands of the Japanese and that he would never betray them and would lead them sincerely, boldly and correctly. Mohan Singh on oath pledged that he was neither playing nor would ever play in the hands of anyone. He said that he was following the dictates of his conscience and emphasized that as long as he was alive he would not allow any one to exploit the Indian National Army and if a situation arose he would sacrifice his very life for the cause. After a frank discussion, four resolutions were unanimously passed.

Those resolutions came to be known as the Bidadari Resolutions which formed the backbone of our determination and inspired us to be the true soldiers of the INA. They were the core of our patriotic fervour and pride. I quote:

1. That we are Indians first and last and we stand for complete national unity.
2. That we stand for the complete independence of India based upon a constitution to be decided by the representatives of India in India.
3. That we are prepared to take any action for India on demand by the people of India in India.
4. That pending further action, we unanimously agree to take all steps in our power to become better Indians so as to bring about national unity.

Bangkok Conference

As resolved at the Tokyo Conference, a representative conference of the Indians who lived in East Asian countries, Burma, Borneo, Canton, Hong Kong, Japan, Java, Manchukuo, Malaya, Nanking, the Philippines, Shanghai, Sumatra, and Thailand was held at Bangkok.

The two-million Indians of these countries were represented by about one hundred delegates. The INA volunteers from among the Indian Prisoners of War were allowed to send thirty, three delegates nominated by Capt. Mohan Singh.

The Conference was held for about ten days. It started on the 15th June 1942. Mohan Singh proposed the name of Shri Rash Behari Bose as President of the Conference. It was inaugurated by the Prime Minister of Thailand, Marshal Phibun Songgram who welcomed the delegates on his own behalf and on behalf of the people and the Government of Thailand. He recalled the age-old ties which bound the people of India and Thailand spiritually and culturally. The opening session of the Conference was attended and addressed by Ambassadors of Japan, Germany and Italy and the Foreign Minister of Thailand. Many messages of greetings and goodwill from friendly countries were read out.

Of all the messages, the most striking was one from Berlin sent by Netaji Subhas Chandra Bose who had exhorted all Indians to take up arms saying, "Indian Independence must be attained by the hands of we Indians." In all, thirty five resolutions, as mentioned in the following pages of this chapter, were unanimously passed.

The Bangkok Resolutions

1. WHEREAS it is the objective of the War of Greater East Asia to destroy British Imperialism in Asia,

   WHEREAS it gives an opportunity for India to realise the goal of complete independence,

   WHEREAS it is the belief of this Conference that a new and regenerated Asia of Free Nations is certain to arise as a result of this said war,

   This Conference expresses its sincere gratification at the war policy of Japan and conveys to the Imperial Government its best wishes for the continued success of the Imperial Japanese Armed Forces.

2. This Conference conveys to all the powers fighting against British Imperialism its sincere congratulations and prays their efforts may meet with complete success.

3. This Conference places on record its sense of deep admiration for the most determined manner in which the Nationalist Leaders at home have been trying to refuse to be drawn into this war on the side of the British and their Allies, and for the frank and definite demand for the withdrawal of the British from India. In the opinion of this Conference, unless the British withdraw from India and the Allied Forces cease to make use of India as a base for war operations and war preparations, unimaginable and innumerable sufferings will be the lot of the people of India.

4. Resolved that a Movement for achieving complete and immediate independence of India be sponsored by this Conference.

Object

5. This Conference endorses the view of the Tokyo Conference held in March 1942 that the complete Independence of India free from any foreign control, domination or interference of whatever nature shall be the object of this Movement, and is emphatically of the opinion that the time has arrived to take necessary steps for the attainment of that object.

Guiding Principles

6. Resolved that the Indian Independence Movement sponsored by this Conference shall be guided by the Principles indicated below:

   (*a*) That Unity, Faith, Sacrifice, shall be the motto of the Indian Independence Movement.

   (*b*) That India be considered as one, and indivisible.

   (*c*) That all activities of this Movement be on a national basis, and not in a sectional, communal or religious basis.

   (*d*) That in view of the fact that the Indian National Congress is the only political organization which could claim to represent the real interests of the people of India, and as such to be acknowledged the only body representing India, this Conference is of the opinion that the programme and plan of action of this Movement must be so guided, controlled and directed as to bring them in line with the aims and intentions of the Indian National Congress.

(*e*) That the framing of the future constitution of India be only by the representatives of the people of India.

(*f*) That a joint Axis policy favourable towards India will be advantageous to India.

(*g*) That the sympathy, co-operation and support of Japan are invaluable in securing the object of this Movement, namely the Independence of India.

7. Resolved that an organization be started for carrying on the Indian Independence Movement and that it shall be known as the Indian Independence League.

8. Resolved that the Indian Independence League shall immediately proceed to raise an Army called the Indian National Army from among the Indian soldiers (combatants and non-combatants) and such civilians as may hereafter be recruited for military service in the cause of Indian Independence.

Constitution

9. This Conference adopts the following Constitution for the Indian Independence League Organization:

(*i*) The Indian Independence League shall consist of :

(*a*) A Council of Action,

(*b*) A Committee of Representatives,

(*c*) Territorial Branches, and

(*d*) Local Branches.

(*ii*) (*a*) Local branches of the Indian Independence League may be formed only at a public meeting of Indians in any locality who shall elect a Committee and a

President.

(*b*) Vacancy of such committee or in the Office of the President may be filled up by the Committee.

(*c*) All Indians above the age of eighteen shall be entitled to be members of such branch on compliance with the rules of the Branch.

(*d*) No such Branch shall be recognized as a Branch unless the Territorial Committee as constituted hereinafter accords and continues to accord recognition, provided however that all Branches of the Indian Independence League now in existence and recognized in the various territories mentioned in article (vi) hereof shall until otherwise decided upon be recognized by this Movement.

(*iii*) Representatives elected by the Committee of Local Branches in each territory shall form a Territorial Committee, and the Territorial Committee shall make such rules as it may consider necessary for the effective working of the Movement within the territory.

(*iv*) The Territorial Committee in each territory shall guide, supervise and control the work of the Movement within its territory and shall also elect representatives as constituted hereinafter.

(*v*) Territorial Committees and Committees of Local Branches under them shall have power to make rules not inconsistent with the rules by the Committee of Representatives or in case of Local Branches by the Territorial Committees.

(*vi*) (*a*) A Committee of Representatives shall be constituted by civilian representatives elected by the Territorial Committees in the territories herein below set out and by representatives selected by the Indian National Army :

Japan and Manchukuo	4
Philippines	2
Thailand	6

Malaya	14
Burma	21
Borneo and Celbes	1
Hong Kong, Canton and Macao	2
Other parts of China including Shanghai	2
Indo-china	1
Java	2
Sumatra	1
Andamans	1
Total	57
Indian National Army	33
G. Total	90

(*b*) The Council of Action shall be at liberty to include in the above list of territories any other territory and fix the number of representatives from such territory to the Committee of Representatives, providing at that event for increase in the representatives from the Indian National Army, equal to two-thirds of the number fixed for such territory.

(*vii*) Every member of the Committee of Representatives shall sign the Oath of Secrecy in the prescribed form before he takes his seat on the Committee.

(*viii*) The Committee of Representatives shall be responsible for the general policy and programme of the Indian Independence Movement and its decision shall in every case be final and binding on each and every member of this Movement.

(*ix*) The Committee of Representatives shall have power to alter, amend or rescind any previous decisions made by it, including any decision arrived at in this Conference.

(*x*) No meeting of the Committee of Representatives shall be valid unless two-thirds in number of the Members of the

Committee are present (either in person or by proxy).

(*xi*) A Council of Action consisting of a President and four (4) members, of whom at least one-half shall be from the Indian National Army in East Asia, shall be appointed by the delegates to this Conference. The first President shall be Shri Rash Behari Bose and the four members shall be :

1. Sri N. Raghavan
2. Captain Mohan Singh
3. Sri K.P.K. Menon
4. Colonel G.Q. Gilani.

(*xii*) Any vacancy in the Council of Action caused by death, resignation or otherwise of Members not exceeding two in number at a time, may be filled up by the other Members of the Council, and in the event of more than two such vacancies, the Council of Action shall call a meeting of the Committee of Representatives to fill such vacancies.

(*xiii*) The Council of Action shall be responsible for the carrying out of the policy and programme of work laid down by this Conference and as may hereafter be laid down by the Committee of Representatives and shall deal with all new matters that may arise from time to time and which may not be provided for by the Committee itself.

(*xiv*) For the proper and efficient carrying out of the work the Council of Action shall have power to create as many departments, as are necessary and to appoint and dismiss administrative officers and staff whenever necessary.

(*xv*) The Council of Action shall have no power to alter or amend the Policy laid down by this Conference without the sanction of the Committee of Representatives.

(*xvi*) The Council of Action may at any time summon a meeting of the Committee of Representatives to be held at such places as the Council may decide provided that necessary facilities to travel to representatives and at least 14 days' notice of such meeting have been given to the Secretaries of the Territorial Committees and to the Headquarters of the Indian National Army. In a requisition by twenty members (Representatives) hailing from more than one territory such a meeting shall be called by the Council of Action and the necessary notices and facilities for travel shall be given.

(*xvii*) The Council of Action shall have general superintendence and control over all Branches of the Indian Independence League in all territories mentioned in article (*vi*) and over the Indian National Army.

(*xviii*) The Council of Action shall keep register of all the territorial and local organizations and may remove therefrom the names of any such organizations and withhold or withdraw recognition of any such organization.

(*xix*) The Council of Action shall have collective responsibility.

(*xx*) The Headquarters of the Movement shall be at Bangkok or such other place as may hereafter be decided upon by Committee of Representatives or the Council of Action.

(*xxi*) The deliberations of the Committee of Representatives and the Council of Action shall be privileged and no action of a disciplinary character can be taken against any member in consequence thereof by any Branch or Territorial Committee or by the Indian National Army.

(*xxii*) Changes in the Constitution of the Indian Independence League may be made only by vote to that effect by three-fourths of the Members of the Committee of Representatives.

10. Resolved that a request be made to the Nippon Government that it may be pleased to place immediately all Indian soldiers in territories in East Asia under their control at the disposal of this Movement.

11. Resolved that the formation, command, control and organization of the Indian National Army be in the hands of Indians themselves.

12. Resolved that it is the earnest desire of this Conference that the Indian National Army from its inception be accorded

the powers and status of a free national army of an Independent India, on a footing of equality with the armies of Japan and other friendly powers.

13. Resolved that the Indian National Army shall be made use of only :

(*a*) For operations against the British or other foreign powers in India,

(*b*) For the purpose of securing and safeguarding Indian National Independence, and

(*c*) For such other purpose as may assist the achievement of the object, *viz.*, the Independence of India.

14. Resolved that all officers and men of the proposed Indian National Army shall be members of the Indian Independence League and shall owe allegiance to the League.

15. Resolved that the Indian National Army shall be under the direct control of the Council of Action and that the said Army shall be organized and commanded by the General Officer Commanding, Indian National Army in accordance with the directions of the Council of Action.

16. Resolved that in the event of military action being taken against the British or other foreign powers in India, and for the said purpose the Council of Action may be at liberty to place the military resources available to it, under the unified command of Indian and Japanese military officers under the direction of the said Council of Action.

17. Resolved that before taking any military action against the British or any other foreign power in India, the Council of Action will assure itself that such action is in conformity with the express or implied wishes of the Indian National Congress.

18. Resolved that the Council of Action shall make all efforts to create an atmosphere in India which would lead to a revolution in the Indian Army there, and among the Indian

people, and that before taking military action the Council of Action shall assure itself that such an atmosphere exists in India.

19. In view of the great urgency and imperative necessity of informing and convincing our countrymen in India and abroad, and friends of India all over the world, of the meaning and purpose of this Movement, and in view of the fact that propaganda in and outside India is one of the most effective means of waging the war for Indian Independence, this Conference resolves to take immediate steps to carry on active and vigorous propaganda by broadcasts, leaflets, lectures and by such other means as may be found possible and practicable from time to time.

20. That all foreign assistance of whatever nature shall be only to the extent and of the type asked for by the Council of Action.

21. Resolved that for the purpose of financing the Independence movement the Council of Action be authorized to raise funds from Indians in East Asia.

22. The Conference places on record its grateful appreciation of the support and encouragement given to this Movement by the Imperial Government of Japan, and resolves that the Council of Action be authorized to approach if and when necessary the said Government with a request to render such monetary help as may be required from time to time for the successful carrying out of the object of this Movement, on the distinct understanding that such monetary help is to be treated as a loan repayable to the Imperial Government of Japan by the National Government of India.

23. Resolved that the Imperial Government of Japan be requested to be good enough to provide all facilities for propaganda, travel, transport and communications within the area under the control of the Imperial Government of Japan, in the manner and to the extent requested by the Council of Action and also all facilities to come into contact

with the National leaders, workers and organizations in India.

24. Resolved that the Imperial Government of Japan be requested to be good enough to arrange with the local authorities concerned that in matters of administration affecting the Indian community, the Indian Independence League in the respective places, and in places where there are no branches of the League, recognized leaders of the community approved by the League branch nearest to such places, be consulted.

25. Resolved that the Government of Thailand be requested to be good enough to consult the Indian Independence League (formerly known as the Indian National Council and the Independence League of India) in matters of administration affecting the Indian community in Thailand.

26. The Conference, while recording its grateful appreciation of the various pronouncements made by General Tojo, the Premier of Japan, expressing the preparedness of the Nipponese Government to give its unstinted support to the cause of Indian Independence, reiterates the Resolution of the Tokyo Conference that in further clarification of the attitude of Japan towards India, the Imperial Government be good enough to make a formal declaration to the effect :

(*a*) That immediately on the severance of India from the British Empire, the Imperial Government of Japan shall respect the territorial integrity and recognize the full sovereignty of India free from any foreign influence, control or interference of a political, military or economic nature.

(*b*) That the Imperial Government of Japan will exercise its influence with other powers and induce them to recognize the National Independence and absolute sovereignty of India.

(*c*) That the framing of the future Constitution of India will be left entirely to the representatives of the people of India without interference from any foreign authority.

27. Resolved that this Conference is committed to a definite policy of close co-operation with Japan, and it shall, on eliciting an official definition satisfactory to this Movement of the term Greater East Asia Co-prosperity Sphere and its implications endeavour to persuade Independent India :

(*a*) To be a member of such Sphere or as member of any other international combine of which Japan is a member, on a footing of equality with Japan; and

(*b*) To confer on Japan the most favoured national treatment on a reciprocal basis.

28. Whereas it has come to the knowledge of this Conference that Indians in the territories which are now freed from the domination of the Anglo-Saxons and their Allies by the Imperial forces of Japan own considerable movable and immovable properties in these territories; and

WHEREAS owing to the exigencies of war a number of Indians had to leave these territories, leaving behind their properties without making arrangements for their care and management; and

WHEREAS the Imperial Government of Japan has promised its unstinted support to the cause of Indian Independence; and

WHEREAS an enormous amount of money is required to carry on and complete the object of the said Movement in East Asia; and

WHEREAS an appreciable steady income is likely to be derived from the said properties in the said territories; and

WHEREAS in the opinion of the Conference, the handing over of such properties to the Indian Independence League by the authorities concerned, on the distinct understanding that the said properties are to be returned to their rightful owners when claimed, will be welcomed as a sign of goodwill and encouragement towards this Movement.

Now this Conference Resolves

That the Imperial Government of Japan may be pleased to arrange with the authorities in the territories now freed from the domination of the Anglo-Saxons and their Allies by the Imperial Forces of Japan, to hand over the properties owned by the Indians (including those owned by Indian Companies, firms and partnership and left by them owing to the exigencies of war), to the Council of Action in this Movement in trust for their rightful owners, to manage and control the said properties, and advance the income thereof for the use of the Movement, to be repaid as and when claimed by the said owners.

29. This Conference having learned with regret that Indians residing in certain countries under the occupation of the Imperial Forces of Japan are being treated as enemy aliens, and suffer hardship and loss in consequence, resolves that the Imperial Government of Japan may be pleased to make a declaration to the effect:

    (*i*) That Indians residing in the territories occupied by the Imperial Forces of Japan shall not be considered enemy nationals so long as they do not indulge in any action injurious to this Movement or hostile to the interest of Japan, and

    (*ii*) That the properties both movable and immovable of those Indians who are now residing in India or elsewhere (including the properties of Indian Companies, firms and partnerships) be not treated by Japan as enemy properties so long as the management or control of such properties is vested in any person or persons residing in Japan or in any of the countries occupied by or under the influence or control of the Imperial Japanese Forces, and to instruct the authorities concerned in the respective territories to give effect to this policy as early as possible.

30. That this Movement adopts the present National Flag of India and requests the Imperial Government of Japan and the Royal Government of Thailand, and the Governments

of all other friendly powers to recognize the said flag in all territories under their jurisdiction.

31. This Conference requests Shri SUBHAS CHANDRA BOSE to be kind enough to come to East Asia, and appeals to the Imperial Government of Japan to use its good offices to obtain the necessary permission and conveniences from the Government of Germany to enable Shri SUBHAS CHANDRA BOSE to reach East Asia safe.

32. That no unauthorized publicity be given to any of the Resolutions adopted at this Conference, but a manifesto be issued by this Conference setting out the purpose and policy of this Movement, and incorporating such decisions and details as may be found proper and beneficial to be made public.

33. This Conference places on record its deepest appreciation of and grateful thanks for the co-operation, assistance and support extended to this Movement and its objectives by the Imperial Government of Japan.

34. This Conference gratefully acknowledges the sincere and friendly attitude the Governments and the peoples of Germany and Italy have adopted towards our struggle for freedom, and places on record its deep appreciation and thanks for the offer of assistance and co-operation extended by them to this Movement.

35. This Conference places on record its grateful thanks to the Government and people of Thailand for the opportunity given to hold this Conference at Bangkok, for their kind hospitality, and for their sympathy and cooperation in India's struggle for freedom.

The Bangkok Conference served as a launching pad of a vast Movement which revolutionized the very psychology of the entire Indian people living in the East Asian countries. There was a new hope, a new aspiration and a will to do something for the noble cause of attaining India's independence from the British Raj. The delegates returned to their countries with the motto of Unity, Faith and Sacrifice on their lips. Shri Rash Behari Bose went round asking Indians, "*Karo sabh nichhawar, Bano sab Fakir*" (Give your all for the cause) and said, "*Jeena hai to marna seekho*" (In order to live, learn to die). Shri Raghavan started enlarging and strengthening the I.I.L. organization. Sh. K.P.K. Menon looked after establishing the Publicity and Propaganda Department. Col. G.Q. Gilani got ready to set up a programme of training the INA.

First Div. Raised

Armed with Bangkok Resolutions, General Mohan Singh went round all the P.O.Ws Camps. He addressed all the officers and men and appealed to them to volunteer themselves for the INA. Their response was so good that some 42,000 POWs volunteered their services. Similarly, I.I.L. leaders impressed upon the civilians who came forward to join the Movement in great numbers. Gen. Mohan Singh's concept was to make the INA 2,00,000(2 lacs) strong. Immediately enough of volunteers were available to raise three divisions. The Japanese showed their inability to provide arms and equipment for such a big army. Their stress was on quality. When we were waiting for the ratification of the Bangkok Resolutions by the Government of Japan, it was decided to go ahead and raise the Ist Division of the INA for which weapons were readily available.

Mohan Singh appointed Lt. Col. Mohammad Zaman Kiani as Chief of the General staff of the INA. Along with a chosen team of capable officers, Zaman Kiani took his job in right earnest with his headquarters at the Bidadari Camp. The work had just started when one fine morning Major Ogawa, an important officer of the Iwakuru Kikan, called on General Mohan Singh. Ogawa informed Mohan Singh that the Japanese had worked out a plan for raising the First Division of the INA in four months. Mohan Singh brushed aside the Japanese proposal and stressed the need of saving the precious time. Mohan Singh told Ogawa that he would not waste such a long time and would like to complete the organization and the forming of the division in a week. Ogawa went back disappointed. Next day he returned again to convey the Iwakuru Kikan's displeasure to Mohan Singh. Ogawa said that a team of Japanese officers had taken a full week to chalk out the plan which General Mohan Singh had so abruptly brushed aside. He challenged Mohan Singh to do the job within a week if he could and the Japanese side would watch if the job could be completed in such a short time.

Mohan Singh took the challenge. He was determined not to waste any precious time when the events in India and the world moved so fast. He also wanted to show the Iwakuru Kikan that the Indian Staff Officers were second to none in their capability and competence. Iwakuru Kikan were surprised to see that the Indian Officers did complete the job within a week. The First Division of the INA was ready in a record time. It was composed of the following units:

I. HIND FIELD FORCE GROUP, 5,000 strong. Raised and commanded by Lt. Col. J.K. Bhonsle and was made up of :

1. 1st Infantry Battalion
2. 2nd Infantry Battalion
3. 3rd Infantry Battalion
4. Heavy Gun Battalion
5. (A.F.V. Bn.) Armoured Fighting Vehicles Battalion
6. Engineering Unit
7. (M.T. Coy) Motor Transport Company
8. Supply Company
9. Signal Company

II. GUERRILLA GROUP comprised three independent Guerilla Regiments, each three thousand (3,000) strong. Its total strength stood at 9,000. The three Regiments were :

1. 2nd Guerrilla Regiment — THE GANDHI BRIGADE, raised and commanded by Lt. Col. I.J. Kiani.
2. 3rd Guerrilla Regiment — THE AZAD BRIGADE, raised and commanded by Lt. Col. Prakash Chand.
3. 4th Guerrilla Regiment — THE NEHRU BRIGADE, raised and commanded by Lt. Col. Aziz Ahmed.

III. Then there were seven Groups. Their total strength was 3,000. They were :

1. BAHADUR GROUP, called the JAN BAZ, the selected personnel who were to fight behind the enemy lines. It was raised and commanded by Lt. Col. Burhan-ud-Din.

2. INTELLIGENCE GROUP, called the SPECIAL SERVICE Group, raised and commanded by Major Jaswant Singh.
3. PROPAGANDA AND WELFARE GROUP — raised and commanded by Lt. Col. M.S. Brar.
4. MEDICAL GROUP — raised and commanded by Lt. Col. Kulwant Rai, I.M.S.
5. REINFORCEMENT GROUP — raised and commanded by Maj. Shaukat Ali Malik.
6. OFFICERS TRAINING SCHOOL (O.T.S.) — raised and commanded by Lt. Col. Shah Nawaz Khan.
7. HEADQUARTERS P.O.Ws under Major A.B. Mirza.

The above formations and units were under the ARMY HEADQUARTERS commanded by G.O.C. General Mohan Singh. The total strength of the INA (1st Division) stood at seventeen thousand strong ready for action.

One National Commission Adopted

It was decided that different categories of Officers created by the British for their own convenience and selfish ends be abolished. Hence K.C.I.Os, I.C.Os, E.C.Os, Indian States Commissions and V.C.Os were amalgamated into one National Commission. Accordingly, all officers who volunteered themselves for the INA service were advised to relinquish their Indian Army ranks and were subsequently gazetted as 2nd Lieutenants of the INA by a Special Order dated 1st September 1942. Gradually, promotions were made to adjust officer ranks according to their seniority. I got my National Commission on September the 1st, 1942 and was promoted as Major on the 10th of September. As I was still not fit for duty and was in hospital, I was attached to the Reinforcement Group.

TRICOLOUR, OUR STANDARD AND HINDUSTANI WORDS OF COMMAND ADOPTED

Synchronizing with other reforms, the English words of command were abolished and Hindustani words of command adopted. The Indian National Congress Tricolour Flag was adopted as the STANDARD of the Indian National Army. Field Officers' badges which were distinctive by the British Crown on the shoulders of a Field

Officer were replaced by Lord Krishna's SUDARSHAN CHAKRA. Considering that the majority of senior officers in the INA were Muslims, it was, indeed, commendable that they proposed and adopted Sudarshan Chakra with pride and solidarity, at once national.

In fact, INA had been raised by Mohan Singh, Mohammad Akram and Giani Pritam Singh with the help of Fujiwara as early as December, 1941 and a Company had actually taken part in the battle of Singapore under Lieut. Allah Ditta, yet officially it was recognized to have been raised as per Bangkok Resolutions on 1st September, 1942.

The first review of the Indian National Army was held at Singapore Padaung in front of the Municipal Buildings on 2nd October 1942, the birthday of Mahatma Gandhi. I attended the function as an observer. Col. Chaudhary was kind enough to grant me permission though I was still weak. It was an unforgettable occasion when Gen. Mohan Singh took the salute at the march past. It was a wonderful show, a moment of national pride.

On Leave to Penang

My progress in recuperating my health was slow. Col. Chaudhary recommended a month's leave for me and I was sent to Penang. Here my health improved under the care of Lt. Col. (later Major General) Alagappan, I.M.S. who checked and screened my chest every week. Many Indians, Chinese and Malays were kind to me because I was an Officer of the Indian National Army. An elderly Sikh, Dr. Jagat Singh, who had a very good business gave me a Baby Austin car for the duration of my stay in Penang. I hired a room at a place above the small sandy beach, called the Miami Beach. It was a beautiful holiday resort called Mount Pleasant.

Miami Beach was the place where Habib and I landed while Alor Star had been captured by the Japanese. It was a wonderful place where waves of the sea sang lullaby to induce me to sleep. The owner of the resort, a Eurasian gentleman was very kind to me. Thereafter he followed my career in the INA with interest and was good enough to send a cable greeting me after my release from the Red Fort in January 1946. Seth Makhan Lal and Sardar B. Singh used to provide me with dry rations. There was a fresh water swimming pool with flowers all around. The Eurasian owner and his wife used to cook for me. I remain indebted to them till today. In spite of the British blood in them, their culture was more Asian than could be imagined.

Shri N. Raghavan, member of the Council of Action and an important Indian leader, was a resident of Penang. He was running Swaraj Institute under the aegis of the I.I.L. It was part of the Secret Service of the Independence Movement. Shri Raghavan invited me twice to address the school.

The Crisis

I returned to Singapore in the middle of November, 1942. The Japanese had not yet ratified the Bangkok Resolutions nor recognized the INA as an independent army. Differences appeared to be growing day by day. Col. Iwakuru's attitude was haughty. The confidence which Fujiwara had built up among Indians was replaced by suspicion. Instead of appreciating our seriousness in preparations for the war, Iwakuru Kikan seemed to be applying brakes to our progress. Col. Iwakuru and his officers started interfering with INA's Internal administration.

The Council of Action which was our Supreme Body was not recognized at places where it did not suit the Japanese Army. When the Iwakuru Kikan was pressed to get the Bangkok Resolutions ratified, Col. Iwakuru did not even send the letter of the President of the Council of Action to his Government. He abruptly told us that as we were not a Government nor had a territory of our own, the Japanese Government could not entertain the request of ratification of our Resolutions nor any demand according to protocol. He felt that the messages of goodwill afforded a sufficient guarantee of the Japanese intentions to help the Indian Independence Movement.

The differences between the Japanese and the Indian sides came to such a climax that all the members of the Council of Action felt that they were powerless and helpless. All of them with the sole exception of the President, Shri Rash Behari Bose, resigned. Iwakuru was known to be a person who wielded a lot of influence in the Japanese Government and military circles. Rash Behari, too, had certain dependable personalities who had helped him admirably in carrying on his struggle for the independence of India. He wished to contact these sources on his own. He advised and appealed to the members of the Council of Action to take it a bit easy and let him try on his own to break the dead lock.

General Mohan Singh had lost confidence in the Japanese. In the beginning of December 1942, the Japanese asked the INA Headquarters to dispatch an advance party to move to Burma so as to prepare camps and accommodation for the main body of the INA. A small party had already left but Gen. Mohan Singh refused to send more troops unless the INA was recognized according to the Bangkok Resolutions. He also took steps to order the advance party of the INA, already in Burma, that they were not to commit themselves into any military action without instructions from the INA Headquarters, Singapore. Earlier in November there were unpleasant discussions between the I.I.L. leaders and representatives of the Iwakuru Kikan in Rangoon, concerning the Indian absentees' property in Burma.

An unfortunate incident that added to the fast deteriorating situation was that Colonel N.S. Gill who had been sent by General Mohan Singh for intelligence work against the enemy was arrested by the Japanese Military Police without Gen. Mohan Singh's knowledge or information. The cause of Japanese action was that Maj. Mahanbir Singh Dhillon, a senior officer of Col. Gill's party had deserted Col. Gill and gone over to the British with a lot of useful information for the enemy. The Japanese blamed Col. Gill for the desertion. General Mohan Singh wanted to investigate the whole matter but he was not allowed to even contact Col. Gill.

Gen. Mohan Singh held that to arrest such an important officer of the INA on suspicion was wrong and improper. As G.O.C. of the INA, Gen. Mohan Singh had the powers to punish any officer for any wrong done by him but the Japanese ignored all reasoning. Naturally, the sincerity of the Japanese stood questioned. Mohan Singh had series of conferences with the INA officers and as a result he decided not to play in the hands of the Japanese to serve their designs. In a conference of his staff officers, an order was unanimously agreed and drafted that in case of Mohan Singh's arrest, which looked imminent, INA would stand dissolved. This order was signed by Gen. Mohan Singh which ended with the famous Chetwodian motto of the Indian Military Academy, Dehra Dun.

This order was passed with the approval of all the officers and it was in conformity with the spirit of the Bidadari Resolutions. We were determined not to be exploited. At the time, it appeared that Mohan Singh might have to pay the price of upholding the honour and integrity of the Indian nation and the Indian National Army with his own life. In those days Mohan Singh daily addressed all INA Officers at Bidadari Hall to keep everybody informed with the fast deteriorating situation. I attended all of his addresses. We were all one with him.

Many unpleasant letters were exchanged between Mohan Singh and Rash Behari Bose. The old revolutionary was still not prepared to give up. At last after a month long crisis, General Mohan Singh was arrested on 29th December 1942 by the Japanese. To save himselves from the blame of Mohan Singh's arrest, Iwakuru took shelter under Rash Behari Bose's letters. Nobody was happy at the turn of the events.

Now Mohan Singh stood dismissed as the G.O.C. of the INA and even as a member of the INA. In recognition of his previous services, Rash Behari Bose sanctioned an allowance for his maintenance and allowed certain conveniences for a man of his status. Yet he was allowed to communicate neither with any member of the Army nor with the public. Iwakuru had added that Mohan Singh was also guilty of a grave crime of suspecting and challenging the Japanese Government's sincerity regarding India's freedom but in view of his burning patriotism and spirit of self-sacrifice for India, the Japanese Government had decided to pardon his life. He was told that he was no more the G.O.C. of the INA but merely Mohan Singh.

After the verdict had been announced, Mr. Senda who had been translating for Colonel Iwakuru told Mohan Singh that Fujiwara was waiting for him at his residence. Mr. Senda was an elderly gentleman with several years of experience as a businessman in India and was Colonel Iwakuru's advisor. When General Mohan Singh came out of Iwakuru's office, he found that his two A.D.C.s Captain Rattan Singh and Lieut. Mohd. Iqbal and his two bodyguards (without arms) were allowed to stay with him. They were Chitra Bahadur Singh (a Gurkha) and Pohla Ram (a Dogra).

INA now stood dissolved but the crises continued. In territories conquered by sword, the Japanese received a tremendous blow to their prestige at the hands of a strong patriot, a young General of the Revolutionary Army of Indians. The Japanese had lost their face. They had failed to create confidence and hence were worried. They were then prepared to concede to anything to regain their lost name, which meant so much to them. They promised that they would do anything in their power to approach the German Government and arrange to get Subhas Chandra Bose over from Berlin.

The period of the INA crisis was one of suspense and indecision. Col. Iwakuru and officers of the Iwakuru Kikan from the Japanese side and Rash Behari Bose from the Indian side were making all-out efforts to resolve the crisis. Major Fujiwara who preceded Col. Iwakuru and was no longer in the Kikan was summoned to talk to the INA officers. Fujiwara had many meetings with us collectively, in groups and individually. One day he called four or five Sikh officers and spoke to us emotionally about how he and Mohan Singh had raised the INA like two parents, he as father and Mohan Singh as mother. He did not wish that his baby should meet a premature death. We had to attain our aim before thinking of leaving the INA, and we should not be worried whether Mohan Singh and Fujiwara were there or not. Fujiwara enjoyed great influence and popularity among Indian officers and civilians alike. His visit influenced most of us, yet the deadlock continued.

Rash Behari Bose went from camp to camp in January 1943. Many ignored him. Some insulted him. He addressed us in public and in Officers' conferences. One day he called us. We were four Sikh Officers — Colonels Gulzara Singh, Gurmeet Singh, Jaswant Singh and myself. Rash Behari Bose asked us if we had achieved the goal for which we joined the INA. We had no right to lay down our arms when the purpose for which we raised them had not been attained. "Individuals will come and individuals will go", he said. He was sorry that Mohan Singh was not there with us, but the purpose for which Mohan Singh founded the INA remained. Our loyalty should not be to an individual leader. Tomorrow we might not be there. He advised us not to be personally loyal to him but to be loyal to the country and to the cause for which the Movement was started. Once that aim was achieved we could leave the INA.

Rash Behari Bose informed us that he was trying his best to get Subhas Chandra Bose brought to South-east Asia. He impressed upon us that our continuation in the INA should not depend on whether or not we had confidence in the Japanese. We had to have confidence in ourselves. If we were armed and any individual or a nation including the Japanese betrayed us, we could then fight. Rash Behari Bose's words impressed me the most and I decided to remain in the INA. I conveyed my decision to all those people whom I could influence to remain in the INA. During January and February along with Col. A.I.S. Dara and Col. A.D. Jahangir I addressed public rallies to put forward our conviction. We went all over the Island and up-country to urge men to remain in the INA.

Meanwhile Netaji was already trying to come to the East. The circumstances were favourable. Rash Behari Bose showed great patience and revived the INA. The old revolutionary had to suffer indignities to keep the INA alive. His conduct during the prolonged crisis after General Mohan Singh's removal makes a story of an extraordinary statesmanship and patience.

Thus, General Mohan Singh's sacrifice and Rash Behari Bose's patience culminated in getting us Netaji, a unique leader. It was unfortunate that before Netaji's arrival, some 5,000 INA troops refused to remain in the Movement. They had been separated from us and sent by the Japanese to the South-west Pacific area as POWs. Had these men known that Netaji would come, they would not have left the INA.

Directorate Military Bureau

In anticipation of Netaji's arrival, the revived INA was reorganized under its new Headquarters known as the Directorate of Military Bureau (DMB) with Colonel (later Major General) J.K. Bhonsle as the Director. This Headquarters controlled the general policy, finance and different branches of the staff directly under the control of the President of the I.I.L., Rash Behari Bose. Under this Headquarters, the Army was commanded by the Army Commander, Colonel (later Major General) Mohammad Zaman Kiani.

I was appointed Deputy Quartermaster General (DQMG) in the "Q" Branch at the Army Headquarters. I had with me Capt. Amir Singh to look after the Technical Branch and Lt. Akbar Ali to supervise the

Non-technical Branch. Major N.N. Khosla and Lt. Mehtab Singh were appointed in the Supply and Transport Department. Lt. Kundan Lal workshops looked after. There were Lt. Girdhari lal, Lt. G.L. Kohli and many more officers whose names I do not recollect presently. The DQMG was responsible for accommodation and the above-mentioned branches. The Army Headquarters was organized by the middle of March 1943 and was duly gazetted on 17th April in 1943.

My immediate task on receiving the appointment was the collection of kit and clothing of those personnel who had decided to leave the INA. They were approached by Colonel Bhonsle, Director of the Military Bureau (DMB), and his respective departmental heads but the non-volunteers did not return their kit and were very rude. The unpleasant job was entrusted to me under the presumption that all the ledgers and the troops were under the Army Commander. The personnel going out of the INA damaged or destroyed the articles but they would not return the items to us. Appealing to their conscience, I suggested that they should not destroy the items because even as Prisoners of War they needed their clothing. I met them half way to the effect that they might keep what was of bare necessity to them and return the rest intact to the INA.

The compromise worked and we managed to collect about fifty per cent of the items. On their part, the Japanese refused to make good the loss of the remaining fifty per cent. When the matter came to the notice of the DMB Colonel Bhonsle, he asked me to explain for the deficiencies. Though he was well conversant with the details of the matter, my explanation failed to satisfy him. In order to save the face of the INA before the Japanese, the DMB ordered a Court of Inquiry against me. Besides Lt. Col. (later Major General) Loganadan as its Presiding Officer, the Court comprised Col. N.S. Bhagat and three other members. The findings of the court vindicated my position and the Japanese agreed to make good the losses.

Those were days, as per saying, when as DQMG we had "to beg, borrow or steal" articles which were not in our stores like the cooking utensils for the men, blankets and certain items of clothing, especially the khaki turban cloth for the Sikhs. I was lucky to purchase large quantities of white muslin for the pugrees but could not get the khaki colour which had to be improvised by dyeing the white cloth in boiled tea-leaves water. As for making utensils, my workshop people managed to get scrapped aluminium from destroyed or discarded British aeroplanes or by removing iron sheets from certain demolished buildings and barracks.

I Become Supply and Transport Officer

One day towards the end of May 1943, a sepoy, batman of Maj. N.N. Khosla, brought me a chit in which Khosla, courteously approaching me as his superior officer, reported that injustice was done to him by placing him under me as Supply and Transport Officer ignoring the fact that he was senior to me in service. He pleaded for justice. The letter had been written to me from his sick bed in the INA General Hospital, Bidadari. I called on the officer during the visiting hours and learnt that he was suffering from chronic asthma. He had recently come from Saigon where he was in charge of INA broadcasting station. He was expected to remain in the hospital for about a month. Asking Maj. Khosla to look after his health, I told him that his case would be put up before the DMB through the Army Commander and justice would be done to him.

When I reported the matter to the Army Commander Mohammed Zaman Kiani, he told me that I had been given the promotion with the full knowledge of Khosla's seniority. He would, however, ask the DMB to reconsider the case. A few days later I was informed that the DMB was not prepared to change the appointment. After about five weeks during early office hours as I was engrossed in my files, I heard a smart clicking of boots. I looked up and found Maj. Khosla saluting me with the words, "Sir, I report for duty." I stood up, left my chair, went over where Khosla was standing and directed him to move towards my chair. He quietly obeyed. When he was standing between the table and the chair I ordered him to sit down. He said, "What are you doing"? I answered, "I am going to give you a duty. Sit down," I commanded. He sat down. I jumped to attention, saluted and said, "Sir, I report for duty under you as your Supply and Transport officer." Khosla responded, "You can't do that." I replied, "I have done it if the DMB cannot do justice. This is my way of delivering justice. Now come with me."

Khosla followed me to the Army Commander whose office was hardly fifty yards away. I introduced Khosla and respectfully informed the Army Commander what I had done. In his characteristic way, Zaman silently looked at both of us, remained quiet for a few moments as if exercising his thought and then said, "Gurbakhsh, are you sure that you will be happy?" My reply was in the affirmative. He again appeared submerged in thoughts and then he said, "If you are happy, I am happy and will recommend the transfer to the DMB". Both of us saluted. He shook hands with the new DQMG. As Maj. Khosla walked out of Army Commander's office I followed my DQMG as his Supply and Transport Officer.

N.N. Khosla

Educated at Oxford and a Bar-at-Law, Narindra Nath Khosla who had spent about five years in England and the Continent, knew his job well, definitely better than I, with his experience of having served in the Royal Indian Army Service Corps. Since our work at the Headquarters was done in English, I found that drafting letters which used to take lot of my time was done effortlessly by Khosla in no time. My position in the Branch remained important as his next senior officer. Khosla never forgot the good turn and we made a very happy friendly team. When Netaji arrived and the Army was enlarged in December 1943, I was transferred to be the 2nd-in-Command of the 5th Guerilla Regiment and Khosla went to Burma with the Ist Div. under the command of Zaman Kiani.

9

NETAJI ARRIVES

The second of July 1943 was the red-letter day in the history of the INA when Netaji arrived in Singapore. In doing so he had taken a very dangerous journey by German and Japan submarines respectively through the waters of the Atlantic and Indian oceans controlled by the British and the American navies. The three-month voyage was undertaken by Netaji at a great peril in spite of warnings from one and all. In this historic journey Netaji was accompanied by Major Abid Hassan Safrani. The German submarine left the port of Kiel. They changed over to a Japanese submarine near Madagascar on 24th April 1943.

Earlier during the voyage, the German submarine had a very narrow escape when an enemy freighter spotted it, and tried to ram it down at full speed. The submarine had just been successful in diving down when the enemy freighter roared past over the submarine. While death scared the crew in the face, Netaji was busy dictating notes to Hassan. So fearless was Netaji even in the face of death that the captain of the German submarine later addressed his crew that they should all take a lesson from their distinguished Indian guest and his adjutant in facing a sudden crisis involving death with such extraordinary composure. I described it in a poem when I learnt about the hazardous voyage.

The Japanese submarine took them to Sabang, an island on the northern shore of Sumatra, and were flown to Tokyo where they arrived on 13th May 1943. Prior to his departure from Tokyo for Singapore, Netaji discussed all the problems facing the Indian Independence Movement with Japanese heads of various departments concerned before he met the Prime Minister of Japan, General Tojo. Netaji met Tojo twice to lay down his demands which were conceded by General Tojo. Then General Tojo invited Netaji to the Japanese Diet (Parliament). Here in Netaji's presence, Tojo made an official declaration affirming full and unqualified support to the cause of India's complete independence. This was the first and the only declaration of its kind by the Head of a Government of a foreign power during World War II. Netaji could not obtain such a declaration from Germany. Neither Gandhiji nor any other Indian leader (pro-British) could extract a similar commitment from the British Government or its Allies at any time during the war.

It was only after getting this declaration from the Government of Japan that Netaji let his presence in Japan be known to the world through an address broadcast from Tokyo. On that day I was in Bidadari where we, the officers and the men, had gathered to listen to Netaji's first broadcast which I translated and explained to the gathering. He made his appearance before his countrymen on 4th July 1943, in the Cathey Building at Singapore which was packed with human beings. The stage had been decorated with Tricolour flags and flowers and with a huge portrait of Mahatma Gandhi smiling at the rising India. Impatient eyes were riveted on the entrance of the hall, when suddenly slogans started resounding and there appeared a man with an upright and erect carriage, with head held high bearing the pride of India, with a serious face but possessing a winning smile.

Amid slogans and songs, "Subhasji ! Subhasji, *woh Shane-e-Hind aagaey*" (Subhas, the glory of India, has come). He was garlanded and welcomed Rash Behari Bose then stood up and handed over the leadership of the Indian Independence Movement to Netaji. The grace with which the old leader, one of the great pioneers of the Indian revolution, parted with his powers offered a rare example of personal sacrifice. It made us emotional. Sitting close to the dais, I could not help admiring it with tears. Equally moving was Netaji's speech as he accepted the great responsibility with an expression of gratitude to the elder leader for his sustained services to the mother country. He warmly appreciated the sacrifices made by the leaders of the Movement who had organized the I.I.L. and the INA. Speaking in Hindustani, Netaji urged the audience to keep up the spirit of the INA for liberation of the motherland. Like the powerful current of light that dispels darkness all around, Netaji charged the atmosphere with hope and fervour. People responded to his call enthusiastically and he was the Man of Destiny, nay the proverbial Caesar who came, saw and conquered.

Netaji Reviews the INA

On the 5th July 1943 Netaji reviewed the INA in a spacious maidan in front of the Municipal Buildings of Singapore. It was here that he gave the war cry of 'CHALO DELHI' to the soldiers and the slogan of Total Mobilization to the civilians. The following day, the 6th of July, General Tojo, Prime Minister of Japan reviewed the INA at the same place. Field Marshal Count Terauchi, the Supreme Commander of the Japanese Armies in the Southeast Asia was also present on this occasion. Tojo, Terauchi and Netaji had a brief but very important dialogue before they left the parade ground. It meant a signal to Netaji to go ahead with his idea of the establishment of the Provisional Government of Azad Hind. The Bonds of mutual respect and cordiality between Count Terauchi and Netaji were further strengthened when Tojo asked Netaji to coordinate with Count Terauchi and the Government at Tokyo regarding the issues which might arise subsequently. Terauchi was one of the few Generals who could talk to Tojo on equal terms.

Provisional Government of Azad Hind (Free India) Created

The speed with which Netaji moved to reorganize and strengthen the Movement dazzled the Japanese and the Indians alike. Things which could not even be thought of before Netaji's arrival started happening before our eyes. On the 21st October, 1943, about 1,000 delegates from all over East Asia, Officers, men and women of the INA and the IIL, Officers of the Japanese Army and Government and distinguished citizens of Singapore gathered in the Cathey Hall at Singapore. They heard Netaji announce the formation of the Provisional Government of Azad Hind to the world. It was here that Netaji took an oath of allegiance to India. He was so deeply overwhelmed by the solemnity and historical importance of the event that he could not utter a single word for some minutes before he took the oath: "In the name of God I take this sacred oath that to liberate India and thirty-eight crores of my countrymen I, Subhas Chandra

Bose, will continue this sacred war of freedom till the last breath of my life".

After this, each member of the Provisional Government came up one by one in front of the big gathering and took oath:- "In the name of God I take this holy oath that to liberate India and thirty-eight crores of my countrymen I will be absolutely faithful to our leader Subhas Chandra Bose and shall be always prepared to sacrifice my life and all I have for the cause."

And Netaji read out the Proclamation which was broadcast simultaneously to the world.

Proclamation of the Provisional Government of Azad Hind

"After their first defeat at the hands of the British in 1757 in Bengal, the Indian people fought an uninterrupted series of hard and bitter battles over a stretch of one hundred years. The history of this period teems with examples of unparalleled heroism and self-sacrifice. And, in the pages of that history, the names of Sirajuddoula and Mohan Lal of Bengal, Haider Ali, Tippu Sultan and Velu Tampi of South India, Appa Sahib Bhonsle and Peshwa Baji Rao of Maharashtra, the Begums of Oudh, Sardar Shyam Singh Atariwala of Punjab and last, but not least, Rani Lakshmibai of Jhansi, Tantia Tope, Maharaj Kunwar Singh of Dumraon and Nana Sahib among others warriors are for ever engraved in letters of gold. Unfortunately for us, our forefathers did not at first realise that the British constituted a grave threat to the whole of India and they did not therefore put up a united front against the enemy. Ultimately, when the Indian people were roused to the reality of the situation, they made a concrete move and under the flag of Bahadur Shah, in 1857, they fought their last war as free men. In spite of a series of brilliant victories in the early stages of this war, ill-luck and faulty leadership gradually brought about their final collapse and subjugation. Nevertheless such heroes as the Rani of Jhansi, Tantia Tope, Kunwar Singh and Nana Sahib live like eternal stars in the nation's memory to inspire us to greater deeds of sacrifice and valour.

Forcibly disarmed by the British after 1857 and subjected to terror and brutality, the Indian people lay prostrate for a while but with the birth of the Indian National Congress in 1885, there came a new awakening. From 1885, till the end of the last World War, the Indian people in their endeavour to recover their lost liberty, tried all possible methods, namely agitation and propaganda, boycott of British goods, terrorism and sabotage and finally armed revolution. But all these efforts failed for a time. Ultimately, in 1920, when the Indian people, haunted by a sense of failure, were groping for a new method, Mahatma Gandhi came forward with the new weapon of non - co-operation and civil disobedience.

For two decades thereafter, the Indian people went through a phase of intense patriotic activity. The message of freedom was carried to every Indian home. Through personal example, people were taught to suffer, to sacrifice and to die in the cause of freedom. From the centre to the remotest villages, the people were knit together into one political organisation. Thus, the Indian people not only recovered their political consciousness, but became a political entity once again. They could now speak with one voice and strive with one will for one common goal. From 1937 to 1939, through the work of the Congress Ministries in eight Provinces, they gave proof of their readiness and their capacity to administer their own affairs.

Thus, on the eve of the present World War, stage was set for the final struggle for India's liberation. During the course of this war, Germany, with the help of her allies, has dealt shattering blows to our enemy in Europe, while Nippon, with the help of her allies, has inflicted a knockout blow to our enemy in East Asia. Favoured by a most happy combination of circumstances, the Indian people today have a wonderful opportunity for achieving their national emancipation.

For the first time in recent history, Indians abroad have also been politically roused and united in one organization. They are not only thinking and feeling in tune with their countrymen at home, but are also marching in step with them, along the path to freedom. In East Asia, in particular, over two million Indians are now organised as one solid phalanx, inspired by the slogan of "Total Mobilisation" and in front of them stand the serried ranks of India's Army of Liberation, with the slogan "Onward to Delhi", on their lips.

Having goaded Indians to desperation by its hypocrisy and having driven them to starvation and death by plunder and loot, British rule in India has forfeited the goodwill of the Indian people altogether and is now living a precarious existence. It needs but a flame to destroy the last vestige of that unhappy rule. To light that flame is the task of India's Army of Liberation. Assured of the enthusiastic support of the civil population at home and also of a large section of British Indian Army, and backed by gallant and invincible allies abroad but relying in the first instance on its own strength, Indian Army of Liberation is confident of fulfilling its historic role.

Now that the dawn of freedom is at hand, it is the duty of the Indian people to set up a Provisional Government of their own, and launch the last struggle under the banner of that Government. But with all the Indian leaders in prison and the people at home totally disarmed, it is not possible to set up a Provisional Government within India or to launch an armed struggle under the aegis of that Government. It is therefore the duty of the Indian Independence League in East Asia, supported by all patriotic Indians at home and abroad, to undertake this task the task, of setting up a Provisional Government of Azad Hind (Free India) and of conducting the last fight for freedom, with the help of the Army of Liberation (that is, the Azad Hind Fauj or the Indian National Army) organised by the League.

Having been constituted as the Provisional Government of Azad Hind by the Indian Independence League in East Asia, we enter upon our duties with a full sense of the responsibility that has devolved on us. We pray that Providence may bless our work and our struggle for the emancipation of our Motherland. And we hereby pledge our lives and the lives of our comrades in arms to the cause of her freedom, of her welfare and her exultation among the nations of the world.

It will be the task of the Provisional Government to launch and to conduct the struggle that will bring about the expulsion of the British and of their allies from the soil of India. It will then be the task of the Provisional Government to bring about the establishment of a permanent National Government of Azad Hind constituted in accordance with the will of the Indian people and enjoying their confidence. After the British and their allies are overthrown and until a permanent National Government of Azad Hind is set up on Indian soil, the Provisional Government will administer the affairs of the country in trust for the Indian people.

The Provisional Government is entitled to, and hereby claims, the allegiance of every Indian. It guarantees religious liberty as well as equal rights and equal opportunities to all its citizens. It declares its firm resolve to pursue the happiness and prosperity of the whole nation and all its parts, cherishing all the children of the nation equally and transcending all the differences cunningly fostered by an alien Government in the past.

In the name of God, in the name of bygone generations who have welded the Indian people into one nation, and in the name of dead heroes who have bequeathed to us a tradition of heroism and self-sacrifice, we call upon the Indian people to rally round our banner and to strike for India's freedom. We call upon them to launch the final struggle against the British and their allies in India and to prosecute that struggle with valour and perservance and with full faith in final Victory - until the enemy is expelled from Indian soil and the Indian people are once again a free nation."

Signed on behalf of the Provisional Government of Azad Hind, Subhas Chandra Bose (Head of the State, Prime Minister and Minister for War and Foreign Affairs); Captain Mrs. Lakshmi (Women's Organisation); S.A. Ayer (Publicity and Propaganda); Lt. Col. A.C. Chatterji (Finance); Lt. Col. Aziz Ahmed, Lt. Col. N.S. Bhagat, Lt. Col. J.K. Bhonsle, Lt. Col. Gulzara Singh, Lt. Col. M.Z.Kiani, Lt. Col. A.D. Longandhan, Lt. Col. Ehsan Qadir, Lt. Col. Shah Nawaz (Representatives of the Armed Forces); A.M. Sahay, Secretary (with ministerial rank); Rash Behari Bose (Supreme Advisor); Karim Ghani, Debanth Das, D.M. Khan, A. Yellappa, A.J. Thivy, Sardar Ishar Singh (Advisers); A.N. Sarkar (Legal Advisor), Syonant (Singapore), October 21, 1943.

After the establishment of the Provisional Government of Azad Hind, events moved with a cyclonic speed all over East Asia. On 22nd October, the Rani Jhansi Regiment was formed and its camp opened at Singapore. Capt. Lakshmi Swaminathan was given its command.

War Declared

On the night of 23/24th October, the Provisional Government during its full session of Cabinet decided to declare war against Britain and the United States of America. When Netaji proposed the resolution,

Col. Loganathan proposed that the U.S.A. should be left out. Replying to the objection Netaji explained that there would be neither ethics nor expedience in avoiding the mention of America. S.A. Ayer argued that it was a grim reality that the forces of the U.S.A. were present on the Indian soil facing the INA and while expelling the British forces, expulsion of the U.S. forces was a part of one and the same operation. The resolution was passed unanimously. The men of the INA including the women soldiers of Rani Jhansi Regiment went mad with joy and enthusiasm when Netaji announced the declaration of war in a public rally the next day.

Provisional Government of Azad Hind Recognised

Within a week of its establishment, the Provisional Government was recognized by nine sovereign States. Germany's Foreign Minister, Herr Von Ribbentrop, was the first to send official felicitation in recognition of the Provisional Government. Other eight countries were Japan, Italy, Croatia, China (Nanking), Thailand, Manchuria, Burma and the Philippines. Mr. Eamon de Valera, the President of the Irish Free State, sent his cordial felicitations to Netaji on the occasion.

Andaman and Nicobar Acquired

During the first week of November, Netaji attended the Greater East Asia Conference held in Tokyo on the 5th and 6th. On the last day of the Conference, Prime Minister General Tojo declared, "I take this occasion to declare that the Imperial Government of Japan is ready shortly to place the Andaman and Nicobar Islands, now under the occupation of the Imperial Japanese forces, under the jurisdiction of the Provisional Government of Azad Hind, as the initial evidence of her readiness to help in India's struggle for independence." He further reiterated earlier promises of Japan's determination to extend all-out cooperation to India in her fight for freedom.

Netaji visited the Islands on 29th December for the ceremonial transfer of the Andaman and Nicobar, renamed by the Provisional Government as SHAHEED and SWARAJ islands. Lt. Col. A.D. Loganathan was appointed as the Chief Commissioner of the islands. With the acquisition of this liberated territory, the Provisional Government had now become a national entity in fact and in name.

During December, the 1st Division of the INA under the command of Colonel Mohammad Zaman Kiani started its move to Rangoon.

Move to Rangoon

Advanced Headquarters of the Provisional Government and the Supreme Headquarters of Azad Hind Fauj as well as offices of the Indian Independence League also moved to Rangoon so as to be as close as possible to the would-be theatre of war. Rangoon, thus, became an extensive camp of Indian War of Independence. We could not have aspired for a better host than the Burmese people whose President Dr. Ba Maw held, "In my view Asia cannot be free unless India is free.... If we wish to destroy anti-Asiatic imperialism, we must drive them out of their Asiatic stronghold which is India. The British Empire cannot be broken until and unless the British domination of India is broken".

Azad Hind Dal Formed

One of the most important organizations formed at Rangoon was the Azad Hind Dal which had both men and women among its cadres. They were the future administrators to be required for running the liberated territory. They were educated and trained to be models of efficient, courteous, fair-minded functionaries of the I.I.L., the executive branch of the Azad Hind Government in the service of a newly-freed people. They were to inspire respect and confidence in the minds of their countrymen. The Rani Jhansi Regiment and the youth organization, Bal Sena, were also busy getting training in their respective camps.

Total Mobilisation Gets a Boost

Netaji's slogan of TOTAL MOBILISATION received a big boost when Habib Sahib of Rangoon donated Rupees one crore and two lakhs to the Netaji Fund. Mrs. H.R. Betai contributed seven lakh rupees. Apart from a cash donation in lakhs, Shri Parmanand donated the 50 square miles of Ziawadi estate along with its sugar factory. The funds collected in Burma alone amounted to about fifteen crores of rupees, while funds collected in other countries were even greater. Azad Hind Bank was established in Rangoon to have funds readily available in the prosecution of the war.

Secret Services

Netaji reorganized the Secret Service of INA and took this delicate task in his own hands. The sacrifices of the members of this organization whom the British Government called "the Enemy Agents" and treated them as such with torture of third degree and death have yet to be recognized by our people and history. Their contribution to the Indian freedom struggle, if not greater than our field regiments, was great and significant in creating that terror among the British which compelled them to quit India when the going was good for them. The greatest sacrifice of these men was to remain unknown.

Tokyo Cadets

Netaji had a characteristic foresight of planning for the future even when busy fighting against the British Empire. As President of the Indian National Congress, he established the National Planning Commission and deputed Pandit Jawaharlal Nehru as its Chairman, an act of eternal benefit to the nation. How aptly Rash Behari Bose had described him as "The born leader of leaders !"

During his first review of the Indian National Army on 5th July 1943 at Singapore, Netaji declared that there were two tasks for the Army — to fight for freedom and then to stand as the defence force of Free India: "It must become a first class modern army of superb morale, its officers fit to form the General Staff of Free India." It was in line with this very aim that Netaji arranged with the Japanese Government to favour us by training our cadets in their Military Academy at Tokyo. The fortunate ones who were personally selected by Netaji for Officer's training at the Military Academy of Japan, came to be known as INA Tokyo Cadets. Netaji used to treat them as his own sons.

In Action

Within three months of the declaration of war in the beginning of 1944, news started reaching us regarding the early encounters of our troops with the enemy in the Arakan sector. After their defeat at the Japanese hands in 1942, the British had planned to launch an attack in the spring of 1944. Appreciating the British move, the INA and the Japanese forces advanced and surrounded the 5th British Indian Division which managed to slip out of the encirclement. Our forces then surrounded the 7th British Indian Division in Maungdaw and Buthidaung area. The heroic deeds and the brilliant achievements of the INA troops of the Intelligence and Bahadur Groups under Maj. (later Lt. Col.) L.S. Misra and Maj. (later Lt. Col.) Mehar Dass, respectively earned acknowledgment and praise of our allies, the Japanese. Messages of appreciation and congratulation were also received from our European allies, Germany and Italy. Misra and Mehar Dass won the coveted decorations of SARDAR-E-JANG awards. More than a Platoon-strong British Indian soldiers came over to join the INA.

By the middle of March 1944, the 1st Division of the INA advanced under its capable and resolute Commander Col. (later Maj. General) Mohammad Zaman Kiani towards Imphal. A battalion from Subhas Brigade was sent to coordinate their action with the Japanese 55th Division against the 31 West African Division in the Arakan Sector. The Commander of this Battalion, Maj. (later Colonel) P.S. Raturi arrived at Kyauktaw in the middle of March and established its base there. The African Division which was advancing towards the south along the river Kaladan was found constructing a bridge to cross the river at a place named Tetma. Raturi had been ordered to check the advance of this Division.

By the time Raturi's Battalion arrived there, the opposing Division had already crossed the river and taken up a defensive position. Without any delay, Raturi attacked the Division at night. Getting a signal from their Commander, Raturi's men jumped into the enemy trenches with fixed bayonets. In a hand to hand fight, the enemy was made to run for his life. In their hot pursuit of the enemy with their machine-guns, Raturi's men succeeded in sinking sixteen enemy boats. INA lost 14 soldiers while 22 were wounded. Besides leaving behind 250 dead, the enemy left their arms and ammunition as well as a large quantity of provisions which our men called "Churchill gift."

Raturi's battalion continued the pursuit. Fifty miles upstream, battles were fought at Paletwa and Daletmi. They chased the enemy right up to Mowdak where another big battle was won. Mowdak being inside India, our men lay prostrate and kissed the soil of Mother India. They cried with joy as their slogans echoed in the Kaladan valley. Mowdak was left under the charge of Captain (later Major) Surajmal as the Mowdak Garrison Commander. As a noble gesture of respect and goodwill, the Japanese Commander left a Platoon of Japanese soldiers under Surajmal's command, a very rare example in Japanese military history to place their men under the command of a non-Japanese Officer. Both Raturi and Surajmal earned Sardar-e-Jang awards.

INA operations continued to threaten Chittagong and continuously harass the enemy lines of communication in the Arakan and Akyab sectors. Meanwhile, our advance continued towards Imphal. Shah Nawaz advanced swiftly along the Manipur road towards Kohima. Colonel Thaker Singh, another officer of the Subhas Brigade, won Sardar-e-Jang award. Capt. Ran Singh (later Lt. Col.) was another hero of Haka and Falam ridge.

Colonel I.J. Kiani and his Gandhi Brigade smashed the main gates of Imphal fortress. It was at Palel. Quite close to it, Major (later Lt. Col.) Pritam Singh very nearly succeeded in taking the aerodrome. His successful assault after assault earned him Sardar-e-Jung award. It was here that, though very seriously wounded, Captain Mansukhlal won the post, very heavily defended by the British to guard the Palel airstrip. While pinning the gallantry medal of Sardar-e-Jang, Netaji said, "You are my Rana Sanga." Mansukhlal had received more than 16 bullets lodged in various parts of his body. I wish I had a list of those heroes who won gallantry awards and sacrificed their lives in this sector.

Tricolour Hoisted on the Liberated Territory

Piercing through the enemy lines, the suicide squads of Intelligence and Bahadur Groups commanded by Col. Shaukat Ali Malik advanced and were the first to hoist the Tricolour flag on the liberated territory of the Mother Country at Moirang on 18th April, 1944. Then they moved towards Imphal and liberated Bishanpur and again to the Red hill within eleven miles of Imphal. Major General A.C. Chatterjee, the Governor-designate of the liberated areas brought up his Azad Hind Dal in order to establish Azad Hind administration. Col. Malik was also the recipient of Sardar-e-Jang award.

Our forces cut off Kohima road and threatened Silchar and Dimapur. Col. Gulzara Singh marched 250 miles, outflanked the enemy with his Azad Brigade. We were virtually knocking at the very gates of the fortress of Imphal. The 14th Army of the enemy was at the verge of surrender. Actually, they had decided to surrender. It was at this crucial stage that two of our important officers, Major Prabhu Dayal and Major J.B.S. Grewal, not being able to endure thirst and hunger any longer, went over to the enemy. It is recorded for the general interest of my readers that both these officers served in the British Indian Army and got promotions. Prabhu Dayal became a Brigadier in free India. Grewal was murdered by some of his men after India attained independence. Chopped and minced, his body was found mutilated in a jungle near Patiala where he was playing shikar.

It was from these two deserters that the enemy learnt that the INA and the Japanese were in a poor state in respect of food and ammunition. Because of the overstretched lines of communication without any air power and with roads gone under water and muddy, our supplies of rations totally failed. Our men were living on jungle roots and leaves. For twelve long days they had fought without a single grain of rice. We had hardly five rounds to a rifle left. Nevertheless, Delhi looked within reach: Imphal was fully besieged; our spirit appeared to have triumphed over steel.

At such a crucial juncture, orders went to the 14th British Indian Army to postpone their surrender. The 5th Division was dropped into Imphal to reinforce the fortress from the air. At the same time monsoon brought contineous heavy rains which cut off even our withdrawal. Yet we did withdraw. The quicksands of the swollen rivers sucked down hundreds of our men. In rains and floods, without food and medicines, many of our valiant soldiers died to join their dead heroes on the various battlefields. Netaji came up to look after them personally. Evacuation of our men under those hazards brought out the best in our men and officers of No. 1 Division under the command of Major General Mohammad Zaman Kiani with his G.l. Col. Raja Mohamad Arshad and Staff Officers and Commanders of various formations of the INA during that retreat which demanded superhuman courage and endurance to survive and continued the fight.

10

The 5th Guerrilla Regiment

In December 1943, I was appointed Second-in-Command to Major J.W. Rodrigues (later Colonel) who retired as Inspector-General of Police, Home Guards, in Madhya Pradesh now settled at Bangalore. Rodrigues raised the 5th Guerrilla Regiment at Bidadari in Singapore. Apart from helping him raise the Regiment I was responsible for training, discipline, morale and welfare of the troops.

Hailing from an eminent Christian family, originally from Goa, but settled at Yeotmal in Maharashtra, Rodrigues was an efficient, hard-working, well-meaning officer, dedicated and devoted to his duties and to the cause of the Indian Independence Movement. He had an independent, non-interfering nature. Having explained his intentions and expectations, he would give his junior commanders and staff officers complete freedom of action. He had a heart which could overlook any fault except indiscipline. It was a pleasure serving under him. One could go all out for the cause.

The 5th Guerrilla Regiment was formed as part of the 2nd INA Division which was organized under the command of Col. N.S. Bhagat consequent on the 1st Division's move to the Front.

The senior-most Indian Commissioned Officer and member of Netaji's Cabinet, Bhagat was the rarest of the rare officers, that the armed forces of any nation could produce. An all-rounder, first-class first in each and every field of life, he was equally at home with a staff job or in command. Of a strong will and character, he was a hard taskmaster with a rough exterior and awe-inspiring personality, reserved, fearless and purposeful. He hated hypocrisy, flattery and falsehood. But he had one weakness; he was straightforward in deed and in expression, for which he had to pay by falling a prey to the intrigues of others. He was removed from the Command in April 1944.

During this period, Bhagat and Rodrigues would be present to watch most of the training, exercises and activities of the Regiment. The whole week, whether day or night, formed one continuous training period.

On March 30th, 1944, the 5th Guerrilla Regiment moved to Ipoh in Perak state of Malaya. I proceeded with the Advance Party to arrange accommodation and make other arrangements for the Regiment and Divisional Headquarters as well as for Ancillary Units. It was quite a job but the Japanese administration and the Indian Independence League as well as the local Indians were so helpful and co-operative, especially Mr. J.A. Thivy and Sardar Sucha Singh Malai that the Camp was well set long before the allotted time. By the third week of April we were well-settled and the training was proceeding enthusiastically.

Then an unfortunate incident took place. I was out in the jungle on a training exercise when Rodrigues, on some grounds, punished the local canteen contractor with a fine of five hundred dollars. On my return to the Camp, the contractor came to me pleading for leniency. I, in turn, approached Rodrigues late in the evening. It was Saturday. He had just come to his room and was in the act of removing his ankle putties and boots. There was nobody else present. Our discussion grew hot. I was hurt that he had not taken me into confidence before punishing the contractor. He was hurt that I had challenged his authority. Never did we have any occasion to differ with each other on any matter of decision and policy whatsoever.

The following Monday, I was produced before the new Division Commander Colonel Aziz Ahmed who asked, "Major Rodrigues ! What have you to say against Major Dhillon?" Rodrigues said, "Sir, I have nothing but good to say about Dhillon." Then after narrating the unpleasant episode, Rodrigues added, "Sir, Major Dhillon is unnecessarily touchy which he should not be. After all, I am the Commander and am not supposed to ask my Second-in-Command every time I take a decision. I do have a right to use my discretion." The Division Commander agreed with him, and asked me to apologise and let the matter end then and there. I wish I had said, "Sorry", but

I did not say the word. I was given time to take a few days to ponder over the matter and apologise, so thoughtful was Aziz.

In the Regiment, nobody knew of this incident. Neither Rodrigues nor I talked about it. The week went on with its full load of work. Nobody felt, not even Rodrigues nor I that anything serious had happened between us. So graceful was Rodrigues! The absurdity of my sensitiveness had ultimately dawned on me and on the following Saturday, having decided to walk over to Rodrigues to apologies, I was on the verge of leaving my office, when Colonel Jaswant Singh, the G-l in the Divisional Headquarters, walked in to invite me to tea. I wish, I had seen Rodrigues before going for tea.

Jaswant or Jessie as I used to call him was a very dear friend. We had worked side by side in the INA Army Headquarters. During the tea, he told me that he had been deputed by the Division Commander to advise me to apologise to Rodrigues, failing which I would be immediately drafted to the Front. Jessie had taken quite some time to approach the subject in as palatable a manner as possible.

The soldier in me could not risk his prestige by making a decision in the face of a threat of the Front. "What else are we meant for?" I asked Jessie, explaining what I was going to do before his invitation to tea that evening. Now, as that very action was beyond me, I would not like to give an impression of being afraid of going to the Front. Jessie tried his best to make me agree to his advice, but my decision was irrevocable. "In that case", he told me, "I should be ready to leave tomorrow by the evening train for Alor Star to report to Colonel S.M. Hussain, Commander No. I Infantry Regiment at Jitra which is on orders to move".

That evening I went to Rodrigues to bid good-bye. I then apologized and assured him that in case I ever got a chance, I would consider it an honour to serve under him and requested him to own me, as and when possible. He was shocked to hear the news of my sudden departure. He told me to withhold departure for a day, as he wanted to keep me. He tried but failed. I left as scheduled, crying and making Rodrigues, Jessie and others cry. Parting is always difficult, but parting from the men I had organized and trained, the men and the Commander I loved and wanted to be with, and fight with and die with, gave me a feeling that I had lost something of myself.

I arrived at Jitra along with Mehar Singh, my batman who had served, nursed and mothered me ever since the Battle of Singapore in February 1942. Jitra was not an unknown place to me. Here, along with my mother Battalion, the l/14th Punjab Regiment—the good old "Sherdil" - I had fought and lost in December 1941. Roads, rivers and rubber plantations with the Elephanta Hill in the background were so familiar and fresh in my memory that the recent parting with the 5th Guerrilla Regiment became all the more difficult for me to bear. I was under an attack of nostalgia.

Colonel S.M. Hussain, the Regimental Commander of the 1st Infantry Regiment, was a wonderfully carefree man with an inborn pleasure of living. He delighted in doing nothing. He neither attended office for more than five minutes a day nor did he attend any parade except once during the period I was with him in Jitra. Some of his Units and all Staff Officers had left for the Front and the remaining were waiting for transportation facilities. Training could have continued, but Hussain did not care. Good food, the best I had during the war for a continuous period and complete leisure with long evenings and nothing to do were not only boring but also agonizing to my conscience when our troops were already in action on the Indo-Burma border. It was a punishment and I accepted it as such, missing Rodrigues and the 5th Guerrilla Regiment all the more.

Tunku Abdul Rehman

During my stay at Jitra, the only relieving factor which I can recall with a sense of pride was the acquaintance made with Tunku Abdul Rehman who was destined to become the first Prime Minister of Malaya, the founder of Malaysia, and the greatest pillar of democracy in the East. At the time, he was Minister for Education in his home State of Kedah of which his uncle was the Sultan. Even at that time his popularity among his people and his concern for the welfare of the common man manifested in all his actions and expressions. It was indeed an honour and a pleasure to enjoy his overwhelming hospitality. The Tunku was a typical example of simple living and high thinking. Patriotism and magnanimity in him were, indeed, inspiring. Here was greatness in an embryo.

11
To Burma

At last the waiting ended and on 15th July 1944, we left Jitra by train for Chumphon for onward journey via Kawashi, Mergui and Tavoy through Thailand and then on to Moulmein and Rangoon in Burma. Hussain had no heart to travel with the troops by road, rail and sea on such a cumbersome journey. He decided to proceed straight to Bangkok, to have a holiday and wait to be flown to Bunna. As I was under him on a special report, he did not consider it proper to leave me behind and took me along. At Bangkok followed another period of prolonged stay and compulsory rest. We were the guests of the Indian Independence League. The League Headquarters were most active here.

Bangkok, the capital of Thailand, the lotus city of the East, untouched by war, bustled in trade and traditions in all its splendour. Shops were flooded with consumer goods which had gone scarce in Singapore and Malaya. The days were cheerful and the nights long and gay. What impressed me the most was the friendly nature of the local people. During my stay at Bangkok to escape from loneliness, I composed a poem, *"Netaji ka Farman Desh Bhagton Se."* — Netaji's commandment to the patriots.

On the 21st of August 1944, we flew over to Rangoon by Netaji's personal aircraft, the "*Azad Hind*". When I got down from the plane at Mingaladon airport, I saw Col. Shaukat Ali Malik moving up and down as if taking a stroll. I went to him and saluted "Jai Hind". He pretended not to look at me even and continued his stroll in a carefree abandon. When he came closer to me again, I repeated my salutation. Col. Malik did not respond to my greetings at all. As he passed in front of me the next time, I went closer to him. We were fast friends and of the same seniority. I addressed him in an intimate and informal tone, "O you bald-headed man. Are you proud of having bagged the coveted medal of Sardar-e-Jang on the battlefield ?"

Malik shouted "Come here". As I approached him he untied the front buttons of his jacket and showed me a bundle of notes of Thai currency stuffed in his inner pockets. Filled with curiosity, I said, "Where did you commit a theft or a robbery ?" He said, "Do you know who gave me these?" On hearing "No" from me, he started narrating, "Netaji gave all the money to me and he has granted me 15 days casual leave. You think that the plane by which you have come was sent to Bangkok from Singapore for your trip. It is Netaji's order by which the plane has been specially chartered to take me to Bangkok."

I wished him a happy holiday. We embraced each other. Suddenly, he took out five hundred rupees worth notes of the Burmese currency and said, "You are new to Rangoon. Take it, you may need it." I was not prepared to accept the money when in his usual authoritative but friendly tone he asked me to shut up and thrusting the currency notes into my bushirt's pocket, Shaukat walked away briskly towards the plane that was waiting for him.

Later I learned that when Netaji held a state banquet to honour the veteran commanders of the Imphal compaign, Dr. Ba Maw, the President of Burma proposed a toast. "Netaji, you hoisted the Tricolour after liberating the Indian territory at Moirang in Manipur state. Here is to your health and future success and glory of the INA." Col. Malik who had already taken some drinks shouted, "Netaji, Netaji, my foot ! I was the man who hoisted the Tricolour after liberating Moirang." Netaji smiled and looked the other way as if he had seen or heard nothing but Col. Habib-ur-Rahman, the Deputy Chief of the Staff, quietly whisked away Col. Malik to a waiting car. Two officers were deputed to escort Shaukat Ali to his residence and to ensure that he took rest and did not come out.

Early next morning Col. Malik felt deeply shocked as he recalled the happenings of the past night. After taking a hurried bath and dressing up in uniform, he took his revolver and drove straight to

Netaji's Bhawan. Netaji used to be at his desk before sunrise. Shaukat met Capt. (later Major) Shamsher Singh, Netaji's ADC and told him that he wanted to see Netaji . When Shamsher Singh reported, Netaji said, "Oh, yes. Where is he? Bring him in." Accordingly, Malik walked in and before he could utter anything, Netaji said, "Jai Hind, Shaukat ! What brings you so early in the morning ?" Standing at attention after saluting Netaji, Shaukat said. "I committed a grave sin last night for which the least punishment that should be awarded to me should be death. Though a Group Commander, I did not award the punishment to me, for that would be an act of suicide and I would be further condemned to hell for the sin."

Thereafter, Col. Malik took out his revolver in both the hands and offered it to Netaji with the request, "Netaji, if you put a bullet into me, I will get my punishment and because of your bullet I shall land straight in the paradise." And he continued sobbing like a child. Netaji stood up, patted his back affectionately and said, "Shaukat, you don't need a bullet. You have been under stress and strain. What you badly need is a few days rest. I will call my plane from Singapore and you will go to Bangkok on 15 days' leave which I grant to you. I will arrange for the wherewithal when the plane is ready."

After my arrival at Mingalodaon, Netaji invited Col. Hussain and me to dinner. That was Netaji's way of knowing his officers who, in turn, also gained from his personal acquaintance. There were three other officers along with us. It was a very frugal dinner. Netaji remarked to his orderly serving us at the table, "We have with us today guests who have come form Singapore. Something special should be served to them."

The orderly said, "Netaji, that is why there are seven green chillies and one banana each for everyone and instead of cooking your khichri, we have made some dal separately and there is some green vegetable also to go with rice." There were neither drinks, soup, nor a sweet course. So simple was Netaji's food!

During the dinner I was pleasantly surprised to see how Netaji looked serene and free from worries, though he was running such a vast organization extended to so many countries. At the sight of the chillies, he gave a loud guffaw of laughter and exclaimed, "Thank

God ! Pundit Sheel Bhadra Yajee is not here otherwise he alone would have consumed all the seven chillies." I did not then know about Pandit Yajee as I know him today. Presently he was the President of the All India Freedom Fighters Organization. When I narrated the incident to Sheel Bhadraji, after the war, Yajeeji said, "It was kind of Netaji to remember me for my chillies which I really relished. In fact, he gave me the name 'Chillie' because of my uncompromising temperament towards injustice."

After the dinner, Netaji took us to the balcony. We had hardly taken our seats when Shamsher Singh came up to report, "Netaji, there is an air raid warning," Netaji replied, "Let it pass." He looked least bothered on that score. And we remained seated on the balcony. Aeroplanes came and flew past overhead without dropping any bomb in Rangoon. Netaji put us certain questions and so did we. It was a very pleasant evening but far more pleasant was the conversation that ensued.

Our Aim

Knowing that Imphal had been lost to us and we had withdrawn from the liberated territories, I asked Netaji that as we and our Allies appeared to have lost the war and there was little hope of our taking to offensive again, what exactly was left for us to fight for? Without the least sign of annoyance, pat came the reply, "To pay the price of India's liberty." His reply was in line with his previous statement: "When the blood of freedom-loving Indians begins to flow, India will attain her freedom."

Thus our National Aim was the attainment of India's freedom and our military objective was to pay the price of India's liberty.

Emboldened by Netaji's receptive and rational attitude, I put him another question, "Presuming that tables are once again turned in our favour and by some miracle we are successful in reaching Delhi and holding our victory parade inside the Red Fort, would Mahatma Gandhi come there to take the salute wearing a military uniform in top boots as he used to wear in South Africa when he led the Indian Ambulance Corps?" I thought I had made a big joke and Netaji would enjoy the humour. Contrary, however, was the effect!

Netaji grew serious and thoughtful. After observing silence that was full of suspense, Netaji said, "No, never, Bapuji is a world reformer first and the Indian leader afterwards, only because he is born in India. It is his creed of non-violence which he has to give to the world. He cannot give up his creed which is the mission of his life." After another long pause in which he appeared to be in a trance, Netaji added: "But I am surprised the way he is helping me. What is there to keep him silent against us? The British Government would gladly and with feeling of gratitude provide him with all the facilities in the Agha Khan Palace where he is imprisoned to broadcast against us. But he is silent. That is the maximum he could do for me. His silence is our greatest help and support. I did not expect so much from him, though on the false news of my death, the message he sent to my mother in 1942, was one of unconditional sorrow. The official message of the Congress Working Committee and other leaders had referred to my differences with them, but not the Bapu."

No wonder, I thought to myself, that Netaji was the first to address him as "The Father of our Nation."

Taking further advantage of Netaji's being so engaging and amiable in discussion, I further inquired as to what would be Pandit Jawaharlal Nehru's attitude towards our victory. Netaji replied, "Pandit ji? Oh! He does not care for violence or non-violence. He will be there to welcome us or oppose us irrespective of whether we are victorious or the vanquished. It all depends upon how he thinks about it at the time."

Today when I look back at the turn of events I wonder how amazingly correct was Netaji's reading of the man. Pandit Jawaharlal Nehru was there at the Red Fort to receive us. We were the vanquished but there stood Jawaharlal Nehru donning the barrister's regalia along with other legal luminaries of India to defend us — Pandit Jawaharlal Nehru after whose name we had one INA brigade, the Nehru Brigade, popularly called "The Nehru." Yet when in power we were to lose Nehru's favour because it did not suit him then, nor did he care to keep the subcontinent undivided. He was for power. Principles? yes when it suited him. India has suffered for half a century because of his mistakes. God knows how long the country will suffer more.

On arrival at Rangoon, we were accommodated in Mingaladon

Camp about fourteen miles from Rangoon city. I was surprised to find Aziz already there waiting for his Divisional Headquarters. Aziz gave me a lot of work and for some time I was the sole Staff Officer looking after all the branches of his Headquarters. My suppressed spirits found an outlet. Aziz was pleased. Hussain, too, had given me an excellent report. Aziz got me appointed temporarily as Deputy Quartermaster General on his staff as the vacancy existed during Maj. Madan's being in transit.

I was also officiating as the Deputy Adjutant General (DAG) and also as the Deputy Quartermaster General (DQMG) in the Divisional Headquarters when the first anniversary of the Provisional Government of Azad Hind came about. As a part of the celebrations of the anniversary, the review of the 2nd Division of the INA was arranged in Mingaladon. It was a part of my duties to make arrangements and issue orders for the ceremonial parade at the vast parade ground. The parade was held on 18th October, 1944.

Netaji Under Fire

Netaji reviewed the parade, addressed the troops and took the salute at the march past. A stage 12' × 12' in dimensions and 5' in height was raised for the occasion. A flag mast about 20 feet high stood in front of the platform. Members of the diplomatic corps, press reporters and special invitees—the Japanese, Indians and Burmans—were seated along the right and left of the stage. In the order for the parade, drafted by me on behalf of the Division Commander, I purposely avoided giving any instructions in respect of action to be taken in case of an air attack. I reasoned out that though the enemy aircraft did cross the Burman skies yet no air raid had taken place for about a year and a specific paragraph on air-raid precautions, if included in the order, would sound to be jittery and superfluous. I was in the wrong.

The parade began in its proper sequence. After the ceremonial review, Netaji stood on the raised platform decorated with red carpet while the Tricolour was fluttering in the air. Some movements of aeroplanes were observed in the sky when Netaji was still addressing the troops. The Japanese planes took off from the nearby aerodrome to intercept the enemy aeroplanes. Behind Netaji, there stood on the stage the Division Commander, Gen. Aziz Ahmad, the Deputy Chief of Staff, Col. Habib-Ur-Rahman and behind him stood Maj. Riaz. on the right hand corner and I on the left hand corner of the plalform.

I stepped forward and softly told my Division Commander to ask Netaji to cut short his speech as the air raid was on. When he stepped forward to inform Netaji, the Supreme Commander ignored his warning as if nothing had happened and continued his speech which was followed by an impressive march past. I watched the proceedings with an added caution as Netaji took the salute of Unit after Unit. It appeared that Netaji was not simply saluting the soldiers passing in front of him but also those in the future free India, the Indian Army of the sovereign state. All this went on when a dog-fight between the enemy and the Japanese planes started overhead.

The march past led by the Rani of Jhansi Regiment and followed by other formations had been half way through when a shrapnel from the air struck one of the men in the last Unit. He fell down and was killed instantly. Shah Nawaz who was present among the visitors sounded a whistle for dispersal. The men dispersed for shelter followed by the invitees and other guests. Netaji, however, did not hasten to climb down from the platform.

I was feeling guilty and held myself responsible for the death of the man. I thought that if I had given the instructions in the order to the effect that the Units would disperse on their own in case of an air attack, I would have neither exposed Netaji nor the spectators, nor the troops on parade to the danger and that man would not have been killed. I escorted Netaji to the nearest trench about a hundred yards away from the stage. Netaji walked with measured steps like a tiger that moves slowly and gracefully without betraying any impression of fear, worry or tension. As I requested Netaji to take shelter in the trench dug under the cover of a tree, he said, "Major Sahib, run up and get report from all the Unit commanders and tell me the fall-out of the air raid on our troops."

The aeroplanes were still in the air and all-clear had not yet been sounded but Netaji did not take to the trench. He kept standing under the branches of the tree till I returned to report that all was O.K. except the man who had fallen dead on the parade ground. Netaji said, "Major Sahib, the death of the man has caused me immense grief but I am afraid I shall not be able to join the funeral in view of the Cabinet meeting which is to be attended by Col. Aziz Ahmad and other Commanders. You will make all arrangements on my behalf to perform the last rites of the martyr with full military honours."

At about four o'clock that afternoon when I was leading the funeral procession, I could not help feeling that I was responsible for that man's death. Then onwards I started fearing whenever any aeroplane, whether hostile or friendly, was in the sky. I thought it had come to punish me. This fear was overcome only later when as a Commander I was under an air attack. Netaji's example of cool and calm demeanour imparted fearlessness that inspired me during the battles to come.

Meanwhile Hussain's Regiment and Division Headquarters arrived. Hussain had got all his machine-guns and most of the equipment of his Regiment sunk en route, somewhere near Moulmein, replacement of which was an impossibility. But that was not my responsibility because the Supreme Headquarters was close at hand to take care of things beyond the approach of the Division Headquarters.

Things appeared to be going fine, when one day I found myself in an awkward situation arising out of the Division Commander's failure to support me against the wrath of the Regimental Commander in the execution of his orders. After the storm was over, I requested Aziz for my transfer. I said 1 did not like to serve on staff. This did make Aziz's position awkward but he was so fair that he asked Netaji for my transfer. When Netaji asked him the reason, Aziz was great enough to say, "I like this Staff Officer but he does not like to serve under me." Netaji remarked, "I would like to see the boy whom the Commander likes and he does not like the Commander."

So Aziz told me and ordered me to go for an interview before Netaji at 1600 hrs. at Netaji Bhawan, Rangoon, the following Sunday. Aziz gave me tips for the interview. "Take your notebook and pencil with you. Netaji does not like to see an Officer without these items on him. Marshal facts and figures concerning your Branch. Do not hesitate to refer to your notes. Netaji does not mind that, but he does mind a wrong answer." Aziz's elderly advice and fatherly concern for one who was running away from him were graceful, indeed. He was magnanimous. There were yet four days to go before the appointed Sunday. Brother Staff Officers, all full of concern for me, kept on serving with various bits of advice till my departure for Netaji Bhawan. I was strongly advised by one and all, against referring to Colonel Bhagat and General Mohan Singh in any way whatsoever, during the interview so that I was not misunderstood.

As for myself, with strange feelings of confidence which only destiny could provide, I looked forward to meeting the Man of Destiny, Netaji Subhas Chandra Bose, the Head of the State of the Provisional Government of Free India and the Supreme Commander of the Indian National Army. I had seen him before, but this was going to be my first formal meeting with him.

12

I Meet Netaji

Meticulously dressed, I presented myself at Netaji Bhawan, Rangoon five minutes before the appointed time on Sunday, the 15th October 1944. A good number of Indian and foreign dignitaries, including two Japanese Generals and General A.C. Chatterjee, the Finance Minister of the Provisional Government of Free India, were already waiting to be received. My turn would take a long time to come, I guessed. It was not so as exactly at 4 p.m. Captain Shamsher Singh, A.D.C. to Netaji, came in to lead me upstairs to a drawing room on the first floor. As I was shown in, Netaji was standing in the door. He acknowledged my "Jai Hind" and shook hands, and asked me about my health.

As soon as we sat down, Netaji started bombarding me with volley after volley of questions concerning the Units under No. 2 Division, their location, strength of arms, equipment, clothing, rations, accommodation, transport, etc. I could gather from his remarks and questions that Netaji was in touch with the latest situation. He was keen to know how the troops relished the changes in different items of food like the red palm oil or the mixed way of cooking everything together with the rice as a "khichri". Having exhausted most of the "A" and "Q" problems of the Division. Netaji asked me a few questions about the training of the troops because for some time I had officiated for the G-1 of the Division as well as for the Deputy Adjutant General (D.A.G.) since the Staff Officers concerned were in transit from Malaya at the time. As advised by Aziz, I did not hesitate to refer to my notebook when I had to check a few figures. I found that I had stood the test well.

And then I was asked a question for which I was not prepared. The dialogue that followed was to the following effect:

Netaji : What is your opinion about the battle-worthiness of the 1st Infantry Regiment ?

I : Very poor; it is not fit for war at all.

Netaji : What do you mean? It is my biggest Brigade.

I : It was, in strength, it still is. But it has had no training during the last four months when I have been with it. It has lost all its heavy arms and machine-guns due to the negligence of its Regimental and Battalion Commanders.

Netaji : How can you blame them for the losses in the face of the enemy air attack ?

I : Surely the attacks were expected. Why did they load all their machine-guns in one boat ? Why were heavy arms not moved with their respective Battalions under their Companies and Platoons so as to be with the men in each Section. We could not have lost all the arms in case they had been suitably dispersed according to the simple procedure of keeping arms with their respective units and sub-units.

Netaji : But this is the only Regiment ready to take part in the coming campaign.

I : Netaji, you may do so only at the cost of your and INA's name and reputation. It is not fair to the men either. Their training has not been carried out since long.

In reply to Netaji's questions I added further details in support of my assessment of the Regiment and specially of its Commander.

After having discussed the Ist Infantry Regiment, Netaji went into the subject that directly concerned me:

Netaji : What had you against Major Rodrigues?

I : I have nothing against him. It was all my fault. I was unnecessarily touchy. I repent having left him and would love to go back to him.

Netaji : And against your present Commander, Colonel Aziz Ahmed ?

I : Again, nothing, I do not get enough scope to use my energies.

Netaji : Under which Commander would you like to be a Staff Officer ?

I : After the removal of Col. Bhagat, I do not see a Commander other than you. I am a combatant but I have been on staff far too long. I like to be a Commander now. If my seniority is not enough to get me a Brigade, I won't mind commanding a Battalion or even a Company. (I had mentioned Colonel Bhagat in spite of and against the advice of my colleagues, yet Netaji appeared to have paid no attention to my remark concerning Colonel Bhagat and he went on.)

Netaji : But if staff job is a must, what will be your choice?

I : I would like to go back to Rodrigues, the 5th Guerrilla Regiment, failing which the Supreme Headquarters is my next choice.

Netaji : I shall see what can be done. Meanwhile I want you to let me have your remarks about the 1st Infantry Regiment on paper. You need not sign it. I just need the details to put up before the Cabinet.

I : I do not mind signing it, Sir. When do you want it ?

Netaji : Captain Shamsher Singh will collect it from your place any time after 4 p.m. on Tuesday. Will it suit you ?

I : Yes sir, I will have it ready by then.

Netaji : How did you come ? Have you a transport to go back ?

I : Netaji, I came by a staff car, which is waiting for me.

Netaji : (Smilingly) Have you enough gas in it ?

I : Yes, sir.

Netaji stood up. I followed suit and saluted "Jai Hind". Netaji responded and shook hands. As advised, Shamsher Singh saw me off. I returned to the Camp where my colleagues and the Commander were waiting to ask me all sorts of questions. My reply had perforce to be evasive. Things were either secret or of too personal a nature to be mentioned. Shamsher Singh came to collect the report on Tuesday evening. I handed him a sealed envelop which contained the letter marked 'Secret' and duly signed by me. I do not know, how Netaji used it but till today my secret has been kept completely and entirely.

A few days after this interview, Aziz sent for me and told me that he had been asked by Netaji to inquire from me whether I would accept the command of the Nehru Brigade, if offered. Aziz went into telling me all the details about the Brigade, specially its weakness. Aziz told me that Netaji had instructed him to be very particular to inform me about the adverse points concerning "The Nehru". Aziz was very frank and he hid nothing. Aziz who had raised "The Nehru" was pleased to learn that I was willing to accept the offer. But he told me that Netaji had given me four days to think and then decide.

I was again called by Netaji on 26th October when he was preparing to leave a day after for a conference in Tokyo. He was in his living room, a very small place with one door. On entering, to the right was a bed and to the left a writing table and a dressing table. There were hardly one and a half paces between the bed and the two tables forming a straight passage to a window on the yonder wall opposite the door. There was only one chair. All these pieces of furniture were covered with spread out files and papers. As I entered, Netaji was standing by the window examining certain documents placed on the window sill. I saluted "Jai Hind". Netaji left the file and advanced to greet me and to shake hands. We remained standing and the conversation was something like the following:

Netaji : Major Dhillon ! After meeting you, I have thought of entrusting to you the command of the Nehru Brigade which is the only one now on the front; so it will give you an opportunity to do something.

I : Thank you, Netaji.

Netaji : Hold on. Before you accept the command, let there be no illusion in your mind because it is a very difficult job. I want you to know that it is under-strength and deficient in arms, equipment and vehicles. It is short of officers and staff. Without a permanent Commander, its discipline is anything but satisfactory. Six hundred of its men are under trial for mutiny. Recently, they have suffered very heavy casualties when the Camp was bombed by the enemy. The coming operations are expected to be more difficult as the enemy is on the advance. You must know, two officers senior to you have not accepted it. Again, the INA is going to get an independent role in the future campaign. It is a very difficult job, indeed. Do you accept it under these circumstances ?

I : Netaji, I accept it. Some one has to do the job.

Netaji : (Shaking hands). Thank you very much.

I : Netaji! May I know how long will it take me to get into touch with the enemy ?

Netaji : Well, you are already on the foremost defended locality. There are no positions held between you and the enemy. It all depends how long the enemy takes to reach the Irrawaddy. The initiative lies with him. You may be lucky to get sixty to seventy days before you are attacked, I guess.

I : If I get that much time, I assure you, "*Keh main ap ki aankhen kisi ke samne nichi na hone doonga*" (I will not let you down before anybody).

Netaji : I have confidence.

I : Netaji, under the circumstances, may I request to be allowed to reorganize my Brigade, without getting prior permission from the Division Headquarters? I ask for this favour with a view to saving time.

Netaji : You may, if you have to, but do keep me and the higher formation informed, with a copy to each.

I : Thank you, sir, I shall do that. Now as I do not have a Second-in-Command, may I ask for Major Jagir Singh to be posted to "The Nehru"? Having worked together in the Army Headquarters, we know each other well. He is cool and calm and a capable officer. I hope we will make a good team.

Netaji : Jagir is the blue eyed boy of Colonel Zaman, the Army Commander. I do not promise but will try to get him for you.

I : Thank you, Sir. May I be given Rs. 10,000/- here in Rangoon, out of the non-auditable funds allowed to a Brigade Commander on his appointment?

Netaji : Yes, but may I know why do you ask for it here when you will get it on your assuming command?

I : I have some "Nehru" troops, sick and wounded in the General Hospital. Some of them are in the Reinforcement Camp waiting to join their Units. So far, whenever I visited them and if they asked for anything, I put it down in the suggestion book and as a Staff Officer I felt, I had done my duty. Now if they ask me for anything, I would like to dig into my pocket and say, "Here, my boy, take it". I want them to feel that they have a Commander to father them. There are a few officers, newly commissioned, ready to join me on their first appointment. A bit of extra money will help equip themselves with certain items which they may badly need and may not be able to get once they are at the Front.

Netaji : Good idea. You will get the amount tomorrow at your bungalow. By the way, your staff car and a truck that had been loaned to the Gandhi Brigade are in workshop. I saw them today. Those vehicles have been repaired and overhauled. Take them with you along with as many of your troops as possible. Have you anything more to ask?

I : No, Sir. Thank you.

Netaji : Then, may I ask you for one thing?

I : Sir.

Netaji : The six hundred or so men who are standing their trial by court martial on the charge of mutiny are South Indians. They are not against the Independence Movement. On the contrary they are more for it, the South having suffered for a longer time under the British than the North. But they do not like to be bullied or ordered about. It is a case of misunderstanding and bad man management on the part of the Commander, and the officers concerned. Whatever the merits or demerits of the case, they are going to get long terms. But I do not want them to suffer even for a day. I have asked senior officers if they would agree to accept these men back in the Army. They have not agreed. I do not wish to thrust these boys on anyone, yet I want them back. Are you prepared to accept them.

I : Yes, Netaji, I accept them.

Netaji : Thank you very much, I feel relieved (Netaji said shaking hands once again and then went on to add).

Let me tell you one thing about our South Indian jawans.' They are second to none where fighting for freedom is concerned. I have often found that if a problem is posed to them, they always volunteer to do the job and then go to any limit to stick to the given word. I suggest that you, too, approach them as I do. Pose or propose a problem. They will volunteer to do the job, appreciating your courtesy and will love to work and die for you. Understanding the nature of men you lead, is the most important factor in commanding them. Once you understand them and they understand you, you can order them about as you like. They will obey you and love to work for you. Look at me, I am at times very harsh with them but they have never let me down. They do anything I ask for.

I : Thank you, Sir. Nobody can reach your standards, but I shall try my best. Can I have Lt. Narayanan to be attached to me to serve as an interpreter ?

Netaji : I am afraid not, I have a job for him. You better find someone else out of your own men. Any other point ?

I : No, Sir. Thank you very much.

Netaji : Well, good luck, my best wishes are with you. Jai Hind.

I sprang up to attention and, saluted 'Jai Hind'. Netaji shook hands and we departed.

The following day, 27th October 1944, Netaji left for Tokyo via Bangkok accompanied by Chatterji, Zaman Kiani, and Habib-ur-Rehman. There was quite a crowd of senior officers and V.I.Ps to bid them farewell at Mingaladon airport. I was also present there. Aziz who was to officiate as Supreme Commander during Neetaji's absence told me on way back from the airport that Netaji had remarked to him pointing towards me, "Look at Dhillon, how happy and smart he looks? Brigade Commander *ho gaya hai na*. Now that he has become a Brigade Commander, I hope he will do well. Do help him for whatever possible?"

13

The Nehru

The 4th Guerrilla Regiment, the Nehru Brigade, popularly called the Nehru, was raised during General Mohan Singh's G.O.C.-ship by Major Aziz Ahmed in September 1942 at Singapore. Originally Aziz Ahmed belonged to and commanded Kapurthala State's Ist Infantry Regiment. He saw active service during Malaya Campaign. He was a staunch nationalist and was one of the first to volunteer for the INA after the British surrender of Singapore. Coming from one of the outstanding landlords of Kapurthala state, Aziz had a very pleasant disposition with a commanding personality. Men and Officers adored him and looked up to him for guidance and help. Of a literary bent of mind, it was a pleasure to be in his company and to work with him. He was a great believer in the cause of independence of India. He enjoyed General Mohan Singh's and later Netaji's confidence. He was one of the prominent members of the Azad Hind Government.

The Regiment was composed of three battalions, the 7th, 8th and the 9th along with Regimental Headquarters, out of the following Indian Army Units:

7th Guerrilla Bn. :	2/16 and 3/16 Punjab	: 4 Coys
	Regt. H.K. S.R.A.	: 1 Coy
8th Guerrilla Bn. :	4/19 Hyderabad Regt.	: 4 Coys
	H.K.S.R.A.	: 1 Coy
9th Guerrilla Bn. :	7/6 Rajputana Rifles	: 2 Coys
	Gurkhas & Garhwalis	: 3 Coys

Further strength was added out of the civilian volunteers, mainly South Indians, after the INA crisis of December 1942. According to the War Establishment, the total strength of the Brigade was 3,000 Officers and Other Ranks as shown below :

	Officers	Other Ranks	Total
Regt. Hqrs.	9	24	33
7th Bn.	25	964	989
8th Bn.	25	964	989
9th Bn.	25	964	989
Total	84	2,916	3,000

"The Nehru" was raised as part of the Sher-dil Guerrilla Group. The other two Regiments were The Gandhi and The Azad. The Group I Headquarters was not formed and each Regiment operated as an independent Brigade directly under the INA Headquarters as far as the chain of command was concerned. These Units later formed parts of No. 1 and No. 2 Divisions. Towards the end of 1943, "The Nehru" was put under the First Division. It moved to Burma in early 1944 and arrived at Mandalay. During the Imphal Campaign it was kept in reserve. In April 1944 Aziz was appointed No. 2 Division Commander in Malaya, relieving Col. N.S. Bhagat. Col. R.M. Arshad, till then the G-l of No. 1 Division, was appointed Commander of The Nehru. Arshad was re-appointed to his original post of G-1 in July 1944. He was succeeded by Major Mohd. Azim Khan Rana.

"The Nehru" did excellent work during the evacuation of No. 1 Division. Though in reserve and not committed to the front line combat, "The Nehru" did undergo all the hardships under battle conditions. Its strength depleted by providing reinforcements to different units on the Front and due to sickness. While at Mandaley, under Rana's command, a serious disciplinary case amounting to mutiny occurred involving about 600 men. The case was yet to be decided when the Unit moved to Myingyan and Rana was replaced by Major (later Colonel) Mahboob Ahmed. Mahboob had just taken over the Brigade and was in the process of getting into grips with the various difficult problems when he was appointed Military Secretary to Netaji at the Supreme Headquarters, Rangoon. I was ordered to replace Mahboob at Myingyan.

I Command "The Nehru"

On getting the appointment orders, I was man in a hurry to go to Myimgyan to take over my command. I handed over 'Q' branch of No. 2 Div. to Major Madan, its respective incumbent who had just arrived from Malaya. I got busy with preparations for my new job collecting here and there whatever I could. Calling on different Units and Headquarters to sort out administrative problems was important before leaving Rangoon. Farewell functions, too, demanded quite a time.

Captain Miss Janki Thever, officiating Officer Commanding of the Rani Jhansi Brigade and the officers invited me to tea. Actually, it was coffee— good old South Indian coffee. On my appreciating the richness of its taste and flavour, they were good enough to send me four pounds of the coffee powder before my departure the next day. In those days it was a very expensive gift with which I served my guests during my stay at Myingyan.

Lieut. Colonel Ogawa, then officiating Head of the Hikari Kikan (the Japanese Liaison Department) invited me to dinner where we discussed various problems. It was during this dinner that Ogawa introduced to me Captain Izumi who was to be the Liaison Officer with me. In Captain Izumi, I discovered a brave, respectful, co-operative and efficient Liaison Officer. He never gave me any cause to complain against Hikari Kikan during the period I was in command of an independent sector. Not that he could solve all the problems facing me, but I had never to doubt his intentions. Our problems were indeed insurmountable, but he did his best to solve them. At times, I was strict with him but he, in return, was always obedient and accommodating.

I had been at Rangoon for a very short time during which I happened to come into touch with Mr. Dina Nath and Sardar Zora Singh, timber merchants, and Mr. S.M. Bashir who owned a rubber factory. In addition to these friends, I met Shri Parma Nand, who donated Ziawadi Estate and Sugar Factory, Mr. and Mrs. Betai who donated seven lakhs of rupees, Mr. Habib who donated one crore and three lakhs rupees apart from all his moveable and immoveable belongings, Shri S.A. Krishnan, formerly an Officer of the Burma Oil

Company and many more V.I.P.s whom I met later in Rangoon Jail. They were among the pillars of Azad Hind Bank and the Supply Department of the Indian Independence League. It was largely due to their efforts that Netaji's call of Total Mobilization became a reality. They were the backbone of the Provisional Government of Free India.

Bashir was a good friend of Aziz. I often accompanied Aziz while visiting Bashir. These casual visits developed into a very precious friendship with Bashir's children. All the ladies and other members of the Bashir family were evacuated to India in 1942. They left behind four children in order to save them from the hazards of the journey across the Indo-Burma border. The eldest amongst them, Balqees was a daughter hardly seven years of age. Like all good children, they hated drinking. Though himself a tee-totaller, Bashir was a generous host and would offer drinks to his guests. As I did not drink then, having taken a vow not to drink until India became free, these children started taking a great liking for me which grew into a very affectionate relationship.

When these children learnt that I was to go to the Front, they gave me a special send-off dinner and prayed for my success and safety in the war. They gave me a T-shirt in khaki colour which I valued as a treasure. Although I lost all my belongings during the war, except the clothes on my body and a few things in a haversack, this shirt was still with me till I arrived at the Red Fort. It always reminded me of those children and their innocent faces praying for me with their open small hands stretched out towards the sky, which elevated my spirits immensely. I was only to see them again when they visited me in Rangoon Jail after the war.

To Myingyan

At dusk on 7th November 1944, a staff car and a 15-cwt. truck left Rangoon for Mandalay carrying about 20 personnel including me, Captain Izumi, 2nd Lieut. Gian Singh Bisht and a Japanese interpreter Private Sakaguchi and Mehar Singh, my batman. I had to report to No. 1 Division Headquarters at Mandalay before joining "The Nehru" at Myingyan which was then under No. 1 Division. Gian Singh Bisht was a young Garhwali officer recently commissioned at the INA Officers' Training School, Neesoon in Singapore. Gian Singh was destined to be the hero and martyr at the battle of Taungzin during the coming March while leading "The Charge of the Immortals".

The enemy was very strong in the air. Our movement was possible only by night and that too without lights. The progress was, thus, slow and straining the nerves. We had to stop dead, every now and then, switch off the engines, check up the sky for the enemy planes and only then proceed. At the slightest hint of a sound of an aircraft we had to pull ourselves off the road, under the trees and remain there till the drone of the planes was dead and gone. There were many a hair's-breadth escape during this journey. We travelled via Toungoo, Pyinmana, Meiktila and Kyaukse. As we got 5 miles short of Kyaukse and pulled up under two solitary mango trees for a routine check up of the skies, we heard no sound and were going just to proceed onward when the car refused to start. This was a very lucky coincidence.

We were pushing the car to start it when an enemy aircraft suddenly appeared from the east out of the sun's rays and started encircling the spot where we were. Leaving the car where it was under the tree, we made for the fields on right and left of the road. There was little cover except small spread out bushes which we kept on encircling along with the movement of the aircraft, thus keeping the bush between us and the aircraft. The aircraft had apparently spotted us before we had stopped. It would surely have bagged us if the car had not let us down or say helped us at the right moment. The plane kept on its search over us for about fifteen long minutes before it went away. Just then we heard it machine-gun and bomb. When the sound had completely died out, we commenced the journey and round the corner saw a bus burning with bodies roasting in it and a nearby hut in flames. Our escape was, indeed, providential.

From Kyaukse I sent the truck and the personnel under Gian Singh direct to Myingyan while I proceeded to Mandalay. Captain Izumi and the Japanese interpreter accompanied me. We arrived at Mandaley on the 11th morning at dawn. Col. R.M. Arshad was the officiating Division Commander, Major N.N. Khosla was the D.Q.M.G. We had worked together in the INA Army Headquarters at Bidadari Camp, Singapore, from where they had come over to Burma and I remained behind to join the 5th Guerrilla Regiment which was then being raised. It was a pleasure meeting old friends and colleagues. This was to be my last meeting with Khosla. He was killed in a bombing raid after a couple of weeks later.

After the formalities of reporting were over, they took me to different camps and the General Hospital where I met some of my jawans. I arranged for their joining "The Nehru" at Myingyan as soon as possible. At the Hospital I met Major Lakshmi (later Lt. Col.), Commander of the legendary Rani Jhansi Brigade. She was at that time commanding a detachment of the Rani Jhansi soldiers serving as nurses in the Hospital. Lakshmi herself was serving as a doctor. Mandalay is famous for its magnificent pagodas, but we were too hard pressed for time to go sight seeing. Even then they did take me to show one pagoda on the top of a hill. Its grandeur was, indeed, astonishing.

The next day, the 12th November we left for Myingyan where we arrived early 13th morning. Mahboob, who had taken over the command hardly about four days ago, welcomed us with his usual grace. The day was spent visiting the three Battalion Headquarters spread out over a twenty-five mile area around Myingyan in which our troops were bivouacked in the villages. After handing over "The Nehru" to me, Mahboob left late at night for Rangoon to join his new appointment as Military Secretary at the Supreme Headquarters replacing Sahgal who got command of the 5th Guerrilla Regiment, later organized as the 2nd Infantry Regiment.

The first thing that struck me on taking over the command was the wearing of civilian clothes by all the Ranks. This they did to avoid being spotted from above, for the enemy enjoyed complete command of the skies. More than a hundred men had been killed here recently. The spirit of the men had suffered and their morale had reached its lowest ebb. There were neither parades, nor training during the day. The digging of trenches for the defence of Myingyan was done only at night and that, too, when there was no moonlight. It was not a happy situation at all. But I was not disillusioned. Netaji had hidden nothing from me. There were no surprises. All the same, it was a great challenge that I had willingly accepted with full knowledge of the state of affairs in the Regiment.

My first action was to address all Officers and jawans, Battalion-

MYINGYAN SETTING

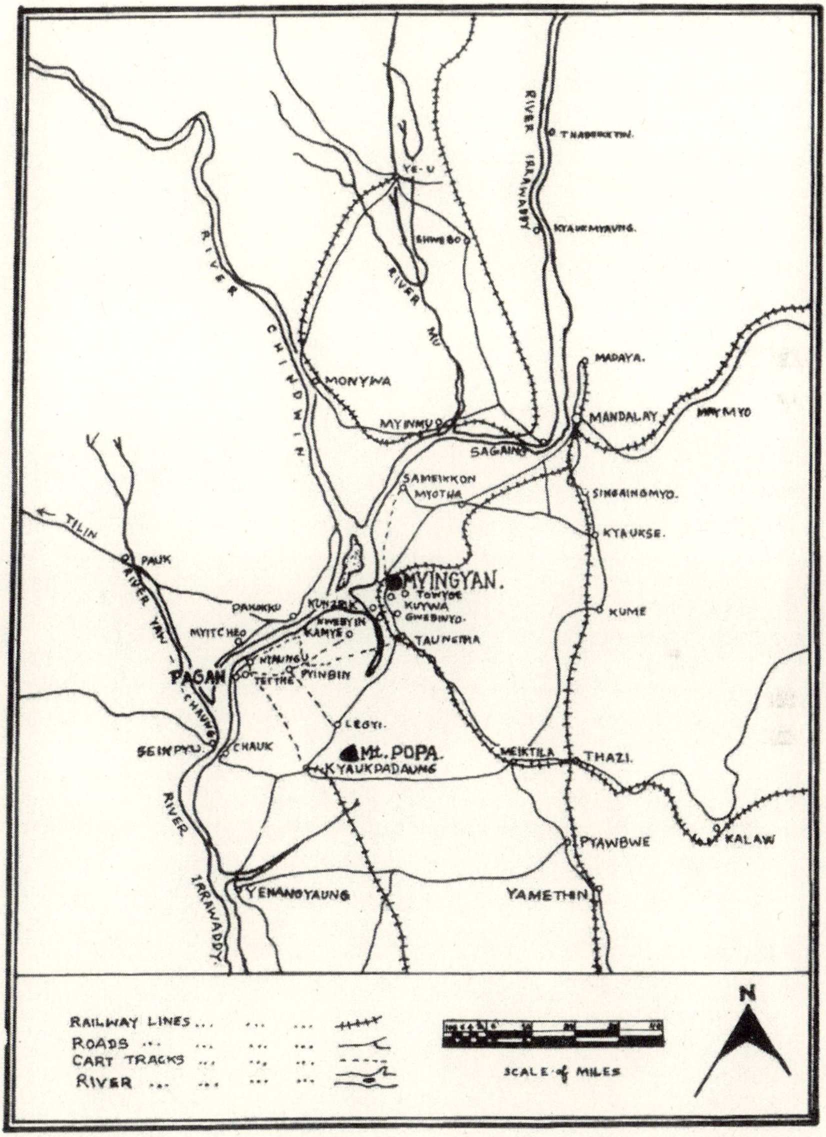

wise within twenty-four hours of my arrival. Their response was encouraging. Their face brightened at the very mention of Netaji's name. They made me feel that they would go with me all the way. Addressing them every month in this way generated a permanent bond between me and my men.

Secondly, I called a Unit Commanders' Conference in which I said that henceforth uniform would be worn by all Ranks at all times. We were already at the battle station. To build up discipline which is the bedrock of morale, foot drill was made compulsory apart from training in tactics and weapons. A Battalion Commander pointed out that it would be too dangerous to put the men on drill in view of the air activities of the enemy. I explained that during a battle we would have to face land forces of the enemy in addition to their aircrafts. How would we do that if we could not train ourselves now ? A Bn. Commander inquired, "Who would be responsible for the casualties ?" Quoting Napoleon's maxim that "Training is war and war is training" I insisted that training would not stop because of the fear of casualties. Confidence can never be built up without training and without confidence you can fight no battle. Training under the prevailing conditions would go a long way to make the jawans battle worthy. Hardship and danger destroy fewer people than indulgence does.

Thirdly, I ordered that I would see all the Officers including Sub-Officers individually, with a view to creating personal contact with them and knowing their problems and grievances, whether personal, political or Regimental. I also granted this privilege to all Other Ranks for ten days if anyone wanted to have an interview with me. I intended to finish interviewing all within this period. This abnormal step was dictated by the prevailing abnormality. Again, personal contact between the Commander and the members of a revolutionary force, I believed, was essential. It was during these meetings that some men came out with such information as proved useful in my day-to-day dealings with them and for making certain necessary changes while reorganizing the Brigade.

Fourthly, I started a daily Battalion Commanders' Conference starting at 2200 hours at my Headquarters. These conferences brought me closer to the Battalion Commanders and their problems. In a week's time, subjects of important and immediate nature were exhausted and daily conferences were accordingly discontinued. The knowledge, thus gathered, was not of a pleasant nature. The Regiment had suffered greatly under Rana's harmful and negative policy unworthy of a revolutionary army.

MYINGYAN, the district headquarters of the Myingyan district situated at the confluence of the Chindwin and the Irrawaddy, had a strategic position as a river port. Both these rivers have been important highways of Burma since the dawn of history. They are navigable by fairly big steamers from the sea as far north as Myitkyina on the Irrwaddy and Tamanthi on the Chindwin. A railway runs through Myithkyina in the north. It is also connected with metalled and motorable roads running in various directions up and down on the east of the Irrawaddy valley. Its very location as an important point on the lines of communication made it conspicuous for the attacker as well as the defender.

"The Nehru" was deployed in the Myingyan area with the object of defending it against enemy attack which appeared imminent consequent on our withdrawal from Imphal. By the middle of November 1944 when I arrived at Myingyan, "The Nehru" was to prepare itself to meet against an attack from all sides except the west, where the waters were wide and stretches of soft sand treacherous and broad, which made the place too formidable to allow any crossing of a mechanized column on a big scale against the defending forces.

Taking advantage of the topography of the area, a long anti-tank obstacle was dug to add to the natural hurdles. Special attention was paid to the road approaching Myingyan from Sameikkon ferry, some twenty mils up north across the Irrawaddy.

This road was joined by another road coming from Kyaukse before it entered the town. By attacking from the north the enemy would have taken advantage of this road because a number of roads running north and south either joined it or crossed it—on the south, the road coming from Taungtha, an important railway station at the junction of the two highways one coming from Kyaukpadaung and the other from Meiktila - apart from other unmetalled roads from the ferry stations of Pakokku and Nyaungu. This area was dominated by hills commanding the plains lying on the west of Taungatha–

Myingyan road. We planned to hold the hills so as to cover the enemy approach from the south and the south-east.

There were no other troops except "The Nehru" in the Myingyan area, neither Japanese nor Burmese nor INA. I was an independent commander within the operational jurisdiction of the Japanese 15th Army, who were responsible for the overall strategy and operations. One of their officers, Major Ogawa designated as the Japanese Garrison Commander - not to be mistaken for Col. Ogawa of the Hikari Kikan—was the only Japanese Officer with a small detachment of about one Section strong who formed a link between me and the Japanese Army Headquarters for the two-way liaison.

He was there to convey to me their intentions and the plans. Ogawa had no authority to interfere in my command; his duty was to convey the orders of the Army Commander. The task of coordination and co-operation among the allies is always a difficult job. Our difficulties were naturally aggravated at times due to our different national outlooks, linguistic difficulties, lack of resources, differences in training and psychological approach. Yet I will submit with all the earnestness at my command that the way Ogawa and Izumi co-operated with me left a very favourable and everlasting impression on me.

After all, the Japanese were not fighting our war, nor were we fighting their's. It was just historical coincidence that we had a common foe to fight. We, therefore, needed Japanese support more than they needed ours. It would amount to ingratitude on my part if I did not appreciate all they did for me and my men. There was only one unpleasant discussion between Ogawa and me in the early stage of my arrival at Myingyan but once policy matters were decided, we commanded each other's reciprocal respect, courtesy and co-operation. Ogawa was an elderly person and of my father's age. I was hardly 29 at that time. We were of the same rank but by virtue of my senior appointment as a Brigade Commander I enjoyed precedence over him.

It did not take me long to understand that if I were to fulfil my word to Netaji, I would have to work round the clock like him. While at Rangoon, I had learnt about Netaji's capacity to work for 22 hours at a stretch each day for weeks together. I thought that being far younger than he, I should be able to follow his example. There was paucity of time but a lot of work to do and time could only be gained by burning midnight oil. There was no other way out. Accordingly, I drew up a fairly tight daily schedule for me.

I would arrive at a Unit location about half an hour before sunrise and remain in the field till sunset moving from one place to another, inspecting and watching my men digging or training. I would manage ten to fifteen minutes sleep. In the evening I conducted my round of interviews held either at my Headquarters or at the respective Battalion or Company Headquarters. Having finished interviews, I would have my dinner to which some of the officers were invited. After dinner, time permitting I would attend to my office work till 10 p.m. when the Battalion Commanders' conference followed which invariably took about two hours. Thereafter I would take up the office work and finish it before retiring for about an hour, so as to start the next day.

I was grateful to my Battalion Commanders and staff officers who warmly responded to the strenuous routine without which, it would have been impossible for me to work. In this connection, I cannot help admiring the never-failing support I enjoyed from the Brigade Adjutant, Captain Darwan Singh Rawat and the Brigade Intelligence Officer, Lieutenant Mohinder Singh, previously both N.C.Os of the 2/18th Garhwal Regiment. They were trained and commissioned at the INA Officers' Training School, Singapore. No less was the part played by my Quartermaster, Lieut. Khan who had to arrange for the distribution of rations and supplies during the night and often catch me for getting signatures in the porch of my bungalow, as I would be sitting in the car to start for the day.

I am sorry for not being able to recall the full name of Khan nor his previous Unit, but I do remember that he too was an INA Commissioned Officer. He was also a good driver and a mechanic. It was due to his resourcefulness that our two 15-cwt. trucks and the staff car were kept on road. He was at the time helped by a Unit of our Civilian Supply Department under Paras Ram, who arranged fresh items of rations, i.e. vegetable, meat, edible oils, fish and eggs locally. Items like rice, sugar and 'dal' were arranged by Izumi from the Japanese stores. Petrol and lubricants were also supplied by the Japanese. The distribution was entirely Khan's responsibility. Having had personal experience of officiating as a Battalion Quartermaster during the British days and as D.Q.M.G. at INA headquarters, I have no hesitation in recording that the supply system notwithstanding the air raids of the enemy at that time worked to my satisfaction.

As I have already submitted, any vehicular movement by day was risky in those days. Enemy planes would not spare even a bullock-cart. To think of moving by a staff car with a flag fluttering on its bonnet was out of question. I was, however, determined to show and prove to my men that with proper vigilance, by posting air sentries along the road, movement could be carried out during day time also. Besides saving time and energy, this action served as a morale booster. Further, it gave me time to sleep while travelling.

A Rape Case

One of the most important factor which helps a guerrilla is the goodwill of the people of the area he has to operate in. No guerrilla can ever successfully operate in an area without the help of the local people, whatever the resources at his disposal. And the easiest way to achieve it is to show respect to the womenfolk and the property of the local people. Three days after my arrival, on 16th November I observed during a Battalion Commanders' Conference that the people of village Kuywa did not receive me with a smile which I received in other villages. I asked the Commander concerned to check up why the villagers were unhappy with us. The Battalion Commander assured me that there was nothing wrong, and that their dealings with the villagers were good.

After the Conference, however, Captain Gurdial Singh, the Brigade Medical Officer, saw me alone and confirmed that my observation was correct. On 11th November there had been a rape case by one of the men of that Battalion. On the basis of this information, the case was investigated, the culprit apprehended and an identification parade held. The offender was recognized by five out of the seven witnesses including the girl. He was a Tamil boy. I asked his Platoon mates as to what punishment should be awarded to him. They all said that he should be shot. When I inquired as to who would shoot him, each one of them volunteered as an executioner. I gave a choice to the offender whether he would like to undergo summary trial by me or be produced before Netaji. The man's reply was that he would prefer to be shot than to be produced before Netaji.

Before going to the village to attend the identification parade, I had arranged to get the headmen of the neighbouring villages and elders invited to a meeting where I intended to address them to apologize for this misconduct of my man. Men of the Battalion concerned were also present there along with the villagers of Kuywa. The offender was produced before me in the presence of all the Burmese gathered there. To this assemblage I announced that having been empowered by the Head of the Provisional Government of Free India and the Supreme Commander of the INA, Netaji Subhas Chandra Bose, I was going to sentence the man to death by shooting. As I made the announcement, I was surprised that the husband, the father-in-law, along with the headmen and a few elders of the village came forward and prostrated themselves before me to beg for mercy for the life of the culprit. When I did not accept their request to pardon the culprit, elders made the girl appeal to me to save the man.

The girl who on recognizing the culprit had shown a feeling of triumph in her eyes for having caught the criminal, was now full of compassion pleading for mercy for the man who had outraged her modesty. Such was the effect of the announcement. I was in a fix. Just before announcing the punishment, I had given awards amounting to two thousand rupees to different persons including the unfortunate girl and her husband for helping me and my staff in unearthing the crime. I made it specifically clear that these awards were in no way any compensation but a recognition of the help rendered to us in digging up the crime. The crime was not of such a nature which could ever be compensated.

The merciful attitude of the Burmese was highly appreciable. Drawing a sharp contrast and comparison between the spirit of humanity shown by the local people and the wickedness of the crime committed, I told my officers and men and specially to the offender, "Look at them and look at your self. What a difference ! What grace ! What mercy ! We are in their country as their guests". Horrified the offender who had been standing still all this time fell down. Captain Gurdial Singh, the Brigade Medical Officer, who ran our Regimental Hospital bivouacked in that very village, knelt down to examine the man. Gurdial told me that there was nothing serious; the man had merely swooned and he would be all right soon.

I announced to the gathering that my verdict was final and the boy would be shot as soon as the Doctor declared him fit. The boy was removed on a stretcher to the Hospital under an armed escort. The village elders kept on pleading for mercy, but I showed firmness in sticking to my judgment and dispersed the meeting. Before returning to my Headquarters, I visited the boy in the Hospital. He stood up as I entered the hut which had been turned into a ward. I asked him, "Do you wish to be shot here or sent to Netaji"? His reply was, "Sir, do whatever you like but for God's sake do not make me show my face to Netaji." The man was repentant. "*Ab mein Netaji Ko Kiya moonh dikhaoonga?* I have no face to face Netaji" The punishment I felt had served its purpose.

His Battalion Commander was ordered that the boy was not to be shot, but posted immediately to a place sixteen miles away. Having made these arrangements, news was issued that the man was shot. Meanwhile, I reported the entire incident to Netaji in a secret letter. He endorsed my action. Here I may submit that as a Brigade Commander I had powers vested in me to try summarily cases of desertion, rape and looting. The penalty included death.

I was obliged by the Burmese and their officials when in the beginning of December, the Japanese Divisional Commander came to visit the area. In the evening there was a dinner at the Deputy Commissioner's residence. In his formal speech, the Deputy Commissioner, an elderly person with a scholarly disposition, praised the discipline of our troops and addressing the General added words to the effect, "Your Excellency, I would like to point out that the Burmese authorities and people are very happy to have the INA troops stationed in our area. They never give us any cause of complaint. On the contrary, I would like to suggest to the young and energetic Indian Commander, that he need not be so strict in dealing with his troops. I understand that recently, he has committed one of his men to death because of a rape case. While we appreciate his stand, we would like to submit that out of thousands of troops, there are bound to be a few black sheep. It cannot be helped. Some cases of indiscipline are bound to occur. I appeal to him in your presence, to remit the sentence and I assure him that I will not report it to my Government nor to his Government and the Supreme Commander."

Thanking the Burmese authorities, specially the Deputy Commissioner, I made it clear in my reply that guerrillas could not operate in an area without the goodwill of the people, which was the greatest and most powerful military asset. The man had been condemned and executed and that I had already reported the matter to my Government and to Netaji. I appreciated from the core of my heart the magnanimity, mercy and elderly advice of the District Head, but at the same time submitted that I would never tolerate any indiscipline amongst my men specially of the nature which was to endanger our existing cordial relations with the Government and the people of our host country.

The dinner was attended, among others, by the Burmese District Officers and quite a number of local leaders. The atmosphere was official and procedures of diplomatic corps adopted, the General representing the Japanese side, the Deputy Commissioner for the Burmese Government and I for the Indian side. Only the three of us spoke. The effect was salutary and our existing relations with the Burmese, which were already cordial, grew better. Shortage of fresh vegetables, meat and milk which could have caused us difficulties started to flow in great quantities. I came to be recognized in the countryside wherever I might go. Children would shout, "*Se-Bhuji Dhillon*, Jai Hind". At times even disputes among the locals were brought before me for settlement. Once a father complained against his son. When I asked them to go to the civil court, the contending parties said that they would prefer arbitration by me, rather than going to the court. I had to be careful not to get involved in local disputes, whatever their nature might be. It was neither my job, nor did I have any time for it. Any interference in the local administration would have annoyed the Burmese authorities for no self-respecting people can tolerate a foreign interference, least the Burmese. It had salutary effect on my men.

Men Did it

Major Ogawa told me that the Japanese Army Headquarters

wanted the defence of Myingyan to be completed within a month. Rana had asked for three months to complete it. Ogawa asked me if I could do it within a month and half. Having had a round of the area, I told Ogawa that I could not afford to spend more than a week on digging trenches and piling up stone defences 'sanghers' on the hills where digging was not possible. I told him that he could ask the Army Headquarters to inspect the work after a week. Expressing his doubts about the time limit, Ogawa remarked that I did not have the power to create miracles. He added that even the Japanese troops could not do the job within a week.

After a long discussion we agreed to ten days. Actually, I had already discussed the issue with my Battalion Commanders and we had decided to finish the job as quickly as possible before we started putting our troops through an intensive course in weapon training and tactics. Our plan was to post air sentries and work round the clock by relief. Apart from finishing the job, this action would serve as practical training in defying the enemy's air power, and thus help in building the fighting spirit of the troops. I did not give more than seven days to the Units to complete their task. The extra three days I kept for checking the completion by me and Battalion Commanders, so as to improve them and rectify any shortcomings, where necessary. On the eleventh day, Ogawa was amazed when I told him to send the completion report to the Army Headquarters. He asked me how I could achieve all this. My answer was, "My men did it". Ogawa reported the progress to the authorities and we were congratulated on the achievement.

Colonel Arshad Visits

Towards the end of November or in the first week of December, Col. Raja Mohammad Arshad, who was the officiating Division Commander, visited us. He knew my problems better than I did. He was not in the habit of talking much. I had always approached him with a feeling of respect and awe. During the inspection, he was so much impressed by our work, specially the anti-air defence arrangements and our movement by road by day and night. When I requested him to spend a few days in Myingyan and help us in training, he very kindly agreed.

Death of a Friend

Unfortunately, early next morning, Izumi brought a wireless message that there had been a heavy air raid at No. 1 Division Headquarters at Mandalay, in which Major N.N. Khosla had been killed. Khosla and I were great friends. The news of his death so deeply shocked me that for once it appeared that the world had come to an end. I would not be able to work, I feared. I could regain self-control only through will power and concentration on the immediate task before me. "The Nehru" was not more than 11,00 strong at the time of my taking over the command; the arrival of 600 South Indian jawans whom I had accepted along with a few more drafts from Mandalay and Rangoon added to my strength and gave me a respectable size.

Anecdote

Troops bivouacking in villages create quite a few problems. Beside Kuywa there was a toddy shop plum on the highway. It required to be watched and placed out of bounds for troops. Once while passing that way, I saw an N.C.O. in a drunken state, trying to cross the road. On getting closer, he was found to be none other than Havildar Sher Singh of the Brigade Military Police posted at the place, especially lo check jawans from going to the shop and drinking. As the car pulled up close on him, he made an effort to come to attention and salute. In the act he was so unsteady that he was falling right and left. Then he drawled out a question, "Sir, may I know why you are not standing still?" A suitable answer was given the following day at the Orderly Room.

Silent Judges

A little bit of interest taken by a Commander in the welfare and well-being of his troops yields rich dividends in the form of emotional attachment, respect and good conduct. Their discipline improves, morale rises and monotony of the work takes shape of a labour of love. The Unit becomes a well-knit family. Its entire activity turns into more or less, a family affair. Reverse is the case when a commander is indifferent. Men lose interest in themselves and in their work. They grow critical of whatever the Commander does. Men are the best judges of their leaders. They are silent like a mirror and reflect the true image of their commanders. Just as a field talks to its farmer without the medium of sound and conveys to him what to do, similarly a visit to the men without any talk is a dialogue. You always come away informed, enlightened and inspired.

The enormity of work would not allow me to visit my men off duty. We used to observe what we called, "*Jawanon ka Din*" every Tuesday. On this day officers dined with their men. It was not expected of an officer to refuse an invitation when invited. Men would save out of their daily rations to make "*Jawanon ka Din*" a real feast, not by spending money alone but also by spending time and taking interest in making various dishes by their imagination and resourcefulness. Cooking good food and serving it properly bring out the administrator in a person. I have often thought that organizing a feast is akin to the art of governance.

Apart from food, there also used to be an item or two of music and song. These feasts could be organized only on a Company or a Platoon basis as the troops were billeted in different villages. At times, village headmen or prominent persons living in the area were also invited to these functions. Though in those days I used to live on one meal a day, yet on the invitation of the jawans I would make it a point to attend at least two places by adjusting timings so that I could be with as many of them as possible.

Health Problems

Medical arrangements within the Brigade too demanded my attention. As a student, I had an ambition to become a doctor but had failed to enter the profession. I showed genuine interest in improving the functioning of the Brigade Hospital. I would visit the Hospital as often as possible specially if a man was reported to be on the dangerously ill or seriously ill list. The patients and the doctors always looked forward to my visits. I saw to it that the financial requirements of our Hospital were met with. But medicines were scarce and money could not purchase them. Our doctors had to depend upon nature. They improvised treatments. For example, they would powder egg-shells to use in place of calcium, give liver in place of an iron tonic and different available fruits, germinated grains and vegetables for vitamin deficiencies. Even fermented rice-water or toddy was one of their prescriptions.

I remember the case of a Dogra jawan who was religiously vegetarian. He had suffered from an attack of pneumonia twice, and was on the way to recovery when he had a relapse. Again he recovered but was so weak that Dr. Gurdial Singh told me that unless he built up some strength, he would not be able to survive. He was too weak to be shifted to the General Hospital at Mandalay. When I visited the jawan he reported against Dr. Gurdial Singh for asking him to eat egg and liver. He was full of anger and sobbed as he talked to me complaining against the Doctor's orders. When I pleaded that the Doctor was acting in his interest and to save his life, he retorted back, "I do not want my life at the cost of my *Dharma*".

Asked if he was loyal to Netaji, his reply was aggressively affirmative, as though I had hurt his self-respect by asking him this rude question. I went on: "So you are loyal to Netaji but at the same time you are killing one of his jawans in you by refusing to abide by the doctor's treatment. Do you want me to go to the battle without you? What type of loyalty is that?" The jawan answered, "In that case, Sir, I shall try." The next day Dr. Gurdial Singh told me that the jawan had tried to eat an egg but vomited. As I approached to see the jawan he said, I assure you that I shall try again." He tried and again failed, but he never left attempting again and again.

Eventually in five days he succeeded in taking an egg, and later could take liver and chicken soup. During his ordeal, I visited him twice, sometimes even thrice, a day. It was a bright day when he joined his Unit fully recovered after one and a half months. As I thanked the Doctor for saving his life, the jawan intervened, "Sir, but for you I would not have eaten egg or meat. You have saved my life and it is not the doctor." Doctor Gurdial Singh stood by smiling. The Doctor had used me as an instrument for the treatment of his patient. His success was his reward and Movement's gain.

Being located as it happened to be in a village, our hospital did provide its services to the local people, though on a moderate scale. The District Officers and their families paid a visit once a month to look up our patients and offer them sweets and fruits which were otherwise so very difficult to get during those days. I remember the visit of a District Officer's daughter who spent a lot of money on making an excellent sweet out of gelatinous rice in a quantity adequate enough to be distributed among more than two hundred persons on the New Year's Day when the Deputy Commissioner and all his officers and their families paid a visit to the hospital. The soldier in a state of illness away from home is an extraordinarily emotional being. The visits by the members of the fair sex and children would always make him feel as if his own mother, sister or daughter have come. These visits go a long way in getting well soon.

Army Commander Visits

In the middle of December, the Japanese Army Commander General S. Katamura visited us. It was a pleasant surprise for me. Along with the General came Colonel I. Fujiwara, the greatest supporter of the INA and one of the originators of the idea among the Japanese. I did not know that he was in Burma. I took his sudden appearance as a good omen. Most of us knew him by face since the British surrender of Singapore at the Farrer Park rally. He looked impressive and dignified. Tall and well-built with his sincere smiling face, he had a conspicuous personality with natural aristocracy, born of the qualities of head and heart. His name and Fujiwara Kikan had become household words among the Indians in Singapore, Malaya, Burma and Thailand. This meeting was indeed pleasant and useful.

Fujiwara consented to have breakfast with me and also to meet my officers. While going round the defences of Myingyan, Fujiwara, leaving the General's group, would go about meeting INA officers. He impressed us as more of an Indian than a Japanese. While addressing him, out of the force of habit, I called him by his old rank of a Major. When I apologized for the mistake, he told me not to apologize for he liked being Major Fujiwara of 1942, when he succeeded in serving the Indian Independence Movement the most by helping General Mohan Singh in raising the INA Knowing that I was that a tee-totallar, he brought me a present of tea, cocoa, chocolate powder and sugar, instead of whisky on behalf of General Katamura. Personal acquaintance counts a lot; it makes you feel important and not lonely in the otherwise solitary world of a Commander.

On completing one month of my command on 13th December, 1944, I again went round addressing all ranks, Battalion-wise, in their respective areas. I repeated this time that the coming campaign was going to be a very difficult affair, and that in case anyone of my troops felt that he was not equal to the situation due to whatever cause, psychological, physical or political, he could inform me in confidence and I would see to it that he was sent to the rear and that no action would be taken or a stigma attached to him in any shape or form whatsoever.

My men and officers were advised to expect the worst so that there was no disappointment later. I reminded them that the time was fast approaching to accept Netaji's offer of "...hunger, thirst, privation, forced marches and death...". I told them that notwithstanding my age I was like their father, a spiritual father, and they should hide nothing from me. And if in spite of all the difficulties facing us and our shortfall in resources to face them, they should decide to remain within "The Nehru", they would have to work hard and be prepared to make the supreme sacrifice.

These talks went a long way in training the spirit of the men. Sharing of danger has a far greater binding influence than promises. So far the only danger to be shared was air raids and machine-gunning from the enemy planes. Men had seen for themselves that to work was better than to rest in suspense under the trees to save themselves from the enemy planes. We had taken to digging what we called foxholes for shelter against air raids. A foxhole was 3 feet by 3 feet by 6 feet deep. These foxholes proved very safe against aerial machine-gunning, howsoever low the enemy planes might swoop to machine-gun.

Once a Company was digging trenches to defend a railway bridge half way between Myingyan and Taunghtha. The digging had just been completed when the place was heavily bombed. The bridge was blown up. The enemy kept up the raid for a considerable length of time, returning again and again to dive on to the bridge throwing bombs and machine-gunning the trenches in the open land. Along with the Battalion Commander I was watching the raid from a hill fearing that there would be no survivors. What we discovered later was simply unbelievable; not a single man got even a scratch. When we met the boys, they were full of joy and laughter. Their comments against the enemy planes were full of fun and humour. The news of the raid and the invincibility of our men put a new heart into us. We felt ourselves superior in spirit and resourcefulness to the enemy might. There was a change for the better; but the change had just began, there was a lot more to be done. It was a great satisfaction to me that the officers and men had taken to training seriously.

A Disciplinary Action

I, however, was not happy to note that the Battalion under the senior-most officer, who was at the time also officiating as the Brigade Second-in-Command, Major Hari Singh, was not showing progress to match with the other two Battalions. He was the same Battalion Commander who, during my first conference, in the beginning had raised the question of casualties, and had brougut my attention to the danger of raids during training. Men of his Battalion were not happy with the quality nor with the quantity of rations issued to them. Later on, it was revealed that Hari Singh was leading an unsoldierly life at the expense of men's rations and their pocket money.

On getting detailed information about his misdeeds, and on a complaint from the people of the village concerned, I raided him on the night of 12-13 December 1944 at 2 a.m. He was caught red-handed with a woman. He was put under arrest and afterwards dispatched to Rangoon. Before sending him to Rangoon, I ran up to Mandalay to discuss the matter with Shah Nawaz, the then officiating Divisional Commander of No. 1 Division. I left Myingyan with Khan, the Quartermaster, Mohinder, the Intelligence Officer, and one escort on the evening of 14th December and was back at the station by the morning of 16th. It was a loss of 33 precious hours. Men always react favourably to a just disciplinary action and so was the case in this instance.

An Enemy Plane Force-Lands

On 21st December, while on patrol duty on the banks of the Irrawaddy, our men saw an enemy plane force-land. They reached the spot and succeeded in making the pilot and the navigator prisoners. The pilot turned out to be Wing Commander L. Hudson of the Royal Australian Air Force, who was the senior most prisoner of war at Rangoon at the time of the British re-entry in May 1945. When I saw the two of them they were badly bruised. Hudson met me again in the Red Fort. I was pleased to find that he had not forgotten a few kind words spoken to him while I interviewed him after his capture. Our booty was a revolver and a few maps. The capture of the two enemy officers boosted the spirit of our men who then were facing frequent air raids.

Christmas Gift

1944 was the most unpleasant Christmas eve I ever had. In the evening just after dark, Myingyan was heavily bombed. Some of my young officers who had recently joined me, went to help the civilian population. As they were helping the air raid victims, another raid came and we suffered 96 casualties, seven killed, others badly wounded. Though these men from an adjoining camp had gone for a good cause to help the civilian population, yet I felt that I was responsible for these causalities. I should have issued a standing order prohibiting troops from going to the town during an air raid.

Some of these casualties were caused by time bombs which exploded on the Christmas morning. Paras Ram from Gujarat was a young handsome Azad Hind Dal Officer looking after our civilian supply system. He found a bomb lying in front of the Supply Stores. With the intention of disposing it off so as to clear the area of the danger, he was in the act of lifting the bomb when it exploded, injuring his hands, legs, thighs and the abdomen. Some of his vital parts had been damaged including the lungs. He was most seriously wounded but was surprisingly serene and quiet. In the evening, as I was seeing him off being evacuated to INA General Hospital at Mandalay, he tried to encourage me and asked me to look after others rather than him. He was sorry for not having been able to complete a certain job which he was to have done that day.

As I was attending to Paras Ram, another man happened to cry. He said to me, "Sir, don't worry about me. Look at that man. He needs your attention more. Please talk to him." Such was the pure, selfless, sacrificial spirit of this young civilian Gujarati officer, who died on the way hardly seven miles away form Myingyan. His handsome face, his consoling tone reflecting concern about others rather than about his own wounds and trying to save me from the worries in spite of his fatal injuries haunted me for days, and I felt as if I had killed him myself. Why could not I avert the calamity? This was the saddest and the most painful Christmas I ever had.

A Decisive Turn

Netaji had not forgotten my request. In the middle of January 1945, Major Jagir Singh (later Lieut. Col.) reported for duty. Myingyan town, by then, was a deserted place, as it had been repeatedly bombed by the enemy. The Burmese District Headquarters were shifted to Towyoe, a small village on the border of a jungle about five miles away from the town. I took Jagir for a courtesy call on the Deputy Commissioner and the Superintendent of Police U. Zawin who was the Deputy Commissioner's son-in-law, tall, fair and handsome. U. Zawin and the Deputy Commissioner had been very helpful to us.

Ever since my taking over the command, I had not been able to snatch a single whole night's sleep. I never got more than two hours for sleep out of the twenty-four. Jagir's arrival gave me such a feeling of relief that my shattered nerves exhausted their power of resistance. I got fever and Jagir had to call the Doctor who advised me complete rest. Jagir left me in the Deputy Commissioner's guest hut where I slept like a log for the next twenty-four hours. Now that I had someone responsible, sensible and dependable to answer for me, I could afford the luxury of having fever and sleep.

The forced rest for twenty-four hours gave me another lease of endurance. Now that Jagir had come, I could think of reorganizing the Regiment which I had not been able to organize in spite of Netaji's permission to that effect. There were two reasons for it. Firstly, I wanted to be fully in the know of the picture to assess the situation for myself before taking any step; secondly, I wanted to take advantage of Jagir's opinion for which I had to wait for his arrival. He had been in charge of the 'A' Branch of the 1st Division, ever since its inception and knew the officer cadre well. By nature, he was so rational that he would not allow his personal feelings to influence his assessment of a man. Again, in case of my becoming a casualty it would have fallen upon Jagir to command the Brigade, and I thought in fairness to him, he should be fully in the picture.

Taking Jagir and Rawat, the Adjutant, into confidence, I shared my assessment of each officer with them. Having placed my proposals before them for the reorganization of the Regiment, I asked them to complete the work on paper for consultation with the Battalion Commanders. I was now able to devote my time to the training of the troops. I could afford to stay out of the Regimental Headquarters and be with the Units longer. The ever-increasing air raids by the enemy and the withdrawal of Japanese forces through our front and from up north were clear indications of the approaching battle of which we had no definite information. Under the circumstances, the completion of our preparations for the battle was of immediate importance. The time for test was fast approaching.

A Dilemma

In spite of the fact that we were working with an extraordinary intensity, I was seized by a dilemma by the last week of January 1945 due to the following reasons:

1. I had no information about the location of our own, the Japanese, or even the enemy forces.
2. I had quite a large number of personnel who were undesirable and could not be depended upon.

I could do little about the first point except asking Izumi, who himself was helpless due to lack of the means of communication and battle conditions beyond his control.

As for the undesirables, I had to take one of the bitterest decision of my life, for which I found myself wavering and indecisive. No method could be foolproof enough to know the true state of a man's mind. Justness of action against any individual could never be accepted as just by the person concerned. I was caught in a strange predicament. Just decisions are seldom pleasant. I decided that I must have men whom I could trust, however, small their number might be, rather than have a larger strength. I was at only 57% strength of my War Establishment. To leave behind 356 officers and men (50% on medical grounds) out of that strength looked too drastic a step besides being unpleasant.

Alarming News

Yet I felt that it was a step in the right direction and I decided to take it against my heart's dictates. I had discussed the problem with Jagir, all the three Battalion Commanders and my Staff Officers. There were differences of opinion about certain individuals, but there was no opposition to my decision as such. I was waiting for an opportune moment to declare my decision, contemplating all the while whether I was right or wrong. Then at the early hour at 3.30 a.m. on 29th January, I received an urgent message from Izumi to go over to him. At that time he was staying in a village about a mile or so from Towyoe where I had set up my Headquarters earlier that day.

Izumi had never called me to his office; this was the first and the only time because he would always come to me whenever he had something to say. There must be a reason for this departure from the rule, and that too at such an odd hour. I hurried up to him taking Jagir along with me. On entering a cattle shed which had been turned into his office, I found Izumi studying a map spread out on an improvised table. Hurriedly, he began to show me the enemy positions on the map and conveyed the following information:

(*a*) That one British Division had crossed the Irrawaddy in the vicinity of Mandalay,

(*b*) that the 2nd British Division had arrived at Sagaing and bridgeheads had been established at Myinmu and at other places in the vicinity and

(*c*) that one Division having advanced from Kalemyo, down the Gangaw valley, was advancing along the Kan-Gangaw-Tilin-Paulroad and was in the vicinity of Pakokku, looking for likely places to establish bridgeheads across the Irrawaddy in the vicinity of Nyaungu and Pagan.

He gave me a copy of the Order which was:

> "No. 4 Guerrilla Regiment will move immediately to Nyaungu and Pagan and prevent the enemy crossing the Irrawaddy at those places. Covering troops will also be sent across to patrol Pakoku-Tilin Road. The Unit should be in position by the 20th January."

Surprise is not the word; I was alarmed ! Striking my stick on the map I demanded explanation for the delayed conveyance of the information and the Order by ten days. I had to be in position by 20th and it was 29th that day. The order must have originated earlier than that date. Why that much delay? Whatever the state of intercommunications, the delay was beyond my comprehension.

Izumi was nonplussed. His explanations could not satisfy me. I was in a rage beyond control. For some time it appeared as if the Indo-Japanese co-operation had come to the end of its tether, but as Jagir intervened and Izumi pleaded his difficulties, I cooled down and asked what immediate facilities were available for the conveyance of my troops to Nyaungu and Pagan. Poor Izumi had no reply. The Japanese themselves had their difficulties. He said that he would go to the Japanese Garrison Headquarters and find out what was possible. I decided that Khan, the Brigade Quartermaster, would go with him. I posed the following problems and told them to bring a definite solution:

(*a*) Transport for an immediate move to Pagan of an Advance Party of Company strength for patrolling the area on the west of the Irrawaddy.

(*b*) Transport for the conveyance of rations to Pagan.

(*c*) Transport for the transfer of patients to Rangoon.

Izumi promised to let me know the answer as soon as possible. I further decided that in the evening I would proceed to Nyaungu and Pagan to reconnoiter the area so as to be in a definite position to order the move of Battalions to preplanned positions. I told Izumi to join me on this reconnaissance also so that I might be able to show him where I wanted Supply Points and my Advance Headquarters located.

On return to my Headquarters, I summoned Battalion Commanders' Conference along with their Staff Officers at Towyoe at 1000 hrs. At Towyoe Conference, I did not tell the Battalion Commanders that we had received the orders late. It is a Commander's burden to swallow much and spit out less. The way Battalion Commanders received the information about the enemy's advance was comforting indeed. Our preparedness for the expected battle did not cause any surprise to them and they took things in their stride. They were in good heart.

The most unpleasant subject of separating the undesirables was taken up for discussion first. With their first-hand knowledge of the unwanted personnel, the Battalion Commanders did not take long to finalize their respective lists. To grant the benefit of doubt in certain cases, the persons concerned were detailed to accompany the medically unfit so that their records were not spoiled. Persons who had taken me into confidence and requested to be sent back were also drafted out on duty on some pretext or the other, which I find difficult now (1996) to enumerate. But I do recall that this thankless task was carried out quite smoothly. Jagir was entrusted with the job of looking after the separated personnel, till their departure from Myingyan for Rangoon, about 57% of whom were unreliable. I felt I had given him a difficult job.

Handling of the patients and medically unfit personnel, however, posed a greater difficulty. Some of them refused to go back and had threatened to commit suicide if not allowed to go to the battle. Dr. Gurdial Singh, the Brigade Medical Officer, was asked to move the hospital to Kunzaik, a village 12 miles from Myingyan on the way to Taungtha, two miles off the road to the west. This was to be their first hop where I would see them and talk to them so as to make parting as natural as possible, if not agreeable.

Meanwhile, Khan and Izumi turned up to inform that it was not possible to get any mechanical transport. The Japanese Supply Department, however, promised to dump our rations for the next week at Pagan at a given point which I should decide during my reconnaissance. They had been able to get only 37 bullock-carts (with bullocks) allotted out of the animal transport abandoned by certain Japanese Units during their withdrawal. These carts were to be collected at the earliest lest some other Japanese Unit grabbed them.

So then, we knew where we stood. After having discussed and decided the administrative issues, the Units were ordered to stand by to move to their respective battle areas on my return after the reconnaissance. Battalion Commander were to make necessary adjustments within their sub-units for the separated personnel. The bullock-carts, the main transport of the Brigade, were allotted as under:

Regimental Commander	1
Regimental Headquarters	6
7th Battalion	10
8th Battalion	10
9th battalion	10
Total	37

A Company from the 9th Battalion was detailed to form the Advance Party. This Company was to proceed that very evening, i.e. 29th January. Their transport was two bullock-carts out of the ten allotted to their Battalion.

A Look before the Leap

Leaving most of the burden behind on Jagir's shoulders, I left for Pagan on the evening of 29th January, accompanied by Izumi and Mohinder (Brigade Intelligence Officer). We proceeded by the direct cart track via Kamye and Pyinbin to Nyaungu reaching there on 31st morning. My staff car was under repairs. The journey was undertaken on foot and by a hired bullock-cart intermittently.

The day of thirty-first January was utilized for reconnaissance of the eastern bank of the Irrawaddy from the cliffs of Nyaungu in the north to the end of Pagan town in the south. When I along with Mohinder and the Advance Party Commander were making this recce, Izumi was asked to arrange for hiring local boats to cross the Irrawaddy the next day so that two Platoons of the Advance Party could cross and take up a covering position to watch any enemy approach from the direction of Tilin.

We crossed the Irrawaddy the next day, the 1st of February, starting from Pagan by dawn. Here the river was wide and there were a few islands in it. Paddy fields with small huts were spotted here and there and smiling people made these little islands wonderfully attractive. The sunrise at Pagan watched from one of these islands gave one the feelings of a lovely dream. Pagan, the capital of Burma during the period of the kings of Pagan, must have been a graceful city. Its ruins and deserted pagodas stood witness to its past glory. Ananda Pagoda, perhaps the largest covered area under one roof in Burma, silhouetted against the first rays of the rising sun with thousands of pagodas of different shapes and hues arrayed along it, created an awe-inspiring effect of its majesty and beauty. To the Indian in me, the scene could not help reminding me of the days of Lord Gautam Buddha, when that Prince preached peace. I for once was lost in the past and the current splendour of the scene until the drone of the enemy planes wakened me up to the stark reality of the prevailing situation.

The west bank of the Irrawaddy opposite Pagan rose steeply into the hills about 800 feet above the river level and well above 1,000 feet above the mean sea level. The breadth of the bank varied here and there where dry streams ran down making little tributaries at their confluence with the Irrawaddy. The hills were closer to the river opposite Pagan and diverged as the river took a north-easterly direction upstream towards Nyaungu. The town of Myitche is situated on a plain stretch of land opposite Nyaungu. The banks were developed into paddy fields, and a line of villages stretched all along north to south connected by a motorable road.

I made for the highest point, a watershed where a pagoda stood overlooking the Irrawaddy in the east and the Yaw Chaungh near to the west at a distance of about 8 miles. The place was crowded with thousands of panic-stricken refugees who had fled ahead of the advancing British forces. On the assumption that the enemy would have infiltrated some agents amongst the refugees, I thought the place was unsafe. As a precaution against being recognised by the enemy, I proceeded to an inconspicuous spot, from where I would have a thorough look at the eastern bank as the enemy would look at us during the battle. It was apparent that it would call for ingenuity on our part to conceal our defences from the enemy's view, who would have the advantage of the commanding heights while the villages and small islands would provide him with cover behind which he could assemble his forces.

Having reconnoitered the west bank and having given full instructions to the covering Party Commander, I bade farewell to the men who by then had assembled at a given point. They were in good shape and high spirits. Having re-crossed the Irrawady as we touched the eastern bank, the sun was about to disappear behind the western hills with a white tall pagoda atop, lit by the golden red rays peeping through the delicate clouds. Holding my breath as if by a reflex action, I sat down to admire and enjoy the priceless vision for the next few seconds before the sun was gone, and I was again left to my problems which at the time were equally engaging, if not more so.

The headman of Pagan served a dinner and we started back for Myingyan by bullock-cart hired through his courtesy. I used to get tonsillitis fever and at other times an attack of an appendicitis. Bullock-cart rides are not a comfortable mode of travel even for a healthy man but with lot of hay spread out as a bedding, did make a difference for the better. During the day I would have to walk in any case due to enemy planes for which I had to save energy as and when I could. Before leaving I checked up once again the task I had allotted to the Advance Party Commander. He had his one Platoon positioned at Nyaungu which to me appeared to be the most likely place for crossing even though at that point too the river was about a mile broad. I had also given him a general idea of the deployment of the Battalions on their arrival when he was to be relieved to go across and lead the covering party himself which even at that time was his baby. He was responsible for gathering information and conveying it to me at the Headquarters through runners.

Prominent personalities at Nyaungu and at Pagan were introduced to the Advance Party Commander and were requested to extend help in the form of hiring boats or procuring rations which he might request. Pagan had struck me as an equally likely place for infantry crossing in the early stages of the enemy assault, but I had little doubt that the only proper place for establishing a bridgehead could be Nyaungu and not Pagan. Pagan being thickly populated. I ordered the Advance Party to avoid entering it till the arrival of the Unit which was to be positioned there. This step was taken to maintain secrecy. As I jolted along lying in the cart returning to Myingyan, I pondered over the Advance Party Commander's problems which were challenging indeed, but the way he had accepted the task assigned to him was reassuring. His job was to look out for enemy movement and to report back. It was not for him to fight except in self-defence. All the same, it was a difficult and responsible job. Through him, "The Nehru" had begun holding the Irrawaddy.

We arrived back at Towyoe by the dawn of 3rd February. Mohinder was asked to make an enlargement of the Nyaungu-Pagan sector as reconnoitered by us. Jagir was asked to arrange Battalion Commanders Conference to which Staff Officers and Company Commanders were also called. I had sufficient time, while returning from Pagan, to counsel myself as to the orders I should issue to my Battalion Commanders which were on the following lines:

1. Information about the enemy was as per Towyoe Conference of 29th January. The flow of refugees from

forward areas showed that the enemy had advanced further.

2. Regarding our own troops, "The Nehru" was the sole force in the Nyanugu-Pagan sector. There was a Japanese Company on the cliffs in the north of Nyaungu which was outside our area. Apparently "The Nehru" had moved out of the Japanese 15th Army Area to the 28th Army Area but I had no information about it then. For all practical purposes, "The Nehru" was all alone in the sector.

3. "The Nehru" was to hold the Irrawaddy from Nyaungu in the north to Pagan in the south, both towns inclusive, and to hold the enemy crossing the Irrawaddy at those places.

4. I planned as under :

   (*a*) The 7th Battalion commanded by Lieut. Hari Ram was to be located at Nyaungu with the immediate object of stopping the enemy crossing by the Nyaungu ferry. All the eight machine-guns of "The Nehru" were pooled and put under Hari Ram to give him maximum fire-power. His unit was approximately 400 strong.

   (*b*) The 8th Battalion under Captain Chander Bhan's command was to occupy the area at Pagan to hold the front from the southern end of Pagan to midway between Pagan and Nyaungu. It was the strongest unit at the time, about 500 strong.

   (*c*) The 9th Battalion under Lieut. Khan Mohd. minus one Company forming advance party and the covering party was to he in reserve at Tetthe.

5. I ordered the move of the Battalions to leave Myingyan by 4th February after dusk, so as to be in their respective positions by the 8th morning. In order to conceal our movements from air as well as enemy agents, Units were to move by different routes, and even then so dispersed as to be nowhere stronger than a Platoon at any one time. All moves were to be made during the night as the enemy enjoyed complete command of the air.

6. (*a*) My Advance Headquarters were to be at Tetthe. I was to proceed by staff car starting on 7th evening having put everybody well on the move except the Rear Headquarters. My route was to be Taunghtha-Popa, Kyaukpadaung and Tetthe. I was to reach Tetthe by the 8th morning so as to synchronize my arrival with that of the Battalions and staff. The Intelligence Officer was to accompany me.

   (*b*) The Rear Brigade Headquarters under Jagir was to move from Towyoe to Popa after clearing all troops up to and out of Taunghtha. This included the sending back of the patients, the medically unfit and the undesirables. Khan, the Quartermaster, was to be with Jagir along with the two 30-cwt. trucks loaded with rations and supplies.

7. The Brigade Hospital under Lieut. Krishnan, 9th Battalion Medical Officer, was to be located at Tetthe in pagodas. Gurdial was to establish the main hospital at Mount Popa after winding up at Kunzaik and seeing off the patients to Rangoon.

8. Ration stores for the Units in the front were to be located in the Ananda pagoda at Pagan. Each man was to carry three days' ration on him.

9. Intercommunication was to be through runners. Each Battalion was to detail four runners, unless otherwise ordered, to wait at the Brigade Headquarters for receiving and conveying messages to their respective units.

10. There were no supporting arms.

11. The 7th Battalion on arrival at Nyaungu, was to relieve the Advance Party (one Platoon) stationed in their area.

After the Conference, copies of written orders were given. The presence of Company Commanders did help in thrashing out all the details and I felt that everybody knew where he stood. Mohinder's map helped a lot during this briefing. Apart from the Battle Orders, all outstanding problems were discussed and decisions taken. That was to be our last conference before leaving Myingyan area. The next day, the 4th February, I visited and talked to as many troops as possible. All Ranks appeared to be in high spirits but the separation of the so-called undersirables kept on weighing on me.

On 7th February, the Deputy Commissioner and U. Zawin invited me and Jagir to a quiet farewell dinner in which no outsider was present. It was a sumptuous meal. The elderly Deputy Commissioner gave me a number of hints for getting support and cooperation from the Burmese people. One of his points of advice was that the Burmese were an extremely simple people. They would never let you down as long as you were sincere to them; but once you betray them, they would never say that they were annoyed with you but would take the revenge when you least expected it. He gave me a few hints about the Burmese armed forces having turned anti-Japanese. Aung San had by then realised that the good of Burma and of the Japanese were incompatible. I was advised to be careful.

At 9 p.m. I left Towyoe having called on everybody, never to see those good affectionate people again. One of the good things of war is that you discover friends. I had discovered one.

14

"The Nehru" Holds the Irrawaddy

The Move

From Towyoe, I walked eight miles to Gwebinyo. Jagir came along for a last minute discussion during the walk. The last party on the move was to wait at Gwebinyo along with my bullock-cart which I often called the "Royal Staff Car". Mehar Singh, my batman, loved this vehicle for its dependability. He had a host of things loaded on it. This was his world from which he would produce anything and everything which I needed. Mehar Singh hated anybody touching anything in it which he might have concealed somewhere in something, God knows where. He would not tolerate even my helping myself to anything except my papers. Coming from the farmer's stock of Hoshiarpur district in the Punjab, Mehar Singh loved his bullocks. Half of the space in the cart was filled with dry grass neatly stacked over the baggage right up to the top on which he spread my hold-all neatly without any fold or a crease so that I could sleep on it.

Jagir arranged for my security by detailing an N.C.O. and a section of men. They had instructions to look after my security without making themselves conspicuous. They had orders to leave me at Gwebinyo and join the rear party. The security N.C.O., however, was found sitting in the staff car on the left front seat as my car moved from Gwebinyo carrying Izumi, Mohinder, and the Japanese interpreter. My driver, Hukam Chand, a Jat from Rohtak district of Haryana was earlier Major Khosla's driver. He was so much devoted to Khosla that Khosla's death badly affected his health and Arshad thought it proper to transfer him to me as he had already worked with Jagir in Burma and with me in Singapore. He was a very conscientious and efficient driver. Mehar

Singh and he were good friends and pulled on very well with each other. Hukam Chand brought Major Khosla's ashes home to India. How he kept the urn safe and secure during the war beats imagination. No wonder I never saw him happy, yet he performed his duties most diligently.

With last minute efforts, Izumi had been able to get us three mortars with a limited number of shells, 20 per piece, which came in response to my request for artillery. Those little things were most welcome but no training in handling them could be imparted by my men because of the late arrival of the weapons. Only verbal instructions were, however, given. The actual firing practice was left to be undertaken in the battle-field so as not to waste any shell. Izumi had also brought me five lakh rupees in Rs. 10/-, 5/- and 1/- denomination notes. My Accounts Officer, a South Indian, was waiting for these precious reinforcements which he took over and leaving a certain amount in the staff car and some with Jagir, got it loaded on to the carts which immediately moved off.

The headman of Gwebinyo had been very kind to me and to our troops during our stay in his area. I owed him a debt of gratitude for his kind and never-failing help rendered to us. Gwebinyo, being plum on the road, was our ration distribution point, and as such liable to enemy air attacks. Not once had this graceful old man denied or grudged us the use of houses in his village for storing our supplies. He called me to tea which I could not refuse in spite of paucity of time. The fried fish which he served that night was to be remembered by Jagir and me whenever we were to eat fish after the war. It was delicious.

The agony of parting was eclipsed by the unknown future ahead. As I moved to enter the staff car, a puff of hot wind blew past making me sad and troubled. Hiding my anxiety, I embraced Jagir and bid good-bye to the headman and all those present. I stepped into the car and it immediately moved off. I was looking at the moving ghost-like trees and dreary hills on which we had been working hard to dig and build defences to defend Myingyan; now I was moving away from it, never to see it and its good folk again. It was a consolation that my emotions lay concealed in darkness.

Having been without sleep for the last five days, I felt weak and tired. I was also running fever at that time. We had hardly moved seven miles away from Gwebinyo and I had dozed off when an enemy fighter plane, diving low, let us have a burst of machine-gun fire followed by another one. Skilfully avoiding the road, the driver took the car off the road, to the left bumping and jumping into and over the pits, ditches and drains. At last the car stopped. Its clutch plate was broken. We came out, all unhurt. I thanked the driver for his presence of mind. He had saved our lives, the car, and its contents. I ordered the Security N.C.O. to walk back to meet the carts, which would have travelled hardly a couple of miles, and divert them to Nwebyin near Kunzaik and wait for me. I would go there next morning and halt for the day before taking the shortest direct route to Pagan.

After arranging this, the Security N.C.O. had to dispatch two jawans to report to Jagir about the accident and the consequent change in my route with instructions to send a 30 cwt. truck to the spot of the accident to tow the car to Mount Popa. Izumi, the interpreter and the driver were told to wait for the truck and accompany it to Popa. From Popa Izumi was to come to Pagan. Mohinder was to remain with me and accompany me after I had taken some sleep which I badly needed. There was a pagoda nearby. Having made these arrangements I went to the pagoda and in a deserted shed in front of it, covering myself with a blanket, I went to sleep as if nothing extraordinary had happened.

I got up before sunrise, without fever and feeling better and immediately started for Kunzaik where our patients were. The sleep had given me some strength. I had promised to visit the patients and medically unfit cases before leaving Myingyan. So far, I had failed to fulfil that promise due to lack of time, and but for the accident, I would not have been able to see these jawans at all. They were, however, still looking forward to my visit, and were happy to see me. Some of them tried to prevail upon me to allow them to go to the battle, but the doctor's verdict had to be obeyed. I advised them to join me when they were fully recovered and strong enough to come to the front. Dr. Gurdial Singh treated us to tea. After spending about an hour with them I took leave of them. They gave me an emotional send-off.

At about 8 a.m. I arrived at village Nwebyin which had been the Headquarters of one of my Battalions. On my second visit to the village, the Battalion Commander told me that a girl by the name of Maiyee wanted to see me. I granted her an interview and she came to see me where I was staying under the headman's hut. Her father accompanied her. Maiyee was a very fair and charming girl of about 25 years of age. She was well-educated and well-informed, but did not know English. Her father could speak good Hindustani and interpreted our conversation. He was a well-to-do person and highly respected elder in the village. During the interview. Maiyee had put me questions about Mrs. Sarojini Naidu, Mrs. Annie Besant, Mata Kasturba Gandhi and Mrs. Vijayalkshmi Pandit. She had the ability to discuss the ladies with knowledge and interest.

The discussion was lively and thought-provoking. She was highly sympathetic and keenly interested in the Indian Independence Movement and her feelings for India were as if she were an Indian herself. I met her once or twice again after our first meeting, but was not able to accept her invitation to visit their home. I promised to do so before leaving the area. The accident now gave me an opportunity to fulfil that word. She, her parents, brothers and sisters along with all the prominent persons of Nwebyin received me and gave me a warm welcome. They had arranged to play host to me along with my party which consisted of about 20 men. Under the trees adjoining Maiyee's house food was being cooked. They had killed a goat for the men. The four bullocks had already been served green fodder and grain, rare in those days.

I was given hot water for a bath, an inestimable luxury which I loved. Meals were served early so that I could have the maximum rest. Apart from mutton and chicken, fish was served along with a number of vegetarian dishes. The Burmese are a very hospitable people. When the guest retires for rest, the whole family would sit around to talk till the guest feels sleepy, when they slowly and quietly melt away. On that day Maiyee who was great admirer of Gen. Aung San told me to consider him as our own irrespective of however things might appear to be. Aung San, she said, was the people's man and a friend of India.

Maiyee put me questions about my family and myself which she had not asked me during our previous meetings. She asked me if I would allow her to adopt me as a brother so that she could tie me an armlet for my safety and success in the war. She was happy when I agreed. The ceremony was to take place at 4 p.m. Before the ceremony, I was asked to take a bath and was made to sit on a small wooden board. A

THE BATTLE OF NYAUNGU & PAGAN

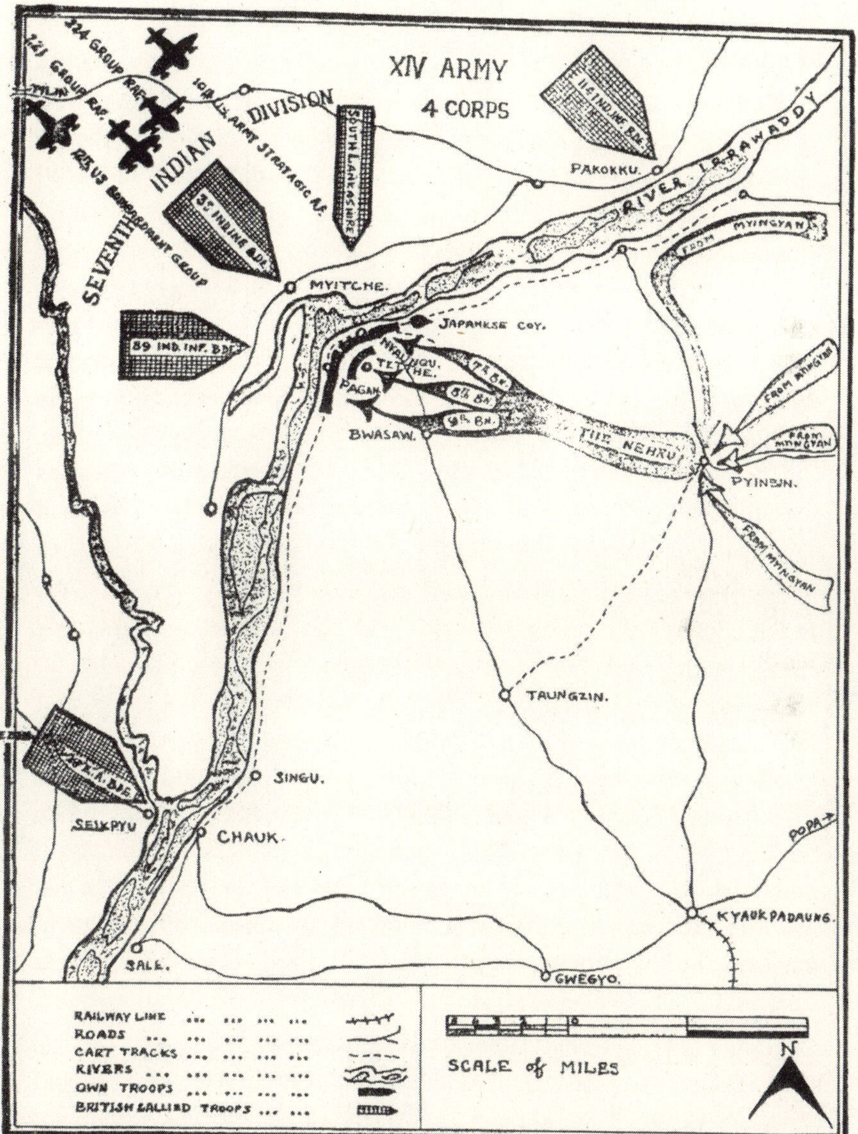

Poonji Buddhist priest had been called to perform the ceremony. Amidst the chanting of sacred hymns, a neat white thread with thousands of knots made in a beautiful circular way was tied on my left upper arm with sprinkling of water and various other rituals. Maiyee's parents and all members of the family watched the ceremony reverentially as Maiyee tied the sacred amulet.

Overwhelmed by sisterly emotions, Maiyee assured me that as long as that amulet was there on my body, I was safe and secure and that no harm, much less death, could befall me. The thread, I learnt, was made of pure cotton and each knot was tied with recitation of sacred hymns. I was filled with emotion and with tears I promised Maiyee that l would always keep the amulet on my arm during the war. I religiously wore the amulet right throughout the war, during the Red Fort trial and also for months afterwards when it eventually had gone old and fearing that it might break and fall off, I gave it to Basant for safe keeping. We used to look at it every now and then during the hour of ordeal in our later life, and at such times, Basant would put it on my arm again. After Basant's demise, I saw it only once. Time has not diminished its value and regard in my heart though I do not know where it is now.

After the ceremony, I was offered food which I could take little and at about 5.30 p.m. our two carts with the party moved off. I took a few minutes to see and thank the villagers who had turned up at the village gate to bid us farewell. Sobbing, I moved off looking at their sad faces with tears glittering in the light of the setting sun towards which our bullock-carts and men were moving silently. I moved on, followed by Mohinder. Maiyee and her parents kept on waving to their brother and the son whom they were never to see again. Distance and time have not dimmed their image in my mind— their waving hands and full-throated good-bye of "Jai Hind". They made me love Hind all the more and be prepared to pay any price for its liberty.

Nightmarish Night

Onward and forward we moved by day and night with a little rest here and there. On 9th February after midnight our carts stopped under a tamarind tree, a mile and half east of Pyinbin. I was lying on my cart suffering from tonsillitis fever and pain caused by appendicitis with a toothache to boot. Knowing that a pond existed just beside the track towards the north spotted during our reconnaissance, Mohinder ordered a halt and was telling our men to fill up their water bottles and water the bullocks. Just then approaching steps were heard. On being challenged, they stopped and passwords were exchanged.

They were two of our jawans. They were on their way to the Rear Headquarters to inform the 2nd-in-Command, Major Jagir Singh, that the Brigade Commander (the present writer) had been killed, that our covering party across the Irrawaddy was either annihilated or captured, and that the enemy had crossed the river and occupied Nyaugu with tanks and infantry. As I heard the news, I sat up on the cart and shouted at the men, "What are you talking about? Who has been killed?" The messengers recognized my voice and apparently puzzled exclaimed, "Sir, what is this?" "Who gave you the message?" I enquired. "Captain Chander Bhan," was the answer. "Where is he?" I asked. The messengers informed me that Captain Chander Bhan was at Pyinbin in a pagoda along with his Officers and other two Battalion Commanders.

Getting down from the cart, I ordered the messengers to lead me to the pagoda at Pyinbin and ordered Mohinder to bring up the party subsequently. On arrival at the pagoda whose entrance had been shaded by a blanket, I found Capt. Chandra Bhan with other Battalion Commanders and Staff Officers seated in a candle light in a mood of mourning. Apparently they were discussing their future course of action after having sent messengers to the Rear Headquarters informing the death of their Commander. They were surprised to see me alive. Their question was "*Sahib, yeh kya bat hai?*" (What is all this ?).

On enquiry, their information was found to be exactly the same as the messengers had reported to me. I wanted to know whether any of their Units had seen the enemy and if so where. There was no satisfactory reply. They had all converged on Pyinbin from their respective routes of advance. I told them that as the news of my death was wrong, there was a possibility of the other information also being wrong. In case the British had crossed the Irrawaddy with infantry and tanks, I saw no reason why they should not have thrown out a covering party at Pyinbin to safeguard themselves from our attack. I decided and ordered a fighting patrol to be sent immediately towards Nyaungu to get correct information about the location of the enemy.

A Platoon was detailed for the purpose. As the Platoon was being given orders, I happened to reach the spot. Standing under a shady tree as I was listening to the Company Commander giving orders to the Platoon Commander, I heard the men talk which showed the lowest ebb of their morale. They were blaming and abusing me for having been killed and left them deserted. On hearing their uncomplimentary remarks, I shouted from under the tree, "Men, who has deserted whom?" I walked up to them and with my walking stick, I drew an arrow on the ground pointing towards Delhi and asked them which way was Delhi, and whether they would go to Delhi with me or I was to be the lone crusader. They immediately apologised and expressed their determination of their onward march to Delhi.

My presence had created a different spirit altogether. I was reminded of the pages of Indian history, when the great Rana Sanga's elephant seen without its rider, was taken as an indication of his death and his forces had fled before the invading armies. After the fighting patrol left, I thought it proper to show myself to my troops. I went around visiting all the Units which had gathered around Pyinbin. I was happy to observe the effect of my visit. Thereafter, I went to sleep under a tree about a hundred yard away from the cart track, where I posted sentries with orders to tell any of the troops who might be passing that way: "The Brigade Commander, Major Dhillon, is alive and is sleeping under that tree." They had instructions to point out the tree and in case anybody doubted the statement, he was to be brought up to me, and I be awakened so that his doubt could be removed. Here was a moment when I preferred living to being a martyr.

I must confess that lying under the tree with a blanket on, which would normally keep me warm, I felt so nervous and weak that I had to ask Mehar Singh to give me another blanket, and then another one, yet the cold did not diminish. I had a sinking sensation in the chest. A strange feeling of depression in the abdomen overwhelmed me. The toothache and the tonsillitis fever rose higher while the appendicitis pain grew. I took clove (ciryazoot) pills and tried to sleep, but without success. The question which haunted me again and again was, "Have I lost the battle without reaching the battlefield?"

I lay restlessly as the time passed. It was dawn when I started walking about to warm myself up. I was all alone. As the first rays of the sun emerged above the skyline, I cried before Netaji's photo that was placed in my map case and begged him to help me in that hour of difficulty. Crying made me feel lighter. Singing the National Anthem all alone to myself, I hurried to Chandra Bhan's pagoda, where I had already called a Battalion Commanders' Conference. After discussing the situation for a while, I decided to advance by 7 a.m. irrespective of the nature of the situation. This was one of those unfortunate moments when I burnt all my diaries and other records which might give out any information that could be of advantage to the enemy.

The head clerk had just finished typing the orders of advance when a messenger came, sent by the Advance Party Commander to report that a British patrol had crossed the Irrawaddy at Nyaungu on the night of 8th February at a point where one of our Platoon was posted. Our sentries challenged the patrol. The patrol fired on our sentries. One of our sentries was killed. Our second sentry killed the attacker who had killed our sentry. The person killed on the enemy side was a British captain of the South Lancashire Regiment whose watch, compass and automatic revolver and a sten gun were brought by the messenger along with a few cartridges. There was also information that the enemy had appeared in strength at Myitche on the western bank of the Irrawaddy.

Our covering troops across the river were hiding on the west of the Irrawaddy with a view to gathering further information about the enemy movements. The news was heartening, indeed. I sent the information to the rear and ordered the Battalion Commanders to push forward to occupy their respective battle areas with all speed. Everybody cleared out of Pyinbin within about an hour. The enemy was very strong in the air but "The Nehru" kept on its advance and all the Units were in their respective positions before the next morning.

On the 10th of February, the morning sun was just piercing out of the sky when I reached Tetthe, my Headquarters. There were clouds, and as I raised myself from prone position in my bullock-cart, I saw the three colours of our National Flag reflected up on the clouds in the east. I shouted to Mohinder to have a look at the beautiful view and to see whether what I saw was not just an illusion. Mohinder pointed it out to other members of the party and all of us felt inspired taking it as an auspicious sign. At last we had reached there in time. Even the skies appeared to be in our favour. "The Nehru" looked forward to the future with confidence. The tricolour would ultimately triumph, I felt.

On the Irrawaddy

Tetthe was a small village. Its people and the headman were of a friendly and helping nature. My Headquarters were set up under a thatched shed open from all sides in the village headman's compound. Khan Mohd., the 9th Battalion Commander had positioned his troops on the outskirts of the village. They had already started digging their defences.

I had a quick bath. Mehar Singh made some tea. The headman's mother, an old graceful lady, infirm with age, came along with a platefulls of hot sweet pancakes made of rice-flour. Like a mother, she compelled me to eat them all up and be strong for the battle. It is amazing how these good little turns cheer up the spirit in an otherwise gloomy situation. I have always accepted such a treat as a blessing from God Himself and felt pleased and elevated.

After a brief inspection of Khan Mohd.'s defences, I went forward to contact the frontline Battalion Commanders to see how they were faring within their respective locations on our side of the Irrawaddy. They had deployed well. I found their plans satisfactory in organising their respective defences within their meager resources. They had started digging trenches. Men were in good shape and their morale was high. Starting with Chander Bhan of the 8th Battalion from the south of Pagan, we checked and discussed the suitability of each and every position on the spot. We ended at Nyaungu with Hari Ram of the 7th Battalion at the northern limits of our sector. Across the Irrawaddy, advance elements of the enemy had already arrived on the west bank. They could not be spotted out from Pagan. But from Nyaungu they could be seen across the river even with naked eye. The enemy was bold, indeed. They could afford to be so in view of their air supremacy.

The very first visit of our defences convinced me that our only chance of success lay in concealment and secrecy. If we could conceal our trenches and our identity as well as the few weapons we had, the opponent was bound to keep on guessing and overestimate our strength and thus commit a greater number of his forces than required. With our limited fire-power we would get an opportunity to inflict maximum casualties on the enemy during their assault en masse and could foil the very first attack. To achieve this objective, strict orders were given on the following lines:

1. Sentries were not to challenge at night by shouting. Our own troops were to stop before approaching each other and be recognised in silence. This could easily be possible as we had no other troops than those of "The Nehru" on our side of the river. Of course, a few sign signals had to be innovated.
2. Slogans like *Chalo -Delhi; Inquilab, Zindabad; Netaji, Zindabad;* and *Azad Hind, Zindabad* were not to be raised except during the big scale assault by the enemy.
3. The National Anthem which we used to sing at reveille and retreat was to be discontinued.
4. Use of firearms except rifles was prohibited. The few automatics and three mortars were to be reserved for the enemy's full scale assault. Even then the fire was to be opened when the opposing boats were not more than 200 to 300 yards from our defences.
5. Enemy patrols at night were to be dealt with bayonets alone. Rifle fire was to be used only as last resort and that too in self- defence only.

During the day, men were instructed and put through practice as to how they were to deal with the enemy patrols at night without firing at them. The enemy was to be allowed to advance as far forward as to be on the verge of landing. This was to be done with the view of causing him an impression that the place of his landing was not manned. Our men were then to start moving slowly and cautiously to disclose their presence and ultimately emerge out of the darkness with fixed bayonets, in an arc-like formation in ghastly silence and try to envelop him by a claw-like pincer movement.

This method, I thought, was bound to make the enemy patrols withdraw. They too had become very cautious after their experience of the night of 8th February. If they did withdraw, they were to be allowed to do so. It was prudent to hold our fire than to give away our positions and disclose our weapons. In case they did not withdraw, they were to be dealt with bayonets with a view to capture or kill. The following nights were to prove the efficacy of this method. Practically each night, the enemy sent forward reconnaissance patrols but as soon as they detected our movements, they made haste to beat a retreat. They were over cautious. My jawans enjoyed this silent game of catch-as-catch can.

The Opposing Forces

I could gather intelligence through following sources :

(*a*) My own troops, who were still across the Irrawaddy and hiding to cross over to join me, were sending useful information.

(*b*) The locals. I had no dearth of funds to employ them for the purpose. They were cooperative.

Putting together the fragments of information I received I could make a broad guess that our probable opponent was the 7th Indian Division with three of its Brigades arrayed on the opposite bank facing us. The only Regiment whose name could be ascertained was that of the South Lancashire Regiment. The presence of the African troops about twenty miles down south outside our sector at Seikpyu facing Chauk was also ascertained. Their strength, however, could not be assessed. Actually, it was 28 East African Brigade under the command of Brigadier W.A. Dimoline, C.B.E., M.C.

I further made a guess that the enemy would launch the initial assault with about ten thousand troops, out of about thirty thousand concentrated on the west of Irrawaddy directly facing us. The only Commanders, whose names I knew at the time were those of Lord Mountbatten and General Sir William Slim. At present, however, I am in a position to state who were being opposed by "The Nehru", at the decisive time of southern crossing of the Irrawaddy by the British forces, which in Slim's words was "the longest opposed river crossing attempted in any theatre of the Second World War."

Today, when the din of the battle is half a century away, I fail to imagine the power which enabled me to stay there and face General Slim. I had with me Captain Chander Bhan, commanding the 8th Battalion at Pagan, Lieut. Hari Ram, commanding 7th Battalion at Nyaungu and Lieut. Khan Mohammed commanding 9th Battalion in reserve at Tetthe, each Battalion posted at about five miles distance from one another. All of them were hardly half of their establishments, about 1,200 strong, all the three put together. They were poorly equipped, armed mainly with rifles and a few light automatics. Fifty per cent of their strength was made up of raw recruits enlisted from among South Indian civilian volunteers mostly from Malaya.

I was lucky to have eight medium machine-guns though four of them had to be condemned two days before the decisive action. The last minute arrival of three mortars with twenty shells each was better than having nothing at all. Our supply of small arms and ammunition also was limited to last for a few minutes of an all-out battle.

We had neither artillery nor air power.

The only means of intercommunication within "The Nehru" was through runners. This deficiency obliged me to leave things to the initiative of my Battalion Commanders far more than I would like to burden them with, or would be advantageous to the conduct of the battle. For me it involved imagining things before hand and catering for eventualities before the events. Imagination is a necessity for a Commander but it must have some limits because you cannot plan everything on imagination alone. Of course, it also meant my personal running about in order to command and control, for which the only means of locomotion were the good old feet.

My readers, I hope, would allow me the luxury and privilege of relying on Field Marshal Sir William Slim's Defeat into Victory and Lord Mountbatten's Report to the Combined Chiefs of Staff to put on record how the Nehru Brigade had to face an array of General Officers Commanding of the British Empire and their Allies.

A) THE LAND FORCES

1. Lieut. General Sir William Slim, C.B.E., K.C.B., D.S.O., M.C., General Officer Commander-in-Chief, fourteenth Army.
2. Lieut. General Sir Frank Messery, K.B.E, C.B., D.S.O., Commander 4 Corps.
3. Major General G.C. Evans, C.B., C.B.E., D.S.O., Commander 7 Indian Division.
4. Brigadier R.G. Collingwood, D.S.O., Commander 33 Indian

Infantry Brigade along with South Lancashire Regiment loaned specially for the crossing from another Brigade as they had experience in boat work and had taken part in the landing at Madagascar; were located at Myitche facing Nyaungu.

5. Brigadier W.A. Crowther, C.B.E., D.B.E., D.S.O., Commander, 89 Indian Infantry Brigade facing Pagan.

B) THE AIR FORCES

1. Air Vice Marshal S.F. Vincent, C.B., D.F.C., A.F.C., Commander 221 Group R.A.F. which consisted of six squadrons of Hurricanes (including one from the Royal Indian Air Force and three squadrons of Thunderbolts P-47) for close support; four squadrons of Spitfires for defence; three squadrons of Beaufighters and Mosquitoes for long-range tactical work; two squadrons of Hurricanes for tactical reconnaissance work; a detachment of night-fighting Beaufighters; and a detachment of Spitfires for photographic reconnaissance. 221 Group was further reinforced, at the end of January 1945, by the U.S. 12th Bombardment Group. Major General Stratemeyer, the American General Commanding Eastern Air Command, also made arrangements for the 10th U.S.A. A.F. and 224 Group (both of these being no longer heavily committed in Arakan), to give as much support as possible whenever 221 Group required it. This arrangement gave 221 Group considerable increased, potentiality at any rate in medium and heavy bomber strength; and it was planned to make the greatest use in the Fourteenth Army's coming operation of 'earthquake' attacks. A special wireless link was opened by Eastern Air Command between its own Headquarters and those of 221 Group, 224 Group and the 10th U.S.A.A.F which was reserved for high priority operational signals relating to Fourteenth Army operations.

Gratefully acknowledging the co-operation extended to him by Air Vice-Marshal S.F. Vincent, Gen. Slim records that the Allied air forces ranged all over Burma as far south as Rangoon to help the Fourteenth

Army: "Our attacks were preceded by devastating 'earthquake' bombardments; our bridge-heads as we clung to them screened by fire from the air. Never, I believe, was air co-operation closer, quicker or more effective; never was it more gratefully appreciated than by the Fourteenth Army and its Commander" (p. 306).

Discussing about "doubt and fear clung in" upon him, Slim has stated, "I drew comfort, too, at this time from quite another thought. I had more than once, in the two Great Wars, taken part in the forcing of a river obstacle, and I had on every occasion found it less difficult and less costly than expected. I had also read some military history. Although I cudgelled my brains, I could not call to mind a single instance when a river had been successfully held against determined assault. As the time drew near for the first crossing, I hugged this thought to me. Historically, the odds were in my favour" (p. 308).

What was favourable to the opponent was bound to be unfavourable to "The Nehru". "The Nehru" holding the Irrawaddy all alone from Nyaungu to Pagan with frontline troops far below a thousand was opposing the southern crossing of the Irrawaddy, which the Fourteenth Army, one of the most modern armies at the time, was now attempting to cross. It was one of that important and "dramatic of all military operations". Its importance was especially enhanced as Slim's plan was to strike a decisive blow at Meiktila. Consequently it was to receive all of Slim's attention and of the Allied Forces cooperating with his Fourteenth Army. He wrote, "As the moment of this all important crossing approached, on which the whole fabric of my battle plan rested, I devoted myself mainly to doing what I could to support Messervy."

"The Nehru" opposing the crossing was, thus, going to be the main recipient of Slim's attention. Never, I believed, the odds were so formidable against the so few, so barely equipped. It was a contest between the steel and the spirit. A sword was being challenged by a needle.

But then enslaved nations have to wait for centuries for such a moment to fight for and pay the price for their liberty. Here was one such rare moment. The strongest weapon on our side, however, was "The justice and invincibility of our cause", which reinforced us with an unending supply of courage and resourcefulness under the inspiring command and leadership of Netaji Subhas Chandra Bose.

The Stage is Set

The British concentration of troops on the west bank of the Irrawaddy was strong enough to have crossed the river at any point at any time, if they had wished it. Their reluctance to do, though because of strategic and operational consideration, was taken by us as a sign of their nervousness. Their intelligence appeared to be faulty and lacking. It helped us to delay their crossing by our elementary tactics.

On the 11th February, as I was inspecting the 7th Battalion's dispositions, I was told that four out of eight machine-guns which we had pooled to increase the Battalion's fire-power, were not dependable for want of spare parts. As a way out, four of the guns were stripped off their parts to serve the remaining four. The defective guns were thrown into the waters of the Irrawaddy. Besides solving our problem concerning the spare parts, this action gave us extra ammunition belts and ammunition for the remaining machine-guns. Previously we had two belts per gun, now each gun had four belts. This ensured double the duration of continuous fire which was considered essential to bring to bear upon the assaulting enemy. Prolonged fire over the surface of water was bound to take a good toll of the advancing adversary.

In the evening, I learnt that the enemy was killing dogs in the villages on the west bank. This meant that they were preparing for a night attack. Their patrolling activities were on the increase, but as previously stated, they dared not land. All the same, the suspense grew.

On the 12th of February, starting from the early hours of morning, hostile planes carried out saturation bombing of our defences by what they called, "earthquake attacks". The raid was kept up throughout the day with such intensity that all hell was let loose from the skies. It ended an hour or so before dusk. Casualties would be enormous, I thought. All medical staff with stretchers were ordered to reach the front-lines for attending to and evacuate the wounded. On arrival, we were surprised that there was no casualty at all. No man got even a scratch !

When I asked Chander Bhan how this could happen, he explained that when in the morning, the enemy started bombing, our jawans were in the rear trenches. This precaution we would invariably take to hide ourselves from the enemy's view from over the hills across the Irrawaddy from the places where the water's edge was visible. The enemy planes initially kept on pounding the front-line trenches with tons and tons of explosives. The bombardment was so intense and unrelenting that our men could not move at all. There was a little respite towards noon. Imagining that the enemy had stopped bombardment with a view to following it up by a surface attack, the jawans were rushed to occupy the front-line trenches. The enemy soon resumed the air attack, presumably after a break for lunch. This time our rear-line trenches were bombed out of existence, but none of our jawans was there. It was a lucky chance.

The "earthquake" bombing was taken by us as a fore runner of a night attack on a big scale, when even dogs would not be there to give us a warning of the enemy's movements in the villages across the Irrawaddy. Apart from patrol activity, the night, however, passed in a suspense. The atmosphere on 13th of February remained tense. There was a comparative lull from air raids. The storm was expected any moment; it was in the air all the time. Late in the evening at about 7 p.m. after I had a round of our front-lines, I decided to discuss the situation and compare notes with the Japanese Company on our right. I called for lzumi and we walked over to the Company Commander, a Major.

His assessment of the situation, I found, was limited to his own immediate front, far up north on the right outside of our sector. There was little that he could add to the information already gathered by my own sources. We did agree on one point that the stage was set for the enemy's main assault which might come any moment. To offset this he had organised a suicidal raid. Actually the Company appeared to have been assigned a commando job more to harass and disturb the enemy erratically rather than fight regular warfare.

On our arrival we found him solemnly addressing two young Japanese Lieutenants. The two officers were being instructed to swim across the Irrawaddy at night on a suicidal mission. They were to set fire to various concentrations of enemy vehicles and dumps. After the instructions were over, the two officers bowed and straightaway proceeded on their mission. They were the ones whom Slim describes as two Japanese shot by the Special Boat Section of his forces during their final reconnaissance of the river bank. The visit to the Japanese

Company, though of little tactical importance, was impressive. Their fighting spirit was, indeed, inspiring. The handsome young faces of the two would-be martyrs with their respectful last bow come vividly before my eyes even today as I write these words.

I returned to Tetthe and met Hari Ram and Chander Bhan. En route Chander Bhan gave me the news that one of his Companies under Lieutenant Dunichand, which had gone seventy miles off track while coming from Myingyan and was believed to have been lost, had reported arrival just then. After enquiring about their battle-worthiness, I suggested to Chander Bhan that the Company be put in the front to strengthen the defences.

Dunichand had followed a circuitous route and entered Pagan from its southern end. Chander Bhan's Battalion Headquarters were situated on the northern end of Pagan. Dunichand marched to reach the Headquarters through the town like a flag march giving the false impression to the enemy that we had received huge reinforcements during the night and had occupied the whole town.

Victory Into Defeat

The night of the 13th/14th February was pitch dark. Just after midnight the enemy launched an assault in front of the 8th Battalion deployed at Pagan. The leading Unit of the enemy headed towards the river-bank where Dunichand had taken up his position late that night. Because of their earlier absence, Dunichand and his men were ignorant of the orders prohibiting the shouting of slogans and firing at night. As soon as there was movement on the surface of the water, Dunichand alerted his men and at the earliest sign of the enemy approach, opened fire with all available weapons including mortars at his disposal. Added to this fire, he led his party in the shouting of slogans, "*Chalo Delhi*", and "*Netaji Zindabad*" along with other national slogans. There was panic among the assaulting enemy waves. A voice was heard shouting, "*Oye! Atma Singh, Come back. They are Chalo Delhi wallas.*"

In their effort to retreat as they wielded their clumsy country boats to turn about, the enemy exposed their flank to the defenders. More than twenty of their boats were sunk. Their casualties mounted as much due to our fire as to drowning and panic. The assault having failed, the enemy had to withdraw. Dunichand's ignorance of orders for silence won us an initial victory and "The Nehru" kept on holding the Irrawaddy. This was our first victory.

After their failure at Pagan, the enemy tried another assault crossing opposite Nyaungu by using outboard motors and rubber boats. This time a British Regiment, the South Lancashires, was put in the field. The employment of a British Unit after the failure of an Indian Unit at Pagan, was taken by us as a sign of lack of confidence by the British in their Indian troops while employing them to oppose the INA. It suited our aim. Though Indian compatriots were fighting against one another on the opposing sides, the feelings of patriotism and nationalism did weigh in favour of the INA in an Indian heart whenever there was a direct clash between the two.

From our side now, it was Hari Ram's turn, the 7th Battalion, to receive the enemy. Here we had the advantage of having the advancing enemy in full view when most vulnerable. To start with, contrary to strict instructions against opening fire, triggers were pressed too early when the enemy was yet beyond our range of fire. Though this early fire could cause no harm to the enemy, it did make his leading boats change their course, which created disorder and confusion among them. Soon our machine-gun belts got exhausted. By now, the enemy started aerial and artillery bombardment of our positions. As our machine-gun crew were recharging their belts, the enemy mistook our silence for having been caused by their artillery and air attack. They continued advancing ignoring our rifle fire.

Meanwhile, the darkness of the dawn disappeared. The sun floodlit the waters of Irrawaddy with its golden rays. The British assaulting troops had advanced within five hundred yards from our trenches when our machine-guns with fully charged belts sprang back into action. The assaulting troops got mowed like grass by a lawn-mower. Their fate was worse than that of the 89th Brigade at Pagan. Hundreds of them were killed or drowned. Even their Commanding Officer had to swim back in under dress to save his life. We estimated that they suffered more than four hundred casualties. South Lancashire as a Regiment were put out of action. Having failed, the enemy had no other choice but to retreat under the barrage of artillery and of air force cover. This was another victory.

On hearing the very first sound of fire on the river, I had left Tetthe for the front. I went to Pagan. Chander Bhan showed me the enemy boats still on the water surface abandoned and upturned floating down the river. Our jawans were naturally in high spirit. Luck often plays a significant role in war. We had been lucky to have Dunichand's sudden appearance on the scene. With all the expectations of the enemy's attack and our precautions, another Company Commander in Dunichand's position might not have differentiated between a reconnaissance patrol and an assault crossing and would have hesitated to open an all-out fire in view of the existing instructions for maintaining silence and secrecy. Due to lack of means of communication, timely directions would not have been possible either.

From Chander Bhan as I moved on to Hari Ram to be with him during the assault on his front, the first phase of the encounter was over. The enemy bombardment from the ground and the air had started blasting our side of the bank. In the noise of the battle, it could not be ascertained why our machine-guns had gone silent. After sometime, however, they started firing. I had left Tetthe with eleven runners, Mohinder, an Intelligence Havildar, a Liaison Officer and lzumi. Up to my arrival at Hari Ram's headquarters, I employed four runners, to send various messages and had deputed Mohinder, his Havildar and the Liaison Officer for various jobs.

I was left with one runner and Izumi only. Under the circumstances, the resumption of fire of our machine-guns sounded soothing and reassuring. By the time I met Hari Ram, the sight on the surface of water was indeed ghastly. It was apparent that in spite of their artillery and air power, the enemy would dare not advance during the daylight hours. Another day was gone, I felt. Unmindful of having suffered heavy casualties, our jawans were in a triumphant mood and in high spirit. As I went round, their ovations made me feel proud of them. Their performance gave me courage. Visibly impressed, Izumi was full of praise for the action.

In the meantime, it appeared that the British had effected a crossing in front of the Japanese towards the north of our sector. It was essential for me to learn the progress of the battle. Accordingly, I set out accompanied by Izumi and one surviving runner to assess the situation personally.

Immediately towards the north of the Japanese position started a range of low-lying hills or cliffs which the enemy had occupied. There was an exchange of fire going on between the British and the Japanese sides. In between these cliffs and ourselves was a solitary hill (knoll) in which there was a cave. Like many other caves in that area, this cave provided an excellent cover from the air and from the ground.

As we neared the cave, an enemy air-attack made us take shelter in it. There were three non-combatant Japanese soldiers already trapped in the cave. They had been cut off from their retreating Company. The cave had an entrance on the western side, through which the enemy was visible atop the hills towards the north and north-east. Their nearest location was hardly three hundred yards from the cave. The air-raid continued with wave after wave and was an unending affair with the difference that instead of heavy bombs now they were throwing anti-personnel explosives. Their dummy flights indicated an approach of their ground forces. Soon we saw that the enemy had lined his machine-guns to cover the entrance of the cave we were in. The exit out of the cave through the main opening thus appeared to be full of risk.

On one side of the cave there was another opening like a ventilator approachable by a steep slope. To ascertain the possibility of an escape through that opening, I sent two of the Japanese soldiers to climb up and have a look. As soon as one of them peeped out of the opening, he was fired upon by the enemy machine-guns and as such had to slide down quicker than he had gone up. Appreciating that any further stay in the cave meant sure captivity, I decided that we must try an escape, come what may. This meant a complete exposure to the enemy machine-gun and mortar fire for about one hundred fifty yards in the open from the exit of the cave to a clump of trees on the south-west of the cave.

Izumi's Devotion

After rushing out of the cave, our safety would hang between our speed and the enemy's capability to shoot us. Having instructed and explained the details of the escape, as I moved towards the exit to rush out, Izumi stepped forward and stopped me saying, "Sir, let me go out first, for if I am killed only a Captain is killed? But if you are killed, a very important person, that is a Commander is lined. Your life is more important for the cause than mine." He had already stepped into the exit and would have rushed out if I had not pulled him back making him nearly fall down. This selfless and heroic expression on the part of Izumi had provoked me to shout out, "No, you will not. I order you to follow me. It is a Commander's privilege to lead". Before he could recover his steps, I rushed out of the cave followed by Izumi and others with the hostile fire following us all. We ran in a zigzig manner to keep on upsetting the enemy's aim. At last we reached the trees and fell down behind their stumps for cover. From the clump of those trees we had to crawl back to be out of danger. My intention was to reach my Headquarters via Hari Ram's defences. On the way, I was shocked to learn that after exhausting all his ammunition and after having fought so bravely, he had lost heart and had put his hands up. He had invited the enemy by a white flag and had offered to surrender along with his troops. Most of the men refused to surrender and withdrew from the battlefield. About one hundred and twenty obeyed him and surrendered.

Thus having got frightened of the overwhelming odds, Hari Ram lost courage and along with it lost the battle which actually he had so bravely won. I wish he had shown a wee-bit more grit. I feel sorry for him because even his inactivity during the hours of darkness would have kept the enemy at bay. It often happens that in a battle when you think you are done for, the opponent also feels the same way. The one who endures wins. But then there is a limit to human endurance against material odds.

The Retreat

Hari Ram's action caused panic throughout his Battalion. Men who did not wish to surrender had no leader on the spot to rally round. They bolted from their posts and made for Tetthe or even for Mount Popa and beyond. There had been some arguments between Hari Ram and his men. Those who refused to surrender were threatened to be shot by him. The result was that Hari Ram got shot instead. Hari Ram's death could not improve the situation, nor was it known at the time.

The fact that Hari Ram had been shot was not disclosed to me during the war. I suspected that Hari Ram had not survived the war but had no definite knowledge. The fact was brought to my notice as late as 23rd January 1973 by the jawan who shot him. The jawan met me during my visit to Trivandrum in connection with Netaji's birth anniversary celebrations.

On arrival at Tetthe, I found that the news of Hari Ram's surrender had created panic among the Reserve Line troops as well. Consequently, I collected all the troops at Tetthe and gave them a pep talk to restore and boost up their morale. The men responded by shouting national slogans and "*Netaji Zindabad*".

My immediate concern was to know how Chander Bhan was faring at Pagan. Two runners were dispatched for this purpose. I sent him a written message to contact me or let me know about the condition at the earliest. I told him to inform me about his Unit immediately. In case he could not contact me by midnight, I would consider that he was in a helpless situation. In that case he would be free to withdraw on his own initiative to Mount Popa and report to the Brigade 2nd-in-Command, Major Jagir Singh. I would wait for him at Tetthe till midnight at all costs. After midnight I too would fall back to Mount Popa.

After the departure of messengers, the hostile shelling of the village on our defences increased. We were surrounded from the north and north-west. The enemy penetrated in between Tetthe and Pagan. Chander Bhan was cut off from me.

Things looked difficult. Realising the responsibility of sending back information about the situation of my sector, I suggested to Izumi to go back to the rear. At that time I did not know that the INA 2nd Division had been ordered to move to occupy Mount Popa. Izumi was reluctant to leave me behind in such a desperate situation. He was determined to go through with me to the end. I reasoned out the necessity and my responsibility to send back the information. Izumi obeyed.

Meanwhile, the situation was worsening every moment. Any further inertia on my part would be disastrous. A suicidal counter-attack appeared to be the only way out. This was the second time that in preparation for facing an expected discomfiture, I had to destroy precious and important documents, diaries and letters to avoid them falling into the enemy hands. A similar precaution was taken to ensure that Izumi did not carry any important papers on his person. I sent Mohinder and most of my Headquarters staff with Izumi. I took this decision because I could not risk my important Staff Officers staying back for suicidal role with me. They would be needed by Jagir for the future conduct of the war. Mount Popa, I thought, was going to be the enemy's next objective. Izumi's departure along with Mohinder and party was deeply moving. We felt we might never meet again.

My next action was to order Khan Mohd. to launch a counter-attack. On receiving the orders, Khan Mohd. along with an elderly Lieut., an engineer, requested me to allow them to be seen alone. I consented. They addressed me in words to the effect, "Sir, are you not contented with having made us fight against such heavy odds ? Are you not satisfied with having sacrificed so many men and having shed so much of blood ? What will you gain by getting the remaining men also killed ? For God's sake have mercy upon us and allow us to surrender rather than condemning everyone to death."

I told them that my heart rebelled at the very thought of surrender but I would let them know my decision within a few minutes of pondering over the situation alone. So I retired behind a cover of haystacks on one corner of the headman's courtyard. Here I burst out crying and asked myself as to what to do and what not to do. I felt the burden heavier than what my shoulders could bear.

Pulling out Netaji's photo out of my map-case I talked to it as though I had gone mad. Reporting the situation to Netaji, as if in person, I asked him for a way out. His serene and determined face with the chin up appeared to be reminding me of his warm handshake and my words to him, *"Main apki ankhen kisi ke samne nichi na hone dunga",*— I will not let you be humbled before anybody —, and his reply " I have confidence." I felt guilty before him even for giving a thought to the word 'surrender'. I cursed myself for not having cursed the two officers who had spoken to me so frankly.

Then I intuitively prayed to Guru Gobind Singh for light and strength. And I saw a vision ! Just above the trees, in the sky there was the Guru, wearing the Golden Crest on His turban, with His Quiver slung over a shoulder and the Golden Hawk perched on His hand. I asked the Guru if I deserved to be disgraced thus, after having tried as I had. I might be a clean- shaven Sikh, a *patit,* the fallen one, yet in history I would go down as Gurbakhsh Singh. I concluded, "History will not record whether I am a good Sikh or a bad Sikh, nor it may record the difficulties surrounding me. But it will definitely record that your one Sikh let down Netaji, the INA and the Freedom Movement at a crucial hour. Now it is up to you to save your Sikh from disgrace. You know the facts better than I do. Grant me courage, O! Guru, grant it before it is too late." I had uttered words to the above effects in sobs as a son before his father. It may be added that a Sikh is supposed to have five K's : (1) kaishas, hair; (2) kanga, a comb; (3) kara, an iron bangle; (4) kirpan, a sword and (5) kachhehra, a pair of shorts. I was a *patit* or a fallen one because I had removed my hair, the most important of all the symbols of Sikhism.

Having unburdened myself, as I emerged out of the seclusion, I was a different man. Gone were tears and the feelings of doubt and fear. I had regained self-confidence and courage. It was a complete transformation. During those few minutes, the proposers of the surrender had already provided themselves with a piece of white cloth to make a flag. As I saw it, I shouted, "Tear it off. There will be no surrender". I collected all the men once again and gave them another talk. I told them that anybody who did not have heart to fight was allowed to withdraw from the south-west of the village and to proceed to Mount Popa. Only those men who were willing to fight up to the last round should stay with me. I would not force anybody to stay back.

As for myself I was committed to stay at Tethhe till midnight as per my instructions to Chander Bhan. I was obliged to inform him about any change in the location of my Headquarters, failing which I might cause disorder and disaster to him. Upon my call the men rallied round and the defences around Tetthe were manned and enemy fire returned. A counter, attack could not be launched due to lack of information about the enemy and due to darkness. The enemy, however, remained at a respectable distance from the village and dared not enter it. They were as much cautious of us as we were of them. Intermittent shelling from their side and of our defences in the village continued.

Here I may record that though Khan Mohd. had proposed to surrender yet neither he nor his co-proposer deserted me. The enemy artillery and mortar fire increased. In the darkness our casualties grew. Most of the bullocks were either killed or ran away because of shelling, leaving many carts without their drafting power.

Looking after the wounded was a job. At about 10 p.m. Dr. Krishnan reported that he had evacuated the wounded by bullock-carts on the way to Popa. With about twenty men, he himself would be available in a pagoda outside the village, if needed. The shelling grew heavier. Sitting alone in an open trench with Mehar Singh at a little distance away, I watched for the enemy and waited for the news from Chander Bhan. Against the enemy's sudden approach I had equipped myself with two grenades tied to my waist belt. I had straightened their safety pins so as to cause no delay while pulling them off during an emergency. I intended to use these grenades as a last recourse to avoid being captured alive.

At about midnight the shelling stopped. I took it as a prelude to an enemy attack. Someone approached in the dark stealthily, presumably a local, used as a spy. He came to me and asked in Burmese if there were any INA troops in the village. I replied that I did not know. He went back leaving me suspicious and warned.

Now it was the time for me to withdraw as it was well after midnight. Chander Bhan had not been able to contact. I presumed he had difficulties of his own. A patrol sent earlier could not bring back any definite information either. Realising the helplessness of the situation I ordered a withdrawal. Bullocks of my cart had been killed but Mehar Singh managed to get someone else's pair and we started withdrawing from the village. I allowed Khan Mohd. to make straight to Mount Popa. As for myself, my conscience could not permit me to withdraw without having a definite information about Chander Bhan's Battalion and the situation at Pagan.

So with my bullock-cart and five personnel as an escort, I started for Pagan. Dr. Krishnan along with his twenty non-combatants volunteered to accompany me. Apparently Krishnan was anxious about my security. Advance towards Pagan had to be by a circuitous route calling for caution and time. By dawn we arrived at Ananda pagoda where we found our ration stores intact. I asked Krishnan to let the men help themselves to as much ration as they could carry and get certain bags loaded on the cart. After doing so, he was to proceed on a particular track leading to a village, Bwasaw. Meanwhile, with an escort I made for the river bank close-by. The sun was just rising, one of the saddest sunrise of my life.

As I stood on the eastern bank of the Irrawaddy near Ananda pagoda, it was strangely quiet on the river front. Taking cover of the sand-dunes and bushes, I proceeded towards Pagan. Half way to the town, I met a Burman whom I recognised. We had met at the headman's residence during my earlier reconnaissance. We greeted each other. He was surprised to find me there, and pointing towards the enemy troops who were hardly two hundred yards away on the eastern bank, he warned me of the danger. I extricated myself out of the perilous situation and before leaving told the Burman to help himself and his people with our rations lying in the Ananda pagoda. Apart from rewarding the villager for his timely warning I got him engaged to keep him away from contacting the enemy for some time.

Krishnan and the party with the bullock-cart had made good progress and were at a safe distance from the enemy. My escorts and I made haste to join them. We reached Bwasaw at about 9 a.m. on 15th February. Through the courtesy of the village headman we had two hours halt in the village. During that time he arranged to help us cook meals. I had a much needed bath and a bit of sleep. We were obliged to leave the village hurriedly for the villagers safety point of view.

But as soon as we left, the enemy planes attacked the village and put it to flames. Those bombs were meant for us. The villagers got punished for giving us a little refuge. I felt guilty and wished we had not stayed there. I decided thenceforth not to enter any village en route. Soon I was to see most of the villages including Tetthe in flames as a result of the enemy air-attacks. We were so much harried by the enemy aeroplanes that perforce our march had to be dead slow and cautious.

After nightfall Krishnan and Mehar Singh urged me to climb up the cart for a ride and rest. Mehar Singh had made my bed, spreading the hold-all with hay underneath. I stretched myself to go to sleep but I could get no sleep. Lying on the bullock-cart half asleep and half awake, I felt such a sense of failure that the whole Nyaungu-Pagan catastrophe appeared to be my personal affair. I asked myself what else I could have done and at what point in the last fortnight I could have made another decision to avert the disaster. How could "The Nehru" hold the Irrawaddy any longer ? I was so keenly pricked by the thought of the defeat that I asked myself as to why I was leading my men to Popa ? Would I get another opportunity to fight ? Would Netaji give me another chance after all that had happened ? My move appeared to be an aimless venture, an exercise in futility. Melancholy and despair enveloped me. Eventually I fell asleep.

By about midnight, the bullock-cart stopped. I was shaken out of a dream which was something like this: "A very senior staff officer of a General's rank informed me that he had specially been deputed by Netaji to receive me and lead me to a place where Netaji was waiting to meet me." The halting of the cart awakened me and the dream was left unfinished. As I asked the reason for the halt, Krishnan told me that they had arrived at a crossroad and he could not decide which way to choose, hence he had called a halt.

The dream had already elevated my spirits. To be received by Netaji, even though in a dream, was auspicious. Krishnan's enquiry following the dream made me feel wanted. Yes, I was wanted. I shall have to shake off the feelings of shame, despair, despondency and defeat. Thenceforth I took the retreat as an inevitable manoeuvre. Mount Popa silhouetted above the sky-line to south-east appeared to be calling. Steadily we kept on advancing towards it.

15

Mount Popa and Kyauk Padaung

Mount Popa rises suddenly and steeply out of a plain country. Its height is nearly five thousand feet above the mean sea level. It is about 50 square miles (49.63 sq. miles) in area. On its western slope there is a plateau at a height of less than two thousand feet, on which Popa village is situated. The village is also called Popayuwa. Near the village there are groves of fruit trees —mangoes, jack-fruit and bananas. The village stands on the highway to Taungtha and Myingyan on the way to Mandalay in the north and Kyauk Padaung in the south leading to Yeenangyaung and Prome on the way to Rangoon. Meiktila where Kimura and Slim were to have the decisive battle of the war in Burma lies about fifty miles east of it. A direct road from Meiktila to Nayaungu passes through Kyaukpadaung. The successful crossing of the Slim's army at Nyaungu had enhanced the strategic value of Kyaukpadaung and Popa.

On the 17th February at about 10.30 morning, I reached the outskirts of village Popa. Jagir, Rawat, Chander Bhan, Khan Mohd., Kartar Singh, Izumi and quite a crowd of Officers received me with apparent relief. Having received earlier information of my arrival they had come out to give me a sad yet warm reception. They made me feel wanted.

One of the Officers who came to receive me was 2nd Lieut. Mangu Ram. This Officer suffered from what I may call air phobia. The very sound of aeroplanes or even the warning of their approach would frighten him so much that he would run away along with his Platoon to hide somewhere miles away from his post and would never be available for any action during or after an air attack. While he was shaking hands with me, perchance, we were attacked by the enemy planes. Mangu Ram started trembling and tried to run away. As his hand was in my grip, I did not let him go, keeping him and myself exposed to the enemy air attack. Mangu Ram struggled hard to get away but I kept him pinned to the ground as if in a wrestling bout. Both of us were in an open harvested cornfield. After the air-raid was over, Mangu Ram lost the fear of aeroplanes and got cured of the malady. Thereafter, he was to be one of my most fearless, brave and dependable Platoon Commanders. He was destined to be one of the heroes of my Brigade in the near future.

Defeat in itself is a very painful affair but demoralisation makes it still worse. The way my men suffered was writ large on their faces. My previous Unit, the 5th Guerrilla Regiment, reorganized as the 2nd Infantry Regiment under its new commander, Lieut. Colonel P.K. Sahgal (later Colonel) had also started arriving at Popa. It was but natural that we were looked down upon by the Officers and men of the sister Unit. At the moment, I deserved nothing better.

It was fortunate that I had sent back Capt. Izumi from my headquarters Tetthe beside Irrawaddy. He had gone beyond Meiktila and met Netaji. He had made an actual report about the situation at Nyaungu and Pagan. He had praised my action as "superhuman effort." Besides Izumi, my greatest support, however, lay in Jagir Singh, my officers and men who stood by me in that adversity.

On the following day, 18th February, Sahgal arrived. He was officiating Commander of No. 2 Division of the INA. It was nice to have someone to approach. Within a couple of days, my officers managed to collect about five hundred of our men. I was at the time anxious about the defence of Kyaukpadaung. It was my feeling that the enemy would try his best to use the Nyaungu-Meiktila road which passed through Kyaukpadaung. That road had to be denied to the enemy if we were to hold Mount Popa. When I discussed the situation with Sahgal, he agreed with my perception and assigned me the defence of Kyaukpadaung and the road running from Kyaukpadaung to Nyaungu.

On 22nd February Col. Shah Nawaz Khan (later Major General), who was to Command No. 2 Division instead of Col. Aziz Ahmad who had been wounded in an air raid on Rangoon, arrived along with Netaji's

Military Secretary, Major (later Col.) Mahboob Ahmad. At the time Jagir, Chander Bhan and I were at Indaw, a village near Kyaukpadaung. Salutations over, Mahboob congratulated me on behalf of Netaji and himself on my promotion to Lieutenant Colonel. Mahboob was a kind-hearted friend. We knew each other since our Indian Military Academy days. He had chosen the occasion to approach me on a pleasant note but I had yet not reconciled myself to defeat at Nyaungu.

On hearing the congratulatory words I got enraged and told Mahboob to take the promotion back. I said, "I do not deserve it and in any case this is not the time for me to take the promotion when I have been just defeated." Mahboob argued that it was not a special promotion; it was according to my seniority. Its coming into effect with my defeat was coincidental. He further pointed out that my refusal to accept a promotion, for which orders had already been published, boiled down to disobedience of orders. I was, however, not in mood to accept any advice from him. Feeling hurt, he reported the matter to Shah Nawaz, who advised him not to argue with me but report the matter to Netaji on his return.

Shah Nawaz had been sent by Netaji specially to assess and report the situation prevailing in my Brigade and at Mount Popa and Kyaukpadaung areas. He took a written report from me about the battle of Nyaungu and Pagan. He interrogated me thoroughly regarding various stages of the battle. He appreciated the difficulties I had been through. I found in him a man of understanding and generosity. His two days' stay helped me to sort out many problems.

Shah Nawaz had brought with him a letter from Netaji in which Netaji had shown his displeasure in the very first sentence thus, "I have heard with grief, pain and shame of the treachery shown by Lieut. Hari Ram and others." The relieving factor in the letter was that Netaji had hoped that, "The 4th Guerrilla Regiment would wash away the blot on INA with their own blood." So Netaji had not lost confidence in us. This was much more than what I had expected. I had read and seen how military commanders were normally given a sack under such circumstances. On the contrary, Netaji had acted with unusual competence in perception and large-heartedness in dealing with us so kindly. Trust is the most powerful morale booster. I collected all my officers and men and read out Netaji's letter to them. They all made me feel that we would live up to Netaji's expectations in our immediate future facing us.

Those of my men who had left me at Nyaungu had gone back even beyond Meiktila and reached Pyinmana where Netaji was camping on his way to the front. They told different stories about me. Some said that I had been killed in action, some said that I had committed suicide, and yet some said that I had surrendered to the enemy. Netaji wanted to know if anybody had actually seen me surrender. When Netaji learnt from Captain Izumi about the True situation, and received my battle report through Shah Nawaz along with his appreciation of the whole episode, and on hearing from Mahboob that I had refused to accept my promotion, Netaji appreciated my position and sentiments. Netaji collected my men and told them that they had deserted me and asked them what punishment should be awarded to them. They all pleaded guilty and appealed to be forgiven and sent back to me. Netaji pardoned them all and sent them to me with a word that I might accept them. They were over three hundred strong and I was happy to get them back. We had lost a lot but gained in experience. Once again "The Nehru" was in a position to go forward.

Meanwhile I received a message of goodwill from a friend at Myingyan wishing me to do something for my country and one day be a well-known person of the world. One of the most beautiful laws of nature is that things do not remain the same for ever. Time changes and it appeared to be changing for the better and I thought nothing was ever so dark as it appeared on the first sight.

Operations Popa and Kyauk Padaung

On 23rd February, 1945, Gen. Shah Nawaz visited the Commander of Khanjo Butai and discussed co-ordination of Indo-Japanese operations in the Popa and Kyauk Padaung area. He held a Regimental Commanders' conference at Popa. No. 2 Infantry Regiment, Col. Sahgal, was given the task to prepare Popa as a strong base with the view to take up an offensive role. My Regiment, the 4th Guerrilla, was assigned the duty to check the enemy advance on to Kyauk Padaung from the west, where the British had established a strong bridgehead at Nyaungu. This was to be achieved by carrying out an extensive and persistent guerrilla warfare in the area between Popa, Kyauk Padaung line in the east and as far forward towards the Irrawaddy as possible so as to deny the enemy the use of Nyaungu-Kyauk-Padaullg-Meiktila metalled road for supplying reinforcements and supplies to his forces fighting in the battle of Meiktila.

In spite of heavy losses they had suffered, my officers and men took up this role with a renewed enthusiasm. They were in the right frame of mind to come up to Netaji's expectations that, "The 4th Guerrilla Regiment would wash away the blot on the I.N.A with their own blood."

Shah Nawaz and Mahboob left for Meiktila on the way to Pyinmana where Netaji was waiting to receive the detailed information about the Popa-Kyauk Padaung situation. I accompanied Shah Nawaz up to Kyauk Padaung where two Battalions of my Regiment were already in position. Col. Jagir Singh along with the two Battalions held the ground. My 3rd Battalion was still in Popa.

On 25th February I received at Kyauk Padaung a reinforcement of about 350 men. They were the very men who had deserted me at Nyaungu and Pagan and met Netaji in Pyinmana camp. They had owned their fault and in his sagacity Netaji pardoned them and sent them to me asking me to accept them back. I welcomed them and posted them to their respective Units. Here I am glad to record that none of them let me down during the ensuing difficult days. Many of them paid the price of India's liberty with their life. I attribute their miraculous transformation to Netaji's personal touch and his unique quality and method of dealing with men in war.

Two days later, two of our patrols met an enemy mechanized patrol escorted by tanks. Our men were armed with mere 303 rifles. Knowing full well that the rifle-fire could not harm the tanks, they fired at them. Instead of returning fire, the enemy hastened to withdraw. This simple occurrence served my men as a morale booster.

On the first of March, a sad thing happened at Popa. Five officers of the 2nd Division went over to the enemy. Sahgal who was officiating as Div. Commander for Shah Nawaz, called me to Popa to take over 'G' Branch of the Div. (which dealt with operations). I had to look after 'A' (Adjutant's) and 'Q' (Quartermaster's) work also. Leaving my 2nd-in-Command Major Jagir Singh to look after the Nehru Brigade Units at Kyank Padaung, I went to Popa. One of my Battalions was located at Popa. Now I had to do two jobs, to Command my own Regiment and to attend to all the staff work at the Div. Hq. Sahgal's hands were similarly full with two commands, of his own Regiment and the Division. Our difficulties increased by regular air raids of the enemy. The enemy had by now got exact information of our locations from the deserted staff officers. Enemy planes dropped pamphlets addressed to the Officers and men of the 2nd Infantry Regiment. These pamphlets were signed by one of the five deserters who belonged to that Regiment. Our casualties in the Popa area were more than 500 killed and many more wounded due to the treachery of our officers. We were forced to keep on changing our Unit locations at Mount Popa.

In my Brigade area, a Company deployed about ten miles to the west of Kyauk Padaung too had an unpleasant experience. Five of its men went over to the enemy. It was not a case of just desertion. After having gone over, they guided the enemy during an attack on our Company by coming along with the enemy to show the spot where our Company was located. Luckily, after their desertion, the headman of the village informed our Company Commander that those deserters had communicated with the enemy through the medium of one of their villagers. The medium had warned the headman that the presence of the INA Company in the village was dangerous, because the British might attack the Indians in the near future. The headman appealed to our Company Commander to vacate the village so as to save the life and property of the innocent villagers. Our Company Commander took immediate steps and left the village. He then took up a defensive position some distance away from the village towards the enemy side.

The next day just after dusk, the enemy came unaware of our readiness to welcome them. The enemy forces were accompanied by our deserters. The enemy was surprised when our Company opened an intensive fire on them. Two of the enemy soldiers and one of our deserters immediately fell dead and the enemy hastened to show their backs. Our men chased the enemy and were successful in capturing four of our deserters who had deserted the previous day. In this encounter it was the Platoon to which the deserters belonged that captured them.

These men were produced before me at Popa. I remanded them for trial by the Div. Commander, Colonel Sahgal who sentenced them to death. Before their execution I had called their Battalion to be present. I asked all the officers and men of the Battalion whether anybody was in favour of forgiving them. Everyone shouted, "No". Then I said, "Who will shoot them ? Take a step forward." Everybody took a step forward. Then I asked who would shoot them. Everybody put his hand up. I selected a squad of four. Poor souls! They were liquidated by the squad.

During his stay in Pyimana, Netaji formed 'X' Regiment out of the able-bodied veterans of Imphal Campaign. Its Command was given to Colonel Thakar Singh, Sardar-e-Jung, one of our heroes of Kohima. From Pyinmana Netaji learnt about the desertion of the five officers from Popa. Netaji was so much hurt that out of shame he did not show his face to anybody for three days. His sole counsel during that time was GITA, the sermon given by Lord Krishna on the battlefield at Kurukshetra to Arjuna, one of the heroes among the Pandavas of the Mahanbharat epic.

Early on the 12th of March at 8 a.m. Shah Nawaz arrived at Popa. He was accompanied by Major (later Colonel) Mehar Dass, Sardar-e-Jung and Major (later Colonel) A.B. Singh, his new Staff Officers. Col. J.W. Rordrigues followed with some reinforcements a bit later. I felt great relief on the arrival of these Staff Officers. Shah Nawaz relieved me forthwith and I went to rejoin my Regiment with feelings of home-coming.

I record it with a sense of gratitude at the way my 2nd-in-Command Major Jagir Singh conducted the activities of the Nehru Brigade during my absence. I owe special thanks to the Brigade Staff Officers, Capt. Darwan Singh Rawat, Capt. Mohd. Khan, and Lieut. Mohinder Singh as well as to my Battalion Commanders, Capt. (later Major) Chander Bhan, Capt. Mohammad Hussain and Lieut. (later Capt.) Kartar Singh and their Company Commanders. We were by then spread out over an area of about 15 square miles west of Popa and Kyauk Padaung right up to Taungzin. I sent back Jagir to Popa to be close to the Div. Hq. so as to keep "The Nehru" well supplied with water and rations.

Water Problem

I moved my Headquarters a bit forward in the revines of the Irrawaddy near a village, KHABOK. Here I was hardly seven miles away from the enemy stronghold of Pyinbin, their harbour on the way to Meiktila. The ground features at Khabok afforded us good cover from the ground as well as from the air. The enemy had complete supremacy of the skies. Besides enemy's constant air raids and heavy bombardments, our greatest problem was the lack of water point in our area. It had to be supplied from Popa by hired bullock-carts which could move only during the night. Often the carts came under enemy air raids and the bullocks would stampede away or get killed. Once we could receive only two barrels of water out of twelve barrels sent by Jagir. Each cart could not carry more than two barrels. Normally cartmen carried only one barrel as the route was uneven. I could only provide a litre per head of water per day.

There were days when I could not provide even that little water and had to depend on the villagers to get us sap from date-palm trees. As this liquid, if left to stay, would ferment and become toddy so men were advised to drink it fresh and not let it turn into an alcoholic drink. As a further precaution, Unit Commanders were ordered to give each man five rupees in the morning and five rupees in the evening for the purchase of a pot at each time. An earthen pot contained about half a litre to three-quarters of a litre of the liquid. It was sweet and cool in the morning. During those days we could get no wash. I often felt lice crawling on my body and when I moved my hand over my head or neck, a small flat wingless insect, louse, would come into my hand. With an all-round white appearance, it had a dark red spot in its centre showing the blood sucked by the parasite.

The nearest water point in our operational area was at Pyinbin which was under the enemy. I was lucky that I had a few Burma-born Gurkhas in the Brigade. Their features and the language were typically Burman. In the garb of villagers they brought us water on carts from Pyinbin. It was a suicidal job which they accomplished day after day without betraying our locations. At times we purchased water from the villagers at the rate of five hundred rupees per barrel of two hundred litres. Certain Phonjis, Buddhist monks, gave us water at the nominal price of five rupees for a barrel. This water was stored during rains in their underground tanks. The Deputy Commissioner at Myingyan had advised me always to call on the local Phonji whenever I entered a new area. This courtesy paid us very handsomely.

The Villagers

Generally, Burmese villagers are simple folks who never like trouble, but only God could save the man who dared trouble them. They would take revenge when least expected. They were very truthful. In their simplicity and innocence they would say, *"Sahib ham jhooth bole na sakta. Aap poochhta American ya Angrez kahan hai ham aap ko sach batlata. Woh poochhta aap kahan hai, ham unko sach batlata.* (Sir we can't tell a lie. You ask us about the whereabouts of the Americans or the British, we tell you the truth. When they ask us about you we also tell the truth)." Thus, their truthful nature helped us to keep our positions changing and we took steps to make the villagers feel that we were spread out all over the area. We exaggerated our strength and the villagers let our enemies believe that we were present everywhere and in overwhelming numbers.

The modus operandi of the enemy was very much dependent on tanks and armoured fighting vehicles. Usually they did not send out a party less than about a hundred. The vehicles carried their troops escorted in front and in the rear by A.F.Vs. On arrival at a place where they had to stop they fixed machine-guns and mortars before debussing the troops. Our men developed such a confidence that they would let a few bullet fly over the enemy. It followed an exchange of fire and invariably the enemy hastened to embuss and withdraw.

During that period, seldom a day passed when we did not raid the enemy. Normally we used to raid them during the night and they raided us during the day. Many a time we attacked the enemy position to find that they had evacuated before our attack went home. There were days when we shared the occupation of places in our area during the night and they occupied it during the day as if their existed a settlement between the two. Many a time our patrols were seen by the enemy patrols or viceversa and firing started on both sides mostly from long range.

One day towards the end of March 1945, an enemy patrol about fifty in strength approached one of our Company positions at 1600 hrs. Our Company Commander Lieut. Ram Nath, warned by his forward observation post, sent two Platoons to encircle the enemy. Before this could be done, the enemy, finding our men trying to envelop them from two flanks, started running back. Our men ran after them for about two miles as if chasing a game during peace time. Our Platoon Commanders had a job collecting their men who shouted, "*Oe! baat tau sun jao* (Please listen to us)." When the enemy opened fire from a distance even then our men failed to take to the ground. They were civilian raw recruits. Their Commanders succeeded in bringing them back to our trenches and when they were told that they should not have done so, the men replied, "Sir, what are we to do when the enemy does not even stop to face us ?" It shows good spirit but bad training. We were hard put to train these men. I used to issue, "Training Notes during War", to my sub-units. I was reminded of Napoleon, "Training is war, war is training."

We learnt from certain villagers that the enemy troops took away young women and kept them for a day or so and then sent them back. Rape cases made the villagers anti-British. Their weakness was our strength. That was why during our stay in the Taungzin area Burmese villagers started co-operating with us. These simple-natured folks turned hostile to the British in spite of the fact that the British gave them food packets and things like socks, shoes, vests and clothes. But honour can never be compensated !

A Gift from Netaji

It was at Khabok that one day I got a case of whisky from the Supreme Headquarters. These were specially sent for me and Col. Sahgal by Netaji. I was surprised to receive such a precious gift from the Supreme Commander and the Head of the Azad Hind Government. My feelings were mixed, happy that Netaji had sent the gift, and sorry that Netaji did not know that I was under a self-imposed vow not to drink till India was free. I gave a bottle each to my Battalion Commanders and one to my 2nd-in-Command, Jagir Singh. I kept two with my batman, Mehar Singh for medicinal use. Out of remaining six bottles, I used to give one as a gift and mark of appreciation when a certain Unit showed good fighting. Once I gave a bottle to go round three hundred officers and men. Having learnt that the bottle had come from Netaji, the men took a few drops each like the sacred AMRITA of immortality with all the solemnity and reverence and shouted Jai Hind, Netaji Zindabad.

I was to learn later the cause of this unusual action on the part of

Netaji. He had sent two cases to Colonel Thakar Singh, Sardar-e-Jung. The story goes that when at Pyinmana, Shah Nawaz produced Thakar Singh before Netaji on the charge of indiscipline, stating that Thakar Singh, the senior-most officer at Pyimnana, had liquor distilled in the camp. Pyinmana camp was composed of the veterans from Imphal Campaign. When it was reported to the Camp Commander, Col. Thakar Singh that the ration of raw sugar, gur, was not good for human consumption, he asked for a sample to check the quality of gur. He found that it was fermented. He ordered the stock to be written off and have fresh gur purchased for issue to the men. He further asked the Quartermaster instead of throwing away the spoilt gur it might be given to him. It was that gur out of which he got alcohol distilled.

When Thakar Singh was produced before Netaji, the following dialogue ensued :

Netaji	:	Colonel Sahib ! *Sunna hai aap ne apni distillery khol rakhi hai?* (It is heard that you are running your own distillery?)
T.S.	:	*Haan Netaji ! Kiya bhi kiya jaye. Yahaan jungle main koi bazar bhi to nahin jo kuchh khareeda ja sake. Apni madad aap hi karni pardti hai* (Yes Netaji ! Here is no bazar in the jungle where anything could be purchased. One has to help one's own self).
Netaji	:	(In English) How is the stuff ?
T.S.	:	Netaji ! It is tolerable when nothing else is available.
Netaji	:	(Appreciating Thakar Singh's helplessness, frankness and straightforwardness). All right, Colonel, you may go.

It was after this episode that when Netaji arrived back at Rangoon, he sent two cases of whisky to Thakar Singh and one case each to Prem Sahgal and me.

In December 1973, I visited the great hero at his home in village Kasso Chahal in the district of Kapurthala in Punjab. I asked Col. Thakar Singh about the above incident. He became emotional and said, "Gurbakhsh ! How great was Netaji." Then he broke down and in sobs said, "Not only the two cases of whisky, Netaji also sent me a leather-cased silver bottle of half a litre capacity and with slightly curved depression so as to fall on the hip conveniently when tied to the waist belt. And more than that he pardoned me, with the result that I never dared break the Camp rules again." He told me that Netaji had got the gift engraved "To Colonel Thakar Singh, Sardar-e-Jang from Subhas Chandra Bose". Then he started crying again and it took me quite sometime to console him. Once an owner of the whole village, Thakar Singh died a pauper but refused to apply for freedom-fighter's Samman pension. His contention was that a person who had given his all should not be humiliated to be asked to apply for help, "Samman, honour is given-not asked."

Samy Gets Specially Made Boots

During my stay at Khabok I also received a pair of service boots for a South Indian sepoy R. Samy. He had very big feet and ever since his joining the INA he could not get a pair of boots which would fit him. I sent a letter along with the footprints of Samy's feet to Colonel K.P. Thimayya, A/Q at the Supreme Headquarters, Rangoon. Netaji saw the letter and told Thimayya to take an immediate action and report to Netaji when the footwear was ready. When I received the pair of boots, there was a small chit along with the issue voucher. On this chit, Netaji wrote to me to personally check that the pair of boots fitted the man properly and send back a report to him. I acted as told by Netaji.

When Samy received his boots and learnt that Netaji had personally taken action to equip him with this essential item, he was overjoyed. Per-chance, he was on the foremost defended locality and an enemy patrol attacked his post. Not caring for the enemy fire he came out of his trench, stood on the parapet of his trench and started firing with his rifle on the advancing enemy. To his good luck, the enemy withdrew. When I went to visit that outpost, his Company Commander reported against the sepoy for exposing himself to the enemy fire. I told Samy that it was wrong on his part. He answered, "Sir how could a bullet hit me today when Netaji had sent me new boots?" So inspired was the man ! So cheerful was his faith in Netaji's blessings even in the face of the enemy bullets.

But for Netaji's personal attention I wonder if "The Nehru" could have held the area for one full month. I confess that it were my men who had inspired me to lead them during that guerrilla warfare. Our troops daily clashed with the enemy and fought many pitched battles.

Employing offensive-defence tactics, Sahgal and the Khanjo Butai attacked the enemy convoys and columns of mechanised troops on their way to Meiktila. Enemy's efforts to occupy Mount Popa were defeated again and again in battles at and around Legyi. The 2nd Infantry Regiment had a head-start when its men wiped out an enemy mechanised patrol who were obliged to leave behind three jeeps and three dead bodies. Two of these jeeps were in working order but the third one had been completely damaged. Lot of information was gathered from the documents and maps found on the dead bodies. Sahgal maintained his Regiment's superior fighting skill in that part of the Popa Mount.

On my side I too had a Company under Capt. Midori Kawa deployed along the area at Taungzin beside Capt. Kartar Singh's Battalion. This Japanese Company was part of Major Watanabe's Battalion of Khanjo Butai. Another Engineering Company of the Khanjo Butai was placed ten miles west of Kyauk Padaung on the road leading to Nyaungu. Both these Japanese Companies and our Units were independent of each other. Our presence in the area was however complementary to both the Japanese and the INA. We acted jointly once only and that was during a night raid near Sade village.

Sade Hill Raid

We learnt from the villagers that Sade hill served as night resting camp for the British. The hill was about 1800 ft. high and had a flat stretch of land on the top. It was steep. Except for one goat track from the north-eastern side of it, there was no route to climb from our side of the hill. This track was narrow and lay through thorny bushes and slippery stones. It could be climbed in single file only. The enemy could not be attacked in force.

In consultation with my Battalion Commander and Major Watanabe I decided to use three Platoons, one from each Battalion of The Nehru Brigade and one from Captain Midori Kawa's Company. The Japanese had one portable infantry gun which could be carried in dismantled parts by four men. It thundered like artillery gun fire. Sade hill was about ten miles away from Khabok. When we were to start for the assembly point at sunset on 16th March, I inspected all three Platoons. I knew that on that day we were short of water and rice could not be cooked. But 1 asked the men whether they had eaten rice. They said, "Yes Sir ! We had rice." I knew that they were not telling the truth yet I found them in high spirits. At the assembly point we had to decide about the selection of the Platoon which would attack the enemy on the hill. My three Platoon Commanders and the Japanese Platoon Commander vied with one another to be the one to go up the hill to attack the enemy. Arguments grew very hot. Ultimately, it was decided by lot and Capt. Khan Mohammad's Platoon won it.

The plan of attack was explained to all the participants on the ground so that each man knew what he was to do and what his fellow participants' job was. It was fully discussed to make sure that a completely foolproof method was adopted before letting the men take up their respective roles in helping the hill-raiding Platoon. The three Platoons supporting the hill raid from below were spread out along the entire length of the hill. All of them including the infantry gun were simultaneously to open fire on the position where main body of the enemy, about a Battalion strong, were resting. The raiding Platoon carried hand grenades and they had orders to launch or throw all the ten grenades which each man had and then withdraw to a given position. The synchronising of the assault was to be done by me by putting a haystack on fire which would serve as a signal to open fire from the foot-hill.

All went well till one of Khan Mohammad's men slipped on a stone and the fall alerted the sentry guarding the track. Luckily at that very moment, our fire from below surprised sleeping enemy. The time was 2 a.m. The British did not expect an attack on such a broad front supported by an artillery gun. They hastened to send up an S.O.S. by firing a very light pistol. The signal went up a bit early and they had not yet withdrawn when their own artillery fire started shelling the hill. An utter panic that followed can be well imagined by the reader. Our assaulting Platoon too had a hard time in disengaging and withdrawing, to join us on the assembly point. It took them full two hours. But by 4 a.m. we hastened to start the return journey to Khabok. We were in a hurry to reach our trenches in the ravines and not to be seen by the early morning enemy planes. Two of our men could not accompany us due to wounds. They joined us by nightfall.

The next day we were to learn that the enemy lost three hundred men killed by our as well as their own artillery fire. Luck did not always favour us like this. In a similar action in that very area we lost seventeen lives.

Another memorable action in Capt. Kartar Singh's 7th Battalion of the Nehru Brigade was performed under one of our great martyrs, 2nd Lieutenant Gian Singh Bisht. I reproduce the description of that glorious action, then written by me as The Charge of the Immortals. The document was produced during the Red Fort trial to show how we waged the war against the King.

The Charge of the Immortals

It was a flat stretch of land without any cover either from view or from fire, except a shallow dry pond near which three roads of great tactical importance met. Four miles north-west of this point was a hill, 1,423 feet high behind which the enemy Artillery was located so as to cover the road junction and the area south of it, the occupation of which would affect the entire plan of operations. At a key point like this was placed a Company of Azad Hind Fauj under the Command of 2/Lt. Gian Singh Bisht trained at the Officers' Training School, Azad Hind Fauj. The Company was only ninety eight strong. They had no machine-guns or even light machine-guns. Good old rifles were their only weapon of defence or offence apart from two A/Tk. mines. Their orders were to check any enemy advance at all costs. They remained in the position for two days, but the enemy dared not advance. Then on 16th of March, 1945 starting early morning, hostile fighting planes bombed and machine-gunned their positions until about 11 a.m. Having got rid of all the load they had, the aeroplanes went away. Then the enemy guns from behind the hill started registering, and behind this barrage of artillery fire advanced a column of motorised infantry consisting of 13 tanks, 11 armoured cars and 10 trucks. Half of this column made its way straight towards the pond where two forward Platoons of the Company were in position. Lead and explosives were being thrown out of the Armoured Fighting Vehicles, but this would not frighten our boys; they waited in their trenches for the infantry to debuss. Tanks and armoured cars like steel monsters creating hell with their fire-power approached so close that they started charging on to our trenches so as to crush and cripple our men under their heavy weight. Two mines were thrown in their way which unluckily did not burst, but they caused the monsters to stop which having stopped became stationary pill-boxes oozing out most inhuman forms of killing materials. There was no communication between this post and the Battalion H.Qrs. When 2/Lieut. Gian Singh appreciated that their rifle fire was no match to the enemy's mortars, machine-guns, light automatics and hand grenades and their staying in trenches meant certain death or captivity with no loss to the enemy, he ordered, "Charge". Leading the assault he shouted slogans of "*Netaji-ki-jai*", "*Inqilab Zindabad*", "*Azad Hindustan Zindabad*" and "*Chalo Delhi*". All the men responded to slogans which echoed above the enemy fire. This was the only support which these heroes had against the superior armament of the enemy. In the name of India and Indian independence they charged into the enemy trucks. The enemy immediately debussed, hand-to-hand fighting ensued which lasted for full two hours, but our heroes would not give in; forty of them sacrificed their lives after killing more than their equal number of the enemy. Their unconquerable spirit harassed the enemy so much that he started retreating. Just then 2/Lieut. Gian Singh called forward his Third Platoon Commander 2/Lieut. Ran Singh and was giving out orders when a bullet struck on his head and he fell down never to give out orders again. 2/Lieut. Ran Singh then collected the remnants of the Company and reorganised. 2/Lieut. Gian Singh Bisht used to tell his men that he would die with them. He fulfilled his promise and remained their comrade in life and death. This was a glorious deed of which the history will remain witness as long as there is world. 2/Lieut. Gian Singh and his men lived up to the ideals of our great leader, the Netaji, and have laid down their lives fighting by their posts to build up a tradition for us to follow. In free India, the spirit of those heroes who knew no defeat would be worshipped for generations to come and would inspire the future sons of India to live up to such high ideals.

Dated 9th April 1945

Commander 801 Unit
Sd/- G.S. Dhillon,
Lt. Col.

A Bouquet from Netaji

Rarest of the rare gift which I ever received was brought to me by Shah Nawaz personally when he came to visit me on the foremost defended post near Khabok on the night of 19th March, 1945. He said, "Here is a bouquet from Netaji for you." It was the following, letter:

SADAR DAFTAR ALA KAMAN, AZAD HIND FAUJ

(Headquarters Supreme Command, Indian National Army).

Rangoon, 12th march 1945

Major G.S. Dhillon, Jai Hind.

I have been following the work of your Regiment and of yourself with the closest interest and I want to congratulate you on the manner in which you have stood up to face bravely the situation that is difficult. I want to express my complete confidence in you and in all those who are standing by you in the present crisis. Whatever happens to us individually in the course of this historic struggle, there is no power on earth that can keep India enslaved any longer. Whether we live and work, or whether we die fighting, we must, under all circumstances, have complete confidence that the cause for which we are striving is bound to triumph. It is the finger of God that is pointing the way towards India's freedom. We have only to do our duty and to pay the price of India's liberty. Our hearts are with you and with all who are with you in the present struggle which is paving the way to our National salvation. Please convey my warmest greetings to all the officers and men under you and accept same yourself. May God bless you and crown your efforts with success?

"Jai Hind".

sd/- SUBHAS CHANDRA BOSE

My reply was:

Beloved Netaji, Jai Hind. Burma, 20th March 1945

I have received your letter of 12th March 1945. Not words, only tears could express my feelings. I thank you with all my heart for expressing your complete confidence in me and in those who are with me. I assure you, our Netaji, on behalf of the Regiment that it does not matter what may come our way, we will continue the struggle according to your ideals, and wishes to earn our Motherland's Freedom as long as a single soldier of this Regiment is alive. As for myself, my last words to you at Rangoon, *"Main ap ki ankhen kisi ke samne nichi na hone doonga,"* have been ringing in my ears ever since I left you, and specially so after I have come back from Nyaungu. I fully realize that in spite of reasons which may be produced I have not only failed to do what I voluntarily promised, but have been the only Regimental Commander to bring humiliation to you and to the Azad Hind Fauj. I have no face to promise again, only my actions will do so. Your letter has put a new spirit into us. All the officers and men present here, and I humbly and with warmest hearts have accepted your greetings. We are confident that with God's grace and your blessing it will not be difficult to achieve success. We all pray for your long life and health to guide us through this Holy War.

Jai Hind.

Your Excellency's Obediently

Sd/- G.S. Dhillon

Then I received a wireless message from Netaji, "I ask you to accept your promotion which you so richly deserve." It was after receiving this letter that I started wearing the badges of the rank of a Lieutenant Colonel.

On 28th March, 1945 I was grieved to learn that Captain Mohammad Hussain was missing. Shash Nawaz thought that he had deserted. On the contrary till today I have not been able to believe that he went over to the enemy. My reason is simple. The enemy was entrenched at a distance of hardly five miles from our trenches. My personal trench was beside a small acacia tree on the front-line. Mohammad Hussain very well knew my habits and modus operandi. The enemy could have easily caught me if Mohammad Hussain had betrayed us. That I did not change our location and continued to stay as we were for over a week after Mohammad Hussain's loss, I am convinced of his loyalty to his Commander and to the INA. I am glad to record that I sent the following message to Shah Nawaz in which I did not use the word desertion; I called it absence. This message was exhibited during our Red Fort trial.

No. D 5, Dated 2nd April 1945

To Colonel Shah Nawaz Khan

From Lt. Col. G.S. Dhillon

Captain Mohammed Hussain's absence has not affected the spirit or morale of the troops at all. We are prepared to continue fighting in the front-line. No need of rest unless objective is achieved. We will sacrifice our lives to maintain the honour of Azad Hind Fauj. Water or no water, rations or no rations will not affect our fighting capacity. Captain Chander Bhan, Lieut. Khan Mohammed and Lieut. Kartar Singh along with my staff join me in assuring you that we will fight up to the last. Jai Hind.

(Sd.) G.S. DHILLON, Lt. Colonel

Commander, 450 Unit, A.H.F.

16

The Retreat

On the 4th of April 1945, I was ordered by my Division Commander, Colonel Shah Nawaz Khan, to return from Khabok to Popa. By then 4th Guerrilla Regiment had been in that area waging guerrilla warfare for over five weeks. The Japanese Company commanded by Captain Midorikawa had already been withdrawn a week earlier. My officers and men during those days did me proud by their acts of courage and perseverance. At times we went as forward as seven miles within Nyaungu bridgehead, the very place from where I had been forced to withdraw in mid-February.

Emotionally, I had become so much attached to the land-features and its people that their memory still lingers with a feeling of gratitude. In fact, I have chosen to make my present abode, Dhillon's Den, at the feet of Hatod hill in the village Hatod near Shivpuri in Madhya Pradesh, because this hill remarkably resembles a hill that stands near Taungzin along the road running to Kyaukpadaung. With a last languishing look, I scanned the area before leaving it. After dusk we left Khabok and arrived at Popa early on the 5th of April where Shah Nawaz had already called for a Brigade Commanders' Conference. Col. Sahgal and I attended it.

Shah Nawaz explained the overall situation that had grown very critical for us and the Japanese. During the last week of March, Meiktila had fallen and fighting was going on at Pyawbe. The important strategic towns of Mandalay, Myingyan, Kyaukse and Thazi had fallen during March. In the Shan States the British had captured Kalaw from where they could outflank the Japanese stronghold of Toungoo on the main highway running between Mandalay and Rangoon via Pegu.

Mount Popa and Kyaukpadaung was one pocket of resistance which had so far defied all British attacks. No. 2 Division of the INA and Khanjo Butai of the Japanese held the area throughout the decisive battle of Meiktila and the British forces were denied the use of the main road connecting Nyaungu bridgehead with Meiktila through Chauk-Kyaukpadaung road. Under our constant raids the British forces were forced to use longer routes (round about cart tracks) north of, and away from Mount Popa. Surely, it caused the British loss of time, greater consumption of petroleum products and frequent breakdowns of vehicles. It was here that Shah Nawaz, Sahgal and I qualified for the joint Red Fort trial.

As mentioned above, the situation had grown very critical for the INA and the Japanese. It was further worsened because of a combination of circumstances on the Burmese political stage. It is but natural for the people who have the misfortune of getting themselves, their hearths and homes and their fields overrun by warring foreign armies that they side with the winner.

In 1942, added to the human instinct of self-preservation was the political prudence which impelled the Burmese people to help and co-operate with the advancing Japanese armies to the extent of attacking the British and the British Indian Army who had held their land. They formed the Burmese Independence Army (B.I.A.) under Thakin Party, a group of young nationalists under the leadership of U. Aung San. Their guerrillas harassed the British retreat all along and took a heavy toll of the British and Indian lives. They even fell on the refugees fleeing Burma, Indians and Burmese alike of whom some thousands fell on the road to India under the Burmese 'Dhaw', axe.

Three years later, in 1945, the story was being repeated in reverse order. For three long years, Burma had her independent Government under the Presidentship of Dr. Ba Maw and the Golden Peacock fluttered proudly over the country, yet she was virtually occupied by the Japanese Army. Though of strategic and operational necessity during the war, the Japanese occupation was intolerable to the Burmese nationalists. They hated the conduct of foreign soldiers on their soil. They found their independence illusory and when the Japanese proved incapable of holding the country against the British they turned against the Japanese.

The Burmese Independence Army which had been trained by the Japanese left Rangoon in early March 1945 under the command of General Aung San with the object of holding the British advance around Prome. They were about 7,000 strong. Arriving at Prome they crossed the Irrawaddy and declared themselves independent of the Burmese Government. They declared war against Japan. To the west of the Irrawaddy, they established a strong base in the district of Thayetmyo and its adjoining areas from where they waged guerrilla warfare along the lines of communication practically all over the country, especially from Rangoon to Toungoo and from Prome to Rangoon, the two most important national highways.

Dressed as ordinary villagers they could not be recognized. They annihilated small Japanese parties who happened to come their way and made it difficult, if not impossible, for the Japanese to supply rations and ammunition to their front-line troops. Here I may submit that the action of Gen. Aung San and his followers contributed significantly to the early collapse of the Japanese resistance, thereby accelerating the speed of the British advance as well as the gaining of independence of Burma from the British.

Looking back at the historical scenario described above, one is amazed as to how on earth it was possible for the Indian National Army to operate against the British and wage a War of Liberation of India. Here I wish to record gratefully that we suffered not a loss of single life at the Burmese hands during the days of our defeat and hundreds of miles of retreat. This pleasant change, miraculous as it was, in the attitude of the Burmese towards the Indians was the result of Netaji's policy of friendship and mutual respect towards host countries and their peoples. He established most cordial relations and maintained personal friendship with Dr. Ba Maw and all Burmese leaders. He commanded as much respect from the peoples of South East Asia as from the Indians living there. In fact, they looked upon Netaji as their own and not an Indian leader alone. From the questions local people often asked about him, it was apparent that Netaji's name filled them with awe and he was respected as a leader of Asia. All the same, the change in the attitude of Burmese Army at that time was a matter of serious concern to us. The Japanese wanted us to be with them against the Burmese and the Burmese wanted us to be with them against the Japanese. Netaji refused to oblige either. We were to remain neutral. This policy of neutrality was to cause us practical problems. As Commanders in the field we had to make some political decisions. This would not have been possible if we had not enjoyed Netaji's confidence. This made us feel responsible for the future relationship between the countries concerned after the war when neither Japanese, Indians, nor British forces would be in Burma.

From the beginning of April the strategic situation began to change rapidly. After winning the decisive battle of Meiktila, General Slim was in a hurry to clear the Irrawaddy valley of all opposition and reach Rangoon before the coming monsoon. With a view to consolidating the gains of his victories, he launched a three-pronged attack on Mount Popa and Kyaukpadaung area. In the north, the 2nd British Division attacked Mount Popa from Taungtha. The 7th Division attacked Kyaukpadatmg coming from Nyaungu in the west. The 5th Division attacked Kyaukpadaung from the east coming from Meiktila.

Battle of Legy

Sahgal's 2nd Infantry Regiment and the Khanjo Butai had a three-day pitched battle seven miles north of Popa at Legy against the 5th Brigade of the 2nd British Division supported by intensive bombing by the R.A.F. and shelling by the 10th Field Regiment. Our side had no air support at all and a little artillery power. In this unequal fight our casualties were heavy, yet on the 4th April Legy remained held by us. During the Divisional Commanders' Conference on the 5th of April, I was allotted the defence of Kyaukpaduang, south of Popa. Sahgal remained committed to his old position, the northern defences of the Mountain.

After giving orders to my Unit Commanders of the move to Kyaukpadaung, I proceeded to Kyaukpadaung in my staff car. Captain Izumi accompanied me. At about midnight we arrived at a Japanese check-post where we stopped to exchange passwords. After we were recognized, the Japanese Guard Commander came to the car, saluted and requested Capt. Izumi to ask me to come out and inspect the guard which had been drawn up as a guard of honour. Surprised at this strange gesture, I asked the reason for this extraordinary courtesy. The Guard Commander said, "We have heard that Dhillon Thai is one of the bravest commanders. We wish to see him and salute him." In the moonlit night, as I inspected the guard, I could feel the genuineness of their gesture. Overwhelmed by the expression of respect I felt rather nervous and asked myself, "O! boy, can you come up to their expectations at Kyaukpadaung?"

The following was a week of daily shelling from the ground and heavy bombing from the air. Under the cover of this barrage the British forces advanced in their heavy tanks and armoured vehicles, but as soon as we opened fire they retreated. There was little fighting of any consequence. Their attacks appeared to be an exercise in probing our weak points. We tried to conceal our strength by withholding our fire as long as possible. On the 10th of April Popa received a very heavy air attack in which high explosive and incendiary bombs were dropped. Casualities were heavy.

In the Kyaukpadaung area we were straffed repeatedly by machine-gun fire from the low-flying planes. For the next two days we were engaged in repulsing several attacks on Kyaukpadaung on the main road about a mile west of the town. Till the morning of 13th of April we remained in occupation of the Popa Kyaukpadaung and Chauk-Kyaukpadaung roads' junction. During the night of the 12th-13th April, our Division Headquarters and the 2nd Infantry Regiment had to fight while withdrawing from Popa through the enemy blockade. They had to leave their transport behind.

Early on the morning of the 13th of April, Shah Nawaz and Sahgal joined me at my Headquarters at Indowakki near Kyaukpadaung. Sahgal had a sprained ankle and was carried on a bullock-cart. His 3rd Battalion under the command of Capt. Bagri had still to join us. So we waited during the day under cover of small scattered thorny bushes. It was late in the evening that Bagri was successful in breaking through the enemy lines and reaching Indowakki. One of his Companies under Lieut. Kanwal Singh failed to extricate itself and was left behind. Having exhausted all his ammunition, Kanwal Singh, one of the bravest officers, was obliged to surrender. The news made us sad.

Advance orders had already been passed that the 2nd Division of the INA was to withdraw to Magwe, a hundred miles south on the Irrawaddy. At Indowakki Shah Nawaz gave us detailed instructions for the withdrawal. The Division was divided into two echelons, viz.

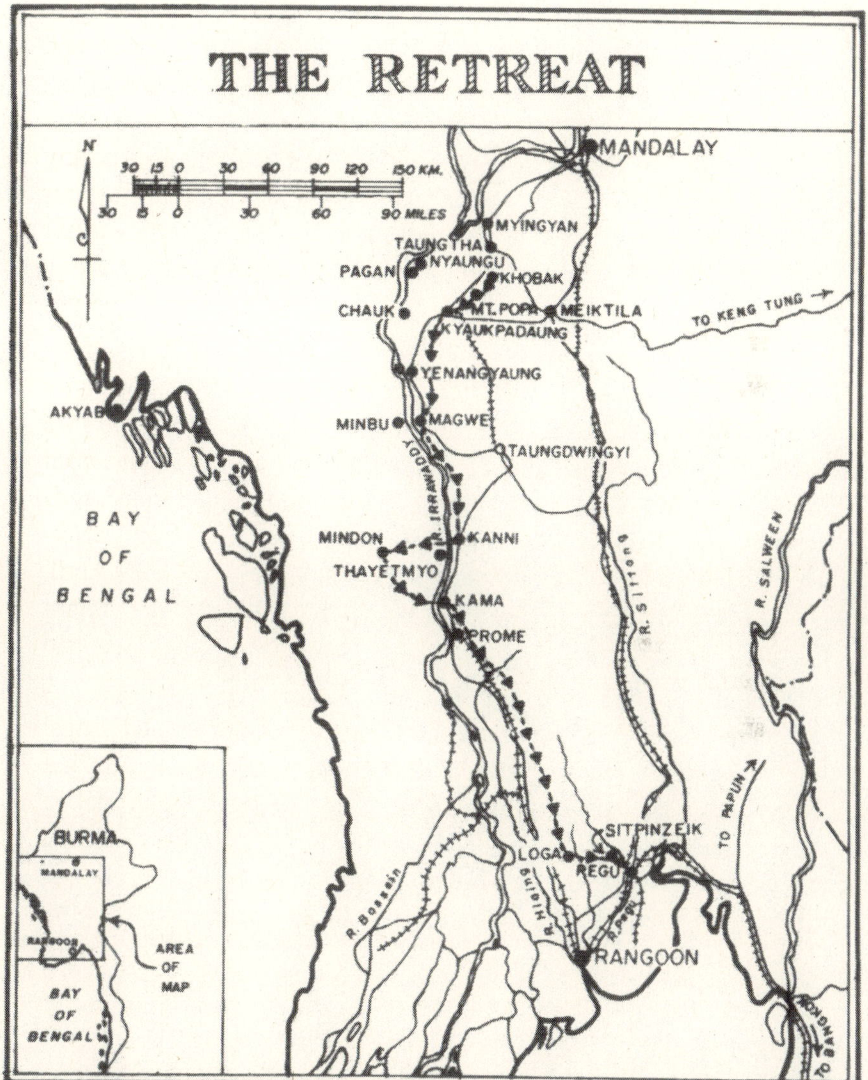
THE RETREAT
N
30 15 0 30 60 90 120 150 KM.
30 15 0 30 60 90 MILES
MANDALAY
MYINGYAN
TAUNGTHA
NYAUNGU
PAGAN
KHOBAK
CHAUK
MT. POPA
MEIKTILA
TO KENG TUNG
KYAUKPADAUNG
YENANGYAUNG
AKYAB
MINBU
MAGWE
TAUNGDWINGYI
R. IRRAWADDY
BAY OF BENGAL
MINDON
KANNI
THAYETMYO
KAMA
PROME
R. Sittang
R. SALWEEN
TO PAPUN
SITPINZEIK
LOGA
PEGU
R. Bassein
R. Hlaing
R. Pegu
RANGOON
BURMA
MANDALAY
RANGOON
AREA OF MAP
BAY OF BENGAL
L. S. MAMANI

(*a*) Div. H.Qrs. along with its ancillary units including the hospital with the sick and the wounded and my 4th Gr. Regt.

(*b*) Sahgal's 2nd Inf. Regt.

We left Indowakki at about midnight. Arranging bullock-carts to carry our sick and the wounded who numbered about three hundred was quite a problem. It had grown all the more serious because of the British attack on Kyaukpadaung and the B.I.A.'s declaration of war against Japan. Most of the main routes going towards oil-fields of Yenangyaung forced us to go through sandy jungle routes. The going was difficult. Our men got tired and had blistered feet. We rested at intervals.

One night after a rest as we marched off, I could not find my 2nd-in-Command Col. Jagir Singh. Greatly perturbed, I ran to the rear of the column but there were no signs of Jagir (Jaggi). I went further back and there I found him all alone searching for his spectacles in the dark. I too knelt down beside him and together we made a thorough search, combing the sand with our fingers. We were lucky to find the glasses and hurried back to take our place in the column.

Shah Nawaz was always careful about our men and officers. One of us always used to lead the column but often he would not allow me to walk and ordered me to get on a bullock-cart. "You are weak with your appendicitis. Take my cart, I shall lead the column. You take rest." In Shah Nawaz I found a great comrade beside being a Commander. It took us six nights to reach Magwe. We were compelled to rest during the day and travel only at night. We had to be very cautious to avoid any detection by the enemy reconnaissance planes which were very active throughout the day. Heavy gunfire all around us appeared to be closing in upon us.

Thoroughly exhausted we arrived Magwe early after sunrise on the 18th of April. Col. Hussain, Commander of the 1st Infantry Regiment of the INA who was responsible for the defence of Magwe, received us cordially. Our supplies of rations were partially replenished. Here we got information from Sahgal that he had arrived Taungdwingyi about 10 miles east of Magwe. The situation was developing very fast and Hussain's Regiment had to repulse an armoured attack on Magwe from five miles east of it on the Magwe Taungdwingyi road. Some of our troops which had lagged behind due to blistered feet and weak health arrived Magwe on the 19th of April, under Col. A.B. Singh.

From midday onwards when the arrivals from Popa were still to be fed and dispersed on an open ground north of the town of Magwe, the enemy reconnaissance planes started hovering above us. Sometime later, paratroops were dropped who were promptly engaged by Col. Hussain's outposts. It seemed that they had dispersed towards the nearby low hills to the north of our camp. At 1500 hrs. aeroplanes dropped a few anti-personnel bombs along with some incendiaries. Our trenches which had been hurriedly covered by hay and old dry branches caught fire. Our bullocks broke loose. It was a chaotic situation.

Then we were surprised by heavy tanks. We simply could not organize any defence. Shah Nawaz and I were at the time at Government Dak Bungalow which was serving as Col. Hussain's headquarters. On the very first sound of aeroplanes we rushed out. We were completely aghast at the sight of the confusion prevailing among our men. Shah Nawaz was for me to withdraw to the Irrawaddy bank and hold it against the enemy. He himself wanted to hold the road in front of the Dak Bungalow. Disagreeing with him I said that it would be suicidal to fight in the open against the advancing tanks. Our discussion grew quite hot. I told him that I could not agree with his committing himself to the battle which we had already lost. We had no other option but to fall back at least five miles south of Magwe along the Irrawaddy and organize our men. I proposed that he should go back south while I would try to help our men withdraw in some sort of order in that utter disorder. Most of the combatant troops belonged to my Regiment and it was for me to command my men. After some heated arguments when Shah Nawaz refused to yield, I said, "Shanu ! you are interfering with my command. You do not appreciate that your life is more important than mine. You are not only a Division Commander but a minister of the Provisional Government of Azad Hind too. If I get killed you can easily control the situation but in your absence who else can?" I requested him to go to the river bank and assured him that I would join him after ordering our men to fall back five miles south of Magwe along the Irrawaddy.

At last Shah Nawaz acceded to my request but told me that he would wait for me to join at the river bank. As Shah Nawaz started going towards the river, I sent runners in all directions with orders for everyone to leave the open ground and fall back along the natural cover of the river bank. What looked a panic few minutes ago had become an orderly retreat. But I was astonished to see my batman Mehar Singh running in the opposite direction towards his trench which was on fire. Near the trench were his bullocks tied to a peg. He set them free and salvaged a bottle of whiskey (for treating feet against blisters) out of the bullock-cart. That was one of the bottles sent to me by Netaji at Khabok. There was also a tin of Australian craft cheese which Bashir Ahmad's niece, Balqees and her siblings had sent to me from Rangoon when I was at Myingyan.

Satisfied to see my men rushing towards the river, I ran to join Shah Nawaz, whom I requested to go further south along the Irrawaddy as already planned. Before leaving he ordered me to withdraw after all our men had been pulled out of the open ground. Shah Nawaz then left satisfied that the situation was under control. Our men were rushing towards the river bank chased by the enemy tanks. About a hundred yards short of the river, the tanks stopped and I saw a British Officer standing atop a tank with his hands resting on his hips, scanning our retreat that must have looked like a stampede.

The British officer seemed to be enjoying the scene in a victorious mood. What would happen next if he ordered his tanks to advance ? As the thought occurred to me, instantly I snatched a rifle from a man nearest to me. From the standing position I fired a bullet aiming about a yard over the head of the Tank Commander. He immediately dived down the turret of his tank and they started withdrawing. That small action saved our troops from being overrun and crushed by tanks in the makeshift trenches where some of our troops under A.B. Singh had just arrived and had taken shelter as an expedient move. I was later to learn that A.B. Singh's trench was saved by a margin of about ten yards.

Meanwhile, in order to show that we were holding the bank, I ordered whoever came my way to take up a position and fire. When Col. Jagir Singh, my 2nd-in-Command arrived, I shouted "Jaggi get down and fire." "Fire into what?" he asked. "Fire into the bloody air," I retorted. "Sir ! Isn't your fire enough?" Jaggi calmly asked and added, "let me save some ammunition for tomorrow." "All right, you go down the river bank and see that Shah Nawaz does not commit himself to a battle. I make you responsible for that." Jaggi said that he would prefer to be where I was and suggested that I should go back to Shah Nawaz. When he found that I was determined to hold the bank so that our men could withdraw, he moved off.

But before doing so Jaggi said, "Sir, make sure that not a single man is left behind." I looked towards Jaggi as if to say, whom he was telling. With a smiling gaze he said, "Even so it is better to remind you." Both of us burst out laughing as Jaggi went away to do the duty assigned to him. His remark brought to my mind an anecdote he used to narrate in lighter moments about a minister who while riding a horse had asked his servant, "Where is the new horse which we had purchased recently ?" The servant replied, "Your excellency presently you are riding on it." "Oh ! even then it is better to ask" (*Phir bhi poochh lena achha hota hai*), the minister had said. Jaggi's sense of humour even under those fearful circumstances served as a great reliever of tension.

Jaggi left on his errand and there came another remarkable character, Sepoy Kandhara Singh, who had volunteered himself for the INA from Shanghai. Actually, he was an old revolutionary of the Ghadar Party. He was carrying on his head an ammunition box, full of currency notes. The box was heavy and Kandhara Singh looked visibly weighted down under its load. I asked him to take some rest. He said, " I cannot rest at such a dangerous place. I must take the public money to a place of safety." I laughed and he carried on doing his duty. I have narrated this small episode to show the feelings of togetherness which existed among officers and men in the INA.

After completing the task of withdrawing from Magwe, I went down to where Shah Nawaz was waiting. He had collected and organized all the retreating men. We went further south and came to a village called

Kanni about eight or ten miles from Magwe. At Kanni we wanted to cross over to the western bank of the Irrawaddy. With Magwe and Taungdwinglyi under British control, Kanni was not a safe spot for us. With its open agricultural fields, it offered neither cover from view nor from fire. The opposite bank had hills and ravines. Our intention was to reach Prome where we could put up some sort of defence.

In view of the Burmese Army having declared war against Japan, the villagers, though courteous, were no longer willing to help us. They were reluctant to provide us boats for crossing the river. The night was passing fast. Shah Nawaz hit around an idea. He pretended to be a British Officer. Taking a village leader aside he showed him some British currency and gave him a couple of rupee coins. Since the villagers had not seen the British currency after the coming of the Japanese, they took the bait and promised to co-operate. As the British motor boats were active patrolling the river with strong searchlights and sending up Very light flares, illuminating the river surface and the surrounding areas, we had to wait till two in the morning when we started crossing the Irrawaddy. The sun had risen high in the sky when our crossing was completed. By that time heavy air reconnaissance started and we were compelled to lie low under bushes, the only cover available till sunset. We had to go without food since leaving Magwe.

In the evening we marched off to the nearest village. We met a couple of Burmese soldiers disguised as villagers. Shah Nawaz had a long discussion with them and was successful in winning their confidence. They told us to wait at some distance from the village and they went ahead of us. We were advised to enter the village after about an hour. When at last we entered the village, it appeared as if the whole village had come out at the village gate to receive us. We were treated to cold water from earthen pitchers and served cubes of date-sugar, and peanuts. We kept going westward, normally travelling by night and resting by the day. We purchased rice and whatever other simple items of food were available. We could hire bullock-carts from one village to another on the way to Prome. The going was so far good.

Our area of retreat was fully under the control of General Aung San's Army under the new name of People's National Army. Their object was "to fight against the Fascist Powers." They had established an effective parallel government extending their hold over about 50 villages with their headquarters at Thayetmyo. They lived in villages dressed as ordinary farmers. Their control in the area was absolute. Without their permission it was not possible to purchase any item of supplies of rations nor hire bullock-carts, the only transport available in those areas.

The villages under the control of People's National Army were well organized against any attack. Each village had a special type of drum, a long hollowed tree trunk which, when beaten, carried sound to a long distance. Sentries guarded each village round-the-clock. On the warning of an approaching enemy, the village would be completely vacated and all men, women and children would disappear into jungles where they had stored away corn and rice. Even the cattle and the poultry were so efficiently dispersed and hidden that not a bird could be found in the village or in its vicinity.

As we had never clashed with the Burmese Army, Gen. Aung San was well disposed towards the Indian National Army. After all, we were fighting for our respective liberty. We found little difficulty in the area through which we were compelled to retreat. Then a snag arose. We had five Japanese personnel with us whom we were asked to surrender to the Burmese. The Burmese considered them as their enemies. Those Japanese were mostly non-combatant liaison staff. When we arrived at a village called Minde, approximately ten miles north-west of Kama, the Burmese captured nine of our men as hostages. They threatened to kill them if the five Japanese were not handed over to them.

Earlier Shah Nawaz had refused to attack the Burmese guerrillas at the behest of the Japanese before the battle of Magwe on the plea that our fight was only for the liberation of India and not against the Burmese. Now he was hard put to save the five Japanese at the risk of losing nine Indian lives as well as the goodwill of the Burmese. He had a conference of his staff officers and the officers of my Regiment. That was the one and the only one occasion when the purchase of supplies of rations was denied to us. Shah Nawaz decided and we all agreed with him that come what may, the five Japanese soldiers who were our allies would not be handed over to the Burmese Army.

A letter was drafted to Gen. Aung San. Its language was diplomatic yet firm. We politely refused to surrender the five Japanese.

That day we could not purchase rations nor were we allowed to leave the village; hence our request to the villagers for hiring bullock-carts to carry our weak and the wounded cases was put off. We spent the night on empty stomachs. Our letter did not receive a ready reply. There was a feeling of great suspense. It was a nightmarish experience for us. We feared that the Japanese might be forcibly taken away from us or attacked in the dark. A clash of arms had to be avoided. Senior Officers were posted as sentries to guard against all eventualities. The Japanese were hidden among the Indians; Shah Nawaz and I took turns to remain awake throughout the night. However, the night passed without any incident.

The next morning the Burmese relented a bit. Gen. Aung San's reply was received. He allowed us to keep the Japanese but to surrender their arms. We refused to give in. Another letter was drafted in which it was argued that surrendering arms boiled down to surrendering the soldiers. We could not agree. I wish the letter had been preserved. It was a piece of diplomatic sagacity and grace which ended with an appeal to the spirit of the soldier's code of honour and the future good relationship between the two independent countries, Burma and India, when neither the British nor the Japanese would be there. We owed it to the future generations of our countries to conduct ourselves in an exemplary manner.

The outcome was a happy one. By the evening our nine men were released. The Japanese were allowed to stay under our protection and keep their arms. It had been further suggested that a meeting be arranged between our Division Commander and General Aung San to plan our future course of action. I opposed General Shah Nawaz Khan's going on such a mission. His life was too important to be risked. I offered to go myself as his representative. It was agreed upon. We moved to village Kama.

The following day I left with a Burmese soldier who came to guide me to their Headquarters. He was dressed as a villager and carried a weapon. I was allowed to take only one man with me, with one weapon only either on me or on my man. A weapon on each of us two Indians was not permitted. It suited me, for otherwise also I did not ordinarily carry a weapon. But on that day it was with strange feelings that at 10

O'clock in the morning I proceeded unarmed to meet a representative of Gen. Aung San at an unknown place. Of course my man carried a rifle.

At about five in the evening we reached a small village humming with life. Hundreds of young men and women were practising weapon training. Even girls were doing bayonet fighting with extraordinary zeal. All of them looked healthy and bright. The sight was pleasing and inspiring. I was received by a young Burmese officer, whose name sounded to be Indian, Major Madan. He was very courteous. We were offered water followed by a cup of tea, and without any loss of time we started the work for which I had come sixteen miles over a jungle hilly track.

Major Madan explained that in order to avoid discussion, he had prepared a questioner which he placed before me. There were eleven questions in all which were to be answered with 'yes' or 'no'. Those were very simple, and direct questions, something like "Are you a friend of Burma ? Are you a friend of the Japanese ? Are you a friend of the British ? Are you prepared to fight against the Japanese ?" It took me very little time to answer the questions. When the Major saw it, he remarked, "So we are in the opposing camps." The conversation was something like the following:

I	:	Unfortunately, it is so.
Madan	:	Do you appreciate that your presence as such in the area of our control is bound to create misunderstanding between us and our allies, the British ?
I	:	We do appreciate that.
Madan	:	General Aung San also appreciates you, that is, the Indian National Army's position.
I	:	We are grateful for that.
Madan	:	How would it be if we leave each other alone? Your leaving our area will not oblige us to act against each other.
I	:	Suits us. As it is, our plan is to withdraw to Prome

on our way to Rangoon.

Madan : Then we are prepared for your recrossing the Irrawaddy by providing you boats and as much rations as your men can carry.

I : Thank you very much. It suits us. Please convey our regards to General Aung San along with our thanks.

Madan : Please convey my regards to your Divisional Commander and thank him for this meeting.

I : Yes, I will. Thank you very much. Now may I go back?

Madan : Not before having a meal with me.

1 : Thanks a lot but let it be a quick one as I have a long way to go.

Madan : It is all ready, we shan't be late.

I had my worries which I could not share with Maj. Madan. Before sending me on this mission, Shah Nawaz had told me to return at the latest by midnight. Any delay after that would be taken by him as a sign that there had been some foul play. He had told me in all seriousness that if I did not return by midnight, he would put the village to flames along with all the inhabitants. And I knew that Shah Nawaz meant each word of his warning to me if I was not back by midnight.

It was a lavish dinner. I can still relish its taste even after the lapse of half a century. After the dinner was over, Major. Madan saw me off at a little distance beyond the village. We thanked each other and said good-bye. Though I did not meet General Aung San in person, I have ever thought of him in gratitude. On the return journey to Kama, I had to make it running at the double to be on time. I feared the consequences of my late arrival. Shah Nawaz was not the man to give empty threats. With thousands of its people, the village would be burnt down by him if I could not reach Kama by midnight.

I feared that I could not make it in time when I heard a horse approaching. It had been sent by Shah Nawaz for me knowing that I was weak. I mounted it immediately and in spite of the darkness galloped to the village. Shah Nawaz had come out on the route to wait for my arrival. He had a bundle of dry grass and matchbox with him. As I got down from the horse to salute him, he fell down on his knees with hands stretched towards the heaven and offered thanks to the Almighty God, saying "O' God, thank You for saving me from committing a sin and for saving innocent lives."

As he stood after thanks giving, his eyes were filled with tears which he wiped with his handkerchief. He told me to make straight for the river bank where our men had already started crossing the Irrawaddy along with the five Japanese. On our way to the river, I reported my doings of the day. Shah Nawaz listened to my report and as we boarded the last boat waiting for us, with a sign of relief he said, "All praise be to Almighty Allah for His blessings and mercies."

After crossing the mile and a half wide Irrawaddy at Kama it took us three days to reach Prome, where we arrived early on the morning of the 1st of May. Here we learnt that most of our officers and men who could not cross the river at Kanni and were stranded on the east bank of the Irrawaddy had already arrived near Prome. From the information which we could gather, it was apparent that we had lost the war. Rangoon had already been vacated. The Japanese were yet holding Toungoo as a way of escape from Burma. It was rumoured that Netaji had left Rangoon and was at Moulmein.

Bagri's Heroic Death

One item of sad news for me was of Captain Bagri's heroic death. His Battalion No. 3 of the 2nd Infantry Regiment was encircled by British tanks some 20 miles south of Taungdwingyi. Following the tradition of the great warriors of the bygone times, he preferred to die fighting an unequal battle than to surrender to the overwhelming odds. He was one of our most valiant officers. I had known him ever since the formation of the 5th Guerrilla Regiment by Col. J.W. Rodrigues under whom I was the 2nd-in-Command. The 5th Gr. Regiment was transformed as the 2nd Infantry Regiment and was commanded by Col. Sahgal at Mount Popa. Capt. Bagri had many successful battles to his credit in which he had fought with valour. Though he died a heroic death, the news struck me as a personal loss.

By the time we arrived at Prome, it was being vacated. We spent the night in an Indian settlement called Kalabasti. Col. Rodrigues and Doctor Maj. Ranganadan had collected most of our sick and wounded and were looking after them. It was a difficult task. Shah Nawaz ordered them to remain there and to surrender on the arrival of the British forces. The next day we came south of Prome. Most of the town was being shelled and bombed heavily. It was at Prome that our Japanese liaison officers and staff were withdrawn and we were left on our own. It was appropriate, for it was not easy for us to look after the safety of the Japanese personnel due to Burmese hostility towards them. We had no wireless sets of our own. So from now onward we could little know what happened around us.

Before leaving Prome I was lucky to find a khaki shirt, a pair of boots and a long waterproof sheet which was a covering for the barrel of an artillery gun. It was about 14 feet long and it became my only piece of bedding. I used to put half of it under me and the other half over myself making a canopy to protect me from the mud underneath and the pouring rain above. As I had lost all my clothes at Magwe, these items came to me as a great boon. Now we had no transport whatsoever, nor even a bullock-cart. However, we were obliged by a Japanese Unit that gave us a lift to a river crossing about twenty miles south of Prome. The bridge there had been destroyed and the Japanese had to leave all their vehicles on Prome-side of the river, a tributary of the Irrawaddy.

Withdrawal through Pegu Yomas

From then onward we took a south-easterly direction to retreat through the jungles of the Pegu Yomas. We used to march during the night and rest in some village during the day. Taking shelter in a jungle during the day or the night was dangerous as we could not light a fire to cook our meals. If the enemy reconnaissance planes found some smoke rising somewhere outside a village, they used to throw a few incendiaries and strafe the area with machine-gun fire. We had to purchase our daily rations from the villagers who were always reluctant to provide us shelter.

If the villagers learnt of any soldiers' arrival, they would leave the village and hide themselves, their animals and belongings in such a way that we could not get even a grain of rice or corn. We did not snatch anything by force either. Their cooperation was one of our vital needs. So we used to arrive at a village before dawn leaving the main body about quarter of a mile away from the village under Shah Nawaz. Dressed in a saffron attire like a Buddhist monk escorted by a few of my soldiers I would go near the gate of the village where I would sit under a tree in a meditative pose counting my prayer beads. My soldiers would capture the first man coming out of the village gate and bring him to me respectfully. They would lie prostrate and touch my feet making obeisance to me.

Gracefully I would ask them through an interpreter (one of my own soldiers) to go back to the village and bring the headman to my presence. I used to whisper in a low murmur so as not to be recognized. When the headman was produced before me, I would tell him that I had some Indian National Army soldiers with me who had to spend the day in their village if he could kindly permit them. They would purchase rice and whatever other items of ration were available. They were Netaji Subhas Chandra Bose's men fighting for the Independence of India. They were all good men and would behave in a most respectful way towards the villagers. They would leave in the evening after nightfall to continue their journey to Rangoon.

I would vouchsafe for their good conduct. I also used to impress upon the headman that if the INA soldiers were not given shelter in the village, they might be spotted by the British aeroplanes which could prove disastrous for them as well as for the village because the British might bomb the area. It was imperative that they should be hidden in the village before the British started their air-reconnaissance. Having won the confidence of the headman, I used to send for Shah Nawaz. He would come and make obeisance to me. I would introduce him to the headman who might ask in his simple way:

Headman : Is he a good man?

I : Yes. He is a very good man and a very big officer too.

Headman : Shouldn't I fear him?

I : Not at all.

Headman : All right then, we don't fear him. You may enter

> the village. (The headman would utter these words facing Shah Nawaz).

Meanwhile, my identity as a Commander became clear.

By nightfall we used to request a guide to take us to the next village, pay in advance for the services to be rendered and gratefully take leave. At times, we hired some bullock-carts to carry some of our weak men. This was the time when I was once again suffering from an attack of appendicitis. Our journey continued without any mishap. Then one day as we were staying in a village, it was reported by some villagers that in a *basti* (dwelling) beside the village some of our soldiers were drunk and were asking the locals to provide them women.

Shah Nawaz and I were resting at that time in the village headman's house on the first floor. My appendicitis caused acute pain and I had fever too. I immediately called all the Commanders down to the level of Platoon and went down to give a talk. I had just finished my talk when a bullet hurled past over my head. As per drill everyone dispersed and my escort took cover in their allotted trenches. I was the only one left standing where I was trying hard to find the source of the bullet. And then I heard the sound of an ejector about three yards to my rear.

Spontaneously and instantly I turned round and before the attacker could reload the next bullet, I fell upon him. He failed to reload but thrust the nose cap of his unbayoneted rifle straight at my heart. He was a strong young man, but I managed to put him down and as I was sitting upon him, Shah Nawaz came running and grabbing his private parts with one hand said, "Bakhshi, leave him." The man surrendered and his hands were tied with a rope. As he was being taken away to his Unit under guard, he managed to escape. He had gone about forty yards from the guards when one of the guards took aim from the kneeling position. The unfortunate man who had failed to hit me from a distance of only three yards, got the bullet plumb in his heart from a distance of forty yards. We had no other incident of in-discipline apart from this. No wonder, the Burmese always helped us.

The blow of the assailant was so hard that it took me more than three months to recover from it. For about a fortnight after receiving the blow I could not move my left arm freely nor could I breathe without pain in the left side of my chest. Appendicitis followed by the recent blow had rendered me quite weak. We had moved onto a densely-forested hilly area where bullock-carts could not go. For some days I used to ride a bullock which was not a comfortable ride at all and this mode of transport had to be given up.

Some of my men who were touched by my physical pain and suffering managed to get hold of a stray mule left behind by a Japanese artillery unit. Though not very comfortable, I started riding the big and strong animal. One day when I was riding the mule, we came under an air raid. I had no saddle. As an expedient arrangement my waterproof sheet was tied on the back of the mule to serve as a saddle. A rope with loops made on either end was made to serve as stirrups. During the air raid, the mule got frightened and as I was trying to dismount with the help of my right hand, for my left hand could not be used due to blow at the heart, I had a fall and thus injured my right foot also. Clumsy though the mule ride was, it kept me on the move and let me be of some use to my men.

Eleven days after leaving Prome, we arrived at a village called Wata about twenty miles west of Pegu. Here we learnt that Germany had surrendered. Japan was being heavily bombed daily. In our immediate vicinity we appeared to have been surrounded on all sides. Pegu had been occupied by the British forces. Rangoon fell during the last week of April. Our rations were exhausted. We had very little ammunition left.

Shah Nawaz gathered all our troops and explained the prevailing situation. He told us that he saw no point in making our men lose their precious lives when we had already lost the war. If we lived we would have a chance to continue our struggle for the Independence of India from within the country. He decided that our surviving force should surrender to the British. As for himself, instead of surrendering he had decided to make a suicidal attack on the British forces encircling us. He called for fifty volunteers for this suicidal mission. Three hundred men came forward. He asked me to select only fifty men out of them. It was a difficult choice to make.

Everyone was keen to go on the suicidal mission. After the selection was over, Shah Nawaz detailed Col. A.B. Singh of his Div.

Headquarters and Col. Jagir Singh of the Nehru Brigade to take the rest of the force to surrender to the British the following day. It was a fateful evening. We were all sad, our throats were choked with emotions and eyes filled with tears when suddenly there were deafening shouts of "Jai Hind" followed by rifle shots. Six of the men who had volunteered to join the suicidal attack but were not selected shot themselves dead.

All the men were collected once again and Shah Nawaz gave them an impassioned speech which he ended by pointing towards his revolver, "If there is any more suicide, I will shoot myself." The situation was thus controlled. The next morning, the 13th of May, Shah Nawaz took the last salute as the valiant men sobbing like children marched past him under Colonels Jaggi and A.B. Singh on their way to the surrender. It was a moment of helplessness and sorrow.

17

The Last Clash

As soon as our men marched off under Col. A.B. Singh and Col. Jagir Singh to lay down their arms were out of sight, Shah Nawaz left Wata with his party of the fifty chosen ones. Lieut. Col. Mehar Dass, Sardar-e-Jung, a hero of many battles, and I were part of this party. Most of the men belonged to my Nehru Brigade. We were sad and the rains further dampened our spirits. Late in the evening of the 14th May 1945, on empty stomachs, we arrived at a small village called Loga. We were obliged to spend the night here as the rains were pouring heavily.

It was too late to get any food. The headman of the village, however, managed to get us some milk. It was boiled and a cup offered to Shah Nawaz who refused to take it saying "Milk ! for me ? No, thanks, How can I ? What right have I to drink when my men had nothing to eat for the last two days? Bakhshi, you take it. You are ill. You need it." When he was informed that there was enough milk, a cup for each, he asked Capt. Kartar Singh, "Where is it? Please show me." He was shown two bucketfuls of milk. Satisfied, he accepted his cup. But he had hardly sipped it when he said, "Have you paid for the milk, Dhillon? Please check it yourself and see that accounts are kept. Public funds must always be handled with respectful care." He was so thoughtful and meticulous even under those chaotic circumstances.

The next day, the 15th of May, the rain stopped. We heard a battle waging some five miles away. Accompanied by four men, Mehar Dass was sent to find out the exact situation. Meanwhile at Loga, stricken with a violent attack of appendicitis, shivering with pain and clutching the abdomen, I lay hunched into a foetal position on a stretcher in front of a hut. I was full of shame for being a burden on my comrades.

Silent and worried, Shah Nawaz sat beside me on a small wooden stool. In the absence of a doctor and any medical aid, an air of helplessness and concern hung about the Divisional Commander. He was at pains to do something for my comfort. God knows from where, he happened to get a twelve-bore shotgun with only one cartidge. He said, "This morning I saw a Siberian duck swimming in the pond beside the village. Let me have a try at it and get some soup made for you." I thought it to be a difficult proposition but he was an excellent sportsman. He went for the duck and bagged it and got some nourishing soup made for me.

As I sat sipping the soup, Shah Nawaz looked happy and satisfied. But deep in him, I could feel he was at a loss for words to say something for which he hadn't the heart. He started recalling how well we had stood by each other in difficult situations, and against heavy odds. Then slowly and reluctantly he said that time had come even for us to part company. He saw no point in making me suffer any longer. He proposed to leave me behind at Loga with four attendants, including Mehar Singh, my batman. He suggested that I should stay there and look after my health. In case of enemy's arrival, he advised me to surrender without offering any resistance. On my part, I, too, appreciated that under those conditions that was the only logical and practical course open to us.

The factor of time and space as well as the war situation warranted an immediate move if Shah Nawaz was ever to reach Netaji by breaking through the enemy encirclement which was constantly pressing upon us with every passing moment. Netaji, as we understood, was somewhere near Moulmein on his way to Bangkok and must be badly in need of news about us. Shah Nawaz had, therefore, planned to go east to join Netaji failing which he said, "I will try to enter India and continue waging the war of India's independence up to the last drop of blood in me."

Mehar Dass had not returned. We feared him lost. In the absence of any definite intelligence about the enemy we were left entirely to base our future course of action on guessing and hypothesizing various possibilities. Eventually, we decided that the party under Shah Nawaz would move off by nightfall. I would stay behind at Loga.

Then I got the shock of my life. As Shah Nawaz was cleaning his revolver, he showed me eight live cartridges and said, "Here are eight bullets left, six for the enemy and the last two for myself. I damn well am not going to fall into their hands alive. Before they can even touch me I will commit suicide or give them suicidal battle which will go down in history like 'The Charge of the Light Brigade,' ever to be sung."

He had hardly uttered the first line of the poem, "Half a league, half a league, half a league onward' when forgetting my pain and breaking all restraint which obliges a soldier to maintain his composure before his Commander, involuntarily I sprang up into a sitting position on the stretcher and shouted, "Shanu ! What did you say? 'Suicide ? By God, I could not imagine you being such a coward !" Equally taken aback by my conduct and infuriated, Shah Nawaz thundered back, "Bakhshi ! Mind your words ! For a soldier, there cannot be a greater abuse than to be called a coward. If you were not in this poor state of health, I would have challenged you to a duel to settle this point of honour. Do you know to whom you are talking ?"

"Yes, Sir, to you, my Commander of whom I am so proud. I never found you fearing death nor even wanting courage, Haven't I seen you under the most difficult circumstances, challenging very death repeatedly ? How could I imagine you contemplating suicide ? Who will compose the poem of our charge ? The British ? Those days of chivalry are gone when poets would sing songs of the valour of their foes. Do you fear torture during captivity ? Surely, they are not going to spare us. They shall kill us. The worst they can do is to torture us before putting us to death. They can't do worse than that, let us be prepared to be tortured and not fear it."

"No, Bakhshi, no. I fear nothing. I fear none except Him (pointing towards heaven), the Almighty God but I do hate to be even touched by these swines— *Main in khanziron ke hath bhi nahin lagna chahta* — Oh ! I cannot tolerate the humiliation of being their prisoner. Bakhshi ! you should not have abused me. I cannot even punish you for your gross insolence. Oh ! Bakhshi, oh ! Bakhshi !" He looked hurt and pained.

Apologizing, I said, "Sir I am sorry, very sorry. I withdraw my words. But Sir, pardon me, for now onward I am not going to leave your company. I am not going to stay back at Loga. I shall come with you and attend on you." I felt he needed to be guarded against himself. I continued, "Sir, you are not just my Division Commander but also the representative of Netaji. You are a member of the Provisional Government of Azad Hind. It is out of appreciation for and duty to the great cause of the Independence of India—the cause for which we have been struggling and will continue to struggle till its achievement—that I cannot imagine being without you. What a great loss would it be to our movement if you were removed from the scene with your own good hands ? I do not know where Prem is (Col. P.K. Sahgal) and what has become of him. At present, we three are the most important part of our Great Movement. We owe it to the INA, to the Indian people and to the freedom-loving people of the world, wherever they may be, to tell them the real story of the Indian National Army, otherwise the British are bound to misconstrue facts to their advantage and against India. I am sure they will kill us. Let them do the dirty job, but before they do that we may be able to tell our part of the story to some of our countrymen. It shall awaken India; our people shall rise and avenge our honour. The noble cause of our Movement demands us to suffer insults and even the humiliation of surrendering to the enemy so as to let the world know that we did not labour in vain. Let us fulfil this important duty. I feel it to be a greater sacrifice than just giving up our lives. Let us suffer living a bit longer for the sake of our cause. Please, Sir, take me along with you. I cannot stay back. I beg of you, Sir."

We had a long and heated argument and discussed the situation from various points of view. Shah Nawaz was a highly self-respecting person and a man of strong conviction. I doubted if I could change his mind. My labours were, however, rewarded for he agreed to take me along. He told me to calm down and postponed the move which was to take place that evening.

The mule which my men had managed to provide me earlier and from which I had fallen during an air raid, injuring my foot, was a huge and awkward animal for my riding. Shah Nawaz felt for me and he asked the village headman to purchase a horse for me. He paid five hundred rupees and got me a small white mare.

We left Loga at dawn the next day, the 16th of May. Having been paid for their wages in advance, the headman and a Burmese guide, accompanied us. An hour after sunrise we arrived on the right bank of the river Pegu which was in flood. Its current was very strong. The flooded Pegu appeared to be an insurmountable obstacle. With the help of the headman we gathered some bamboo poles from an abandoned hut and built a raft which could carry four men at a time. We had five good swimmers in the party who could guide the raft across the river. The current of the Pegu was so strong that the raft would float downstream more than five hundred yards away from the intended landing point. This obliged us to haul the raft against the current every time on each bank before we let it go across. It was a strenuous and time consuming task, made dangerous by the enemy planes hovering very low above us.

Himself a good swimmer, Shah Nawaz crossed with the first lot. I crossed the last. The mule and the mare tied to the raft swam across with great difficulty. The mare was so exhausted that having crossed the river she fell down in a helpless manner. I remained dependent on the mule. It took us the whole day to cross the Pegu. There were a good number of the Japanese on the left bank from whom we gathered a lot of information about the prevalent situation. The enemy was all around us and we felt trapped expecting clash with them at any moment. We cleaned and oiled our rusty weapons. At nightfall we set off for the nearest village.

It was a bright moonlit sky when by midnight we halted under the cover of tall teak trees in the vicinity of a village, Sitpinzeix. Leaving me behind with the main party and taking with him the Burmese guide and two jawans, Shah Nawaz went ahead to ascertain if the village was occupied by the enemy. I had just taken up a defensive position and had finished issuing orders to different sections of the party and was still on the back of the mule which was loaded with two bags of currency notes worth three lakh rupees when suddenly heavy machine-gun and rifle fire opened up from the direction of the village. Shah Nawaz and three men were no more, I feared.

Under fire, the mule got frightened and became uncontrollable.

Feeble as I was with an injured left shoulder, sprained right foot and appendicitis to boot, it was quite a job for me to dismount. Eventually, I got dropped with my sprained foot entangled in the loop of a rope which I had made to serve as a stirrup. With one foot on the ground and the other in the loop I dangled along with the mule precariously. I lost quite some precious time before I could disentangle myself. The mule ran away with all its loaded effects.

After recovering myself, my immediate action was to open an overhead fire so that Shah Nawaz or any of his party, if alive, could extricate themselves. Our fire, I was to learn later, killed seven of the enemy. This caused a lull in firing, but soon after this the enemy opened heavy mortar and machine-gun fire to which we replied by light machine-guns and rifles. And then over the din of the battle, I heard Shah Nawaz come as he shouted, ''Bakhshi, Bakhshi! Where are you ?" With a great sigh of relief I answered, " Here, Shanu." "Get back. I shall hold the front, you organize the rear till I withdraw" ordered Shah Nawaz.

And then he attacked the British position. After the enemy was silenced by an exchange of heavy fire, he withdrew and took over the line which had then become the front and asked me to get back. Thus with successive leap-frogging backward with Shah Nawaz always keeping himself forward we extricated ourselves from the vicinity of the village. The engagement cost us three lives—all three who had accompanied Shah Nawaz. It was miraculous how Shah Nawaz survived to tell the story in his own words :

> "As I reached the entrance to the village, someone shouted in Hindustani, '*Tum kaun ho* ? - Halt ! Who are you ?' I replied that we were Indians.
>
> They again shouted, "*Tum kaun ho* ?"
>
> I shouted back, "*Tum kaun ho* ?" and I told them that we were the men of the Indian National Army thinking that they were probably our own men who had refused to go and surrender to the British. As soon as they knew that we were men of the INA, I heard a British officer shout, 'Rapid Fire !'
>
> "From a range of approximately fifteen yards,

> intensive rifle and machine-gun fire was opened on us. All three of my companions who were on my right, left and one in front were killed outright, and a leather handbag which contained my diaries (that was produced at the time of our trial by Court Martial in the Red Fort) was shot out of my hand. I remained untouched through some miracle. I walked back to my party and brought them up and attacked this British position and forced them to abandon it. Since our route was blocked, I decided to go back a few hundred yards and took up a defensive position."

The mule had run away with so much cash that during normal times it would have been a very serious matter, but under those extraordinary circumstances, my greater worry was the loss of my waterproof sheet which the mule had carried away leaving me shelterless in those tropical rains. As for money, I was lucky to have seventy-five thousand rupees still with me in my haversack.

After our disengagement with the enemy, we came to a little hill and took up a defensive position. There was an abandoned hut with a well in front of it. Perhaps the well had not been in use for some long time, for when a cup of water was offered to me it gave a stinking smell. Thirsty as I was, I just had a sip of it and I felt hundreds of maggots and worms crawling in my mouth. Even after spitting out the water, I kept on having a nauseating sensation for hours.

The next day, the 17th of May, we were surprised to find ourselves hardly 500 yards away from an enemy artillery gun post. It was apparent that we were encircled by the enemy. Shah Nawaz's immediate reaction was to plan an all-out last charge and get killed. I opposed a suicidal attack. Shah Nawaz was good to listen to me and having full confidence that all our men would back him up agreed to decide the issue in a democratic way.

A conference of our officers and men, about forty-five in all, was called. Shah Nawaz told us that there were three ways by which we could choose our death. The first and perhaps the easiest one was to commit suicide by shooting ourselves. He did not favour this method as it was a cowardly act. The second method which he proposed was to charge into the nearest artillery guns of the enemy and destroy them or get destroyed ourselves. This he explained would be a glorious death, an ideal death a soldier could wish for.

The third method, he said, was to allow ourselves to be captured by the British and shot by them. He told us that in his own mind he had no doubt whatsoever what the British would do if they captured him alive. The advantage of this, he told us, would be that we might be taken to India, court-martialled and then shot. There was a faint ray of hope that we might have an opportunity of placing the full facts about our Movement before our countrymen. And then, of course, there was a hope that we might get our graves in India on the soil of the beloved Motherland. He left the final choice to all the officers and men.

I then spoke. I ruled out the first method of committing suicide. The second method, I said, was a glorious method of dying in action all right but at that late stage of war, it would end up without any advantage to the Movement. The third method, I said, was the best. If we had to die, it was better to let the British do the dirty job of shooting us; but before they could do so, we might be able to tell our countrymen and the world how we wanted to pay the price of India's liberty with our very lives. Let us live a bit longer so as to awaken Indians, who will surely rise to avenge our death, bring independence to India and inspire enslaved people all over the world to fight for their freedom.

I, therefore, favoured the last course of action. And the majority supported me. Though troubled to the core of his heart, Shah Nawaz accepted the decision with silent grace. I shall remain eternally grateful to Shah Nawaz for his large-heartedness in surrendering his prerogative of a Commander to the combined will of the officers and men under his command. It is here that the revolutionary and democratic character of the great INA Movement stands out conspicuously.

The conference was held in an area abounding in trees under which we sat unmindful of the enemy artillery fire which boomed past above us at random. After the meeting was over, a quarter of a pound tin of Kraft cheese was produced by Mehar Singh. It was opened and a small slice of cheese was given to each member of the party. That bit of cheese with rain water from a nearby depression in the ground was our last breakfast as free men of the INA.

At about 10 a.m. Lieut. Rai Singh along with a local man was sent to contact the opposing Commander. They carried a flag of truce and a letter. They returned after about four hours with a message that we should lay down our arms and place them in a line about fifty yards away from us across a small brook and wait till 4 p.m. for them to collect us. I carried no side arms, but when Shah Nawaz was asked to give his revolver to hand it over, he said, "I shall not surrender my revolver." Sitting on the bank of the brook, he slowly took out cartridges and one by one dropped them in the water below. Lastly he took out his revolver, kissed it and bidding it a tearful farewell threw it into the water.

Away from other members of the party as we two sat waiting for the enemy troops to come to take us, Shah Nawaz scrawled with his fingers circles on the wet ground aimlessly. He was so overcome with grief that at times he would burst out into sobs saying, "Bakhshi, O' Bakhshi you have made me act cowardly. How can I surrender ? Oh, Bakhshi !" Sensing his agony, but unable to console him, I sat there dumbfounded, At times, I picked up courage to submit that our intentions were neither cowardly nor selfish, and I had confidence that in our loss lay the gain of our country. While Shah Nawaz drew circles on the wet earth, made wetter by his falling tears, he repeated poet Iqbal's verse:

Us mauj ke matam mein
Rotee hai bhanwar ki aankh
Darya se uthi lekin
Sahil se na takrai
(The vortex wails
over the wave
That originated
In the river
Yet reached not
The river bank !)

At the appointed time, a convoy of two heavy trucks headed by a jeep arrived where our weapons had been stacked. Trucks stopped while the jeep advanced to where Shah Nawaz and I were sitting. We stood up. The jeep was being driven by an English Major on whose right sat an Indian Major who was the Unit Commander. He recognized Shah Nawaz and gave him a smart salute which Shah Nawaz accepted with matching smartness in the INA fashion saying "Jai Hind !"

"Jai Hind, Sir ! How are you ?"

They shook hands. Shah Nawaz then introduced me.

"Meet Col. Dhillon, Commander of the Nehru Brigade." We shook hands. The Indian Major then ordered a Subedar to get the party boarded and weapons loaded on the trucks and be ready to move. The Indian Major was a junior cadet to Shah Nawaz in the Indian Military Academy at Dehra Dun while Shah Nawaz was an under officer. Again, they happened to come from the same part of India, the Punjab.

There was no formal surrender ceremony. As the Subedar reported that they were ready, the Indian Major asked Shah Nawaz, "Let's move." He then ordered the English Major to get back. He offered Shah Nawaz the right hand front seat and asked me to sit in the rear opposite the English Major. It was after getting us seated that he moved over to the left to take his seat behind the wheel. Apart from four of us there was no escort nor any other personnel in the jeep. We were taken to the nearby artillery position and offered water. As the gunners served us much-needed water many Indian troops gathered around us and asked many questions. Their attitude was friendly and inquisitive. They felt happy to talk to us and so did we.

From there we were taken to the Divisional Headquarters. Enroute the Indian Major and Shah Nawaz had a continuous informal conversation mostly concerning the INA and Netaji's personality and qualities of leadership. The respectful attitude of the Indian Major and his remarks of admiration for Netaji made us feel happy. Looking ill at ease, the English Major remained silent. The way Shah Nawaz replied to each question with perfect case and dignity made me feel that the shock of surrender had been considerably absorbed and Shah Nawaz had regained his natural poise. The change was heartening.

The convoy stopped at a big playing field where a Captain of the British Military Police took us over. As soon as the two Majors drove away, the Captain shouted, "Fall-in a line." It was evening and hundreds of enemy soldiers, mainly Indians leaving their games, gathered around us. Making full use of the opportunity, Shah Nawaz told us to hold our heads high and push our chests out and show a bit of the stuff we were made of. Going about twenty paces forward he shouted in Hindustani words of command as loud and deliberate as if he was commanding a big formation at a ceremonial parade. He said, "*Azad Hind Fauj! Dehne se Sidhai Lenge, Azad Hind Fauj! Dehne se Sidhai lo*" (The INA will take dressing from the right, INA Right Dress). Even in our dirty and old uniforms with the INA badges of ranks, our appearance and drill were so impressive that someone remarked, "Oh ! they have their own words of command in our national language".

Capt. Kartar Singh had just said, "*Samne Dekh*" (Eyes-Front) when the Military Police Captain feeling nonplussed, said, "That will do, that will do. We are getting late." and without any further ado we were told to board the waiting vehicles but Shah Nawaz was whisked away in a separate jeep. While on the move, Shah Nawaz remarked in Punjabi, "Good show, keep it up. The enemy is nervous and flabbergasted. Don't worry about me. Maintain your dignity, Jai Hind !"

Late at night we were herded into the jail at Pegu. From a distant cell came the familiar voice of Shah Nawaz, "Jai Hind, Bakhshi! I am here with Ram Saroop (Lt. Col., Sardar-e-Jung, hero of Arakan operation)." Before we could exchange any more words, a curt British voice shouted, "Don't talk !" Relieved to know about Shah Nawaz's and Ram Saraop's presence, I quietly lay down on the crowded bare floor and soon much-needed sleep overpowered me.

18

INTERROGATION

My stay in Pegu Jail was of one night. Early next day, the 18th May 1945, Shah Nawaz and I were picked up by Major C. Ore and taken to No.3 Field Interrogation Centre under his command. An elderly man, Major Ore was of pleasant demeanour. Courteously, he offered a front seat to Shah Nawaz and sat on his left to drive the jeep. I was asked to sit in the rear where sat two armed security guards and a Subedar. Ore took us straight to his headquarters. On the way he talked to Shah Nawaz in an informal manner.

Anxious as he was about my ill health, Shah Nawaz requested Ore for my treatment at the earliest possible opportunity. Apart from appendicitis, swollen right ankle injured by my fall from the mule during an air raid, a stiff painful arm, I had pain in the heart-area which made breathing difficult. This was due to a direct blow during hand-to-hand combat in which the attacker had thrust the nose of his rifle on my chest. Ore told Shah Nawaz that he would, in that case, take me for interrogation first so that I could be sent to the hospital soon.

The No. 3 Field Interrogation Centre (No.3 F.I.C.) at Pegu was billeted in a few bungalow-type buildings raised around an open rectangular space. The general layout of the land was of an even slope. There were luxuriant trees abounding all around. Before the war it might have been an elegant residential area. In one of the buildings were lodged some twenty of our officers under strict security arrangements.

Major Ore occupied one of the bungalows on the higher side of the slope. This bungalow was his office-cum-residence. Shah Nawaz was provided a chair on the verandah and asked to wait while I was ushered in. As I was leaving, Shah Nawaz advised me in Punjabi to take it easy and be cool, calm and collected and also to remember that we were now prisoners. Inside Maj. Ore sat alone in his office. There was one spare chair facing his table. Having entered the room, I remained standing as the following dialogue ensued between us :

Ore	:	Your name is ?
I	:	Gurbakhsh Singh Dhillon (I spelt out Gurbakhsh).
Ore	:	And your rank ?
I	:	Colonel
O	:	Your real rank ?
I	:	That is my real rank.
O	:	I mean your actual rank ?
I	:	What is the difference between actual and real ?
O	:	(After a pause) What is your British rank ?
I	:	I am not a British Officer.
O	:	Your Indian Army rank ?
I	:	Nor am I an Indian Army Officer. I am an Officer of the Indian National Army and I have told you my rank.
O	:	(Thinking aloud) How should I put it, Now then ? What was your rank in the Indian Army before you joined the Indian National Army ?
I	:	Acting Captain: substantive Lieutenant.
O	:	Oh! Thank you. May I put it Lieutenant.
I	:	As it may please you (He wrote down Lieutenant).
O	:	I suggest that you may put on the badges of the rank of a Lieutenant and remove the badges you are wearing.
I	:	Is it a suggestion or an order?
O	:	Well, as for putting on the British badges of rank are concerned, you may take it as a suggestion but I am afraid you may not keep on wearing your INA

badges, I am sorry. (Major Ore's courtesy was impressive. I took my right hand to my shoulder in an effort to remove the badges but Major Ore interrupted).

O : There is no hurry. You need not do it here. You may do so later on your own.

I : Thank you but please do not mind if I do not wear the British badges.

O : I shan't force you but in your own interest let me suggest it that wearing the British badges will give you recognition as an officer and hence shall get you the courtesy and deference due to an officer.

I : Thank you for the suggestion. I do see the point but I am afraid I just can't bring myself to wear British badges whether I get courtesy or not. I do not mind how I am treated.

O : But why do you refuse when it won't bring you any harm ?

I : Because when I wore these badges (I pointed to my shoulders) I kissed them. When I removed the British badges I kicked them. With what conscience can I wear them again?

O : You need not take it that way. Don't take a hasty decision. There is plenty of time for you to ponder over it. You have nothing to lose nor is there any obligation, yet your gain is there.

I : I wish I could agree with you but my decision is final and irrevocable.

O : Well, it is up to you to decide but that is my earnest advice to you. You are looking tired. Do please sit down. (He pointed to the vacant chair in front of him).

I : Thank you. I do need it. May I rest my arms on the table ?

O : Please do, be at ease. (He asked his batman to bring water and as it was offered to me, I was pleasantly surprised as I looked at the transparent glasses of clean and clear water, for I had become so accustomed to drinking dirty muddy water that I had ceased to remember that clean water did exist in nature!)

Major Ore gave me a sheet of paper and a pencil and told me to take it with me and write down my bio-data at my own convenience. Then he said:

O : Mr. Dhillon, I know you more than you can imagine that I do. About 1,200 officers and men whom I have interrogated so far have told me all about you. I know you are a responsible and an honourable officer capable of looking after yourself. I do not want you and Shah Nawaz Khah to be kept under security guard. A word from you shall be enough to let you live independently and unguarded so that you may move about as you please.

I : I cannot decide when my Commander is here. You may please ask General Shah Nawaz Khan. His decision shall be binding on me.

O : Care to have a cup of tea before you go?

I : Oh ! thank you, I would love it. (Tea was brought by his batman which we shared helping ourselves to milk and sugar to our taste. It was an excellent Darjeeling tea, so delicious and refreshing. I enjoyed each sip of it.)

Observing my meager and mud-splashed outfit with all my worldly belongings on my person, Ore asked me if I needed any item of bedding. I asked for a mosquito-net but he gave me a ground sheet (*durri*) and a blanket also. Then I asked him if I could get a comb. Not being an issue of Government stores he gave me one of his own which I gratefully accepted. He advised me to take some rest and report the next day at 8 a.m. along with my bio-data. He also asked me to bring official documents and photographs if I had any. Then he told me to wait outside and send in Shah Nawaz.

While asking Shah Nawaz to go in, I cautioned him about Ore's proposal of looking after ourselves which meant denying ourselves the right to escape. Shah Nawaz added, "How can we accept preferential treatment when our colleagues are being guarded as criminals ?" Sitting in the verandah as I waited for Shah Nawaz I could not help pondering over Major Ore's courteous dealings bordering on cordiality. Was it interrogator's strategy ? I counselled myself to be cautious.

After Shah Nawaz came out, we were taken to a nearby bungalow where we were to stay during our interrogation. Our meals came from a common kitchen. There was no furniture nor did we need any. We had become so accustomed to living under open sky in all weathers that the dry, bare, wooden floor was a boon to us.

On his rejection of the proposal relating to any preferential treatment for both of us, Shah Nawaz was told by Ore that in case we were prepared to take the responsibility of the conduct of our colleagues during their stay in the 3 FIC., he would be prepared to place them under Shah Nawaz's charge. Shah Nawaz accepted the responsibility and all of us started living together in a reasonably free atmosphere within the 3 FIC Camp. In the evenings, we could go on long walks unattended by any security personnel. There was no close watch on us.

Before the start of the interrogation the next day, the 19th of May, 1945. I handed over my bio-data and a few documents including:

(*i*) Charge of the Immortals, an account of a battle under Lieut. Gian Singh Bhisht who achieved martyrdom.

(*ii*) A letter of appreciation from Netaji to me.

(*iii*) My reply to Netaji's letter.

(*iv*) A photo of Netaji.

Major Ore guessed my feelings and returned Netaji's photo. He was so impressed with it that he said, "I wish I could have a copy of it. It is so majestic, but I haven't the heart to deprive you of it. Can you barter it with any photo of your choice out of my collection ?" I chose one and he gave it to me in exchange. I possess it even today (1996). As I am writing these memoirs, I feel indebted to Major C. Ore for putting my documents on record which got preserved because they were subsequently produced against me during my trial.

With a genuine concern for my health, Major Ore took only five days to complete my interrogation, that embraced all aspects of my life during the war, with a particular reference to my activities in the INA. I found little necessity to hide anything concerning me. On the contrary, I thought it proper to disclose the truth because in that, I believed, lay the service to the cause for which we had laboured and lost while thousands of our men and women had paid the price with life. Their sacrifices gave me immense moral and spiritual strength and made me fearless. So much so that even death appeared to be of no consequence; nay, rather a pleasant duty to join those heroes who had paid the price of liberty in full measure. This boundless courage, however, did not make me oblivious of the safety of my comrades, especially of those who had been under my command.

On the first day after a daylong interrogation, before letting me off Ore accosted me thus:

O : Mr. Dhillon, from what I know of you I am afraid you may be put on trial for waging war against the King and the trying court may have no choice than awarding you capital punishment, that is death. And when the time comes do ask for clemency and I am sure, it shall be granted.

I : Ask for clemency, to whom?

O : To His Majesty the King Emperor.

I : Ask for clemency from my enemy ? Oh, No I shall never do so. I cannot.

O : The King is not your enemy. He has nothing personal against you. He does not even know you. Asking for clemency is only a formality and His Majesty has the prerogative to pardon. I am sure

His Majesty would graciously grant His pardon.

I : But I do not deserve any mercy from Him after all that I have done against His Empire. I do not expect any clemency.

O : Field Marshal Smuts also acted as you have and he was awarded the death penalty. He asked for mercy and the King pardoned him. It was later that he rose to be a General and then a Field Marshal. He served as the Prime Minister of the Union of South Africa and today is a world figure.

I : I am not Smuts. He is a big man. I am too small to be compared to him. Again I am not a white man, You have different scales of justice while dealing with the coloured people. Don't you think so ?

O : Dhillon, you do not understand yourself. There are very few Indians like you. And India needs sons like you. India needs you, my son. India needs you (He had tears in his eyes).

I : Thank you, Sir. You make me feel great. (It was the first time for me that I addressed him, Sir).

O : I mean what I say. You deserve to live. India needs you. Please try to understand me. I have no ulterior motive. I am just stating how I feel. Go, have a good rest. I have taxed you so much for so long. Let's call it a day. We shall continue tomorrow.

The next day the first thing that Ore did was to place a typed statement before me and asked me to go through it and let him know if it was correct. The statement described the execution of four deserters of my Regiment at Popa Hills where I was present and had ordered the shooting of those unfortunate men. In the long evidence, I searched for my name and when I could not find it in an otherwise quite an elaborate and fairly accurate report by Nursing Sepoy Abdul Hafiz Khan, tears rolled down my cheeks. Ore, who had been keenly observing my reactions, said, "I do appreciate your feeling of sorrow and repentance." I shouted back :

I : Oh, no! Not at all ! These are not tears of regret nor of repentance. These are tears of pride and of gratitude for the loyalty of a man to his Commander. How cleverly this man had avoided mentioning my name in order to save me though I ordered the execution. !

O : I did not ask you about yourself. I only wanted to know whether this statement is right or wrong.

I : This statement is wrong.

O : Do you mean to tell me that the four men were not executed?

I : They were.

O : That's all. Now don't tell me anything more. Why do you volunteer information against yourself ? That boils down to committing suicide. Can't you just keep quiet ?

I : And let my men go to the gallows ! This man had mentioned so many names in his report, officers and men, who are not responsible for the execution at all.

O : But why should you offer your own name when it is not there?

I : Because I was there. I was the senior-most Commander on the spot. I am simply owning my responsibility by telling the truth. My men have been loyal to me. How can I be disloyal to them and the Movement and to its leader, Netaji?

O : Netaji does not come into the picture at all as far as this episode is concerned. As for the Movement, it belongs to the past. You have done what you could. Now stop looking to the past. Look to the future and try to save your precious life. Don't commit suicide which won't help any one, not even your men.

I : How can I safeguard the future by disowning the past? Should I withhold telling the truth to save my life? Why are you advising me to tell a lie? Don't you want me to make an honest statement ?

O : Dhillon, I am not asking you to tell a lie. I am just asking you not to volunteer information against yourself. Can't you just keep quiet ?

I : I am sorry. I can't. Keeping quiet means withholding the truth, that is telling a lie.

O : Dhillon, Dhillon, don't be a pig-headed fool, my boy. Listen to me and let bygones be bygones.

I : I appreciate your fatherly concern for me. I am grateful to you but I am sorry I cannot tell a lie by keeping quiet. I am sorry, the security and safety of my men is my responsibility. It is my duty. If in the discharge of it my life goes how can it be called suicide?

Getting annoyed Ore roared back.

O : You are not in your senses. Get out. I don't want to talk to you.

Stunned, I remained seated while Ore kept on looking into the void. Then he spoke in a soft voice:

O : I am sorry, I wish I had not shown you the statement. Now please leave me alone. I shall call you later.

Overwhelmed by his concern for me, I slowly moved out. After lunch I was called back and the interrogation resumed without any reference to the morning incident. We worked late till dark.

During the night it rained heavily and a Japanese Unit broke through the British lines. The din of the encounter rumbled throughout Pegu town. The next morning we found ourselves guarded by a body of soldiers who had occupied the verandah of our bungalow. We felt offended. As I was leaving for my interrogation, Shah Nawaz told me to convey his displeasure to Maj. Ore and to warn him that henceforth we would take no responsibility of looking after ourselves.

On presenting myself at Ore's office as I delivered Shah Nawaz's message, Ore lost no time in removing the guards and then he went to Shah Nawaz to apologize and explain that it had not been posted under his orders. It was the work of a junior officer who was on duty at night and who felt jittery due to the inclement weather and the Japanese attack. The guards had occupied the verandah in front of us as a precaution. He regretted the action and assured Shah Nawaz that it would not be repeated and there the matter ended. We continued as we were.

Altercations between Ore and me continued to occur throughout the interrogation. Each passing day brought us closer to each other and yet we maintained our respective positions. Many a time the old man shed tears for me and shouted at me calling me names as a father to a son.

On the last day of the interrogation Ore asked me about prominent personalities in the Movement. The first name on his list was of Netaji Subhas Chandra Bose. He said, "I know you won't like to be asked any question about your supreme leader Netaji, and I shall ask you none. I also know your view about Mr. Rash Behari Bose and General Mohan Singh. You hold them both in the high esteem. Most of the senior officers and colleagues you have worked with have been dealt with in the course of your interrogation. Perhaps you have never worked with Col. Ehsan Qadir, but you must have formed an opinion about him. May I know what you think of his role in the Independence Movement ?" This simple question put me on my guard. Why had Ore singled Ehsan out from all the INA Officers to evoke my opinion? And that too knowing that the two of us had never worked together ?

I knew Ehsan from a distance only. He was son of a great man, a knight, Sir Abdul Qadir of Lahore. Ehsan was a very senior Officer and a member of the Cabinet of the Provisional Government of Azad Hind and of the War Council. He belonged to 5/2 Punjab Regiment and was its adjutant when captured by the Japanese in January 1942 near Kuala Lumpur during the Malayan Campaign. He joined the

Movement in its early stages before the surrender of Singapore. Capt. Mohan Singh then sent him to take charge of the Radio Station at Saigon. During the INA crises he came to Singapore. It was during the crisis that I met him for the first time. He had an intellectual's bearing and was a scholarly person who read a lot, thought a lot and possessed an ever scheming brain.

During the difficult days of the Imphal Campaign, Ehsan had plotted an anti-Movement demonstration at Maymyo where Netaji had his Advance Headquarters. His object was to incur Netaji's displeasure and thus earn a disciplinary action against himself so as to show the British that he was in the Movement to down it. Netaji was too great to be outwitted. Instead of awarding him any punishment, Ehsan was given the portfolio of the Minister for Manpower and Recruitment. Now that we had lost the war and the dire consequences of defeat stared us in the face, I feared Ehsan's capacity of projecting anti-Movement stance so as to bail himself out even at that late stage. His father's knighthood might be of some help in salvaging his career. I praised him to the skies. That was my way to counter his plausible move.

The stratagem worked. Ore disclosed how Ehsan had laboured during his interrogation to show that he was against the Movement and was in it because of fear of Netaji and remained in it under compulsion. The disclosure made me go a step further and at the risk of giving a poor impression of my own faculties I played the simpleton by giving all the credit of my remaining in the I.N.A. after the crisis to Ehsan's canvassing. Actually, as mentioned in the earlier pages, my decision was my own and it was the result of an interview with Rash Behari Bose. Giving all the credit to Ehsan did hurt my ego for denying myself the credit of an important decision in my life at a crucial stage of the Liberation Movement.

However, my satisfaction lay in roping in Ehsan along with us. I can claim at least a little share in Ehsan's failure in gaining his objective of being categorized white or grey. Going scot free of such a senior officer was bound to give a poor lead to officers and men in captivity and cause demoralization. After dealing with Ehsan, Ore went into my personal life.

O : Do you have any friends in Burma ?

I : Yes, many. How could I wage guerrilla warfare against a victorious British Army if I had no friends among the locals ? Without their friendship I could not stay for a single day on their soil. It was vital to my very existence and actions.

O : Did you have any intimate friends ?

I : Yes.

O : Men only ?

I : No, women, too. The easiest way to get people's co-operation is to respect their womenfolk.

O : Did you have any love affair ?

I : I was too busy and a responsible person to afford having an affair. A Commander's lot is a lonely one. Yet I confess I did have some very close relationships but there was no sex involved. Those connections were so simple and pure that it was their love which inspired me to act good and be brave so that they might be rightly proud of me and of my actions. They gave me courage to overcome many an impossible situation. I owe them a lot for their relationships, so simple and sacred transcending all physical desires.

O : Platonic love ?

I : Yes. Something like that.

O : Where are they ?

I : Balqees is seven years old Muslim girl, niece of Mr. S.M. Bashir, one of our leaders in Rangoon and a Director of the Azad Hind Bank. I can vividly imagine her innocent face with both little hands raised in prayer for my safety and success. This T-shirt I am wearing is her gift to me. How I wish to see her again and to be seen alive by her?

O : Who is the other one ?

I : A Burmese student, unselfish and sacrificing who helped me a lot.

O : Where is she?

I : Don't know.

O : Do you believe in democracy or dictatorship ?

I : Democracy.

O : Do you respect Mahatma Gandhi ?

I : Yes, his very name is synonymous with the Indian freedom struggle.

O : Do you think he will appreciate your violent action ?

I : Well, our methods may differ but our aim is the same, the independence of India.

O : Do you think he will support you if you are put on a trial?

I : Can't say. He may or may not, but we never banked on his support.

O : The INA and the Japanese very nearly succeeded in Imphal. It was a matter of touch and go between victory and defeat. Now that you have lost the war and thousands of you have fallen prisoners, it is a problem for the British to deal with you. You cannot just be let off. Not all of you, and we cannot drown you all, nor hang so many. You cannot even be shot. To put such a big number of you on trial is not an easy task. What do you think should be done to you ?

I : From the British point of view or ours ?

O : Of course from the British viewpoint.

I : The worst punishment you can give us is to take us all back to our Units and then one by one send us home on some pretext or another. Back home when we tell our people that we have been thrown out of the service for having waged a war of liberation against the British Empire, nobody will take us seriously. They won't believe us. Whatever the victorious British may say will be believed. Our people will think that we were cooking up stories to cover up our individual misconduct. We shall be nowhere. It shall be a great punishment to us and real defeat. Some of us may even get disowned by our own people. It's the victor's word which will have the sway and not what we say.

I : The Government can never agree to such a suggestion. Some disciplinary action is called for and an example set to serve as a deterrent.

I : I shall welcome it.

O : What do you think will be the effect on the Indian people if some of you were tried by an open public trial ? Even Mahatma Gandhi won't favour you.

I : But the people will. They will immediately go in our favour and against the Government.

O : Well, thank you, Mr. Dhillon. That finishes your interrogation. I can't say as yet about Shah Nawaz but so far among the officers and men including very senior commanders and ministers whom I have interrogated, you stand out as the most likely one to be tried by a General Court-Martial. And it is my sincere advice to you that when you are put on a trial, do ask for an official defence and when you are awarded punishment, please do not hesitate to ask for King's clemency. While appearing before the court, do wear the British badges of rank. Please do look after yourself. India needs you, my son. God bless you. Do write to me in case you need any advice or help.

Ore looked moved; his eyes were wet and so were mine. Kindness had removed the sting in me. He asked me to take some rest. After tea time at about 5 p.m. on 22nd May 1945 I bade farewell to Gen. Shah Nawaz Khan. Col. Jagir Singh, my Second-in-Command, Col. A.B. Singh and other colleagues and with a heavy heart sat in the jeep beside Maj. Ore who took me to No. 14 C.C.S., Casuality Clearing Station where he got me admitted to the Officer's Ward. His fatherly attitude and concern for me left an everlasting impression on me.

19

HOSPITALISATION

Notwithstanding the tension of interrogation, the courtesy and consideration displayed by Maj. Ore at 3 FIC were remarkable. Having got me admitted to the Officer's Ward of 14 C.C.S. (Casualty Clearing Station), Ore left me wishing good health. I kept on feeling that in spite of an unpleasant duty to which he was so honest, Maj. Ore was basically a kind-hearted man. 14 C.C.S. at Pegu was located in a spacious building. The Officer's Ward was commodious enough to accommodate about forty beds which were all occupied. There prevailed an atmosphere of peace and plenty. Clean white linen and a soft comfortable bed took little time to induce me to an early sleep and I slept undisturbed throughout the night.

The next day there was quite a commotion in the Ward marking preparations being made for a visit of a General, probably the 4th Corps Commander, Sir Frank Messervy. The General was followed by a train of commanders and staff officers as he approached each patient with an infectious smile, exchanging pleasantries and asking the welfare of each patient in a manner radiating good humour and cheer. He recognized some officers and greeted others asking about their Units with reference to battle locations, putting in a word of praise here and there.

When the General came to my bed, he asked me in his typical manner, "And where were you ?" "At Nyaungu and Pagan facing you with the Nehru Brigade of the Indian National Army at the southern crossing of the Irrawaddy. "Obviously taken aback, the General collected himself instantly and then said, "Oh! And how are you?" "I am very well, thank you," I replied and the General hurried on to the next patient.

Some time after the General had left, I was taken to the office of the Officer Commanding the hospital, an Englishman with Lt. Colonel's rank. He spoke politely, "For me all patients are alike, but even a doctor has to obey orders. I am sorry I am obliged to send you to the P.O.W. Ward. However, it will make no difference in your medical treatment." "Thank you", was my reply as I was escorted out and taken to the P.O.W. Ward.

The P.O.W. Ward was located beside the imposing hospital building in two small tents heavily fenced by barbed wire. It was on a low-lying muddy ground where rain water collected and leaches abounded. There were neither beds nor any linen; bare stretchers were the only item other than the tentage of the Ward. In one corner of the tent I occupied a stretcher. Other occupants in the Ward were a Japanese Captain and three Japanese Other Ranks. It was a miserable accommodation for a hospital ward. But then it was the place to which I belonged. Here I found solace what the Officer's Ward lacked in spite of all the physical comforts. I was with my comrades.

The Medical Officer (M.O.) in charge of the P.O.W. Ward was an Indian Captain. Dull and cold, he even feared talking to me. He was so raw that without making any investigation he administered a dose of saline but made no arrangements for providing me the facility of a bedpan, which resulted in causing me a tortuous night. In the morning I had to write the following letter to the M.O.

To

The M.O. I/c,

P.O.W. Ward.

Subject :- Reports.

I am extremely sorry to report to you that last night, i.e. 24/25 May at 0100 hrs. I made a request to the sentry to allow me to go to the latrine or to let me call for the Ward orderly who might arrange to get me a bedpan. The sentry not only stopped me from doing so but was very rude and threatened by reloading his rifle and informed me that by orders patients were not allowed to go out to the latrine area at night.

As you know, I was given a dose of purgative yesterday. I feel it most unnatural that one be given a dose of saline and then not allowed to pass motions. I wonder whether this is part of the punishment to a P.O.W., yet I doubt very much that it is under your orders or within your policy.

It is a great humiliation for me to report against a sentry and that too on a matter like this one, but I am afraid unless there are proper latrine arrangements it will be very difficult for me to receive treatment against a stomach illness. Under the circumstances I request that I may please be given facilities to answer the call of nature or my treatment may be suspended and I be sent back to the cage. Unless proper arrangements are made, I am afraid I may have to refuse to take any medicine.

The case may be referred to the Commanding Officer of the Hospital, if need be.

With apologies,

Sd/

G.S. Dhillon/25.5.45

Colonel, Indian National Army

How on earth could my anatomical system control itself and save soiling my only clothes which I was wearing was something miraculous ! It saved me from the disgrace and shame of damaging my name and causing mental agony. On receiving my letter, the M.O. came rushing to apologize and begged for the withdrawal of the letter to save him from getting into trouble. Taking the letter back from him, I tore it up. This dramatic move changed the attitude of the doctor, Ward orderly and the guards. It also disclosed my identity to the Japanese POWs. When the Indians saw me being respected so profusely by the Japanese, they became inquisitive and eager to know the facts about me and the INA.

The sentry who had been threatening me with the bolt action of his rifle during the night did not only make it up by apologizing but brought me a cake of Lifebuoy soap. His Guard Commander, a Jemadar by rank, brought me a tin of cheese and biscuits. Another sepoy gave me a toothbrush and a tube of Colgate tooth-paste. Whenever these precious gifts were refused by me, the givers looked so miserable that

I had no choice but to accept them. Indian soldiers from different units started calling on me. Their admiration for Netaji Subhas Chandra Bose and for us, the members of the INA was growing day by day. The change was heartening. I felt stronger and happier.

The Japanese POWs kept on pouring into the Ward. Soon the Ward was full to capacity. Their crowding did not disturb me for they were so well-behaved and disciplined. They respected me as if I was their own Regimental Commander and sought my advice in solving their problems. Without any authority or command, this distinguishing position among the patients was gratifying and I thoroughly enjoyed it.

On the morning of 26th May I was still asleep when I felt something soft crawling on my face. On opening my eyes, I was surprised to find two young Japanese nurses in men's uniform trying to wash my face and brush my teeth. One of them held a jugful of water while the other had a kidney-tray in her hand. On my refusal to be thus served, they started crying and were adamant to wash my mouth and give me a sponge bath. I had no other go but to surrender to their wishes. The special service, they told me, was out of respect for my status. They did not serve any other patient in the Ward.

During the day they came once again to inquire whether the news of the bombing of Tokyo by the Anglo-American aeroplanes was true. They had tears in their eyes as they put questions to me. Keen not to hurt their feelings, I told them that those were false rumours. They felt better and said, "British were bad." Then with reverence they asked me how the Emperor Tenno Haika was. On hearing that he was safe, their faces lit up with smiles. They bowed several times and then said, "*Arigato Goziamashita. Sayonara, odaijini*" (Thank you very much, farewell. Look after your health), and they left.

They never came again. Possibly, they were not allowed to visit the Ward any more. I have not forgotten those beautiful young faces adorned with tears of concern for their country, people and the Emperor. They were distressed when they had to don men's clothing to their utter disliking, just to safeguard their womanhood in all pervading hostile atmosphere. Their very thought gave me strength and boosted up my courage and morale during my days of captivity.

On 27th May my chest was X-rayed and blood tests taken. My

right ankle was put into a crepe bandage. On the 29th I was taken to No. 1 Indian Beach Medical Unit at Rangoon. By now my appendicitis had considerably subsided. I spent only two days of solitary existence in the Indian Beach Medical Unit. Apart from an Indian doctor of the rank of a Captain, cold but courteous and a nursing sepoy, I did not see any other human face in that hospital. It came as a relief to me when on 31st of May I was discharged from the Beach Medical Unit and taken to the Rangoon Central Jail.

20

Rangoon Jail

Dominated by the golden-spired Shiwe Dagon Pagoda, Rangoon, the capital city and chief port of Burma lying on the river Rangoon near its entrance into the Gulf of Martban, had the distinction of hosting the Headquarters of the Provisional Government of Free India and the Supreme Command of the Indian National Army in the last war of India's Independence against the British Raj during World War II.

In Rangoon rests Bahadur Shah Zafar, the last Emperor of India, who died in exile as a captive of the British, away from his beloved Delhi. Pining for his native land, the poet in him cried, *"Hai kitna badnaseeb Zafar daffan ke liye/Do gaz zamin bhi mil na sakki kooay yar mein."*

"How unfortunate is Zafar !
That for his burial,
He could not get
Even two yards of land,
In his beloved's lane."

It was under Bahadur Shah Zafar's flag that Indians had fought their last war as free men for their independence in 1857-59, called "Sepoy Mutiny" by the British. Since then some of our tallest freedom fighters including Netaji Subhas Chandra Bose had during their incarceration passed through the portals of jails in Burma, including the Central Jail of Rangoon.

With that historical background and feeling a bit important I looked forward to entering the Central Jail at Rangoon, little expecting the unpleasant surprise which awaited me. As I entered the big hall beside the main gate of the Jail I saw Major Malik Fateh Khan seated in the Jailor's chair on a raised platform beside an English Captain. Malik wore British badges of a Captain's rank. Ignoring this change in him I greeted my old colleague, "Jai Hind! *Major Malik*." He replied. "Good morning, Mr. Dhillon," and then hastened to order a Gurkha Subedar to take me to the Officer's barrack inside the Jail. I met Malik after quite a long time. He was my junior brother officer. His curt behaviour and the change in his badges of rank were a jolt to me.

Flabbergasted, carrying my few belongings under my arm, I limped on to the inner door of the jail under the Subedar's direction. He left me at the door of the Officer's barrack located within the jail. It was a low room where INA Officers were held. It had one door only. There were about twelve stringed cots jammed in two rows with little elbow-room in between. Near the door, a few odd shaped old chairs and low tables were placed to serve as a sitting place. At the time of my arrival, only half of the cots appeared to be occupied. I chose one on the farthest corner away from the door.

On arrival I was greeted by a young Flt. Lieut. Gurbachan Singh of the Royal Indian Air Force. He had joined the INA after his survival in an aircrash. He was very courteous and helpful. Having been in the INA Supreme Headquarters in Rangoon for quite sometime, he appeared to be knowing about my doings on the Front. Out of regards, he gave me a clean white bed-sheet of his own and helped me make my bed.

Gurbachan gave me details regarding the civilian communities and the INA in Rangoon. It was heartening to learn how the INA troops under the command of Maj. Gen. A . D. Loganathan with Colonel R.M. Arshad as his G-1 had successfully maintained law and order in Rangoon without a single mishap when the INA was the only army left in the city during the intervening period between the withdrawal of the Japanese Army and the arrival of the British forces of occupation. The period covered about two weeks as the British took quite some time in taking over the town from the INA.

Gurbachan Singh was full of praise for Gen. Loganathan after whose removal to India demoralization set in among the Officer cadre. Some of these officers stressed that they had done their duty but now that they had lost the war, it served no purpose to boast about the past.

If by disowning the past, one could save one's head on one's shoulders, why should not one save it? Would it not be foolish to keep on bragging about the past at life's cost and for nothing to gain ? Why be so foolish? Had not the British won the war and were we not the vanquished ? It was as simple as that, they said!

Against this way of thinking stood out in bold relief Netaji's words which he addressed to us through a message while leaving Burma on 24th April, 1945:

> Comrades ! At this critical hour I have only one word of command to give you, and that is that if you have to go down temporarily, then go down as heroes. Go down upholding the highest code of honour and discipline. The future generations of Indians who will be born, not as slaves but as free men because of your colossal sacrifice will bless your names and proudly proclaim to the world that you, their forebearers, fought and lost the battle in Manipur, Assam and Burma but through temporary failure you paved the way to ultimate success and glory.
>
> My unshakable faith in India's liberation remains unaltered. I am leaving in your safe hands our National Tricolour and the best traditions of Indian warriors. I have no doubt whatsoever that you, the vanguard of India's liberation, will sacrifice everything, even life itself, to uphold India's national honour so that your comrades who will continue to fight elsewhere may have before them your shining example to inspire them at all times.

In order to feel the pulse of the men I took a round of the Jail in the afternoon. As I moved from one barrack to another where the INA troops were lodged in different compounds, I was saluted half-heartedly in the old communal fashion of the British Indian Army saying, "Ram Ram, Salam and Sat Sri Akal" and so on. Bereft of the power of speech from sheer astonishment, I acknowledged their salutations like a dumb man without uttering a word. Their sad woe-begone stony faces spoke world of troubles suppressed deep down in their beings. Then as I went to another barrack I found my tongue and spoke:

I	:	Jawans ! Have you forgotten Jai Hind?
They	:	No Sir.
I	:	Then why don't you say Jai Hind?
They	:	Sir, we have been ordered not to say Jai Hind. We have been told that the INA exists no more.
I	:	Who gave you that order?
They	:	Our own senior officers. They even said. "*INA Fai NA koi nahin Jai Hind Fai-Hind koi nahin*." (There does not exist anything like the INA nor Jai Hind etc. etc.)
I	:	If some of your officers go traitors and offer their bottoms to the British, would you too lose your manly grace and submit passively ?
They	:	No, Sir, never.
I	:	Then, hold your heads high, Jai Hind !

They all shouted Jai Hind and as I moved on, INA slogans started reverberating throughout the Jail. Men kept on shouting and crying the war cry of "*Chalo Delhi*" and other slogans of the INA.

Azad Hind	*Zindabad!*
Azad Hind Fauj	*Zindabad !*
Netaji	*Zindabad!*
Chalo	*Delhi !*
Inquilab	*Zindabad*

They even hailed my name, Colonel Dhillon Zindabad

Troubled, hungry and exhausted, by sunset, I returned to the Officer's barrack where altogether a different atmosphere greeted me. Major Malik and the INA officers living in the barrack had arranged a small get-together for my welcome. There was Scotch for everybody, but for me a soft drink of lime juice *nimbupani* had been specially arranged to cater to my taste. It was a thoughtful gesture and in spite of all the happenings of the day, I looked forward to a comparatively relaxed evening. With the pleasant aroma of fresh lime from the glass offered to me as I waited for others to get their glasses charged for the toast, an unfortunate incident brought the party to an abrupt end.

One Field Officer addressing me said, "Sir, you kept the morale up at the Front but when Bose ! he (uttered 's' in Bose like z) left Rangoon we..." His casual reference to Netaji's name as 'Boze' was so offensive that without letting him complete the sentence, I intervened resulting in the following altercation :

I	:	Who? Who left Rangoon?
He	:	Boze.
I	:	I beg your pardon ?
He	:	Mr. Bose.
I	:	Thanks for the improvement. Can you do a bit better?
He	:	Mr. Subhas Chandra Bose.
I	:	How did you refer to his name before the fall of Rangoon ?
He	:	Netaji.

"Oh ! Thank you, you bloody traitors. You ...." I cursed and abused them all in the foulest loud language, telling them that I could neither drink nor dine with traitors. With all my force I smashed the glass on top of the nearest table scattering the liquid and splinters of glass all around the place. Then I walked off to my bed. After about fifteen minutes Gurbachan Singh came to offer meals which I refused. On his persistence to serve me something, I asked him to fetch a glass of water and then let me be alone.

Feeling concerned about my safety, Gurbachan informed me that Malik had gone to report to the British authorities against me. Thanking him for the information, I told him not to worry about me for I cared little about my self. Gurbachan was good enough to leave me alone. I started pondering over happenings of the day and came to the conclusion that what ever happened was in the interest of the Movement. I was at peace with myself and had the satisfaction of letting the British learn that the revolutionary soul of the INA was indestructible. Before long I fell asleep.

An hour before dawn, on the 1st of June, 1945 I was in sound sleep when I was awakened and taken out of the Jail by a Black Maria to No. 2 Field Interrogation Unit. Here I was produced before the 2 F.I.U. Commander — Major W.P.G. Maclachlan. He asked me if I had a girlfriend in Rangoon. I told him that I did have one. He inquired about her identity. When I informed him that she was niece of a friend and was of seven years age whom I loved as a daughter, Maclachlan showed remorse for having used the world girl-friend. But then he added that he could not allow me to visit her. I retorted, "I never asked you for that. Did I ?"

Major Maclachlan ignored my reaction and politely concluded the meeting. That was the first and the last time. I saw him, I was impressed by his demeanor. It was a surprise to me that there was no mention of yesterday's happenings. From there I was taken to a nearby bungalow where junior officer interrogators were billeting. Here I was given a hero's welcome. They provided a feast fit for a gala occasion with many delicious Indian dishes including fried chicken and hot *jalebees*. My sojourn there was of a day only, and late in the evening I was taken back to the Jail and put in solitary confinement.

The Central Jail of Rangoon was a big place. It had various enclosures and compounds. Its towering double-storey buildings were built like spokes of a wheel converging at an open space which formed the hub. At this focal point were located an administrative post and a small Medical Room attended by a doctor. It was an assembly and dispersal point for fatigue parties going to and coming from work. I was detained in an upper storey room overlooking this focal point. It was a room big enough to accommodate about thirty persons, a hall about 60 feet long and 20 feet wide with large windows from where I could look out and be seen, making a farce of my so-called solitary confinement. Below me on the ground floor were held Japanese POWs. Some prominent Burmese and Indian leaders were also confined in the same compound a few rooms away from me on the same storey. All these rooms and corridors in front were kept locked to keep different categories of prisoners apart.

I got no food for the first two days of my detention, not even tea, as if they had forgotten me. I did have cheese with me and used to fill my water-bottle while taken to toilets early in the morning and late in the evening, all alone. Except for this attention I was left alone, undisturbed, unattended and uncared for. My appendicitis now was not so painful but weak health did at times cause a strange sinking feeling. The rest and sleep brought me quite a relief. Missing tea more than food, on the third day, I wrote to the Officer-in-Charge of Cage No. 110: "This is just to ask you to please let me know whether along with solitary confinement, I am also supposed to be given no food. For the last 36 hours it has not been provided. I request you to please convey my report to the higher authorities."

On receiving my letter, the O-I-C of the Cage, an Indian Captain, called on me. He straightaway apologized, accepting responsibility for the act of omission. He confessed that he had completely forgotten to make any arrangements for my meals. His frankness totally disarmed me and the matter was just laughed away. Thereafter, I started getting regular meals and tea twice daily. The following day I was even taken to the Medical Room within the Jail. I knew that my ailments needed no immediate treatment other than rest, which I was getting in plenty.

My main trouble was that of sinking feelings due to debility. I had become peevish in temperament. Taking advantage of my visit to the doctor, I asked him if he could prescribe something like a nerve tonic which might help me control my temper. He precribed phosphoric tablet, though he did not have any. He, however, told me that it was available in the market. I took the prescription, though I did not have a single coin with me to get the medicine.

An Unknown Soldier

Late that night I awoke to the sound of a soft prolonged knocking at the door. "Who are you?" I inquired. "Sir, I am your Guards Commander" was the reply in a whisper. "Jemadar Sahib! At this time? What is the matter ?", I spoke in a low voice. "Sir, may I open the door?" "*Jemadar Sahib*! Why are you asking me ? I am under your security, just a prisoner." "Sir, I know who you are. Sir! there is one of your jawans downstairs. He requests to see you, *Hazoor*." "*Jemadar Sahib*, do you understand how risky it is for you to bring in a man to see me? How deterimental it is for your service?" "*Hazoor*! You have sacrificed your career and staked your very life for the freedom of Mother India, BHARAT MATA, and yet you are advising me not to be brave enough to take a petty little risk. Sir, I have already brought the man downstairs."

My words of caution sounded hollow in comparison to the Gurkha Guard Commander's action. I kept quiet. The Guard Commander unlocked the door. He went down and sent the visitor up. The visitor turned out to be a Sikh young man of twenty-five, whom I could not recognize in the pale moonlight filtering through the windows of the hall. He came to where I was sitting on the floor and sat down in front of me. As he started talking, I recognized him. Born and brought up in Rangoon, he had donated a substantial sum of money to the Netaji Fund, discarded a peaceful settled civilian life and volunteered to join INA on Netaji's call for Total Mobilization.

He had joined me when my Regiment, the 4th Guerrilla, was stationed at Myingyan and had been through battles on the Irrawaddy and Popa Hill areas. He lit a candle and in its light I could see his face clearly. He gave me a cake of soap, a loaf of bread and some bananas. Then he gave me a small envelope containing five hundred rupees in the British currency notes of various denominations. The Japanese currency, having been completely devalued, was not worth the paper on which it had been printed. The only use it could be made of was to light a fire or for keeping as a souvenir. Five hundred rupees in British currency at that time was a lot of money, and here was a sepoy of the INA giving it as a gift to his Brigade Commander.

How could the Commander in me accept it? And how could I? Hence I returned the envelope. The sepoy refused to take it back. I told him that in the jail I was getting everything enough for my needs but outside the Jail he had to provide for himself. The sepoy became emotional and said, "Sir, you used to tell us that irrespective of age you are our father. Now why do you deprive me of the pleasure of serving my father ? Sir, am I no more your son ?" "You are my dear son but I am sorry, I feel your need is greater; take it back." I handed over the envelop to the sepoy.

While taking the envelope, he said, "I brought it because I could easily afford it. I did not bring it to take it back and I am determined that I will not take it back." After saying so, he brought the envelope near the flame of the candle and was about to set it on fire when in a flash I flipped his hand away from the flame saying, "My son, you have won. I stand defeated. I accept it. Please give it to me." And I thanked him. "Thank you Sir, thank you very much. You have made me happy," he uttered in a choked voice.

The young man gave his address and took leave. I stood up to embrace him and kissed his turbaned head and having patted his back blessed him. Then we exchanged a formal salute saying, "Jai Hind !" And he left. Our meeting lasted for hardly five minutes but his memory has lingered on with me for over half a century and it shall eternally remain with me as an instance of a revolutionary comradeship of an INA solider. I had to destroy his address when I learnt that British C.I.D. were hounding and arresting our men in the town. Bad as I am in remembering names, it is a shame that I have forgotten his name. Perhaps it is better this way, for good soldiers remain THE UNKNOWN.

The next day I rose feeling rich because providing myself with phosphoric tablets was no more a problem. It cost just five rupees. What was I to do with so much money on me ? I got the answer instantly. That very evening another jawan visited me with his pathetic story of illness and non-availability of the medicine prescribed by the Jail doctor. In the bazaar its cost was thirty rupees. He asked me what he was to do. As I gave him the money, the jawan went back happy and hopeful of his recovery. I was equally happy that I was in a position to operate a small welfare fund of my own.

On Thursday, the 7th of June, I had a very pleasant surprise. Without any warning at ten in the morning, I was taken to a room outside the Jail in front of the main gate. I could scarcely believe my eyes when I found Balquees with her siblings along with uncle Bashir waiting for me. The children had brought a backutful of food, fruits and sweets along with a cotton T-Shirt of dark blue colour. On top of the basket was placed a packet of two hundred rupees in British currency. By chance I was wearing the khaki T-shirt which they had given me on my departure from Rangoon to the Front in November, 1944. I had always carried this T-shirt as a charm on my person. I could see that the children did not fail to notice it as they moved their soft fingers blessing it anew.

The children wore Churchill's victory sign "V" except Balquees who still displayed the INA badge. I asked the children, "Have you gone pro-British?" With tears in their eyes, in silence, they unbuttoned their shirts to show Netaji's badges pinned inside. Our meeting was of a short duration. We spoke very little and departed with hugs and kisses as we said, "JAI HIND".

Back in my room, I was reminded of Bahadur Shah Zafar's verse which he had composed on the farewell visit of one of his dear ones who had come all the way to Calcutta when the Emperor was being brought to Rangoon as an exile:

"Jo whoh aeye bhi to khare khare

Na woh baithey na main bitha saka!"

(Unexpectedly they came but for a while,

They kept standing for I could offer no seat.)

Balquees and the children left me richer not only in love and happiness but materially too. My little welfare fund increased thereby enhancing my capacity to serve the needy jawans, which made me feel blessed.

The kindness and understanding of the Captain in-charge of the Cage and the courtesy and co-operation of Gurkha guards kept increasing with time and in spite of my weak health my days passed happily. My room was locked no more during the day. It used to be a pleasure to wash and bathe in the rain. I could visit civilian prisoners in the neighbouring rooms on the same storey. They suffered overcrowding and scarcity of water in addition to other living facilities. Here I met most of our leaders of the I.I.L. who were the pillars of our Movement in Burma. My most cherished memory of those days is a meeting with the great Burmese leader U. Nu.

Habib Sahib

One day Habib Sahib came to visit me. He was the most prominent donor who, by contributing one crore and three lakhs of rupees in cash, jewelry and property in a lump sum, had boosted the fund-raising drive of the Netaji Fund Committee in Burma and had also volunteered his personal services as an ordinary worker in the freedom struggle. Netaji used to liken his contribution as HABIB MIXTURE, tonic for the health and growth of our Movement. Habib was older than my father. I took his visit in my captivity as a singular honour.

However, the pleasure of meeting him was marred by his hysterical sobs. He took a long time to collect himself and with sobs he uttered his anguish and shame for having succumbed to the wrong advice of certain weak-hearted and cunning colleagues and threats of dire consequences by the British. Under duress, he made a statement that he had not donated funds to Netaji of his own free will and that the donation had been forcibly extracted from him. He regretted that having sacrificed so much for the Movement, he undid all the good by his false statement, thereby betraying Netaji and thus forfeiting his trust for which there could be neither reprieve nor pardon.

Habib Sahib asked me to inform Netaji, as and when I met him, that Habib was sincerely repentant and begged to be pardoned. We were together for about two hours. His face showed the anguish of his soul. I consoled him and promised to approach Netaji to ask for his forgiveness. But, above all, I counselled him to rest assured of Netaji's capacity to understand human nature, on his own. I believed, Netaji was capable of appreciating Habib's difficulties and helplessness. He should, therefore, be at ease having full faith in Netaji's judgment and benevolence. I wonder how much solace my words brought to the old man but he looked composed and relieved, when he left me.

On the 9th of June, Shah Nawaz was brought from Pegu and put up with me for the night. He was taken to India the next day. It was nice for both of us to be together once again. He told me that we were kept away from each other as they thought that we had mutually inspired each other to attain martyrdom. He advised me to take it easy and not invite trouble. I agreed with him but my patience would come crumbling down the moment someone behaved in an arrogant and disparaging manner in dealing with me. Though I could always deal with such rude visitors with matching capability, I would feel depressed after the event.

It hurt me all the more if the visitor happened to be an Indian trying to pose more royal than the King himself. One day there came such a bloke who asked me with a queer twist of the tongue, "Are you one of the JIFS?" (Japanese Inspired Forces). In return I said, "And who the hell are you, a bloody BIF?" (British Inspired Forces). The Officer made a hurried retreat as I gave him a bit of my mind in an expressive English. But the moment he left, I got annoyed with myself for having lost my temper and thought, "Weren't I also a BIF before joining the INA? Why should I lose temper with a fellow countryman who is oblivious of his slavery ?"

As a freedom fighter, I thought, I should be humble and courteous. "After all, who am I?" I kept on posing the question to myself. I got the answer in the form of a poem, MAIN KAUN HOON, WHO AM I ? The poem makes it abundantly clear that I am merely a petty solider of Netaji, just one among his innumerable followers. I am fortunate to be one of those kindred souls who love to live and die for the native land.

My problem, however, was not how to put up with the arrogance of the British or the British Indian Army officers which was understandable for, after all, I was a prisoner. Had I been in Singapore, things might have been far worse because of my Changi Garrison Command. What really troubled my mind was the attitude and actions of a few INA officers who, lacking courage to face the consequences of their actions for having joined the INA, were now behaving in a manner unbecoming of the freedom fighter's code of honour.

Taking the line of least resistance was one thing but to blame the Movement, its leadership or one's colleagues for one's own actions was unpardonable. I could neither tolerate nor understand it. There were officers who held responsible jobs in the Headquarters and had not been even to the field. My mind was always engaged in the thought as to how I should deal with such colleagues. To show how I pondered over the problem, I reproduce a specimen of what I scribbled on the 19th of June, 1945 as :

Code of Honour

> I wonder whether there can be any Code of Honour in the present-day world. If one thinks of self-respect, one gives an impression of being proud. Only weak people can be proud. Strong people are not. Losing one's temper gives strength to your opponent and you simply

> make a fool of yourself.
>
> What you think 'right', others may call wrong. There must be a reason for it. Think, think, think and find out the reason. To think is never dishonourable, even if you think of things against a certain code of honour. This may make you realise that your code of honour regarding certain things is based on something false and if it is not, then you can be justly proud of it.

By the middle of June I was transferred to a compound in a secluded part of the Jail where some three hundred segregated INA personnel were detained. Most of these men had fought in the Popa area. The majority of them belonged to my Regiment. It was pleasant to be among one's own men once again and especially so under the circumstances when one could inspire them and get inspired in return. Mehar Singh, my batman since the days of Singapore (1942) was also there. He took up catering to my little needs.

The facilities for basic needs like water, cook-houses, baths and lavatories were adequate. We cooked our meals in a common kitchen. Rations were issued at the field scale of the British Indian Army which were good in quality and plenty in quantity. The standard of rations of the British Indian Army had improved remarkably since the Malayan Campaign (1941-42). In the INA we never had it that good.

From this compound, a door opened into an inner compound where about ten of I.I.L. leaders were interned. They were all very important persons, mainly from Burma, who had contributed much to the Indian independence movement. Dina Nath, Bashir Ahmad and Habib Sahib were among them. They were kept in rooms which during normal times were meant to keep prisoners of special categories or those of security risk to the Raj. We were not supposed to mix with them.

Within the compound we were left free to look after ourselves. Our rooms and barracks were never locked. Sentries remained posted outside the compound wall. My room was a narrow cell away from and facing the main barrack. The confines of the cell never let me have the feelings of being squeezed into it. I could always keep my door open which let me enjoy the open space of the compound extending before me. The monsoons had given the place dark green grass imparting a natural touch to an otherwise dreary jail outlook. But for the sense of captivity, it was a simple, clean and healthy life, camp-like, but without any excitement or recreational thrill of a camp. It was dull.

Yet excitement of a sort was there. It was provided by a senior officer of the British Intelligence, Major H. Bowes who, while on his rounds, would often scold and bully the inmates of the inner compound. He had chided one of our civilian leaders in a threatening loud tone, "And, so you are the one who removed Bose's boots on his visit to the grave of Bahadur Shah. Did you ?" As if it was a great anti-British crime ! When I learnt about this episode I got greatly disturbed, yet I could not advise our civilian friends to pay Major Bowes in his own coin.

Placed as they were, they had no other alternative but to stomach it in silence. Yet in my heart of hearts I wished to face Bowes personally, but he never came my way. Then as luck would have it, one day I got a chance. I was sitting under a shed, in the humid weather wearing only underwear, absorbed in reading a book, *One Thousand One Nights,* given to me by some friend, when I heard someone approach in a deliberate manner. As I looked up from my sitting position, I could guess that my visitor was Major Bowes, though we had never met. And as we accosted each other, the following altercation occurred:

B : Who are you ?

I : Colonel Dhillon.

B : You are not a Colonel.

I : I am a Colonel.

B : You bloody well are not. You are just a Lieutenant.

I : I bloody well am a Colonel and a very bloody one for persons like you.

B : Do you know who am I ?

I : Just a bloody Britisher (I said snapping my fingers).

B : Do you think just any person can come here ?

I : O, yes, many fools can come to disturb a prisoner. I do see you are in a Major's uniform and think a hell of yourself, a Field Officer !

B	:	And you think you are a hero ?
I	:	Of course, I am. Have you any doubt ?
B	:	Do you know, India won't own you and Mahatma Gandhi will spit at your very name ?
I	:	I know my people. They shall be proud of me and even Mahatma Gandhi will adore me when he comes to know me.
B	:	Gandhi hates violence. Don't you know it ?
I	:	I know him better than you do.
B	:	Do you know what can happen to you ?
I"	:	I care less. May be a bullet.
B	:	No.
I	:	A loop (encircling my neck with my both hands).
B	:	No.
I	:	Tortured death.
B	:	No.
I	:	Transportation for life.
B	:	No. Can't you think of something else, something better ?
I	:	No. I don't expect anything better from you folks.
B	:	Are your married?
I	:	Yes.
B	:	Do you love your wife?
I	:	Yes.
B	:	Mother ?
I	:	Yes.
B	:	Father ?
I	:	Yes.
B	:	Sister ?
I	:	Yes.
B	:	Brothers ?

I : Yes.

B : Don't you want to see them ?

I : I have no hope.

B : Don't you want to go back to India?

I : It makes little difference whether I am in jail in Burma or in India. The jails are alike.

B : You are going to be released.

I : I am not a fool to believe it.

B : What will you do if you are released ?

I : Do the very thing I have done before.

B : Do you mean you will again take up arms against His Majesty the King Emperor ?

I : Of course.

B : I take it as a challenge.

Boiling with rage Bowes picked up his cap and made a hasty exit.

Most of the inmates of the compound attracted by the uproar of the war of words between Bowes and me, had gathered around us to watch the bout. Bowes sudden move left them guessing what might fall on me. My officers and men out of deference could show their concern only by their silence, but the civilian colleagues of the inner compound, though happy for the much-needed treatment meted out to Bowes, advised me to avoid any future trouble. However, I had no regrets and was satisfied that I could do what I could not advise others to do.

All the same, I did apprehend that some action against me was in the offing, but contrary to all expectations nothing happened. The only apparent result of the episode was that Bowes stopped coming on his rounds and the prisoners were, thus, spared his harassing them which in itself was quite a relief. Meanwhile, we learnt that a good number of prisoners were being taken to India. After about ten days as I stood in front of my cell at nine in the morning, I saw Major Bowes enter the compound. He had come to visit the inner enclave, I thought. I was wrong. He made straight for me and the following conversation ensued between us :

B : Good morning, Mr. Dhillon.

I : Good morning, Major Bowes.

B : How are you this morning ?

I : I am very well. Thank you and how are you ?

B : I am very well. Thank you. How is your health now?

I : Better than before.

B : Do you still feel pain ? (Bowes asked, having knelt down to touch my bandaged foot).

I : A little, it is much better now. Thank you.

B : You are very courteous this morning, Mr. Dhillon !

I : Aren't you so affectionate, Major Bowes?

B : I have come to talk to you. Can you give me some time ?

I : You are welcome.

B : Where can we sit ?

I : You mind coming to my room ?

B : That's good. Thank you.

Mehar Singh had placed a small wooden case of discarded packing in my room which used to serve me as an all-purpose item of furniture.

I : May I offer you this box for a chair ?

B : Thanks but where will you sit ?

I : I am accustomed to squat on the floor.

B : I can do that too.

I : No, I do not want to get the crease of your trousers spoilt and then it is my room.

We both laughed. Sitting down on the box, Bowes felt composed as Mehar Singh served tea.

B : Do you know what happened that day was because of an argument we had in the mess that nobody could bully you. I made a bet that I would, but instead got bullied and lost a bottle. I had to hurry away lest some JAI HIND WALAS should break my head. But I am sorry I reported against you.

I : Well, you did your duty.

B : But, did you really mean what you said about taking up arms again ?

I : Yes, I did mean it.

B : Do you still mean it ?

I : I am afraid, I do India must attain freedom.

B : Don't you really want to go back home ?

I : Aren't you kidding ? As if you have to ask a prisoner before sending him anywhere ! My answer remains the same. It makes no difference to me whether I am in a jail here or in India.

B : I don't agree with you. Do you know that members of the Congress Working Committee have been released and the Viceroy has invited representatives of all the political parties to a conference in Simla on the 25th of June, that is tomorrow. These developments do concern you and here you are in utter darkness. You might be able to keep abreast of current affairs if you were in India and thus assess the situation for yourself. It shall also soften your attitude.

I : I do see your point. If I have to go one day, why not now ?

B : Do you want to go by sea or by air ?

I : Can a prisoner have a choice ?

B : I ask you as a friend.

I : Oh ! Thank you, then let me go by air. I do not like the sea voyage in this season.

B : I am glad you have made the choice. Now I can arrange to send you within a week. Meanwhile, I will bring you some newspapers to read.

The following day Bowes brought some recent copies of *The*

Statesman of Calcutta edition. He again was with me for a cup of tea and before leaving gave me a very pleasant surprise. He told me that he would send Captain Rashid Yusaf Ali to take me to visit Balqees and other children at Mr. Bashir Ahmad's house in the evening. He asked me to be ready to go out at 4 p.m. It was, indeed, a very kind thought on the part of not only Major Bowes but also of Major Ore and Major W.P.G. Maclachalan's for which I shall ever remain indebted to them.

Captain Yusaf Ali was punctual. An evening drive in an open jeep driven by courteous Captain Yusaf Ali through the town of Rangoon was a rare treat. Sitting on the front seat I felt a soul-lifting whiff of fresh air bathe my face. At Bashir's house my joy was further enhanced to find him among the children. I did not expect him at home, he being an internee in the inner compound where I had met him only the day before, when along with others he had counselled me to take it easy.

Balqees and her siblings treated us to tea. I was with them for about an hour and a half. The joy of this wonderful visit was constantly attended by a sad sensation of the separation to come. War had made the children wiser than their years. Back in my cell, I wondered whether I had made them happy or unhappy.

21

To Delhi

On first of July in 1945 at ten in the morning, six British officers entered the compound. One of them, Captain of the Military Police, called for me. I came out of my cell to hear him shout, "Get ready immediately ! You are going to India. Hurry up, otherwise the plane will leave. I give you five minutes to move." I could have moved out instantly for there was nothing to be readied, yet the curt manner of the Captain shouting like a drill instructor disregarding the very presence of a Field Officer, a Major, amongst them forced me to answer, "I can't get ready to go to India within five minutes. If the plane can't wait, let it go. I don't care." My reaction resulted in a small row and the Captain was obliged to yield. "O.K. Take your own time and let us know when you are ready."

I got ready within no time. I spent a few minutes meeting officers and men in the compound who had gathered to wish me farewell. I wore my haversack over a shoulder and put a rolled up ground sheet containing all my belongings under an arm and announced my readiness to move. The Captain said, "You have taken only five minutes." I looked at my watch and said, "Not five, ten minutes." The Major who till then had been a silent observer came forward and guided me to the front seat of a jeep parked outside the compound in the middle of a long line of more than ten vehicles carrying armed soldiers. He himself took the driver's seat beside me and the convoy started moving. After having gone about two miles away from the Jail, the escorting vehicles started falling out one at a time at regular intervals.

Soon the jeep carrying me was left alone on its way to Mingladon Airport. I was guarded by only four armed Gurkhas of the Major's Unit.

They sat silently at the rear of the Jeep, alert and ready to act, if needed. There was tension. The Major looked ill-at-ease. Sensing his uneasiness I broke the silence, "Major ! you may please rest at ease, assured that no harm is going to come to you because of me. I appreciate your responsibility." My words surprised the Major and with a sign of relief he said, "Oh, Sir ! Thank you, thank you very much."

Suddenly there was no more tension. We started conversing and I learnt that Major Anderson had been abroad for more than six long years, mainly in Nagaland. He had developed great liking for the land and its people and had a lot to say about them. He had collected a rich treasure of Naga souvenirs. Now that the war had ended he was going back to his home in Scotland and had been assigned to escort me up to Calcutta. His longings to reach home were so intense that he could brook no delay on the way.

A typical Regimental Officer, even otherwise he had little liking for an extra-Regimental stint and hated running into an unnecessary problem. Escorting a prisoner who had waged war against the King Emperor was not a pleasant task, yet he took me at my word and felt at ease. At the airport he left me alone under a canopy as he went to contact the embarkation authorities. After some time he returned looking agitated and said, "Sir, the plane chartered for you is being used by so many officers and men that I am not being allowed to take along my baggage. Could you, Sir, help me ?"

His dilemma put me into a strange predicament. What could I do ? I could only advise him that war having ended, it was but natural that soldiers would long to go home at the earliest opportunity and they did deserve accommodation. In my position I could not help him, and my being under his custody, any action or request from me might be taken as a dereliction of duty by him apart from causing embarrassment to both of us. I proposed that he should try once again and see if the authorities concerned would yield a bit. Anderson tried, and having achieved what he wanted, returned with a smile on his face and a Naga spear on his shoulder.

The space under the canopy soon got crowded with officers and men from different Units of the 14th Army in their olive-green uniforms. In my worn-out khaki outfit without any badges, I wondered whether they knew who I was and why I was among them. They all ignored me and I ignored the whole lot of them except a British Brigadier who was the only one to exchange greetings with me. He was the senior-most officer on that journey. In the plane he sat next to me. I found him pleasant to travel with.

The plane left Mingladon in Rangoon at 1400 hrs and arrived Dum Dum in Calcutta at 1900 hrs. En route we landed at Akyab for refuelling and tea. Tea at Akyab was a lavish affair with many eatables to go with it. The Brigadier and Major Anderson looked after me well. When the call to embark the plane was sounded, everybody rushed to catch the plane. When I tried to catch up with them with a pronounced limp, Anderson said, "Sir, you need not hurry. This plane is for you. It can go without anybody but not without you."

On arrival at Dum Dum, there was no one to receive Anderson and me. While all other passengers left instantly for their respective destination, we were the only ones stranded at the end of a deserted military landing strip beside a small canteen. Anderson took out a big padlock and a pair of handcuffs from his trousers, bulging pockets and said, "Sir, those bloody fools in Rangoon gave me these cuffs for you. They know not a gentleman from a criminal."

Putting forward my both hands, I said, "Please put them on. You should have handcuffed me. These are ornaments to a freedom fighter." He responded, "No, Sir, never; I can't do that to you. You are a thorough gentleman, but in case I am asked why I did not cuff you, I shall reply that I have just released you for letting you go to the toilet." "Why risk it ? I do not mind being handcuffed." I pleaded, but Anderson paid no heed. He left me alone standing about fifty metres away from the canteen and went in to ring up the Allied Land Forces Advance Headquarters to report our arrival.

It took him a long time to contact the officer concerned whom he found in a down town cinema hall half way through a movie. Anderson returned to inform me that we would be picked up when the officer returned from the town after the end of the picture. It was a pleasant evening. Standing in the open we enjoyed the gentle, cool southern breeze blowing in our faces coming from over the Bay of Bengal. Anderson invited me to join him for a drink of whisky and soda in the canteen.

It was indeed a pleasing invitation and I felt grateful but when I told Anderson about my vow not to drink till India got free, he was disappointed. I asked him to get a soft drink when he could have the good old Scotch. He happily agreed. However, anxious not to cause any harm to him, I asked him to let me stay where I was and bring out the drinks. Anderson agreed and brought out a glass of lime juice and soda for me and another of Scotch and soda for himself with which we toasted each other's health standing in the open under the beautiful Indian sky.

Late in the evening, a jeep drove up straight to us. A tall and handsome officer jumped out of it and introduced himself as Major Allen of the ALFA HQ. He was profusely apologetic for having made us wait for long for a bit of personal pleasure in seeing the picture through and not giving it up in the middle. Anxious to offer us something to eat, he took us straight to the Officers Mess. On Sundays most of the officers liked dining out and Major Allen was apprehensive of its early closure. As we entered the dining hall we found that it was on the verge of being closed. Allen got a table specially laid for us two and moved about to see that we were served a good hot multi-course meal. Having dined out he joined us only for coffee.

After the dinner, Allen took us to his suite, a two-room single officer's accommodation built during the war with slanting corrugated cement sheets for roof over one brick-thin walls. It was modestly furnished. Allen instructed his servant to make my bed in his bedroom. He personally checked that the bed was properly made and mosquito net correctly tucked. He and Anderson shared the drawing room to spend the night. The only bathroom connected with the bed room was left entirely for my use. Before wishing good night, I was asked timings for my bed tea and for bath. The next morning, the 2nd of July, I was pleasantly surprised to find that the room where I had spent the night opened out to a vast grassy space with dark green trees waving in the wind. "Was I a prisoner ?" I asked. They had not posted any guard on me either.

The bearer brought in the bed-tea on a tray in the English manner. After an interval, the bearer announced that he had laid hot water for my bath. I could not help recalling that the last time I had enjoyed having the luxury of a hot bath was at village BAWASA near PAGAN through the courtesy of its headman during my brief halt on way to POPA on 15th February 1945. The villagers had to pay the price for sheltering us in getting the village put to flames by the British planes a short while after we had left the village.

After I had finished my bath, Anderson and Allen took turns to bathe. Allen took us to the Mess for breakfast. After the breakfast Anderson left us. We parted like friends of long standing. I felt sad. Anderson having gone, Allen himself carried my few belongings to a waiting jeep and took me straight to his office. His office was in an old stately building with a prominent porch, a broad verandah and a very big central hall which in the past would have seen many banquets and balls. After a brief introduction to the members of his staff amongst whom I met Major Hayat of the CSDIC (Combined Services Detailed Interrogation Centre of India) for the first time, Allen took me to a wall of the central hall which was covered with a big quarter inch-to-a mile map of Burma.

On the map were shown battle positions and routes of the different formations of the INA by means of various tapes of different colours pinned on the map. Pointing out a particular colour he said, "This is how we followed you. Could you please tell us how far we have been right ?" Some officers of his staff were keenly following our dialogue. I replied, "You deserve to be congratulated on your accuracy in following me except from Magwe to Prome where you have shown me on the east of the Irrawaddy while we had crossed over to the west and then recrossed to the east at Kama." Allen got the tape realigned and asked me to have a look at the routes of other formations.

Meanwhile, all the members of his office including ladies surrounded me to ask a number of questions about Netaji and the INA. Their queries showed that they were very well-conversant with my role in the war. Their questions about Netaji were quite intriguing. It was pleasing to note that none of them referred to him by any other name than Netaji. A Bengali girl said, "Did you ever shake hands with Netaji?" "Yes, many a time", I said. "May I shake that hand?" she asked. "You are welcome," I replied as I offered my hand.

Then another girl asked me, "How did he look in the military uniform?" In response I asked them to open my bedroll and see it for themselves. I produced a photo. As they all stood admiring the photo, a Corporal of the British Military Police turned up. They helped me to roll up the bedroll which was again picked up by Major Allen as he said, "I am sorry we have to part now. They have come to take you." Allen carried my bedroll up to the door of the hall and handing it over to me bade me farewell. As we shook hands, I thanked him for his hospitality and courtesy. My last words to Allen were, "Kindness kills, your kind courtesy has destroyed the sting in me."

Out in the verandah looking at the Black Maria parked in the porch, I felt I had come to a different world as I heard the Corporal shout impudently at me with an obnoxious gesture of a hand, *"Challo, challo, jaldi, jaldi,"* Go go, quick, quick. He got hold of my bedroll at the corner of it with one hand and flung it towards the rear of the Black Maria falling just short of it. I picked it up and got into the vehicle where I was made to sit down on the floor betwixt three British guards who stood with loaded rifles and bayonets fixed at the ready. The Corporal closed the door of the vehicle from outside with a bang.

I had never been to Calcutta before. Seated on the floor with the outside view denied, I could little guess where I was being taken to. Ultimately, the Black Maria stopped and on coming out of it, I learnt that I had been brought to the British Military Police Lock up in the town. The place was meant to detain British Other Ranks (B.O.Rs) arrested by B.M.P. for offences committed outside their unit lines. The offenders would be kept in the lock-up for the barest minimum time and then handed over to their respective Units for necessary action for trial and punishment by their Unit Commanders.

The lock-up was set up in a double-storey building in the market area beside a cinema hall called, 'Elite'. The ground floor of the building had been turned into a prison with small cells arranged in rows. The office of the P. M. (Provost Marshal) was on the top floor. On arrival I was taken to the P.M. On the way, the arrogant Corporal pushed me as I was limping due to my bad foot which was still under a bandage. He shouted, "*Challo, challo, jaldi, jaldi.*"

Taken aback by his rudeness I stopped impulsively. Caught unaware by my sudden halt, the Corporal stumbled on me. As he was trying to regain his balance, I said, "Corporal, I can't go fast and don't touch me." The Corporal reacted, "I can't go slow. I am going ahead, you take your own time." Having said so he went forward to the base of the staircase leading to the P.M.'s office hardly ten paces ahead of me. My presence before the P.M. was of a routine procedure after which I was taken to a cell. It was about 10 feet by 8 feet square with a strong iron door with thick bars. There was a narrow bare wooden bench without a back placed in the centre of the cell to serve as a bed.

Immediately on entering the cell, the Corporal started a search on my person and of my effects. His method of search was not only peculiar but also insulting. He picked up one thing at a time and tossed it high into the air to let it fly to an upper corner of the cell and then got hold of another item and flung it likewise to a corner diagonally in the opposite direction. He, thus, went on throwing my few precious belongings. Non-plussed, I stood watching the show which was so provocative yet ludicrous.

I was reminded of my childhood days of watching a juggler display his objects out of a bag to the spectators gathered around him in the village square. As though to justify his performance, the Corporal had the cheek to say, " I cannot help it. This is my way of doing the job." "Carry on, Corporal, carry on, you do it well" was my response with a forced smile. When he saw my pen, he started observing it minutely and then shouted, "It is a Japanese pen, dangerous enemy property. You can't keep it. It must be surrendered." "It is not a weapon, it is a simple pen," I replied. "It is as dangerous an instrument as a sword, you can't keep a Japanese pen." To his charge I answered that it was not a Japanese pen. He showed me some letters embossed on it which he took for Japanese letters. It took me quite sometime to tell him that KANJI characters were common to both the Chinese and the Japanese languages.

Confused by my arguments, the Corporal gave in but then turned his eyes to my watch and started murmuring., "*Gharee, gharee, gharee* give me *gharee,*" (Watch, watch, watch give me watch). I told him that

I could not part with the watch and implored him to let me keep it. After some time he relented and then asked me to bundle up all my belongings including the clothes I was wearing in one single package. Having done so, I was told to carry the bundle to a store room where it was deposited. The only items left with me were the watch, the underpants and a small hand towel.

At last, the Corporal locked me up in the cell and left without any further ado. Heaving a sigh of relief I stretched myself on the bare wooden boards for a bit of rest. I had hardly laid my back on it when hordes of bedbugs mounted an assault on all those parts of my body which were in contact with boards of the bench. When I got up to locate my tormentors, they just vanished into the crevices of the bench and waited there nonchalantly to attack me again and again whenever I dared to lie down on the bench. They were completely invulnerable. I had no option other than to watch, vex and suffer impotently. The menace was made all the more unbearable by lack of a fan in that hot and humid July climate of Calcutta. As if that were not enough, a blinding glare from a powerful bulb in the ceiling, apart from making the cell hotter caused a burning sensation in the eyes. Yet an awful noise from the adjacent cinema hall was a further complement to the hellish state of things prevailing in the cell, notwithstanding reasonably good meals from the BORs' mess and general cleanliness of the cell.

Late in the evening as I sat pondering over the happenings of the day, I was startled by painful shrieks and obscene shouts from nearby, just one cell away from me. The Military Police were torturing two African soldiers. In utter helplessness, I felt distressed and rather guilty for having not even shouted against the barbaric treatment meted out to those poor souls who had come all the way from their homes to fight for the defence of the British Empire. That was the time when I appreciated Major Ore's proposal of wearing the British badges of rank. But then I too was a bloody nigger and a prisoner at that!

Yet another episode occurred after midnight when four Japanese POWs were brought and pushed into a cell next to my cell. On arrival they were beaten and cursed and then made to do strenuous physical exercises like sitting, standing, jumping with parting of legs and clapping hands over head etc. etc. Tommies shouted, "*Ichi, ni, ichi, ni*" (one, two, one, two). They appeared to have picked up only these two words of the Japanese language. Whenever the Japanese movements got slack, they were thrashed and cursed in the filthiest words. Their torture continued throughout the night. The Japanese conducted themselves with dignity and bore up under each blow so bravely that neither a word nor a moan ever escaped their beings. When this treatment was being meted out to them, I waited apprehensively for my turn, fully prepared to face the eventuality gracefully. But it did not occur.

In the morning, two tommies naked above their wastes turned up outside my door and stood there clutching bars in a childish manner peeping in at me. I could little guess the purpose of their visit. After sometime, without any greetings, they engaged me in a brief dialogue, reproduced below, speaking one at a time.

They	:	Are you an officer ?
I	:	Yes, so I am.
They	:	And a Brigade Commander ?
I	:	Yes
They	:	This is no fuckin' place for officers. It is for us fuckin' Other Ranks. Why the bloody hell have they kept you here ?
I	:	Because I fought against the King Emperor for the freedom of India, my country.
They	:	Oh! Did you Sir, did you ?
I	:	Yes, I did.
They	:	(In excitement) You are a great man, Sir, a very great man. And a bloody good Indian.

Completely thrilled, their bodies quivered like the strings of a musical instrument while they spontaneously sprang up to attention, fully stretching their arms along their bare bodies, straining each muscle as they said, "Good morning Sir." I stood up to respond to their salute in all solemnity. Then they left.

After a while they returned bringing a packet of cigarettes for me. When I showed my inability to accept it displaying my iron bangle, they said, "Oh ! you are a Syeikh, Syeikh are damn good Indians and bloody good fighters." They apologized for having offered cigarettes to a Sikh and left. After about a quarter of an hour they came again and gave me a nice big chocolate bar. Once again they came for the last time at lunch hour to give their share of custard pudding and told me that they were being taken to their Unit and wished me good health and said good-bye like friends of long standing.

They went away leaving me lost in thought about the nature of the soldier who dies fighting for the boundaries of his country. Yet his simplicity, innocence and large-heartedness would cut through all barriers, national and international. At about nine in the evening I was made to collect my belongings and asked to get ready to move.

Soon after, guarded by British Military Police I was carried in a Black Maria to Howrah Railway Station and taken straight to a third class compartment of a Troops train under the command of Captain Khan of the Bahawalpur State Forces. The move from the lock-up to the railway train was made under such perfect security arrangements that I could not have the slightest glimpse of any place or a person. The train immediately steamed off as soon as I boarded it. Captain Khan courteously apologized for having accommodated me in a third class compartment. He explained that there was only one class in that train which was meant for the I.O.Rs (Indian Other Ranks) only. Thanking him for his courtesy, I told him that I was happy in their company and that a higher class made little difference to me.

It was a small compartment and I was given a central berth, obviously for reasons of security, and Captain Khan and a Subedar and a Jemadar and a Section-strong personnel to guard me. Though cold and reserved, their attitude was courteous. We talked little that night. And after the nightmarish experience of suspense, nearby torture, intolerable light, and bugs that polluted the British Military Lock-up, I was happy to get much needed rest and sleep.

Next morning after tea, Captain Khan and his men opened up and started asking me about myself. As I started telling them about the INA, its aim and objects, they listened to me with rapt attention. They were discovering something which had been kept secret from them throughout the war. They were pleasantly surprised to learn that from their State, the Ist Battalion Bahawalpur State infantry under command of Lieutenant Colonel G.Q. Gilani had en block joined the INA, and its officers and men had played very important roles in India's last war of independence.

Lt. Col. G.Q.Gilani (Colonel INA) was elected a member of the Council of Action along with General Mohan Singh. The Council of Action with Rash Behari Bose as its President was the Supreme INA Executive Body of five members. Major M.S. Barar (Colonel INA) had been Commander of the Propaganda and Welfare Group during Gen. Mohan Singh's period. One of their officers, Captain Shaukat Ali Malik (Col. INA) distinguished himself as being the fist Indian officer to hoist the *Tricolour*, National Flag on the liberated territory of India after having won it from the British in April 1944, at *Moirang* on the banks of Loketak lake in Manipur State. Colonel Malik was honoured by Netaji with the award of *Sardar-e-Jung*.

They were enthralled to know that the Provisional Government of Azad Hind had been recognized by nine countries and that we had our own Azad Hind Bank and various administrative departments. The branches of the Indian Independence League existed in all the countries of Asia in the East.

In a moment they put me on a pedestal and I was no more a prisoner for them but an honoured guest. I was no longer guarded and they even let me have long walks all by myself whenever the train halted for long intervals. In spite of arrangements for the provision of field rations in the train, Captain Khan took me to dine at the Ist Class Refreshment Room at Allahabad Railway Station. The standard of food and service at Railway refreshment rooms used to be of five-star luxury in those days.

The special troops train by which I was taken to Delhi ran once a week between Howrah and Rawalpindi via Delhi and Lahore. It carried its own field rations in the charge of a Quartermaster Havildar who catered to the troops needs. When the Havildar learnt about me, he took special care to look after me. He picked out chocolate and fruit bars from airtight food packets to give me. Some of these packets contained small coffee tins fixed with a combustible stuff which could be ignited by a match stick (also provided in the packet) and was just enough to make the delicious coffee boiling hot. Tasting these field rations I wondered what we could have achieved if we had a bit of these rations in the INA.

The Quartermaster Havildar was a Pathan, Aziz Allah Rich Khel from UTTAMANZAI, a village in Peshawar district of the North-West Frontier Province (N.W.F.P.). He was of intense patriotic outlook. After asking me many questions concerning my person, my people and my village, he came out with a proposal to visit my folks and inform them that I was alive and well. My village Chak No. 32 was two miles from Chhanga Manga railway station, forty-five miles south of Lahore on the main North Western Railway running to Karachi.

Aziz Allah's move to my village and back was full of an unnecessary risk for Aziz. If detected, he could be charged as an espionage agent and court-martialled for which the punishment was certain death or transportation for life. I could not allow him to take that big risk. And then for what ? I argued, but Aziz was determined and adamant to visit my parents to pay his homage and convey the news of my welfare. He called it a 'Pilgrimage', and cared little for any consequence. He was prepared to pay any price for it. I could see the freedom-loving Pathan in his eyes and radiant face. I asked him to let me sleep over the idea and I would talk to him the next day.

On the following day, I was further surprised that Captain Khan, his Subedar and the Jemadar along all their men supported Aziz Allah's proposal. I could clearly see that Aziz was taking too much of a risk for my family's pleasure. Ultimately, I yielded. Aziz further suggested that instead of a verbal message I should give him a letter and anything for safe-keeping or as a mark of memory. Eventually, I gave him four letters, one each for mother, father, eldest brother Gurdial Singh and for my wife Basant. I had written these letters while I was in solitary confinement in Rangoon Jail.

I also gave him two notebooks in which I had scribbled a few dates and names for safe-keeping. I had childlike things, an empty talcum powder tin and a small hand towel which had been given to me by a Burmese friend for my foot care and a worn-out T-shirt given to me by

Balquees and children of Bashir family. These simple little things were a mark of precious innocent love which I had always carried in my haversack. Those items had been a great source of inspiration to me so as to be worthy of their admiration in the performance of my duty to my country.

I shall ever remain grateful to Aziz for taking those articles to my home. And yet Aziz Allah was just one and not the only one. There were Capt. Khan and his men too who had treated me, a vanquished adversary, with overwhelming respect and love. How would have they treated and welcomed the INA, had we entered India as a victorious army ? How correct and confident was Netaji in giving a call to the Indians in the British Army of occupation to join us "in the sacred struggle for India's freedom"? Engaged in these thoughts I was awakened out of my reverie as the train stopped just short of Shahdara Bridge over the Yamuna, opening a grand vista of the skyline of Delhi with the glow of the Red Fort in the soft light of the sunset.

It was after dark when the train steamed into Delhi railway station. Its dreary outlook was made all the more gloomy due to the shaded dim lights of the blackout. Bidding farewell to my guards as I stepped down from the train carrying my belongings, a Section-strong British Military Police with bayonets fixed on their rifles surrounded me. Surprised by a show of arms around a single person, passers-by stopped to look with curiosity only to be chased away by the Military Police, *"Chalo, chalo"* with a crude gesture of hand.

Equally curious to observe my own countrymen, I heard someone say, "What a strong force to guard one man"? Another person said, "Come along, must be a murderer or a dangerous criminal. What have we to do with him?" When they were being chased away by the tommies of the Military Police, I mused over the harsh reality. "Poor souls! They know not who I am. O' my beloved ones, you are still in the dark. You have yet to arise. And arise you will definitely. Arise you must."

22

The Red Fort

From Delhi railway station I was brought straight to the Red Fort, thoroughly searched and lodged in a cell. Here prisoners were kept in complete solitary confinement and were guarded by British military personnel. The cell was small and furnished by a bare Indian cot placed in the centre. High above in the ceiling was an electric light controlled from outside. The Guard Commander, a Sergeant, showed me a pitcher of drinking water placed in a corner and an empty bucket for use at night. With these formalities and a cold "Good night", the Sergeant locked me in and left.

The sound of footsteps of the Sergeant and his guard slowly faded away. When it had died out, I heard someone tap softly from the adjacent cell. I heard a familiar voice in an extra-cautious tone, "Jai Hind ! Gurbakhsh! How is your appendicitis ?" "Jai Hind ! Sir, I am much better, thank you, and how are you, Sir?" I whispered. "I am well, now let's not talk for they watch us through hidden microphones in these cells. Jai Hind ! Sleep well." "Jai Hind, Sir !" It was comforting to find Shah Nawaz so close in that strange atmosphere.

Left to the company of my thoughts in that silent, dark, humid and hot cell, it took me long to get to sleep, but when I did sleep, I slept like a top till I was awakened by the jingling of keys on the padlock outside my cell. The Sergeant opened the door and beckoned me to come out. Thus dawned my first morning in the Red Fort of Delhi, the 6th of July 1945.

The sergeant looked markedly different from the uniformed Guard Commander whom I had seen the previous night. Bare-bodied except for a pair of short underpants hanging to his knees and a wet towel placed on his shoulders, he looked more like an Indian who had just come out of a holy dip from a nearby brook on his way to the place of worship. He took me to the toilet area which had a few Indian style lavatories and separate bathrooms where prisoners were locked in for ablutions one at a time. Here I was locked in a lavatory, where I heard someone taking a bath in the adjacent cubicle. From the sound of clearing his throat I guessed that he was Jagir. Though I could not talk, I was happy that he was there.

When he was taken out and moved away, the door of my lavatory was opened and I was shut in the same bathroom. Here I found Jagir's pair of glasses in a small recess in the wall meant for holding soap and toothbrush, etc. I recognized those glasses, and when I was taken out of the bathroom, I handed them to the Sergeant and said, "Sergeant these glasses have been forgotten by Colonel Jagir Singh." The Sergeant retorted, "How do you know these glasses belong to whom?" "Just by guess," I said. "Be careful, here you do not try to know who is who." All right, Sergeant," I replied. Without uttering another word, he took the glasses and guided me back to my cell where I was locked in again.

At 8 O'clock I was taken to a nearby office within the security area but outside the gate guarding our cells. Here I found a civilian gentleman in thin white shirt-sleeves who welcomed me courteously and introduced himself as Mr. Bannerjee of the Central Intelligence Department. His rank was of a Deputy Superintendent of Police and he was at the time a member of C.S.D.I.C. (I) (Combined Services Detailed Interrogation Centre, India).

Mr. Bannerjee had my interrogation file before him. Starting my detailed interrogation he said, "Here in your first interrogation at Pegu, you had stated that if you were tried by an open public trial, the Indian people would immediately go against the Government in your favour. Now that you have reached India and quite sometime has passed since you made this statement, may I know if there is any change in your statement?" I replied, "Yes, please replace the word 'immediately' with 'definitely'." "May I know the reason for this change ?", Bannerjee asked. In reply, I told him that the British Government had been successful in keeping their subjects, the people of India, in the dark about our existence and operations. They had even succeeded in concealing the very name of the INA from their own troops fighting against us.

Our successful operations, I continued, were attributed to our allies, the Japanese Army, and the British feared calling us even by our name, the Indian National Army. They had coined a new label, calling us JIFs (Japanese Inspired Forces). They dared not call us even Indian or National. It was only after the end of the war in Burma that our compatriots fighting for the British got to know about us and our work, and treated us with some understanding and warmth. Though we were the vanquished, Indians, by and large, appreciated our efforts. Referring to the ignorance of the general public in India, I told Bannerjee about my last night's experience at the railway station when an inquisitive passerby, seeing me, had asked his companion, "Why such a strong force to guard a man?" I opined that our trial was bound to awaken the people in our favour.

After two hours of interrogation, Mr. Bannerjee got a cup of tea and a toast for me and himself. The toast was crisp, hot and buttered with salty flavour. It was a delicious treat made all the more enjoyable as I had no breakfast.

At midday I was taken back to my cell. On entering the cell I was surprised to notice the loss of a cake of Lifebuoy soap which I had yet not used and a new, unworn blue cotton T-shirt missing from the shelf where I had neatly placed them in the morning. It was beyond me to imagine how a thief other than a member of the British guard could operate in the area where the security measures were so strict. Though deeply hurt, I decided to keep quiet and bear the loss in silence. I was still under the shock caused by the loss of those precious things when the door of my cell was flung open by a British Corporal who was followed by two Indians carrying buckets containing dal and chapatis.

The Coporal said, "Will you have a Hindu or a Muslim khana?" "Any would do," I replied. "Does your khana have no religion?" he asked. "Food has no religion," I remarked. "Who are you, a Hindu or a Mohammedan?", the Corporal asked. "An Indian", I answered. The Corporal stared at me in disbelief and then added, "I too don't understand why you Indians call your food by religious names, though it is the same bloody dal and chapatis without any distinction. You Indians even divide water on the basis of religion. Why the hell cannot you call it just water and Indian khana ?" I could only stare at him in silent appreciation while one of his men put some dal and a couple of chapatis in my plate and I was locked in again.

I was provided with the daily newspaper, *The Statesman*, and after reading it I utilized it as a hand pankha (fan), which was quite a boon in that closed cell. Bannerjee normally held two sittings a day for about three weeks. He was cordial and full of understanding in his dealings. I had little to hide or change in what I had already stated before Major Ore at Pegu. Detailed interrogation in Delhi was comparatively an easy affair. It was like a cross-examination of my previous statements and actions of what had been said by others about me.

Bannerjee gave me the impression of being an admirer of Netaji and told me with some sense of pride that though altogether in another context he too had an opportunity to serve him when Netaji was the Congress President and Bannerjee as a young police officer was detailed to shadow him during his tours. Bannerjee urged me to acquaint myself with the fast-moving political events in the country. He often gave me a copy of the daily *Hindusthan Times* which had a national outlook. *The Statesman* provided to the prisoners was more of a Government organ in those days (1945) and not as objective as it is now (1996).

The solitary confinement weighed little on me as the interrogation took most of the working day while the rest of the wakeful hours were spent in reading newspapers. Bannerjee never failed to treat me with his standard cup of tea and buttered toast during every sitting. This luxury I enjoyed all the more due to the poor quality of Indian meals served cold.

During this period of captivity I was let out for a walk and exercise only twice into an enclosure just opposite my cell. It was about fifteen feet wide by fifty feet long with a ten feet high barbed wire fence around it. The fence had a covering of bamboo mats lined with thick dark blue cloth which prevented observation from within as well as without. It was open above. On my first airing I was thrilled to see treetops waving in the late afternoon breeze. What delighted me the most was the sight of a kite (hawk) hovering leisurely high in the sky. I could not help feeling envious of its graceful gliding and freedom. This bird was the only living being other than my captors that I happened to see during those twenty-one days of my solitary captivity.

By the last day of the third week of July, my interrogation by Mr. Bannerjee was over and with it ended my solitary environment. I was taken out of the cell and handed over to two unarmed Gurkha guards waiting at the exit of the inner area guarded by the British troops. They escorted me out of another guarded gate and within a couple of minutes of walk I found myself on the road running in the centre of the Red Fort connecting the main gates on the north and the south. I was led out of the gate which opened on to a bridge spanning the moat of the Fort and a National Highway. The bridge ended at a railway level crossing just in front of the entrance to Salimgarh, the magazine-cum-prison wing of the Red Fort which had been turned into a cage for the INA. The prison was secured by a double row of tall barbed wire fences covered by opaque mats and guarded by troops from a Gurkha Unit.

Here I was interned in one of the cages meant for INA Senior Officers. At the time of my arrival there were about thirty inmates. It was quite a relief to find Major Generals A.D. Loganathan, Aziz Ahmad, Shah Nawaz, Khan and Colonels Ehsan Qadir, R.M. Arshad, Prem Kumar Sahgal and Lieut. Colonels Jagir Singh and A.B. Singh among them. It was a one-room barrack type accommodation with a verandah running on three sides, which eased congestion to some extent. The compound to the cage was about forty yards wide and seventy yards long. There were communal latrines and washing facilities about fifty metres away on the southern end. Each one of us had a cot and chair. There were four tables which served as dinning tables.

Besides a radio, we were provided the daily *Statesman* that kept us in touch with what was happening in the world around us. We were provided cooked meals from the Indian and British kitchens of Other Ranks. At the beginning of the detention, each officer was given the choice to opt for the British or Indian meals. The meals were brought to the gate of the cage where we would go to collect our respective food in cups and plates through the barbed wire gate. We tried to bring meals for our senior members but they rarely allowed us to serve them. They believed in the doctrine of 'self-help', not only in theory but in practice also.

We organized ourselves roughly into four dining groups corresponding to the number of tables. The food collected by each member was brought to his respective table where it was shared jointly within the group. Meal times used to be a period of fun. I was in Gen. Loganathan's group. Though suffering from an ulcer of the stomach, the old man was always in good humour and would sit with us throughout a meal with his lively anecdotes. A darling of a man, we all used to call him uncle. Normally, he ate very little and if we tried to make him eat a bit more he would say, "Don't you like this food that you are dumping so much on my plate? Am I the dustbin of you all ?"

Our number in the cage kept on fluctuating due to fresh arrivals from abroad, and from the camps within the country and departure to camps outside Delhi like nearby Bahadurgarh in Punjab (now Haryana) and Bairagarh near Bhopal. A few days after my arrival, Major General J.K. Bhonsle arrived wearing British badges of a Major's rank. Most of us could not appreciate that our Chief of the Army staff should appear in enemy's badges, but then General Bhonsle was a man with a deep sense of humility and believed in keeping a low profile.

"What we had to do we have done, now why boast and keep on blowing our own horn?" was General Bhonsle's way of dealing with the situation. The morning after his arrival on the way to the toilet I accosted him greeting, "Jai Hind, Sir." He answered with a "Good morning," and added, "don't be a fool. I want to keep my head on my shoulders." Feeling pity for him and not to spoil my own morning anymore I kept quiet but stopped greeting him therefore. Fools, too, have a role to play, I thought. It did not take him long to fall in line with us all and he also gave up wearing the Major's crown (badge) on his shoulders.

Lieut. Colonel Mehar Das, Sardar-e-Jung, one of our great heroes, arrived few days later. He looked so thin and withered that I could hardly recognize him. We were separated in Pegu Yomas. When asked what he had done to himself, he told me that to avoid being interrogated he had poisoned himself by taking ground glass but doctors saved his life. So far he had been successful in avoiding his interrogation. He said, "I don't care for my life but I am yet not sure whether my statement, when I make one, would be good or harmful for our Great Movement or for any one of my men or brother officers." He asked for my advice.

After some deliberations with him I told Mehar Das that his actions had been so noble that he could speak out the truth without caring for the result. He was a man of great integrity and of unmatched courage. I had seen him on the battlefield. Though a Staff Officer in a higher Headquarters, he volunteered to work as a scout for me. Now he was asking me many searching questions in order to work out his strategy for the pending interrogation. It was a great relief to find a smile of understanding on his face. I requested him to look after his health.

Though it was a period of suspense for us at Salimgarh, it had its own charm. We were kept fairly busy by our interrogators who often called us for some further interrogation or clarification. When the presence of one of us was required for the purpose, two baton-bearing Gurkhas with a chit carrying the number of the required prisoner would appear at the gate and shout out the number. Those numbers had been allotted to us at the time of interrogation in one of the Field Interrogation Centres. It used to be quite an outing as we walked up and down from the cage to the CISDIC office practically all the way to the other end of the Fort escorted by the Gurkhas. Though very reserved and cold in the beginning, they grew more respectful and friendly when they learnt all about us. This attitude kept on improving with the passage of time.

The experience of living together gave us an added advantage of exchanging notes with each other. It taught us the importance of these interrogations. Our statements went a long way in making or unmaking the future of our comrades. One evening at about 9 p.m., someone told me that Major Hari Singh who was the senior-most Battalion Commander in my Regiment and was also acting as the 2ndin-Command of the Regiment at Myingyan in November 1944, wanted to see me. I had sent him back to Rangoon on disciplinary grounds.

As I approached the intervening fence screened by mats, Hari Singh talked to me through a gap saying that he had used the Myingyan incident as a proof of his being pro-British. He said, "I was going to be released and sent back to rejoin my Indian Army Unit, but Shah Nawaz Sahib had told that to Major Hugh Toye and now my reinstatement in service has been cancelled. Sir, I have six daughters, all of marriageable age. Sir, I am an old man, and I beg of you to help me by endorsing my statement. Sir, I beg to you for mercy in the name of my daughters." I assured Hari Singh of my help.

Early next morning, I discussed the matter with Shah Nawaz. He had already told me about a talk he had with Hugh Toye. Discussing about me, Hugh Toye had said that I had punished Hari Singh for being pro-British. On Hugh Toye's remarks, Shah Nawaz had laughed and said, "If womanizing means being pro-British, Hari Singh was really a strong pro-Britisher." Thus Hugh Toye had learnt the whole story in detail and reversed his decision. After Hari Singh's previous night's approach to me, I decided to review the case on compassionate grounds. Though we now had no powers, Shah Nawaz allowed me to do whatever I could to help Hari Singh.

A couple of days later, Shah Nawaz returned from a round of interrogation looking worried. Calling me aside, he said, "Something terrible is going to happen today. Colonel Hussain is being released and reinstated before this evening. If by any chance you are called today for an interrogation, do try to see Major Hugh Toye and put in a few good words about Col. Hussain. If he is released it will be catastrophic for the Movement. He is the senior-most Regimental Commander. His release will demoralize officers and men alike."

As luck would have it, within a few minutes my number was called at the gate and I was taken to Major Hayat's office. I had just arrived when there entered a brilliant young Major of medium height to ask for a paper when Hayat said, "Toye, meet Col. Dhillon." "Oh! so you are the famous Colonel Dhillon?" Hugh Toye said with a glee, rubbing his hands as if he had caught his prey. "No. The famous

Colonel Dhillon came to you much earlier," I replied.

Hugh Toye: Who do you mean ?

I : The one you decorated.

H.T. : Do you mean Mahanbira, that bloody cheat who cheated you and cheated us.

I : Cheating us under the circumstances was understandable, but you love being cheated.

Hugh Toye surprised me by putting another question.

H.T. : Now then, what is your opinion about our Colonel Hussain ?

I : I do not know anything about any Col. Hussain of yours but we did have one Colonel of that name under whom I had the honour of serving for three months. I know him very well. He commanded our strongest Brigade, the Hind Field Force, later designated as the 1st Infantry Regiment of our 2nd Division.

H.T. : Yes, yes, that is the one I am referring to. What do you think of him ?

I : I admire him. A wonderful Officer. One of our intellectuals, a lovable man.

H.T. : Do you know he was in our pay ?

I : I can't believe it.

H.T. : I am telling you.

I : Really ! How incredible !

H.T. : Are you surprised ?

I : Yes, I am.

H.T. : Now, then, may I ask you what you think of him ?

I : O, I admire him all the more. How wonderful? You paid him and he served us. May I know how did he serve you ?

H.T. : He joined us at the first possible opportunity at Magwe.

I : Yes, when you overwhelmed him from the air and on the ground surrounded him by tanks, he surrendered.

H.T. : You and Shah Nawaz were also there with him at Magwe. Why did not you surrender ?

I : Because we were damn fools. Did not have brains enough to fool you while he could. May I ask you what we achieved after Magwe ? Could we inflict any great casualities on you ? He saved his men and himself from the hardships of retreat. He commanded the strongest Regiment of the INA. From his Regiment he sent the maximum number of cadets to the O.T.s (Officer's Training School). In other words, gave us the maximum number of officers to fight against you. He gave an exemplary report in my favour when I served for three months under him on a special report asked for by the Divisional Commander. It was because of his good report that I got command of the Nehru Brigade. In fact, he gave you an adversary in me. His services to the cause of the INA make a long list. He was also a member of the Provisional Government of Azad Hind. In his surrender, too, he succeeded in making a fool of you. Oh, yes, I admire your Colonel Hussain who was, indeed, ours.

H.T. : Why did you punish Hari Singh ?

I : Which Hari Singh ?

H.T. : One of your Dogra Officers, your 2nd-in-Command at Myingyan. Major Hari Singh whom you sent back to the rear.

I : Because I could not trust his loyalty. He was pro-British. I could not risk keeping him at the Front.

H.T. : (Smiling) Because you caught him with a woman ?

I : That was an excuse I made use of. I could have overlooked his weakness for women and would let him off with an admonition if I could trust his loyalty to the cause. But how could he be loyal to me with his pro-British stance ? I could not trust him.

We talked, all the while standing beside Hayat's table and sipping tea offered by him. Hugh Toye excused himself as casually, as he had come. He was a man in hurry. I wondered whether his meeting was accidental or had been planned, for Hayat had little to discuss with me except an incident on the Irrawaddy in which one of my sentries and a Captain Commander of a British patrol were killed.

On my return to the cage, I gave Shah Nawaz a resume of the dialogue between me and Hugh Toye. Shah Nawas showed satisfaction at my performance.

Hugh Toye acted fast. That very day at about five in the afternoon, wearing a newly-made full uniform and escorted by two Gurkhas carrying his bag, new leather suitcases and sundry belongings, Hussain entered the cage. He was welcomed by us all. Shah Nawaz was happy that all his Command group, Hussain, Sahgal, and Dhillon were with him. We had never been together at one time during operations. Shah Nawaz greeted Hussain with a warm hug. Hussain had lived in the freedom of an Officers Mess set up by CSDIC within the Red Fort where those INA officers were accommodated who had been classed WHITE and whose former privileges and services were to be restored.

Col. Hussain took with surprising ease to the change of living in the cage marked for those who had been classed black and the blackest, and for whom law was to take its course resulting in imprisonment and even death, as if he belonged to this cage. He did not let anybody feel whether he was even slightly sad for this sudden change. He joined General Loganathan's dining group of which I was already a member. Though coming from a highly respected and rich Sayyad family owning vast agricultural lands in Lyallpur district of the Punjab, Hussain was by nature a combination of sophistication, simplicity and adaptability with a multi-cultural bent of mind. He read a lot. It was a pleasure to be with him.

Summary of Evidence

On the 6th of August, 1945, Shah Nawaz, Sahgal and I were jointly summoned to the CSDIC for the first time. Here under a makeshift accommodation, Major E. Beaton, Deputy Assistant Adjutant General from the Adjutant General's Branch of the General Headquarters, assisted by Staff Captain (Legal), Capt. M.P. Pariser of the A.G.'s Branch, started recording Summary of Evidence in case of the three of us. The process was the beginning of the first INA trial at the Red Fort. Here I may record that we three were not the senior-most officers in the INA Seniority-wise I was the junior-most Regimental Commander among all the three Divisions of the INA.

The first Prosecution Witness (PW) for recording the Summary of Evidence was Subedar Major Babu Ram of 1st Battalion of 14th Punjab Regiment. He was a Major in the INA and had been Battalion Commander of the 1st Battalion of the Hind Field Force Group. He had been an active member of the INA from the very beginning. He was one of General Mohan Singh's most trusted officers. He was pretty well-known to all three of us. I had known him since May 1933 when I joined the 10/14 Punjab for training as a recruit at Ferozepur where he was an Instructor of Education in the Regimental School. He had, thus, been my teacher.

After my graduation from the Indian Military Academy, Dehra Dun in March 1940 when I joined the 1st Battalion, 14th Punjab Regiment, my first attachment was with the Dogra Company where he was the senior-most Warrant Officer and later Viceroy Commissioned Officer and I was the junior-most I.C.O. The bond, thus begun, kept growing stronger and stronger with the passage of time. We had joined the INA together to fight for the freedom of the country. Although he had left the INA after the arrest of General Mohan Singh and had suffered a lot in New Guinea, his appearance as a deponent against me was incredible. Sitting on an opposite bench, his downcast posture made me feel that he was not happy in his present predicament. The recording of his evidence lasted three days, the 6th,

7th and 8th of August. He did not say anything which was not true. I declined to cross-examine him.

The next PW, Lieut. D.C. Nag was another responsible and Hon'ble Officer who had been a First Class Magistrate at Raj Shahi in Bengal before being granted Commission in the A.I.R.O. (Army in India Reserve of Officers) and called for active service in the Indian Army. After the surrender of Singapore he had joined the INA and was given charge of its legal department as the J.A.G. (Judge Advocate General). It was he who had drafted the INA Act.

Babu Ram and Nag were objective in their evidence, showing all the salient features of the Indian Independence Movement and the INA—its aim, formation, organization, administration, command and control at various stages including the battlefield. Nag produced most of the documents that were exhibited in the case. Their objectivity suited us and the British alike. We could not have wished for a better testimony of our actions. In the early stage, the Summary of Evidence consisted of only 29 witnesses, though, the prosecution kept on bringing more and more witnesses as the case progressed.

The Summary of Evidence of PWs numbers 1 to 4 was taken down by Major Beaton in our presence on the 6th, 7th, 8th, 9th, 10th, 11th, 13th, 14th, 15th, days of August and in the case of PWs 5 to 29 by Capt. M.P. Pariser on the 28th, 29th, 30th and 31st of August and on the 1st, 3rd, 4th, 5th and 6th days of September 1945. Owing to the exigencies of service, the attendance of three British Officers could not be readily procured. They were Lt. Col. A.D. Mac Conachie, Commanding Officer of 4/5th Royal Gurkha Rifles, Capt. B. Fanshawe M.C. 2 S. Lan. Regiment and Lt. Col. J.A. Kitson, Officer Commanding 4/2 Gurkha Rifles. They had fought against Sahgal's and my Regiments. Duly signed written statements from each one of them purporting their respective claims were read to us. As we showed no wish to call any one of them for cross-examination, their statements were attached to the Summary of Evidence.

At the end of the Summary of Evidence, having been cautioned by Major Beaton in accordance with and in terms of the Indian Army Act, Rule 15(F), we declined to make any statement at that stage. On 17th September 1945 we, the three accused - Shah Nawaz, Sahgal and

I—were each served with a copy of charge-sheet duly signed by Col. Commanding, CSDIC (I) Delhi dated 17th Sept. 1945. Along with the charge-sheet we were also provided with a copy of the Summary of Evidence. The news of our trial was made public through the press and All India Radio the same day.

On our return to the cage, brother officers clustered around us eager to study the charge-sheet. Overwhelmed with the joy of being one of the first to be tried in the Red Fort, on which we had intended to hoist the National Tricolour, I extricated myself from the crowd and, clutching my charge-sheet like a toy in the hands of a child, I ran to General Loganathan who was lying on an old sagging cot in a verandah. On that day he was suffering from a severe abdominal pain due to a stomach ulcer. I shouted, "Uncle ! Look what we have got ! I am going to be senior to you now. Charges against us are of waging war against the King. Other charges against me are the gravest. I shall die earlier than you and thus become your senior. Look Uncle, here is the charge-sheet."

Forgetting his pain with a great effort, clutching both sides of the charpoy on either side with his bony hands, slowly, very slowly but surely without any help (Loganathan loathed to accept a help), the old man sat up in an inclined position corresponding to the curve of the sagging cot. He got hold of the charge-sheet and started reading it as I reverently stood by in utter silence. As he read through the charges, big tears started rolling down onto his sunken cheeks and then in a choked voice he shouted, "No, no, no ! My son, they can't do that to you when I am living. Being the senior-most among you, I must be held responsible for all what you did. I must be tried and punished first. I must die earlier so as not to see you suffer." It was this very ulcer developed during the INA days which was responsible for his early death—a martyrdom on the altar of the freedom of India.

Netaji, a Martyr

It was during the period when the Summary of Evidence was being recorded that on 21/22 August, 1945 we heard over the All India Radio that Netaji died as a result of an air crash involving the plane in which he was travelling. We took the broadcast as a British trick to demoralize us. We just did not believe the news. It was much later that the truth dawned upon us through Col. Habib-ur-Rehman, Netaji's Deputy Chief of the Staff who was in attendance on Netaji on that fateful journey, and still later from the Indian and Japanese sources in the East.

I have no doubt that Netaji died a martyr's death in Nanmen Army Hospital, Taipeh in Formosa along with four Japanese Officers. Lieut. General Shidei, Chief of Staff, Burma Army Command and a Japanese Major were killed instantly when the plane crashed. Netaji and the other casualties were removed to the Hospital where they breathed their last on the 18th night. Netaji was cremated the next day and his ashes were taken by Col. Habib to Tokyo where the last remains of the martyr were guarded by Tokyo Cadets of the INA till their removal to Renkoji Temple. Netaji died in harness while in uniform; he met a soldier's death during the war. The ashes of the Supreme Commander of the INA lie in Renkoji Temple (Tokyo) till today (1996).

A couple of weeks before the end of the war, Netaji laid the foundation of Shaheed Memorial in honour of the brave soldiers of the INA who had laid down their lives for the freedom of their motherland. The memorial was unveiled on behalf of the Provisional Government of Azad Hind by General Mohammed Zaman Kinai. What an irony that the *shardhanjali* (homage) of the most tragic death of our Supreme Leader had to be performed at the very unveiling ceremony? The memorial was dynamited and destroyed under orders of Lord Mountabatten after the occupation of Singapore when the INA personnel had been disarmed and kept in captivity. On the spot, the Government of Singapore were kind to install a plaque to preserve the sanctity of the historical monument in 1995.

Netaji's ashes remain in Tokyo where the Japanese veterans of war go to pay homage to the hero on 23rd of January, Netaji's birthday and 18th of August, his martyrdom, every year. How sad and tragic that our Government and the people have yet to acknowledge the martyrdom of the Greatest General who fought for the liberation of the subcontinent of Hindustan!

I Meet My Father

After serving the charge-sheet we had been told that we could contact and call our next of kin to visit us if we so desired. For this purpose, the facility of a State telegram was made available to us. I sent a telegram to my father who came to see me on the 19th or 20th September. It was about 9 o'clock in the morning when escorted by two Gurkhas, I was taken to the CSDIC, little expecting that father could come so soon. When I saw him standing outside the gate of the CSDIC in the company of a British Major, I rushed forward to make obeisance to him. As I knelt down and touched his feet, my father tenderly picked me up in an affectionate hug, patting me and showering his blessings. The Major guided us to a nearby meeting place in an open barbed wire compound adjoining the CSDIC, where three chairs had been laid for our use. Two of those chairs facing each other were occupied by father and me. The Major sat on the third chair on one side of us as close as we were to each other.

I was meeting my father after an interval of four long years, years of suspense and uncertainty. The last time when I left for overseas in 1941, father had a robust bearing with an awe-inspiring presence. It was no more so that autumn morning of 1945. The old man had changed a lot, his dark black beard had gone grey and he looked careworn, aged and hopelessly sad. We sat silent for a while and then with some courage I asked father about mother and everyone's welfare at home. The weather-beaten old soldier and peasant could not control himself and burst into sobs.

When he was able to recover his composure and control, he said, "Bakhshi ! Your younger brother Amrik is suffering from a terrible disease of the stomach and has been in and out of hospitals for the last two years, giving us some very anxious moments. There is yet no sign of his recovery. His will-power has gone very low. And as if it were not enough, the news of your trial has landed us in another worry. I fear I am going to lose two young sons, one by illness and the other by capital punishment. Bakhshi ! Only you and you alone can save us from this tragedy. You have done what you had to do. Now just ask for an apology and you can save your life. This action on your part may make Amrik pick up his spirits, for he loves you so much. We all love you, Bakhshi. The lives of my two sons are in your hands. I beg of you, my son, to be merciful to me and to your mother at this time of our age. Look at my tears and my grey hair !"

To witness father imploring me for what I could not do was so painful that I felt distressed. To pity him who had been always a tower of strength for me was not so easy. It was one of the greatest trials of my life. Feeling at a loss for the proper way to say 'no' to father, I kept quiet. My father went on to tell me that the Deputy Commissioner of the district of Lahore, the very representative of the Crown, had sent an English Officer, an Assistant Superintendent of Police, all the way to our village to see father and assure him that if the old Sardar could make *chhota* (young) Dhillon Sahib (that is me) ask for an apology, I would not only be pardoned and released but would also be reinstated in my due seniority in spite of all the charges against me and on top of all that father would be granted a jagir (reward by Government for services rendered).

In case I refused to apologize, my father was given a second alternative; to make me apply for a defence to the Government and not to the INA Defence Committee set up by the Indian National Congress. As a third alternative, my father was told that being a Sikh I should apply to the Akali Party for my defence but under no circumstances I should accept defence by the Indian National Congress "which was a Hindu organization." Even for this indirect service on my part at that stage, the Government would deal with me leniently, my father was assured.

At long last I told my father that I was very sorry for being unable to concede to the British points and co-operate with them in their anti-Indian designs of dividing our ranks. I told father that the basic principle of our INA Movement was that, "We are Indians first and last and we stand for complete national unity.'' We had recognized the Indian National Congress and the Tricolour Flag which embraces all communities irrespective of their religions. I could not undo all our achievements and gains for which thousands of our men and women had given their all, including life. I could not be a traitor to the cause of the Independence of India just to save my life.

"What may I tell your mother when I go back home?" father asked. "*Bhayaji* ! (I used to address my father Bhayaji) What can I tell to the mothers of those soldiers of the INA who under my command and on my orders advanced, charged and laid down their lives ?

Bhayaji, what shall I have to tell their souls when one day I too leave this world ?"

My father said, "Bakhshi, if my tears do not melt your heart, I shall see how long you can hold against your mother's tears and wails when she beats her breast before you." And before I could utter a word, my father removed his *paggri* (turban) and was about to place it on my feet when I immediately stood up and replaced it on his head and said, "*Bhayaji* ! Please don't do that. I am your son, let me not be a sinner."

Visibly moved, the Major attending our interview said, "Why don't you listen to the old man and do what he is telling you ? Everybody will be happy." I did not consider it proper to say anything to the Major but father, a retired V.C.O., a Jemadar, could not possibly overlook a remark of a British Field Officer.

Father : See, what Major Sahib Bahadur has said. Take his advice.

I : *Bhayaji* ! What advice can he give me ? I shall always remain small before you but I am two ranks higher than he and have commanded a Brigade against hundreds of officers of his rank and of ranks much higher than his on the battlefields. *Bhayaji*, your Bakhshi is very big by your blessings.

Father : All right Bakhshi, if you don't see my tears and do not listen to me I shall come again and again and bring your mother too.

I : *Bhayaji* ! I beg of you not to bring mother to see me nor try to come yourself for I won't come out to see you.

Father : What will you say when you are told that your father has come to see you ? What excuse can you make?

I : I will say he is not my father.

Father : (Father was shocked) Have you gone that far ? Do you understand what you have said ? (I saw that awe- inspiring light in his eyes. He seemed to be again a self-respecting Jat.)

I : I am sorry, father, but what am I to do when you are trying to pull me down from the noble path of a hero in the history to that of a traitor to the country ?

Father : You are trying to take a very dangerous step, Bakhshi.

I : Not going to take it I took it long ago, and am now close to my goal. India is going to be free, *Bhayaji*. You should be proud that your son is going to be an important maker of that Free India.

Father : Are you sure that you will not waver from your chosen path ?

I : Yes, *Bhayaji*, no power on earth can change my mind, come what may. Neither your tears nor mother's wails can change my way. Your efforts to change me will only fail and will have no effect on me other than increasing my distress, for I do not like to disappoint you. *Bhayaji*, it is not easy for me to disobey you.

Father : Are you determined.

I : Yes, *Bhayaji*, more than a rock.

Father : Right Bakhshi, I promise not to get in your way from now onward, but do allow me to come and watch your trial. And if at any time you happen to see a tear in my eyes, please do not mind it, and don't hate me for that. My heart is not as strong like yours. Again love makes me weak, my son, I love you.

Surprised at father's statement, I could hardly believe my ears. Now it was my turn for tears. I broke down. I touched father's feet and begged him:

I : Then please bless me *Bhayaji*.

Father : (Patting my back) God bless you, my son. Now

may I mortgage one or two squares of land in order to pay for your defence ?

I : No, *Bhayaji*, your blessings are enough. The whole of India is on my defence. I do not need a single pai.

Father : But may I ask you, how do you feel ? Will you survive the trial

I : *Bhayaji*, I will survive (I said in order to console him).

Father : Will you say so touching my body ?

I : Yes, father, they can't kill me. The entire India is at my back. (I said touching father's hand).

Father : May I give you some money for your personal needs ?

I : No, *Bhayaji*, we are not supposed to keep any money. Again, all our needs are provided for. You need have no worry on that score. How is Basant?

Father : She is at her parents' place and does not come to Chak No. 32. I will send a message to her to come and see you. Do tell her to come to the village. She is angry with me.

I : Yes, *Bhayaji*, I will tell her to come home when she comes.

I touched father's feet. He took me in his embrace and uttered words of blessings. As the meeting was over, the Major bade farewell to my father and asked the Gurkhas to take me back to the cage. My father had left a couple of minutes earlier but when he saw me coming on the road from a distance, he stood there under a tree watching me come escorted by two Gurkhas. When I reached the spot where he was standing, I asked the Gurkhas if I could talk to my father. They saluted him and stood back. I asked father If he had received any letters which I had sent through a Pathan Havildar. He confirmed that he had received letters along with a packet. My father praised Havildar Aziz Allah — so good was the Pathan, patriotic, fearless and true to his word.

Once again, my father asked me to take some money. I refused but on a second thought as a mark of respect to father and to please him I picked up twenty rupees out of a pile of notes which he had taken out of his pocket to give me. Once again I assured father that I was well and gratefully happy to have received his blessings. I saluted, "Jai Hind,'' and touching his feet got his blessings again. He remained standing under the tree as long as he could see me going away to the cage with the two Gurkhas. Overwhelmed with the transformation in father's attitude, I was so full of joy that I wept, though silently, walking ahead of the Gurkhas to hide my tears. I felt I had won a great victory. How could I thank father ? How ? That was the thought which kept me awake long into the night.

My father had been great in dealing with me so generously. Could I talk as boldly with mother as I had done with father ? Would it not be only crude but cruel too? Would even my silence be not only discourteous but also distressing to her and an expression of impending doom? So I thought, and hence decided to avoid meeting mother as long as possible. But facing Basant would not be so easy either. How could I tell her to be prepared to lose me and learn to live without me, most probably for ever ? Next to my parents and my teachers, Basant had contributed the maximum in building my career. I was soon to find that my fears were unfounded.

I Meet Basant

Basant came within a week after father's visit. She was accompanied by her cousin Sardar Anokh Singh Sidhu and his wife. I had expected her father to come with her. Missing the old man, when I asked about his welfare, sadly I had to learn that he had died some two years ago. Bapuji, as I used to call him, was one of the most enlightened and well-read persons among our relatives. He knew Gurmukhi, Urdu, Hindi, Persian, Pushtu and English. He was a staunch supporter of Guru Ghar (the Sikh Mission) and the Guru Vani, the holy scriptures of the Sikh Gurus, believing in the oneness of the humankind irrespective of religious, geographical or racial distinctions. He used to sing:

Awal Allah noor upaya. Qudrat de sab bande,
Ek noor te sab jag upjeaa kaun bhale kaun mande.

(From the very start God made us all alike. We are all born of one light without any distinction of good or bad.)

Bapuji, Sardar Wassan Singh had joined the Indian Army as a Sowar in a Cavalry Unit and rose to the rank of a Dafedar. He had quite a bright future in the Army, but, being a nationalist, he realized that serving in the Indian Army was incompatible with the freedom struggle and hence sought an early release. Basant's mother died when Basant was still a child of about six years. Bapuji never married again and lived a lonely life. He was fond of music and had a melodious voice capable of holding an audience for hours. It was an irreparable loss. I was too shocked to say anything.

Appreciating my predicament, Basant broke the silence to tell me that during the Quit India Movement in 1942 she had taken part in an anti-British demonstration by leading a procession carrying the Tricolour through Anarkali bazaar at Lahore. When the Police lathi-charged the procession, most of the participants dispersed but she was arrested and had been behind bars for some days till my father (*Bhayaji*) was called. My father told Basant that her action would be detrimental to my career, and that being an Officer's wife she should not have taken part in the demonstration. My father urged her to make an apology for my sake, which she did and was released.

I congratulated her and told her that now a bigger test awaited us. She assured me that she would not be found wanting in any way and would gladly stand by me, come what may. I told her all that had transpired between father and me and expressed my worry about mother. How would she endure the trial? Basant told me to leave that responsibility to her and pledged to look after her. She said, "Mother is stronger than Bhayaji and I will bring her when she understands that you have done the right thing." When I told her to go to our village, Basant agreed without any demur. Our meeting was not attended by an official observer as in the case of father's visit. Basant fortified my spirits all the more. It was a happy meeting.

I discovered in Basant a staunch patriot, cast in the heroic mould. Her utterances and conduct during the days of our internment in the Red Fort and the subsequent trial were amazingly bold and inspiring. Speaking at a reception accorded at Delhi on November 19, 1945 to

Maulana Noorudin Bihari, a member of the All-India Congress Committee and vice-president of the Delhi Provincial Congress Committee who had been released after 39 months detention, Basant felt proud of the heroic deeds of INA officers and declared that she would unhesitatingly sacrifice her husband for India's freedom. The proceedings of the meeting, presided over by Pandit Nekiram Shanna and attended among others by Lala Deshbandhu Gupta, were widely covered by the press. I reproduce extracts of her maiden speech from the report published in the *Hindustan Standard* dated 20th November 1945.

> Addressing a largely attended public meeting held yesterday (10-11-45) evening, Mrs. Dhillon, wife of Lieut. Dhillon of the INA, now under court martial trial, asked the people to make all possible sacrifices for liberation of their country. She declared that she would unhesitatingly sacrifice her husband and asked all Indian mothers and wives smilingly to send their sons and husbands to fight for the liberation of their mother country.
>
> Indians were not cowards but brave people, and the undaunted courage of Indian soldiers in the battlefields won admiration all over the world. She said that she was thankful to the British Government for putting three INA Officers on trial thus giving opportunity to the world for knowing about the heroic deeds done by them.
>
> Concluding she said that indiscriminate firing and bombing by police and military on unarmed people could not last any longer and people would emerge out stronger.

It was perhaps in the light of such sentiments that Bhulabhai told me a few days later, "Basant has surpassed you." Dr. Katju said, "Gurbakhsh, you had made a very big hole in my heart but Basant has further enlarged that hole. I acknowledge Netaji's oft-repeated statement that India cannot be kept under bondage any longer. It has been confirmed that Netaji foresaw the awakening which would come to the Indian armed forces and the people. Basant comes from a village and this shows how the message has gone deep and when the simple village womenfolk are so awakened, men cannot remain behind."

Then there followed a period of interviews with our relations—Col. Sahgal's father, mother, sisters and other members of his family; Shah Nawaz's uncle who had brought him up along with Shah Nawaz's younger brother Captain Nawaz Khan who had fought against us on the Imphal front. My two elder brothers Gurdial Singh who had resigned to be beside me during the trial and Balwant Singh whose jeep had been attacked somewhere by my men in the Popa Kyauk Paduang area and many more relatives kept on visiting us. We, the trio, met all the three families as our own.

The most important visitors who started meeting us were the members of the INA Defence Committee organized by the Indian National Congress with Raghunandan Saran and Maulana Asaf Ali as the joint conveners. Shri Saran rarely talked to us except asking us if we needed anything. He looked simple and serene. Asaf Ali was one of the most meticulously dressed persons in *khadi* I had ever seen. On each of his visit he would be wearing a different combination with his Gandhi cap matching his sherwani and the churidar. Asaf Ali had about five pairs of glasses, some mono-glasses to read different sizes of the printed words.

With his refined language and polished expression, Asaf Ali was a gentleman of graceful personality who drew people towards him like a magnet. Asaf Ali was invariably accompanied by Sultan Yar Khan and four or five junior advocates. When he put us questions, he would go into the minute details and appeared to be digging for the predisposing causes of raising the INA, apart from the narrative of actions in which we took part.

About a week after Asaf Ali's arrival on the scene, Prem's father Mr. Justice Achhru Ram, a sitting Judge of the Punjab High Court, Lahore started visiting us each weekend, with a team of advocates from the Punjab High Court bar including Kanwar Sir Dalip Singh and Bakhshi Sir Tek Chand (ex-Judges of Punjab High Court) and Inder Dev Dua. Sometimes both the teams led by Asaf Ali and Achhru Ram turned up simultaneously but generally they came independently. Out of Justice Achhru Ram's team, the most revered personality of the legal profession from the Punjab was Rai Bahadur Badri Das. Clad in white *khadi,* he looked like Prince Yudhishtra of the Mahabharata epic, kind yet awe-inspiring whose thoughts could not be fathomed. He would neither look serious nor show happiness or appreciation when he listened to our answers. He was always calm and serene.

Later Dr. Kailash Nath Katju and still later Mr. Bullabhai Desai began to join our interviews and interrogations being conducted by different lawyers. I do not remember them taking any notes. Dr. Katju was to be the next senior-most Counsel for us during our trial. Pandit Jawaharlal Nehru also visited us once during those days. When Shah Nawaz told Panditji that we had a Brigade after his name called the Nehru Brigade and I was sharp enough to say that I commanded the Nehru Brigade, Panditji smiled.

One day Shri Bhulabhai Desai visited three of us alone and addressed us thus, "I have got picture of your case. Details can be filled in easily. But before I start, I would like to know from you personally whether you wish me to take up your case or am I only forcing myself on you. In case you do want me, then I would like to know as to how much you wish to compromise between your personal safety and the cause which you fought for?"

Replying on our behalf, General Shah Nawaz said, "Sir, when we joined the INA we pledged our lives to the cause. Today, the pledge stands, as it ever did. We tried our best to be nearest to death. It never came. The honour of the nation, of the Azad Hind Fauj and of Netaji has to be saved and if in doing so these three lives go, it is just proper."

Shri Bhulabhai Desai said, "I am glad you have said so. You have made my job easy for I would rather have you hanged than to defend you ignobly on the first, the most honourable charge of waging war against the King. As regards other charges, I worry little for they are actually a part of the first one. I take it that your trial is the trial of the INA under all stages and of all men, and that is what we will fight for, of course, never forgetting about your persons which are equally precious to us. If you have confidence in me, then as Mahatmaji says 'Leave everything to me.'

Later on as he was leaving I talked to him, "Sir! The days of our trial are the grace days of our life. I want to pass them gracefully." With a small pat on my shoulder, Desaiji said, "Don't have a morbid feeling." And he left.

23

The Trial

The winter of 1945 was just setting in when on Monday, the 5th of November, our trial by a General Court Martial began at the Red Fort of Delhi. It was our last battle, and was led by Shri Bhulabhai J. Desai, the leader of the Defence Counsel made up of the topmost legal luminaries of India. Early that day we, the three accused, Shah Nawaz, Sahgal and I were medically examined by the M.O. (Medical Officer) in-charge of Salimgarh M.I. Room (Medical Inspection Room). We were found fit to undergo the trial.

The day began on a rather desultory note. When I was returning from the M.I. Room to my cage, some of our junior officers detained in an adjacent cage informed me that the British Captain Commander of the Gurkhas who guarded Salimgarh as well as the INA Detention Camp at Bahadurgarh treated our men in a rough and a cruel manner. Some of the officers who recently came from Bahadurgarh told me that the Captain made our men run round the camp in between two lines of barbed wire fence. When our men slowed down out of sheer fatigue, the Captain ordered a section of the Gurkhas to chase the detainees with bayonets poked into their backs to make them run faster.

Our officers sought my advice whether they should go on a hunger strike or not. Though the British Captain was behaving in an inhuman way, I advised our officers to exercise restraint. I thought that I should personally wreak vengeance on that Captain and teach him a lesson. I could not advise my men to invite any further trouble for themselves. And I had not to wait long for an encounter with the Captain.

At about 9.30 a.m., three vehicles came to our cage. One of those vehicles was parked right in front of and close to its barbed wire gate. The other two vehicles carried fully armed British Military Police guards which were positioned one in front and the other in the rear of the vehicle nearest to the gate. They had come to take us to the court. It being the first day of the trial, all INA officers of our cage stood in a formation under Major General J.K.L. Bhonsle to give us a ceremonial send-off. Though we, the three accused, were not the senior-most officers, this kind of courtesy was indeed touching. It made us feel that we were going to the trial not as three individuals but as three representatives of the INA. When we were acknowledging the greetings with "Jai Hind," that very Captain against whom I had earlier received the complaint had come to hand us over to a Captain of the British Military Police and three British Subalterns who were to escort us to the court. The Captain shouted arrogantly, "Stop that bloody nonsense". Shah Nawaz took no note of it but Sahgal asked him, "What do you mean by that ?". The Captain curtly responded, "*Chalo, chalo* before you are in trouble".

I was the third to come up. When I approached him where he was standing in the middle of the gate I said, "What the hell did you mean by insulting our national greetings ?" He rudely said, "Come along" and tried to push me. I put my hand forward and told him not to touch me. He gave me a blow with his knuckle. He wore a ring that struck my forehead which started bleeding. Unmindful of the blood oozing out of my forehead, I took my leather file case from my right hand to the left and started boxing the Captain with my right hand. Sahgal tried to separate us. Shah Nawaz shouted, "Stop that Dhillon ! Stop it". The Captain called for his Gurkhas to come up to help him. The Gurkhas remained standing where they were about ten paces away. They did not come forward to help their Company Commander. Meanwhile the Captain and I had quite a boxing bout.

Afraid of getting late the Military Police Captain and three escorting officers said, "Please come out, we are getting late". We came out of the cage and along with the escorting officers sat down in the vehicle meant for us. I felt that the Gurkha Company Commander deserved to be punished otherwise he would continue to torture our men at Bahadurgarh. My anxiety was visible in my face. One of the escorting officers observed, " Now please cool down". I responded,

"You are not here to see that I don't attack anybody, you are also to see that nobody attacks me". In his typical way of fair play the officer answered, "Well, I am sorry but then you did give him what he asked for". His remark eased the situation. All of us laughed

We were brought at the breakneck speed to the venue of our trial which was not more than two hundred yards away from our cage. Perhaps this speed was because of a demonstration which was going on outside the Red Fort in front of the main gate—Lahore Gate—facing the Chandni Chowk. People were shouting:

Lal Qile se aaee awaz,
Sahgal Dhillon Shah Nawaz,
Teenon ki ho umar daraz,
Netaji! Zindabad,
Inquilab! Zindabad,
Qaumi Nahra! Jai Hind,
Hamara Nahra! Jai Hind,
Jai Hind! Jai Hind,
Lal Qila Tor Do,
Azad Hind Fauj Chhor Do.

(Sahgal, Dhillon, Shah Nawaz, comes the voice from the Red Fort. May the Trio live long? Long live Netaji, Long live Revolution. National slogan Jai Hind. Our slogan Jai Hind! Demolish the Red Fort. Set free Azad Hind Fauj).

The court was held on the second floor of a three-storey block of a British military barrack built eleven years after 1857. It stands in north-eastern corner of the Red Fort. On the northern end of the top floor where the Court was held was set aside a place marked "Accused Marshalling Room". There were three chairs placed in the room for us.

As soon as we entered this room, I told the escorting officers, "I refuse to attend the Court unless I am heard." Shah Nawaz, Sahgal and the escorting officers pleaded with me not to take such a step. There was a lot of sense in their advice but I could not accept it. They did not know about the complaint which the junior officers had made to me that morning against the Captain's inhuman treatment of our men at Bahadurgarh Camp. I did not have the time to share the information with anybody. Events moved so suddenly that I did not wish an opportunity to slip out of my hands to put the conditions of Bahadurgarh Camp before the higher authorities. So I did not yield. Hence the Colonel Commanding C.S.D.I.C. appeared on the scene. He was accompanied by some of his staff officers. The Colonel informed us that the Court had already assembled and we were getting late. He asked me what my complaint was. Whereupon without going into details I told him that the man (the Captain) who at the time stood behind him had hit me. And I showed my forehead where the blood had coagulated. The Colonel assured me that he would see to it in the evening after the adjournment of the Court., and asked me to come out. I also saw that the Captain wore no belt which meant that he was already under arrest. Without any further ado, I stepped out of the Accused Marshalling Room and quietly followed Shah Nawaz and Sahgal. We were marched off to the Court Room. On arrival we saluted the Court and the Defence Counsel and sat down on chairs provided for us, one behind the other in the order of our seniority.

In front of us, on a three feet high platform sat the members of the court behind simple wooden tables. The President of the Court, Major General Blaxland, C.B., O.B.E. who could easily be singled out because of his badges of rank and a striking personality sat in the centre. He was flanked on his right by :

1. The Judge Advocate, Col. F.C.A. Kerin, O.B.E., Deputy Judge Advocate General (D.J.A.G.) Central Command.
2. Brigadier A.G.H. Bourke, and
3. Lieut. Colonel Nasir Ali Khan, Rajput Regiment.

On the General's left sat.

4. Lieut. Colonel C.R. Stott, M.C, I.R.R.O.
5. Lieut. Colonel Stevenson, C.I.E., M.B.E., M.C. Royal Garhwal Rifles.
6. Major B. Pritam Singh, I.A.C.
7. Major Banwari Lal, 15th Punjab Regiment.

Behind them along the wall stood three waiting members :

1. Lt. Col. C.H. Jackson, I.R.R.O. Incidentally Col. Jackson was the one to whom I owe my Commission. He recommended me for Kitchener College, Nowgong when he was the Officer Commanding, the 4/14th Punjab Regiment.
2. Major S.S. Pandit, I Punjab Regiment.
3. Captain Gurdial Singh Randhawa, 13.D.C.O. Lancers.

Below the court's platform immediately to our right in two rows sat the members of the Defence Counsel :

First Row

1. Bakhshi Sir Tek Chand, former Judge of Lahore High Court.
2. Kanwar Sir Dalip Singh, former Judge of Lahore High Court.
3. Pandit Jawaharlal Nehru.
4. The Rt. Hon. Sir Tej Bahadur Sapru.
5. Shri Bhulabhai Desai
6. Shri Asaf Ali.
7. Dr. Kailash Nath Katju.

And in the second row

8. Shri Jugul Kishore Khanna
9. Shri Manik Lal S. Vakil
10. Shri Gobind Saran Singh
11. Shri R.C. Soni
12. Shri Inder Dev Dua
13. Shri Shiv Kumar Shastri
14. Shri Sultan Yar Khan
15. Shri Rai Bahadur Badri Dass
16. Shri P.N. Sen, former Judge of Patna High Court

Mr. Justice Achhru Ram, Col. Sahgal's father, was conspicuous by his absence among the Defence Counsel. Being the sitting judge of the Lahore High Court, he was not allowed to appear as a counsel.

On our left, with a passage in between, sat the Counsel for Prosecution consisting of Sir Naushirwan P. Engineer, Advocate General of India and Lieut. Col. P. Walsh, Military Prosecutor along with a couple of his assistants.

In front of the Prosecution Counsel on the platform, on the right hand corner end of the Court, sat the stenographers and the interpreters.

Behind us was the visitor's area separated by a rope stretched across the barrack room. Here sat the representatives of the Press and the public including our relatives. The area had an accommodation for about one hundred and sixty chairs. Entry was permitted by passes.

Sharp at 10 a.m. the Judge Advocate, Col. Kerin called out names of the members of the Court and of its stenographers and the prosecution counsel who answered to their names with "present".

After this formality was over, the President of the Court, Maj. Gen. Blaxland said, "Sir Tej! May we start the proceedings?" Sir Tej Bahadur Sapru answered, "Yes please" and then added "Owing to my ill health I have asked my colleague Mr. Bhulabhai Desai to conduct the case". He then introduced all the members of the Defence Counsel.

Gen. Blaxland: "I take it, you are all qualified to appear in terms of the Indian Army Act ?"

Mr. Desai: "Yes".

The Judge Advocate: Addressing us, "Do you object to be tried by the President or any member of the Court?"

Capt. Shah Nawaz Khan, "No Sir."

Capt. Prem Kumar Sahgal, "No Sir".

Lieut. Gurbakhsh Singh Dhillon, "No Sir".

Thereafter the Judge Advocate administered the following solemn oath to the members of the court:

> I swear by Almighty God that I will duly administer justice according to the Indian Army Act without partiality, favour or affection, and if any doubts shall arise, then according to my

> conscience, to the best of my understanding and the custom of war in like cases, and that I will not divulge the sentence of the court martial until it shall be published by authority and further cover the vote or opinion of any members of this court martial unless required to give evidence thereof by a court of justice or a court martial in due course of law. So help me God.

Similarly though a bit different, an oath was administered on the stenographers also. The Christian members took oath with the Bible in hand. A Pandit, a Maulvi and a Garanthi handed over their Holy books to the members of their respective religions.

After the oath taking ceremony, the Military Prosecutor, Lt. Col. P. Walsh read out the charge-sheet. This charge-sheet had been served on us, the three accused, on the 17th of September, 1945.

CHARGE-SHEET

THE ACCUSED No I C 58 CAPT. SHAH

NAWAZ KHAN - 1/14 Punjab Regiment, No. I C 226 CAPT. P.K. SAHGAL - 2/10 Baluch Regiment and No. I C 336 LIEUT. GURBAKHSH SINGH DHILLON -
l/14 Punjab Regiment, all attached C.S.D.I.C. (I), Delhi, Indian commissioned officers, are charged with :

Ist CHARGE	Committing A CIVIL OFFENCE that is to say
I.A.A.Section 41	WAGING WAR AGAINST THE KING contrary to
(against all three	Section 121 of the Indian Penal Code
Accused jointly)	- In that they together

at Singapore, in Malaya, at Rangoon, in the vicinity of Popa, in the vicinity of Kyaukpadaung, and elsewhere in Burma, between the month of September 1942 and the 28th day of April 1945 did wage war against His Majesty the King Emperor of India.

2nd CHARGE I.A.A. Section 41 (against the said Lt. Gurbakhsh Singh Dhillon alone)	COMMITTING A CIVIL OFFENCE, that is to say, MURDER contrary to Section 302 of the Indian Penal Code - in that he- at or near Popa Hill in Burma, on or about 6th March 1945, by causing the death of Hari Singh, did commit Murder.
3rd CHARGE I.A.A. Section 41 (against the said Capt. P. K. Sahgal alone)	COMMITTING A CIVIL OFFENCE, that is to say, ABETMENT, contrary to Section 109 of the Indian Penal Code, of an offence punishable under Section 302 of the Indian Penal Code -in that he- at or near Popa Hill, on or about 6th March 1945 did abet the offence of the murder of Hari Singh as specified in the 2nd charge thereof, which offence was committed in consequence of such abetment.
4th CHARGE I.A.A. Section 41 (against the said Lt. Gurbakhsh Singh Dhillon alone)	COMMITTING A CIVIL OFFENCE, that is to say, MURDER, contrary to Section 302 of the Indian Penal Code -in that he- at or near Popa Hill in Burma, on or about 6th March 1945, by causing the death of Duli Chand, did commit Murder.
5th CHARGE I.A.A. Section 41 (against the said Capt. P.K. Sahgal alone)	COMMITTING A CIVIL OFFENCE, that is to say, ABETMENT, contrary to Section 109 of the Indian Penal Code, of an offence punishable under Section 302 of the Indian Penal Code -in that he- at or near Popa Hill, on or about 6th March 1945 did abet the offence of the murder of Duli Chand as specified in the 4th Charge hereof, which offence was committed in consequence of such abetment.

6th CHARGE I.A.A. Section 41 (against the said Lt. Gurbakhsh Singh Dhillon alone)	COMMITTING A CIVIL OFFENCE, that is to say, MURDER, contrary to Section 302 of the Indian Penal code -in that he- at or near Popa Hill in Burma, on or about 6th March 1945, by causing the death of Daryao Singh, did commit Murder.
7th CHARGE I.A.A. Section 41 (against the said Capt. P.K. Section Sahgal alone)	COMMITTING A CIVIL OFFENCE, that is to say, ABETMENT, contrary to Section 109 of the Indian Penal Code, of an offence punishable under 302 of the Indian Penal Code -in that he- at or near Popa Hill, on or about 6th March 1945 did abet the offence of the murder of Daryao Singh as specified in the 6th Charge hereof, which offence was committed in consequence of such abetment.
8th CHARGE I.A.A. Section 41 (against the said Lt. Gurbaksh Singh Dhillon alone)	COMMITTING A CIVIL OFFENCE, that is to say, MURDER, contrary to Section 302 of the Indian Penal Code -in that he- at or near Popa Hill in Burma, on or about 6th March 1945, by causing the death of Dharam Singh, did commit Murder.
9th CHARGE I.A.A. Section 41 (against the said Capt. P.K. Sahgal alone)	COMMITTING A CIVIL OFFENCE, that is to say, ABETMENT, contrary to Section 109 of the Indian Penal Code, of an offence punishable under Section 302 of the Indian Penal Code -in that he- at or near Popa Hill, on or about 6th March 1945 did abet the offence of the murder of Dharam Singh as specified in the 8th Charge hereof, which offence was committed in consequence of such abetment.
10th CHARGE	COMMITTING A CIVIL OFFENCE, that is to say,

I.A.A. Section 41 (against the said Capt. Shah Nawaz Khan alone)	ABETMENT, contrary to Section 109 of the Indian Penal Code, of an offence punishable under Section 302 of the Indian Penal Code -in that he- at or near Popa Hill in Burma, on or about 29th March 1945, did abet the murder by one Khasin Shah and one Aya Singh of Gunner, Mohd. Hussain of H.K.S.R.A., which offence was committed in consequence of such abetment.

Place: Delhi Col. Sd. Comdg.,

Date 17th Sept. 1945 C.S.D.I.C (I)

DELHI

After the charge-sheet had been read to us the three accused, each one of us was asked by name, "Do you plead guilty or not guilty?" Our reply one after the other was, "Not guilty".

The Defence Seek Adjournment

At that point the Judge Advocate, Col Kerin took up to deal with the application submitted for adjournment by the Defence Counsel.

Col. Kerin : Gentlemen, do you wish to apply for an adjournment on the ground that any of the rules relating to procedure before trial have not been complied with and that you have been prejudiced thereby or on the ground that you have not had sufficient opportunity for preparing your defence ?

Shri Bhulabhai Desai : We are asking for adjournment on the latter ground.

Shri Desai then read out an application for three weeks' adjournment of the case. He listed three substantial grounds for adjournment:

(*i*) That within the last few days a summary of fresh witnesses, numbering seven, has been given just now;

(*ii*) The charge has been made just now: and

(*iii*) That out of 112 witnesses, 80 have not been interviewed at all.

Further Desaiji argued that it was a case which was unprecedented in the recorded history as far as one was able to study the matters relating to the military law. It would also save the time of the court if those witnesses who had not been interviewed were interviewed before the trial began. What he meant was that if the preparation was made, probably a good deal of time would be saved, because the essential and unessential would have been separated from the evidence which would be necessary and useful to put before the court. For these reasons Desaiji submitted that they should be granted three weeks' adjournment which they had sought in the petition.

The petition for adjournment was opposed by the Prosecution Counsel Sir Naushirwan, but he did not altogether reject the contention of the Defence Counsel. His considered opinion was that an adjournment, if at all was to be given, it should be allowed only after he had presented the case, called formal evidence relating to the position of the accused in the Indian Army and after he examined one witness who would also be producing most of the documents to be exhibited in the case.

The Judge Advocate conceded that the Indian Army Rule 70 did grant the court power to adjourn from time to time and from place to place. But it also imposed another duty upon the members of the court that once the court had assembled and the accused were arraigned, the court should continue and sit from day to day. Col Kerin however thought that some adjournment was called for, but as to the length of that adjournment was for the court to decide.

After listening to the opposing counsels and the Judge Advocate, the Court had a short break. When they reassembled the President, General Blaxland ruled that the Court Martial had to continue its proceedings in accordance with the provisions of the Army Act and hence could not be adjourned like a civil court but an adjournment would be made after Sir Naushirwan had opened the case and the evidence of the first witness had been recorded.

Just as a passing reference, I recall that before General Blaxland went to his chamber to discuss the matter of the adjournment with the members of the Court, he came down to where Sir Tej Bahadur Sapru was sitting beside us. He inquired about Sir Tej Bahadur's health. This simple gesture of Blaxland showed his sense of propriety.

Opening Address by the Counsel for Prosecution

Addressing the President and the Members of the Court, the Advocate General of India, Sir Naushirwan P. Engineer began by telling that the charges against us, the three accused were under Section 41 of the Indian Army Act. All three of us were jointly charged with "Waging war against the King Emperor of India, contrary to Section 121, of I.P.C." I, Lieut. Gurbakhsh Singh Dhillon (alone) was charged with the murder of four men and Capt. P.K.Sahgal (alone) was charged with the abetment of murder of those very four men. Capt. Shah Nawaz Khan (alone) was charged with the abetment of murder of one man.

Sir Naushirwan informed the Court that we were all Indian Commissioned Officers. The Advocate General told about our dates of birth, and the notices of the grant of regular Commission pertaining to each one of us as published in the Gazette of India and when we were posted to our respective Regiments.

At the very outset while dealing with the charge of "waging war against the King Emperor", the Advocate General stated that Section 41, Indian Army Act, provided that every person subject to the act who, either within British India or at any place beyond British India, committed any civil offence should be deemed to be guilty of an offence against the military law, and, if charged therewith under the section, should, subject to the provisions of the Act, be liable to be tried for the same act by the Court martial. Civil defence was defined in Section 7(18) as an offence which if committed in British India would be triable by a criminal court.

While explaining the liability of our trial by the Indian Army Act, the thrust of Sir Naushirwan's argument was on the act. He said, "The motive with which the war is waged is immaterial whether the persons charged with the offence did the act with what they considered to be a patriotic motive or with a mercenary motive, the offence is nevertheless committed according to law. The question is whether according to law applicable to the accused (in this case, the Indian Army Act read with the relevant provisions of the Indian Penal Code) the offence with which they are charged is committed. The offence in question is committed against the 'duty of allegiance'. This allegiance the accused owed to the Crown at all times and in all circumstances. The allegiance remained with them wherever they might be. They were bound by this allegiance even when they were prisoners of war".

He then went into the details of how the INA was raised, its composition and expansion, move to the front and our actual act of waging the war under the auspices of the Government of Azad Hind and Netaji Subhas Chandra Bose. The Advocate General laboured at length to narrate our individual acts from the very start of the raising of the INA. He informed the Court that he would produce oral and documentary evidence in the case. He referred to some of our individual acts based on various documents which came into the possession of the British Army in Burma. He cited some of the documents to impress upon the court how we had acted.

After a lengthy opening address, Sir Naushirwan concluded :

"It is submitted that the aforesaid acts of the accused amounted to murder and abetment of murder. If the accused seek to rely upon any general or special exception or upon any proviso in the Indian Penal Code, the burden of proving the existence of circumstances bringing the case within such exception or proviso is under Section 105 of the Indian Evidence Act upon the accused and the Court shall presume the absence of such circumstances. The prosecution will submit that any plea that they were bound or justified by law in doing what they did cannot avail them. Joining with rebels in an act of rebellion or with enemies in acts of hostility makes a man a traitor. An act of treason cannot give any sort of rights nor can it exempt a person from criminal responsibility for the subsequent acts. Even if an act is done under a command where the command is traitorous, obedience to that command is also traitorous.

"It is submitted that the accused cannot in law seek to justify that they did as having been done under the authority of the Indian National Army Act. No authority purporting to be given under that Act can be recognized by this Court or indeed by any court of this country. The assumption of any such authority was illegal from the beginning.

"Any tribunal or authority purporting to be established under that Act could be in repudiation of the allegiance which is inherent in a court of the country. Those who instituted or took part in the proceedings were themselves liable to be punished for offences against the State. All orders under the INA Act or by any tribunal or authority purporting to be established by it are without sanction. They cannot protect the persons who made such orders or who acted upon them".

After the Advocate General of India's opening address, the evidence against us was started.

First witness for the prosecution Lt. Col. P. Walsh having been duly sworn in, produced documents to verify our biographical details and service records in His Majesty's Indian Land Forces. Our Defence Counsel did not think it necessary to cross-examine Lt. Col. Walsh who had laid merely the facts before the Court to show that we had been and were according to the Prosecution Regular Indian Commissioned Officers in His Majesty the King Emperor's Land Forces. It was this fact which held us liable to the Indian Army Act under the law.

Then there was a break for lunch. We the accused joined the members of the Defence Counsel for lunch. This privilege was enjoyed by us throughout the duration of the trial. Lunch was arranged on the verandah at the back of the court room. Shri Raghunandan Saran, Shrimati Sarla Saran, Sahgal's mother and his sister Raj were the organizers behind the scene, who would see to it that the lunch provided was the best which Delhi could produce. Shri Desai never ate lunch. His daughter-in-law, Shrimati Dhirubhai Desai would bring coffee and Monaco biscuits especially for Desaiji. On the first day we were pleasantly surprised when Brigadier Thorat (later Lieut. General) and Colonel Misrichand (later Lieut. General) somehow managed to sneak in to meet us during the lunch. They both were K.C.I.O.S. and belonged to the 1/14th Punjab Regiment.

During the lunch, Pandit Jawaharlal Nehru took me aside and referring to the morning incident said, "Gurbakhsh, what happened?" I briefly narrated the occurrence and then added, "The Captain hit me and I hit him back". Panditji pondered for a while and then said, "I might have done the same". Earlier Bhulabhaiji had asked me the same question. His response was, "*Thik hai, koi baat nahin*" - It's allright. It matters little. I was to learn long after the trial that the one who did not approve of my action was Kanwar Sir Dalip Singh. But he was so magnanimous that he never let me know about his disapproval.

After the lunch when the Court reassembled, the Counsel for Prosecution, Sir Naushirwan started the examination-in-chief of the most important prosecution witness, Lieut. D.C. Nag. It was he who had drafted the Indian National Army Act. He had been in the INA from the beginning to the end and was the Judge Advocate of the INA. He was in a position to make an authentic statement on the story of the INA. Yet when he was asked about the strength of the INA. and how it was armed, Mr. Desai, Col. Kerin and even the President, Gen. Blaxland had to impress on him, "It must be your own personal knowledge and not a hearsay". Actually Lieut. Nag told little which we the three had not already owned.

To show the attitude of the leader of Defence, Shri Bhulabhai Desai, the Judge Advocate, Col. Kerin and the Advocate General, Sir Naushirwan P. Engineer, Counsel for Prosecution, I give a sample of their approach in their own words as under :

Sir Naushirwan : I do not know if you want me to read the whole of the document or the relevant parts of it. There are a number of documents to be put in. My only anxiety is to save time.

Mr. Desai : Some of these documents have to be read.

Sir Naushirwan : If you want any particular portion to be read, I will gladly do it.

Mr. Desai : My only submission is that if all the three minds work together it would be better.

Sir Naushirwan : If you have any portion which is considered to be material and which I have not read, I will read it.

Col. Kerin : Our primary object is, of course, to do justice and our secondary object is to save time.

The deposition by Lieut. Nag had started well on its way when at 5 p.m. the court adjourned until the next morning at 10 a.m.

Yet the day did not end for us the three accused. We were taken to a part of CSDIC where a Lieut. Colonel, most probably the Battalion Commander of the Gurkha Unit to which the Company Commander, guarding Salimgarh belonged was present. I had my 'friend of the accused' Major Hardial Singh Randhawa as well as Shah Nawaz and Sahgal's friends of the accused also present.

The Colonel heard and recorded my complaint against the Captain. He summarily removed the Captain from the command of the Company. The Colonel added that further disciplinary action against the officer would follow. Thereafter we were lodged back into our cage where we were being long awaited by our colleagues.

Friend of the Accused

I gave Major (later Brigadier) Hardial Singh Randhawa's name as my Friend of the Accused. Randhawa's superior officers failed to prevail against his acceptance of my request. Ultimately Randhawa was invited by the Adjutant General to a dinner which stretched from an early evening into late night. The General tried his best to persuade Randhawa to reject my request. Randhawa's simple reply was, "It would be very unofficer-like on my part to reject the request of an accused brother officer. I am sorry I cannot do that. My conscience doesn't allow me". And he stuck to his word.

On the first day of the trial Randhawa noticed that I didn't have warm clothing on. The news was flashed in the press. Hardial took immediate steps to provide me with a woollen ready-made battledress. When General Fujiwara and other Japanese Generals and diplomats arrived to appear before the Court in our defence, they were accommodated under tents in a barbed wire cage inside the Red Fort near the Delhi Gate. They were treated as prisoners. I told Randhawa how helpful they had been to our freedom struggle, and that they deserved to be better looked after. Knowing Fujiwara's liking for Scotch I suggested to Randhawa if he could provide them with a few bottles somehow. Randhawa, a generous host as he is, saw to it that Scotch whisky and some eatables reached our Japanese friends as far as possible.

On the second day of the trial, 6th of November, we were pleasantly surprised, when we found Mr. Justice Achhru Ram seated among the defence immediately behind Shri Bhulabhai Desai. Later we learned that Pitaji, as we three used to call him, had intended to resign his judgeship in order to take part in our defence. When the Punjab Government came to know about his intention, they prevailed upon the Central Government who in their prudence allowed Mr. Justice Achhru Ram to sit with the Defence Counsel.

The deposition of Lieut. Nag continued on the second day of the trial also. He recalled his meeting all the three of us, Shah Nawaz, Sahgal and I at different occasions and at various places. He informed the court about our appointments from time to time. He produced most of the important documents and orders of the Supreme Commander of the INA and of the Head of the State of the Provisional Government of Azad Hind (Free India), Netaji Subhas Chandra Bose. The papers dealing with the I.I.L. and INA from the beginning to the end were fairly exhaustive. He produced diaries, battle reports, intelligence summaries, charge-sheets etc. signed by one of us three or other officers. All these exhibits were marked and kept.

At the end of the examination in-chief of Lieut. Nag by Sir Naushirwan, the Judge Advocate, Col. Kerin announced that the cross-examination of Lt. Nag was being postponed. The court wished to deal with the period of adjournment which the defence had asked for. He said that the adjournment which the defence had asked for was for three weeks. The court wanted to know the number of defence witnesses then available and how many of them had been examined till then.

Then followed a discussion among the Defence Counsel, the Judge Advocate, the Prosecution Counsel, the Military Prosecutor, Col. Walsh and the President of the Court, Gen. Blaxland. Desaiji informed that the defence had interviewed twenty-three witnesses and the number of witnesses had been reduced to 112. That meant that 89 witnesses remained to be interviewed. They discussed about the availability of Col. Hunt who had proceeded on sick leave. The question of the report by Field Marshal Wavell on the Malayan Campaign which was asked for by Desaiji was also discussed. The Judge Advocate Col. Kerin said, "We are all men of the world and we know that if unpublished official documents are asked for, privilege may be claimed in respect of them". Desaiji added, "Then it will have to be decided on the basis of the Indian Evidence Act. As regard the admissibility of the affidavit or otherwise in support of the privilege, it will be for the court to decide." At this stage the Court adjourned to consider the plea for adjournment. Eventually the Court decided to adjourn until Wednesday, November the 21st.

It was late in the evening of the 6th November when we three returned to our cage in Salimgarh and broke the news of the adjournment of our case for two weeks. The information gladdened all our colleagues.

There was however an officer whom I would not name had this to say, "So it means fourteen more days in this wretched bloody piggery". His statement shocked me. He was a former K.C.I.O. His habits were easy going. His cot was next to mine in the barrack. Out of compassion and courtesy I used to share my morning tea with him. From the following morning I stopped serving him bed tea. Over and above that in the evening I took the officer to the back of the barrack and gave him a bit of my mind. For the next three days I neither greeted him nor talked to him. On the fourth day after dark he took me to the same spot where I had told him what I thought of him. There he said, "Gurbakhsh, God has given you a big heart while I am a bloody coward. Why do you hate me for my weakness?" His words melted me so much that with folded hands I begged for his pardon and started serving him tea as before.

The two weeks' of adjournment were spent by members of the Defence Counsel to interview witnesses who were made available by Col. Walsh. Shah Nawaz, Sahgal and I were present during these interviews.

When the Court reassembled on 21st November, the 1st Prosecution Witness, Lieut. Nag was cross-examined by Shri Bhulabhai Desai. From Nag Desaiji gathered a lot of evidence which proved the integrity of the Indian National Army, its aim and its actions through all its stages from its very inception. For instance, Nag deposed that General Mohan Singh had told the Indian prisoners of war that if needed they would fight against the Japanese in addition to the British. Mohan Singh did what he preached. He also recalled and testified a statement made by Netaji, "When the Azad Hind Fauj launches its fight, it will do so under the leadership of its own Government and when it marches into India, the administration of liberated tracts will automatically come into the hands of the Provisional Government. India's liberation shall be achieved by Indian effort and sacrifice through our own Fauj". The copy of this statement was kept as an exhibit. Similarly many exhibits produced by the defence were testified by Lieut. Nag. Nag also did depose to individual actions of us three accused during our INA service, showing that we did wage a war against the Crown.

At the close of the cross-examination of the first prosecution witness, the Court called upon Sir Naushirwan to show a relevancy under the Indian Evidence Act in respect of further evidence to be called.

The counsel for Prosecution said that he had divided his evidence into various groups. The first group pertained to the recruitment in the INA from among the Indian prisoners of war who lived in various camps. He stated that we the accused made speeches and were aware of atrocities that were committed in those camps. Sir Naushirwan argued at length that recruiting for war was if not actually waging war, it was making preparations for war which came under the Evidence Act and that we tried to win over the P.O.Ws from their allegiance to the Crown in order to join us for waging war against the King. He stressed that he would produce evidence to show the conditions that prevailed in the P.O.W. camps. He said that the accused were aware of atrocities in those camps.

Mr. Desai rebutted Sir Naushirwan's statement: "I have never yet heard of any law that merely because you know that somebody has done something, that knowledge constitutes an offence. It is an extraordinary argument made before this Court, and I know the reason. The reason is that they cannot bring home to these accused any dishonourable conduct. Failing that, they now hopelessly try to do this: somebody did something and they heard about it. If my friend thinks that a great deal of padding is necessary, he can well have it, namely, that they made speeches asking them to join the INA."

Mr. Desai continued, "My case is that in some cases the alleged

Netaji (Tokyo, 1944)

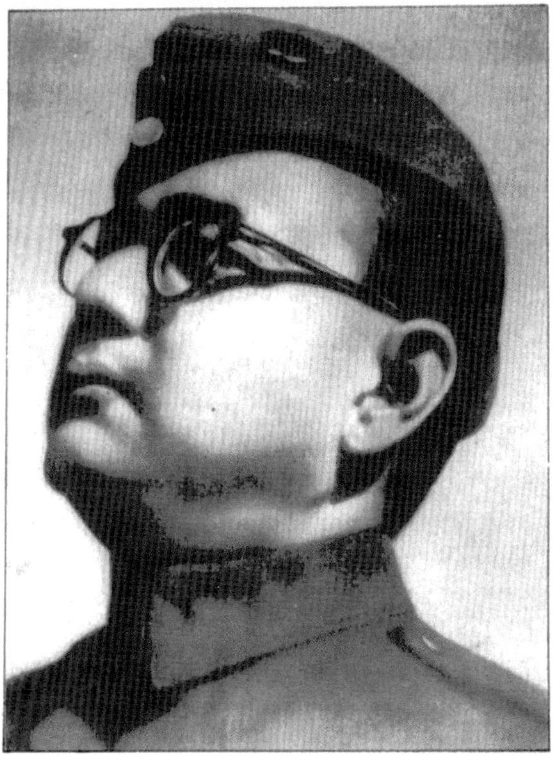

Netaji Subhas Chandra Bose

Mrs. & Mr. Rash Behari Bose

General Mohan Singh (1948)

General Mohan Singh

Lt. General I. Fujiwara

General Fujiwara and the author (1973)

INA officers salute the Father of the Nation

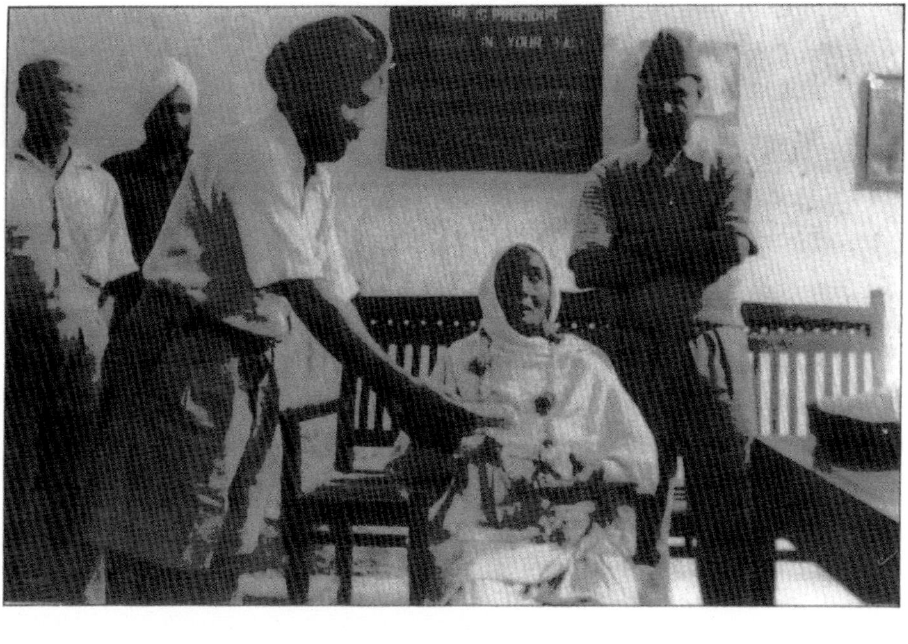

Author's mother handing over a purse for INA Relief Committee (Lahore)

Mr. Bhulabhai Desai

Major General Blaxland and members of the Court Martial

Shri Bhulabhai Desai (leader) and members of the Defence Counsel

On the first day of the trial; Mrs. Naidu with Mrs. Dhillon on her left; sister and mother of Capt. Sahgal on her right

Shah Nawaz Khan after release

Prem Kumar Sahgal after release

G.S. Dhillon after release

The three INA heroes at a public reception (January; 1946)

Crowds at Lahore Railway Station

Crowds gathered at Lahore

Punjab High Court Bar Association receives the Trio

Reception at Shri Bhimsen Sachar's House

With Dr. Radha Krishnan during world Agriculture Fair (1960)

With Dr. Shankar Dayal Sharma (Indore, 1965)

Escorting Queen Elizabeth at Agriculture Fair (Calcutta)

Azad Hind Expedition (1995-96): Members before flagoff.

Azad Hind Expedition (1995-96): At Mount Popa
(Headquarter Cave of 1945)

Col. Dhillon at his den in Shivpuri

Working on his memoirs

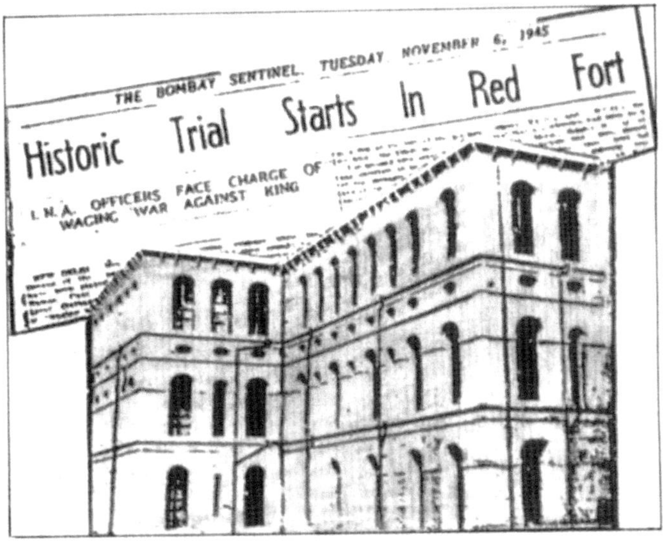

Special postage stamp issued on the trial of the three INA heroes (On the occasion of 50 Years of India's Independence, 15-8-1997)

speeches were not made and in some cases they were made at different periods of time. If my learned friend thinks that part of the case has any value in proving the waging of war, he is entitled to that satisfaction, and if the court thinks that the matter should be extended to that plane. They have put in documents that they joined that Army and that Army waged war: but now to go back and say that their great-grandfathers did something, is something which does not appeal to reason. The Crown cannot plea res gestae. That is a matter which is essentially so connected that it is necessary for the court to know whether actual relevant acts were done.

"Even so, my learned friend cannot say anything more than they had knowledge of it. He has cited nothing, and nothing can be cited. That because a man has knowledge of some act, the person knowing it is guilty of any offence.... My submission is that it is totally irrelevant and should not be allowed. It is to create a prejudice against honourable men, who on their own showing took no part in any of the atrocities. I take it a tribunal of this kind will set its face against such an attempt to prejudice it. By all means, let those who committed torture be brought before this or any other tribunal.

"Therefore, my submission is that the first part may stand, but the second part is totally irrelevant. Waging war itself is great enough. But if he thinks he can add that by mere knowledge that somebody else committed it, I submit it is totally irrelevant. If a witness is called and he deposes, for example, that a speech was made, it may be allowed, but when he proceeds to talk about somebody else having committed something else merely on the ground that he came to know about it, I trust the Court will rule it out."

There followed arguments between the Prosecution and the Defence Counsel. Then the Court adjourned for taking a decision on the point. The court decided that evidence of torture and hardships undergone by Indian prisoners of war in Malaya and Burma should be admitted.

On the following day, 22nd November Captain K.P. Dhargalkar of the 3rd Cavalry was examined. He was a K.C.I.O. I remember what a poor show he put up when the Defence Counsel cross-examined him. To many questions asked by Shri Desai, Dhargalkar showed lack of memory.

The 3rd Prosecution Witness, Subedar Major Babu Ram contrary to his hostile attitude during the Summary of Evidence, deposed in quite a sympathetic manner. Cross-examined by Shri Desai he admitted that he joined the INA to fight for the freedom of India.

Desai : Then why did you leave the INA.?

Babu Ram : After the arrest of General Mohan Singh I saw no strong leader to lead the INA.

Desai : What did you think of Netaji Subhas Chandra Bose?

Babu Ram : He was very big and a strong leader.

Desai : Then why didn't you rejoin the INA.?

Babu Ram : Because I had been already removed to New Guinea by the Japanese before Netaji arrived.

Desai : Did you love the freedom of India ?

Babu Ram : (In a loud and determined tone) *Ji haan. Main aaj bhi Hindusthan ki aazadi se piar karta hoon.*—Yes Sir, Even today I love the freedom of India.

Sir Naushirwan: Answer to the question.

Babu Ram : (In an emphatic loud voice with stress on each word) *Yeh usi sawal ka hi to jawab hai* - This is the answer to that very question.

Desai : That is our first victory (and he sat down).

The forceful deliberate answer of Babu Ram caused a spontaneous laughter among the public. General Blaxland visibly annoyed warned the public to keep quiet so that he was not obliged to make them clear the Court. This was the first time that the President of the Court had to take such a step. The only other occasion of the kind was when Maj. General Tudashi Katakura, one of our witnesses for defence spoke in the Japanese in a commanding tone. Apart from these two occasions proceedings throughout the Court sittings were solemn and serious.

It was some days after the trial that I learned about Babu Ram. He had about 20 years meritorious service and a long tenure in the rank of a Subedar Major, yet immediately after his deposition that he loved the freedom of his country, he was released from the service on a paltry pension of Rs. 36/- per month only. That was the price of loving the liberty of his country that Babu Ram paid.

In all there were thirty witnesses for the prosecution and twelve for the Defence who deposed before the Court. In order to be brief I propose not to give out all the details of our trial. I shall confine my narration to our full statements before the Court and gists of Shri Bhulabhai Desai's Defence Address, Sir Naushirwan's Prosecution Address: Col. Kerin the Judge Advocate's summing up and then Findings of the court, apart from a few anecdotes.

My Dilemma

Making a statement before a military court is a privilege of the accused. We were at liberty whether to make a statement or not. Yet if a statement is made, it can go against an accused as an evidence though it is not made under an oath. My colleagues Shah Nawaz and Sahgal had already written and submitted their statements to Defence Counsel for legal advice. One day Mr. Justice Achhru Ram, asked me, "Gurbakhsh! When are you going to submit your statement?" I said, "Pitaji I have not been able to make up my mind whether I should tell a lie or the truth in case of the four persons of my Brigade who were executed."

Pitaji said, "Gurbakhsh, that is very simple. Why should you admit it ? It is a question of saving your own and Prem's life."

I said, "Pitaji, my conscience does not allow me to tell a lie. I did not fear telling the truth during my interrogation when I was all alone. Should I fear to tell the truth when you and the whole of India are at my back ? When I do not care for my own life, why should I care about Prem's life?" This curt reply by me to one who treated us all three as his own sons has ever since troubled my mind and it troubles me even today for the discourtesy shown by me, a son to Pitaji, the father.

When I talked to Pitaji, Shri Bhulabhai Desai, Dr. Kailash Nath Katju and Rai Bahadur Badri Das were present. When I asked Rai Bahadur Badri Das, he said, "Say what your conscience tells you". I turned to Shri Desai to know what his opinion was. Desaiji said, "You say whatever you like. The second charge is no charge in my opinion".

During those days Dr. Kailash Nath Katju often used to take me away from the crowd of visitors and lawyers and would ask me to recite some of my poetical compositions like, CHALO DELHI and NETAJI KA FARMAN DESH BHAGTON SE. I took him aside and asked, "Sir what is your advice?" He said, "Gurbakhsh, say whatever your conscience tells you". I said, "Doctor Sahib, you are my counsel. Can't you help me to make a decision? Isn't it a part of your duty? Please advise me whether I should tell the truth or a lie."

It was most probably Saturday when the aforesaid conversation took place. Dr. Katju told me that he would think over it and advise me on Monday after the sitting of the Court. Monday came and when I approached him, Dr. Katju said, "Sorry, I haven't been able to make up my mind what to advise you". I said, "Doctor Sahib, can I ask you after two days?" He said, "Yes". He was happy that I left him alone.

During the next two days I decided not to admit the charge. When I met Dr. Katju I asked him, "Sir, what is your advice?" He said, "Gurbakhsh it is a difficult problem. I have not been able to make up my mind". I added, "Sir, I have". Like a child who wants to know what's in the bag, Dr. Katju asked me imploringly. "What is it? Let me know what you have decided and how?" I answered, "I am going to tell a lie." Impatiently he asked, "Why?" I could see that his inquisitive face showed as if he had lost something.

Trying to explain the working of my mind, I said, "Among the principles of war, there is one: 'Mystify and mislead the enemy'. I take it that the Court Room is the prolongation of the battlefield where I had been fighting and the members of the Court are as good my enemies now as they were on the field. As a Commander taking refuge under that principle of war I have the right to mystify and mislead them. Again, the motto of the Indian Military Academy enjoins me to give priority to the honour, welfare and comfort of my men over my own ease, comfort and safety. Hence my first duty remains to save my men. It is immaterial whether in doing so, Sahgal and I live or go. I cannot please my conscience by telling the truth and as a result endanger the lives of my junior officers and men who participated or attended the execution of those unfortunate four fellows: Thus my decision".

Dr. Katju attentively listened to me and said, : "I am glad you have taken a decision". "Do you agree with me?" I asked. Dr. Katju repeated, "I am glad you have taken a decision". And he walked away. I felt I had fallen low in his estimation. How great, noble and upright were those legal luminaries who would not advise their clients to withhold truth even in the face of a certain capital punishment!

In the evening after last post I retired to a tent in the compound of the cage which served as a dining place. Closing the flies of the tent, I sat down to write my statement. By the daybreak my statement was ready. I handed it over to Pitaji during the day. In a way, the statement was an expression of my repentance over my crude bitter reply to him earlier in the week. Today as I write these memoirs after a lapse of half a century, I confess that in spite of all arguments I should have told the truth. I do feel sorry for having told a lie.

On 7th December, 1945 after the close of the Prosecution, we the accused read out our written statements.

Statement by Capt. Shah Nawaz Khan

Mr. President and members of this Honourable Court:

In this statement I am going to lay before you, very frankly, the considerations and motives that have impelled me from the day of my surrender in Singapore on February 15, 1942, to the day of my capture by the British forces at Pegu on May 16, 1945.

Before touching on the actual period, I would like to throw some light on my early history and Army career.

I was born in a family of Janjua Rajputs in Rawalpindi. My father who was the leader of the Tribe in the District served in the Indian Army for 30 years.

In the First and Second World Wars, every able-bodied member of my family joined the Army. At present there are over 80 of them serving as officers in the Indian Army. In short, I belong to a family in which loyalty to the Crown has always been a valued tradition.

I was educated at the Prince of Wales Royal Indian Military College, Dehra Dun.

In 1933, I passed out into the I.M.A., Dehra Dun, and received the undermentioned scholarships:

(*a*) King Emperor's Cadetship;

(*b*) Sir Partap Singh Memorial Prize for being the best cadet and for belonging to a family having the best military services to its credit.

I passed out of the I.M.A. as an under-officer and was attached to a British Battalion for one year, after which I was posted to Ist Battalion 14th Punjab Regiment in February 1937.

In short I was brought up in an atmosphere which was purely military and up to the time of meeting with Netaji Subhas Chandra Bose at Singapore in July 1943, I was politically almost uneducated. I was brought up to see India through the eyes of a young British Officer, and all that I was interested in was soldiering and sport.

In March 1941, my Battalion went overseas to Malaya. At that time I was left behind in command of a Company at the Training Centre at Ferozepore.

Early in November 1941, my Officer Commanding, Lt. Col. L.V. Fitzpatrick, wrote to the G.H.Q. India, asking for my being sent out to join the Battalion. The Officer Commanding the Training Centre, however, refused to allow me to go on the grounds that my services could not be spared. He also protested about it to the G.H.Q. and an Indian Army Order was published stating that in future the active Battalions should not ask for any officer by name.

Col. Fitzaptrick, however, again applied for me through Malaya High Command, but his request was again turned down.

Early in December 1941, he wrote a private letter to the Officer Commanding the Training Centre, stating that it was imperative in the interests of the Battalion that I should be sent out to join it.

On receipt of this letter I was allowed to proceed to Malaya and join my Battalion.

I was very proud of my Battalion, and was very happy to join it in the fight against the Japanese.

On January 16, 1942, I sailed from Bombay, determined to live up to the good name of Sherdil battalion and to uphold the martial traditions of my family.

I arrived at Singapore on January 29, 1942, when the situation had become very critical. In spite of this, I was determined to put up a brave fight.

In the battle of Singapore on February 13, 14 and 15, 1942, when the British Officers, on my right and left flanks, had disappeared with their Units, I held onto my position until ordered by my Commanding Officer to surrender.

I resented this order very much especially because I felt that I had not been given a fair chance to fight the enemy. To have brought me to Singapore so late in the fight, only to be ordered to lay down my arms, and to surrender unconditionally, I considered it to be extremely unjust to myself and to my sense of honour as a soldier.

Surrender and the Concentration at the Farrar Park

On the night of February 15-16, 1942, the day of surrender, we received orders that all Indians, including the King's Commissioned Officers, were to concentrate at the Farrar Park: and all British Officers and Other Ranks were to concentrate at Changi.

All of us, especially the officers, were surprised to hear this order, because according to the laws of civilized warfare, all captured officers, whether Indian or British, are kept together, and separate from rank and file.

We had heard of the Japanese methods and atrocities before, and felt that our British brother officers were leaving us in the lurch to face it all by ourselves.

On the morning of February 16, 1942, when we were marching off to our concentration area, our Commanding Officer, Maj Madum, along with other British Officers, came to see off the Battalion. When shaking hands with me, he said: "I suppose, this is the parting of our ways". These words confirmed my belief that we, the Indians, were being left in the lurch. These were the feelings and the state of mind in which I went to the Farrar Park.

Handing over Ceremony

At the Farrar Park we were handed over to the Commander of Japanese Intelligence Department, Major Fujiwara, by Col. Hunt, the Representative of the British Government. When handing over, Col.

Hunt called the parade to attention and said:

"Today I, on behalf of the British Government, hand you over to the Japanese Government, whose orders you will obey as you have done ours".

Major Fujiwara then brought the parade to attention and said:

"On behalf of the Japanese Government I take you over under my charge." He then went on to say: "I, On behalf of the Japanese Government, now hand you over to G.O.C. Capt. Mohan Singh,. who shall have the power of life and death over you." After this Col. Hunt departed.

Major Fujiwara made a speech in which he declared that we would not be treated as prisoners but as brothers by the Japanese and expressed a hope that all of us would join the army which would be raised for India's freedom under the leadership of Capt. Mohan Singh.

After this Capt. Mohan Singh came to the stage and made a similar speech.

These speeches came to me as a complete bombshell. The very idea of joining hands with our former enemies to fight against our own kith and kin was fantastic. I as well as most of the other officers had a feeling of being completely helpless at being handed over like cattle by the British to the Japs and by the Japs to Capt. Mohan Singh whom they gave powers of life and death over us.

With all due regards to Capt. Mohan Singh's sincerity and leadership which he displayed later - I had known him well for the last 10 years—he had always been an efficient, but very average officer. The mere fact of being handed over to him, and his announcement as the G.O C. made me feel suspicious of the Japanese intentions, as among the Indian prisoners of war there were some very senior and brilliant officers like Col. Gill and Col. Bhonsle with at least 15 to 20 years' service in the Army, whereas Capt. Mohan Singh had only 8 to 9 years' service.

I was fully convinced, knowing Capt. Mohan Singh so well, that politically at any rate, he would not be able to cope with Japanese political intrigues and we would be exploited by them for their own ends. I, therefore, firmly made up my mind not to have anything to do with such an organization and in spite of the feeling of frustration and helplessness, the element of traditional loyalty to the King triumphed and not only did I make up my own mind to keep out of the INA., but as the head of a famous military tribe I felt it my duty to warn others, especially the men I commanded and the men that came from my area, to keep out of it. The advice that I gave them at that time was that if any of them is asked to shoot at his brethren he should turn round and shoot at the person asking him to do so.

The period from the time of my surrender in Singapore in February 1942 to the time of my capture by the British in May 1945 can be divided into three distinct parts.

Part I—February 15, 1942, to the end of May 1942: During this period I was against the very idea of the coming into existence of such an organization and fought against it as vigorously as was possible, under the unfortunate circumstances in which we were placed.

Part II. June 1942 to July 1943: Realizing that I had failed in my first object I decided in the interests of my men, to volunteer for the INA with full determination that I would do every thing possible to break it or to sabotage it from within the moment I felt it would submit to Japanese exploitation.

Part III. July 1943 to May 1945: I was fully convinced that it was a genuine army of liberation.

I would like to give some details and important events that took place in each of the above-mentioned parts.

In the first part I was against the idea of creating an Indian National Army because:

(*a*) I realized that the Japanese were out to exploit us, and none of us was politically capable of dealing with them;

(*b*) The handing over of all the Indian prisoners of war to Capt. Mohan Singh by the Japanese made me feel even more suspicious of their intentions, and so I felt it my duty to fight against it.

On February 17, 1942, I went with my Battalion to Neesoon Camp, and after a few days I was appointed Camp Commandant.

There were approximately 20,000 prisoners of war in that Camp. The accommodation there was sufficient only for approximately 8 to 10 thousand men; there were no sanitary arrangements, there was no water supply; and hospital arrangements were very poor and we had no medicines. As a result of this, dysentery and other epidemics broke out in the camp.

The discipline of troops had gone completely, and so I had a very difficult task to perform, but thanks to the strenuous effort of the Camp Medical staff, particularly Col. Chaudhri, Maj. Elahi Bakhsh and Major Gillani, the disease was controlled, and by the efforts of an S & M. Unit, electricity, water and sanitary arrangements were completed.

After the events in Farrar Park, I was fully convinced that the Japs were going to exploit us, and so on reaching Neesoon Camp, one of the first things I did was to organize a block of officers, with the object of preventing the formation of the INA.

I commanded the Neesoon Camp from March to June 1942, during which period my only concern was to improve the unfortunate lot of the men under my command.

During the time, I was commanding Neesoon, the largest Indian prisoners of war Camp in Singapore, not a single person was ever sent to any Concentration or Detention Camp. I allowed everyone to have and express his opinion freely and to decide for himself, without any outside pressure, whether or not he wished to join the INA.

By the end of May 1942 it had become quite evident that in spite of all our efforts the INA would come into existence.

In the same month we had to decide whether or not we would volunteer for the INA and volunteers and non-volunteers were to be separated. I received orders from the Headquarters to forward lists of volunteers and non-volunteers to them, for allotment of separate camps to each category.

In view of this new situation I held several meetings of the "Bloc" and it was decided that since we had failed in our first object to prevent the formation of the INA the next best thing was for senior officers to join it with the object of:

(*a*) Giving protection and help to prisoners of war,

(*b*) To stop its being exploited by the Japs, and

(*c*) To sabotage and wreck it from within, the moment we felt that it would submit to Japanese exploitation.

I, however, advised the rank and file to keep out of it. This at the time concerned mainly the Muslims.

In accordance with this decision, in the middle of May 1942, at Neesoon, in the presence of all officers of the camp, I declared myself a volunteer, but gave everyone a free choice to decide for himself. I also gave orders that anyone trying to persuade anyone else to join the INA would be punished. I also asked for the list which had to be forwarded to INA Headquarters on the following day.

The same afternoon I called a meeting of all Muslim officers in the mosque and told them my reasons for joining the I.N.A, I also told them that they would be separated shortly, and I asked them to give me an assurance that they would not become volunteers, through any force or coercion used against them by the Japanese. They all agreed and said "*Dua-Khair*"— a religious confirmation of the decision taken.

Early in June 1942, Capt. Mohan Singh called a conference of all senior officers at his residence to discuss the plans for the forthcoming conference to be held at Bangkok. He revealed that he had to take 90 delegates there on behalf of Indian prisoners of war. He went on to say that he proposed to take only 30 delegates and 60 proxy votes.

My own feeling was that at Bangkok we were likely to be committed too far and I was not in favour of Indian P.O.W.s participating in such a conference. In the discussion that followed some misunderstanding arose over the selection of delegates and from Neesoon, the biggest prisoners of war Camp in Malaya, only one delegate and not a single proxy vote was sent to the conference.

On account of this misunderstanding the same evening I was relieved of the command of Neesoon Camp and was ordered to proceed to Kuala Lumpur, with working parties of prisoners of war.

I arrived at Kuala Lumpur by a goods train early in June and was appointed Commander of all prisoners-of-war parties in Malaya.

My duty was to tour all prisoners of war stations in Malaya and put their grievances to the Jap G.H.Q. which was at Kuala Lumpur.

At Kuala Lumpur, I was ordered by the Japanese to assemble all troops for the Garrison Commander's inspection. The Jap Commander addressing the prisoners of war said: "I welcome you all and am very pleased to have you under my command. We regard you not as Prisoners of War but as our brothers as we are all Asiatics. It is the most ardent desire of all Japanese people that India should achieve its independence as soon as possible and to enable you to participate in the freedom fight we have made arrangements for rearming and training you for that purpose". I realized that the Japs were out to exploit the Indian prisoners of war who resented taking up arms.

I explained to the Japanese Commander that the question of Indian Independence was an affair of the Indians and that the Japs had no right to force any Indian against his wishes to participate in. He agreed with me and it was decided that in future the Indian prisoners of war would be asked to do only labour, and other prisoners of war duties.

A similar trouble arose at Seremban, where on refusal of the POWs to take up arms, the Japs fixed machine-guns all round their camp, put the Camp Commandant Lt. Ghulam Mohd. 3/16 P.R. in a cell and gave the POWs 24 hours to think about it and decide, after which, if they still insisted, they would all be shot.

I heard about it and at once rushed to Seremban. With the Jap G.H.Q. decision given at Kuala Lumpur, and after a great deal of persuasion I was able to make the Japs see our point of view and future trouble was averted. In a similar manner I visited all Indian POWs camps in Malaya and ensured that they were not coerced to take up arms and undergo any form of military training under the Japs.

At Kuala Lumpur the Japs tried to teach the Indian POWs Jap Foot Drill, words of command and saluting. I refused to allow them to do so, although it will be interesting to know that the English prisoners of war in Rangoon did this.

While holding this position I managed to secure for the Indian POWs excellent living conditions very likely the best given to any POWs in the Far East:

(*a*) Food was excellent. It included eggs fish, chicken and vegetables.

(*b*) Work was moderate and pay was given regularly.

(*c*) There were adequate arrangements for the recreation of troops. They played hockey, football etc. Cinema shows were given in camps and troops could go out and see any picture by paying 10 cents.

(*d*) POWs soldiers could go out of their camp on a pass given by their Unit Commanders from 10 a.m. to 4 p.m. daily and on holidays officers could go out in mufti and visit any civilian friends from 10 a.m. to midnight.

(*e*) On Fridays, Muslims were allowed to go and say prayers in the Jumma Masjid, and Hindus and Sikhs could go to their respective religious places in the town on Sundays.

On one occasion when I was out of station on tour, the Japs took away 23 N.C.Os belonging to 42 Fd. Pk. Coy R. Bombay S and M, on the accusation that they were too pro-British and selected some of them for execution and made them sign their last will. When I returned from tour I found this I at once went to the Jap G.H.Q. and requested them to hand over my soldiers to me. I told them that I was supposed to be the Commander of Indian troops and that in principle it was wrong for the Japs to deal direct with my subordinate officers and take away the men under my command without my knowledge.

Finally, I told them that if they insisted on doing this I would resign from my appointment. They told me that I could take away 15 of them and the rest they said they must execute as they were too "Pro-British" and being Japanese prisoners they were still insisting that they had taken an oath to be loyal to the British King. They said they could not allow such Indians to live.

I explained the full significance of this oath to them and told them that the normal procedure for dealing with any serious offence in the Indian Army was to hold a court of inquiry, and I assured them that I would go very thoroughly into the case, and if in the end the court found their offence of a serious nature, I would myself hand them over to the Japs for punishment. They eventually agreed to this and I brought back all the 23 N.C.Os safely to their Unit, held a court of inquiry and released all of them.

In September 1942, I was recalled to Singapore during the period of my stay at Kuala Lumpur as Commander of P.O.Ws in Malaya.

(*a*) I served them to the best of my ability. Many a time I had to travel by goods train without food and had to face insults and humiliation from junior Jap officers for the sake of the men I commanded.

(*b*) I refused to allow the Japs, to exploit the Indian P.O.Ws. in any way and at the same time secured them good treatment.

(*c*) I always upheld the honour and prestige of my country and refused to accept any racial superiority of the Japs.

(*d*) I also induced the Japs not to arrest any Indian soldiers who had turned civilian during the war and were honourably earning their living. The case of one Sy Abdul Matlab of 2/.16th P.R. who had opened a tea shop at Seremban railway station is a typical one.

(*e*) At Kuala Lumpur I helped the Indian destitutes as much as I could. There were scores of them dying of starvation. I requested all POWs to fast for one day in a week and send all the food thus saved to them. The Jap Commander on coming to know of this was so impressed that he gave 20 bags of rice per month for the destitute camp which we were supporting.

(*f*) At Singapore in May 1943 the Japanese ordered officers of 2/12th F.F.R. to provide three hundred men to do guard duties over Jap aerodromes. The men refused to go, but the Japanese insisted and it looked as if a serious situation would develop. Sub. Fazal Dad Khan of 2/12 F.F.R. then approached me

> and informed me of the critical situation that had arisen. I went to the Seletar Camp with Sub. Fazal Dad Khan, talked to the Jap officer and succeeded in convincing him that it was wrong to persuade POWs to take up arms. After this the Unit was never troubled by the Japs.

I was recalled to Singapore in September 1942, and one of the first things I did was to go and pay a visit to all the POW camps in Singapore, where there were large numbers of men from my area. All along during my stay in Singapore I had been most concerned about the welfare of the POWs whom I quite often used to visit and distribute among them my INA pocket money, clothing and medicine.

There was the case of one POW Jem. Mirzamam, 2/10th Baluch Regt., who had an ulcer in the stomach. The doctor said that he would not survive. I took him to my bungalow, kept him with me for over 4 months and through good nourishment, completely cured him and then sent him back to rejoin his Unit which was still a POW unit. There are several such instances.

On recall from Kuala Lumpur, I was appointed Commandant O.T.S. which had to be disbanded after a few days by order of Capt. Mohan Singh, who had some misunderstanding with the Japs.

I took full advantage of this situation and together with other members of my "Block" persuaded Capt. Mohan Singh to disband the INA I did so because I knew the Japs were trying to exploit us.

I joined the second INA in February 1943, on being told that Netaji Subhas Chandra Bose would be coming to Singapore to take over its command.

At this time I also realized that whether we liked it or not, the Japs were definitely going into India.

I also realized that the fight would in all probability be carried into Indian territory as I did not think that the British forces were able to stop their advance.

I had also seen with my own eyes the indiscriminate looting and raping that the Japanese had done in Malaya, and did not wish it to happen in India. I felt that by going into India with them we would be able to stop this, or at any rate, I would be much more useful to my country with a rifle in my hand to save the life, property and honour of Indians than as a helpless prisoner of war in Malaya.

I, therefore, set about to collect such men for the INA who would be prepared to fight even against the Japs if they proved dishonest, and this fact has been established beyond doubt even by the prosecution witnesses.

When Netaji arrived in Singapore, I watched him very keenly. I had never seen or met him before, and did not know very much about his activities in India. I heard a number of his public speeches, which had a profound effect on me. It will not be wrong to say that I was hypnotized by his personality and his speeches. He placed the true picture of India before us and for the first time in my life I saw India, through the eyes of an Indian.

I was most impressed by Netaji's selflessness, his absolute devotion to his country, his frankness and his refusal to bow before the Japanese wishes. I knew that in his hands India's honour was safe; he would never barter it away for anything in the world. Also when I heard him give a free choice to everyone in the INA to leave its rank if they were not prepared to make extreme sacrifices and his warning to those who stayed on in the INA to be prepared to face thirst, hunger, forced marches and, in the end, death and when with my own eyes I saw the enthusiasm of thousands of poverty-stricken Indians in the Far East, who gave to the INA all that they possessed and the whole families joined the Azad Hind Fauj and became "*Fakirs*" for the sake of their country, I knew we had a real leader; and when he in the name of millions of poverty-stricken, unarmed and helpless Indians, appealed to us to come forward and sacrifice our lives for their liberation, no honourable Indian could have refused this much to him.

I found a leader and decided to follow him, and for me it was the greatest and the most difficult decision of my life, i.e., of fighting against my kith and kin, who were in the British Indian Army in very large numbers, and whom I was certain, I could never induce to see eye to eye with me.

At the back of my mind was the traditional urge of loyalty to the King. I owed all my education to him. My family and my tribe were one of the privileged classes in India; they were all prosperous and contented. This too we owed to the British Government and I knew that no change in India would bring them any more prosperity. In fact they were likely to suffer by it.

But on the other hand when I thought of the "starving millions" who were being ruthlessly exploited by the British, and were being deliberately kept illiterate and ignorant to make this exploitation easier, I developed a great hatred for the system of rule, in India, which to me it seemed was based on "injustice" and to remove this injustice, I decided to sacrifice my everything - my life, my home, my family and its traditions. I made up my mind to fight even against my brother if he stood in my way, and in the actual fighting that followed in 1944, we actually fought against each other. He was wounded. My cousin and I were fighting each other in Chin Hill, almost daily for two months.

In short the question before me was my King or the country. I decided to be loyal to my country and gave my word of honour to my Netaji that I would sacrifice myself for her sake.

Another thing which has always upset me has been the difference of treatment between an Indian and a British soldier.

I saw with my own eyes that as far as fighting was concerned there was no difference. The Indian soldier stood his ground and fought to the last; why then there should be so much difference in their pay, allowances, food and living conditions, I have never been able to understand. It seemed to me to be extremely unjust.

Secondly, I would also like to point out that the INA was raised, organized, trained and led in the field entirely by the Indians. Comparatively junior officers commanded Divisions and Brigades, V.C.Os, commanded battalions, and under the circumstances they did not do it "too badly". But on the other hand, out of two and a half millions of Indians in the Indian Army, not a single officer was given the command of a Division, and only one Indian was given the command of a Brigade.

There were some very senior and competent Indian officers in the Army, and it appeared to me that the lack of talent could not have been the reason for more Indians not getting higher commands. This also appeared to my mind to be very unjust.

I was a soldier and once I had taken the decision I concentrated on fighting from the first to the last.

In September 1943, Netaji decided to select a picked regiment consisting of the cream of INA and send it into action to form the spearhead of the advance into India. It was known as "Subhas Brigade" and I was selected to command it. The Brigade took part in fighting in the Arakan, Haka-Falam and in the vicinity of Kohima.

In December 1944, I was appointed Commander of No. 1 Division which was at Mandalay then.

In February 1945, when No. 1 Division H.Q. was at Pyinmana, Netaji came there and told me that No.2, a fresh Division of the INA, was moving to the front in the vicinity of Popa, and that unfortunately its Division Commander Col. Aziz Ahmed, had been injured in an air raid. He, therefore, ordered me to take over its command. I did so, but in April 1945 I had to fall back to Pegu, where I was captured by British forces.

In joining the INA, I was prompted only by motives of patriotism. I fought a straightforward and honourable fight on the battlefield, against most overwhelming odds. I was further handicapped by lack of proper medical, transport and ration supplies and for long periods I with my troops had to live on paddy and jungle grass, and even salt was a luxury for us.

During these operations I with my men marched over 3,000 miles in Burma.

From the Japanese we could expect nothing, and they proved more of a hindrance to us than of assistance; and on some occasions I had even to open fire at them. These facts are all in my diaries which are before the court.

I gave good treatment to the British troops that my soldiers captured, and expected to receive the same treatment for my troops when they surrendered as prisoners of war.

Finally, Sir, I wish to bring to your notice, and to the notice of my country that no mercenary, or puppet army could have faced the hardships as the INA did. We fought only for India's Independence.

I do not deny having taken part in the fight but I did so as a member of the regular fighting forces of the Provisional Government of Free India who waged war for the liberation of their motherland according to the rules of civilized warfare. I therefore committed no offence for which I can be tried by a court martial or by any other court.

As for the charge of abetment of murder, even if the facts alleged by prosecution were true, I could not be held responsible to have committed any offence. Mohd. Hussain, who had voluntarily joined the INA and submitted himself to its discipline, admittedly attempted to desert and to induce others to desert at a very critical juncture. If he had succeeded in his attempt he would have carried all information about the force under my command to the enemy which would have meant complete disaster for us. Under the Indian National Army Act and under the Military Codes of all civilized nations the offence attempted to be committed was the most serious and heinous offence, punishment for which was death. It is however, in fact wrong that I sentenced him to death or that he was shot in execution of a sentence passed by me. Mohd. Hussain and his companions were only informally produced before me, there being no crime report drawn up. I only very strongly admonished Mohd. Hussain and told him that he had committed an offence for which he could and should be shot. I however left the matter there and asked the case to be put up again before me or the Regimental Commander who had, in the meanwhile, been vested with the power to try such cases, if the men concerned attempted to misbehave a second time. The case never came up before me again presumably because the contemplated contingency never arose.

Statement of Capt. P.K. Sahgal

I deny being guilty of any of the offences with which I have been charged. I also maintain that my trial before this Court Martial is illegal.

After serving one year's attachment with a British Regiment, I joined the 5th Battalion of the Baluch Regiment in February 1940. In October 1940 the Officer Commanding of my Unit was asked to send a suitable officer to fill the vacancy of a Company Commander in the 2nd Battalion of the same Regiment which was proceeding overseas on active service. I was specially chosen for being posted to the 2nd Battalion.

I disembarked at Singapore with my new Unit on November 11, 1940. A fortnight later we were sent to Kota Bharu in Kelantan State, where we were entrusted with the task of the preparation and manning of beach defences. Major General Murray Lyones, then Commander of Northern Area in Malaya, Major Gen. Barstow, Commander of the 9th Indian Division, Lt. Gen. Heath, the Corps Commander, and Lt. Gen. A.E. Percival, G.O.C., Malaya Command, inspected our work and complimented me on the very remarkable work done by my Company.

During the Malaya campaign, the Company that I commanded distinguished itself in more than one encounter with the Japanese. Although, generally, we were fighting a retreating battle, on occasions we were able to take the offensive and inflict heavy losses on the enemy. On one occasion my Company annihilated a Japanese force approximately 500 strong and captured a large quantity of enemy arms and equipment. This incident was noticed in the Press.

During the night of January 30/31, 1942, we crossed the Johore Bharu Causeway and reached Singapore. Although my Battalion had been in action without a break from the day hostilities started and had suffered heavy casualties and its officers and men were completely exhausted and their morale was low owing to constant withdrawals and intense enemy air activity, they had immediately to undertake the defence of Singapore.

The Japanese landed in Singapore on February 8, 1942, and on February 10, we marched out to counter-attack the enemy and drove them back into the sea in the woodlands area. Unfortunately, the next day we were ordered back to relieve the Australians in the Mandai Hill area. While we were moving along the Mandai Road, the Japanese launched an attack. The Australians abandoned their positions and ran away and the Japanese got possession of the high features on both sides of the road. We were caught on the road and my Company, which was the leading Company of the Battalion, suffered most heavily. My Company Subedar and three other men of the Company H.Qrs. were killed within five minutes.

The Company Headquarters were cut off from the rest of the Company and although the Japanese beckoned my men to go over to them, I managed to reassemble in an hour or so the whole Company except three or four men whom the Australians had taken away with them. The Company was completely separated from the rest of the Battalion and we continued fighting on our own until the afternoon when we managed to rejoin the Battalion. The same night we were withdrawn to Neesoon where we stayed for 24 hours. The Japanese made three or four determined attacks to break through our positions but we did not allow a single Japanese to go through and the enemy lost three medium tanks in the engagement. During the night of February 12/13 we were withdrawn to Bidadari where we eventually surrendered.

As we were withdrawing southwards on the mainland of Malaya, I was often approached by the Indians living in those areas. They all asked me the same question: "You are leaving us behind, what is going to become of us. We contributed all we could for the defence of Malaya and now why do you leave us at the mercy of the enemy? The Chinese and Malayas all hate us. They will loot and plunder our property, disgrace our women and murder us". There was little that I could do, or even say, to help them. The only thing that I could tell them was to trust in God, and to hope for the best. My heart went out in sympathy to them but I felt helpless and ashamed because I was unable to do anything for them.

On February 17, 1942, in a meeting held at the Farar Park in Singapore, Lt. Col. Hunt, as the representative of the British, handed over the Indian Officers and men to the Japanese like a flock of sheep. This came as a great blow to us all. The Indian Army had fought bravely against the heaviest odds, and in return the British High Command had left them completely at the mercy of the Japanese. We felt that the British Government had, on its own, cut off all the bonds that had bound us to the British Crown and relieved us of all obligations to it. The Japanese handed us over to Capt. Mohan Singh who was styled as the G.O.C. of the Indian National Army and we were left free under him to fashion our own destiny. We bon a fide believed that the British Crown having ceased to provide any protection to us could no longer demand allegiance from us.

After formally taking over the Indian Officers and men, Capt. Mohan Singh proclaimed his intention of raising an Indian National Army for the liberation of India. He was acclaimed by all those who were present there and they all raised their hands to show their willingness to join the Army.

When call for volunteers was made by Capt. Mohan Singh, a large numbers of officers and men came forward to enlist. There were however, some who, while equally desirous to see their motherland free from all foreign domination, were skeptic of the intentions of the Japanese in encouraging the formation of the Indian National Army, and I was one of them. I had a feeling that the Japanese only intended to exploit the propaganda value of the proposed Indian National Army but had no desire of helping the cause of Indian freedom. I, therefore, in spite of my most ardent desire to see my country free at the earliest possible moment, refused to volunteer. In May 1942, volunteers were separated from non-volunteers and I with my Battalion was sent to the Tengab Aerodrome Non-volunteer Camp where I stayed as a non-volunteer till the end of August 1942. During this period no pressure of any kind was brought to bear upon me or other officers or men in my camp numbering about 10,000 to volunteer for the INA The rations provided to us were, considering the prevalent circumstances, quite good and medical aid was satisfactory.

In June 1942, I was invited to attend the Bangkok Conference but I declined the invitation. However, during the period between June and the end of August 1942, events of very far reaching importance took place which compelled me to revise my earlier decision to keep out of the Indian National Army. In the first place, the Japanese forces met with the most astounding successes in every theatre of the war, and an attack on India appeared to be imminent. Everyone thought that the Indians would soon be exposed to a Japanese onslaught and even the B.B.C. London sent them messages of sympathy in their coming misfortune. The last Indian drafts that had arrived to reinforce Singapore consisted only of raw recruits and gave one a fair indication of the type of men available for the defence of India. Officers who came to Singapore shortly before its surrender told us that there was no modern equipment available for the army in India. I was told that the soldiers were being trained with wooden rifles and light machine-guns and that the defences of the North Eastern borders of India were almost non-existent. Everyone of us felt convinced that if the Japanese invaded India, there was none to resist their advance. This was a most distressing thought for all of us. In the second place, on August 8, 1942, the Congress Working Committee passed the famous "Quit India" Resolution. Country-wide demonstrations followed the passing of this Resolution. The All India Radio, Delhi, and the B.B.C. drew a curtain over the happenings in India. However, certain secret stations, supposed to be functioning somewhere in India, and the Japanese and other Axis-controlled Radio Stations outside India broadcast freely about these happenings and the measures taken by the Government to suppress the freedom movement. From the details broadcast by these stations a veritable reign of terror, similar to the one that had followed the revolt of 1857 seemed to have set. In view of the complete reticence of the British and the Indian Press and the official broadcasting agency on the subject, we had no reason to doubt the correctness of these broadcasts. Needless to say that they filled us with most terrible anxiety concerning our near and dear ones whom we had left behind and with the bitterest resentment against the British Imperialism which seemed to be bent upon keeping our country under perpetual subjection.

I and those of my friends, with whom I was on intimate terms, every day discussed amongst ourselves the very critical situation then existing in India and the best way in which we could help her. We knew only too well the fate that would be in store for our countrymen—when a new foreign power invaded India. The British Government claimed the sole responsibility for the defence of the country and had with contempt rejected the offer of her own leaders to take charge of and organize such defence. The information we had about the state of the defence in India was by no means encouraging and the most optimist amongst us could not be sure of the ability of the British to stop the Japanese advance. The civilian population could not even think of organizing any resistance and must submit to untold sufferance and hardships. The "scorched earth policy" which the British Government had already decided upon, and even begun to follow, must add very considerably to the disaster. After protracted discussions the only solution that we could think of for our country's problems was the formation of a strong and well-disciplined armed body which should fight for the liberation of India from the existing alien rule, should be able and ready to provide protection to their countymen against any possible molestation by the Japanese, and to resist any attempt by the latter to establish themselves as rulers of the country in place of the British. This being also the avowed object of the Indian National Army, the question that began to agitate the minds of us, who had so far stayed away from that Army was whether it was not our duty to join that Army for securing the freedom of our country—not so much from the British who could hold her no longer but from the Japanese who were bent upon invading India. The protection that the Indian National Army had already been able to give to Indian life, property and honour in Malaya and Burma seemed to furnish another very strong argument in favour of joining it.

For days I passed through a terrible mental struggle. On the one side was my loyalty to my former comrades with whom I had fought shoulder to shoulder and on the other was the urge to save my mother country from the horrors that stared her in the face. After a great deal of careful thought and deliberation I came to the conclusion that I must join the Indian National Army, which must be built up into a stong, well-armed, well equipped and disciplined force, dedicated to the cause of India. Every soldier of the Army must be prepared to make supreme sacrifice for the sake of India and the Army must be prepared to fight even the Japanese if they attempted to harm the Indians or to establish themselves in India.

I did not join the INA through any fear of Japanese ill treatment or from any ulterior or mercenary motives. In September 1942, as an INA Captain, I only received eighty dollars a month, whereas if I had stayed out of the INA. I would have received one hundred and twenty dollars a month.

I joined the INA from purely patriotic motives. I joined it because I wanted freedom for my motherland and was ready to shed my blood for it. Another reason why I joined it was that I wanted to safeguard the honour of Indian women and the lives and property of my unarmed countrymen in Burma, Malaya, and India. I joined the INA for a noble cause and I never stooped to coerce or even to persuade any one to join the INA. The recruitment to the INA to my knowledge was purely voluntary. The evidence given by the prosecution on this point is false.

In any event, I had nothing to do with any of the alleged atrocities and have no knowledge about them. From the very beginning I was convinced that our strength lay in our selfless devotion to our cause and my aim was that our army should be composed of only those who were willingly prepared to shed their blood for Mother India. For this very reason, before proceeding to the front, I explained at great length to the officers and men under my command the noble ideals for which the INA had been raised and I also told them the grave dangers, difficulties and hardships that lay in the way of the fulfilment of those ideals. I warned every man that if he was not willingly prepared to fight and suffer for those ideals he need not proceed to the front. Many who did not consider themselves physically or mentally fit to participate in the operations decided to stay behind. They were not subjected to any force or humiliations nor were they punished in any way. They were all transferred to the Reinforcement Group and left behind in Rangoon. On arrival on the front line, I gave another chance to those who did not wish to continue in the front line to return to the base. Those who took advantage of this offer were returned to Rangoon without being punished.

When I arrived in Popa, as I did not consider it honourable that any man should be kept in the ranks of the Units under my command and made to fight against his wishes, before going into action, I expressly and publicly told all the men under my command that such of them as were desirous of going over to the British could do so at that time provided they left arms behind and went in one organised party whom I assured a safe conduct through our lines.

I count a number of Englishmen and women among my very best friends. Against the English people, I never cherished any enmity. To the officers and men under my command, I had issued explicit instructions that any prisoner of war captured by them, be he of any nationality, was to be treated kindly.

Till the end of November 1944, I was Military Secretary in the Headquarters Supreme Command, INA, and for a time officiated as Assistant Chief of Staff. In December, I was given the command of a Regiment which fought in the Popa area. I took part in this fight as a member of the regularly organized fighting forces of the Independent Provisional Government of Free India which fought according to the rules of civilized warfare for the liberation of my motherland from foreign rule. I claim that in doing so I committed no offence. On the other hand, I have served my country to the best of my ability. I claim further that I am entitled to all the privileges of a prisoner of war. In my Note of April 28, 1945, to the Commander of the British forces to whom I and the Officers and men fighting under my command surrendered (the receipt of which Note is admitted by the Headquarters, Bahadurgarh Area in their letter no. J. 900/50 dated 12/10/45, but which was stated in the letter to be "unavailable") I said quite plainly that we were ready to surrender only as prisoners of war. On receipt of this Note, surrender was accepted without objection to the terms on which we had offered to surrender, and after the surrender we were actually treated as prisoners of war. Had we been told that surrender on the terms offered by us was not acceptable to the British Commander, we were determined to fight on and were in a position to do so because we were nearly six hundred strong, fully armed and equipped and each one of us was prepared to shed the last drop of his blood for the sake of his country.

From February 13 to March 12, 1945, I was officiating as Divisional Commander in the absence of Col. Shah Nawaz Khan. In my capacity as Divisional Commander I had to try on March 6, 1945, four Sepoys—Hari Singh, Duli Chand, Daryao Singh and Dharam Singh—who had been committed for trial by Col. G.S. Dhillon for offences of desertion and attempting to communicate with the enemy, under Sections 35 and 29 (c) of the Indian National Army Act. They were found guilty and were sentenced to death. The sentence was, however, not carried out, the convicts, like many others who were similarly tried and sentenced about that time, having been pardoned on their expressing regret and giving an assurance not to misbehave in future. The fact of the sentence having been passed, was, of course, used for its propaganda value in order to deter others from deserting.

Even, however, if the sentence had been carried out, I could not be charged with the offence of abetment of murder. The four culprits had voluntarily joined the INA and had submitted to its discipline, and had voluntarily and willingly agreed to participate in the coming fight. They, having shamefully deserted while in action and in the face of the enemy, had committed an offence punishable with death under the

Indian National Army Act and under the Military Law all the world over. The information which they sought to convey to the enemy would have meant the complete annihilation of the entire force under my command. The sentence was passed after proper trial in the exercise of authority lawfully vested in me.

Although, the Indian National Army failed to achieve its primary object of liberating India, every one of us has the satisfaction that it fully accomplished its objective of protecting Indian life, property and honour in Malaya, Burma and other parts of South East Asia against all aggressors. The telegrams that I have received, after the commencement of this trial from the President of the Indian Christian Association, Rangoon, and the President of the Burma Indians' Association and which I am attaching to this statement bear ample testimony to this.

TELEGRAMS :- 13.11.45

DLT NIL. R128/13 RANGOON 12 VIRC.

30 LT SAHGAL INA PRISONER

RED FORT DELHI

BURMA INDIAN ASSOCIATION SENDS YOU GREETINGS HOPE YOU WILL BE RELEASED YOU SERVED INDIA AMK PITCHAI PRESIDENT BURMA ASSOCIATION.

NLT NIL 13/13 RANGOON 12 IRC 7 NLT SAHGAL INA PRISONER TRIAL ON NOV. 5 BURMA SYMPATHISES WITH YOU. GOD WILL HELP YOU. YOUR INA SAVED THOUSANDS OF INDIAN LIVES FROM BEING BUTCHERED BY ARMED MEN WHILE THEMSELVES LEFT UNARMED INA SAVED ENTIRE INDIANS FROM ABJECT SLAVERY. TELEGRAPHING VICEROY AND JAWAHARLAL NEHRU.

MISS. S.A. AREN PRESIDENT INDIAN CHRISTIAN ASSOCIATION

56 126 MN STREET KALABASTI.

Statement of Lieut. G.S. Dhillon

My story is a simple one. I was enlisted as a sepoy in the 4th Battalion of the 14th Punjab Regiment on May 29, 1933. In 1936, on the recommendation of Lt. Col. C. Hungerford Jackson, I was selected to do a prospective cadet's course at Kitchner College, Nowgong. Before this I had a long struggle in the ranks, Eventually, I was selected to do a Gentleman Cadet's course at the Indian Military Academy, Dehra Dun.

It was in this institution that I learnt to serve my country above everything else. There I read written in Chetwode Hall in block letters of gold:

THE SAFETY HONOUR AND WELFARE OF
YOUR
COUNTRY

COME FIRST ALWAYS AND EVERY TIME.
THE HONOUR WELFARE AND COMFORT OF
THE
MEN YOU COMMAND COME NEXT.

YOUR OWN EASE COMFORT AND SAFETY
COME
LAST

ALWAYS AND EVERY TIME.

Ever since I read this motto, the sense of duty towards my country and my men has under all circumstances reigned supreme in my thoughts. It was with this motto in front of me that I served my country as an officer in the Indian Army. After joining the 1st Battalion 14th Punjab Regiment as a 2nd Lieut on April 30, 1940, I remained throughout with my Unit, and moved overseas with it. We arrived at Ipoh in Malaya on March 18,1941. Then we went to Sungei Patani. Here I had the privilege of officiating under my C.O. Lt. Col. L.V. Fitzpatrick as Adjutant for about two months. In June 1941, I came back home to do an All Arms Signal course at Army Signal School, Poona.

Just before the outbreak of the war in East Asia, I rejoined my Unit at Jitra on December 5, 1941. During the Malaya campaign I was the Battalion Signal Officer. My Battalion was the foremost unit in Jitra Sector to contact with the Japanese forces. We held them for three days. After a battle at Changlun, as we were withdrawing to Jitra, which was to be our main defensive line, we were surprised by the enemy tanks. The C.O. and most of the officers and men were cut off. On December 12, 1941, after a day of roaming about I managed to contact Capt. Habib-ul-Rahman who was also in a similar plight. We managed to collect about 80 men of different units including the British. The main road being in the Japanese occupation, we had to cut our way through jungles and paddy fields.

On the 13th early in the morning, we were attacked by the enemy and most of the men were cut off except about 26 of our own Unit. During the day, however, we managed to gather some more stragglers and in the evening when we were about two miles from Alor Star we were informed by some civilians that Jitra and Alor Star had fallen. We could not believe this and Habib instructed me to follow him by bounds while he with a small party proceeded towards Alor Star to find out the situation for himself. We had hardly advanced a mile when we saw certain people running away from the town. They too told us about the fall of Alor Star and asked us to withdraw. We did so, and on the 14th evening sailed in small coastal boats for Penang from Kuala Kedah. On arrival at Penang we with our party reported at 3 M.R.C. Within 15 minutes of our arrival we were ordered to leave Penang. On the 16th morning we arrived at Nibong Tibal, about 26 miles from Penang on the main land. Here Habib and myself were given the command of a Company each and were ordered to defend two bridges. I was placed in command of a Gurkha Company formed out of the M.R. C. and a detachment of the 1st Bahawalpur Infantry. I remained in position until all our troops north of that point had withdrawn. Eventually, on December 19, we were ordered to withdraw. We fell back to Taiping and then to Ipoh, where I rejoined the remnants of my Battalion.

I had not had a single whole meal ever since the war had started on December 8. Rest was out of question during such a retreat. I had an attack of fever and was admitted into a hospital and then evacuated to Singapore. On my discharge from the hospital I reported for duty at 7 M.R.C. I tried to rejoin my Unit but red tapism caused so much delay that by the time arrangements were made for my conveyance, the battle of Singapore had begun. During my stay with 7 M.R.C., I officiated as the Indian Wing Commander and Adjutant. The situation became such that the Commandant of 7 M.R.C. wanted my presence in order to control the Indian troops who were getting dissatisfied due to discriminatory treatment. The Commandant said that he had great confidence in my way of handling the troops.

By February 11, 1942. we began hearing rumours that Singapore was going to surrender. I could not believe it. While evacuating Bidadari Camp where 7 M.R.C. was stationed, on the way to town I saw thousands of Indians gathered in an open space. They had hoisted many Indian National Flags. I pointed this out to the British Colonel who was with me. He said, "I don't blame them. If we cannot defend them they have to look after themselves".

On the 13th evening we were told officially that 500 of our aeroplanes would arrive by the 15th morning and that the Americans were going to land at Penang and come down south. But they never did. On the l5th at about 22.00 hours, the C.O. called for me and told me that Singapore had surrendered unconditionally. This came to me as a great shock. With a heavy heart and tears in my eyes I dropped my revolver, and ordered my men to collect their arms. A still bigger shock came when the C.O. told me that the Indians would march off to Farrar Park and the British to Changi. At Farrar Park, Lt. Col. Hunt, representing the British Supreme Command, handed us over to Major I. Fujiwara, a representative of the Japanese Army who in turn handed us over to Capt. Mohan Singh who was introduced to us as G.O.C. Indian National Army. I felt like one deserted by the British in a state of utter and tragic helplessness.

Mohan Singh expressed his intention of raising an Indian National Army for the liberation of India. His declaration was received with great enthusiasm and a feeling of hope and joy by all of us present at Farrar Park.

I had known Mohan Singh before as we belonged to the same Unit. He was one of my dearest friends and I had confidence in him. However, it was after a long mental struggle that I could persuade myself to accept him as G.O.C. With my knowledge of the recent events and of the state of Eastern defences of India, I felt convinced that Singapore, the biggest naval base in the world, having surrendered so quickly, there was no possibility of the British being able to defend or hold India against Japanese invasion.

Mohan Singh's task was a hard one. He had never even imagined that one day he would have to handle 75,000 officers and men under circumstances unprecedented in the history of the world. Discipline had to be maintained amongst a demoralized, defeated and disappointed Army. Freedom of political thought had to be given as the INA was entirely based on a voluntary basis. On top of all this, lives of officers and men suspected by the Japanese had to be saved. Our civilian nationals had to be protected against all sorts of dangers. And all this had to be done consistently with India's national honour and laws of humanity. And in doing all this he had constantly to deal with highly suspicious people like the Japanese.

I had seen how people in Malaya had suffered as a result of the Japanese invasion in consequence of the utter lack of preparation on the part of the British Government which had undertaken responsibility for her defence and I shuddered to think of the plight of my own countrymen on invasion of India. It was at this time that I got to realize the full significance of the havoc done to my unfortunate country by the one and a half century of the British rule. While the British had exploited all our material resources for their own benefit and had freely drawn upon our manpower to fight their own imperialistic wars, they had not only done nothing to prepare us for the defence of our motherland in case of need but had, in order to keep us in bondage for all time to come, completely emasculated us. I felt that if India had been free and in a position to look after her own defences no aggressor could have thought of crossing her borders. In the Indian National Army proposed to be organized by Mohan Singh I saw a new hope for India. I felt that if a strong and willing National Army could be raised at that juncture, it could not only liberate India from foreign rule but could also resist the Japanese in case they should try to go back upon their word and instead of helping us to win our freedom, should seek to exploit our country for their own purpose. Such an army could also give protection to our Indian brethren in the Far East against aggression by people belonging to other nationalities. Mother India seemed to be calling me and I decided to respond to her call and threw in my lot with Mohan Singh.

I co-operated with Mohan Singh in the organization of the Indian National Army till June 29, 1942, when I became very ill and had to go to hospital. On being discharged from the hospital on October 2, 1942, I was sent to Penang for reasons of health. I was still not quite well and fit for work. I returned from Penang about the time when very sharp differences had arisen between Mohan Singh and the Japanese culminating in the arrest of the former and dissolution of the INA by him. On receiving the assurance that Netaji Subhas Chandra Bose would come to lead the movement I decided to continue in the second INA.

Recruitment to the INA at all times was on a purely voluntary basis. To my knowledge no coercion or force was ever used to induce any prisoner of war to join the INA. In fact, use of force or coercion for such purpose was wholly unnecessary because we always had a very large member of surplus volunteers whom we were unable to arm or put under training for want of equipment. The evidence given by some of the prosecution witnesses that prisoners of war were sent to Concentration or Detention Camps to coerce them into volunteering is absolutely false. There was no Concentration Camp in existence at all. There was a Detention Camp to which only persons found guilty of indisicipline or other offences were sent by way of punishment. That camp had, however, nothing to do in any shape or form, with enlistment in the INA. On the contrary, persons confined in the Detention Camp were not accepted as volunteers even if they offered to do so, because detention in that camp for any period indicated some defect of character which was a disqualification for membership of the INA. These witnesses have told false and distorted tales to save their own skin or to curry favour with the Government. In all lectures delivered by me I warned my audience in the clearest possible terms that they should volunteer only if they loved their country and were willing and able to bear all kinds of hardships and sufferings in her cause. At the time of going into action I again warned the men under my command that we had to fight against an enemy much better equipped and far superior in men and materials and that anybody who, either for want of courage or otherwise, did not wish to go to the front need not do so and could, if he so desired, be sent back to the rear areas. Some of the officers and men did show their unwillingness and about 200 such men were sent back to Rangoon before my Regiment left Myingyan. This option I gave to my command at every stage of the campaign and it was due to this particular reason that although for weeks I stayed within two miles of the enemy lines yet none of my men ever went and reported my location to the Allies.

Many a time I had to go without water for 20 to 30 hours and without food for two or three days. If as a Brigade Commander I had to undergo these hardships, my men must have suffered much more and yet they accompanied me. No men who had joined under duress or coercion could have done so.

It is true that I committed four men for trial on charges of desertion and attempting to communicate with the enemy. It is however quite untrue that those men were shot at my instance or under my orders. On the day and at the time they are said to have been shot I was confined to bed and unable to move. In fact, the sentences of death passed on these men were subsequently remitted by the Divisional Commander and were never executed.

Whatever I did, I did as the member of a regularly organized force fighting under the Provisional Government of Free India and am, therefore, not liable to be charged with or tried under the Indian Army Act or the criminal law of India for any offence on account of any act done by me in the discharge of my duties as a member of such force. I am further advised that in point of law my trial by the court martial is illegal. I joined the INA with the best and purest of motives. As a member of the INA, I was able to help a number of prisoners of war with money and materials. The INA was able to protect life, property and honour of the Indians residing in the Far East. It saved the lives of many civilians and prisoners of war who had been sentenced to death by the Japanese on different charges. I successfully persuaded the Japanese to refrain from bombing civilians and their properties in Indian towns. The Indians in the Far East showed their appreciation of the services rendered to them by the INA by contributing crores of rupees to the funds of the Provisional Government.

I respectfully maintain that the INA rendered distinguished services to two and a half millions of Indians who owed allegiance to the New Provisional Government of Free India and was actuated by the most patriotic motives.

Defence Witnesses

Members of the Defence Counsel interviewed more than a hundred persons and Shri Desai chose ten out of them to put before the Court. They were high rank dignitaries.

Mr. Teruo Hachiya was the Japanese Minister accredited to the Provisional Government of Azad Hind. His statement showed how independent was Netaji in running the affairs of the Azad Hind Government. Mr. Hachiya disclosed that when he reported at Rangoon Netaji refused to see him because he did not bring his credentials. Hachiya was obliged to send a telegraphic message to Tokyo and his Government despatched credentials duly signed by the Emperor of Japan.

Mr. Hachiya's statement was corroborated by Mr. Renzo Z O Sawada who was Vice Minister of Foreign Affairs from October, 1944 to May, 1945. Cross-examined by Prosecution Counsel, Mr. Sawada gave full details of the Hachiya episode.

Mr. Saburo Ohta who belonged to the Japanese Foreign office stated what he knew about the Provisional Government of Free India. He gave details of its Proclamation and testified statements and documents pertaining to the occasion of its establishment.

Mr. Shunichi Matsumato, Vice Minister for Foreign Affairs from November 1942 to October 1944 deposed about the formation and the recognition and statements of various Governments.

Major General Tudashi Katakura who had planned the Imphal Campaign on the orders of the Southern Army Commander, General Count Terauchi gave details of the INA role during the Campaign. He gave testimony that there were two separate proclamations, one signed by Netaji and other signed by Lt. General Kawabe. The Japanese proclamation said that they were to fight the British and not the Indians and that whatever booty and liberated territory they obtained would be handed over to the Provisional Government of Free India. Netaji's proclamation declared that we were fighting for the Independence of India and all the territory captured by the Japanese would be handed over to the Indians.

General Katakura gave details of the INA units which took part in the Imphal Campaign under No. 1 Division commanded by Colonel (later Maj. Gen.) Mohammed Zaman Kiani. To Prosecution's cross-examination Katakura replied in a deliberate manner in an authentic way. Asked about the status of the INA he deposed that the INA was an independent army as an ally with equal status with the Japanese Imperial Army based on reciprocal relationship.

I appreciate the good offices of the British Government for bringing the Japanese VIPs from Japan and other places. At the same time I feel sad that we were unable to offer them Indian hospitality. These Japanese, about eleven in number including Lieut. General 1. Fujiwara were kept as prisoners under tents in the Red Fort for about 6 months. I remain under a debt of gratitude to them for ever.

From the Indian side, Desaiji examined two ministers of Azad Hind Government, Maj. Gen. Loganathan who was the Administrator of Andaman and Nicobar Islands, Shri S.A. Ayer, Minister for Propaganda, Shri Dina Nath a Director of Azad Hind Bank, Rangoon and Shri Shiv Singh who had an assignment at Ziawadi Estate handed over by Shri Parmanand to the Provisional Government of Azad Hind. These dignatories gave testimony to the working of the Azad Hind Government, its various organizations, its assets, and problems.

Shri Dina Nath disclosed that at the end of the war when the British sealed the Azad Hind Bank, INA had a credit balance of 4 lakhs of rupees. Ziawadi Estate had an area of 50 miles square. There was a sugar factory fed by its own sugarcane fields. The Estate provided accommodation to various establishments of the I.I.L., the I.N.A and the Azad Hind Dal.

Shri S.A. Ayer among many other disclosures stated the functioning of four Azad Hind Radio stations. Those were at Singapore, Saigon, Bangkok and at Rangoon. He told the Court that Netaji arranged and offered to the British Government of India a gift of ten thousand tons of rice for the relief of famine stricken Bengal if the British Government would take the responsibility of safe conduct of our ships under the Red Cross flag. There was no response from the British side.

Colonel Raja Mohammed Arshad was our last defence witness. Col. Arshad had been G-1 of No. 1 Division under Col. Zaman Kiani. Arshad was the senior-most Staff Officer from the INA side in Imphal

Campaign. He was in a position to reply to all questions put by the defence as well as the prosecution. He earned Court's appreciation because of his concise, direct and authentic way of giving evidence. Shri Desai was so impressed that while dealing with the question of allegiance in his Defence Address he quoted Col. Arshad's sentence, "We believed that the only allegiance we owe is allegiance to our country."

VVIPs at the Trial

Besides the members of the Defence Counsel which included some of the top ranking personalities of India, the prominent leaders who attended the opening day of the trial were: Sarojini Naidu, Liaqat Ali Khan, the General Secretary of the All India Muslim League and later the first Prime Minister of Pakistan, and Master Tara Singh, the undisputed leader of the Sikhs. Master Tara Singh wanted to meet me personally but the authorities could not oblige him. He however was allowed to send his trusted secretary, Sardar Ajit Singh Sarhadi to see me alone. The meeting between Sarhadi and me took place in the Accused Marshalling Room. Sarhadi conveyed Masterji's blessings to me. He told me that Masterji was disappointed to see me without beard but appreciated that at least I did wear the Kara—an iron bangle, one of the five symbols of Sikhism. I was touched by Master Tara Singh's magnanimity in sending me his blessings rising above the religious confines.

Another Dilemma

It was during the days of the trial that while addressing a Women's Conference in Calcutta, the Nightingale of India, as Sarojini Naidu was called, declared in her characteristic poetic style, "If mothers could select sons, I would have chosen these three, Shah Nawaz, Sahgal and Dhillon". When I read her statement in a newspaper, I was filled with pride. But it soon ebbed away as I thought that Mother Sarojini was an acknowledged world figure. How would my mother feel when instead of me, my body were delivered to her? Undoubtedly she would rend the sky with beating of her breast and wailing, "*Vey mere putra tenoo kidhar diaan puthiaan wag gayaan?*" (O my son what made you do the wrong?)

I pondered over the idea increasingly. Would my supreme

sacrifice for a cause as the freedom of my motherland go unrecognized and unblessed by my own mother ? In spite of an apparent care for the devil attitude, deep down in me I was a nervous wreck. I feared to face my mother lest she might cry on meeting me. That was why I withheld meeting my mother so long. Basant was the only one to whom I could confide my weakness.

During the trial, Basant resided at the house of Dr. Jiwan Lal Maleri of Nabha, in Darya Ganj. The doctor and his wife had adopted Basant as their daughter. In spite of having a big family of their own, their doors were always open to Basant and all our relatives who came to see me. Maleris' generous hospitality under those circumstances when the C.I.D. were on the lookout to watch and note our sympathizers was admirable. I remain eternally indebted to Maleris.

Their house was about two kilometres away from the Red Fort. Basant used to make to the Fort on a push-bike. Her pictures often appeared in the newspapers and magazines. People recognized her. She was warmly and respectfully cheered by crowds on her way up and down to the Fort. By her speeches and the way she conducted herself Basant attained a status of prominence in her own right. It was under those circumstances that Basant went to Battichak, our village to bring my mother to see me.

While on the way to Delhi, the train was overcrowded but the passengers recognized Basant and offered her an accommodation. Basant thanked them and said, "Please do not worry about me. I have Colonel Sahib's mother with me. I need some room for *Maaji*". In no time passengers vacated a berth exclusively for mother and started shouting:

Lal Qila se aai awaz

Sahgal Dhillon Shah Nawaz

Mata Dhillon Zindabad

Netaji Zindabad

Someone ran to fetch a garland of roses for mother. On arrival at Delhi, Basant took mother to Shri Gurudwara Sis Gunj in Chandni Chowk. There too mother was received as a VVIP and offered Saropa, traditional mark of recognition by the Sikhs. The old lady was accorded standing ovation wherever she went, with slogans of "Dhillon, Sahgal, Shah Nawaz!" At the residence of Dr. Maleri, mother was treated as a guest of honour where crowds specially came to pay respect to her. Mother would have seriously pondered over what her son had done that entitled her to such a spontaneous flow of goodwill and affection wherever she went.

I Meet My Mother

The much dreaded event of my imagination took place in the evening of a day in the second week of December 1945. It turned out to be one of the most pleasant and invigorating experience of my life. As we three, Shah Nawaz, Sahgal and I walked into the Visitor's Enclosure where my mother and Basant stood waiting for us, mother hugged Shah Nawaz and Sahgal, kissed them on their foreheads and blessed them in prayerful words.

As they moved to meet their folks, I moved up. As I touched my mother's feet, I felt having been lifted up by her as she hugged me. Her hands moved all over my body from head to foot as if she wanted to feel and ascertain that I was her own Bakhshi all intact, safe and sound. I felt, I was a tiny little chick overwhelmed and enveloped in her sheltering wings. It was a strange feeling which I feel even today (1996) but cannot describe. It was a pure bliss.

We sat down on a nearby bench. I was speechless. Ma said, *"Put dhan hain toon. Toon meri kukh saphal kiti ai. Main taan ik pind di ruree da dher saan. Menoon ki pataa see ke mere tey terey jeyaa lal peyaa hoya hai. Put toon bara naam raushan kita ai. Dhan hain toon jine meri kukh saphal kiti ai"*. (Son blessed are you. You have blessed my womb. I was just a dunghill in a village. Little did I know that a gem like you were resting on me. Blessed are you. You have earned a great name and glorified my womb). Mother's words made me dumb. Mother continued, "Son you need not fear. The British Government cannot harm you. *"Government tuhada val vi vinga nahin kar sakdi. Put angrezaan ne tuhade bare bande lal qiley vich mare. Par hun pura desh tuhade pichhey hai. Bilkul fikar na karna."* (The Government cannot harm even a hair on your body. The British did kill many of your (INA) men in the Lal Qila. But now the whole country is supporting you. You need not fear anything, my son).

Mother's words made me all the more emotional. On the day father met me, he had asked me, "I do not have a strong heart like yours. From where did you get all that strong heart"? During my interview with mother, I got the answer, "I had my mother's heart" and tears rolled down from my eyes. That was the speechless expression of my joy. As my mother moved the soft corner of her *chunni* (head cover) to wipe off my tears, I burst out crying and said *"Maan main aj bara Khush haan"*- (Maa I am very happy today). Perhaps Basant felt happier. Dumb founded and overwhelmed I went away to my cage. I did not even utter, "Thank you Basant".

Defence Address

In his defence address Shri Bhulabhai Desai took note of the evidence bearing on the two charges of waging war against the King and murder or abetment of murder in respect of the deserters for which we three accused had been arraigned before the Court. In his matchless style, Desai submitted that there was only one charge before the court, that of waging war; charge of murder could not stand the legal scrutiny and the test of cross-examination.

Appearing in his best as a lawyer gifted with a penetrating vision. undisputed grasp of facts, thorough comprehension of law, oratorical skill and a deep commitment to the national cause, Shri Desai addressed the court as a teacher addresses a class. He said :

"There are one or two matters which I am bound to mention to the Court before I come to the actual facts of the case. This case raises issues which are not of the normal type which a Court Martial is called upon to decide, because most, if not all, of such cases are generally cases of individual dereliction of duty or individual offences. Here is a case in which, I venture to say and the evidence supports it that it is not at all a case of what you might call three individuals waging war against the King. The evidence amply bears out the fact that these men charged before you were a part of an organized army which waged war against the King even according to the Prosecution. Therefore the case before the Court is not a personal case of any kind or sort. The honour and the law of the Indian National Army are on trial before this Court.

"WHAT IS NOW ON TRIAL BEFORE THE COURT IS THE

RIGHT TO WAGE WAR WITH IMMUNITY ON THE PART OF A SUBJECT RACE FOR THEIR LIBERATION. I shall be able to cite authorities on International law that A NATION OR A PART OF A NATION DOES REACH A STAGE WHERE IT IS ENTITLED TO WAGE WAR FOR ITS LIBERATION, and I shall be able to prove that point to your Honour's satisfaction.

"There is another thing I wish to say, and I say it with a certain degree of earnestness. This case has naturally aroused a considerable amount of public interest. It is not for me to say whether it is right or not but the fact remains that it is so, and opinions have been expressed from the point of view of the public and from the point of view of what I might call 'official sources' beginning with the Viceroy of India. You, Sirs, having sworn to do justice to these men on the evidence before you, will, I have not the smallest doubt, come to your own decision guided by your conscience and entirely unaffected by opinions for or against them. For in all trials of this kind and in a few of them I have had the honour to be engaged it is very difficult for the human mind to maintain that detachment which justice requires. In the case of Juries I have had to caution them against the use or abuse of the effect of public expressions of opinions on matters which it is for them to decide. In this case what I wish to say is this. Having studied the rules which guide the proceedings before this Court I find that you, Sirs, are the judges both of law and of fact. I am aware that the Judge-Advocate who is your advisor will take care to do justice to everything that myself or my learned friend on the other side will place before you on questions of law and fact, and while you will very seriously regard his advice in the end, the final decision is your privilege and your responsibility. Therefore what I might have done in another place I do not do before you and that is, I cannot say that I will address the Judge on law and the Jury on the facts. There it is an easier process because I must confess that before a trained Judge it is easier to deal with the question of law than before a tribunal of this character. At the same time I have this consolation that sometimes if the law is plain as I submit it is in this case, it will probably be much easier, appealing to commonsense, to establish the law on which I rely, and I desire to ask your indulgence and your attention in the somewhat difficult task which I am undertaking.

"My next submission to the Court is that I desire, as far as possible, to state categorically the conclusions of fact which are established in this case. Having done that I will proceed to deal with the law applicable to them. In dealing with any single item, should any doubt arise in the Court's mind, I trust that you will be pleased to tell me, so that, if it is necessary, I will go into the details of evidence, because as at present advised, I do not desire, unless there is a real doubt about it, to weary you with reading over 250 pages of evidence and about 150 pages of exhibits, which are before the Court. A few important ones I will certainly read where necessary. Having regard to the attention which the court has paid to the evidence as it was recorded. I will avoid reading them in extenso."

As a preamble to the main thrust of his arguments, Shri Desai enumerated the important events in its proper sequence which formed the history of the case—the declaration of war by Japan against Britain and America (December 1941), the surrender of the British Indian forces at Singapore (15-17 February at Farrar Park); the formation of the first Indian National Army (September 1942), its dissolution and the arrest of General Mohan Singh (December 1942); the arrival of Netaji Subhas Chandra Bose in Singapore (July 1943); the Proclamation of the Provisional Government of Free India (October 1943); the Declaration of war by the Provisional Government on Great Britain and America; the movement of this Government from Singapore to Rangoon; the movement of the INA from Burma into the territories of India; and the retreat of that Army.

Referring to the first conclusion of facts justified by evidence, Shri Desai asked the Court to accept that the Provisional Government of Free India was formally established and proclaimed, that it was an organized Government with the Indian Independence League as its executive organ. Refuting forcefully the remarks of the Prosecution Counsel who facetiously called it 'a set of rebels' or 'a desultory sort of crowd of no consequence', Shri Desai quoted exhibits that in Malaya alone 230,000 persons actually took the Oath of Allegiance to the Azad Hind Government; that this Government was duly recognized by nine sovereign states including the three Axis powers. It was the recognition that established statehood, argued Shri Desai.

Dealing with the issue whether our Government had attained that degree of Statehood which gave it the power to declare war, Shri Desai observed, "Once you have a state which can and is entitled to declare war, the war itself is its own justification. There is no question that only two independent states have a right to declare war." He emphasized that any act done in the prosecution of a war is justified by the mere fact of the war itself. In support of this statement Shri Desai cited quotations after quotations from books of international law on the question of right to make war.

Shri Desai quoted from Wheaton's *International Law,* 1945 Edition, Vol. II, page 98, which states "War in the absence of any international authority competent to suppress effectively international wrongs, has always been legal by international law."

Shri Desai went on to quote many authorities from seventeenth century to date (1945) and he deduced that international law in the question of war was not static. It had grown from time to time with the progress of civilization. "Therefore the question was, once it comes to war, there is no question of justification. Now in the global war a great many events have occurred of which international conscience takes note."

Referring to certain statements by Mr. Winston Churchill and Mr. Eden, Shri Desai said, "The position now is that international law has reached this stage that if liberty and democracy are to have any meaning all over the world, and not merely just for a part of it, and this is not politics, it is law that any war made for the purpose of liberating oneself from foreign yoke is completely justified by modern international law. And it will be travesty of justice if we were to be told as the result of any decision arrived at here or otherwise, that the Indian may go as soldier and fight for the freedom of England against Germany, for England against Italy, for England against Japan, and yet a stage may not be reached when a free Indian State may not wish to free itself from any country, including England itself. We maintain that this particular war, according to the decisions, requires no justification. If one State can declare war, then the other State can also declare war and fight, and anything done in its due prosecution has no civil consequences of any kind. In other words, not one of these men now charged before you can be called upon to account for his actions. We can show that they have done nothing outside the scope of the due prosecution of war on a civilized basis. That is an emphasis which I always wish to put. It is not alleged against these men that there was any question about the acts with which they are charged. They were acts carried out in due prosecution of the war, under what you may call civilized rules. Therefore the question before the Court is a very narrow one."

Shri Desai remarked, "There was at one time the old idea that you had to be an independent State or a sovereign State in order to be able to declare war. Of course that created a vicious circle, that a subject race will remain in perpetuity a subject race. It can never make a legitimate war for the purpose of liberating itself. Hence modern international law has now recognized the right of subject races which are not for the time being or at the moment independent, to be so organized, and if they are organized and fight an organized war through an organized army, the individual members of that army are unanswerable before any municipal court for what was done in due prosecution of that war.

"It seems to be now settled that it is unnecessary in order to constitute a war that both parties should be acknowledged as independent nations or sovereign states. A war may certainly exist between a State and its suzerain as the Boer War. May I appeal to this Court and all of you who are familiar with British history what about Charles I and his death? What about the Magna Charta? What about James II? It is all recorded history. In other words, you do reach a stage where the organization, call it rebel if you like, call it insurgent; insurgents or rebels may reach a stage of organization for the purpose of liberating themselves when what they do after declaring war is subject to the laws of war.

"A war may certainly exist between a State and a suzerain as in the Boer War. Moreover, a war may exist where one of the belligerents claims sovereign rights as against the other, whether in a federal or a unitary State. . . . .

"But it is quite an unnecessary requisite. If even a subject race finds itself in a position where its organization is able to declare war, then acts done by the armies on either side come under this. I put a very simple question; What about the acts of those who fought on the side of the British in this war? They killed lots of people. Would they be put up before this Court under Section 302? Most amazing ! It was a properly fought war, no doubt as in other wars one or the other side lost, and the fact that a war is lost has no effect on the immunity from the consequences in acts done in due prosecution of the war."

After giving many examples from the history of various countries Shri Desai quoted, "As President Grant said in his message of June 13, 1870: The question of belligerency is one of fact not to be decided by sympathies for or prejudices against either part. The relations between the parent State and insurgents must amount, in fact, to war in the sense of international law. I call upon you to do the same. It is not a question of prejudice; it is not a question of prestige or what happens to the Army, to this or the other person. Please remember that you are here as judges; you are not politicians, I agree, and I do not want you to be such. If you find that there is a de facto political organization sufficient in numbers, sufficient in character and sufficient in resources to constitute itself capable of declaring and making war with an organized army, your verdict must be in favour of these men no more and no less than the verdict on your own men for killing others, of which act you are justly proud.

"That is the position in law.

"Then I wish to call attention to another book on International Law, an accepted book and what is more it is borne out by all the earlier cases in which war was waged by what you may call insurgents against their own sovereign, if you must use that expression. This book is by Lawrence, page 309. The whole question before the Court under this particular head is whether or not there was a properly declared war in prosecution of which the accused before you did the acts which they did. And if they did that in due prosecution of that war, then there can be no question of any civil offence, as I think all of you in your own person will easily realize. I am not obliged in my civil life to kill anybody except on pain of conviction, but you are."

Shri Desai felt grateful to the Prosecution for having spared him the necessity to prove the proposition that the aforesaid state had an army which was properly organised, having its own distinctive badges and emblems, functioning under regularly appointed officers. The documents exhibited in the Court and the cross-examination of the witnesses clearly established that the Indian National Army was regulated by an Indian National Army Act.

Continuing his arguments, Shri Desai explained that the Indian National Army was formed with two purposes. The main purpose was securing the liberation of India. The other object was the protection of the lives, the honour and the property of the Indian inhabitants of Burma, Malaya and other Asian countries. The evidence tendered by the witnesses had proved the two objectives for which the I.N.A was formed. As was evident from the record, the Indian State had its own Azad Hind Bank. It had also a Civil and Army Gazette of its own.

"It was, thus, the formation and functioning of the Free Government of India which entitled it to make war. The prosecution of the war was outside the pale of municipal law or the Indian Penal Code", said Shri Desai.

The next issue taken up by Shri Desai was the question of allegiance which he held was closely linked with the right and freedom of the people to liberate their own country which was recognized among the civilized community of the world. Shri Desai explained that when an organized force was fighting under an organized government for its freedom, they were entitled to fight. He cited in this context the statement of Colonel Arshad: "We believed that the only allegiance we owe is allegiance to our country." Delving deep into the evidence tendered by the witnesses Shri Desai tried to convince the Court that the Indian National Army was an independent and a voluntary army which owed its allegiance to India.

Dealing with the charge of murder pertaining to four persons alleged to have been shot on one occasion and another subsequently, and the evidence produced thereof, Bullabhai Desai pointed out the absence of the crime report, any other documents bearing on the case or a casuality report, in the latter case. Referring to the evidence purporting that I had signed the crime report and watched the sentence carried on the four persons, who had deserted to and communicated with the enemy, Shri Desai produced an exhibit to show that I was in a state of complete collapse of health. Shri Desai argued that though the order had been passed, the execution of the sentence was not proved. In view of the failure of the Prosecution to prove the actual execution of the sentence, our Counsel stressed that we, the three accused, were entitled to the benefit of doubt.

The evidence tendered by the Prosecution to the effect that I was physically present at the time of shooting, Shri Desai pointed out, that I was suffering from grievous infirmities. The state of my health that day could not be disregarded or ignored. Moreover, there was no identification of the persons alleged to have been shot with the persons mentioned in the crime report. Shri Desai made a submission that the prosecution had entirely failed to prove the charges of murder and abetment of murder. His alternative submission was, assuming that the Court agreed with in that this was done in due course of the execution of the duty of an officer in the INA governed by its own code, there was no question of any liability.

Relying on the Indian Army Act that "A civil offence means an offence which, if committed in British India, would be trailed by a Criminal Court," Shri Desai critically and analytically interpreted and examined the phrase "trailed by a Criminal Court" and observed that the Criminal Procedure Court was not competent to try the offences and that the joint trial of the two sets of offences was completely illegal. He was emphatic that no rule would allow any court to charge people collectively in one trial unless they had committed all the offences collectively.

Summing up his extempore Defence Address that went on for two full days, Shri Desai submitted that here was a case of men as part of a regular organized army, accepted as such by their opponents, fighting a war under the directions of a regularly formed Government. As such, he contended, that we the accused were subject to the ordinary laws of war and were entitled to all the rights and immunities of belligerents. Secondly, the question of allegiance was irrelevant to the issue. Thirdly, the Indian National Army was a voluntary organization. The complaint of torture following conscription was not upheld by the evidence recorded. Fourthly, the charges of murder could not be proved.

Fifthly, Shri Desai argued, there was an organized Government enjoying allegiance of Indians settled in the Far East which was recognized and it was by this Government that war was declared and the Indian National Army fought this campaign. Sixthly, the Indian National Army was governed by a Code which was substantially the same as the Indian Army Act. The question of alleged atrocities for getting enrollment to the INA was not true. Shri Desai pointed that we, the three accused, were neither charged with atrocities nor had we anything to do with the crime. Seventhly, the execution of the sentence regarding the alleged charge of murder and abetment had not been proved. Lastly, the trial was wholly illegal.

Shri Desai closed his Address with a request that he should be given another chance to speak in case the Counsel for the prosecution raised any new point that had not been hitherto covered. The plea was not granted. Shri Desai clinched the issue in his characteristic clarity and frankness: "If my friend thinks that he is supporting the cause of justice by saying that I cannot reply to a new matter in the case is law, that is a new law. Unless he is prepared to submit to this restriction, I submit the law lays on him the duty merely to reply to what I have said. I have nothing more to say, justice or no justice. I hope my friend cites nothing that is not strictly relevant to what I have said."

Prosecution Address

In his second Prosecution Address read out in the Court on December 22, 1945, the Advocate-General, Sir Naushirwan Engineer sought to rebut the arguments presented earlier to the Court by Shri Desai. He reiterated his point that we, the three accused, joined the INA immediately after the fall of Singapore and tried to make other prisoners of war forsake their allegiance to the Crown and that we had fought against the forces of His Majesty the King. Atrocities were committed, Sir Naushirwan contended, openly and notoriously on those men and officers of the Indian Army who had refused to join the INA. There was ample evidence to establish, the Prosecution Counsel continued, the fact that we, the three accused, held out veiled threats of tortures, etc. to the prisoners as an inducement to join the INA.

Sir Naushirwan argued that international law did not come into the case regarding the jurisdiction of the Court or the Law to be administered by it. It was his contention that the Court was duly constituted under the Indian Army Act to try the accused for offences under the Indian Army Act and the Indian Penal Code. Commenting on the plea of Mr. Desai regarding the recognition of the Provisional Government of Free India by Japan and her Allies, the Prosecution Counsel pointed out that the recognition of Japan was for its own object of winning the war. It was Japan, he suggested, who made arrangements with Germany to bring Subhas Chandra Bose to Malaya. Sir Naushirwan held that it was also misleading to suggest that the liberated territories were administered by the Provisional Government as Japan had never ceded the Andaman and Nicobar Islands or any other territory to the Provisional Government.

Disagreeing with the Defence Counsel that there was only one charge, that of waging the war, as the second charge of murder was a part of it, the Prosecution Counsel asserted that the charge of murder was distinct and separate. Waging a war does mean fighting and killing the opposing army but it does not necessarily mean killing a man on the same side. He further argued that the Provisional Government of Free India was itself an illegal body and the formation of that body was in itself an offence against the State. Neither that body nor any tribunal constituted under it nor any order or authority derived from such a body could be recognized by the Court. In conclusion, the Prosecution Counsel submitted that all the charges against all three of us stood proved beyond any reasonable doubt and that there was no defence in law to the charges against the accused.

Judge-Advocate's Summing Up

In his summing up tendered before the court on December 29, 1945, Col. F.C.A. Kerin, the Judge-Advocate suggested that the finding of the Court should be based only on the evidence placed before it, together with unsworn statements of the accused, excluding all extraneous reports and opinions. Raising a preliminary objection to the plea made by Shri Desai, the Defence Counsel, regarding the jurisdiction of the court, Col. Kerin remarked that the issue should have been raised at the commencement of the trial. It was, however, his considered opinion that the court was legally constituted and its jurisdiction was valid and that the question of the applicability of the

International Law was not relevant to the case. Col. Kerin also held that the offence of waging war was an offence against the duty of allegiance to the State.

I have in the foregoing pages produced only the summaries of addresses of the Defence, the Prosecution and the summing up by the Judge-Advocate. All these addresses were at length, in detail and relevant to the point, delivered in an atmosphere of rapt attention from all sides. Even as an accused, while listening to Shri Desai I could not help telling myself, "O boy aren't you lucky to have got such an opportunity to listen to such a masterly speech?" I confess, I felt for Sir Naushirwan for having an adversary of Shri Desai's calibre to oppose under the circumstances when the whole of the country was for us. His was an unpleasant and thankless job.

To show how objective was Col. Kerin, the Judge-Advocate, I produce hereunder two extracts from his summing up address :

(*a*) While dealing with the question of ill-treatment of Indian prisoners of war Col. Kerin said, "I must preface my remarks by emphasizing the fact, which is common both to prosecution and defence alike, that whatever be the relevancy of this subject of the case, there is not, and there never has been, the least suggestion that these three accused before you were personally engaged in the ill-treatment of prisoners or even that they were at any time present when men were tortured or ill-treated".

(*b*) While closing up his summing, Col. Kerin advised the Court and showed appreciation of the various participants who fought the case in these words:

> Before you close the Court to consider your verdict on the charges before you, I would once again remind you that the onus of proof is upon the Prosecution and that it is upon them to establish the various charges before the Court, beyond reasonable doubt. By reasonable doubt I do not mean every possible or fantastic doubt, since in criminal proceedings absolute or mathematical certainly is not required and is seldom

obtainable; but you must not convict the accused on any charge unless you have that degree of certainty which as prudent and careful men of the world you would require when acting in important affairs of your daily lives.

"Finally, I would like to express my appreciation to Counsel for the Defence, and to Mr. Bhulabhai Desai in particular, for their assistance to me at all times, and for the extremely lucid manner in which the case for the defence has been put before the Court. To the Advocate General and Lt. Col. Walsh also I would like to express my appreciation of the fair manner in which the case for the Prosecution has been conducted throughout.

"Would you now, Sir, close the Court for consideration of your findings ?"

Evidence of Our Character

The New Year Eve 31st December 1945 was the last day of our trial. On that day when the Court assembled at 10 in the morning, Col. Kerin, the Judge Advocate, called upon the Military prosecutor, to give evidence as to the character and particulars of service of us, the accused.

Col. Walsh put in our records in the order of our seniority as under:

Capt. Shah Nawaz Khan. Age 31 years and 11 months. Length of service, 9 years and 11 months and served as a commissioned officer throughout having been captain for 5 years and one month. Apart from the trial his general character was very good. He had no military decorations or award. There was no previous conviction.

Capt. P.K. Sahgal. Age: 28 years and 11 months. Length of service 5 years, all as a commissioned officer and as Captain. Had no military decorations or awards. His general character was very good with no previous conviction.

Lieut. G.S. Dhillon. Age: 30 years 9 months. Total service, 5 years and 9 months. Commissioned service as Lieutenant, 4 years and 3 months. No previous convictions nor decorations. General character very good.

The Judge-Advocate, then asked the Defence Counsel if they desired to cross-examine Col. Walsh, Mr. Soni, acting for Shri Desai said, "No".

The Judge-Advocate then asked the Defence Counsel if they wanted to address the Court. The reply again was "No".

Lastly we the three accused were asked if we wished to address the Court. Each one of us replied, "No".

The President, Maj. General Blaxland then declared that proceedings in the Open Court were closed to consider the sentence.

The moment, the members of the Court left the Court Room to go to their Chamber and before our removal under the regular security, we three individually met all the members of the Defence Counsel for the last time to pay our gratitude and say good-bye. With the knowledge of the Indian Army Act we had no doubt that with our owning the main charge of waging war against the King Emperor and the Defence Counsel upholding our privilege and right to act as we did, we had left no alternative for the Court other than to declare us guilty and sentence each one of us, the three accused, to death. The least the Court could do was to award us transportation for life. Parting with graceful, top ranking legal luminaries of India and men of the world was in itself a great privilege, made all the more memorable under those emotional moments. Stoic personalities in all appearance like Rai Bahadur Badri Das, Dr. Kailash Nath Katju, Kanwar Sir Dalip Singh, Shri Jugal Kishore Khanna along with their junior colleagues, who were later to occupy the chair at one of the High Courts or the Supreme Court of India, Shri Inder Dev Dua, Manak Lal Vakil, Shiv Kumar Shastri, Sultan Yar Khan, Ranbir Soni, Rajindra Narain, R.P. Khosla and Asaf Ali and so many more along with them who had laboured hard for the last four months for the national cause and to save us were there to bid us farewell. Their composed faces, their affectionate words and friendly gestures, have never deserted my memory ever since that last day of December 1945.

The last to meet me was Kanwar Sir Dalip Singh. At first he held my right hand with his right one, then he held it with his both hands. I followed suit. And he said, *"Dil nahin bharya."* (My heart is not yet content). And he gave me a long, affectionate hug. At last he said, "I am glad, by serving you I got a chance to serve our country. Jai Hind!"

The security men who stood waiting by then took me along with my senior colleagues Shah Nawaz and Sahgal to Salimgarh.

The trial was over.

24
THE VERDICT

There was a chill in the air on that beautiful sunny New Year Day of 1946. Appendicitis like a faithful friend never left me alone throughout the crucial year of 1945. It kept on recurring and subsiding again and again. The doctor at the Red Fort arranged for my removal to the Military General Hospital in Delhi Cantonment. He told me to be ready to go to the hospital by 4 p.m. on the 3rd of January. I bade farewell to all the brother officers in the cage and was waiting for an ambulance to take me to the hospital.

A bit earlier than 4 o' clock, three military vehicles carrying fully armed troops arrived at the gate of the cage. A Captain shouted, "Captain Shah Nawaz Khan, Captain Prem Kumar Sahgal, Lieutenant Gurbakhsh Singh Dhillon ! Get ready to move to an unknown destination. And bring along all your belongings."

All the brother officers in the barrack were stunned. They felt that we were being taken to some jail to be executed. That was it, we thought. I was already prepared for the move to the hospital. Shah Nawaz and Sahgal were helped by friends to pack up their belongings in a hurry. The British Captain of the Guards shouted from outside, "Please hurry up."

We were given a hurried and an emotional farewell. Brother officers embraced each one of us. General Aziz Ahmed gave Shah Nawaz a jar of Pond's cold cream. And when he was handing it over to Shah Nawaz, he thrust a guinea coin deep under the cream. Helped by everybody, our belongings were loaded on the central vehicle, parked nearest to the gate. As soon as we boarded the vehicle, we were rushed to the Trial Barrack at breakneck speed. The security arrangements on that day were heavier than ever before during the trial. The presence of the civilian police in strength was specially noticeable.

We were taken straight to the Accused Marshalling Room of the trial days. Here we were made to wait. Shah Nawaz asked me, "Gurbakhsh! What about your appendicitis? You were to go to the hospital today?"

I replied, "Sir, why worry, any jail would be more comfortable than the battlefield. And if we are executed there will be no need to go to the hospital at all".

We were all calm and composed and prepared for the eventuality.

After sometime we were produced before Lt. Col. Walsh in his office on the same floor next to the Court Room where we had stood our trial. Escorted by two Lieutenants, one in front and one in the rear with swords drawn under the command of a Captain, we were ordered, "Quick march. Halt. Right turn. Salute." Formalities over, we remained standing at attention. Walsh opened a big sealed envelop. He read out our charge-sheet. Then he started reading out the findings of the Court pertaining to each charge one by one. Having finished that, he read out the sentences passed by the Court for each one of us. The procedure of reading out each item was full of suspense.

All three of us were found guilty of waging war against the King Emperor.

Shah Nawaz was found guilty of the charge of abetment of murder.

Sahgal was not found guilty of the charge of abetment of murder.

I was not found guilty of the charges of murder.

The Court sentenced all of us:

1. To be cashiered from service.
2. To be transported for life.
3. To forfeit all the arrears of pay and allowances and other sums.

The confirming authority, the Commander-in-Chief in India, General Sir Claude Auchinleck confirmed all the findings and sentences of the Court but remitted the sentence of transportation for life, for all of us.

After Col. Walsh finished reading the verdict, there was a moment's lull before he ordered the officers guarding us to withdraw. He said, "Well gentlemen make hay while the sun shines. Where do you like to go so that I may arrange to provide you Railway warrants to your respective home stations?" Col. Sahgal spoke on our behalf, "We would like to go to Mr. Raghunandan Saran's house in the Civil Lines in Delhi." "In that case you may go by the same truck which brought you here," said Walsh.

Without any further formalities we on our own walked down into freedom.

Simultaneously, on that very day, the 3rd of January 1946, the following communique was published in the Gazette of India Extraordinary:

Capt. Shah Nawaz Khan, Capt. Sahgal and Lt. Dhillon have stood their trial by Court martial on charges against all three of waging war against the King-Emperor, Lt. Dhillon being also charged with murder and the other two with abetment of murder. The findings of the Court are that all three are guilty of the charge of waging war, while Capt. Shah Nawaz Khan is also convicted of the charge of abetment of murder, Lt. Dhillon is acquitted of the charge of murder and Capt. Sahgal of the charge of abetment of murder.

Having found the accused guilty of the charge of waging war, the Court was bound to sentence the accused either to death or to transportation for life: no lesser sentence was permissible under the law. The sentence of the Court on all three accused is transportation for life, cashiering and forfeiture of arrears of pay and allowances.

No finding or sentence by Court-martial is complete until confirmed. The confirming officer, in this case the Commander-in-Chief, is satisfied that the findings of the Court are in each instance in conformity with the evidence and he had therefore confirmed them.

The confirming officer is, however, competent to mitigate, commute or remit the sentences. As already stated in the Press, it is the policy of the Government of India to bring to trial in future only such persons as are alleged, in addition to waging war against the State, to have committed acts of gross brutality: and it has been announced that in reviewing sentences in any trials the competent authority will have regard to the extent to which the acts proved offended against the canons of civilized behaviour.

Lt. Dhillon and Capt. Sahgal have been acquitted of the charges of murder and abetment of murder, and it has not been alleged that they were guilty of other acts of brutality. Although Capt. Shah Nawaz Khan has been found guilty of abetment of murder and the acts proved against him were harsh, the prevailing circumstances have been taken into account by the confirming officer.

The Commander-in-Chief has decided, therefore, to treat all three accused in the same way in the matter of sentence, and to remit the sentences of transportation of life against all three accused. He has, however, confirmed the sentence of cashiering and forfeiture of arrears of pay and allowances, since it is in all circumstances a most serious crime for an officer or soldier to throw off his allegiance and wage war against the State. This is a principle which it is essential to uphold in the interests of the stability of any governments by law established, present or future.

Our release was of momentous significance both on the personal and the national level. Whereas it came as a relief to our near and dear ones, it was a moment of triumph for our Defence Counsel who fought the case with devotion to the nation as well as to save our lives. The man in the street felt that our release was his victory. His slogans, *"Sahgal Dhillon Shah Nawaz, Zindabad! Lal Qila Tor Do, Azad Hind Fauj Chhor Do"* had gained him our release by throwing open the heavy gates of the Red Fort. The unprecedented publicity in the national papers and the media during the proceedings of our trial enhanced the credibility and legitimacy of the freedom struggle launched by the Indian National Army. It made heroes of us.

Netaji, already an acknowledged and popular leader, now stood the tallest leader in the history. His words, *"Tum mujhe khoon do, main tumhain azadi dunga"* came to be household words. And Netaji Zindabad was on the lips of everybody. His conviction was that the conscience of the nation would be stirred by the blood of the martyrs and that would make it impossible for the British to keep awakened people under bondage any more. And that was exactly what happened when in the battlefield the brother fought against brother, the Indian Army of the British got transformed from a mercenary to a nationalist and a patriotic Army of India. The British were prudent enough to read the writing on the wall.

As I write the above words I am reminded of Shri Desai, who in some rare moments during the trial, would share his loud thinking with us. Once he said, "Do you think that I need more time to argue your case? I ask for adjournment for the people to get time to grasp what you did, how, why and what for. I have not to plead your case before these Jhonnies (the judges of the Court). Their powers are limited by the Indian Army Act. They are bound to declare you guilty, for you confess and we confirm that you did wage war against the King for the liberation of India. So what I am to do, is to plead your case before the bar of the public opinion and of the world." That was exactly what he did and his strategy transcended the boundaries of the Imperial law. His address even jolted the very conscience of the members of the Court. Our crime of waging war against the King was a crime of the nature which called for the heaviest punishment, that is, death. But General Blaxland and his fellow judges of the Court instead of awarding us death sentence tempered it with mercy and sentenced us to transportation for life, cashiering and forfeiture of arrears of pay and allowances.

General Sir Claude Achinleck, the C-in-C, went a step further and having confirmed the punishments was sagacious and gracious enough to remit the sentence of transportation in case of all of us in view of the "prevailing circumstances".

Forfeiture of pay and allowances was fair enough an award, for we did not serve or belong to the Indian Army when we waged the war against the King. Sentence of transportation having been remitted by the C-in-C, the only punishment we had to suffer was that of cashiering which I have been enduring for the past fifty years and shall have to endure till the last breath of my this life for having fought for liberation of India as an INA man. The sentence of cashiering carries with it the stigma of disgrace which still shadows us. It was due to this very stigma that we the I.C.Os who joined the INA, including

General Mohan Singh, the founder of the INA were denied the privilege of an Old Cadet from being invited to Dehra Dun for participation in the Golden Jubilee celebrations of the Indian Military Academy, our alma mater. I am afraid the stigma still prevails against us though the night of TRYST WITH DESTINY occurred half a century ago.

Government's Predicament

The secret official papers and documents pertaining to the period of our trial in the Red Fort published subsequently in *The Transfer of Power* offer loud and unambiguous testimony to my faith when during interrogation at Pegu I had stated that if I were tried by an open public trial, the Indian people would immediately go against the Government in our favour. When I was asked the same question by the interrogator in the Red Fort, my reply was in the affirmative but I changed the word "immediately" to "definitely."

In an official correspondence, D.O. 80/V-I/II/56 dated 24 November, 1945, marked Top Secret and Personal, General Auchinleck writes to the Viceroy, Field Marshal Viscount Wavell: "The representatives of Provinces expressed considerable uneasiness about the political situation which might result from a continuance of the present agitation. They felt that a decision to execute any of the accused in the present trials might result in unrest on a scale more serious than in 1921 and 1942. (p. 530). It was suggested that there should be no further trials, except for murder and atrocities and the charges of waging war against the King-Emperor should be dropped in future trials. Arguing that the stability or the reliability of the Indian Armed Forces would not be undermined in the process, the proposed course would create confidence in them: "With the existing Armed Forces recruited from all parts and all classes of India and modern means of communications and the growth of nationalist feeling in the country, it is quite impossible to isolate the Armed Forces from the rest of the country. There is evidence to show that there is no general resentment in the Indian Army against the INA", (p. 532).

The issue was dealt more precisely and clearly in the document (Enclosure 2 to No. 233 signed by C.M. dated 17/11/45), that was submitted by the Punjab Government for consideration at the highest level. The Governor of Punjab proposed that if the trials of Shah

Nawaz, Sahgal and Dhillon could not be stopped as that would betray weakness and a lack of courage on the part of the Government, it was not desirable and prudent to sentence the accused to death: "If Government intend to carry out the death sentence, they must be prepared to face unparalleled agitation, more widespread than in 1919 and 1942, and to use ruthless force to suppress it. Another 'fast unto death' by Gandhi as a protest must also be taken into consideration" (p. 535). Fearing that the agitation which would follow the execution of the three men (Dhillon, Sahgal and Shah Nawaz) and the force which would have to be used to suppress it would prejudice any hope of a settlement with India, the Punjab Government made a proposal that was finally accepted in our case: "In these circumstances, the only practical solution would appear to be to carry on the trials and for the Commander-in-Chief to commute the death sentence if imposed. Their commutation should be announced simultaneously with the announcement of the death sentences themselves. There should be no time-lag in which to work out violent agitation" (p. 535).

The document further stresses the need to speed up the trials as the delay would aggravate the internal situation seriously. The public was not likely, it was stated, to attach much importance to the prosecution story. The INA people were popular heroes and treason charge would only increase their popularity: "The defence will concentrate entirely on the 'Patriotism' of Bose and the INA will draw freely on sentiment and racial feelings. The press will follow its lead. Already its tone is worse than it has ever been before. The result will be that a thoroughly dangerous and explosive situation will be worked up" (p. 536).

In another document enclosure to No. 424 dated 12th February, 1946 circulated to the Army Commanders, marked, "Strictly Personal and Secret: Not to be passed through any Office, General Auchinleck shared his perception of the general effects of the action taken in respect of the INA trial on the Indian Army as a whole. He admitted to have commuted the sentences of transportation on Shah Nawaz, me and Sahgal in the interest of discipline, solidarity and reliability of the Indian Army. The three officers were applauded as patriots and nationalists who, though misled, should be treated with clemency as true sons of India. He showed no hesitation in observing that all Indians, including the Indian Commissioned Officers, were nationalists, though not necessarily anti-British: "In this connection, it should be remembered, I think, that every Indian worthy of the name is today a 'nationalist', though this does not mean that he is necessarily 'anti-British'. All the same, where India and her independence are concerned, there are no 'pro-British' Indians" (p. 940).

Content with the punishment of "cashiering" which carried a stigma of disgrace, the General expressed the feelings shared by the Indian officers of the Indian Army that "My attempt to enforce the sentence would have led to chaos in the country at large and probably to mutiny and dissension in the Army culminating in its dissolution, probably on communal lines." The overriding object of commuting the sentence, the Commander-in-Chief, stated (p. 944) was "to maintain the stability, reliability and efficiency of the Indian Army so that it may remain in the future a trustworthy weapon for use in the defence of India, and we hope, of the Commonwealth as a whole."

No wonder, that in a statement published in *The Statesman* dated 4th march, 1946, Pandit Jawaharlal Nehru revealed that Shah Nawaz, Sahgal and (Dhillon)—the three INA officers, were not released owing to demonstrations in India, but the Indian Army had demanded their release.

What an irony that when Nehru came in power, the INA soldiers were not taken back into the Indian Army! However, I do remain indebted to him for he visited us once during our detention in the Red Fort and again for his presence during the first two days of our trial. His appearance for two days in a barrister's gown after an interval of 26 years earned him the credit for having defended our case.

25

Aftermath

After our sudden release, unescorted we walked down to the waiting truck and boarded it. The truck did not carry any guard. Apart from us three, Shah Nawaz, Sahgal and I, the driver was the lone occupant. The area around the barrack where our trial was held and the roads leading to it were very heavily guarded by armed police and the Army. I did not know how my two senior colleagues felt but I thought that we might be rearrested at some point within or outside of the Fort. I was in the wrong. Nothing of the sort happened. In fact, the deployment of a strong force was to cope with an unforeseen situation which might have arisen in case of our getting capital punishment.

On arrival at Raghunandan Saran's house we were informed that both Mrs. Sarla Saran and Mr. Saran were in their office of Piaray Lal and Sons at Connaught Place. Meanwhile Saran's mother who was on the top storey of the house observed the military truck and asked who were we ? Col. Sahgal answered, "Maji I am Prem along with Gen. Shah Nawaz and Col. Dhillon". The old lady said, "But you were in the Lal Qila. How can you be here?" "We ran away from the Red Fort. We need to be sheltered", replied Sahgal. The mother made haste to come down.

At the same time, Sarans entered along with a crowd of people. They had heard the news of our release over the All India Radio. In the process our joke was lost on the old lady. She hurriedly brought *ladus* (sweets) for the driver and gave him a handsome reward. We three were ushered into the drawing room of the Sarans. It was a big hall but the crowds made it look small. We were served tea and refreshments which we could little take. Everyone was so anxious to shake hands with us that we could not even hold a cup. Col. Misri Chand of 1/14th Punjab Regiment was one of the crowds who had come to greet us. He later retired as Lieutenant General. At the time it was bold of him to come to see us who were guilty of violation of allegiance towards the British sovereign.

I was anxious to go to meet Basant. She lived at Dr. Jiwan Lal Maleri's residence in Darya Ganj. The crowds kept on increasing and I found it nearly impossible to leave Saran's house. Ultimately Shri Saran prevailed upon some of his friends to escort me to Darya Ganj. When we arrived at the INA Defence and Enquiry Office in 82, Darya Ganj, I got recognised and the crowd which had already assembled there started shouting:

Sahgal Dhillon Shah Nawaz

Teenon ki ho umar daraz

*(*May the trio Sahgal, Dhillon,

Shah Nawaz live long*)*.

Basant too had come to the INA Office. She heard me being hailed by the crowd. She came out of the office and there at the threshold of 82, Darya Ganj we met for the first time outside the Red Fort. We hugged each other as the people cheered us. From there we were taken in a procession to Dr. Maleri's house where we received a parental welcome. Maleris treated Basant as their daughter. It was from their house that every day during the trial Basant had ridden to the Red Fort on a bicycle.

On the following day, Saturday, the 4th of January, 1946 Shri Raghunandan Saran took three of us to several places and to some friends. Wherever we went, it was roses, roses all the way. We were loaded with garlands and bouquets. In the evening, a big rally was held at Gandhi Grounds beside the City Hall. It was presided over by Mr. Asaf Ali, the convener and a member of the INA Defence Council. A wooden stage about 15 ft. high was specially made on which along with some dignitaries sat Shah Nawaz, Sahgal, Basant and I. It appeared that the whole of Delhi and its neighbourhood had turned up to receive us. Even today after a lapse of half a century, old people who participated in that rally recall that never in the history of Delhi did they ever see such a stupendous and spontaneous show of national sentiments and solidarity. The participants in that joyful meeting belonged to all the creeds, classes, communities and political parties.

Apart from Mr. Asaf Ali's welcome address, Shah Nawaz, Sahgal and I spoke. The public heard us with rapt attention and in pin drop silence. But at the end of the rally we found it difficult to get down from the stage. We were mobbed. Everybody was eager to reach us and shake hands with us or at least touch us. Some enthusiasts climbed the stage and it broke down under their weight. Somehow we remained unhurt but Basant fainted. Shah Nawaz and Sahgal helped me to lift her up so that she could be saved from being trampled over by the crowds. It was quite a job to keep her lifted over the heads of the mob. People pulled down our hands for shaking and in the process Basant kept on falling over our heads. It took her quite some time to recover. By that time people had learned about Basant's condition and they helped us to a car which was waiting to take us to Delhi Railway Station. When we arrived at the station we found that most of our tunic buttons were missing. People removed them to keep as souvenirs. Shah Nawaz lost all the buttons of his jacket.

We caught the Frontier Mail for Lahore. A first class compartment had been reserved for us. It was bedecked with flowers, flags and buntings. It was jammed with autograph seekers. Young women and men had occupied all berths and they were adamant to travel with us. If some of them yielded to go out of the compartment, another lot came in to occupy the vacated space. At last we got our respective seats/berths when the train started. My problem was my appendicitis. Basant tried to protect me as much as she could but the young college girls cared less. I was obliged to protect my abdomen by keeping my elbows on the guard. An eight-hours journey which should have taken us to Lahore by daybreak of Sunday 5th January, 1946 took more than double the time to travel the same distance. People made the train stop at each wayside station. We were asked to come out on the platform. People wanted to see us, touch us, hear us, speak and garland us. They had gone mad with the joy of our release. Young girls cut their fingers with razor blades and applied blood to our foreheads instead of *sindhur* vermilion. At Amritsar a special stage was put up at the railway platform for our reception. The members of the Golden Temple Managing Committee came all the way to accord us a ceremonial welcome. They honoured us with the sacred *saropas* and swords with gold plated hilts. The function lasted for over an hour. And the train got that much more delayed. It was thrilling and gratifying to hear "Jai Hind" and "*Bole so Nihal Satsiri Akal*" which echoed through that holiest of the holy town of Amritsar. Netaji, INA slogans and our names were hailed along with Inquilab Zindabad as the train steamed off towards Lahore, the capital city of the Punjab.

Meanwhile uncontrollable multitude coming from all over the Punjab surged towards Lahore Railway Station. In order to avoid a risk of stampede, the civil administration asked the city fathers to get us off from the train some miles ahead of the Main Railway Station and then bring us by car to the frontage of the main station of Lahore so that the crowds who had occupied every available place inside in front and atop the station buildings might be able to see us from various vantage points. The plan worked though en route some young enthusiasts managed to climb on top of the car of Mr. Justice Achhru Ram, Colonel Sahgal's father in which we were travelling and its roof caved in. On arrival in front of the main station we were taken out of the car and made to go on top of a truck which had been turned into a stage fitted with loudspeakers. Expression fails me and I cannot describe the joy of the people on seeing us. How aptly a poet said,

Haqeekat ki haqeekat moonh se batlai nahin jati

Ishe samjha to jata hai yeh samjhai nahin jati

(Reality of a fact cannot be told by a word of mouth. It is understood all right but cannot be described).

Slogans rumbled through the sky like an unending boom of thunder. From our vantage point crowds saw us and we three waved to the crowds who were all around us as far as the eyes could see.

It took General Shah Nawaz quite some time to make the multitude stop slogan shouting and listen to us. Three of us spoke in the order of our seniority. Those were words of thanks for the people's support, which had resulted in our release and granted us a new life, words to congratulate them on their victory to save us from the gallows, words of gratitude for their overwhelming love for Netaji, INA and the cause of freedom, words of concern for those of our men and women who were still under detention in the Red Fort and in various jails and camps within and outside India and of course a salute in homage to our glorious dead who would never come home.

When I was speaking I saw my parents being brought out of the crowds with the help of police in plain clothes. I was later to learn that my mother was saved from being trampled under the rushing crowds. I owe my gratitude to those men who took my mother and father to a place of safety by making a cordon around them.

After the public reception in front of the railway station, we were taken to the house of the most venerable Rai Bahadur Badri Dass. Here in the presence of our parents and relatives, revered Shrimati Badri Dass applied *tilak* on our foreheads, garlanded us and put sweets (*laddus*) with her own hands in our mouths.

The most pleasant surprise of the day especially for Shah Nawaz, Sahgal and me was that Netaji's elder brother, Mr. Sarat Chandra Bose's release from the jail synchronised with our arrival at Lahore. And at Rai Bahadur Dass's place we met him for the first time. Each one of us three cried like kids as Sarat Bose took us one by one in his embrace. The moment was full of emotions. I felt as if Netaji had sent his elder brother as his proxy to welcome us on our home-coming. Netaji was missed all the more. At night a big rally was held at the Municipal grounds. It was a cold winter night. The public meeting went on and on late into the night and yet people wanted to listen to the INA story more and more. The public asked Netaji's brother to speak in English for his accent reminded them of Netaji's way of speaking.

Shah Nawaz, Basant and I remained with Sahgal for another three days. We were kept busy with various public meetings and college receptions. The Punjab High Court Bar Association gave a reception. We called on prominent personalities of the Punjab, parties and all newspaper offices. We visited to thank those members of the INA Defence Counsel who belonged to Lahore. They, apart from Pitaji, Colonel Sahgal's father Mr. Justice Achhru Ram, were Rai Bahadur Badri Dass, Kunwar Sir Dalip Singh, Bakhshi Sir Tek Chand, Shri Ranbir C. Soni, Shri Inder Dev Dua, Shri R.P. Khosla and Shri Shiv Kumar Shastri.

His Holiness Shri Guru Partap Singh of the Namdhari (Kuka) Sikhs specially invited us. His Holiness honoured us with *saropas* and blessings.

One of the strange incidents which we had to often face was that the commercial bands engaged to welcome us at functions gave us the British Royal salute on our arrival. Most of those bands had Army veteran band-masters as their conductors. The moment we arrived on the stage they would say, "Royal Salute" and the band played, "God Save the King". On the first such happening though we three had taken the salute standing rigidly at attention, after the meeting we told the bandmaster, a retired Havildar Major that we did not deserve the Royal salute. The bandmaster replied, "Sirs, you deserve a higher salute than the General salute and I could not think of a salute higher enough for you than the Royal salute." His predicament was understandable but Shah Nawaz remarked, "Surely God only can save the King with people like us in the British Empire." All the same, the status quo continued. I do not know about General Shah Nawaz, Col. Sahgal or other INA officers' feelings but as I stood at attention when the British national anthem was played I could not help admiring the democratic nature of the British people and their Royalty. My salute was to the British people. I respect their anthem even today.

One of those three days we went to Jallianwala Bagh to Amritsar. A taxi driver specially volunteered to drive us to Amritsar in his cab. He wanted to exhibit his driving skill to impress upon us that he could drive really fast. Half way through to Amritsar, the car skidded and we three were picked up by another car. We had received minor injuries which were attended to at the Medical College, Amritsar. We arrived half an hour late at the Jallianwala Bagh. The public having learned about the accident felt relieved as they saw us walk to the stage in our normal gait.

The next day Shah Nawaz left for his village Matoor in district Rawalpindi. Basant and I went to Chhanga Manga, our home station for Batti-chak. After Lahore we three, Shah Nawaz, Sahgal and I seldom got a chance to travel together. We had so many invitations from different parts of the country that in order to visit maximum places we went single. Though we were three distinct individuals, even while travelling alone people would say, "There goes Sahgal, Dhillon, Shah Nawaz". On Netaji's birthday, January 23, 1946 Delhi invited Sahgal, Calcutta invited Shah Nawaz and I was invited by Bombay.

Basant and I were at Karachi in Sindh when we received a telegram from Amrik, Col. Sahgal's brother-in-law about the invitation to go to Bombay. Amrik got two berths reserved for Basant and me by Frontier Mail that was to leave Lahore for Bombay on 21st January. Accordingly we left Karachi by Karachi—Lahore Mail so as to be on time to catch the Frontier Mail at Lahore. The Government did not wish us to reach Bombay on time. The train was delayed for over seven hours and we failed to catch the Frontier Mail for Bombay. However, we caught a local train and arrived Delhi on the morning of 23rd January. We went straight to Airline offices in Connaught Place to take a chance on catching a flight for Bombay. We were disappointed to learn that no seat was available on any Airline. Perchance a gentleman by the name of Shri Natha Lal Parikh met us at an Airline office. He was Netaji's friend. It was at his house that Netaji used to stay while in Bombay. He asked me, "What are you doing here in Delhi when the whole of Bombay is waiting for you?" He told me that a rally had been arranged on Chaupati beach that evening and it would be a great disappointment to the people if I did not arrive. He offered his own ticket to me and told me to proceed to Bombay and he would bring along Basant. Luckily another friend of his turned up and offered his ticket. So Basant and I arrived Bombay though very late.

When we arrived at Chaupati I heard Bhulabhai Desi announce, "Dhillon is not the man to disappoint us. I am sorry that due to some unknown circumstances he has not been able to come. I don't want you to wait any longer so—" On hearing those words over the loudspeaker I rushed towards the stage and before Desaiji could disperse the meeting, I said, "Jai Hind, Sir. I am sorry for being late."

Desaiji addressed the public, "Didn't I tell you that he was not the man to disappoint us. You have waited so long for him that now I will not stand between you and him. Here I introduce him to you by reciting a verse from his own poetry :

Chalo delri agar rastey mein lakhon musklein aein
Chalo delri ke apne khoon se tarikh likh jaein.

And now I present to you the writer of history with his blood, Colonel Gurbakhsh Singh Dhillon" and sat down.

The crowds went mad with joy. There was an enthusiastic

applause for quite some time but as soon as I started to speak there was a pin drop silence. At times I had to request them not to cheer and clap too often if they wanted to hear the story of the INA, its Netaji, its heroes and heroines of the Rani of Jhansi Regiment. People sat at every perceivable place on the beach, on the trees, on the roads, and buildings towards the Marine Drive of Bombay as far as visible from the stage at Chaupati beach. I spoke for about two hours telling them about Netaji and the INA—the story of the heroes who gave their blood, flesh and bones to build the road to Delhi our glorious dead who never came home and paid the price of liberty in full measure. The meeting ended after 10 at night. Exhausted as we returned to Desaiji's palatial house, our greatest honour was that we were guests of not only our saviour but one of the forerank builders of modern India.

Saving CPI Office

I had just gone to sleep when Dhirubhai Desai, son of Bhulabhaiji Desai awakened me. He was accompanied by Shri S.K. Patil who was then General Secretary of the Bombay Indian National Congress Committee, later Minister for Agriculture in the Central Government. They told me that crowds were trying to put the office of the Communist Party of India on fire because of their 'anti-national' policy during World War II. Actually the C.P.I. were supporting Russia, though with the Allies Russia was engaged to save her own fatherland. She was never anti-India. That was why Netaji did not include her among those against whom we declared war.

I was rushed to the CPI office. Mr. S.K. Patil announced over a microphone that I had come. It took me quite some time to reach the office of the CPI, but because of Mr. Patil's announcement of my arrival, the crowd's attention was diverted from the CPI office to me. I stood up on a sort of makeshift platform and with folded hands requested the people to disperse. The people shouted "*Netaji Zindabad, INA Zindabad, Sahgal Dhillon Shah Nawaz! Zindabad*" and dispersed. The CPI office was saved. 1 returned to Desai Sahib's house at about 4 in the morning, Netaji's birthday ended successfully and peacefully.

Once again people gathered to attack the CPI office at 4 in the afternoon of 24th January 1946. The Mayor of Bombay, Mr. Nigan Dass T. Master who was also the President of Bombay Congress Committee took me to control the crowds. I stood on the bonnet of the Mayor's car. People were kind enough to listen to my appeal and as I was thanking them, a British Police Sergeant fired at me. The bullet landed near my feet and went through the bonnet of the car. People were enraged but the Mayor and I were successful in restoring peace. The next day a Press Conference was arranged at Jinnah Hall in the Congress office and with the overwhelming support of the Bombay Press, public remained unprovoked by the action of the police.

My stay in Bombay was prolonged by more than a week. I had to attend many receptions in different parts of the city of which I will describe only two. A Labour Union invited me for a rally. Basant and I were taken on a platform on wheels for about two miles from the site of the rally. This platform was about fifteen feet long and eight feet wide. Basant and I were seated on a sofa. The only other person on the platform was Mr. S.K. Patil, General Secretary of the Indian National Congress of Bombay. Mr. Patil squatted on the platform in the left hand corner in front of us. The platform was being pulled by eighteen pairs of gorgeously decorated bullocks. On either side of the bullocks, men and women wearing ornaments and magnificent clothes were dancing their native folk dances with overwhelming joy. I was enchanted. I looked toward Basant. Her face was filled with tears of joy. I said to her, "Basant, could the King Emperor or Viceroy of India's presence import this much joy to these people?" That very night, the RSS also gave us a secret reception as they were a banned organization at that time.

A meeting at Shivaji Park was the biggest in size second only to the Chaupati rally of January 23rd. As I was speaking at the Shivaji Park rally, someone talked on the stage. I requested him to keep quiet and when he did not listen to my request I told him to leave the platform. He refused. I got hold of his hand and showed him the stairs and he gently obeyed. I didn't know that he was one of the Block President of the Indian National Congress in Bombay. Before I left Bombay I went to call on Sardar Vallabhbhai Patel, known as the 'Iron Man of India'. Mr. Parikh and Mr. Patil escorted Basant and me. Sardar Patel was a man of few words. Everybody in the Congress feared him. When I sat down, his first question was, "Did you throw out someone from the stage at Shivaji Park?"

I replied, "Not only one man, quite a few of them."

"Why did you do that ?"

"Because they were talking and disrupting the proceedings."

"Do you know that one of them was a very important person, a Block President of the Indian National Congress ?"

"Was it so ? I am happy that I did it, because I can't teach politics. I can only teach discipline. Such an important person must know how to behave on a stage."

Sardar Patel laughed. Every one present laughed, and the matter ended. My conversation with Sardar Patel was as under :

I : Sardar Sahib, I have been making so many speeches, as might have come to your notice. Can you tell me if I have made any mistakes so that I may make amends ?

Sardar Patel: No. I don't think you made any mistake.

I : Sardar Sahib, people have been very kind and have given me a lot of money for the relief of the INA. Since you are the Treasurer of the All India Congress Committee and of the INA Inquiry and Defence Committee as well, may I hand over the funds to you "?

Sardar Patel: Yes, that would be proper. What is the amount ?

I : I have not counted. The money is with the General Secretary of the Congress Committee, Shri S.K. Patil and Shri Parikh. It is about five lakhs and unaccounted coins in two bagfuls.

Patil and Parikh handed over the bags to Sardar Patel and we left.

After we left Sardar Patel's residence, Parikh and Patil told me that they were surprised that Sardar Patel who was not happy with the Shivaji Park incident could be dealt with so bluntly by me for they were feeling very nervous because they knew, that the complaint had been made against me. They felt greatly relieved.

Shri Bhulabhai Desai advised me to stay with him at Bombay and write my memories. He said, he would get my appendicitis operated and help me publish my book. Again my colleague Shri Mani

Bhai Doshi, his mother Shrimati Ujamma and his wife Shrimati Vilasben made a similar offer. But I had to go visiting places as per public demand. I wish I had accepted one of the above invitations. On the contrary I left Bombay though with a heavy heart.

My next destination was Ahmedabad, the present capital of Gujarat. My hostess there was Miss Mridula Sarabai. She was a very important member of the All India Congress Committee. She was the hardest working woman I have ever come across in any political circle.

After my return from Gujarat I was taken to Sukhar and Hyderabad Sindh and to various places like a show-piece. Each day I had to deliver at least a dozen speeches and I have forgotten even the names of those hundreds of places I was made to visit. Everywhere crowds mobbed me with love and affection. Young girls carried razor blades to cut their fingers and put blood on my forehead as a *tilak*. I was loaded with flowers so much that I used to feel their load. Since that time I became allergic to marigolds, and even today whenever I am garlanded I hasten to remove them as soon as possible. How strange for a neck which was prepared for a hangman's rope.

My most rewarding visit was to Montgomery D.A.V. High School from where I had passed Matriculation. This school was an Arya Samajist institution where the staff was deeply nationalist. Every Saturday they held a havan (sacred fire) and after the havan we were given a talk by the Headmaster or a visiting Swami with a view to making us self-respecting independent Indians. I owe a lot to this school for my having become a freedom fighter. Our Urdu and Persian teacher was Shri Nathuram, a tall slim person who had retired after a long period of forty years from Government service and was teaching in that school on an honorarium of only one rupee a month. He was a dedicated and committed teacher. During my visit to Montgomery I learnt that he had become too old to teach. He was living in retirement. I went to his house to pay my respects. That afternoon, the school which had grown into a college during the war had arranged a special reception for me on the college premises. Thousands of guests had been invited to tea. The Reception Committee took me to the college by car in a procession. On the way, I saw Master Nathuram walking slowly with his cane along the shaded roadside. I had the car stopped, went to Shri Nathuram, touched his feet and said, "Sir, I went to call on you at your house so that you would not have to take the trouble of coming to the reception. Would you mind sitting in the car to avoid this hot sun ?"

Nathuram replied proudly in a majestic tone, "*Tum aey they hamarey haan, hamein khushi deney, ham pedal chal rahey hain tumhain IZZAT bakhshne*" – (You came to our house to give us joy. We will walk to the reception to grant you honour.)

That was the greatest honour I could receive from my teacher. A similar honour I was to receive from my father. I started doing relief work for the INA men who were being released daily from various jails and detention camps in India. I set up my office under a tent at Bradlaugh Hall on the premises of the Punjab Indian National Congress Office. Hundreds of people visited me daily. I employed a few INA men to control the crowds. People were asked to form a queue. I was always short of time. Most people brought donations for the INA. Some came only for my autograph, others to invite me to their districts. One day during my interviewing hours I had to go out of my tent to receive a phone call in the Congress Secretary's office. When I came out, I was surprised to find my father standing fortieth in the long queue of visitors. I stopped and said, "*Bhayaji*, you needn't stand in the queue. You can come in straight to see your son."

My father answered, "Son I know I could have done that, but I wanted to enjoy the feelings of an ordinary visitor who comes to see a national hero."

I felt father could not have done me a greater honour. I knelt to touch his feet and hastened to go to answer the telephone.

Another occasion of receiving a similar honour was when the revered Principal of Gordon College, Rawalpindi Rev. Dr. Stuart presided over a reception given to me by the college. And again when I went to see Mahatma Gandhi. The Mahatma was living in the Bhangi Colony in Delhi at the time. Two INA officers accompanied me, Dr. Major Bawa and Dr. Major Puri. Congress volunteers guarding the colony could not allow us in because we had no appointment. I requested them to inform Pandit Jawaharlal Nehru that I had come. Pandit Nehru ran out of the thatched hut where Gandhiji was living and ushered us into the hut. He told us on the way that Bapu was observing silence (*Moan*). I told Nehruji that we had come only to have his darshan and we had no other business or request to make. As we entered the hut we found that most of the top leaders of the country were seated there. The Mahatma sat with his statue of three monkeys in front of him. We entered, and saluted "Jai Hind!" which the Father of the Nation acknowledged with folded hands and radiant smile. Everyone was silent. We three also sat down in front of Gandhiji silently. Panditji told me that we could speak and Bapu would break his silence after five minutes. He had already given an appointment to Mr. G.D. Birla, the famous industrial magnate. I used the five minutes to introduce the two officers and informed Bapu that we would not take any of his time, as we had come only to pay our respects.

When Mahatma Gandhi broke his silence he took out his watch and said, "It is time now for Shri Birla's appointment, but you are our Netaji's soldiers. Sorry, officers, so I dare not refuse to meet you. Do you know Brahma, Vishnu and Mahesh ?"

I said, "Yes, Sir."

He said, "I have seen two of them already. May I know which one are you of the three ?"

I replied, "Bapuji, I do not know who I am. You have given me such a high place. Only you may know who am I."

Bapu laughed. Everyone laughed. We three stood up and saluted "Jai Hind."

Bapu with folded hands accepted the salute, saying "*Bande Mataram*!", Then hastened to add, "Now 'Jai Hind' has become prevalent everywhere." He repeated "Jai Hind!" - *Ab tou sabh Jai Hind hi hogaya hai.*

Panditji escorted us out and embraced me affectionately.

This incident demonstrated the high regard in which Gandhiji held Netaji and the INA.

In spite of all these honours, when Basant and I went on house-hunting in Lahore, we could not get a room. People were afraid that British Intelligence would be watching their premises. We were obliged to continue living in Sahgal's house for quite some time. Then Mr. Inder Dev Dua, who had been an apprentice under Sahgal's father and one of the most active advocates during our trial, came forward to offer lodging in their home. Dua's eldest sister, Kumari Lajyavati, Principal of one of the premier women's colleges in the north, Kanya Mahanvidyalya in Jallandur, was one of the most eminent women in the Punjab. She was Secretary to Lala Lajpat Rai, known as "The Tiger of Punjab." She had given protection to Bhagat Singh and had been the convenor of their defence committee during the trial.

Dua's younger sister, Dr. Shiva Dua, was a Professor of History. Their house became my home till the partition of India for over a year. I will ever remain indebted to them for their overwhelming hospitality not only to Basant and me but to most of the INA persons who visited us and they were not a few.

One night I returned very late from a public function and had just gone to sleep at about two a.m. when I heard a knock at the door. I was too exhausted and weak to get up and open the door. Basant did it instead. The visitor entered the room, saluted "Jai Hind" and spoke:

Visitor	:	Have you recognized me, Sir ?
I	:	I am sorry, I have not.
Visitor	:	Don't you know I am one of those men whom Netaji sent on a secret mission by submarine ? I was dropped on the Orissa coast, south of Calcutta.
I	:	I am sorry, I do not know of any such mission.
Visitor (sobbing):		I have been doing such a risky job, and you, such a senior officer, do not even know anything about me. Didn't Netaji tell you that I was given the task of organizing an anti-British underground unit in Lahore Cantt.?
I	:	You seem to have enjoyed Netaji's confidence more than I did.
Visitor	:	This evening during the public meeting you advised all the INA officers and men to follow Gandhi's non-violent method to struggle for the independence of India. Didn't you say that ?
I	:	Yes, I did.
Visitor	:	Don't you think that is contradictory to Netaji's

		ideology ?
I	:	I don't think so. Now we are in India. Netaji respected Mahatma Gandhi, calling him the Father of the Nation. It is only proper that the person from whom Netaji sought blessings should be our guide while in India.
Visitor	:	Are you saying this only to please the government or is it your sincere advice to us INA people ?
I	:	It is my sincere advice.
Visitor	:	For your information I have made arrangement to destroy the senior British officers' bungalows in Lahore Cantt: by 4 a.m. tonight. Do you think I am doing the right thing ?
I	:	Not at all, my dear boy, not at all. It will serve no purpose.
Visitor	:	Do you advise me to dismantle the arrangements I have made ?
I	:	Of course. You are so far from the Cantonment. Please haste and go to order your group not to carry it out.
Visitor	:	Is it your advice or an order ?
I	:	If this destruction can be stopped by my order I order you to rush to the Cantonment and dismantle whatso ever you have done.

The visitor kept on crying throughout the above discussion. He touched my feet and asked if he could embrace me. I embraced him and asked him to see that this destruction did not take place.

He assured me that he would do as told, shouted "Jai Hind" and left.

Basant sat on the cot with tears running down her cheeks, and she said, "What a wonderful person the INA had who could undertake such a risky job."

I said, Basant, "he is not an INA man."

Basant asked, "Then who was he?" I replied, "A person of the

CID, to find out whether the INA ever had any terrorist network in different parts of India."

The man never came again.

I had to face such probing inquiries at many places, and at many odd hours. Once a visitor came to me pretending that he was Shah Nawaz's maternal uncle. He met me in an affectionate manner and asked me in confidence if I needed some weapons to continue the underground struggle for independence within India. Most of these interviews took place during the months of January, February and March after our release from the Red Fort. I was always followed by CID officers and men wherever I went. At our residence at Dua's house, there were always a few CID informers posted near the outer gate of 8, Muzang Road, Lahore.

I was convinced that these activities of the CID were meant to find out if we had any underground anti-British movement in India. The British authorities could not risk to release our senior officers until they were convinced that we were running no underground movement.

Senior officers like General Mohan Singh and Major General Mohammad Zaman Kiani were the last to be released by the end of March 1946.

Those officers and men who after release called at Bradlough Hall were provided Rs. 100 per officer and Rs. 50 per Other Rank. I found it difficult to have the cash ready to make these payments, however small. I was given a lot of money by the public and that money I should have deposited with the Indian National Congress Committee in the Punjab but I had to use it for relief to the INA personnel returning to their homes without a single coin.

I flew to Delhi to discuss the problem with Sardar V.B. Patel. It was very difficult to get an appointment with him. When I approached his daughter, Mani Behn Patel she told me that the Sardar was not well and she refused to give me an appointment. Luckily, another very senior Congress leader Shri Piaray Lalji recognized me and I got an appointment. Miss Patel advised me to turn up at 9 p.m. at Birla House and wait in the drawing room to meet the Sardar as he came out of the dining room. She advised me not to take more than five minutes. Sardar Patel came out exactly at nine. I asked him to permit me to use the funds directly as I received them from the public and not send them to him and not seek his permission to help the INA personnel. I said I would keep accounts and render them to him. He said, that would be the proper way to save time and inconvenience to the INA men. I thanked him and my problem was solved within two minutes.

I told Sardar Patel's daughter that my interview was over. Sardar Patel said, "Your interview is over, but won't you give some time to me now?" He told his daughter and a few other Congress leaders who were standing nearby to go away and addressed me, "I have to listen to everyone's troubles. Nobody listens to my troubles." He gave me the news that, that morning Mahatma Gandhi had expressed his desire to visit the INA officers and men still detained in the Red Fort and in Kabul Lines in the Cantonment. Patel said that for him or Nehru it was very easy to make a visit, but for Mahatma Gandhi, permission was required from the Viceroy and the Commander-in-Chief. He had to approach the Adjutant General, who made arrangements for the interview and was good enough to accompany Mahatma Gandhi to the Fort and Kabul Lines. Sardar Patel also complained that there was too much criticism against him and Maulana Abul Kalam Azad for their having advised the Royal Indian Navy mutineers to lay down their arms. I said that the purpose had been served and that by advising them to lay down their arms, he had saved their lives and avoided the destruction of Bombay city and the harbour.

After the interview I came away thinking that greater the man, the greater were his responsibilities and worries. Patel was known as 'the Iron Man of India' but even a strong man has to pay attention to public opinion.

The question of employment was the main problem facing the INA men after their return home. Immediately after our release I was offered five thousand per month by a businessman for a job. I asked Mr. Raghunandan Saran for his advice. He said, "Gurbakhsh, wait for five months and then go to ask the same man if he wants to hire you. If at that time he offers you five hundred a month, accept it. But if you accept it now he will throw you out as soon as he has gained some publicity."

I was operated upon for appendicitis during the month of March.

Most of the senior officers were released during the last week of March or in April. I got an opportunity to hand over the relief work in the Punjab to Colonel Gulzara Singh and returned to my home in the village Batti Chak.

In May I went to Lahore and called on the businessman who had offered me five thousand a month job. I was not surprised when he did not hire me even for five hundred. I thought I would do well as a film actor. I got a letter of introduction to the great actor and film producer Shri Prithviraj Kapur from Shri Raghunandan Saran and was on the verge of my departure for Bombay when my mother came to me at Lahore. She informed me that my father had suffered dislocation of shoulder by falling from a horse and was laid up, or he would have come personally to prevent me from going to Bombay. He sent his turban to advise me not to become a screen hero for my status was of a genuine hero in the history of India. My mother told me that father had said that if I did not listen to his advice she should place his turban at my feet. I was left with no option but to cancel my trip to Bombay. That was the end of my idea of becoming a film actor.

Instead I went with mother to my village to see father who was laid up after his fall from horseback. Later on, a friend approached me about becoming his partner in owning a truck which he would finance. My father rejected that proposal as well. He thought to become a truck driver was not a respectable occupation. It involved bribing the police and at times carrying goods that might be contraband knowingly or unknowingly. If I were caught in any wrong doing I would lose my name which did not belong entirely to me but to Netaji and to India.

At the time Basant was expecting a baby. Basant had lost five earlier infants. I took her to Simla to divert her attention from the past and look forward to the future with hope. Amrita came into the world on April 15, 1947 at Simla Lady Harding Hospital.

1946 and 1947 were turbulent days. Riots erupted in 1946 in Multan before the Partition. I was approached by the Punjab Provincial Congress Committee to go to Multan to pacify both the Hindu and Muslim communities. I stayed there for about a fortnight and visited most of the affected villages of the district. Here the Muslims were in majority. The leaders of both the communities listened to me but Partition had been agreed upon by the Congress Working Committee and this had demoralized the Congress-minded people. The Multan riots were followed by riots in western Punjab. Many people were killed; there was arson and rape. The destruction was indescribable and women were the main victim of inhuman torture.

I formed area-wise defence and peace committees in Multan, talked to various men and women's assemblies and returned to Lahore. As I look back, I feel that the time for talk and advice was over.

Before the Congress Working Committee passed the resolution for the partition of India I went to Pandit Nehru at his residence. He was Prime Minister in the Interim Government. I implored him not to support the partition resolution. In retrospect, I feel that I was too naive to discuss with him a subject which had already become our fate and Nehru was one of the main actors in it. We had a heated discussion to no avail. I returned disappointed. I kept away from Panditji as much as I could.

In August 1947 when the newly formed Governments of Pakistan and India were celebrating their respective independence, the Punjab, Sindh and Bengal were burning. The apostle of non-violence and peace, Mahatma Gandhi, was trekking Noakhali to try to stop the bloodshed, arson and rape wherever the majority was attacking minority communities.

My district of Lahore too was partitioned and it became part of Pakistan and we became refugees without our land and belongings. I was at Simla at the time. From Simla I went in search of my parents and found them in a refugee camp near Amritsar. I took them to my residence in Simla. The people of Punjab were demoralized and were escaping eastward from the newly created Indo-Pakistan border. The Jammu and Kashmir problem arose out of the late decision of the ruler of Kashmir, Maharaja Hari Singh and Pandit Nehru.

The armies of Pakistan and India were poised against each other over the issue of Kashmir. The Indian Government and its leaders gave the impression of incompetence and helplessness. The people suffered and the soldiers bore the brunt of riots.

General Mohan Singh, Colonel N.S. Gill and I, together with a number of our INA veterans, felt that we owed it to the people of Punjab to restore some semblance of order and self-confidence in the people. Accordingly, we raised an unarmed volunteer force, the Desh Sewak Sena. We went to Delhi before raising it to seek the blessings of Mahatma Gandhi, Pandit Nehru and Sardar Patel. We explained to them that though we had no arms, we would impart military training without arms to foster discipline and a sense of security among the populace. We hoped they would remain in Punjab rather than leave it. We emphasized that our object was to help the local administration in maintaining law and order and looking after the welfare of the refugees who had come from across the border as well as safeguard the passage of those who were going across the border to Pakistan.

My Fast

The Central Government and the Punjab Government appreciated our move. We had our units in each village and town of Punjab. Our popularity irked the Congress Government of Punjab and after a year of our activities, the Punjab Government banned us accusing General Mohan Singh of trying to subvert the Punjab Government. We did not mind the ban, now that order had been restored and our purpose fulfilled to some degree, but the accusation of subversion was a stigma to our organisation and to us which suggested disloyalty to the nation.

I took the matter too seriously and went on fast for an indefinite period. I laid down two conditions for ending it: one, that the Punjab Government should withdraw the accusation or try us in a court of law, and two, some sort of volunteer force be raised by the Government. The Government did not yield for a long time. During my fast, I had resolved to take only water, salt and bicarbonate of soda. During my fast the people of Punjab used to come to where I was fasting under a tent in Majitha House at Amritsar. Daily I had thousands of visitors coming to show their support. When my health started deteriorating and our popularity grew, the Government of Punjab yielded.

The Punjab Home minister, Sardar Swaran Singh, came down from Simla to Beas Dak Bungalow on the banks of the river Beas. Swaran Singh, the Punjab Congress Committee President, Shri Gurmukh Singh Musafar, Sardar Ishar Singh Majhail on one hand and General Mohan Singh and Col. N.S. Gill on the other held prolonged discussions. The Government withdrew the accusation unconditionally and promised that they would find ways and means to establish a National Volunteer Force in due time. Then all three of them came to my tent in Amritsar. I was offered orange juice and thus ended my fast in triumph after two weeks' time. I was happy when ultimately National Cadet Corps (NCC) was started in 1948 for students, both boys and girls, and still later B.S.F. came into being.

Following the success of my fast we raised the Desh Sewak Party. The Desh Sewak Sena was non-political organisation, while the Desh Sewak Party was political in character. It captured the imagination of the national leadership of the Forward Bloc. We felt that the Desh Sewak Party was only a regional party. The Forward Bloc appealed to us because it had been raised by Netaji. Pandit Sheel Bhadhra Yajee invited us to join the Forward Bloc. We dissolved Desh Sewak Party and joined the Forward Bloc. The Forward Bloc by that time had split into two separate parties. One party was called the All-India Forward Bloc (Marxist). The other was called the All-India Forward Bloc.

INA veterans enjoyed popularity among both the segments of the Forward Bloc. In course of time General Mohan Singh was elected President of the Marxist wing and I was elected General Secretary. Our All-India headquarters at that time were located in Calcutta where the party had been founded by Netaji. At Calcutta Netaji's elder brother Shri Sarat Chandra Bose invited us and all the progressive parties of India to join together in the socialist organization of India. Sarat Bose was elected President. General Mohan Singh, Shri S.S. More, Yajeeji and Yajnik were elected as Vice-Presidents. After the death of Sarat Chandra Bose, this organisation became defunct.

We continued in the Forward Bloc till the Chinese attacked Tibet. A meeting of the All-India Forward Bloc was called in Calcutta. The political resolution under consideration dealt mainly with the Tibetan issue. The majority of Working Committee members, including Mohan Singh and Yajee, were in favour of the Chinese occupation of Tibet. Some members even went to the extent of saying that Netaji was returning to India via Tibet to save India from the pro-British Nehru Government. I had no love for the Nehru Government, but I did not agree with the contentions of the majority. So I opposed the resolution. My opposition to the resolution was construed by the youth wing of the Forward Bloc as opposition to Netaji.

The next morning I was mobbed by about fifty students at the residence of my host, Shri Nirmal Chandra Ghosh. A heated discussion ensued. As a result, the resolution, when brought before the Working Committee that day, could not be passed. The students had switched on to my view. Yajeeji and General Mohan Singh took me aside to plead that I should withdraw my opposition or at least not speak at the meeting so the resolution could be passed. I told them that I had utmost respect for them but if I were present I could not keep silent and would oppose the resolution. Therefore, I would not attend the Working Committee meeting at all. I further told them that they should kindly allow me to resign from the Forward Bloc. They objected to my resignation and advised me not to take such a step as the party would be weakened. I told them that unlike politicians I would quietly leave the party without making any statement. I left politics, but remained for about a fortnight with Mr. Ghosh, a Forward Bloc supporter since the time of Netaji.

My stay in Calcutta was prolonged because I wanted to find a means of livelihood there. I decided to become a taxi driver and approached the Chief Minister of West Bengal, Dr. B.C. Roy, one of the great men of India. I requested him to grant me a licence for a small owner driven taxicab and also sanction a loan for its purchase. I would repay the loan in instalments. Dr. Roy promised to help me and asked me to call on him at his residence the next morning. When I called on him the next day, he had just finished his daily routine of examining his patients. He was a doctor of most outstanding reputation. In spite of his age and administrative responsibilities as Chief Minister, he used to examine patients at his residence without charging any fee. As usual, a large crowd of people was waiting at his residence. He took me to his consultation room, gave me two thousand rupees and said, "Take this money instead of a loan and apply for a car and you will get a permit. I will talk to the boy who looks after the Transport Ministry." Dr. Roy was in the habit of referring to his ministers as '*chhelas*' (youths) instead of ministers.

I returned to Ghosh's house to announce the success of my meeting with Dr. Roy. In the evening about two hundred young men and women of the Forward Bloc came to tell me that they would not allow Netaji's Colonel Dhillon to do such a lowly job of a taxi driver on the roads of Calcutta where Netaji had grown up. They said they would burn my car. They refused to leave the house until I promised that I would not become a taxi driver nor own a taxicab.

The next day I learnt that my father had died (June 1952) in an accident in Ludhiana under suspicious circumstances. He was about seventy-four years old at the time. The newspapers of Calcutta flashed the news. I flew back to Punjab, and the money given by Dr. Roy became very handy in that difficult situation.

During 1951 I had met Kavi Ghasi Ram Jain when we were travelling together from Bombay to Delhi. I had boarded the train at Bombay during the night. Kaviji along with two friends had boarded the same train at a suburb of Bombay. In the morning I asked the people on the lower berth if I could climb down and sit beside them. They made room for me and I sat there for quite a long time looking at the landscape and marvelling at the sight of small fortresses. Pointing to a suitcase bearing the name G.S. Dhillon, Kavi Ghasi Ram asked me courteously, "Is that your suitcase?"

I replied, "Yes, it is mine."

"Is your name G.S. Dhillon?"

"Yes".

"There is one Col. G.S. Dhillon who was in the INA. Do you know him?"

"Yes, I know him very well."

"Is he related to you?"

"Yes."

"Where is he these days?"

"*Is waqat woh mujhi mein brajman hain*" (At the moment he is residing in me).

Immediately all three of them left their seat, touched my feet and were so overjoyed that they started asking questions about me, the INA and Netaji. After some time Kavi Ghasi Ram wanted to know why I was so absorbed in looking at the landscape. I answered that a soldier's job is to observe the lie of the land from the point of view of defence, and as most of the soldiers come from farming stock they are interested in the land from the agricultural point of view too.

"Where is your farm?", he asked.

I answered that I had left it in Pakistan.

"Are you in need of some land?", he asked.

"Yes."

"Of what kind? Can you describe where and what type of land do you need?"

I said, "About ten miles away from a town which should have educational and hospital facilities. It needs to be connected by road to the town and be beside a brook or a river, with a hill nearby. The seller of the land should not charge me any down payment as I have no money now. I will earn and pay by instalments. "

Ghasi Ram said that he had a piece of land that fulfilled all my requirements.

After my father's death I received a letter of condolence from Kavi Ghasi Ram inviting me to visit Shivpuri in case I still wanted to purchase some farm land. About two months later, I went to visit Shivpuri. Shri Ghasi Ram received me at the bus stand along with a crowd of people carrying garlands in their hands. Later on, he took me to the proposed land. I liked it very much and we struck a deal with the two owners, Shri Jasram and Shri Damodar Dass. Later on Hafiz Nisar too gave me land without any price. The land in Shivpuri in those days was much less expensive than in Punjab. I had to lead the life of a pioneer in thatched huts for eighteen long years. Basant was my biggest support. She died on March 19, 1968, when the land had started just to support us.

In the fifties, Dr. Panjab Rao Deshmukh, Deputy Minister for Agriculture, Government of India formed a farmers' organisation, Bharat Krishak Samaj. He was kind enough to take me on the Governing Body of the B.K.S.

In 1959, under the aegis of the Bharat Krishak Samaj, a World Agricultural Fair was organised on the Fair Grounds on Mathura Road, New Delhi. I was assigned the job of Chief Security Officer of the Fair which was inaugurated by Gen. Eisenhover, the President of the United States of America. During that period I had an opportunity to escort several Heads of States and many world figures, apart from Indian dignitaries. They included General Dwight David Eisenhover - President of U.S.A., Nobel Laurete Albert Einstein - the great physicist, Her Majesty Queen Elizebeth the 2nd and Her Royal Consort Prince Philips, Nikita Sergeyich Khurushchev - the Soviet First Secretary of the U.S.S.R., President Vorchelov of U.S.S.R., Lady Mountbatten, His Majesty the King of Bhutan, His Majesty the King of Nepal, Chouen Lai, the Prime Minister of China, Field Marshal Lord Montgomery of Alamein from Great Britain. A National Agricultural Fair was also held in Calcutta the following year which secured the participation of international farmers' bodies also.

One of the blunders of my life was that when I was leaving Punjab for Shivpuri, some of my relatives, political colleagues and friends wanted to accompany me and I allowed them to come. I got fifty acres of unreclaimed land granted by the Government for each one of them. All those who came with me had neither means of cultivation nor funds to provide them. The Government at that time favoured the formation of co-operative societies. The piece of land I had purchased through Kavi Ghasi Ram was the only productive land under irrigation. We formed Dhillon's Co-operative Joint Farming Society. According to our by-laws we pooled our lands. A part of the land was in the name of my wife and it was kept out of the co-operative as a precautionary measure. None of the members except me had funds to put in the pool and mine, too, were borrowed from Kavi Ghasi Ram or through him. As debts began to mount, members started deserting the Co-operative Society because they could get land elsewhere and keep it in their names. The idea of joint pooling of land in the name of the Co-operative Society was not viable.

In 1957, I went to the United States. The visit was arranged by the Farmers' Forum of India and the U.S. Department of Agriculture, which sponsored the exchange programme. One of the lessons I learnt from the farmers in the U.S. during our three-and-a-half months visit was that the farmers there made their budget before investing in their crops. They kept accounts. On return from the States, I had a balance sheet made for my personal as well as the Co-operative's accounts, which for all practical purposes were in my name. I was shocked to find that I was under a debt of ninety-seven thousand rupees. I calculated that in case I had to clear all the debts and the interest on the principal, it would take the rest of my life to do so. In order not to increase the interest I disposed of half of Basant's land to clear the debts. Only fifty per cent of the debt was cleared.

When China attacked India in October 1962, I wrote a letter to the Prime Minister Pandit Jawaharlal Nehru and offered my services unconditionally, anywhere in any capacity at any time to serve my country. It resulted in a three-year stint for me in the National Cadet Corps (N.C.C.) at the Madhya Pradesh N.C.C. Directorate at Indore from 1964 to 1967. I was taken in the rank of a Lieutenant. But Brigadier Hardial Singh Randhawa, Director N.C.C., Madhya Pradesh, got me promoted to the rank of an acting Captain. Though it was humiliating to be an acting Captain, I accepted it as I had volunteered my services unconditionally. By the time I got this appointment, Chinese aggression had become a story of the past. I spent those three years at Indore. I was lucky to have kind officers under whom I had to serve. I shall ever remain grateful to the N.C.C. My gain was that I could have my children, Amrita, Amarjit and Sarvjit to be with me at Indore. This helped me to continue their education. My gain was that I got to know, the Director General of N.C.C., Major General Virendra Singh who was very kind to me. Brigadier Randhawa was my "friend of the accused" during the Red Fort trial and Brigadier P.R. Dewan was known to me since my Indian Military Academy days at Dehra Dun. I got some very good friends in the persons of Wing Commanders V.R. Malik, D.B. Mahindra, Colonels V.S. Chitnis, S.R. Mohan, Major Kunwar Abhey Singh and Major Professor Gurdev Singh Deol and above all Major Rajendra Nath Mehrotra, my son-in-law.

I had to work for the MANNES MANN, a German construction company that was laying a pipeline from Assam to Bihar. This necessitated that I had to go to Bengal for one year. I was the Chief Security and Administrative Officer responsible for liaison work between the German Company and the Indian Government. I was also expected to supervise labour. I succeeded in paying about ten thousand rupees against my Society's loans by the end of the year. I was compelled to sell some of the Co-operative's land and thus managed to repay all the debt and dissolve the Co-operative. In the process, seven landless families including four Adivasis got lands. I was left with hardly eighty acres of land which I divided among my daughter Amrita and two sons Amarjit and Sarvjit. I had no land of my own after the division. So I purchased five and a quarter acres of land where I built my present residence which I call Dhillon's Den.

I am grateful to the people of my village Hatod and the people of Shivpuri and of Madhya pradesh for their love and kindness without which I could not have been able to settle down honourably.

I am further indebted to certain son-like friends who do not allow me to mention their names but helped me to build my Den at the feet of Hatod Hill—BETI MAYYA KI PAHARI—in the lap of Mother Nature.

26

MEMORABILIA

Quit India Golden Jubilee

On 9th August in 1992, the Golden Jubilee of the Quit India Movement was celebrated under the aegis of the Central Government's Ministry of Human Resource Development, the Department of Culture. The main function was held in *Dewan-e-Aam* at the Red Fort of Delhi. Thousands of veteran freedom fighters from all over the country participated by special invitation. Some chosen leaders addressed the huge gathering on behalf of their movements. Col. P.K. Sahgal spoke for the INA. The Prime Minister Shri P.V. Narasimha Rao dedicated a part of the Red Fort to the Nation as a mark of homage to the freedom fighters who struggled, suffered and sacrificed for the freedom of the motherland.

Shri Arjun Singh, Minister Human Resource Development, during his address declared that the barrack in which the General Court Martial was held to try the INA officers for waging war against the King as well as the barracks where they were kept as prisoners would be acquired from the Ministry of Defence and made into a Museum of the Freedom Struggle. Shri Rajesh Pilot, Minister for Communications spoke on the freedom struggle and announced certain facilities for installation of telephone connections at concessional rates to freedom fighters.

Swatantrata Sangram Sangrahalaya

Eventually on 2nd October 1995, 125th Birth Anniversary of the Father of the Nation, Mahatma Gandhi, Prime Minister Shri P.V. Narasimha Rao inaugurated a freedom struggle museum called SWATANTRATA SANGRAM SANGRAHALAYA at the Red Fort.

The venue of the inaugural ceremony was again the historic *Dewan-e-Aam*. This time Shri Madhav Rao Scindia was the Minister for Human Resource Development who welcomed the veteran freedom fighters and V.I.P. guests. Shri Shashi Bhushan spoke on behalf of the All India Freedom Fighters' Organization. Col. Lakshmi, Commander of the legendary Rani Jhansi Regiment of the INA who was a minister of the Provisional Government of Azad Hind was on the dais. In the absence of Col. Sahgal and General Shah Nawaz and most of the INA Commanders and colleagues, when I was asked to speak, 1 found it difficult to address the gathering. I was lost in the past about which I spoke with emotion.

The Prime Minister Rao said :

> The establishment of the Swatantra Sangram Sangrahalaya has come not a day too soon. The Museum will be a tribute to those great sons and daughters of India who participated in the freedom struggle and who have left a lasting legacy, for generations of Indians to admire and emulate. The Museum will capture the events of those momentous times. Every individual who walks into the Museum will be able to experience the spirit of the freedom struggle and the trials and tribulations of those known and unknown leaders and men and women across the length and breadth of India to whom we owe our freedom today.
>
> Millions of people from India and abroad visit the historic Red Fort and get a glimpse of India's heritage. It is only fitting that the Swatantrata Sangram Sangrahalaya should be located in the Red Fort. It saw the beginning of the first war of independence in 1857. It was also in the barracks of the Fort that the freedom fighters were tried. There is history in every brick of these buildings.
>
> On the auspicious Birth Anniversary of Mahatma Gandhi, I dedicate the Sangrahalaya to the nation and to the memory of the heroic men and women, peasants

> and workers, students and professionals who participated in the attainment of Swaraj.

Kumari Selja, the Minister of State for Education and Culture thanked the participants, institutions and organizations and individuals who helped in various ways in organizing the Museum which is divided into thirty episodes of the freedom struggle from 1857 to 1947. It embraces practically all the waves of the freedom struggle. There are seven dioramas in fiber glass depicting:

Rani Lakshmi Bai of Jhansi, Bahadur Shah Zafar, Gandhiji's Dandi March, Netaji Subhas Chandra Bose taking salute at an INA Review, Jalianwala Bagh Massacre, INA Trial of Shah Nawaz, Sahgal and Dhillon and Pandit Nehru speaking from the rampart of the Red Fort. There are many historical paintings in oil and colour, busts of great men and women, photographs of historic events and persons. Going through the Museum is a walk through history of the freedom struggle.

Salimgarh Swantantrata Senani Smarak

It is located to the north of the Red Fort and is connected with a bridge in the fortress of Salimgarh. It was built by Islam Shah also known as Salim Shah - son and successor of Sher Shah Suri (1540-45). After the death of Salim Shah in 1552, Salimgarh remained neglected for a long time and then passed through good and bad days. During the reign of Aurangzeb (1658-1707) Salimgarh served as a state prison. Prince Murad Bakhsh and Prince Sulaiman Shikoh spent parts of their incarceration here. During 1857 Salimgarh was one of the strongest bulwarks of the national forces under the command of Mohammad Bakht Khan against the British.

It was in Salimgarh that General Mohan Singh, Maj. Gen. J.K.L. Bhonsle, Maj. Gen. A.D. Loganathan, Maj. Gen. Aziz Ahmad, Maj. Gen. Shah Nawaz Khan, Colonel Ehsan Qadir, Col. S.M. Hussain, Col. Raja Mohammad Arshad, Col. J.W. Rodrigues, Col. P.K. Sahgal, Col. Jagir Singh, Col. Mehar Dass, *Sardar- e-Jung*, Col. A.B. Singh, Major Abdul Qayum, Maj. Abdul Rashid, myself and many officers and men were imprisoned. General Mohan Singh had the distinction of being kept in a small solitary cell throughout his incarceration in the Red Fort. The rest of us lived together in barracks. We were not even aware of his presence in Salimgarh for a long time, so strict was the security.

It was in Salimgarh that two of our good and brave officers Major Maghar Singh and Major Ajmer Singh committed suicide. They both belonged to the Intelligence Group of the INA. They were caught in the Kohima sector and brought to Red Fort. They were daily tortured but they refused to disclose any information about the INA and the Japanese dispositions. When they felt that they might not be able to keep the secret under daily torture, they planned to snatch a guard's rifle one night and committed suicide.

Here on 26th November 1995, the President, Dr. Shankar Dayal Sharma inaugurated a museum called Salimgarh Swatantrata Senani Smarak. During his inaugural address, the President paid rich tributes to the selfless and undaunted contribution made by the freedom fighters to the achievement of independence of the country. He recalled that it was at Salimgarh that Shah Nawaz, Sahgal and myself and hundreds of the members of the Azad Hind Fauj of Netaji Subhas Chandra Bose were imprisoned. During my speech, I suggested that a tower, tall like the Qutab Minar be built at the Red Fort in memory of Netaji, the liberator of India. I also suggested that the defenders of Independent India after August 1947 deserve a special memorial at a different place than India Gate which the British made to the memory of those who died to defend the British Empire. The President said that the values of the freedom movement were our proud heritage and the memorial would remind the sacrifices made by freedom fighters and serve as an inspiration to strive hard to realise their dream of a strong, united and prosperous India.

The President of the All India Freedom Fighters' Organisation, Pandit Sheelbhadra Yajee, an associate of Netaji since the twenties, spoke about Netaji, his experiences and trial at the Red Fort as a soldier is court-martialled. He said that Azad Hind Fauj had become so popular that though Pandit Nehru did not see eye to eye with Netaji, he could not help being attracted by the public opinion. No wonder he donned a lawyer's gown to attend the INA trial of Shah Nawaz, Sahgal and myself.

In his welcome address, the Minister for Human Resource Development, Shri Madhav Rao Scindia explained and appreciated how Salimgarh was developed by the Archaeological Survey of India after it was taken over from the Armed Forces. He described the inauguration of the memorial as a new chapter in our history which would constantly remind us of the sacrifices of our freedom fighters. The Minister of State for Education and Culture, Kumari Selja thanked the freedom fighters and all the participants in the inaugural function. "Salimgarh Fort is now Delhi's latest landmark", said a news reporter.

Being one of the surviving prisoners of the Red Fort and the Salimgarh fortess, I offer my gratitude to the Prime Minister Mr. Narsimha Rao, the Ministry of Human Resource Development, the Department of Culture and Education and Archaeological Survey of India and to all those artists and organisations and individuals and workers who contributed, laboured round-the-clock to establish this museum.

Enemy of Empire

History has ways of its own. It unveils buried and forgotten events of bygone days. On 29th May in 1995, I received a telegram from Ms. Anuradha, a Delhi-based representative of the British Broadcasting Corporation (B.B.C.) that Mr. Charles Bruce wanted to phone me from London. She asked for my phone number. Consequently Mr. Bruce rang me from London on 2nd May. He asked me for an appointment of an hour or two at my place. I told him that I would be happy to meet him at Delhi to avoid him inconvenience of coming to an out of the way place only for two hours involving 4 to 5 hours of journey by train from Delhi to Gwalior and then another two to three hours from Gwalior to Hatod by road, over and above his journey from London and back. Mr. Bruce said, "I want to see where a veteran of INA lives". "You are welcome," said I. Bruce visited me on 6th May 1995. Rajendra, my son-in-law, received him at Gwalior and left him at Gwalior to return to Delhi the same day. Bruce interviewed me and told me that he would bring his crew to make a film on Netaji.

As planned, the B.B.C. crew arrived on 17th May. They were received at Gwalior railway station by Rajendra and my grandson Maneesh Mehrotra and were brought to my Den in village Hatod. The crew comprised: Mr. Charles Bruce - the Producer, Mr. Nigel Davey - the cameraman, and Mr. John Parker - the sound recorder. They started their work immediately on arrival. They spent full two days shooting my place and interviewing me. Maneesh and Om, my maid servant, were of great help to me in looking after this hardworking B.B.C. crew. They had already shot the story related to Netaji at various places in Singapore and South East Asia, Japan and India before coming to me. They had yet some more persons and places to go. The film thus made was telecast on Channel - 2 of the B.B.C. London at 8 p.m. on Sunday, 13th August, 1995 under the title, Enemy of Empire. Mr. Bruce kindly sent me a tape through Ms. Shanaz of the B.B.C. stationed in Delhi. There was a small note along the tape in Charles' own hand, "It's a tall order to tell the life of Subhas Chandra Bose in 50 minutes, but I hope you will enjoy it." Yes, I did enjoy seeing the film. It was objective. When they were shooting the film, I had asked Mr. Bruce, "You are recording so much, how much will you telecast?" His answer was, "Only that much which can be contained within 50 minutes. The rest of the story will be kept in archives."

My son-in-law and grandson drove them back to Gwalior. They were gone but I kept on pondering for quite sometime over the British ways of keeping historical records. Thank you Charles and thank you B.B.C.

Azad Hind Expedition

While the Ministry of Human Resource Development were busy developing museums of the freedom struggle in the Red Fort and Salimgarh, I was approached by Shri Akhil Bakshi, President of Yuva Shakti and Lt. Col. S.S. Singh, a retired Army Officer with an invitation to join them on Azad Hind Expedition under the auspices of Yuva Shakti - a national organisation of the Indian youth. The proposed expedition, they informed me, was to traverse the routes taken by Azad Hind Fauj when Netaji Subhas Chandra Bose ordered them, "*Chalo Delhi* - On to Delhi". The expedition sought to refresh the national memory with the spirit of patriotism demonstrated by INA on the battlefields for the attainment of the Indian independence. The expedition was to instill the will amongst the people especially the young men and women of India to live up to the slogan of INA—UNITY, FAITH, SACRIFICE.

My immediate reaction to the invitation was that I should be left alone due to my weak health because of running irregular pulse for the previous three years. Bakshi and Singh were not prepared to accept 'No' from me. Ultimately their will prevailed. I accepted their kind invitation. I am glad that I did go on the Expedition.

The Expedition was composed of 18 members including Mr. Bakshi, the leader and Lt. Col. S.S. Singh, the deputy leader. Members were chosen on merit. We had Lt. Col. V.J.S. Grewal, a military historian and Burmese interpreter. Born, brought up and educated in Myanmar, he was of great assistance with his knowledge of Myanmar, her people, their nature and culture. There was Mr. Sunil Dutt, Member of the Parliament and an eminent film artist, a darling of the masses. I have been his fan ever since I saw him act along with late Nargis in the film, *Mother India*. There were three INA veterans including myself, the other two were Col. Lakshmi Sahgal, Commander of the legendary Rani Jhansi Regiment of the INA as well as the member of the Cabinet of the Provisional Government of Azad Hind of which Netaji was the Head of the State. The third INA veteran was Captain S.S. Yadava, presently General Secretary of the All India INA Association. We had Ajmal Shah Nawaz Khan, younger son of General Shah Nawaz, who apart from reminding us of his father, was a great helping hand to us especially to me. We had Dr. Darchhawana, Professor of Modern History from Meghalaya with us. We loved to call him Dara. Dr. Chhiring Dorji of the Archaeological Survey of India from Lahol Spiti is a serious research scholar of History and Geography. We had another matchless personality with us - Shri Narindra Srivastava, a graphic artist and Jawaharlal Nehru Fellow with us, quick-witted, outspoken and a very keen observer. Dr. Rajendra Jain, M.S. was the Expedition Medical In-charge. He is presently Medical Superintendent, KTS Cottage Hospital, Gondia. I was down with an acute attack of malaria just before going on the Expedition. I was very weak. But for Dr. Jain's presence and treatment I could not have continued to remain in the Expedition. There was a four-member film crew comprising Mr. Kabir Khan, Cinematographer and Mountaineer, Ms. Navaz Bhatena, Production co-ordinator and Rally driver, Mr. Vineet Sabharwal, Cinematographer and Adventure Film-maker, and Mr. Raj Kumar, Sound Recordist and Maintenance Engineer. The Expedition had five Armadas which kept us on the move during the 8,000 km. long route of Azad Hind Fauj from Singapore to Delhi through Malaysia and Myanmar. These Armadas were loaned to us by Messrs Mahindra and Mahindra. They also let two of their seasoned maintenance engineers accompany us. They were M/s Nazir Chagla and Gavin Herts.

The Expedition departed from Delhi for Singapore by an Air India flight on 14th December 1995. Before our departure we had a farewell dinner hosted by Colonel Harsh Kaul, the Commandant and the Officers of 6/5th Gurkha Rifles. Mr. Ashish Ray, grand nephew of Netaji and Chief of South Asia Bureau of CNN gave us a dinner at the India International Centre. It was attended by quite a number of Ministers, members of the Parliament, Members of the Press and many national celebrities headed by the Vice President of India, Shri K.R. Narayanan presently President (1997) and his wife. Captain Satish Sharma, Chairman of the Azad Hind Expedition and Minister of State for Petroleum and Gas treated us to tea followed by a Press Conference. Before our departure we called on the Prime Minister Shri P.V. Narasimha Rao who wished us godspeed.

Late on the night of 14th December, 1995 we landed at Changi International Airport, the best of its kind in the world. Singapore has grown into a city beyond recognition of its colonial past. In search of living space it has expanded skyward yet retained its natural environmental greenery. It is admirable, the way the people and the Government of Singapore have maintained the historical monuments of foreign nations irrespective of any bias of any sort.

It is gratifying to note that landmarks related to Indian National Army stand today as they were half a century ago during the history-making days of the Azad Hind.

Farrar Park : Where the Indian troops were surrendered to the Japanese Major (later Lieutenant General) Fujiwara by the British and in turn Fujiwara handed them over to Captain (later General) Mohan Singh. This is the place where Mohan Singh expounded his idea of raising the INA. It was at this Park where mammoth rallies were held where we heard and cheered leaders of the Indian Independence League (I.I.L.) and the INA speak. This place can be called the birthplace of the INA, though it was conceived up north in the jungles of Jitra by

Giani Pritam Singh, Maj. Fujiwara, Capt. Mohan Singh and Capt. Mohammad Akram.

Cathay Building was, during the war, the tallest and the most prominent landmark of the town of Singapore. It had a large cinema hall. It was in this hall that Rash Behari Bose had handed over the leadership of the Indian Independence movement to Netaji Subhas Chandra Bose on 4th July, 1943. It was here that Netaji proclaimed to the world the formation of the Provisional Government of Azad Hind on 21st October, 1943. Col. Lakshmi, the Commander of Rani Jhansi Regiment, who was also one of the members of the Expedition, is the honoured surviving member of Netaji's Cabinet who took oath of office along with Netaji on that historic day. Azad Hind Radio used to broadcast from this very building. It is remarkable that the people and the Government of Singapore have retained and maintained this historical landmark in its originality. They have put up a distinctive bronze plaque on the open lawn on one side of its front with an inscription informing about the formation of the Azad Hind Government by Netaji on 21st October, 1943.

Rani Jhansi Camp was located in the middle of the town of Singapore. It was in the northwesterly direction of Cathay Building at a distance of about 500 metres. There were hurriedly made makeshift barracks with enough of open space which served as training grounds. The camp was secured by a screen of planks and wire around it. During our visit in the middle of December 1995, we found the place well maintained as open playing fields. It was a pleasant sight to see children practising football. Little did those lovely young Singaporeans know the great contribution of their playing field to the Indian Independence.

Padang, a large open ground - maidan - in front of the City Hall is the place where General Mohan Singh held the inaugural parade of the INA on Mahatma Gandhi's birthday, 2nd October, 1943. It was at this very place that Netaji reviewed the INA for the first time on 5th July, 1943 and during his address gave us the slogan of "*Chalo Delhi*". Following this historic occasion, on the 6th of July, the Prime Minister of Japan, General Tojo reviewed the INA. In a corner of the Padang, Netaji laid the foundation of the INA Memorial to our martyrs. This memorial was unveiled by Major General Mohammad Zaman Kiani, the Supreme Commander of the INA. Before leaving Singapore on his last journey, Netaji had appointed General Kiani to be the Supreme Commander. When the British reoccupied Singapore, the INA Memorial was destroyed by the British under the orders of Lord Mountbatten. Today there stands a bronze plaque, put up by the Government of Singapore to mark the place. The plaque has an inscription stating the history of the Memorial.

During our brief stay at Singapore, we the three veterans of the INA, Col. Lakshmi, Capt. S.S. Yadav and I, visited the above places. An experienced film crew composed of Ms. Nawaz Bhatena, Mr. Raj Kumar, Mr. Vineet Sabharwal and Mr. Kabir Khan took us for shooting documentary film concerning the spots connected with the INA history. This crew was amazingly active throughout the Expedition. They were very keen to capture all the moods of the nature during various times of the day with technical mastery. Their days always began an hour before sunrise and ended long after sunset. Again when the day was gone they would be awake for hours during the night to dig books to gain knowledge of history, places and the persons whom they were to interview on the following day. Their patience and sense of objectivity in dealing with their subject were admirable.

Our stay in Singapore was only of about 60 hours' duration. During this period we along with the Indian High Commissioner paid a courtesy call on the Minister for Parliamentary Affairs who received us on behalf of the Prime Minister of Singapore, who at the time was out of the country on a foreign visit. The leader of the Expedition, Shri Akhil Bakshi delivered a letter of thanks and goodwill on behalf of the Indian Prime Minister. Exchange of courtesies between the two sides was a pleasant experience. We had a press conference. It was arranged at the office of India's High Commissioner - a rather poor building with neither enough of accommodation nor furnished well enough to match the dignity of a national mission of our country. The disappointment was however made up by the courtesy and cordiality displayed by the High Commissioner and members of his Mission. The response of the Press was indeed encouraging. The following day, 16th December, the High Commissioner gave a buffet reception at his residence where the Indian gentry of Singapore were invited to meet the members of the Expedition. It was a happy gathering. It included the three surviving Singaporeans of the Indian Independence

Movement. They were Lieut. John Jacob of INA, Mr. Ram Prakash of I.I.L. and Mr. S. Sokalingarn of the Bal Sena. In spite of being a heart patient, Jacob joined the Expedition from Yangon onward up to Delhi on his own expense.

By 1100 hrs. on Sunday the 17th December, 1995, Singaporean Indians, members of the High Commissioner's office in Singapore, local veterans of the INA and I.I.L. and the members of the Azad Hind Expedition assembled in one corner of Padang. Here we paid homage to the hallowed ground where once stood the INA Memorial to our glorious dead. Wreaths were laid by the High Commissioner and the leader of the Azad Hind Expedition and rose petals sprinkled by all of us on the sacred bronze plaque inscribed with *"Itefaq! Itemad! and Kurbani!"* (Unity - Faith - Sacrifice). In full-throated emotional voice we sang the Azad Hind National Anthem :

> *Shubh sukh chain ki barkha barse, Bharat bhagya hai jaga!*
>
> (May the auspicious shower of happiness, peace and prosperity pour on the glorious fate of the rising India).

And the slogans of:

> *Chalo Delhi!*
>
> *Azad Hind Zindabad!*
>
> *Inqilab Zindabad!*
>
> *Netaji Zindabad!*
>
> (On to Delhi! Long live Free India! Long live Freedom! Long live Netaji! Long live Revolution!)

echoed across the buildings as the High Commissioner of India, Shri Prem Singh flagged off the Expedition composed of five white Armadas formed up like a fleet of "Warships". Each Armada bore the emblem of the Azad Hind Fauj, The Leaping Tiger and a title of one of its Field Regiments, Subhas, Gandhi, Rani Jhansi, Nehru and Jai Hind. With the drop of the flag by the High Commissioner, the fleet rolled on or I may say charged on to the Chalo Delhi trail of eight thousand kilometres long laid by Azad Hind Fauj during its War of Liberation half a century ago. This was the trail on which many of our glorious dead had marched onto the battle to pay the price of India's liberty in full measure, when Netaji had said, *"Tum mujhe khoon do, main tumhe azadi doonga!"* (Give me blood, I will give you freedom).

The advance of Armadas was full of nostalgia. I could not help recalling the days when Netaji personally used to bless and see off his soldiers go to the front. The nomenclature Armada reminded me of the days of the Middle Ages when British Admiral Nelson's armada advanced on to Trafalgar and secured Britain from invasion by the Spanish Armada and her allies. The scenes of such a distant history passed on the screen of my mind's eyes as Armadas passed through the Singapore battlefields of 1942. And I recalled the plight of Singaporeans which I had actually seen half a century ago:

Woh dordte the jis taraf, thi maut hoti us taraf,
Theen auratain bache liye, behosh firti ik taraf,
Sar pur uthaye bojh the, bache kisi ki goud the,
Paon mein chhaley pad gaaey
Halat buri mein kesh the
Sehme hue chehere liye, ye auratoun ke bhes the,
Ehsas ka mada na tha, hum desh ya pardesh the!
(Whichever way did people sway,
Death was there awaiting.
Women had loads on their heads,
And children folded in their arms.
Thus weighed down they treaded the ground,
With tired and blistered feet.
Their ruffled hair and frightened looks,
Spoke world of woes around them.
With feelings benumbed they couldn't discern
Where on earth were they,
In their own their native land,
Or on an alien soil?)

After crossing the causeway of Johr Bahru we entered the mainland of Malaysia. Our destination that evening was Kuala Lumpur. In Malaysia live the maximum number of INA veterans. The

Ambassador of India in Kuala Lumpur invited all of them and the prominent citizens of the capital to meet the members of the Expedition at dinner. About seventy five, of the INA veterans turned up. Some of them were too aged and sick even to walk. Amriek Singh of the Secret Service of the INA was one of them. He was brought in a wheel chair. They were headed by the legendary figure of the Rani of Jhansi Regiment's 2nd-in-Command Captain Janaki Thever. They were all honoured by an award of a certificate of merit.

From Kaula Lumpur, the Expedition moved on to Penang from where it sailed off for Moulmein in Myanmar. The route from there to Yangon is a difficult one. In regard of our age, Col. Lakshmi Sahgal, Capt. S.S. Yadav and I were left behind at Kuala Lumpur. Capt. Janaki played the host.

Captain Janaki is a very generous host. Our stay at Kuala Lumpur from 18th to 28th December came to me as a boon for I could fully recover my health, which had gone very weak due to malaria. Then I took the opportunity to go to Ipoh with Dr. Perdamen Singh and Manjit, his wife who is my niece. Their daughter Harjit is also a doctor. They all looked after me as a convalescent but I was determined to visit all those places around Ipoh which were a reminder of war days. I am grateful to Perdamen for taking me to Jitra, Alor Star and Penang.

At Ipoh a veteran of the INA, Lal Harcharan Singh took me to Kuala Kangsar to show me the place where 6th Guerrilla Regiment under Col. Gurmit Singh was stationed. Gurmit was a famous hockey player of Dhayan Chand's Olympic team. I celebrated the Christmas at Ipoh and on the following day, 26th December, 1995, Perdamen and Manjit dropped me back at Kuala Lumpur at Janki's place. On 27th Lakshmi, Janaki, Sumathi (a young enthusiast of Netaji Centre, Kuala Lumpur), Yadav and I flew to Yangon to join the main body of the Expedition. We were in Yangon till 9th of January 1996. This stay in Yangon was used to visit the INA Supreme Headquarters and various camps, right up to Ziawaddi and Pegu. We also visited the golden-spired pagoda, Shwedagon and paid homage at Bahadur Shah Zafar's grave and General Aung San's memorial.

The Ambassador of India Mr. L.J. Pudaite and Mrs. Pudaite honoured us by inviting us to a dinner where most of the Indian gentry was present. He also gave us a New Year Eve banquet. In Yangon we called on Shri Dina Nath who was one of the pillars of I.I.L., presently disabled because of paralysis. He cannot even speak. There are about 11 INA veterans living in Yangon in utter poverty. They deserve some kind of support from the mother country.

On Tuesday, 9th January 1996, five members of the Expedition consisting of Kabir, Nawaz, Rajkumar, Lakshmi and I flew to Bagan. We visited the battlefields of Nyangu and Bagan, where the 4th Guerrilla Regiment of INA had opposed the southern crossing of the Irrawady by 14th Army under General Slim. From Bagan we drove on to Kyaukpadaung and visited Mount Popa. This was the area where Shah Nawaz, Sahgal and I (Dhillon) had qualified for a joint trial at the Red Fort in Delhi. That was the trial which turned our defeat into victory.

This is the place in Myanmar which I hold sacred. Here during the youth of my life I could serve my country the most. It was here that my men on the call of Netaji paid the price of liberty with their blood. In gratitude and homage to their memory and to the ground all around hallowed with their flesh, blood and bones I prostrated on that holy land and kissed it. I wept. I missed all my comrades in arms and the local folks - real good friends in need. It was something to be there after a lapse of fifty years. It was something to greet them "Jai Hind" again.

I am grateful to Lt. General S.L. Menezes PVSM, SC for his observations on page 395 of his book - *THE INDIAN ARMY* (published by Penguin Books India [P] Ltd. 1993). It pertains to this very place:

> This period in the INA story is portrayed in a GHQ (India) Intelligence Summary." "A measure of courage cannot be denied to the Leaders of the INA front-line units in Burma in 1945 when ....they faced up to British equipment, tanks, guns and aircraft with rifles and bullock-carts and empty stomachs.

In the following para on the same page (395), General Menezes writes, "Toye encapsulates the INA operations thereafter based on his war time interrogations: Dhillon's regiment suffered heavy casualties in actions near Taungzin on March 15th to 17th in which it showed persistence and gallantry."

> I am further obliged to General Mohan Singh, the founder of the INA who in his book - *Soldier's Contribution to Indian Independence* (Army Educational Stores, 22 / 1 - A Naraina Industrial Area Phase I, New Delhi 1100028), Pages 336-37, wrote: They had become the fellow-travellers on the journey of death suffering woes and tortures of the last chasm of life in the last scene of the Burma tragedy. Dhillon, Sahgal and Shah Nawaz, who were destined to be the heroes of the Red Fort trial, fought with remarkable tenacity along with several other officers. But the play had reached the end and the last curtain was to be drawn. The major brunt of the fighting fell on Dhillon's Fourth Regiment. I raise my hat to him for the way he withstood blow after blow and this, despite his failing health and shattered nerves. Let us pause for a moment to think of those hundreds of martyrs, and heroes, who fought and perished in those battles without anyone knowing their names and recounting their deeds of heroism. History continues to remain cruel by denying them the glory of their sacrifices. Perhaps it has always been so - the names of the men who really make history are often kept out of it.

From Popa we came to Myingyan visiting the battlefield of Legy en route where Sahgal's Regiment had held the enemy Division till 10th April, 1945, and made straight for Mandalay. Mandalay Central Jail has the distinction of keeping some of our greatest men like Bal Gangadhar Tilak, Lala Lajpat Rai, and Netaji Subhas Chandra Bose during their incarceration. Mandalay served as the INA base camp during Imphal Campaign. Having visited most of the historical places around it we drove to Mamyo, the Advance Headquarters of Netaji. Here we saw the house where Netaji stayed during some of the most crucial days of the war. Dr. Montu Banerjee, a lone survivor of those days took us to show Rani Jhansi Camp and the INA Hospital where Col. Lakshmi had seen action. We returned to Mandalay going through the memory lane of the days when Azad Hind Fauj had to withdraw to the Irrawaddy line. From Mandalay we flew to He Ho in Shan States and visited Inlay and Taunggyi. This is the area where Mr. Yellappa, one of the stalwarts of the I.I.L. achieved martyrdom. It was in that area that Lakshmi was arrested.

On 18th January, we flew back to Yangon and from there to Calcutta, in order to join the main body of the Expedition which had been on an extensive tour of North-Eastern states of India. They visited some of the bloodiest battlefields of World War II around Kohima and Imphal. At Calcutta, Janaki was further joined by two other enthusiasts of Netaji Centre, Kuala Lumpur, Ms. Pramodini Menon and Ms. Ramalu. We had to wait for the main body till 22nd January. Meanwhile we participated in the seminars organised by Netaji Research Bureau at Netaji Bhawan - the house from where Netaji had escaped in January 1941 to go on the great mission of his life.

On 22nd January, the main body of the Expedition arrived. Colonel Raja Mohammad Arshad who was G-1 of the 1st Division of the INA which took part in Imphal operations arrived from Lahore along with his wife to be with us on Netaji's 100th Birthday. Colonel Arshad was awarded Netaji Award for 1996 by Netaji Research Bureau. On Netaji's Birthday on the afternoon of 23rd January, 1996, after attending various celebrations in Calcutta, the Expedition continued on its march to Delhi.

The Expedition passed through the states of Bihar and Uttar Pradesh. At Patna, the capital of Bihar, we paid homage to an INA hero — Col. Mahboob Ahmed. He died a few years ago. He had willed that his grave should be simple without any brick or stone work. We laid a CHADDAR on his earthen grave. His wife had come to Calcutta to welcome us back from the Expedition. At Patna, their elder son, Imran joined the Expedition from Patna to Delhi

It was like roses, roses all the way. Members of the Yuva Shakti and the public turned out in overwhelming numbers to greet us on the way. There were arches and gates decorated with flowers, flags and buntings hailing Netaji and Azad Hind Fauj at every village and town en route. Apart from the INA veterans we had a magnetic personality, Sunil Dutt with us. The Armadas carrying us must have been made of some special metal for at times the people apart from being all around us also climbed on top of the vehicles. Often the bonnet of an Armada served us as a stage from where we addressed the public. Each road side meeting was a test of strength of the Armadas and of our power of endurance. It was miraculous that Armada roofs did not cave in. Public ovation appeared to enhance their quality of performance on rough and rugged, steep and level roads alike.

We were 18 members of the Expedition but I would count the Armadas also as five members. For it were they who kept us on the move. And behind them unseen by us were the sponsors of the Expedition and the Government who made the move possible. After half a century in oblivion, it was a pleasant reality to be appreciated by one's own people and the Government.

The Expedition gave us an opportunity to convey the gratitude of our people and the Governrnent to the peoples and the Governments of Singapore, Malaysia and Myanmar whose forebears had helped our war effort for the liberation of our Motherland. But for their willing co-operation, generous hospitality and all possible support, notwithstanding their own wartime ordeals, Azad Hind Fauj could not have been able to wage war of independence against the British. We could also pay homage to our glorious dead on the spot of their martyrdom.

At Kanpur, five of us were given one lakh rupees each by the Governor of U.P., Shri Moti Lal Vora as award on behalf of the U.P. Government. I was one of the awardees. I gratefully accepted the award. It came as a great help in the autumn of my life.

On arrival at Delhi on 28th January 1996, we went straight to Subhas Park to unfurl the Azad Hind Flag and to salute Netaji's statue which points towards the Red Fort, our historic destination. En route we went to the nearby grave of Gen. Shah Nawaz Khan to pay homage to the great hero.

At the Red Fort we had a grand welcome where INA veterans, members of our families, our friends, national dignitaries, representatives of the Press, the All India Radio and Doordarshan headed by Shri P.S. Sangma and Shrimati Margaret Alva welcomed the Expedition back home. Begum Shah Nawaz Khan came all the way from her village in Pakistan with her daughter Hamida Khan to be with the Azad Hind Expedition and INA families to welcome us and also say KHUDA HAFIZ — farewell. Begum Shah Nawaz had a tryst with death on the following day 29th January, 1996. Helped by Shri Akhil Bakshi and Shri Sagar G. Suri, permission was obtained from the Government and Begum Shah Nawaz Khan was laid to rest beside her husband LAJO (Shah Nawaz Khan's pet name). Apart from the surviving members of the INA in Delhi and surrounding area, Col. Raja Mohammad Arshad and Begum Arshad from Pakistan, Lieut. John Jacob from Singapore, Captain Janaki Thever, Ms. Sumathi, Ms. Pramodini Menon, Ms. Ramalu from Malaysia, all the members and the families connected with the Azad Hind Expedition, including Gen. Shah Nawaz's family, members of the Yuva Shakti and of various organisations were there to offer FATEA. Blessed are the General and Begum Shah Nawaz Khan that even death could not prevent them from reaching Delhi for their eternal rest near Netaji's statue between the Red Fort and the Jama Masjid.

Words fail me to thank all those who made it possible for us to relive the memorable fifty years of our glorious past in forty-six days during the Azad Hind Expedition (1995-1996). Thank you very much, my dear countrymen, members of the Yuva Shakti, and the Narasimha Rao Government.

Further I shall remain beholden to the Prime Minister Shri I.K. Gujral and to the Minister of Communications Shri Beni Prasad Verma along with all the Officers and the staff of his Ministry for the release of the Commemorative Stamp for the 50th Anniversaryof India's Independence on 15th August 1997. The Stamp depicts the 1st I.N.A. Trial at the Red Fort in 1945. I take this stamp as a tribute not only to the Trio of the Trial but to all the known and the unknown Freedom Fighters and to our glorious dead who made the Independence of the Sub-Continent of India a reality.

Jai Hind !

AZAD HIND ZINDABAD.

27

NETAJI

Before closing this manuscript I wish to respond to two questions which I am often asked. One question deals with Netaji's personality. What was so exceptional in his ability which attracted and inspired those who came in touch with him? Whenever I am asked this question, I am reminded of the fable of, "The elephant and blind men". Like one of those men I could not scan that great man Netaji Subhas Chandra Bose in totality. So before saying what I could perceive, let the reader allow me to look at him through the eyes of those who had better vision than I.

Mr. S.A. Ayer, Minister for Publicity and Propaganda had this to say in his book - *Unto him a witness :*

> The title of Supreme Commander, if it truly fitted any commander on the battlefields of Europe or Asia, fitted Netaji most superbly. HE LOOKED SUPREME, every inch of him. The way he talked and moved with the soldiers on or off the war front was one of supreme dignity and self-confidence.
>
> The word personality assumed a meaning when Netaji, in his Supreme Commander's uniform, stepped on to the saluting base and faced the serried ranks of the INA. And yet, the uniform itself was the simplest in the world — no bright red cloth, no shining metal, no ribbons, no medals in a row, no shining leather belt or shoulder straps, nor a sword in its scabbard hanging from his waist, nor a horse to ride. Whatever clothes he wore, he wore them smartly. Normally he wore

> khaki cotton cloth except when he visited Japan. There he had to use khaki woollens as a protection against the severe cold weather. His forage cap with two tiny well polished brass buttons in the front sat majestically on his bright and broad forehead, the face beneath the cap of a rosy wheat complexion, now inscrutable, immobile, dignified, now wreathed in a charming smile, now reminding one of the Bengal Tiger as when he roared an inspiring exhortation to soldiers or civilians at mammoth gatherings.
>
> It was impossible to take one's eyes off his face. Whenever he ascended the platform, he held one spellbound by its compelling magnetism. . . .

Now let me show readers another glimpse of Netaji's creative qualities when he drafted the Proclamation of the Provisional Government of Azad Hind. After a long busy day, a day just earlier to 21st October 1943, it was past midnight. This is what Mr. Ayer says:

> Then I witnessed a phenomenon. I had glimpse of the great man. He took hold of a bunch of quarter-sheets of blank paper, took pencil in hand and started writing, 'After their first defeat at the hands of the British in 1757 in Bengal_____.'
>
> He did not lift his eyes from the paper in front of him, silently handed it to me the first page as soon as he finished it, and I walked out of the room and sat at the typewriter. Abid and Swami went to his room in turn and brought me the Proclamation manuscript, sheet after sheet, as Netaji finished it.
>
> What amazed me was that he never even once wanted to see any of the earlier pages that he had written. How he could remember every word that he had written in the preceding pages, how he could remember the sequence of the paragraphs. In the entire script there was not one word corrected or scored out, and the punctuation was complete.
>
> That he wrote out the whole proclamation sheet after

> sheet without a break and at one sitting was some measure of Netaji's clear thinking, remarkable memory and grasp and facile pen ! The entire historic proclamation was written with the ease with which a brief letter could be penned.

The proclamation shows Netaji's extraordinary grasp of history.

Herr Alexander Werth, one of the important Liaison Officers at the Free India Center, in Chapter Four - Planning for Revolution - 1941 - 1943 in the book, *A Beacon Across Asia,* edited by Sisir K. Bose, Alexander Werth and S.A. Ayer and published by Orient Longman, has observed (page 127):

> Those who observed Bose during these years were all greatly impressed by the fact that he succeeded so well in convincing all his co-workers - both Indian and German - about the great importance of the work they were doing and inspiring them with a sense of mission, common objectives and mutual co-operation. Whenever there were differences of opinion or misunderstanding or even quarrels amongst his colleagues, he knew how to settle them without difficulty. He showed his remarkable capacity of keeping the thread of all the activities of his political, military and technical co-workers in his hands so that the overall control of the whole organisation remained with him. He was the driving spirit behind all the activities of the Free India Center. He succeeded in doing so much in spite of the fact that the organisation he built up was something between an official mission and a provisional government and not so fully recognised association of a group of exiles from India.

Earlier after his arrival in Berlin, Netaji went under the name Orlando Mazzota for quite sometime. He intended to remain in anonymity till he could bring round the Axis Powers to declare that the independence of India was among their war aims. He also did not wish to let the British know about his whereabouts. Without going into details of how difficult his task was, let me quote Shri H. N. Pandit's work - *Netaji Subhas Chandra Bose from Kabul to Battle of Imphal*—Sterling Publishers Private Limited (page 38) :

For the whole story we have to turn to the narration of Mr. M.R. Vyas who was one of the first four associates of Netaji in Germany when Bose was still known as Orlando Mazzotta.

> It seems an emissary of the Foreign Office went to Badgastein (where Bose was staying) with the German government's request for co-operation. Subhas thanked the German government for the proposal and added that the collaboration would have to be based on a very well defined agreement. His terms were :
>
> 1. For all purposes of negotiation, India should be regarded as a completely sovereign state of which he would be the representative until such time as the Indian people could finally constitute their own Government on their own soil.
> 2. While India remained in subjugation, he (Netaji) should have facilities for a separate free establishment of his own with the status of a diplomatic representative attached to the head of a sovereign state.
> 3. For the finances of such a set-up, the German government would advance an interest-free loan which would be repayable by free India after the termination of hostilities.
> 4. The loan so granted must be without any condition and the expenditure for the same must be subject to diplomatic immunity.
> 5. Any broadcasts, any publications or any publicity to be carried on by the establishment so contemplated, must not be subject to any German censorship even though the same may have to be carried on from Germany or territories under her occupation.
> 6. Recruitment to any Indian National Army to be

raised would be made solely by Indians or representatives duly approved by the head of the state, *i.e.* Subhas Chandra Bose.

7. The oath of allegiance by the members of the Army would be to Subhas Chandra Bose who, as the Head of the Sovereign State of India, would also be the Commander-in-Chief of all Indian armed forces.
8. Though apparent from above, still it must be specially agreed that the Indian forces, while operating in any joint sub-command, must not be deployed on any front other than against the British or other troops under British command subject to any unforeseen military entanglements.
9. While the free India establishment and its forces would support all anti-British actions, it would not ipso facto consider itself at war with other allies of Great Britain.

The Nazis were flabbergasted to see the terms. Were these conditions of a powerless one-man state for co-operation with the Reich? The man must be cut to size. The task was assigned to one of Ribbentroph's senior officers who came to meet Bose in the Foreign Office with an S.S. Colonel accompanying him in the mission. The following account of the conversation which took place has been given by Mr. Vyas:

> "Your Excellency", Ribbentrop's officer began, "while we realise your anxiety on many questions, don't you think that after your having come here, there could be no activity of any kind unless the German government voluntarily agrees to it ?"
>
> Subhas Chandar Bose replied: "Do you mean that you could put me in prison if I do not agree to work on your terms?"
>
> "Certainly not, Your Excellency", the S.S. Colonel interposed, "but you would be incapacitated and will have to remain inactive."

> Bose, "If I wanted to remain inactive I would have remained in a British prison. But this war provides a unique chance for my country to be free. So I would rather go elsewhere or even back to India and fight from there, come what may."

The Foreign Office representative commented sarcastically, "But Your Excellency, even for leaving Germany, you will require our permission. Isn't it ?"

Apparently the officer bargained for more than he could afford, because the reply that came stunned him. "Sir, I have heard a lot about your Gestapo. Probably the gentleman here is a representative of that body. But believe me, the British C.I.D. in India is no less efficient and ruthless. And if I have foiled them and escaped, I shall do the same here. I have not come here to live the life of an exile. Gentlemen. I think we shall leave it at that."

The meeting came to an end abruptly.

This happened in the second half of October 1941. For two days nothing happened. Then Ribbentrop (the Minister for Foreign Affairs) had a meeting with Subhas Chandra Bose in a very friendly way. Shortly afterwards an official communication arrived that Fuhrer (HITLER) had approved the civil parts of Netaji's terms from points 1 to 5. The decision on the military points too followed in due course of time with some minor modifications. Mr. Vyas says that although there was tough bargaining in the beginning, once the agreement was signed, the Germans honoured it in letter and spirit.

The Free India Center with status of a diplomatic mission was established with its office in Lichtensteiner Allee, opposite the Spanish Embassy in Berlin's diplomatic enclave. After having lived in various hotels, Subhas Chandra Bose was allotted a villa in the Charlottenburg area of Berlin. Previously this house was occupied by the military attache to the American Embassy before the outbreak of the war.

The work at the Free India Center began with a few Indian volunteers, mainly students. To start with, they were M.R. Vyas, N.G. Gunpulay, N.G. Swamy, Habib-ur-Rehman, Abid Hassan Safrani and one or two more. It can be said that more than a diplomatic mission, the Free India Center worked like the secretariat of a Government-to-be. Free India movement came to be called Azad Hind, with its emblem of TRICOLOUR with the springing tiger and *Jana Gana Mana* adopted Hindi words - *Subh Sukh Chain Ki Barkha Barse* - without any alteration in the tune. Jai Hind was adopted as the greetings among the Indian nationals. It gave us a special identity as members of one nation irrespective of our many religions and races. Our leader Subhas Chandra Bose was addressed by the members of Azad Hind as Netaji. This title owes its introduction to the members of the Azad Hind Free India Center. In Hindustani, Neta means a leader, the suffix "ji" is a common word of respect and courtesy used among equals and among the high and the low alike. It sounds of closeness between the person addressed and the addresser in contrast to words like *Hazoor, Sahib, Janab, Janab-e-Aala, Janab-e Aali, sahib Bahadur, Shriman, Sarkar, Alijah, Hukam,* etc. etc. The word Netaji became so popular that it immediately reminds one of Netaji Subhas Chandra Bose. There have been netas, there are netas, many of them will come and go but Netaji will remain only one and one only - Netaji Subhas Chandra Bose.

In her book - *Jungle Alliance*, Dr. Joyce Lebra has this to say about Netaji's early days in Tokyo.

Bose in Tokyo

> After several weeks on a submarine Bose was exhausted and in need of rest. But he had one aim in Tokyo, an obsession. He had to meet Premier Tojo. Yamamoto after a few days arranged meetings with Army Chief of Staff Sugiyama, Foreign Minister Shigemitsu, Navy Minister Yonai, and various section chiefs of the Army, Navy and Foreign Ministries. Bose's opening words to Sugiyama took the Chief of Staff by surprise. "The war will end in victory for Japan!" Bose boomed. Japan was in the midst of adverse circumstances in Guadalcanal and the campaign was obviously not going well for Japan. Perhaps Bose's statement was a reflection of his faith in Japan's human and material resources. Bose continued, without waiting for a response from the bemused Chief of Staff, "Will Japan send soldiers to India or not ? We are going to fight our way to India

step by step. If we don't push on with determination we won't be able to achieve independence."

The immediate reaction of Sugiyama was that Bose had none of the humility or reserve a Japanese would have shown in such an interview. But there was no doubting his sincerity or his aims. He was a known quantity, whatever the Operations Bureau of IGHQ thought of his value to Japan. Sugiyalna, despite his interest and sympathy derived from two years' experience in India, could only respond to Bose with a briefing about Japan's current military position. Bose, dissatisfied with Sugiyama's general discussion, explained with great fervour his hope of first taking Chittagong, then pushing on into Bengal. Sugiyama assured Bose of his sympathy with Bose's aspirations, and Bose's first interview in Tokyo ended more calmly than it had begun. But Bose was dissatisfied. He had to meet Tojo and get a Japanese commitment.

Yamamoto, meanwhile acting as guide for Bose, for ten days escorted him through factories, schools, and hospitals, trying to distract his attention from Tojo and keep him occupied. Bose was impressed with what he saw but not deterred from his object.

Why was Tojo putting Bose off ? In the first place, there were many more pressing military problems than India, and Tojo's pleas that he was too busy were not simply excuses. Secondly, there was a group in the Operations Bureau of IGHQ which took a dim view of India and the INA. The INA had no direct relevance to military strategy and operations in the Pacific or even in Southeast Asia. And there was no proof of Bose's propaganda impact within India in any case. But the main reason for Tojo's reluctance to meet Bose was Tojo's own attitude. Tojo was a man of strong prejudices and often formed an opinion of a man before meeting him. The INA had been only a headache so far as Tojo was concerned. The trouble between Mohan Singh and Rash Behari Bose had disposed Tojo unfavourably towards the INA. And the demands in the Bangkok Resolution Tojo regarded as presumptuous. How could a small revolutionary group which did not even represent a government presume to make demands on the Imperial Government of Japan ? There was no need for Tojo to meet another Indian, even if he had just come from Berlin.

It was persuasion by Sugiyama and Shigemitsu which at length prevailed on Tojo to meet Bose. On 10 June the first of two meetings took place. The magic of Bose enchanted Tojo immediately. It had been the same with Sugiyama, Shigemitsu, and nearly everyone Bose met, whether Japanese or Indians. Apart from the impact of Bose's words and passionate devotion to Indian independence, there was something about his face, his voice and his eyes that captured the minds and hearts of men. Tojo was enthralled. The meeting was brief but Bose had succeeded, and Tojo promised another interview four days later. This time Shigemitsu and other officials were also present, and there was a brief but fruitful exchange of views between Bose and Tojo. Tojo explained Japan's ideas on the Greater East Asia Co-Prosperity Sphere. Bose, with his customary frankness, asked Tojo, "Can Japan give unconditional help to the Indian independence movement ? I would like to confirm that there are no strings attached to Japanese aid." Tojo immediately gave Bose an affirmative reply. Bose continued, "Can the Japanese army push its operations into India proper?" This time there were complex military matters involved, and Tojo was unable to answer as decisively. But Bose had been favourably impressed and was grateful he had made a friend in Tojo. If Bose was to secure meaningful help from Japan for the INA Tojo's sympathy and co-operation was the crucial point. In this Bose had succeeded admirably, and Tojo

> was ready to make public his official support of Bose and the INA.
>
> On 16 June Bose visited the House of Peers in the 82nd Extraordinary Session of the Diet. Tojo made an historic address on the Greater East Asia Co-Prosperity Sphere which attracted attention outside Japan. Bose listened intently in the audience to interpreters as Tojo said, "India has been for centuries under England's cruel rule. We wish to express righteous indignation at their agony and sympathy for their aspirations for complete independence. We firmly resolve that Japan will do everything possible to help Indian independence. I am convinced the day of Indian freedom and prosperity is not far off. . . ." Tojo spoke too of the emancipation of all of East Asia and of the welfare of the people of Greater East Asia. This was not Tojo's first mention of India in the Diet. Early in 1942 he had spoken of the Pacific War as an opportunity for India to rise against British rule. But this time when Tojo promised aid and co-operation for Indian independence Bose was listening in his audience and felt Tojo was making him a personal promise which he would follow through.

In 11th chapter of this treatise I narrated how cool, fearless and graceful was Netaji under fire. Now I wish to portray in Gen. Shah Nawaz Khan's own words from his book - *My Memories of INA & Its Netaji* (Rajkamal Publications Delhi) - page 179, another picture of Netaji under fire :

> He listened to me very calmly, because he knew that all that I said came from the very depths of my heart, and was prompted by my extreme anxiety for his safety. He just smiled and said, 'Shah Nawaz, it is no use pleading with me. I have made up my mind to go to Popa and I am going there. You do not have to worry about my safety, as I know England has not yet produced the bomb that can kill Subhas Chandra Bose.' This last statement appeared particularly true,

> as Netaji seemed to lead a charmed life. That afternoon the place he was living in was heavily bombed by sixty B-25. They caused terrible devastation all around, and it was difficult to imagine how Netaji escaped without even a scratch. All of us had failed to persuade Netaji not to proceed any further, but once he had made up his mind, no one could make him change it.

Dr. Ba Maw, the War-time President of Myanmar wrote a paper which was read out on his behalf at Netaji Research Bureau, Calcutta on one of the Netaji's Birthdays. I reproduce some excerpts out of it as under:

> Taking a historical view now that the time has made it possible, Netaji is by any measure an Asian figure whose shadow stretched out across the whole of this part of the world during the last war and has remained there ever since. As one who was with him throughout most of the war years, I assure you that what I have just said is true. I myself have seen it happen. I witnessed almost from beginning to end Netaji's work and achievements during those years, how he moulded out of the rawest possible materials lying scattered throughout all Southeast Asia an Independent Indian State and Government and Army and made them a positive force in the World War. A single mind and will turned a dream into a reality. It pursued the Indian dream across half the world, through the Middle East, and then into Russia and Germany, then to the farthest edge of Asia, then back again to Southeast Asia, and finally to Burma and for a few delirious weeks across the Indian border into India itself. Very soon the man and his dream set aflame the hearts of three million of his countrymen who answered his call from every office and bazaar and workshop throughout Southeast Asia and gave him practically everything he asked for. Within an year of Bose's coming Azad Hind was a full-fledged state recognised by nine other states; it

> had acquired a large piece of territory; its armies were fighting on eight sectors of the Burma-India border and soon set foot on Indian soil, proudly planted the flag of Free India on it and came within a few inches of winning a decisive victory there, when all that reality forged out of a single dream crashed together with half of the world.

Dr. Ba Maw goes on,

> "However to say something, I asked Netaji what he intended to do next. 'Why', he replied calmly lighting a cigarette, 'start again and go on fighting when ready. What else can we do? The fight certainly has to go on.' These words echoed my own thoughts so much that I nearly wept to hear them. In my case of course, with Burma and Burmese Army in the hands of the British and nothing ready in my hands I would not be able to do anything, at least for some time. I explained that to Netaji and he understood completely. Later I heard that he told his men, 'Now that Germany and Italy are out of the war, we must continue it with the Japanese as long as they are still in it; and if they too are knocked out we must fight on by ourselves.' Those words spoken during the greatest crisis of his life sum up the essential spirit and character of the man. Time passes and powerful men in their day come and go, and a few of them, a very few, leave behind memories which live on and even grow by themselves with the years. Such men become part of the ultimate story of their people. There is every reason to believe that Subhas Chandra Bose is among those few men. I need not say more.

Netaji's personality appealed so much to us that he will ever remain and live as a superhuman hero in the imagination of not only us who had the good luck to work with him but also in the imagination of our people. His spirit of patriotism is bound to manifest itself in the future generations and serve not only India and Asia but also the world.

His very name commanded our subconscious mind without knowing and thus brought out the latent good lying deep down in an individual. Imagine a jawan having been awarded death punishment for committing a heinous crime, *i.e.* rape and when given the option to appeal to Netaji against my award, the man cried out, "No Sir, shoot me here rather than sending me to Netaji. Now I have no face which I can show him." *(ab main netaji ko kiya moonh dikhaoonga* ?)

I am reminded of the man who when admonished by his Section Commander for exposing himself to the enemy fire, the raw recruit retorted, "How can I be killed today when Netaji himself has sent me a pair of boots?" It was that confidence in Netaji which made us face an enemy superior to us in all respects.

In his book - *Builders of Modern India - Subhas Chandra Bose* - Dr. Girja K. Mookerjee (Publications Division, Ministry of Information and Broadcasting, Government of India) on page 104 says,

> The question to all of us is then: Will Subhas be remembered by the generations to come? I think he will. At least it was for this recompense that his restless soul traversed oceans and foreign lands in search of an answer to India's freedom. It is too horrible to think that he is no longer amongst us. To his colleagues he will remain ever alive, ever green and immortal. He imposed on them his vivid personality so well and they at least will not forget him as long as they live, but I hope those who will come after them will also gratefully remember this magnificent man, born to be a 'grand signeur' who lived and died so that India could be great and so that men and women of our race may have not to be born into this world with the stigma of being a subject people and not free and independent as we are today.

Long back in the thirties, Dr. Rabindra Nath Tagore called Netaji, Deshnayak - Leader of the Country. During the INA crisis when General Seizo Arisue, Second-in-Command of the Japanese Imperial Army General Staff invited Rash Bihari Bose in order to know his mind about Netaji's coming and discreetly asked, "Netaji is desirous of coming over here and I wonder how you would treat him.'' The old revolutionary quietly replied, "Netaji is a born leader of leaders. I shall of course be quite pleased to ask him to take over from me." I am also reminded of a conversation with General Fujiwara during my visit to Japan in the autumn of 1974. We were passing along General Tojo's house reminiscing of the war days. I asked the General about Prime Minister Tojo's opinion about Netaji. Fujiwara replied that General Tojo was so much impressed by Netaji that he said, "If there exists a man of the Century, he is one whom I met today." Fujiwara believed that if Netaji had arrived in the East a year earlier, we would have won the war.

After citing above impressions of some of the great men who happened to see Netaji from a close range, now I will try to sum up my answer to the question as under :

Netaji practised what he preached. There was never any difference in his words and deeds - *unki kathni aur karni mein koi farq na tha.*

Netaji cared not only for the honour, welfare and comfort of his soldiers but also respected their feelings. He had a compassionate nature. He overwhelmed us with his concern for us individually and collectively, like sending a pair of boots to a sepoy with instructions to Regimental Commander to see personally that it fitted the man and report back to Netaji, offering a cigarette case to a veteran commander from Imphal, helping his own staff officers to wash hands by pouring water and offering his own towel to scrub hands, shedding tears with a lump in his throat on hearing about our difficulties and taking immediate steps to supply relief. Such spontaneous feelings coming out of his heart, made him extraordinarily a rare leader of men in war. His men felt happy, proud and lucky to do and die under his command. It was this relationship which kept up our morale in spite of all our difficulties and deficiencies.

Netaji's knowledge of history of wars fought on different battlefields of the world could easily surpass the knowledge of any seasoned General. He read a lot and did his homework on the subject he had to deal with. When he had to see anybody he would learn all about the person and his problems before the interview. The result was that the man could go back happy and contented that the Supreme Commander knew him intimately. An interview with Netaji went a long way in creating that confidence without which it is impossible to wage a revolutionary war.

He had a gift of judging the character of the man which served him to put the right man at the right place at the right time and on the right job. He picked up some of us from the dust and made heroes out of us.

He never failed to appreciate when appreciation was due. A good word from him made us to strive to do our job well. He had a very kind heart, so kind that he never punished anybody. He always gave a defaulter an advice so that the defaulter could improve himself.

He had remarkable power of observation and could predict an eventuality correctly. Once he wrote a small note to me on the margin of a routine order. It was scribbled in his own hand. He told me that as the mail was getting ready to be dispatched, he wanted to advise me that instead of expecting the enemy at a particular point which I had reported in my previous report, I should also watch at a point. He gave 6 figured map reference. The note was written in Rangoon about 500 kilometres away from me. When I received it I was surprised at the accuracy of Netaji's judgment. I was already facing the enemy where he had told me to watch. This was a measure of Netaji's skill at generalship. Again, I am reminded of my conversation with him when he gave me the command of The Nehru Brigade - 4th Guerrilla Regiment. I said, "Netaji may I know how long will it take me to get into touch with the enemy?"

Netaji's reply was, "Well, you are already on the foremost defended locality. There are no positions held between you and the enemy. It all depends on how long the enemy takes to reach the Irrawaddy. The initiative lies with him. You may be lucky to get sixty to seventy days before you are attacked, I guess."

Netaji's guess was accurate. I took my command in mid-November 1944. I got to grips with the enemy early in February 1945. Another example of Netaji's military foresight is when in March 1939 during the annual session of the Indian National Congress at Tripuri (Madhya Pradesh) he proposed that the Congress should at once send an ultimatum to the British Government demanding independence within six months and should prepare immediately for a national struggle. The proposal was opposed by the rightist leaders. Netaji's proposal was based on his appreciation of the European situation which was something beyond the understanding of our political leaders. But Netaji's prediction turned out to be correct. The war did break out within six months on 3rd September, 1939. Similarly Netaji's oft repeated statement, "There is no power on earth that can keep India enslaved. India shall be free and before long." The enemy officers used to mock at the statement which they thought was illusory and a face-saving device. Actually Netaji had a plan which was beyond the comprehension of professional soldiers. He kept the INA in the field even in the face of defeat. He wanted us to pay the price of liberty not only when we were on the advance but also during the retreat while going away from India not to win a territory but to continue fighting against the British forces who were holding India in perpetual bondage. These forces consisted of a greater number of the Indian soldier who paused and pondered as to why the INA with their poor strength and poorer equipment yet higher spirit were fighting against the British. It created a psychological revolution. The war ended and with it ended the slavish mentality of the Indian soldier. When the British started INA trials in the Red Fort they thought that the Indian people especially the soldiers would appreciate the British action against the INA officers. Reverse was the case. As soon as the first INA trial of the three front-line commanders started on 5th November 1945, within a week disturbances broke out in Lahore, then in Lucknow and in Calcutta where hundreds of demonstrators were injured and twenty killed by police firing. Even after the first INA trial in which the three accused officers were released by the Commander-in Chief, the public demand to stop the future INA trials continued. Anti-British Raj feelings kept on rising unabated. The climax came with the mutiny of the Royal Indian Navy in Bombay during February 1946. There were further disturbances in the Royal Indian Air Force in Karachi and certain units of the armed forces at Jabalpore. The British top brass were for a strict action. The British were however lucky that Field Marshal Sir Claude Auchinleck, the Commander-in Chief in India could read the writing on the wall. Netaji's stratagem had transformed the British Indian Army into the INDIAN ARMY. The days of the

British Raj in India were close to their end.

Having shown Netaji's powers of generalship which turned the defeat of the INA into the defeat of the British Raj, let me record that another great asset in Netaji's being was that he was at once secular. Whatever our religion and the area or the station of our birth, we had full confidence that we would get absolute justice from him and his Government - the fore runner of our Government today. To show how his mind worked in this direction, his brief but an all-embracing idea of independence is shown in distilled form in the last but one para of the Proclamation of the Provisional Government of Azad Hind. I quote:

> The Provisional Government is entitled to, and hereby claims, the allegiance of every Indian. It guarantees religious liberty, as well as equal rights and equal opportunities to all its citizens. It declares its firm resolve to pursue the happiness and prosperity of the whole nation and of all its parts, cherishing all the children of the nation equally and transcending all the differences cunningly fostered by an alien government in the past.

The second question is about his person. Where is Netaji? Is Netaji alive?

When I heard about the death of Netaji in August of 1945, I was a captive in Salimgarh part of the Red Fort in Delhi. The recording of the Summary of Evidence against Gen. Shah Nawaz Khan, Col. Prem Kumar Sahgal and me had already started. That showed that our trial was in the offing. We took the news of Netaji's death as a British ploy to demoralise us. That was our first reaction. We kept on hoping against hope and wished Netaji were alive. By the time we were released from the Red Fort, a lot of controversy had already started regarding Netaji's death. Later on when a committee was set up under Gen. Shah Nawaz Khan, its finding was that "Netaji met his death in an aircrash, and that the ashes now at Renkoji Temple, Tokyo are his ashes' Thousands of Indians did not believe it. The controversy kept on gathering weight and because Netaji did not turn up to contradict the evidence that he did die in the air crash in Taiwan, the myth of his living carried on. Today, some of the members of his family, his colleagues, his admirers and even those who never saw him are not prepared to hear that Netaji is not in this mortal world. They believe it as a faith that Netaji is alive. They become aggressive to hear anything against their belief or faith. I feel, it is not proper to argue or debate the question of Netaji's death and thus hurt anybody's feelings.

But I look at the problem as an INA man. I know Gen. Shah Nawaz and Colonel Habib-ur-Rehman because we belonged to the same Unit, the 1st 14th Punjab Regiment. They were both loyal to Netaji and to the INA movement. Their contributions to the INA cause were outstanding. I was at Delhi when a relative of Col. Habib happened to call on Gen. Shah Nawaz in the late seventies. He brought a message from Habib that we the INA officers must try and bring the ashes from Renkoji Temple to Delhi. He said those were Netaji's ashes and whatever Habib had stated ever since the Taiwan air crash was the truth. Habib pleaded that Netaji was the greatest martyr of the freedom struggle and deserved to be honoured as such.

My submission is that whatever the statements and inquiries, one fact cannot be denied that the Japanese war veterans and the priest Rev. Mochizuki of Renkoji Temple of Tokyo have been keeping the ashes in the Temple and looking after those ashes as a deity with the daily worshipping rituals for the last now over half a century. The Japanese war veterans think very low of us, the Indian people in general and the INA people in particular for not bringing home the sacred ashes of such a great man as Netaji. They feel we are an ungrateful people to Netaji and the INA people are disloyal to their martyred Supreme Commander. Their Generals have been pleading to us with sobs and tears to bring home Netaji's ashes. They say that they are too old and passing the last days of their life. They know Netaji through personal touch. They saw Netaji in the public rallies and parades. They saw him on the war fronts. But what would their future generations know. And they cry. They beg us to understand that for the sake of the future generations of Indians, Netaji's ashes must be brought home in a ceremonial manner befitting such a great leader and a martyr.

I visited Japan in 1974 and again in 1984. General Katakura's wife had died during my visit in April 1984. General Fujiwara and I went to condole General Katakura on his bereavement. I was shocked and pained to see the General crying like a baby not on his own bereavement but to plead that Netaji's ashes must be taken to Delhi.

Now my appeal to those of my countrymen and women who believe that those ashes are not of Netaji may kindly allow us who believe those ashes are of Netaji, that we may bring those ashes home. Netaji deserves to be honoured as the greatest martyr of the nation. Netaji deserves a memorial worthy of his greatness and sacrifices and his ashes should be placed preferably in the Red Fort.

As a compromise, let those ashes be called ashes supposed to be of Netaji or so-called ashes of Netaji brought from Renkoji Temple of Tokyo in Japan. The visit of the younger generations to Netaji's ashes is bound to inspire them to be great and noble Indians. Let the future generations not be deprived of that physical touch with the ashes of such a great man as Netaji.

Once again I submit that the ashes in Renkoji Temple are being worshipped not in anybody's name, but Netaji. It is Netaji's name which is revered. The international courtesy and gratitude to the Japanese requires that we take the responsibility of looking after the ashes which bear Netaji's name. It is the name which counts and that too of Netaji.

I remain reminded of Netaji's speech of 5th July, 1943 when he reviewed the INA in Singapore. He ended it thus :

> I have said that today is the proudest day of my life. For an enslaved people, there can be no greater pride, no greater honour, than to be the first soldier in the army of liberation. But this honour carries with it a corresponding responsibility and I am deeply conscious of it. I assure you that I shall be with you in darkness and in sunshine, in sorrow and in joy, in suffering and in victory. For the present, I can offer you nothing except hunger, thirst, privation, forced marches and death. But if you follow me in life and in death, as I am confident you will, I shall lead you to victory and freedom. It does not matter who among us will live to see India free. It is enough that India shall be free and that we shall give our all to make her free. May God now bless our Army and grant us victory in the coming fight !

Inquilab Zindabad! Azad Hind Zindabad!

Netaji fulfilled his promise and gave his all to make India free. Today we are all free. I wish I could also be free to worship Netaji's ashes on the free soil of our country !

Netaji Zindabad!

Jai Hind!

AZAD HIND ZINDABAD!

Afterword

By

Professor Harbans Lal Agnihotri

Colonel G.S. Dhillon of the I.N.A. has lucidly recounted his memories in detail but the account, I am afraid, remains incomplete till it is supplemented and corroborated by Gurbakhsh, the poet whose response to the stirring times was marked by an all pervasive emotional experience, as reflected in his poetical compositions bearing on the times.

Fighting a battle involves killings which a poet detests but a patriotic soldier fights to liberate his motherland. He is an inspired being motivated by a cause. The patriotic soldier and the poet are, thus, kindred souls. There is a kind of compelling urgency, inevitability and spontaneity in their waging a war, be it with a gun or with a pen.

Gurbakhsh Singh Dhillon is surprisingly two in one - revolutionary patriot and poet. Though not a prolific poet, his poems vividly capture some of the momentous happenings of recent history. His lyrical outpourings compel re-readings and entitle him to place among the votaries of the Muse. It is not difficult to reconstruct a convincing story of the struggle and its aftermath from his poems.

What follows is not a critical evaluation of Gurbakhsh, the poet or a rendering of the literary merits of his selected works but an appraisal of the saga of struggle as suggested in the poems.

The struggle for the liberation of India carried on from across her frontiers in the East gained new dimensions with the arrival of Netaji on the scene. Gurbakhsh makes us visualize the dangerous journey undertaken by Subhas Chandra Bose in German and Japanese submarines through the waters of the Atlantic, the Indian and the Pacific oceans controlled by the British and American navies. Death stared him in the face but the Man of Destiny remained unruffled and serene.

"*Netaji ka dubkni kishti ka safar*" : Netaji's voyage in the sub marine offers a brief but moving account of the journey and the composure of Netaji threatened by death. It was a game of hide and seek played between life and death. Any moment could be the hour of collision and the distance to be covered from Germany to Japan was frightfuly long. Committed to a cause, Netaji was least bothered about the dangers. He was courage personified and a living picture of grace and dignity :

Har lamha dhundhta tha jahan maut ko
Maut thi dhundhti har lamhey ko jahan
Zindgi khelti thi wahan Bose ki
Maut thi khelti zindgi se jahan
Socheye to zara Germany hai kahan
Yeh kahan se gaye they kahan aur kahan
Germany aur Japan to ik tarf
Sagron ka safar dubkni kishtiyan
Sar ko apney sar-e-dast thamey hooye
Netaji Bose they aagey aagey rvan
Qadam uthtey they kiya fakhro andaz se
Karna azaad tha jab ke Hindustan
Piara Hindustan, Nyara Hindustan

Netaji accepted the leadership of the Indian Independence Movement and electrified the Movement with his clarion call '*Chalo Delhi*' which became the war cry of Azad Hind Fauj. The twice smutted sensibility of Gurbakhsh, by the love of his country and no less by the magnetic pull of Netaji, clothes the magic of the Colonel in a captivating short lyric bearing the caption "*Chalo Delhi*".

The poet reminds the volunteers of their leader's call to reach Delhi to hoist the national flag after getting their motherland liberated. Delhi which was then ruled by the English had to be brought under "*Hindi Raj*". The brave soldiers should defy all impediments, write a new chapter in history with their blood and raise "Jai Hind" from the Red Fort:

Chalo Delhi jawano Hind ko Azad karwayen

Chalo Delhi ke jhandha shan se hum apna - lehrayen

Chalo Delhi usi Delhi jahan hai Raj Angrezi

Chalo Delhi ke Hindi Raj apna phir se hum layen.

Chalo Delhi, jahan Jamna kinarey hai quila apna

Chalo Delhi, wahin saff bandh kar Jai Hind hum gayen

Chalo Delhi, usi Delhi Jahan Minar -e- Qutbi hai

Chalo Delhi, Nishan-e-Hind ko hum us pai lehrayen

Chalo Delhi, agar rastey mein lakhon mushkalenin aayen

Chalo Delhi, ke apney khoon se tarikh likh jayen.

"Netaji ka pharman" (desh bhagton se) is a stirring poem that unfolds Netaji's commandment to the compatriots to awake, arise and break asunder the chains of slavery. Composed in August 1944 at Bangkok, the poem eloquently proclaims Netaji's revolutionary message that no price should be too great for the liberty of the land. The soldiers of the Azad Hind Fauj should become formidable warriors and inflict a crushing defeat on the enemy. No force should withhold the thrust of their forceful advance that would usher their beloved Motherland into a period of independence and prestige. They should continue unmindful of starvation, inconveniences, obstacles and wounds sustained in the fight. The Red Fort and Qutab Minar of Delhi were inviting the volunteers of Netaji to hoist the Tricolour there and rend the sky with the greetings of Jai Hind sounded in the liberated India:

Utho soye Bharat ke nasibon ko jagaa do.

Azadi yoon latey hain jawan laey key dikha do.

Khoonkhar bano sher merey Hindi Sipahi:

Dushman ki safein torh do ik thalkha macha do.

Haan Hind ke badley mein adoo cheez hi kiya hai

Restey mein ho Bhai to usey mar gira do.

Kar yaad Shaheedon ka lahu desh ki khatar

Ik toli bhi dushman ke hazaron se larha do.
Ho bhook, ho takleef rukawat ko thakawat;
Kha zakham -e- giran maut ko bhi hans ke dikha do
Kyon Lal Qila yoon rahey Dushman ke hawaley ?
Phir lashkaraye-e-Hindi ki wahan dhoom machaa do.
Minar-e-Qutab dekhta hai rah tumhari
Chal uski bulandi ko tarangey se sajjaa do.
Kuchh aur tamanna hai na khawahash merey dil mein:
Azad watan Hind mein Jai Hind bulaa do:
Utho soye Bharat ke nasibon ko jagaa do

Netaji wrought marvellous transformation in the psyche of soldiers and civilian volunteers. They stood committed to the cause of freedom and showed unflinching loyalty to their Supreme Commander. The soldiers thought it a privilege and good luck to be reckoned as the followers of Netaji who gave them identity. An idea of Netaji's mass appeal is projected in the poem "*Main Kaun Hoon*?" (Who am I?). Written in June 1945 in Rangoon Jail, the lyric registers the representative character of the men and officers who constituted Azad Hind Fauj. Gurbakhsh modestly claims to be a petty soldier of Netaji. He deems himself to be lucky to have found a place among thousands of Netaji's combatants who defy enemy's cannons and bombers with unbarring fervour. They live for the sake of their country and would lay down their lives at the altar of her freedom. They remain undaunted by physical privations and the might of the enemy :

Hoon ik adna sepahi apney Neta ke hazaron mein;
Mili ho jis ko kismat se jagah un khaksaron mein;
Hain jeetay watan ki khatar hain martey watan apeny par;
Museebat se rahen larh kar museebat ke paharhon mein.
Kabhi bhookhey kabhi pyasey kabhi bimar bey-bistar;
Fikar phir bhi nahin dil par nazar aayen baharon mein,
Na unko khauf topon sey, na dar bombar jahazon ka;
Liye sangeen ja hamla karein lakhon hazaron mein.

Larhai key waqat josh-e-watan josh-e-samandar say:

Barhey jinka sepahi hoon main ik unki kataron mein

All lovers and saviours of humanity who appear on the stage of the world from time to time vindicate the eternal truth that human spirit cannot be subdued indefinitely by the oppression or repression of the tyrants, dictatorial ruling hierarchy or the imperialistic powers. What we ordinarily call the rising of the Messiah is an expression of the social reaction against the prevailing tyranny and the denial of justice. The emergence of the martyr is a manifestation of the spirit of freedom-consciousness that percolates to the grass-roots. That accounts for the repeated occurrence of martyrdom and resurrection resulting the redemption of the suffering humanity. Gurbakhsh, the revolutionary poet, beautifully brings out the continuity of the freedom struggle in a poem that enshrines of glowing tribute paid to Tantia Topey. Gurbakhsh identifies Rani Jhansi, Tantia Topey, Bhagat Singh, Chander Shekhar Azad, Bismal, Ashfaq, Udham Singh, Madan Lal Dhingra, Savarkar, Netaji Subhash Chandar Bose and his I.N.A men as individuals inspired by the same spirit:

Aa jata hai woh kabhi kabhi;

Jab zulam hai hota tabhi tabhi.

Kabhi Bhagat Singh ban jata hai

Chander Shekhar ho jata hai

Azad wohi Bismal bhi wohi

Ashfaq wohi kahlata hai

Kabhi Udham Singh bun jata jai

O'Dyre mar mukata hai.

Kabhi Madan Dhingra banta hair

Waily ko khatam karata hai

Savarkar Vir Bahadur ban

Sagar mein chhalang lagata hai

Azad Hind afawj larha

Wohi Netaji kehlata hai

Talwar leeye jab aata hai

Larh mar kar zulam mitaney ko
Bigrhi taqdeer bananey ko
Jai Hind ki jai bulwane ko
Talwar liaey nirbhay yodha.

The Indian National Army fought the war of liberation in alien lands. They knew that their destination was not easy to reach and the odds were placed heavily against them but they went ahead with their ceaseless struggles. The Red Fort of Delhi constantly goaded them on:

Dur thi manzal dur watan tha;
Dur bahut Jamna ka kinara.
Dur Qutab Minar Kharha tha;
Dur Qila tha Lal Hamara.

The sacrifices made by the heroic soldiers and freedom fighters bore fruit but the country stood partitioned. The lot of the common man continues to be miserable. The poet's dream of a united India is still a distant dream. He is simply disillusioned at the turn of events when the sacrifices of the soldiers, known and the unknown, have not been recognized and people fight for their narrow domestic walls raised in the name of religions, castes, communities, languages or provinces. Our political independence is yet to be translated into social justice, equality and economic prosperity of the masses. How poignantly the poet realizes that the destination continues to be distant as ever ? The shock of the shattering of the cherished dream is too deep for words:

Dur thi manzal; dur hai manzal;
Dur nahin go Jamna kinara
Jumna kinarey ghoom raha hoon,
Ghoom ghoom kar dhoondh raha hoon;
Toot gaya jahan sapna pyara.

Gurbakhsh, the poet, has a message for the sub continent, nay for humanity, that the path of peace, progress and prosperity lies in banishing hatred and war :

Jaag musafir, jaag!

Jaag musafir Hindustani,
Bangali aur Pakistani:
Nafrat sey na miley kinara
Prem bina na koi chara
Jung hai barbadi ka darya.
Prem bina na koi chara
Jaag, musafir, jaag!

The poet and the revolutionary in Colonel G.S. Dhillon cannot approve of the system that breeds sycophancy, corruption, nepotism and opportunism. The powers that he disdain independent thinking and exploit the masses to perpetuate their authority. The Britishers left India but the new rulers are faring no better. Gurbakhsh finds himself an exile or an alien in his own land:

Nahin aaj Angrez gaddi ke oopar;
Hamarey hi leader hamarey hain sar par.
Magar khud-prasti ke chakkar mein aa kar,
Hamari hi kismet ke chakkar phira kar,
Hamin se hamari raza mangtey hain,
Ajab kamsini hai ye kya mangtey hain
Dimaghi ghulami nahi hai gwara,
Nahin sar jhukana kabhi sar ko pyara.
Mera desh hai main ye kehta jabhi hoon;
Mera desh hai main yahan ajnabi hoon.

INDEX

Abottabad, 28

Achhru Ram, Mr. Justice, 59, 425, 426, 432, 443, 444, 449, 510, 511

Adams, Maj., 85

Agha Khan Palace, 224

Agnihotri, Prof. Harbans Lal, 572

Ahmedabad, 517

Ahmednagar, 112

Ajmer Singh, Maj., 537

Ajmer Singh, Naik, 79, 104

Akali Party, 418

Akbar Ali, Lt., 199

Akyab, 391

Alagappan, I.M.S., Maj. General, 194

Algon (birth place), 3, 4, 10

Ali Mohammad, 48-51

Allah Ditta, Capt., 97, 194

Allen, Maj., 392-394

All India Forward Bloc, 527

All India Radio, 85

Alor Star, 86, 87, 89, 111, 218, 546

Alva, Margaret, 550

Amarjit (Son), 532, 533

Amar Singh, Baba, 176

Amir Singh, Capt., 199

Amman, 164, 174

Amriek Singh, 546

Amrik, (Sahgal's Brother-in-law), 513

Amrik Singh, (Brother), 8, 11, 13, 19, 417

Amrita, (Daughter), 512

Amritsar, 4, 509, 510, 512

Ananda Pagoda, 265, 296, 297

Andaman & Nicobar Islands, 210

Anderson, Maj., 1/14th Punjab, 69, 81, 83, 85

Anderson, Major, The Escort, 390-393

Arakan, 212, 213, 349

Arisue Seizo, Lt. General, 564

Arjuna of Mahabharata Epic, 305

Arjun Singh, Lance Naik, 38

Armadas, 541, 544, 545, 549, 550

Asaf Ali Defence Counsel, 425, 432, 497, 508, 509

Ashok Kumar, 86

Atma Singh, 288

Auchinleck, Sir Claude General, 500, 503-05, 567
Aung San, General, 270, 274-76, 319-20, 328-32, 546
Aurangzeb, Emperor, 536
Ayer, S.A., 209-10, 481, 554
Azad, Maulana Abul Kalam, 523
Azad, Chander Shekhar, 576
Azad Hind, 558
Azad Hind Aircraft, 220
Azad Hind Bank, 211, 361
Azad Hind Dal, 211, 214, 240
Azad Hind Expedition, 539-551
Azad Hind Radio, 481, 542
Aziz Ahmed, Maj. General, 209, 217, 225, 227, 229, 231, 232, 237, 238, 240, 300, 406, 464, 499, 536

Babu Ram, Naik, Sub. Major, later Major INA., 68, 165, 448, 449
Boden Powell, Lord, 18
Badri Das, Rai Bahadur, 426, 432, 449, 497, 511
Bagan (Pagan), 547
Baghat State, 20
Bagri, Capt., 322
Heroic death, 333
Bahadurgarh Camp, 407, 428, 429, 431
Bahadur Shah Zafar, Emperor, 206, 370, 379, 383, 536, 546
Bahadur Singh, Subedar, 45, 46, 51
Bahawalpur Infantry Regiment, 105, 172
Bairagarh, 407
Bakhshi/Bashki, 10
Bakshi, Akhil, 539-40, 543, 551
Balqees, 240, 326, 361, 378-79, 388, 400-01
Balwant Singh (Brother), Subedar, 10, 13, 18-20, 24, 27, 65, 66, 425
Balwant Singh, Major, 163
Ba Maw, Dr., 211, 221, 319-20, 562-63
Bamfield, Major, 57
Bande Matram, 25-26
Banerjee, Montu, 548
Bangkok, 164, 165, 220-21, 340
Bangkok Conference, 177-78, 468
Bangkok Resolutions, 178-90
Bannerjee, Interrogator at Red Fort, 403-06
Bansi Lal, 61, 62, 72, 75
Banwari Lal, Major, 431
Barog, 20
Barstow, A.E. Brigadier, 63, 64
Basant, 38-44, 48-49, 52, 66, 68, 70-73, 75, 76, 78, 84, 85, 276, 400, 421, 422-425, 483-485, 508-509, 512, 513, 515-21, 524, 530, 532
Bashir Ahmad S.M., 239, 240, 326, 361, 378, 382, 388, 401
Batti Chak, 13, 32, 50, 483
Bawa, Dr. Major, 518
Beaton, E., Major, 413, 414
Begums of Oudh, 206
Besant, Annie, Mrs., 274
Betai, H.R., Mrs., 211, 239

Bhagat, N.S., Col., 209, 216-17, 228, 231, 238
Bhagat Singh, the Martyr, 25, 520, 576
Bhago, 2
Bharat Krishak Samaj, 530
Bhim Singh Chaudhry, 5, 6
Bhonsle, Appa Sahib, 206
Bhonsle, J.K., Major General, 192, 199, 200, 209, 407, 429, 454, 536
Bidadari, Conference, 177
  Resolutions, 197
  Camp, 204, 241, 476
Birla, G.D., 519
Birla House, 522
Bishanpur, 214
Bishan Singh, Colonel, 163, 169
Bisht, Gian Singh, 2nd Lieutenant, 240, 241, 313-14, 354
Blaxland C.B., Major General, 431, 433, 438, 442, 448, 497, 503
Boer War, 489
Bombay, 10, 12, 76
Bose, Rash Behari, 175, 178, 190, 195, 197-99, 204, 209, 212, 359-60, 399, 542, 564
Bose, Sarat Chandra, 511, 527
Bose, Netaji Sabhas Chandra—
  Escape from home, 74
  Message to Bangkok Conference, 178
  Conferece invites S.C. Bose to come to East Asia, 190
  Dangerous journey arrives Sabang, 203
  Tojo invites to Diet, 204
  Appears in Cathey Building Singapore, 204
  Reviews INA, Provisional Govt. of Azad Hind Created, 205
  Proclamation, 206-209
  War declared, 209-10
  Govt. Recognised, Andaman & Nicobars acquired, 210
  Move to Rangoon, Azad Hind Dal formed, Funds by Habib, total mobilisation, 211
  Secret Services, Tokyo Cadets, 212
  In Action, 212, 213, 214
  Tricolour hoisted on Liberated Territory, 214
  Imphal besieged, 215
  The Retreat, 215
  Our Aim, 223
  Under fire, 225
  Sends a gift, 308, 309
  Takes pains to provide boots to Samy, 310
  Sends a letter, 315
  Address while leaving Burma, 372
  Air Crash, 415, 416
    Where is he ? 568-71
Bourke, A.G.H., Brigadier, 431
Bowes, H., 383-88
Bradlaugh Hall, Lahore, 518, 522
Brar, M.S., Major, 105, 163, 193, 399
Brooke-Popham, Sir Robert, 79

Bruce Charles, 538-39
Buddha, Lord, 15, 19
Budh Singh Baba, 163-64
Burhan-ud-Din, Colonel, 192
Bwasa, 296, 297, 393

Chander Bhan, Major, 268, 277, 279, 280, 293, 295, 296, 299, 301, 305, 317
Changi Garrison, 105-74
Changi Airport, 541
Changlun Battle, 88
Charge of Immortals, 313
Charlottenburg, 557
Chatterji, A.C., Maj. General, 177, 209, 214, 229, 236
Chaudhury, B., Lt. Colonel Later Maj. General, Indian Army, 100, 105, 132, 134, 161-62, 169, 174-75, 194, 456
Chauk, 282
Chetwode, Sir Philip Field Marshal, 56
Chhaja Singh, Sardar, 5, 6
Chhanga Manga, 7, 17, 31, 400, 512
Chhatra Bahadur, 79, 197
Chindwin, 245
Chitnis, V.S., Colonel, 532
Chittagong, 214, 559
Chouen Lai, 531
Christ, Lord Jesus, 19, 27
Churchill, Sir Winston, 30, 129, 169, 379, 488
Col. Raja Mohamad Arshad, 215, 238, 241, 252, 271, 371, 406, 481, 482, 491, 536, 549, 551
Collingwood, R.G., Brigadier, 283
Corfield, 2nd Lieutenant, 69
Croatia, 210
Croft, Sergeant Major, 58
Crowther, W.A., Brigadier, 284

Daletmi, 213
Dalhousie, 50
Dalip Singh, (Brother), 16, 17, 19
Dalip Singh, Kanwar, Sir, 425, 432, 442, 497, 498, 511
Damodar Dass, 530
Dara Ali Iqtadar Shah, Colonel, 163, 199
Darchhawana, Dr., 540
Daryo Singh, 436
Das Debanath, 209
Davey, Nigel, 538
Dayananda, Swami, 19
Dehradun, 33, 43, 56
Deolali, 10, 11, 13
Deol, Gurdev Singh, Prof. Major, 532
Desai, Bhulabhai, 59, 60, 424, 426-28, 432-33, 437-38, 441-42, 447-49, 480-82, 485-97, 503, 513-14, 516
Desai, Dhirubhai, 441, 514
Deshmukh, Panjab Rao, 530
Desh Sevak Sena, 525-27
Desh Sevak Party, 527
Dewan-e-Aam, 534-35
Dewan, P.R., Brigadier, 532
Dharm Singh, 436
Dhargalkar, K.P., Captain, 447

Dhian Chand, Major, Hockey Wizard, 72, 546
Dhillon, Gurbakhsh Singh,
  Birth, 4
  Heritage, 5-9
  Childhood, 10-16
  Education, 17-28
  Decides Army career 29-31
  Father's advice, 32
  A Recruit, 31-36
  Attestation oath of allegiance to the British King, 36
  Drafted to active Battalion 4/14 Punjab Regt. at Lahore, 36
  Pay of Sepoy, 37
  Mule Driver, 37-38
  Basant enters life, 38
  Father enters, 42, 43
  Taming the mule, 43
  N.C.O's Cadre, 43-44
  Family Lines and humiliation 44, 45, 46
  Promoted Acting Unpaid Lance Naik, 47
  Pole vaulting, 47-50
  Kitchner College, 50-54
  A British Sergeant advises, 54
  Selected for I.M.A., 54
  I.M.A. Dehra Dun Chetwode Hall, 56
  Long vacation and Father's gift, 60, 61
  Commissioned Officer, 1/14th Punjab, 61
  Public indifference to war, 62, 63
  Colonel Barstow enters, 63, 64, 65
  Owns a Car, 65, 66, 67
  Colour bar, 67, 68
  Battalion moves to Secunderabad, 68
  Acted as Battalion Quarter Master, 69
  Basant joins, 71
  Battalion Depot Commander, 73, 74
  Colonel's advice, Punishment be Minimum, 73, 74
  Subhas Chandra Bose Escapes, 74
  Vow not to drink while abroad, 75
  Baggage Officer and British Sergeant's intolerable conduct, 76
  Bombay Skyline, 76
  Colonel's criticism, 77
  Ipoh, 77-79
  Proper Expression, 79, 80
  Officiating Adjutant, 80-82
  Indian food problem, 82
  Colour Bar, 82-84
  Gratitude to Col. Fitzpatrick, 84
  Rejoins Battalion, 86
  Order to go to northern Frontier of Malaya-Battle of Changlun, 87-88
  Japanese tanks attack, 88
  Signal truck burnt, panic caused stampede, 88, 89
  Alor Star fell, 89

Escape to Penang, 3 MRC, 89
Guarding bridge at Nibong Tabol, Colour Bar even in War, 90
Adjutant of 7 MRC. and Move to Raffles Square, Singapore falls, 90, 91
To Farrer Park, 92
The Surrender, 93-96
Early Formation of INA, 96-97
First INA Action, 97
Neesoon Camp, 100-102
Move to Changi, 102-104
Changi Garrison, 105-106
The Camp, 107-110
The Changi area, 115-119
Garrison duties, 119-120
British attitude, 120-22
An Australian P.O.W, 127-29
Shooting case, 130, 131-34
The Hut, 135-36
Insults, 136-38
Religion, 139-42
A Desertion, 142-51
Meet the G.O.C., 151-54
Men are generous, 155-57
Neighbours, 157-59
Illness, 159-63
A Christmas Cake, 163
Baba Budh Singh, 163-64
Pala Singhs Boldness, 166
General Mohan Singh visits, 167
P.O.Ws, 167-71
Garrison in Retrospect, 171-73
Our Glorious Dead, 173-74
Vive La Garrison, 174
Convalescence, 175
First Division raised, 191-94
Penang on leave, 194-95
I.N.A. Crises, 195-99
Appointed D.Q.M.G., 199-201
Supply and Transport Officer, 201-202
5th Guerrila Regiment Second-in-Command, 216-19
With Ist Infantry Regiment, 219
Meets Tunku Abdul Rehman, 219
To Burma, 220
Meet Col. Shaukat Ali Malik, 220-22
Dined with Netaji, 222-23
Our Aim, 223
Conversation with Netaji, 223-25
Netaji under Fire, 225-27
Meet Netaji, 227-36
A Brigade Commander, 235
To Myingyan, 240-70
A Rape Case, 248-51
My Men, 251-52
Colonel Arshad visits, 252, 53
Silent Judges, 253
Jawanon Ka Din, 254
Health Problems, 254-56
Army Commander's visit, 256-58
Disciplinary Action, 258

Saddest Christmas eve, 259
Col. Jagir Singh Comes, 260-61
A Dilemma & Alarming News, 261-70
Irrawaddy operations, 271-98
Mount Popa and Kyauk Padaung, 302-17
Gift from Netaji, 308-10
Samy gets Boots, 310
Sade Hill Raid, 13, 311
The Charge of the Immortals, 313-14
Letter from Netaji and My Reply, 315-16
Message to Shah Nawaz Khan, 317
The Retreat, 318-38
Battle of Legy, 321-22
Magwe, 324-28
Relations with Burmese Army, 328-33
Bagri's Heroic Death, 333
Withdrawal through Pegu Yomas, 334-38
The Last Clash, 340-49
Interrogation, 350-64
Hospitalisation, 364-69
Rangoon Jail, 370-88
An Unknown Soldier, 376-78
Habib Sahib, 379-80
Code of Honour, 381-82
Meet Bashir Children, 378-79
Altercation with Maj. Bowes, 383-88
To Delhi, 389-401
Kindness Kills, 389-94
British Military Police Lockup, 394-99
Special troops train, 399-401
The Red Fort, 402-27
Major Hayat and Hugh Toye, 409-12
Summary of Evidence, 413-15
Charge Sheet served, 414-15
General Loganathan's tears, 415
Meet my father, 416-22
Meet Basant, 422-25
Defence Committee Members start visiting us, 425-26
Bhulabhai Desai's visit before taking up our case, 426-27
The Trial, 428-98
The Verdict, 499-506
Aftermath, 507-533
Memorabilia, 534, 551
Quit India Golden Jubilee, 534
Swatantrata Sangram Sangrahalaya, 534-36
Salimgarh Swatantrata Senani Smarak, 536-38
Enemy of Empire, 538-539
Azad Hind Expedition, 539-51
Netaji, 552-71

Desh Sevak Sena, 525-27
Desh Sevak Party, 527
Deolali, 10-14
Dhillon, Gurdial Singh, (Brother), 10, 400, 425
Dhillon, Joginder Singh, Lt. Gen., 85

Dhillon, Mahanbir Singh, Brigadier, 196
Dhillon's Den, 318, 533
Dhingra, Madan Lal, Shaheed, 576
Dicky, 2nd Lieut., 69
Didar Singh, Naik, 131, 133, 142, 149
Dina Nath, 239, 282, 481, 547
Dipalpore, 17-19
Dimoline, W.A., Brigadier, 282
Directorate Military Bureau, 199-201
Dorji, Chhiring, Dr., 540
Dua, Inder Dev, Mr. Justice, 425, 432, 497, 511, 519, 522
Dua, Shiva, Dr., 520
Duly Chand, 435, 472
Duni Chand, Lieut., 288, 290
Dutta, Sunil, 540-49

Egypt, 13
Eisenhover, Dwight David, President U.S.A., 530-31
Elizebeth the 2nd, Her Majesty Queen of England, 219
Elahi Bakhsh, 456
Emerson, Lt. Colonel, 51-54
Engineer, Sir Naushirwan P., 433, 438, 439, 442, 444, 493, 495
Evans, G.C., Maj. General, 283

Fairbank, Major, 53, 54
Falam, 214
Fanshawe, B., Captain, 414
Farah, Mrs., 144-48, 150
Farrer Park, 92-96, 154, 541
Fatimah, 19
Ferozepur, 9, 10, 31, 34, 85
Field Interrogation Centre No. 3, at Pegu, 350-51, 365
Field Interrogation Centre No. 2, Rangoon, 375
First War of independence, in 1857, 25
Fitzpatrick,. L.V., Lt. Colonel, 63, 68, 71, 73-74, 77, 80, 82-85 88, 111, 432, 474
Fourth Battalion of the 14th Punjab Regiment, 31-32
Fuhrer, 557
Fujiwara, Iwaichi, 93, 94, 98, 154, 176, 194, 195, 197, 198, 256, 443, 453, 454, 476, 481, 542, 565, 569
Fujiwarakikan, 91, 98, 101, 137, 153, 176

Gandhi Brigade, 234
Gandhi, Kasturba, 274
Gandhi Mahatma, 18, 102, 194, 204, 207, 223-24, 362-63, 384, 505, 558-61, 573
  125th Birth Anniversary of, 134-35
  Netaji first to address 'Father of our Nation' to, 224
Garret, Brigadier, 80, 87, 88
General Officer Commanding, Lahore Area, 50
Geneva convention, 131, 150
Ghani, Karim, 209

Ghoragali, 28
Ghasi Ram Jain, 529-30
Ghosh, Nirmal Chandra, 528
Ghulam Mohd, Lieut., 458
Gian Singh, Sepoy, 48-50
Gilani, G.Q., Colonel, 172, 183, 191, 399, 456
Gill, Naranjan Singh, Colonel, 94, 102, 103, 176, 196 454, 525
Girdhari Lal, Lieut., 200
Gita, 305
Goho, S.C., 175-176
Golden Peacock, 319
Gordon Mission College, Rawalpindi, 17, 26, 28, 518
Govind Singh, Shri Guru, 19, 294
Graer, 2nd Lient., 69
Grewal, Jang Bahadur Singh, Major, 165, 215
Grewal, V.J.S., Lt. Colonel, 540
Guadal Canal, 558
Guerrilla Group, 192
4th Guerrilla Regiment, 237, 318
5th Guerrilla Regiment, 216-19, 241, 300
Gulzara Singh, Colonel, 96, 198, 209, 210, 524
Gupta, Deshbandhu Dass, 424
Gurdial Singh, Capt. Dr., 248-50, 255, 264, 269, 273
Gurmeet Singh, Col., 198
Gurucharan Singh, Lieut, 85, 161
Gurudwaras Reform movement, 18
Gwebinyo, 271-73
Habibur Rahman, Col., 88-90, 96, 163, 194, 221, 226, 236, 416, 475, 557, 569
Habib Sahib of Rangoon, 211, 239, 379, 380, 382
Hachiya, Teruo, 480
Hafeez Jalandhari, 23
Hafiz Nisar, 530
Haider Ali, 206
Harbhajan Singh, 6
Harcharan Singh, 546
Hargreeves, Capt., 88
Hari Ram, Lieut., 280, 282, 298-90 292-93, 301
Hari Singh, Maharaja of Kashmir, 525
Hari Singh, Major, 258, 268, 408, 409, 411, 435, 472
Harjit, 546
Harnam Singh, 112
Haro, 7, 8
Haryana, 5
Hatod Hill, 318, 533
Hayat, Maj., 393, 409, 412
Hazara Singh, Subedar, 64, 69
Heath, Lady, 168
Heath, Lieut General Sir L.M., 86, 168, 466
Herts, Gavin, 541
Himalaya, 21
Hind Field Force Group, 192
Hirao, Sgt., 125, 164, 166
Hitler, 557
Hongenji Temple, 176

Hospitalisation, 365-69
Hotel Majestic, 78
Hudson, L., Wing Commander, 258
Hunt, Col., 93, 444, 453-54, 467, 476
Hussain, S.M., Colonel, 102, 218-20, 222, 225, 227 324-25, 409-12, 536
Hyderabad, 68
Hyderabad Sindh, 517

Imphal, 214, 215, 223, 245, 480, 549
Imran, 549
Indaw, 301
Ingle, Lt. Col., 69, 85
Indian Evidence Act, 445
Indian Independence League, 176, 180, 220
Indian Infantry Bridage, 80
Indian Military Academy, Dehradun, 30, 51, 54, 56, 57, 68, 413
INA Defence Committee by Indian National Congress, 418, 425
Indian National Army, 84, 95-202
  Intellegence Group, 193
  INA Detention camp at Bahadurgarh, 428-30
INA Trial at Red Fort, 60, 82, 132, 536
Indian Penal Code, 491
Indian Prisoners of war in Malaya, 94, 97, 105
India's High Commissionar, 543
Ipoh, 76-78, 90, 217, 546
Iqbal, 21-23, 347
Irrawaddy, 245, 258, 265-66, 277
Ishar Singh, 209
Islam Shah, 586
Italy, 210
Itoh, 104, 106
Iwakurokikan, 176, 192, 195-98
Izumi, Capt. 239-41, 246, 262-65, 271-73, 287, 290-94, 299-300, 302, 321

Jackson, C. Hungerford, Lt. Colonel 44, 50, 432, 473
Jackson, Mrs., 45, 46
Jacob, John, Lieut., 13, 544, 551
Jagat Singh, Dr., 194
Jagir Singh, Lt. Col., 234, 260-61, 263-65, 267, 269-73, 277, 293, 299, 301, 303, 305, 308, 324, 326, 338-39, 364, 403, 406, 536
Jain, Ghasi Ram Kavi, 529-31
Jain, Rajendra, Dr., 540
Jai Singh, Subedar, 36
Jallianwala Bagh, 63, 512, 536
James, Major, 164
James II, 489
Jasram, 530
Jaswant Singh, Col., 163, 193, 198, 218
Jawahar Singh, 6
Jitra, 86, 87, 111, 219-20, 475, 541, 546
Johore Bharu Channel, 91, 545

Kabir, 19
Kaladan, 213
Kalaw, 318

Kalka, 20
Kandhara Singh, 327
Kanni, 328, 333
Kanpur, 552
Kanwal Singh, Lieut., 322
Kapoor, Prithvi Raj, 524
Karam Chand, Head Master, 22
Karnail Singh Sepoy, 39, 48
Kartar Kaur, 24, 27
Kartar Singh, Subedar, 37, 38, 40, 44, 46-47, 49, 299, 305, 311, 313, 317, 339, 349
Katakura, Tudashi, Maj. General, 448, 480, 481, 569
Katamura, Maj. General S., 5, 256
Katasraj temple, 28
Katju, Kailash Nath, Dr., 426, 432, 449, 450, 451, 497
Kaul, Harsh, Colonel, 541
Kawabe, Lieut. General, 480
Kawanishi, Sgt., 114
Kawashi, 220
Kerin, F.C.A, Col., 431, 433, 437, 442, 444, 449, 494-96
Khabok, 305-06, 310, 312, 318, 326
Khan, Lieut., 247, 263, 264, 305
Khan, Abdul Hafiz, Sepoy, 356
Khan, Abdul Rashid, Major, 101
Khan Ajmal Shah Nawaz, 540
Khan, D.M., 209
Khan, Subedar Fazal Dad, 460, 461
Khan, Hamida, 550
Khan, Kabir, 540, 543
Khan, Malik Fateh, Major, 371, 373, 374
Khan, Mohd., Lieut., 268, 280, 282, 294-96
Khanna, Jugal Kishore, 432
Khan, Shah Nawaz, Maj. General, 103, 193, 209, 214, 226, 258, 300-03, 305, 309, 316, 318-19, 322, 324-51, 353-54, 359, 363-64, 380, 402, 406, 409, 411-14, 425-26, 428-31, 433, 443-45, 449, 451, 482-84, 496, 498-500, 504-09, 512, 535-37, 550, 561, 568-69
Kharak Singh, Baba, 18
Khosla, N.N., Major 200-02, 241-42, 253, 271-72
Khosla, R.P., Mr. Justice, 497, 511
Khurana, Madan Mohan, Major, 165
Khurushehev, Nikita Sergeyich, 531
Khushi Ram Jemadar, 111, 112
Kiani, I.J., Colonel, 214
Kiani, Mohammad Zaman, Maj. General, 72, 80
Kikan, Hikari, 239
Kimura, Lt. General, 299
Kingsley, Brigadier, 54
Kitchner College, Nowgong, 50-52
Kitson, J.A, Lieut. Colonel, 414
Kohima, 214, 549
Kohli, G.L, Captain, 200
Kota Bharu, 86, 87
Krishna, Lord, 7, 19, 194, 305
Krishnan, S.A, 239, 269, 296-98
Kuala Kangsar, 546
Kuala Kedah State, 91
Kuala Lumpur, 76, 98, 457, 545

Kuka movements, 25
Kulwant Rai, Colonel, 193
Kundan Lal, Captain 200
Kunizuka, Lieut., 94
Kunwar Abhay Singh, Major, 532
Kunzaik, 264, 273
Kut-al-Amara, 33
Kuywa, 248
Kyauk Padaung, 245, 299, 317, 319, 321, 322, 324
Kyaukse, 241, 245, 318
Kyauktaw, 213

Lady Mountbatten, 531
Lacy, R.C., Prof., 28
Lahore, 6, 13, 61-63
Lajpat Rai, Lala, 520, 548
Lajyavati, Kumari, 520
Lakshmana, 12
Lakshmi, Captain, 209, 242, 535, 542, 543, 548, 549
Lal Din, Captain, 111, 112,136, 173
Lebra, Joyce, Dr., 558
Legy, 311, 321, 548
Liaqat Ali Khan, 482
Loga, 339-40
Loganathan, A.D., Maj. General, 200, 209, 210, 371, 406-07, 412, 415, 480, 536
Longwill, Lieut., 69
Lt. Col. A.D. Mac Conachie, 414
Lyon, Murray, Maj. General, 80, 87, 466

Maalaan, 7
Mac Carthy, Lieut., 69
Maclachlan, W.P.G. Major, 375, 388
Madagascar, 203
Madan, Maj., 225, 239, 331, 332
Madhya Pradesh, 318
Madum, Maj., 453
Maghar Singh, Maj., 537
Magwe, 322, 324-28, 410-11
Mahabharata, 28
Mahavira, 19
Mahboob Ahmed, Col., 96, 288, 292, 301-03, 549
Mahindra, D.B., Wing Comdr., 532
Maiyee, 273-76
Majhail, Ishar Singh, 526
Makhan Lal, Seth, 194
Malai, Sucha Singh, 212
Malaya, 76, 86, 89, 98, 550
Malik, Shaukat Ali, Col., 193, 214, 220-22, 399
Malik, V.R., Wing Comdr., 532
Mamyo, 548
Manchuria, 210
Mandalay, 238, 240-42, 318, 548
Mangu Ram, 2nd Lieut., 299, 300
Manipur, 214, 399
Mansukhlal, Capt., 214
Master, Nigan Dass T., 514
Matsumato, Shunichi, 480
Maulana Iltaf Hussain, Halli, 21
Maungdaw, 213
Maymyo, 360
Mehar Dass, Col., 213, 339, 340, 407-08, 536

Mehar Singh, Sepoy, 103-04, 108, 110, 128, 161, 241, 271, 278, 290, 296-97, 308, 325, 340, 346, 382, 386
Mehrotra, Maneesh, 538-39
Mehrotra, Rajendra Nath, Major, 532
Mehtab Singh, Lieut., 200
Meiktila, 241, 245, 285, 300, 303, 318-19
Menezes, S.L, Lieut. General, 547
Menon, K.P.K., 176, 183, 191
Menon, Pramodini, 549, 551
Mesopotamia, 33
Messervy, Lieut. General Sir Frank, 283, 285, 365
Miami Beach, 89, 194
Midori Kawa, Capt., 311, 318
Miller, A.B., Major, 46, 47, 50
Minde, 329
Mingaladon air port, 220, 222, 224, 389
Mirza, A.B., Maj., 193
Misra, L.S., Colonel, 213
Misri Chand, Lt. General, 85, 441, 508
Mohammad Prophet, 19
Mohammad Ashraf, Hav., 79, 83
Mohammad Bakhsh, 12
Mohammad Bakht Khan, 536
Mohammad Hussain, Capt., 305, 316, 317
Mohammed Akram, Capt., 82, 83, 88, 91, 93, 111, 152, 153, 176, 194, 542
Mohd Iqbal, Sir, 197
Mohan Singh, Naik, 33-34
Mohan Singh, General, 79-81, 91, 93-99, 105, 111, 113, 147, 151-53, 165, 167, 176-78, 183, 191-94, 196-99, 228, 237, 256, 359-60, 399, 413, 445, 448, 454, 457, 461, 467-68, 476-78, 487, 504, 522, 525-17, 536, 541-42, 548, 560
Mohan, S.R. Col., 532
Mohinder, Lieut., 265, 267, 269, 271, 273, 276-77, 279, 290, 293-94
Mohinder Singh, 247, 305
Moirang, 221, 399
Montgomery, 17, 19, 22, 25, 517
Montgomery of Alamein, Field Marshal, 531
Mookerjee, Girja K., 564
More, S.S., 527
Morrey, 2nd Lt., 69
Maulmein, 220, 333, 340
Mountbatten, Lord, 282, 283, 411, 543
Mount Popa, 273, 293-94, 296, 298, 299-317, 321
Mount Popa and Kyauk Padaung, 299-317
Mowdak, 213, 214
Multan, 524
Murad Bakhsh, Prince, 536
Murata, 132-34
Musafar, Gurmukh Singh, Giani, 526
Muzang Road, Lahore, 522
Myanmar, 540, 541, 550

Myingyam, 238, 239, 241-42, 245, 266, 273, 302, 308, 318, 409, 411, 548
Myitche, 266, 279
Myithyina, 245

Nag, D.C., Lieut., 414, 442, 444-46
Naidu, Sarojini, 72, 274, 487
Nana Sahib, 206
Nankana Sahib, 18
Nanmen Army Hospital, 416
Napolean, 244
Narasimha Rao, P.V., 534-535, 541, 551
Narayanan, K.R., 541
Nargis, 540
Nasik, 12
Natha Singh, 6, 12, 13
Nathiagalli, 28
Nathu Ram, Master, 23, 24, 517-18
National Agriculture Fair, 531
National Cadet Corps, 527, 532
National Planning Commission, 212
Neesoon Camp, 96, 98, 100-04, 105, 240, 456-57, 545
Nehra, R.N., Lt. General, 62
Nehru Brigade, 224, 237-70
Nehru, Jawaharlal, 212, 224, 426, 441, 506, 518-19, 523, 525-27, 532, 536, 540
Netaji Fund committee, 379
Netaji Research Bureau at Netaji Bhawan, 549, 562
Netaji Statute at Subhas Park, 550
Neazbeg, 46, 48
Nibong Tabol, 90
Nilakanta Aiyra, 176
Nippon govt, 184, 187, 207
Nizam of Hyderabad, 68
Noakhali, 525
Noorudin Bihari, 424
Nowgong, 50-52, 55
Nwebyin, 273
Nyaungu, 245, 263-67, 277, 280, 289, 300, 318, 365, 542

Ogami, Lt. Col., 150, 162
Ogawa, Maj., 191, 239, 246, 251, 252
Ohta Saburo, 480
Okazaki, Lieut., 105, 106, 109-10, 112-14
Om, Maid, 539
Ore, C., Maj., 350-65, 388
Orlando, Mezzota, 554, 555
Otaguro, 176

Padang, 542
Pagan, 263-67, 280, 296-97, 300, 365
Pakistan, 5, 525
Pakokku, 245
Pandavas, 28
Pandit, H.N, 554
Pandit, S.S., Major, 432
Pandit, Vijayalkshmi, 274
Panja Sahib, 28
Panjwar, 5
Paras Ram, 247, 259
Parikh, Natha Lal, 513, 515, 516
Pariser, M.P., Captain, 413, 414
Parker, John, 538

Parmanand, 211, 239, 481
Partap Singh, Satguru, 24, 25, 511
Patani, 86, 87
Patel, Mani Behn, 522
Patel, Vallabhai, 515, 516, 522, 523, 526
Pegu, 318, 343, 349, 350, 403, 546
Pegu Jail, 350
Penang Island, 76, 77, 89, 194
Percival, A.E, Lt. General, 86, 91, 109, 121, 168, 466
Perdamen Singh, Dr., 546
Peshwa Baji Rao, 206
Peter, Private, 142, 144, 146-51, 164
Philippines, 210
Piaray Lal, 522
Pilot, Rajesh, 534
Pohla Ram, 197
Poonji Buddhist, 276
Porter, Dr., 27
Prabhu Dayal, Maj., 215
Prem Singh, High Commissioner of India. 544
Prince Philips, 531
Prince of Wales, 87
Pritam Singh, Giani, 91, 95, 153, 175-76, 194, 542
Pritam Singh, Col., 214
Pritam Singh, B., Maj., 431
Private David, 142, 144-51
Prome, 320, 328, 333-34
Provisional Govt of Azad Hind, 205-09, 399, 542, 553-54
  Proclamation of 206-09
  Recognised, 210
Pundaite, L.J., Ambassador, 546
Punjab High Court Bar Association, 511
Punjab Regiment, 33, 413
  1/14, 14, 61, 87-88, 101, 111, 151, 167, 219, 413
  3rd Battalion file 14th, 62, 85
  3rd Battalion on 16th, 169
  4th Battalion of the 14th, 62, 85
  6/14th, 69
  8th, 87
Puri, Major, 518
Puri, Satyananda, Swami, 176
Pyawbe, 318
Pyinbin, 265, 276-78, 306
Pyinmana, 241, 307- 09

Qadir, Abdul, Sir, 359
Qadir, Ehsan, Col., 96, 209, 359, 360, 406, 536
Qayum, Abdul, Maj., 536
Quit India movement in 1942, 423, 469
Qutab Minar, 85, 574

Raffles Square, 91
Raghunandan Saran, 425, 441, 507, 508, 523, 524
Raghvan, N., 176, 183, 191, 195
Rai Singh, Lieut., 347
Rajendra, Son-in-law, 538
Raj Guru, Martyr, 25
Rajindra Narain, 497
Rajkumar, 540, 543
Raj, Sister of Sahgal, 432
Rama, Lord, 12, 19

Ramalu, 549, 551
Ram Nagar, 6
Ram Nath, Lieut., 307
Ram Prakash, 544
Ram Sarup, Sadar-e-Jung, Lt. Col., 96, 349
Ram Singhji, Shri Guru, 25
Ram Singh, Major, 95
Ram Tirath, Swami, 19
Rana, Mohd. Azim Khan, Lt. Col., 165, 174, 238, 245
Rana Sanga, 214, 278
Randhawa, Gurdial Singh, Captain, 432
Randhawa, Hardial Singh, Brigadier, 62, 67, 75, 81, 82, 443, 532
Ranganadan, Maj., 334
Rangoon, 220, 333
Rangoon Jail, 370-88
Rani Jhansi camp, 542, 548
Rani Jhansi Regiment, 209-10, 226, 239, 242, 514
Ranjit Singh, Maharaja, 6
Ran Singh, Lt. Col., 214
Rashid Yusaf Ali, Capt., 388
Rattan Singh, Capt., 79, 197
Raturi, P.S., Col., 213, 214
Rawalpindi, 17, 28
Rawat, Capt. Darwan Singh, 247, 260, 299, 305
Ray, Ashish, 541
Red Cross Society of Singapore, 91
Red Fort, 85-86, 99, 223, 240, 258, 276, 402-27, 430, 574
Renkoji Temple, 416, 568-70
Riaz, Maj., 226
Ribbentroph Herr, 556, 557
Rodrigues, J.W., Col., 216-18, 230-31, 305, 333, 536
Royal Indian Navy, Mutiny, 523
Roy, B.C., Dr., 528, 529
R.S.S., 515
Ruldu Ram, Lala, 15
Russia, 514

Sabang, 203
Sabharwal, Vineet, 540, 543
Sade Hill raid, 311-13
Sadhu Singh, Captain, 167
Safrani, Abid Hussain, Major, 203, 557
Sahay, A.M., 209
Sahgal, Lakashmi, Col., 540
Sahgal, Prem Kumar, Colonel, 59, 242, 300, 302, 304, 308, 311, 318-19, 320-21, 449, 482-85, 496, 498-501, 504-09, 512, 534-37, 568
Saji, 144-46, 164
Sakaguchi, 240
Salimgarh, 406, 408, 428, 443, 498, 536-38
Salimgarh Swantantrata Senani Smark, 536-38
Salim Shah, 536
Sameikkon, 245
Sampuran Singh, Sardar, 79
Samy, R. Sepoy, 310
Sangma, P.S., 550
Sant Singh, Lieut. General, 62
Santa Singh, Sepoy, 48-49

Santa Singh, Capt., 71, 103, 104, 113, 130-31, 141, 161, 172-73
Sapru, Tej Bahadur, Sir, 432, 433, 439
Sarabai, Mridula, 517
Sarda Nand, Lt. General, 73-74
Sarhadi, Ajit Singh, 402
Sarkar, A.N., 209
Sarup Singh, Havildar, 37, 38
Sarvjit, Son, 532-33
Satya Nand, Swami, 153
Savarkar, Vir., 576
Sayed Sahib, 38-40
Scindia, Madhav Rao, 535, 537
Secundrabad, 9, 68-70, 73-76
Seikpyu, 282
Selatar, 105, 132, 134, 175
Selja Kumari, 536, 538
Senda, Mr., 197
Sen, P.N., Justice, 432
Shalimar Garden of Lahore, 39
Shamsher Singh, Maj., 222, 223, 229, 231, 232
Shanaz, 539
Shanghai, 327
Sharma Nekiram, Pandit, 424
Sharma, Satish, Captain, 541
Sharma, Shankar Dayal, President, 537
Shashi Bhushan, 535
Shashtri, Shiv Kumar, 432, 497, 511
Sher Singh Havildar, 253
Sher Shah Suri, 536
Shidei, Lt. General, 416
Shigemitsu, Foreign Minister, 558, 560
Shivpuri, 318 530, 531, 533
Shiwe Dagon Pagoda, 370
Shonan town, 166
Shyam Singh Atariwala of Punjab, 206
Sidhu, Anokh Singh, 422
Sidhu, Wassan Singh, 52, 423
Simla, 20, 71, 524
Singapore, 85-87, 90, 93, 222, 542, 550
Singapore Falls, 91-92
Singh, A.B., Col., 305, 325-26, 337-39, 364, 406, 536
Singh, B. Sardar, 194
Singh, Govind Saran, 432
Singh, P.P., Lieut., 84
Singh, S.S., Lieut. Col., 539, 540
Singora, 86, 87
Sirajuddoula, 206
Sita and Lord Rama, 12
Sitpinzeix, 343
Slim, Sir William, Gen., 282-85, 287, 299, 321, 547
Smuts, Field Marshal, 356
Sokalingarn, S., 544
Solan, 17, 19
Songgram, Phibun, Marshal, 178
Soni, R.C., 432, 497, 511, 517-19, 534-37, 568
South Africa, 223
Srivastava, Narindra, 540
Stott, C.R., Lieut. Col., 431
Stevenson, Lieut. Col., 431
Stracey, C.J., Col., 69
Stratemeyer, Maj. General, 284

Stuart, Rev Dr., 518
Subhas Brigade, 464
Sucha Singh, Dr. Capt., 141, 142, 161, 162, 131
Sudarshan Chakra, 194
Sugiyama, Army Chief of Staff, 558-60
Sukarchakys, 497
Sukhdev, Martyr, 25
Suleiman Shikoh, 536
Sultan Yar Khan, 425, 432, 497
Sumathi, 546, 551
Sumatra, 203
Sunaswa, 106, 109, 110, 119, 131, 164
Sungei Pattani in South Kedah, 80, 83, 86, 87, 120
Surajmal, 213, 214
Surat Singh, Capt., 68
Suri, G., Sagar, 551
Sulakhan Singh, Hav. Major, 35-37, 50
Swamy, N.G., 557
Swaran Singh, 111, 125, 132, 136, 141, 144, 168
Swaran Singh, Sardar, 526
Swatantra Sangram Sangrahelaya, 534

Tagore, Rabindra Nath, 564
Taipeh, 416
Talib Din, Maj., 96
Tamamori, Cpl., 114, 122, 136-38, 143-47, 149, 155, 164
Tantia Tope, 206, 576
Tara Bai, 11
Tara Singh, L/Nk, 131, 133
Tara Singh, Master, 482
Taro Bibi, 11, 13
Taundwigyi, 325, 328
Taunggyi, 549
Taungtha, 245, 269
Taungzin, 241, 305, 308, 547
Tavoy, 220
Taylor, J.F.L., Maj., 24, 29, 71-73, 75
Teja Singh, N.K., 35
Tej Kaur, 10, 12, 13
Tek Chand, Bakhshi, Sir, 425, 432, 511
Tenno Haika, Emperor, 368
Terauchi, Field Marshal Count, 205
Tetme, 213
Tetthe, 269, 279, 290, 293, 297, 300
Thailand, 86, 87, 210
Thakar Singh, Col., 7, 214, 309, 310
Tahakin Party, 319
Thapar, Premvati, 84
Thayetmyo, 320, 329
Thazi, 318
Thever, Janki, Capt., 239, 544, 551
Thimayya, K.P., Col., 310
Thivy, A.J., 209
Thorat, Kusum, 85
Thorat, Leela, 70, 85
Thorat, S.P.P., Lieut. Gen., 32, 61, 68, 74, 85, 441
Tilak, Bal Gangadhar, 548
Tipu Sultan, 206
Todar Mal, Raja, 18
Tojo, General, 102, 176, 187, 204-05, 210, 542, 558-61, 565

Tokyo, 203, 368, 558
Tokyo Cadets, 212, 416
Tokyo Conference, 175-76
Toungoo, 241, 318, 320, 333
Towyoe, 260, 267, 269-70
Towyoe Conference, 263
Toye, Hugh, 409-12, 547
Trial, 428-98, 536
- Counsel for Prosecution, 433
- Court Composition, 431-32
- Cross examination of Babu Ram, 448
- Cross examination of Dhargalkar, 447-48
- Cross examination of Nag, 444-46
- D.C. Nag witness, 442, 444
- Defence address, 485-93
- Defence seek adjournment, 437-49
- Defence witness, 480-82
- Evidences against us, 441-43
- Evidence of our character, 496-98
- First Row of Defence Council, 432
- Friend of the accused, 443
- Indian Army Act, 433
- INA Detention camp at Bahadurgarh, 429-30
- Judge Advocate administrated solemn oath to members of court, 433-34
- Judge Advocate's summing up, 494-96
- Meet mothers during, 484-85
- My dilemma, 449-51
- Opening address by Counsel for prosecution, 439-41
- Prosecution address, 493-94
- Prosecution opposed Defence adjournment, 438
- Lt. Col. P. Walsh witness, 441
- Raja Mohammed Arshad witness, 481-82
- Saburo Ohto witness, 480
- Second Row of Defence Counsel, 432
- Shunichi Matsumato witness, 480
- Statement by G.S. Dhillon, 473-79
- Statement by P.K. Sahgal, 465-73
- Statement by Shah Nawaz Khan, 451-65
- Teruo Hachiya witness, 480
- Trial over, 498
- Tudeshi Katakura witness, 448, 480

Tricolour Flag, 193, 418, 558
Trivandrum, 212
Tunku Abdul Rehman, 219

Udam Singh, 576
U. Nu., 379

Vakil Manik Lal S, 432, 497
Viceroy's commission, 46
Virendra Singh, Maj. Gen., 532
Vincent, S.F., 284
Vir Singh, Capt., 62
Vivekananda, Swami, 19

Von Ribbentrop, Herr, 210
Vorchelov, (President U.S.S.R.), 531

Walsh, P., 433, 434, 441, 444, 445, 496, 497, 500, 501
Watanbe, Maj., 311
Wavell, Field Marshal Viceroy, 444, 504
Werth, Alexander, 554
Women Conference in Calcutta, 482
World Agriculture Fair, 530
World War I, 10, 13, 35, 41, 65
World War II, 62, 549

X Regiment, 305

Yadava, S.S., Capt., 540, 543, 546
Yajee, Sheed Bhadra, Pandit, 223, 527, 528, 537
Yajnik, 527
Yamamota, Col., Maj. Gen., 558, 559
Yamashita, Tomoyuki, Lt. General, 92, 109, 121, 168
Yangon, 544, 547, 549
Yaw Chaung, 266
Yellappa, A., 209, 549
Yenangyaung, 324
Yeotmal, 216
Yonai, Minister for Navy, 558
Yudhishtra, 426
Yuva Shakti, 539, 551

Zamzama, 6
Zawin, U., 260, 270
Zaiwadi, 211, 239, 481, 546
Zora Singh, 239
Zulekha, 13